Basic Criminal Law

The Constitution, Procedure, and Crimes

Basic Criminal Law

The Constitution, Procedure, and Crimes

Third Edition

Anniken U. Davenport

Harrisburg Area Community College

Prentice Hall

Boston   Columbus   Indianapolis   New York   San Francisco   Upper Saddle River
Amsterdam   Cape Town   Dubai   London   Madrid   Milan   Munich   Paris   Montreal   Toronto
Delhi   Mexico City   Sao Paulo   Sydney   Hong Kong   Seoul   Singapore   Taipei   Tokyo

Editorial Director: Vern Anthony
Senior Acquisitions Editor: Gary Bauer
Editorial Assistant: Megan Heintz
Director of Marketing: David Gesell
Marketing Manager: Leigh Ann Sims
Marketing Assistant: Les Roberts
Senior Managing Editor: JoEllen Gohr
Production Editor: Christina Taylor
Project Manager: Susan Hannahs
Senior Art Director: Jayne Conte
Cover Design: Suzanne Behnke
Cover Image: Alan Williams © Dorling Kindersley
Full-Service Project Management: Chitra Sundarajan, Integra Software Services Pvt. Ltd.
Composition: Integra Software Services Pvt. Ltd.
Printer/Bindery: Edwards Brothers
Cover Printer: Lehigh/Phoenix Color
Text Font: 11/13, Minion

Credits and acknowledgments borrowed from other sources and reproduced, with permission, in this textbook appear on the appropriate page within the text.
Photo Credits: Anniken U. Davenport, pp. 8, 145, 208, 227, 350.

Library of Congress Cataloging-in-Publication Data
Davenport, Anniken U.
   Basic criminal law : the constitution, procedure, and crimes/Anniken U. Davenport. — 3rd ed.
     p. cm.
   Includes bibliographical references and index.
   ISBN-13: 978-0-13-510946-5 (alk. paper)
   ISBN-10: 0-13-510946-9 (alk. paper)
1. Criminal law—United States.   I. Title.
   KF9219.85.D38 2012
   345.73—dc22

2010034552

10 9 8 7 6 5 4 3 2 1

Prentice Hall
is an imprint of

PEARSON

www.pearsonhighered.com

ISBN 10:   0-13-510946-9
ISBN 13: 978-0-13-510946-5

Brief Contents

Contents

Preface

Ask any American his or her view of the justice system and you will receive a lengthy, passionate answer deeply rooted in that person's social, political, and legal experience. You will hear stories of police heroism or corruption, wise judicial decisions or ridiculous ones, an opinion of the Supreme Court based on news stories, but almost never actual court decisions. A quick glance at television listings shows that Americans are fascinated by the inner workings of the law from cops and robbers to prosecutors and defenders. That fascination leads hundreds of thousands of students to pursue careers in the American justice system. The third edition of *Basic Criminal Law* attempts to put flesh to the bones of the amorphous concept of the American justice system each of us carries in our minds.

For those pursuing careers as legal professionals, *Basic Criminal Law*, third edition, provides a comprehensive, organized approach to understanding key legal concepts and to developing real-world skills students will need when they enter the workforce.

Third Edition Tools

Like the second edition, the third edition uses a "crimes first, procedure second" approach to criminal law. We have retained and updated the popular **"You Make the Call"** sections to spur lively classroom discussions. Additionally, we have also revised the **"Historical Highlights"** that appear throughout the book. These highlights illustrate pivotal events in American legal history, events that remain influential today and continue to inform legal and public debate. The "highlights" provide students with a historical context and provide a legal cultural literacy necessary for legal professionals to succeed.

The third edition contains many new additions to enhance both the teaching and learning experience, including:

- **Evidence concepts for each crime chapter** show how prosecutors, police, paralegals, defense attorneys, and other criminal justice professionals can use the rapidly changing technologies in court
- **Expanded sections on defenses to crimes**
- **An entirely new chapter on sex crimes** reflects the growing complexity and prevalence of such cases in the criminal justice system
- **An all new appeals section** walks legal and criminal justice professionals through the appeals process
- **Expanded use of examples** illustrate each key learning concept
- **More state statute examples** show how individual states handle crimes
- **An increased emphasis on procedure** provides legal and criminal justice professionals the key skills they will need in the workplace
- **More charts and diagrams** show key trends in the field

- **New hands-on case portfolio-building applications** allow legal and criminal justice professionals to build their skills. Students who complete the end-of-chapter materials will have a portfolio they can present to prospective employers that illustrates their research and analysis skills and serves as a valuable personal reference guide as they begin their careers

New Concept Reinforcement and Skill Building End-of-Chapter Exercises

The third edition's end-of-chapter material has been completely revamped to focus on key concepts and their application. The material begins with a **Concept Review and Reinforcement** section that focuses the student on the chapter's key concepts. Next, a **Key Terms** section provides a list of critical terms used in the chapter. **Concept Review Questions**, simple questions meant to confirm that students understand the major concepts in the chapter, provide the grounding the student will need to tackle the **Building Your Professional Skills** section. Here students will encounter two to three **Case Applications** per chapter that illustrate the chapter's most important concepts. **Critical-Thinking Exercises** follow where students confront at least one hypothetical situation for each learning objective and critical variations discussed in the chapter. Finally, a **Portfolio Building** section features hands-on exercises that walk the student through creating a document, simulating what the paralegal will do in a law office.

Basic Criminal Law, third edition, is designed to provide legal professionals with a thorough grounding in criminal law, its history, how it is practiced today, and what trends will take it into the future. The third edition's new features allow students to get the hands-on experience and develop the key skills necessary to enter the legal profession ready to perform on day one.

Student Resources

Companion Website

Go to www.pearsonhighered.com/davenport to access links to additional resources, download a PowerPoint review of chapter concepts, and test mastery of concepts by taking the self-grading quizzes.

Instructor Resources

To access supplementary materials online, instructors need to request an instructor access code. Go to www.pearsonhighered.com/irc, where you can register for an instructor access code. Within forty-eight hours of registering you will receive a confirming e-mail including an instructor access code. Once you have received your code, locate your text in the online catalog and click on the Instructor

Resources button on the left side of the catalog product page. Select a supplement and a log in page will appear. Once you have logged in, you can access instructor material for all Prentice Hall textbooks.

Instructor's Manual

The instructor's manual contains sample syllabi and chapter notes including a chapter outline, brief overview of topics, instructional ideas, additional readings and occasional viewing recommendations, and suggested answers to discussion questions.

Test Generator

The test generator allows you to generate quizzes and tests composed of questions from the Test Item File, modify them, and add your own.

PowerPoint Lecture Presentation

The PowerPoint Lecture Presentation includes key concept screens and exhibits from the textbook.

CourseConnect Online Criminal Law Course

Looking for robust online content to reinforce and enhance your students' learning? CourseConnect courses contain customizable modules of content mapped to major learning outcomes. Each learning object contains interactive tutorials, rich media, discussion questions, MP3 downloadable lectures, assessments, and interactive activities that address different learning styles. CourseConnect courses follow a consistent twenty-one-step instructional design process, yet each course is developed individually by instructional designers and instructors who have taught the course online. Test questions, created by assessment professionals, were developed at all levels of Blooms Taxonomy. When you adopt a CourseConnect course, you purchase a complete package that provides you with detailed documentation you can use for your accreditation reviews. CourseConnect courses can be delivered in any commercial platform such as WebCT, BlackBoard, Angel, Moodle, or eCollege. For more information contact your representative or call 800-635-1579.

Acknowledgments

No work of this length and complexity is done alone. I would like to thank those who helped make this edition possible. My researchers, Albert Davenport, Morgan Horton, and Eric Horton, all pitched in to do much of the legwork necessary to update and enliven this edition.

I would also like to thank Stephanie Lingle, Esq., who contributed much to the first edition—initially as a legal assistant student at Wilson College and later as a law student at Case Western Reserve University School of Law. I am proud to say that she is now a criminal prosecutor in Ohio and may soon embark on teaching, too. Thanks also to Elizabeth Gonzalez, who contributed to the second edition.

There were also a number of criminal law teachers from paralegal and criminal justice programs across the country that provided very helpful feedback in the preparation of the third edition. I want to give them special recognition and my personal thanks for constructive commentary that informed and inspired this revision.

Elmer Criswell, Harrisburg Area Community College

Lisa Morris Duncan, Central Carolina Community College

Mark A. Hallal, Bridgewater State College

I would also like to thank reviewers of past editions. Their help has made this a far better book than it would have been without their assistance.

Sally Bisson	College of Saint Mary
Teresa Blier	Northern Virginia Community College
John Burkoff	University of Pittsburgh
Sylvia Caballero	Miami Dade College
Teresa Carlo	Pierce College—FS
Carol Chase	Pepperdine University
Lora Clark	Pitt Community College
Nigel Cohen	Richard Stockton College of New Jersey
Ernest Davila	San Jacinto College North
Kathleen DuBois	St. Louis Community College at Meramec
Lisa Duncan	Central Carolina Community College
Garry Elliott	Reedley
Duane Everhart	Wayne Community College
Harold Ferguson	Montclair State University
Phyllis Gerstenfeld	California State University—Stanislav
Pam Gibson	Rockford Business College
Christopher Godialis	Iona College
Tim Hart	College of the Sequoias
Darren Henderson	Remington College

Warren Hodges	Forsyth Technical Community College
David Jaroszewski	Lee College
Edan Jorgensen	University of Nebraska—Lincoln
Alan Katz	Cape Fear Community College
Prahlad Kedia	Grambling State University
David Kemp	Amarillo College
Mark Lloyd	Ivy Tech State College
Patricia Marcus	Consolidated School of Business
William Marino	Hesser College
Susan McCabe	Kellogg Community College
Maya Mei-Tal	West Virginia Wesleyan College
James P. Murphy	Union Institute & University
Kathryn Myers	Saint Mary of the Woods College
Michael Napolitano	City University of New York
Judith Olean	Central New Mexico Community College
Jeffrey Penley	Catawba Valley Community College
Alex Poyuzina	Maric College
Peter Puleo	Harper College
H. L. Raburn	Florida Metropolitan University
Doris Rachles	South University
Anana Rice	Metropolitan College
Cliff Roberson	Washburn University
Thomas Sarver	Ivy Tech Community College
Brian Schorr	Briarcliffe College—Interboro Institute
Michael Seigel	University of Florida
Scott Silvis	Griffin Tech
Howard Sokol	Athens Technical College
Andrew J. Sosnowski	Elgin Community College
Claire Summerhill	Utah Career College
Susan Sutton	Durham Technical Community College
Leo Villalobos	El Paso Community College
Michael J. Watanabe	Arapahoe Community College
Lorrie C. Watson	Orangeburg-Calhoun Tech
Charlotte A. Weybright	Brown Mackie College—Fort Wayne
Mary Wilson	Northern Essex Community College
John Woodruff	Bay Path College
David Woods	Limestone College
Alvin Zumbrun	University of Maryland

My "partners in crime" at Pearson Prentice Hall also deserve many thanks, especially Gary Bauer, my editor, and Christina Taylor, who had the unenviable task of keeping me on schedule. I hope I didn't cause you too many headaches, Christina.

About the Author

 Anniken Davenport holds a J.D. from the Dickinson School of Law of the Pennsylvania State University and has served as an assistant district attorney in Mifflin County, Pennsylvania, where she handled numerous criminal jury and bench trials, as well as appellate work. In addition, she was a prosecutor for the Bureau of Professional and Occupational Affairs at the Pennsylvania Department of State, where she worked with state and federal agencies on cases involving physician insurance fraud, drug and alcohol abuse, and misuse of DEA registration.

Ms. Davenport also holds an MA in Writing from Johns Hopkins University and serves as an adjunct instructor of legal subjects at Harrisburg Area Community College. She has also taught at Penn State University and directed the Legal Studies Program at Wilson College. It was at Wilson College that she first developed *Basic Criminal Law* and first tested it in the classroom.

Chapter **one**
WHAT IS CRIMINAL LAW?

We hold these truths to be self-evident, that all men are created equal, that they are endowed by their Creator with certain unalienable rights, that among these are life, liberty and the pursuit of happiness.

Declaration of Independence (1776)

Introduction and Historical Background

Every society, from the most remote tribe to the most technologically advanced culture, has rules by which it operates. Most societies have written rules governing behavior and a set of punishments for those who break the rules. These can be called the society's laws. The **law** is defined as the body of rules of conduct created by government and enforced by governmental authority. Without any rules of behavior, life in a group would be difficult, if not impossible. **Jurisprudence** is the study of law. Criminal law is a specialized part of the study of jurisprudence.

In order to master criminal law, you must understand the context in which criminal law exists. In this chapter, we will take a look at the American legal system as a whole. Once you have a good grasp of that system's structure and form, you will find it easier to visualize the criminal law system as a subpart of the whole.

As the original English settlers arrived in the New World, they brought with them a well-developed system of justice known as **Common Law.** The law was common to all persons and all areas in the English Empire, hence the name. At its core, Common Law operates on the premise that if one set of facts yields a particular decision in one case, the same set of facts should yield the same decision in the next case. So, if a judge in Essex ruled that entering another's house after sunset and removing goods belonging to the owner was

CHAPTER OBJECTIVES

After studying this chapter, you should be able to:

- Explain what law is
- Explain the concept of English Common Law
- Explain *stare decisis*
- Explain the term *jurisprudence*
- Explain *mala in se* and *mala prohibita*
- List and explain the major theories of law and schools of jurisprudence
- Explain the difference between criminal and civil law
- List the three categories of crimes
- Explain the federal court system and federalism
- Explain checks and balances
- Explain the Supremacy Clause
- Explain the Commerce Clause
- Explain police power
- Explain how a criminal case is processed through the criminal justice system
- List and explain the sources of American law
- Understand how the criminal justice professional fits into the criminal justice system

Law
The body of rules of conduct created by government and enforced by the authority of government.

Jurisprudence
The study of law.

Common Law
The system of jurisprudence, originated in England and later applied in the United States, that is based on judicial precedent rather than legislative enactments.

Stare decisis
To stand by that which was decided; rule by which courts decide new cases based on how they decided similar cases before.

Precedent
Prior decision that a court must follow when deciding a new, similar case.

Schools of Jurisprudence
Various theories concerning how societies develop, maintain, and change laws governing individual behavior.

Consensus theory
A theory developed by Emile Durkheim that postulates that laws develop out of a society's consensus of what is right and wrong.

Referendum
The enactment of a law through a popular vote rather than a legislative action.

the crime of burglary, a judge in Londonderry faced with the same facts should rule the same way. Under Common Law, judges look to similar cases decided before and decide new cases the same way. This helps make the legal system predictable and stable. Using previous decisions in similar cases to decide a current case is called following the rule of *stare decisis*. *Stare decisis* means "to stand by the decision." The earlier case on which the court relies is called a **precedent.** Thus, in our previous example, the Essex judge's decision serves as the basis—or precedent—for the Londonderry judge's decision.

Theories of Law and Schools of Jurisprudence

Law's role in society varies from era to era, culture to culture, country to country, region to region, and sometimes even town to town. Different cultures have different ideas of what is right and wrong and what should be legal or illegal. Recall that jurisprudence is the study of law. Over the years, philosophers, lawyers, and social scientists have developed theories about how laws develop and are accepted by cultures. These theories of law are referred to as "**schools of jurisprudence.**" As you study these, ask yourself how each theory is reflected in the laws that affect you daily. For example, which theory do you think best reflects the almost universal prohibition against sexual relationships between blood relatives? Which theory explains laws against jaywalking or spitting on public streets?

Durkheim's Consensus Theory

Emile Durkheim (1858–1917) was a Frenchman who is often referred to as the father of sociology. Durkheim developed what he called the **consensus theory.** He thought that laws develop out of a society's consensus of what is right and wrong.

According to Durkheim, crimes are crimes because the society decides they are, not because certain actions are inherently right or wrong. In his classic work, *The Division of Labor in Society,* Durkheim wrote:

> Even when a criminal act is certainly harmful to society, it is not true that the amount of harm that it does is regularly related to the intensity of the repression which it calls forth. In the penal law of most civilized people, murder is universally regarded as the greatest of crimes. However, an economic crisis, a stock-market crash . . . can disorganize the social body more severely than an isolated homicide. (T)he only common characteristic of all crimes is that they consist . . . in acts universally disapproved of by members of each society. . . .[1]

In Durkheim's view, society's collective membership decides what is a crime and what isn't. Consequently, laws may change over time to reflect changing societal attitudes or technological advances. For instance, prior to the mid-twentieth century, smoking marijuana was not a crime simply because most people had never heard of marijuana. When smoking it became popular, many states passed laws barring its use. Later, when societal attitudes began to change, the behavior was decriminalized in some states. For example, some states now permit individuals to grow marijuana for personal consumption and others allow its use for medicinal purposes while others still criminalize cultivating, selling, or using it. In some cases, these laws were passed by **referendum** (a change in the law that occurs when the majority of voters vote to make the change) showing that society has made a collective judgment that growing marijuana isn't worthy of being considered a crime. Similar changes have occurred in attitudes toward gambling, prostitution, slavery, and racial segregation.

Marx's Ruling Class Theory

While Durkheim saw criminal laws as agreed upon societal norms, the sociologist Karl Marx (1818–1883) saw things very differently. He taught that laws are a reflection of the interests or ideology of the ruling class. Under Marxist theory, laws are a manifestation of ongoing class conflict. They exist merely to protect property interests of the **bourgeoisie,** or the group that controls industrial production. Private property rights are viewed as a tool of oppression of the **proletariat,** or the working classes.[2] This theory is referred to as the **elite or ruling class theory.** Related to this theory is the **Command School** theory.[3] The Command School believes that law is a set of rules developed by the ruling class or elite and imposed on the society.

For example, Marxists or Command School adherents would view the Toxic Assets Relief Program (TARP) used to bail out large banks as a pure reflection of the ruling class' interests because it moved assets from the middle class to the upper class. Both the Marxist and Command School teach that laws will only change when those in power change.

Blackstone's Theory

The great English legal analyst Sir William Blackstone (1723–1780) theorized that there are two different types of crime. Some acts are crimes because the behavior is inherently bad or evil. A crime that is bad in and of itself is defined by the Latin term **mala in se.** Other acts are crimes because society has chosen to criminalize specific behaviors. Such crimes are called a **mala prohibita.**[4] For example, murder is *mala in se*, or inherently evil. Driving a car with an expired inspection sticker, however, isn't inherently evil. Most traffic and auto code violations are *mala prohibita*.

The Natural Law School of Jurisprudence

The **Natural Law School** believes that people have natural rights and that laws are based on what is right. They adhere to the **moral theory of law,** the belief that law is based on morality. Much of English law reflects this school.[5] The English political philosopher John Locke (1632–1704) spoke of the natural rights of man. According to Locke, man possessed these rights in the "state of nature," a state that theoretically existed prior to any government. Since man naturally possesses these rights, government has no right to abridge them. Locke profoundly influenced Thomas Jefferson (1743–1826) in the writing of the Declaration of Independence. Both the Declaration of Independence and the U.S. Constitution reflect the Natural Law School of jurisprudence. For example, the introductory quote in this chapter is from the *Declaration of Independence*. Note the references to self-evident truths and unalienable rights. These are hallmarks of the Natural Law School of jurisprudence.

The basis of a democratic state is liberty.

Aristotle, *The Politics* (343 B.C.)

Bourgeoisie
In Marxist theory, the class in society that controls the means of production.

Proletariat
In Marxist theory, the working class who must sell their labor in order to survive.

Elite or ruling class theory
Also known as the "ruling class" theory, it is the theory put forth by Karl Marx that postulates laws exist only as a means of class oppression.

Command School
The school of jurisprudential thought that posits that laws are dictated to the society by the ruling class of that society.

Mala in se
According to Blackstone, a category of crimes that are bad in and of themselves.

Mala prohibita
According to Blackstone, a category of crimes that are crimes because society has decided they are crimes.

Natural Law School
The school of jurisprudential thought that teaches that laws are based on morality and ethics, and that people have natural rights.

Moral theory of law
A theory subscribed to by Natural Law adherents stating that laws are based on the moral code of the society.

Let us consider the reason of the case. For nothing is law that is not reason.

John Powell, English judge (1645–1713)

The Historical School

Historical School
The school of jurisprudential thought that believes that law is an accumulation of societal traditions.

The **Historical School** of jurisprudence states that law is merely the accumulation of a society's social traditions. Historical School legal theorists believe that laws evolve to accommodate changes in society.[6] Historical legal scholars will look to previous decisions and then determine if the norms reflected by those decisions are still the norms of the society. In other words, precedent is only relied on if the society's current social norms support the rationale underlying the decision in the case.

The Historical School would likely support overturning precedent if times have changed. For example, assume that the courts have regularly ruled that children born out of wedlock can't inherit from their fathers. The Historical School would look to society's current views on illegitimate births. If such births have become commonplace and accepted by a large segment of society, the Historical School would support overturning precedent. Like Durkheim's consensus theory, the Historical School recognizes that society influences what is or should be legal and illegal.

The Analytical School

Analytical School
The school of jurisprudential thought that believes laws are based on logic.

The **Analytical School** of jurisprudence holds that logic determines what is law. Analytical philosophers will apply theories of logic to the facts of a case to make a decision.[7] Emotional appeals hold little sway. Analytical adherents will tend to focus on the logic of a legal decision rather than on popular opinion or changing values.

The Sociological School

Sociological School
Adherents of the Sociological School of jurisprudence believe that the purpose of law is to shape societal behavior. Believers are called realists.

Realists
Belonging to the Sociological School of jurisprudence. Realists believe that the purpose of law is to shape societal behavior.

The **Sociological School** of jurisprudence holds that law is a way of achieving sociological goals within a society. Also known as **realists**, sociological theorists believe that the purpose of law is to shape societal behavior.[8] Because of their activist approach, they are unlikely to place much emphasis on prior decisions. Realists propose new laws designed to shape behaviors they consider desirable for society. For example, realists seeking to encourage religious tolerance might urge the passage of laws banning religious hate crimes such as church burnings and the desecrations of houses of worship. In effect, realists decide on a public policy and then mold laws to achieve that policy.

The Crit and the Fem-Crit School of Jurisprudence

Crits
The school of jurisprudences that believes the legal system is arbitrary and artificial, that legal neutrality and objectivity are myths to maintain the current status quo, and that the legal system perpetuates social inequality and oppression of those not in power.

Fem-Crits
A school of jurisprudence that holds the legal system perpetuates the oppression of women in society.

Another theory of jurisprudence that emerged in the twentieth century is the Critical Legal Studies School, or the **Crits.** Crits believe that the legal system is arbitrary and artificial, that legal neutrality and objectivity are myths to maintain the current status quo, and that the legal system perpetuates social inequality and oppression of those not in power. The **Fem-Crits** are an offshoot of the Crits. Fem-Crits apply the Crit theory of oppression and control to women, arguing that the legal system perpetuates the oppression of women in society.[9]

Which Theory Fits the American System?

No one theory of jurisprudence explains or describes the American legal system perfectly. There are elements of each theory in our legal system. For example, the introduction of a new bill to encourage more fathers to pay child support can be seen as the work of realists who want to encourage more fathers to support their children by penalizing those who don't. The law could also be the work of Analytical School proponents who see increased child support as logically reducing dependence on government aid. Or the law could be the work of proponents of the Historical School who see increased child support collection as a necessary measure in a society that accepts a high divorce and illegitimacy rate. Or the law could be the work of proponents of the Natural Law School, who see a child's right to support as the natural and moral obligation of his or her father. Finally, the Realists and Fem-Crits would see the law as a way of addressing a societal problem of children living in poverty and a correction of the unequal earning power of single mothers.

Criminal Law Vs. Civil Law

Legal proceedings are classified as either criminal or civil. Criminal and civil law each have a unique set of functions, procedures, and consequences. Generally speaking, criminal law is designed to protect and vindicate public rights, while civil law is used to resolve private disputes. Criminal law seeks to protect society as a whole from the aberrant (as defined by the law) behavior of some members of that society. A **crime** is a wrong against society.

Crime
A wrong against society.

Criminal Law Protects Public Rights

When a person commits a murder, assault, rape, or other crime directed at another person, a victim is harmed, and the public order disturbed. Since a civilized society values its citizens' physical safety, any action that threatens an individual's physical safety is a crime.

Similarly, societies that believe that property can be owned (and that's not a universally held belief) value property rights on the assumption that stable property rights produce a stable society. When members of the society appropriate property for their own use without permission or payment, it threatens social stability. Theft of property is therefore a wrong against society.

Because criminal laws protect public interests, criminal prosecutions are brought on behalf of all of us through a state actor. The prosecutor is always a public figure, not a representative of the victim of the crime. Thus, a Pennsylvania rape case is prosecuted by a district attorney and the case is captioned "*Commonwealth of Pennsylvania v. John Doe.*" A federal case is brought by a U.S. attorney and is captioned as "*United States v. Jane Doe.*" Both the district attorney and the U.S. attorney represent society as a whole.

Civil Law Protects Private Rights

While criminal law deals with crimes, civil law deals with **torts,** contracts, estates, and family matters. A tort is a private or civil wrong, or injury resulting from a breach of a legal duty. Torts may be intentional, such as an assault, or unintentional, such as an automobile accident. A person who commits a tort is called a **tort feasor.** Individuals seeking redress of private grievances file civil lawsuits over personal injuries, breach of contract, divorce and custody actions, or the administration of estates.

Sometimes one act can be both a crime and a tort. For example, a physical assault is both a crime and a tort. The criminal law seeks to punish the assailant

Tort
A private or civil wrong or injury independent of contract, resulting from a breach of a legal duty.

Tort feasor
A person who commits a tort.

on behalf of all of us, and the civil law seeks to reimburse the assault victim for any loss he or she had because of the assault. Because different rights are at stake, the assailant can be sued in both criminal court and in civil court for the same assault.

Perhaps no event in American history better explains the rights vindicated by the criminal and civil system than the terrorist bombings of the Pentagon and World Trade Center on September 11, 2001. The aftermath left the entire nation in grief and feeling less secure than before. Clearly, the terrorists' acts harmed us all. Those same acts also killed almost 3,000 innocent men and women, whose survivors each have a potential civil tort action against the terrorists, those that financed their operations, and perhaps other parties responsible for security.

Criminal Law Penalties and the Burden of Proof

Defendant
In a civil case the person against whom a suit is filed. In a criminal trial, the person accused of a crime.

Crimes are punishable by imprisonment or death. Sometimes the convicted **defendant,** the person charged with the crime, must pay a fine in addition to serving the prison sentence. Criminal punishments are meant to vindicate the public interest by either removing the convicted criminal from society for a period of time, or permanently in the case of death or a life sentence. Of course, not every convicted criminal will serve a prison sentence. He or she may be allowed to pay a fine instead or otherwise be restricted in where he or she may go for a period of time, including house arrest or other forms of monitoring. Punishments are supposed to be a **deterrent** to crime, meaning that individuals are less likely to commit crimes out of fear of punishment.

Deterrent
An action that discourages an individual from committing a crime. Fines, imprisonment, and death are considered deterrents to crime.

In the American criminal law system, it is always the government that has the **burden of proof,** or has to prove that the allegations against the defendant are true. The criminal defendant is presumed innocent until proven guilty.

Because the consequences of conviction are so great, the prosecution bears a heavy burden of proof. In criminal cases, prosecutors must prove **beyond a reasonable doubt** that the defendant did commit the criminal act he or she was charged with. (See Chapter 12 for a full discussion of the meaning of "beyond a reasonable doubt.")

Burden of proof
The duty to go forward to prove an allegation with facts.

Beyond a reasonable doubt
The burden of proof the prosecution must meet in a criminal case in order to convict the accused.

Tort Penalties and the Burden of Proof

The remedy in tort actions is a payment of money to the victim, an order to stop doing something (such as polluting a stream), or an order to do something (such as clean up an industrial waste site). A tort feasor stands to lose money if he or she must pay a damage award or stop production. The loser in a civil trial is in no danger of imprisonment. Because only money is at stake, a different burden of proof is used in civil trials. A **plaintiff** (the person bringing the suit) in a civil case need only prove his or her case by a **preponderance of the evidence.** This concept can best be explained by picturing a blindfolded statue of justice holding her scales. If the scales tip under the weight of evidence ever so slightly to one side or the other, the side to which it tips wins the case.

Plaintiff
The party who files a lawsuit.

Preponderance of the evidence
Evidence that is more convincing than the opposing evidence; enough evidence to tip the scales of justice.

Unlike criminal cases, which are prosecuted by a representative of the state or federal government, civil cases are brought by private attorneys retained to represent the plaintiff. As in criminal cases, the person bringing the suit has the burden of proving the case.

Types of Crimes

Crimes are often classified as **summary offenses, misdemeanors,** and **felonies.** The exact terminology varies from state to state. Summary offenses are generally minor violations such as speeding tickets, parking violations, and littering. They carry only the possibility of a short prison term, generally less than ninety days, and are usually punishable by the payment of a fine. Summary offenses are often tried at the lowest level of the judicial system, usually before a district magistrate or justice of the peace, and often use a streamlined procedure. A person charged with a summary offense may not receive all the procedural safeguards a defendant charged with a more serious crime would receive. For example, he or she will not have the case tried before a jury.

Summary offenses
Minor offenses such as parking tickets, or minor traffic violations.

Misdemeanors
Crimes punishable by relatively short prison sentences, or fines. Misdemeanors are less serious than felonies.

Felonies
The most serious classification of crimes punishable by long prison sentences or death.

HISTORICAL HIGHLIGHT

Different Burdens of Proof—Different Verdicts

On June 12, 1994, Nicole Brown Simpson and Ron Goldman were brutally murdered outside of Nicole Simpson's condominium in the Brentwood section of Los Angeles. Nicole was the former wife of football star and sportscaster O. J. Simpson. Bloody footsteps led from the scene. When police arrived at O. J.'s house, they found his white Ford Bronco parked on the street with bloodstains trailing from it toward the house. Scaling the fence, Detective Mark Fuhrman claimed he found a bloody glove matching one recovered at the scene of the crime. Simpson was not home, having left earlier in the evening for a business trip to Chicago.

Upon his return from Chicago, Simpson was questioned. Suspicion quickly fell on him because the police were familiar with the violence of the Simpsons' marriage. The police made arrangements for Simpson to turn himself in, but he didn't show up. That evening a low-speed chase took place on the freeways of Los Angeles. The chase was televised live across the United States. Simpson's friend A. C. Cowlings drove the white Ford Bronco as a despondent Simpson threatened suicide in the back seat. The nation watched as the chase ended peacefully at Simpson's house when he surrendered.[10]

Simpson retained a legal "dream team" of high-profile attorneys to defend him against the charges. The prosecution expressed confidence in its ability to convict Simpson. The evidence presented by the prosecution was at first compelling. Bloody footprints at the crime scene matched exclusive, high-fashion shoes belonging to Simpson. Bloodstains in the haphazardly parked Bronco and a bloodstained sock found in Simpson's bedroom all pointed to Simpson's guilt.

The "dream team," however, found holes in the prosecution's case. The Bronco was left unsecured in police custody. In a dramatic in-court demonstration, the prosecution had Simpson try on the bloody glove, and it was too small. That led Simpson's attorney Johnny Cochran to say in his summation, "If the glove doesn't fit, you must acquit." A DNA expert testified that DNA belonging neither to Simpson nor the victims was found in the blood removed from under Nicole's fingernails. And when Detective Fuhrman was called to testify about the circumstances under which he found the glove, he refused to answer on the ground that the answer might incriminate *him.* In a stunningly short deliberation, the jury returned a "not guilty" verdict. The district attorney had been unable to prove beyond a reasonable doubt that O. J. Simpson had murdered his ex-wife.

Months later, Simpson was sued civilly by Nicole's parents and the family of Ron Goldman. Much the same evidence was presented. But this time Simpson lost. A judgment for $33.5 million was entered against Simpson. Why the different verdicts? The answer lies in the different burdens of proof required for criminal and civil proceedings.

Misdemeanors are more serious than summary offenses, but less serious than felonies. A defendant convicted of a misdemeanor offense may serve a prison term, generally less than one year. The length of possible imprisonment varies

The U.S. Capital.

from crime to crime and state to state. Most theft offenses are misdemeanor offenses unless they involve several thousand dollars.

Felonies are the most serious crimes. Murder, rape, and robbery are typically considered felonies. Felonies are punishable by long prison sentences or death. A convicted felon faces lifelong consequences. Felons generally cannot serve in public office or on a jury, and often cannot hold professional licenses. They also can't vote while imprisoned, and sometimes for long periods after release. They may also lose other important benefits such as access to student grants and loans for college.

The American Judicial System

The Federal System

Federal system
A system of governing where government is divided into different levels.

The American government is a **federal system** where the task of governing is divided between different governmental levels. The United States has a national government, fifty state governments plus the District of Columbia, and numerous local governments. In addition, Puerto Rico, Guam, the Northern Mariana Islands, and the U.S. Virgin Islands are governed by American law.

The U.S. Constitution lays out the federal government's structure, including the framework for its court system. In addition, the Constitution guarantees that American citizens and legal aliens shall enjoy liberties such as freedom of speech and religion and equal protection under the law. In many instances, these rights extend to those in the United States illegally. The Constitution provides important procedural safeguards for individuals charged with crimes, including the right to counsel, right to a jury trial, and freedom from cruel and unusual punishments. You will learn more about these guarantees in later chapters.

Men being . . . by Nature, all free, equal and independent, no one can be put out of this Estate, and subjected to the Political Power of another, without his own consent.

John Locke, *The Second Treatise on Government* (1690)

The Constitution establishes three branches of government: the **legislative,** the **executive,** and the **judicial.** The legislative branch makes laws, the executive branch enforces the laws, and the judicial branch interprets the laws. The **U.S. Supreme Court** heads the judicial branch. The Supreme Court has the last say on the constitutionality of laws and its decisions establish the law of the land. For example, no law specifically states that the police must inform a suspect of his rights upon arrest, but the Supreme Court interpreted the Constitution to compel law enforcement officers to do so. (Read more about the *Miranda* decision in Chapter 11.)

The U.S. Supreme Court hears appeals from the federal court system and from state court systems if the issue concerns the interpretation of federal law or the U.S. Constitution or a conflict between states or citizens of different states. Generally, the Supreme Court only hears cases it considers important to the national interest. As a result very few of the many cases presented to the court are actually heard. A litigant who wants to take his or her case to the U.S. Supreme Court must file a **petition for *certiorari,*** requesting that the court hear the case. If the court decides it wants to hear the case, it issues a **writ of *certiorari.***

The court's ability to declare laws unconstitutional is part of the **checks and balances** system between the branches of government. The legislative branch consists of the Senate and the House of Representatives. Together, these two bodies are referred to as Congress. Congress makes law. The Senate must also approve all judges appointed to the federal bench, including to the Supreme Court, in a process called **confirmation.**

Supreme Court justices and all other federal judges are appointed for life. A federal judge or a justice of the Supreme Court can only be removed from office through **impeachment.** The Constitution specifies that a judge or justice can be impeached if he or she is convicted of "high crimes or misdemeanors." Charges are brought in the House of Representatives; if enough evidence of wrongdoing is found, the House can pass a bill of impeachment. A trial is then held in the Senate. If the judge is convicted by a two-thirds vote of the Senate, he or she is removed from office.

The executive branch of the government enforces the laws Congress enacts and constitutional protections. The president of the United States heads the executive branch, which contains numerous agencies, each responsible for enforcing laws under its **jurisdiction.** For example, the Department of Justice enforces federal criminal laws, the Department of Labor wage and hour laws, and the Food and Drug Administration laws governing foods and pharmaceuticals.

The Federal Judiciary

The Supreme Court sits atop the federal judiciary with the **Courts of Appeal** at the next level and **U.S. District Courts** beneath them. Federal crimes are tried in the U.S. District Courts and appealed to the U.S. Courts of Appeals, and ultimately to the U.S. Supreme Court if that court agrees to hear the case. Federal courts try cases when federal laws are alleged to have been broken, and in other areas where the federal government has been given **exclusive jurisdiction.** For example, the federal court system has exclusive jurisdiction over patent cases, federal crimes, disputes between the states, most admiralty cases, and federal bankruptcy cases.

Legislative
One of the three branches of government; the one charged with making the law.

Executive
One of the three branches of government; the branch charged with enforcing the law.

Judicial
One of the three branches of government; the branch charged with interpreting the law.

U.S. Supreme Court
The highest court in the United States.

Petition for *certiorari*
Request by a litigant that the U.S. Supreme Court hear his or her appeal.

Writ of *certiorari*
Notice from the Supreme Court that the court will hear a case.

Checks and balances
The system of restraints built into the U.S. Constitution that prevents one branch of government from dominating the others.

Confirmation
The process of approval of presidential nominees by the Senate.

Impeachment
The process by which Congress may charge a sitting judge, president, or vice president with "high crimes and misdemeanors" and convict that person in a trial before the Senate. A conviction results in removal from office.

Jurisdiction
The power to hear and decide a case. Jurisdiction can be divided as to subject matter, parties, or territory.

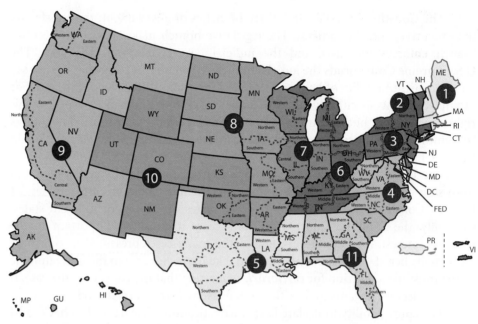

Geographic Boundaries of U.S. Courts of Appeals and U.S. District Courts.

U.S. Courts of Appeal
The federal court system's intermediate appellate courts.

U.S. District Courts
The federal court system's trial courts.

Exclusive jurisdiction
A court with exclusive jurisdiction is the only court that can hear the case.

Concurrent jurisdiction
Jurisdiction shared by two or more courts.

Federal Circuit
One of 13 federal judicial districts, each with a U.S. District Court and a U.S. Court of Appeals.

War on Terror
The term commonly used to refer to the aftermath of the September 11, 2001, attacks and efforts to bring the masterminds of the attacks to justice.

Executive Orders
Orders given by the president or governors that have the weight of law within the operation of executive branch of the federal or state government.

Federal courts also have **concurrent jurisdiction** with state courts over some matters. For example, a federal court can decide a civil lawsuit filed by a citizen of one state against a citizen of another state—cases which can also be heard in state courts.

The federal system is organized into thirteen **Federal Circuits.** Within each circuit, there is at least one U.S. District Court and a U.S. Court of Appeals. The number of U.S. District Courts in a circuit depends on the size of the geographic area covered by the circuit. Within each circuit, the District Court must follow the law as interpreted by the Court of Appeals for that circuit, and the rulings of the U.S. Supreme Court. That is, it must abide by *stare decisis* and rely on precedents if any are available.

The Circuit Courts of Appeals must follow the rulings of the U.S. Supreme Court but don't have to follow the decisions of the other twelve U.S. Court of Appeals. That means that there can be up to thirteen different interpretations of a law. These differences are referred to as "splits in the circuits." The U.S. Supreme Court often accepts cases for review to resolve these splits.

There are also special federal courts that handle specific subject matter. The U.S. Tax Court handles federal tax questions, the U.S. Bankruptcy Court handles bankruptcy cases, and the Armed Forces Court adjudicates military-related matters.

After the terror attacks of September 11, 2001, first the White House, and then Congress (after input from the U.S. Supreme Court) created a separate judicial process largely outside the federal court system to deal with alleged terror suspects caught in the armed conflicts in Afghanistan, Iraq, and other battlefields in the **War on Terror.** The Military Commissions Act of 2006 was passed by Congress and signed into law by President George W. Bush on October 17, 2006 and provides detainees and unlawful enemy combatants with an alternative judicial process. Shortly after taking office in 2009, President Obama issued a series of

Executive Orders designed to try more terror suspects in civilian courts.[11] (See Chapter 8 for more information on military tribunals and enemy combatants.)

The Constitution gives specific powers to the federal government. All other powers are reserved to the states and their citizens. It is a common misconception that powers flow from the federal government to states. In fact, all power originates at the state level. The powers given by the states to the federal government are called the **enumerated powers.** These powers are primarily in areas of national and international interest.

The Supremacy Clause

The **Supremacy Clause** of the Constitution establishes it as the supreme law of the land. The concept that federal law must take precedence over state and local law is called the **preemption doctrine.** When the U.S. Constitution or a federal law addresses an area within the federal government's exclusive jurisdiction, federal law is said to preempt the state or local law.

All states have their own constitutions, but state constitutions can't give the state's citizens fewer rights than given under the U.S. Constitution. In other words, states can give their citizens greater rights than the U.S. Constitution gives, but never fewer rights. The U.S. Constitution serves as the minimum standard below which the states may not go.

For example, long before the 20th Amendment to the Constitution provided women with the right to vote, several states already permitted it. Once the 20th Amendment passed, all states had to allow women to vote.

The Commerce Clause

Initially, federal court jurisdiction was very limited. However, as transportation and communications linked the states more closely, some standardization of laws was necessary. The Constitution gives the federal government jurisdiction over matters of **interstate commerce.** In the early days of the republic the Constitution's **Commerce Clause** was interpreted narrowly. However, as commerce grew more complex, the federal government assumed jurisdiction over anything affecting interstate commerce. For example, Congress passed the Civil Rights Act of 1964, which guarantees equal civil rights to all regardless of race, sex, religion, or national origin, under the authority of the Commerce Clause.

As the federal government's role expanded, so did the number of federal laws. Crimes that involved interstate flight posed problems for state and local law enforcement. The advent of the automobile made flight easier, and created a whole new category of crime—auto theft. Interstate flight problems became so large that a federal law enforcement body was needed. This organization eventually became the Federal Bureau of Investigation.

Police Power

What does it mean when we say a government has the right to regulate an activity? We mean that a government has the power to enforce existing laws, and punish those who break them. This is commonly referred to as the government's exercise of its **police power.** A state's police power allows it to regulate the health, safety, morals, and the general welfare of its citizens.

Enumerated powers
The powers explicitly given to the federal government in the U.S. Constitution.

"We the People" tell the government what to do, it doesn't tell us. "We the people" are the driver, the government is the car. And we decide where it should go, and by what route, and how fast.

Ronald Reagan, farewell address (January 11, 1989)

We may define a republic . . . as a government which derives all its powers directly or indirectly from the great body of the people, and is administered by persons holding their offices during pleasure, for a limited period, or during good behavior.

James Madison, *The Federalist* (January 16, 1788)

Supremacy Clause
The clause in the U.S. Constitution that states that the Constitution, federal law, and treaties are the supreme law of the land. Article VI, Section 2.

Preemption doctrine
This concept that federal law must take precedence over state and local law.

The people made the Constitution, and the people can unmake it. It is the creature of their own will, and lives only by their will.

John Marshall, *Cohens v. Virginia* (1821)

Interstate commerce
Commerce that occurs between states as opposed to strictly within a state's borders.

HISTORICAL HIGHLIGHT

Birth of a National Police Force

Until 1908, there was no national law enforcement agency. States and cities all had their own police forces. But as travel became easier, crime became more mobile. Criminals could now easily cross state lines and elude prosecution. Local police departments often lacked training and were unable to coordinate investigations that crossed county and state lines. In some cases, police corruption also interfered with the ability to effectively control crime.

President Theodore Roosevelt and his Attorney General, Charles Bonaparte (a descendant of Napoleon I), realized the need for a law enforcement body that could cross state lines to apprehend criminals, coordinate the investigations of local police forces, and do it in a professional way with no trace of corruption. Bonaparte created a corps of special agents who were chosen strictly on the basis of their qualifications.

The force was small and tightly controlled by Congress. The idea of a national police force was very controversial. States were wary of this federal intrusion into an area that was traditionally the purview of states, counties, and municipalities. Many feared a national police force as a first step toward widespread federal control of state affairs.

Gradually, events led to a widening of the special agents' jurisdiction. In 1910 the Mann Act was passed into federal law. It is also known as the "White Slave" Act. White Slavery refers to the practice of abducting or luring away rural Southern girls and forcing them into prostitution in Northern cities. Since White Slavery abductions took place across state lines, local police forces were ill-equipped to stop these lucrative operations. Special agents became adept at investigating the trade in young girls.[12]

During World War I, the force was again expanded and charged with investigating violations of the Espionage, Selective Service, and Sabotage Acts. After the war, a series of bombings highlighted the need for the Bureau of Investigations, as the agency was now called. On the evening of June 2, 1919, U.S. Attorney General A. Mitchell Palmer heard a thud at his front door as he was going upstairs to bed. A second later an explosion ripped through the front of his house. No one in the Palmer household was injured, but the bomber was killed. The explosion scattered the anarchist political leaflets the bomber was carrying throughout the neighborhood. America's first "red scare" was on.

The explosion was the first in a series of bombings to take place across the country. The Bureau of Investigation began large-scale arrests of immigrants believed to be communists. These mass arrests became known as "Palmer Raids." The Palmer Raids were organized and carried out by an ambitious law school graduate, J. Edgar Hoover.

Hoover would rise very quickly to assume control of the Bureau in 1926. Until his death in 1972, Hoover would run the FBI with the shrewd ability to manipulate, cajole, and influence Congress and the White House to gain increased funding and greater power. Although some of his methods have been criticized, he managed to build a law enforcement agency that has garnered national and international respect and praise. Today the FBI remains a vital part of the nation's policing forces and an integral part of the nation's homeland security.

Commerce Clause
The clause of the U.S. Constitution that gives the federal government the right to regulate interstate commerce. Article I, Section 8, Clause 3.

Police power
The power of a government to enforce laws and regulate the health, safety, morals, and welfare of the population.

Intrastate
Occurring within a state's border.

Most states have an extensive system of laws and regulations that govern how business is done within the state. Additionally, anytime a state passes a criminal law, it exercises its police powers. Whereas federal criminal laws cover crimes affecting interstate commerce or interfering with an individual's constitutional rights, state criminal laws cover **intrastate** crime, or crime that occurs within the state's borders.

States are also free to delegate some of their police powers to local governments like counties and municipalities. These entities can then pass laws, usually called ordinances, to protect health, safety, morals, and the general welfare of people in the county or municipality. Ordinances are sometimes classified as criminal laws. For example, it is fairly common for cities to have in place extensive building codes designed to protect its citizens from faulty or dangerous conditions—violating these may be a summary offense.

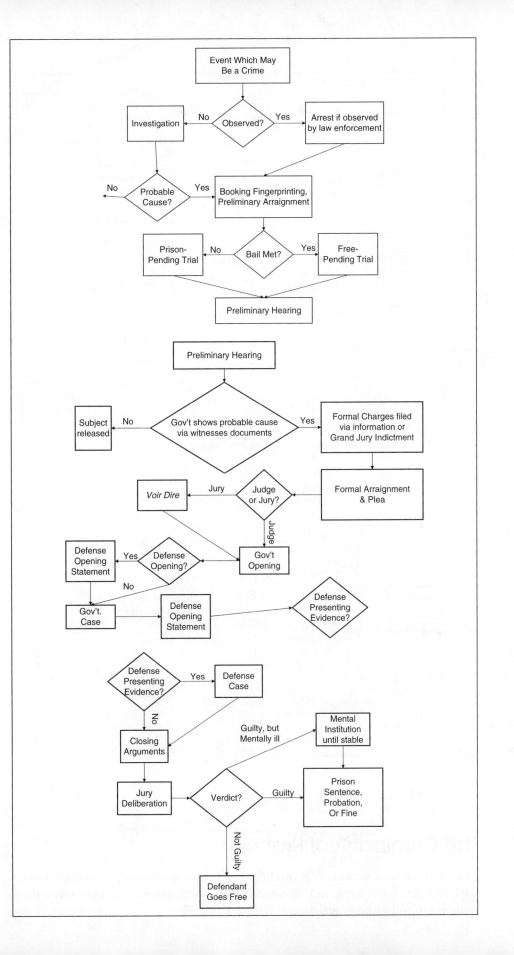

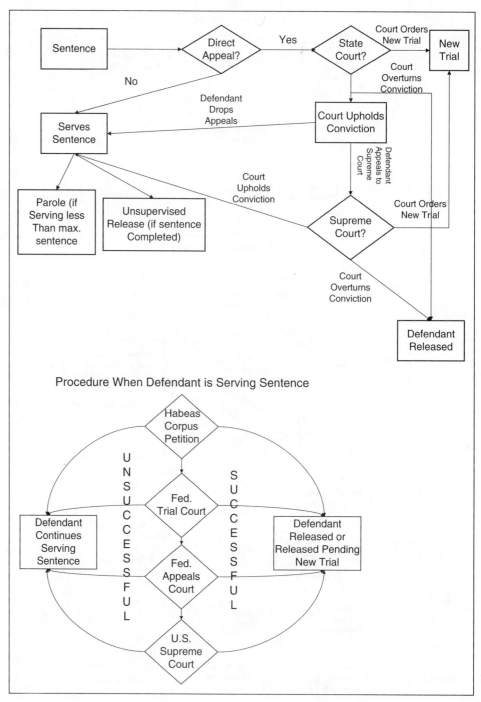

The Criminal Justice Process.

The Criminal Trial Process

The criminal trial process is a carefully orchestrated journey from suspicion to trial and possibly conviction or appeal. Convicted defendants may serve their sentence in full or be granted early release or *parole* after serving just part of the sentence. They may go through a lengthy period of post-release supervision. In addition, convicts frequently must pay fines and penalties and make restitution to victims. This is where theory meets practice, where concepts of punishment, rehabilitation, and restorative justice come together as a convicted person serves his sentence, emerges (one hopes) rehabilitated, and pays his debt to society and the victim.

The criminal process falls into four distinct phases:

- Investigation, arrest, and pretrial
- Trial
- Appeal
- Serving the sentence

Investigation, Arrest, and Pretrial

The criminal process begins when authorities are alerted to the possibility that a crime has taken place. This may be something as simple as a police officer observing an illegal act or as complicated as an auditor questioning a company's financial transactions and alerting appropriate authorities. Either way, the criminal process begins.

Once the relevant law enforcement officer for the offense has enough information to institute criminal proceedings, an arrest may be made. In the case of an officer observing an illegal act, the arrest may take place immediately. Because probable cause must be present for all arrests, the officer will have to justify his decision with a sworn statement or complaint after the fact. The officer need not, however, wait for a magistrate to authorize the arrest. This, of course, is based on the practical reality that the offender might be long gone before a magistrate's permission could be obtained. For example, a police officer who witnesses an attempted burglary may make the arrest without consulting a judge.

A police officer may also issue a citation for minor offenses. If you've ever been caught speeding or running a stop sign, you were probably issued a citation. Citations usually allow the defendant to plead guilty and send in a fine or elect to have a hearing before a district justice or magistrate. If the officer finds illegal narcotics or the driver fails a sobriety check, it's more likely that the driver will be arrested on the spot rather than cited, given the more serious nature of the offense.

Naturally, police officers don't catch every defendant "red-handed" so that an immediate arrest or citation is possible. Sometimes an arrest is made only after a long investigation, weeks or months after the offense was allegedly committed. In that case, the arrest is usually carried out by the use of an **arrest warrant.** To get an arrest warrant, a police officer must apply for one with the local judiciary—usually a district magistrate or other judge assigned to oversee arrest warrants. The application includes a police officer or investigator's sworn statement or affidavit about what he or she believes happened and who committed the offense. Before an arrest warrant is issued, the magistrate or judge must be convinced that there is probable cause to believe the offense took place and the defendant committed it based on what the officer alleges in the affidavit or statement.

Armed with a signed arrest warrant, police officers can arrest the defendant and bring him or her to a central processing center, usually located at the police

Arrest warrant
Document approved by a magistrate or judge attesting that there is probable cause to believe that someone has committed a specific crime and authorizing that person's arrest.

[handwritten margin notes:]

① Alerted to possibility that a crime has been committed.

② Arrest made once enough info is obtained to institute crim proceedings (can be a long or short investigation)

②a Get warrant from local judiciary - sworn statement by officer or affidavit

station, municipal building, or local jail. There, the defendant is held temporarily while being processed. Processing may include fingerprinting and a thorough search. If the police officers haven't already done so, they will inform the defendant of his or her constitutional rights by reading the ***Miranda* warning.** (For a thorough discussion of *Miranda* warnings, see Chapter 11.) The officers may then also question the defendant—who, of course, is free to refuse to answer or to demand an attorney be present during questioning.

In most jurisdictions, the defendant will be brought before a magistrate soon after arrest at a **preliminary arraignment.** At that point, the magistrate may rule on whether **bail** should be granted. Whether and how much bail is set depends on the seriousness of the charges and the likelihood that the defendant will appear for trial if he is released. The more serious the offense, the less likely bail will be granted and the higher bail is likely to be. In some cases, bail may be nothing more than the defendant's promise to appear for trial. This is usually referred to as being **released on one's own recognizance.** Defendants with close ties to the community and no prior criminal convictions are most likely to be released on bail or their own recognizance. Sometimes conditions are attached to bail, such as surrendering a passport to prevent flight to another country.

Next, the defendant attends a **preliminary hearing,** which is the first stage in the criminal process where the government must present evidence. In most cases, the arresting police officer represents the state. He or she will act as the government's representative and call any witnesses needed to prove that there is probable cause to hold the defendant over for trial. Sometimes, especially in cases where the defendant is mounting an aggressive defense, the district attorney or prosecutor will represent the government at the preliminary hearing.

In high-profile cases, preliminary hearings may become something akin to a mini-trial. For the defense, the preliminary hearing may be a good opportunity to look at the evidence the state has against a client. The defense can also gauge how well a witness handles being on the witness stand. At this point, the defense gets a transcript of the witnesses' statements to use later if the witness' story changes later. The defense usually does not present any evidence at the preliminary hearing. If the government's case is weak, the case may even be dismissed after the preliminary hearing.

The evidentiary standard the government needs to meet at the preliminary hearing is simply that there is **probable cause.** Put succinctly, the government needs to prove that it is more likely than not that an offense took place and that it was the defendant who committed it. If the magistrate or district justice hearing the case believes the government has met those standards, the defendant will be ordered bound over for trial.

Even after the preliminary hearing, the defendant has not been officially charged with a crime. The government must jump yet another hurdle—it must convince either a **grand jury** or a prosecutor that the defendant committed a crime. A grand jury is a body of citizens whose job it is to determine if a crime has been committed and if a person should be charged with that crime based on probable cause. In many jurisdictions, the decision to formally charge a defendant with a crime is left to the district attorney or state attorney. He or she has the authority to file an **information,** which formally charges the defendant with a crime and begins the next phase of the process—the actual trial phase. The information is very specific and names the penal sections of the law that the defendant is accused of violating. Very often it will include the most serious crimes the defendant is

---

Miranda **warning**
The warning given to suspects that they have the right to remain silent and the right to counsel named for the Supreme Court case that requires police officers to read the right to suspects (*Miranda v. Arizona*).

Preliminary arraignment
An accused's first official notification of the charges against him or her. The preliminary arraignment generally occurs shortly after arrest.

Bail
Money or other guarantee posted to assure a defendant who is released from custody pending trial or appeal will appear when called or forfeit the security posted.

Released on one's own recognizance
The situation that occurs when the court does not require the defendant to post bail at the preliminary hearing. Despite the lack of bail, the defendant is obligated to return for further proceedings.

Preliminary hearing
A formal hearing that is the first occasion at which the government must produce evidence against the defendant. The prosecutor must convince the judge or magistrate hearing the case that it is more likely than not that the defendant committed the crime he or she is charged with.

charged with as well as any other lesser included offenses. For example, a defendant may be charged with rape, indecent assault, aggravated assault, and simple assault. If the prosecution is unable to prove the more serious crime, he or she may still get a conviction for one of the lesser offenses. In addition, the inclusion of the lesser offenses allow some room for maneuvering if the prosecution and the defense decide to engage in **plea bargaining.** Plea bargaining is the practice of negotiating with a defendant and his attorney concerning the terms of a guilty plea. For example, a defendant might be persuaded to plead guilty to indecent assault but not rape because he knows if convicted of rape he faces a much longer sentence than if he is sentenced on the indecent assault charge.

If the jurisdiction uses a grand jury to commence criminal trials, the charging document is referred to as an **indictment.** There is great flexibility in whether a defendant is charged with a crime. A district attorney has the discretion to decline to prosecute cases in most jurisdictions. The district attorney also typically can drop a case at any stage if he or she believes that would be in the interest of justice. This is done with a *nol pros* motion, which stands for the Latin *nolle prosequi,* translated loosely as no prosecution. Requiring an indictment or an information before people can be tried for a crime is another way to assure that innocent persons are not subjected to the power of the state without good reason. It is another of the checks and balances on state power.

After the defendant is formally charged by indictment or information, he or she is then formally **arraigned.** At arraignment, the formal charges are read to the defendant and he or she must enter a formal response to the charges, or a **plea.** The plea may be not guilty, guilty, *nolo contendere* (meaning no contest), or not guilty by reason of insanity.

All jurisdictions have strict time limits requiring the government to move the criminal process forward in a timely fashion. Those limits are designed to prevent the government from holding defendants for extended periods of time without having the opportunity for a trial on the charges. For example, in many states, defendants must be brought to trial within 180 days of being charged if imprisoned or 360 days if free on bail. Any continuance requested by the defendant is excluded from the count. If the case isn't brought in a timely fashion, the government must dismiss the charges.

There are some exceptions, most notably for those who have been detained on the battlefield in Afghanistan in the War on Terror or are suspected terrorists picked up elsewhere in the world, such as the battlefields of Iraq, and held at Guantanamo Bay in Cuba. In addition, Americans suspected of terrorist activities and picked up on the battlefield or even in the United States have been designated as "enemy combatants" by the president of the United States before being transferred to civilian authorities for trial. (For a more detailed discussion of the developing wartime criminal justice system put in place after the September 11 attacks, including the treatment of terror suspects, see Chapter 8.) This is an area of criminal procedure that is in flux.

Trial

As a practical matter, most criminal cases never make it to **trial.** Most cases are disposed of by guilty pleas through plea bargaining. Plea bargaining in one form or another takes place in every jurisdiction. If the defendant doesn't plead guilty or no plea bargain is entered into, the case will proceed to trial.

Probable cause
A low standard of proof in a criminal case used to justify an arrest or hold a defendant over for trial after a preliminary hearing. The standard requires that there be sufficient proof to convince a reasonable person that it is more likely than not that he or she committed the crime charged.

Grand jury
A body of citizens whose job it is to determine if a crime has been committed and if a person should be charged with that crime based on probable cause.

Information
A formal document signed and filed by a district attorney or prosecutor that charges an individual with a specific crime.

Plea bargaining
The practice of negotiating with a defendant and his attorney about the terms of a guilty plea.

Indictment
A formal charge by which the defendant has been charged with a crime, usually as the result of a grand jury inquiry.

***Nol pros* motion**
An abbreviated form of the Latin *nolle prosequi,* which roughly translates as "no prosecution"; it is a motion filed by a prosecutor indicating that justice is better served by not prosecuting the defendant.

Arraignment
The stage of a criminal case at which the defendant is first formally charged with a specific crime.

Plea
A formal response to criminal charges. A plea may be not guilty, guilty, nolo contendere, or not guilty by reason of insanity.

Nolo contendere
Latin for "I will not contest this," also called "no contest"; a plea entered that admits no wrongdoing but allows the court to sentence the defendant as guilty.

Trial
The examination of facts and law presided over by a judge, magistrate, or other person with authority to hear the matter.

Trial by judge
A trial where the presiding magistrate renders the verdict.

Trial by jury
A trial where the verdict is determined by a jury.

Jury
A group of men and women from the community selected to determine the truth; while the judge is responsible for interpreting the law, the jury is charged with the task of finding the facts of the case. The right to trial by jury is guaranteed by the U.S. Constitution in all serious criminal cases. A jury decides what the facts of the case are and applies those facts to the law. Juries must be convinced beyond a reasonable doubt that the defendant broke the law.

Voir dire
From the French meaning "to speak the truth," it refers to the examination of citizens to ascertain their fitness for serving on a jury; during the *voir dire* phase of a criminal trial, the attorneys ask questions of the jury pool. These are designed to ferret out jurors who cannot be impartial or who can't serve on the jury because of illness or other obligations and to help the attorneys in the case decide where and when to use available peremptory challenges.

Most jurisdictions hold special sessions of criminal court. Defendants who want a trial may select either **trial by judge** or **trial by jury.** Which type of trial a defendant chooses depends on many factors such as the reputation of the judge who would hear the case and the type of crime with which the defendant has been charged. A separate **jury** pool is called from the community for each criminal session with jurors for individual cases selected from the pool. Jurors called to jury duty may hear several cases.

If the defendant chooses a jury trial, he or she may assist in the selection of jurors from the jury pool. Sometimes the defense will even hire jury consultants, who are specially trained psychologists or sociologists well versed in human psychology who predict which jurors may favor one side over the other and who understand group dynamics.

The process of selecting jurors starts with *voir dire,* which involves asking potential jurors questions to determine whether they can judge the case fairly and impartially. *Voir dire* also helps to eliminate jurors who know too much about the case or who are related to the defendant, the victim, or any of the witnesses or attorneys or police officers involved in the case.

Both the prosecution and the defense help choose the jurors. Either side may challenge the selection of a juror. The attorneys have unlimited **challenges for cause.** For example, a juror who admits he has followed the case closely in the press and has already concluded that the defendant is guilty will be dismissed for cause. Judges may also dismiss a juror for cause. Attorneys may also reject potential jurors using a **peremptory challenge.** Peremptory challenges are essentially wild cards available to either side. When used, the attorney need not state a specific reason. Usually, there are a set number of peremptory challenges allowed. For more information on the jury process, see Chapter 13.

After a jury has been selected, the prosecution and the defense address the jury through **opening statements.** Because the government has the burden of proof to show the defendant is guilty beyond a reasonable doubt, the government makes its opening statement first. The government's opening statement usually outlines what the prosecutor expects to prove and whom the jurors can expect to hear testify for the prosecution. Essentially, the government tries to orient the jury by giving them a road map of the case.

The defense may make its opening statement next, or it may choose to wait until after the prosecution has rested its entire case. Many defense attorneys think it's better to wait until later, when they have already heard the government's witnesses and evidence. They can then tailor their opening to the weaknesses in the government's case.

After opening, the government presents its witnesses for **direct examination** and the defense **cross-examines** them. Either party may then ask questions again by **redirect exam** and **recross exam.** Redirect and recross questions are limited to subject matter raised in the last cross or direct exam.

Because the government has the burden of proof and the defendant is considered innocent until proven guilty, the government must prove each element of the crime charged. That is, they must prove beyond a reasonable doubt that the defendant intentionally committed the act charged. Many prosecutors use a checklist of the elements of the crime charged and cross off each element as the evidence is presented. For example, in a theft case, the prosecutor would have to present evidence of who owned the stolen goods and that the item was taken without the owner's permission.

Finally, the prosecution would have to show that it was the defendant who physically took the owner's property, intending to permanently deprive the owner of it.

At the end of the prosecution's case, the government rests. If the defense thinks that the prosecution failed to prove an element of its case, it may ask for the charges to be dismissed. If the motion is denied, the defense may present its case. It is not required to do so, since the burden is on the prosecution to prove the case beyond a reasonable doubt. If the defense does present evidence or witnesses, the prosecution has a chance to cross-examine them. The defendant is not required to testify against himself, and therefore may not testify. The jury will be instructed that it cannot consider the defendant's decision not to testify as evidence of guilt. The decision to testify or remain silent depends on the case and on the defendant. If his or her testimony is likely to be sympathetic, it may be best to testify. However, the prosecutor has the right to cross-examine the defendant and will most likely attempt to question the defendant's credibility. Generally, unless the defendant is very sure he can persuade the jury and withstand cross-examination, the best option may be to stay silent. If the defense does have witnesses testify, the prosecution may present rebuttal evidence to disprove the evidence.

Once the prosecution has presented its case, the defense may make a motion for a judgment of acquittal. Under the Federal Rules for Criminal Procedure, a judge must "enter a judgment of acquittal for any offense for which the evidence is insufficient to sustain a conviction."[13] Most states have similar provisions. Judges have the option of waiting until the jury has rendered a verdict until ruling on the motion.

Finally, the attorneys present closing arguments. The prosecution goes first; usually outlining what it believes its evidence has proven. The defense then closes. In some jurisdictions, the prosecution may again address the jury to rebut issues made by the defense.

The jury then retires to the jury room and elects a foreperson to help direct its deliberations. In high-profile cases, jury members may be barred from returning to their homes during the trial and deliberations to avoid tainting their process with outside news or opinions by an order of **sequestration.**

If the jury is unable to reach a decision, the jury is said to be *hung*. The jury can judge the defendant guilty or not guilty. Its decision is the **verdict.** In a case in which the defendant has raised insanity as a defense, the jury can also find the defendant not guilty by reason of insanity. In some states, they can also find the defendant guilty but mentally ill. For more on the insanity defense, see Chapter 10, Common Law Defenses.

After the jury renders a verdict, the court will enter the judgment in the record. In those cases where the judge is deciding the case, he or she will announce the verdict and enter judgment.

The defendant may be sentenced immediately or after presentence investigation and recommendations. There may be sentence guidelines or mandatory sentences. In the case of a capital crime tried by a jury, there will be a sentencing phase of the trial.

Appeal

Every defendant is entitled to an appeal of some sort. In state criminal cases, those appeals go though the state system and may include a trip to the state's highest court or even the U.S. Supreme Court. Except in very rare circumstances,

Challenges for cause
An attorney's (either prosecution or defense) request that the judge dismiss a potential juror from serving on a jury by providing a valid legal reason why he or she shouldn't serve. Judges may dismiss potential jurors for cause as well.

Peremptory challenge
The right to dismiss or excuse a potential juror during jury selection without having to give a reason. Each party to a lawsuit is allowed a fixed number of peremptory challenges.

Opening statement
A statement made by an attorney or self-represented party at the beginning of a trial before evidence is introduced. The opening statement outlines the party's legal position and previews the evidence that will be introduced later.

Direct examination
The initial questioning of one's own witness.

Cross-examination
Questioning a witness put on the stand by the other side following direct examination.

Redirect examination
Questioning of one's own witness following cross-examination.

Recross examination
Questioning of a witness called by the other side following redirect examination.

Sequestration
The confining of jury members for the duration of a trial to prevent any outside influences.

Verdict
A judge or jury's decision at the end of a trial. The verdict in a civil case must be by at least a preponderance of the evidence, while the verdict in a criminal case must be beyond a reasonable doubt.

Habeas corpus
Literally meaning "you have the body," a judicial process for determining the legality of a particular person's custody. The "Great Writ" which orders another authority to bring a person to court. It was originally used to prevent kings from simply making enemies disappear.

Writ of habeas corpus
An order by federal court to "bring the body" of the prisoner to the court.

and only before the defendant has "been placed in jeopardy", the prosecution may not appeal.

If the jury concludes that the defendant is not guilty, that is the end of the matter. Appeals generally must be filed within thirty days of sentencing, though some states set a shorter appeal period.

The defendant's appeal may attack any defect in the trial or evidence. Generally, however, the issue appealed must have been preserved during the trial by an objection on the record. For example, if the defense believes a piece of evidence should not have been admitted, it must have challenged the admission at the time to preserve the issue on appeal. (For a more detailed examination of appeals, see Chapter 14.)

Once all direct appeals are exhausted, the defendant may still have an opportunity to be heard. He or she can do so through a process called **habeas corpus.** A **writ of habeas corpus** is an order by federal court to "bring the body" of the prisoner to the court. It is an old right designed to protect citizens from abusive government practices. A *writ of habeas corpus* may be filed years into a defendant's sentence and raise issues that weren't raised earlier, such as ineffective counsel. It may also be raised if there is new evidence of innocence, such as a DNA test, that clears the defendant or proof of some form of corruption during the trial.

Serving the Sentence

The defendant may begin serving the sentence immediately after trial or may be free pending appeal. Once direct appeals are over, the defendant will have to start his sentence. He or she will get credit for any time already served while awaiting trial.

Most defendants will serve a minimum sentence (generally half of the bottom range of the sentence). In some cases, no deviation from the sentence range is permitted. Parole boards generally rule on when the defendant may be released. Defendants may also ask the parole board or the governor (or president) for a pardon under limited circumstances.

Once parole is granted or the defendant has served his sentence, the defendant is released. In the case of parole, he or she will be supervised for as long as the maximum sentence would have been. If he or she has served the maximum sentence, there is no additional supervision unless he or she is a sexual predator as defined under that state's laws. (For more on restrictions on sexual predators see Chapter 4.)

Sources of Law

As you have already learned, the Constitution and the laws Congress passes pursuant to its powers are the supreme law of the land. But they aren't the only sources of law in the United States. Law is also created by treaties signed with foreign governments, laws enacted by state and local legislatures, regulations of administrative agencies, executive orders, and judicial decisions.

Constitutional Amendments and the Bill of Rights

The original Constitution provided little to safeguard civil rights. Anti-federalists, the group opposed to ratifying the Constitution, feared the new American Constitution would create too strong a federal government, and the freedom gained by overthrowing British rule would be lost. To address these fears, federalists agreed to ten amendments to the Constitution known as the Bill of Rights.

The Bill of Rights provides protections for:

- Freedom of religion
- Freedom of speech
- Freedom of the press
- The right against self-incrimination
- The right to be free from cruel and unusual punishment
- The right to due process and others

Subsequent constitutional amendments abolished slavery, provided women the right to vote, and legalized federal income tax. Clearly, some amendments are better than others.

> Governments . . . deriv(e) their just powers from the consent of the governed.
>
> Thomas Jefferson, *Declaration of Independence* (July 4, 1776)

English Bill of Rights
A precursor to the U.S. Bill of Rights, it guarantees due process and bars cruel and unusual punishment.

HISTORICAL HIGHLIGHT

The English Civil War and the English Bill of Rights

The American Bill of Rights owes much to the English Bill of Rights adopted 100 years before in 1689. By the seventeenth century, England had been using the concept of Common Law for over 400 years. But the first kings to sit on the throne in the seventeenth century believed in the "divine right of kings." In other words, kings ruled through a God-given mandate without regard to the rule of law.

Tensions grew until a long, bloody civil war broke out in 1642. Charles I was executed, and replaced by Oliver Cromwell, who trampled English rights as effectively as the kings had done. Ultimately, parliament agreed to restore the monarchy, putting Charles II, a protestant who did not believe in the divine right of kings, on the throne. Charles II agreed to many limits on his power.

Charles II died in 1685 and his brother James II, a Roman Catholic, became king. James II also believed in the divine right of kings, and England once again seemed poised for internal strife. The English did not want another civil war, and tolerated James. The Protestant majority in England placed their hope for peaceful transition in James's daughter, Mary, who was a Protestant. But then James had a son and Mary was no longer next in line for the throne under the laws of primogeniture.

Parliament invited Mary and her husband, William of Orange, the ruler of the Netherlands, to invade England with an army and assume the throne. When William and Mary invaded, James left the country without a drop of blood being spilled. Because the change in monarchs happened without violence, it is referred to as the "Glorious Revolution."

Parliament, however, did not intend to import an absolute ruler. Part of the deal was that William and Mary had to agree to a "Bill of Rights." The **English Bill of Rights** of 1689 would prove to be a very influential document in the evolution of the American legal system.

The English Bill of Rights reiterated the king's subservience to the law and the limited role of Parliament. Because monarchs had frequently abused the judicial system to silence political foes, Parliament inserted the following provisions to protect those accused of a crime:

- That excessive bail ought not be required, nor excessive fines imposed; nor cruel and unusual punishments inflicted.
- That jurors ought to be duly empanelled and returned, and jurors which pass upon men in trials of high treason ought to be freeholders.
- That all grants and promises of fines and forfeitures of particular persons before conviction are illegal and void.

The provision about excessive bail became the Eighth Amendment to the U.S. Constitution. The provision about jurors carried over into American law as well. The fines and forfeitures provision refers to the accused being innocent until proven guilty. No fine is due until the person has been convicted of a crime. You will learn more about these and other important constitutional protections provided to persons accused of a crime in later chapters.[14]

Treaties

Treaty
An agreement with a foreign government, that to be enforceable must be ratified by a two-thirds vote of the Senate.

Advise and consent
The constitutional relationship of the Senate to the president regarding the selection of federal judges and other duties.

Extradition
The process of returning an accused criminal to the jurisdiction in which he or she is charged.

Napoleonic Code
The French System of laws developed by Napoleon I; it is the basis of Louisiana law.

Treaties with foreign governments have the force of law. Any **treaty** negotiated by the president or his representatives must be ratified by two-thirds of the U.S. Senate to become law. This is part of the Senate's **advise and consent** duty under the Constitution. The most common way treaties affect criminal law is through the power of **extradition.** Countries with an extradition treaty with the United States have agreed to send an accused criminal to the United States where he or she can be charged with a crime and tried. Likewise, the United States is the signatory to many treaties that obligate it to return persons accused of a crime in another country to that country for trial. Not all countries have extradition treaties with the United States.

Extradition treaties may be limited in scope. For instance, since the European Union has no death penalty, it will not extradite an accused person facing a death sentence to any country including the United States.

The Napoleonic Code

Most of our discussion has centered on the tradition of English Common Law. However, there is another major influence on current American criminal law—the French system of civil law based on the **Napoleonic Code.**

The Napoleonic Code was written under Napoleon I. The goals of the Napoleonic Code were to make criminal penalties more consistent and to bring the French government under the rule of law in much the same way the Magna Carta and Common Law tradition made the English government accountable to the people.

Napoleon had seized power in the aftermath of the French Revolution. The French Revolution had taken place in large part in response to the excesses of the French monarchy. Under the French monarchy, an influential person could issue a *lettre d'cachet*—a document that directed that a person be imprisoned indefinitely without trial, or even without ever being charged with a crime. The Reign of Terror followed the Revolution during which many French nobles and members of the middle class were beheaded. After reeling between the extremes of Royal tyranny on one hand and mob terror on the other, Napoleon recognized the need for an open and fair legal code.[15]

In the United States, only Louisiana relies heavily on the Napoleonic Code tradition. The U.S. government in 1803 purchased Louisiana from France. Its customs and laws were much more influenced by the French and Spanish than the English.

Differences between the Napoleonic Code and English Common Law

The way courtrooms are organized and run is very different under the two systems. Under the Napoleonic Code or civil law, criminal trials resemble boards of inquiry rather than the adversarial arrangement we are familiar with. Judges in civil law cases may cross-examine witnesses to gather facts. In contrast to the English system, plea bargaining is unknown. The judge does not ratify "deals" made between the prosecuting and defense attorneys. Rather the judge's duty is to conduct an investigation into the circumstances surrounding a crime and render a just verdict.[16]

Many of the legal maneuvers in American criminal trials are designed to protect the rights of the accused and the state. Our system attempts to balance the rights of the individual and the state in an adversarial setting. The civil law system seeks to discover the truth about a crime with all parties participating in the search. Critics of the civil law system charge that it does not offer the same safeguards of individual rights that the English system provides. This may be why so many Louisiana criminal cases reach the highest court of the land, the Supreme Court. (See, for example, Chapter 13 on the right to trial by jury.) In many ways, the Napoleonic Code tradition is at odds with the English tradition of trial by jury and the right against self-incrimination.

Codified Laws

Whenever the U.S. Congress or a state legislature passes a law, it becomes part of the federal or state code. Laws passed by the U.S. Congress become part of the U.S. Code. These laws are collected and classified by topic. For example, most laws dealing with crimes and criminal procedure are in Title 18 of the U.S. Code. Similarly, state laws are published in the various state codes. Local governments are said to be "creatures of the state" in that they draw their power from state governments. They may pass local laws or ordinances within the bounds of their charters.

In each case, the government uses codes to organize all the laws passed by their legislative bodies. The codification process ensures that contradictory laws do not appear on the books. For example, when a law comes before Congress that changes existing law in the U.S. Code, it must specifically state which words in the code it seeks to change.

YOU MAKE THE CALL

Treaty Obligations and Criminal Law

Under the U.S. Constitution, ratified treaties have the same force of law as the Constitution, meaning that theoretically, treaty provisions should have priority over state laws. But states have seldom been willing to abide by treaties to which they were not a party.

A case in point is the execution of a Paraguayan national by the name of Angel Francisco Breard (pronounced BRAY-ard). Breard was arrested for the stabbing death and sexual assault of Ruth Dickie, his neighbor. Under the Vienna Convention, an international treaty signed by 130 nations including the United States and Paraguay, police are required to notify the consular office of a nation if they arrest a foreign national. Virginia police never did so.

Mr. Breard confessed to the crime, but claimed that the reason he committed the stabbing was that his father-in-law had put a satanic curse on him. Breard had the benefit of court-appointed attorneys who advised him not to testify at his trial, and probably didn't endorse the satanic curse defense. Breard testified anyway and was sentenced to death. The government of Paraguay sued Virginia officials in federal court complaining that Breard had been denied his rights under the Vienna Convention.

continued

The case worked its way through to the Supreme Court. The Court ruled in a 6–3 decision that because Breard had not raised the Vienna Convention violation in his initial defense, he could not raise it now. Paraguay presented the case to the International Court of Justice. The International Court of Justice hears cases involving international treaties. It is also known as the World Court and is a part of the United Nations. The International Court of Justice agreed to hear the case and scheduled argument for the fall of 1998, well after Breard's date with the Executioner.

Secretary of State Madeline Albright personally requested that Virginia authorities delay Breard's execution until the International Court could hear the case. She cited possible repercussions for Americans charged with crimes overseas. After all, if the United States refused to comply with the treaty, why should other signatory nations? Virginia refused and executed Breard on April 14; hours after the Supreme Court denied his final appeal for a stay of execution.[17] Eventually, Paraguay dropped the case and no final decision was ever rendered by the International Court of Justice.

YOU MAKE THE CALL: If you were the Governor of Virginia, would you have stayed the execution until the International Court of Justice had a chance to rule? What would the political fallout have been for doing so?

Regulations

Regulations

A rule, adopted under authority granted by a statute, issued by a municipal, county, state, or federal agency. Although not laws, they have the force of law and often include penalties for violations. Regulations may be challenged as either exceeding the authority granted by the underlying statute or as being unconstitutional.

Regulations are written by administrative agencies. At the national level these become part of the Code of Federal Regulations (CFR). When Congress passes a law, it often instructs an appropriate administrative agency to develop regulations to give guidance on how the law should be enforced. For instance, regulations dealing with counterfeiting are developed by the Department of the Treasury, the agency that is responsible for the legitimate printing of bills and coinage. Regulations that are consistent with the law under which they are promulgated are also law.

Model Penal Code

Model Penal Code and Commentaries

Code that attempts to unify state penal codes. Legislatures often look to it when drafting legislation.

Although not a law, the **Model Penal Code and Commentaries** is an attempt to standardize conflicting penal codes among the states. The code was developed in 1961 and provides commentary and advice to state legislatures, judges, and students of the law. State legislatures commonly refer to the Model Penal Code when drafting new legislation.

Executive Orders

The president and the governors of the states have the power to issue executive orders. The power to issue executive orders comes from the power delegated by legislatures to the executive branch to enforce the laws. President Obama's order to move terror suspects into civilian courts and close the prison at Guantanamo Bay (mentioned in this chapter) is an example of an executive order.

Judicial Decisions

As you learned earlier in this chapter, the doctrine of *stare decisis* is employed by judges to create Common Law. Much of American Common Law can be traced back to English Common Law.

Stare decisis lends uniformity and consistency to legal decisions, at least within a state. A court is bound to follow a precedent of a higher court in its system. For example, a state trial court is bound to follow the decision of that state's supreme court. But a state does not have to follow the precedence of another state's highest court. Thus, *stare decisis* promotes uniformity within a jurisdiction, but not necessarily across different jurisdictions.

Priority of Law

The U.S. Constitution is the supreme law of the land. Any treaty ratified by the Senate carries the same weight as the Constitution. Federal statutes take precedence over federal regulations; federal law will take precedence over state law.

Most state legal systems are a mirror image of the federal structure. The state constitution is the highest state law. State statutes supersede state regulations, and state laws take precedence over local laws and ordinances. Most state court systems also mirror the federal judicial system. Each state has a set of courts that are responsible for trials and another set that handles intermediate appeals. All fifty states also have a state supreme court, although it may go by another name.

Criminal Justice Professionals

Our legal system could not function without specially trained professionals at every level of the system. From the police officers who investigate crimes and make arrests to the justices of the U.S. Supreme Court, each has a crucial role to play in protecting the public and assuring that the legal foundation on which the system is built remains strong. Soon you will join these professionals for whom the U.S. Constitution serves as the guidepost.

Here are some of the professionals you will encounter in your criminal justice or paralegal career and the role they play:

Attorneys Attorneys are licensed professionals who can appear in court to represent individuals. Attorneys typically earn an undergraduate degree in any topic before attending law school for an additional three years of education in the legal system and the law. After earning a Juris Doctor (JD), they must take and pass an additional state-sponsored bar examination and meet moral and fitness for practice standards set by their state in order to practice law.

Each state sets its own requirements for granting a license to practice law, though in practice those requirements do not differ significantly. Some attorneys may hold several state licenses. There is, however, no federal licensing requirement. In order to practice in federal court, attorneys must file a brief application with the circuit court in their jurisdiction. Attorneys may also earn advanced degrees in specific areas of the law such as taxation or trial practice.

Attorneys
Licensed professionals who can appear in court to represent individuals.

Judges
The presiding officer or officers at judicial proceedings. Judges at the trial level and above are attorneys.

Judges

Judges at the trial level and above are attorneys. Federal judges, including the justices of the U.S. Supreme Court, are appointed and can serve for life if they choose. Federal judges are nominated by the President of the United States and confirmed by the U.S. Senate. Most state judges are elected to office and serve a fixed term—such as ten years—before having to seek reelection.

Minor judiciary
Magistrates, justices of the peace, or municipal judges who are commonly called members of the minor judiciary.

Minor Judiciary

Many disputes are decided by magistrates, justices of the peace or municipal judges who are commonly called members of the minor judiciary. These judges usually aren't required to hold a law degree and may be elected or appointed, depending on their state law. For example, a justice of the peace may very well be a former police officer or other legal professional.

Magistrates and justices of the peace are crucial to the criminal justice system, as they often handle initial criminal matters. For example, their job often includes approving or rejecting arrest or search warrants sought by police officers or other authorities. They may also set initial bail levels, inform defendants of the charges against them, and hold preliminary hearings to determine if there is enough evidence to send a defendant on to trial.

In addition, the minor judiciary hears low-level criminal and civil cases such as traffic violations, disorderly conduct, and other minor offenses and disputes involving less than a dollar amount set by the state.

District or prosecuting attorney
District attorneys (sometimes referred to as prosecuting attorneys) are lawyers who typically have been elected to try criminal cases on behalf of the people.

District or Prosecuting Attorney

District attorneys (sometimes referred to as prosecuting attorneys) are lawyers who typically have been elected to try criminal cases on behalf of the people. Most states elect their district attorney on a county-by-county basis. He or she then administers the operations of criminal prosecutions within that county, including hiring and supervising other attorneys who serve as assistant district attorneys.

States also typically have a statewide office for handling criminal matters within their office of the Attorney General. A state's attorney general is usually elected. He or she then appoints assistant attorneys general.

At the federal level, criminal prosecutions are conducted by the direction of the U.S. Attorney General. He or she has ninety-three U.S. attorneys stationed across the country, each appointed by the president of the United States and confirmed by the Senate. Within each federal judicial district, the U.S. attorney is the chief federal law enforcement officer.

Public defenders
Attorneys provided by the state to defend individuals who cannot afford to hire a private attorney.

Public Defenders

Public defenders are attorneys provided by the state to defend individuals who cannot afford to hire a private attorney. Some states have a statewide public defender and others handle the matter on a county basis. The federal criminal justice system also has a public defender's office, which works with indigent defendants charged with a federal crime.

State and local law enforcement officers
Police personnel, sheriff's deputies, and other officers who work for state and local law enforcement agencies.

State and Local Law Enforcement Officers

Law enforcement officers are legal professionals who are responsible for a wide range of criminal law enforcement work. Some jurisdictions hire law enforcement officers with a high school degree, but many agencies require an associate's, bachelor's, or even an advanced degree for specialized positions within a local law enforcement agency.

State or local uniformed police officers have general law enforcement duties such as patrolling a neighborhood, making traffic stops, responding to a call about a burglary, or rendering other general emergency assistance such as first aid at the site of an automobile accident. Uniformed police officers may also serve in specialized units such as a motorcycle unit or a SWAT (special weapons and tactics) unit.

Sheriffs, who are typically elected, serve their communities by enforcing the law at the county level. They may provide security for county courts and prisons.

Most states also have a statewide law enforcement system, usually called the state police, highway patrol, or state troopers. These uniformed officers may also patrol the highways, assist in rural areas where there is a small law enforcement presence, and provide logistical support and expertise for local police departments.

Detectives are law enforcement officers who typically work in plainclothes and specialize in a specific criminal activity such as homicide, arson, or child abuse.

Federal Law Enforcement   Just as there are local, state, and federal judges and prosecuting attorneys, there are federal law enforcement officers. The principal law enforcement agencies are the Federal Bureau of Investigation (FBI), the U.S. Bureau of Drug Enforcement (DEA), the U.S. Marshall Service, the Bureau of Alcohol, Tobacco, Firearms and Explosives (ATF), and the Department of Homeland Security (DHS).

The FBI investigates organized crime, public corruption, financial crime, bank robbery, kidnapping, terrorism, espionage, drug trafficking, and cybercrimes. The law enforcement officers who work for the FBI are called agents and may conduct surveillance, monitor court-authorized wiretaps, examine business records, investigate white-collar crime, or participate in sensitive undercover assignments.

DEA agents enforce federal drug laws and policies, federal marshals provide security for the federal court system, and ATF agents enforce explosives and alcohol and tobacco laws.

The DHS is the newest cabinet-level federal agency. Its agents are responsible for securing our borders, inspecting cargo, providing protection for the U.S. president, providing airline security, and enforcing counterfeiting laws, among an expanding list of responsibilities.

Such positions usually require a degree in psychology, social work, or criminal justice. Officers may visit those they supervise at work, at home, or in county offices and may assist in developing plans for vocational training, drug and alcohol treatment, and other programs to help the parole or probationer become a productive member of society who will not re-offend.

Paralegals or Legal Assistants   Paralegals or legal assistants are legal professionals who assist attorneys and others involved in the legal system. There professionals can perform many of the tasks usually reserved for attorneys, with the exception that they may not represent clients in court or give legal advice. The educational requirements for such positions depends on many factors, including location, but typically includes either a two-year degree in paralegal studies, or a four-year degree in another field followed by specialized training in legal assisting.

The Role of the Criminal Justice Professional

So far, you have learned quite a bit about some of the players in the criminal justice system, including judges, district attorneys, U.S. attorneys, and attorneys who represent defendants. These and other professionals play crucial roles in making

Federal law enforcement Law enforcement officers who work for the Federal Bureau of Investigation (FBI), The U.S. Bureau of Drug Enforcement (DEA), the U.S. Marshall Service, the Bureau of Alcohol, Tobacco, Firearms and Explosives (ATF), and the Department of Homeland Security (DHS) or other federal agencies.

Paralegals or legal assistants Legal professionals who assist attorneys and others involved in the legal system. These professionals can perform many of the tasks usually reserved for attorneys, with the exception that they may not represent clients in court or give legal advice.

our system work as effectively and efficiently as possible while protecting the rights of defendants, victims, and the society in which we live.

Whether you are a paralegal working in the district attorney's office, a parole officer working for the county, a police officer working for a city or town, or an investigator working with defense attorneys, you will be dealing with people who are facing some of the darkest hours of their lives. Those who haven't "been in trouble with the law" before may (rightfully so) be very frightened. For the first time in their lives, they are staring at the power of the state.

The process awes even the rich and famous. For example, before her trial on charges she lied about her sale of Imclone stock, Martha Stewart told Larry King on his show *Larry King Live* that " . . . no one is ever strong enough for such a thing . . . you have no idea how much worry and sadness and grief it causes."

Others who are more "experienced" may seem nonchalant or even unconcerned about the criminal process. Either way, as a criminal justice professional, you may be one of the few sources of reliable information for defendants facing criminal charges. How you handle questions about the process may help reduce anxiety and let the defendant better help in his or her defense.

CONCEPT **REVIEW AND REINFORCEMENT**

Every society has a body of laws. Laws govern the behavior of members of society. Laws are created and enforced by government. The United States has a system of law derived from the English Common Law.

Common Law relies on *stare decisis* and precedent to decide cases. Courts must follow earlier decisions when faced with a new case. This makes the legal system predictable and stable.

Jurisprudence is the study of law. There are many theories of law, or schools of jurisprudence. The consensus theory holds that society decides what is and isn't a crime. The Ruling Class and Command School theories posit that the ruling classes decide what is legal and what is illegal. Blackstone classified crime into two types: those that are *mala in se,* or inherently evil, and those that are *mala prohibita,* or illegal because society decides they are. The Natural Law School believes that people have natural, inherent rights and that laws are based on what is right. The Historical School sees laws as changing to accommodate changes in the society. The Analytical School claims laws are based on logic. The Sociological School (also known as the realists) asserts that law should be created to shape societal behavior. Finally, the Critical Legal Studies School and the Fem-Crits believe that laws are arbitrary rules to enforce the status quo and oppress and control those not in power.

A crime is a wrong against society. Criminal law differs from civil law in several important ways.

First, criminal law seeks to protect all of society from lawbreakers while civil law deals with vindication of individual, private rights. Secondly, criminal cases are always brought in the name of the people by a representative of the government, while litigants' private representatives bring civil cases. Thirdly, in order to win a criminal case, the prosecutor must prove the case beyond a reasonable doubt, a very high standard. Private plaintiffs need only prove their case by a preponderance of the evidence, a much lighter burden of proof.

Crimes are classified in order of their relative seriousness. Summary offenses are minor violations, usually punishable by either a short period of imprisonment or a fine. Misdemeanors are more serious offenses and carry a penalty of up to a year in prison. Felony offenses are the most serious, and are punishable by a long prison sentence or death.

The American judicial system is part of a federal system of government. The United States has a national government, fifty state governments, and numerous local governments. The framework for our federal system is found in the U.S. Constitution. It established three branches of government: the legislative to make law, the executive to enforce laws, and the judicial to interpret laws. Each of the three branches serves as checks and balances to the other two.

The Supreme Court, federal laws, and treaties are the supreme law of the land. The U.S. Supreme

Court heads the federal judiciary. The system is divided into thirteen circuits. Each circuit has trial courts called U.S. District Courts and an intermediate appellate court called the U.S. Court of Appeals. Justices of the Supreme Court and other federal judges serve for life. They can only be removed by impeachment. Federal courts have exclusive jurisdiction over some subject matter and concurrent jurisdiction with the states over other matters. Some areas of exclusive jurisdiction include patents and federal tax cases.

State court systems parallel the federal judicial system in many ways. Each has a trial court, at least one intermediate appellate court, and a supreme court. State courts follow the same hierarchy as federal courts. That is, the lower courts must follow the decisions previously handed down by the Supreme Court and the intermediate appellate court. The intermediate appellate court must follow the state Supreme Court's decisions. And all state courts must abide by decisions made by the U.S. Supreme Court.

The Constitution's Supremacy Clause establishes that federal law takes precedence over state and local law. The Commerce Clause allows the federal government to pass laws that regulate interstate commerce. Both the federal government and state and local governments have police powers. Through its exercise of police powers, government can regulate the health, safety, morals, and welfare of its citizens.

The legal system provides many safeguards for persons thought to have committed a crime. These safeguards exist at every level of the criminal process. For example, persons can only be arrested for a crime if a law enforcement officer has either observed the accused committing the crime or has enough probable cause to convince a magistrate or judge that the accused committed the crime to issue a warrant. The defendant must then be formally charged with the crime and be given an opportunity to defend against the charges within a reasonable period of time.

A defendant is entitled to a trial at which the prosecution must prove beyond a reasonable doubt that he or she has committed the crime. The convicted defendant may then appeal the verdict. He or she can also challenge the verdict later under some circumstances such as newly discovered evidence.

There are many sources of American law, most importantly the Constitution. Others include treaties, codified laws, regulations, ordinances, executive orders, and judicial decisions.

Criminal justice professionals play critical roles in the criminal justice system ranging from police officers and paralegals to parole officers, prison administrators, lawyers, and judges. Because the American system is an adversarial system, each criminal justice professional must be well-educated and vigorously carry out his or her duties to ensure the system's checks and balances perform their job of protecting the public and those accused of crimes.

KEY TERMS

Advise and consent	Crits	Grand jury
Analytical School	Cross-examination	Habeas corpus
Arraignment	Defendant	Historical School
Arrest warrant	Deterrent	Impeachment
Attorneys	Direct examination	Indictment
Bail	District or prosecuting attorney	Information
Beyond a reasonable doubt	Elite or ruling class theory	Interstate commerce
Bourgeoisie	English Bill of Rights	Intrastate
Burden of proof	Enumerated powers	Judges
Challenges for cause	Exclusive jurisdiction	Judicial
Checks and balances	Executive	Jurisdiction
Command School	Executive Orders	Jurisprudence
Commerce Clause	Extradition	Jury
Common Law	Federal Circuit	Law
Concurrent jurisdiction	Federal law enforcement	Legislative
Confirmation	Federal system	Mala in se
Consensus theory	Felonies	Mala prohibita
Crime	Fem-Crits	Minor Judiciary

Miranda warning
Misdemeanors
Model Penal Code and
   Commentaries
Moral theory of law
Napoleonic Code
Natural Law School
Nol pros motion
Nolo contendere
Opening statement
Paralegals or legal assistants
Peremptory challenge
Petition for certiorari
Plaintiff
Plea
Plea bargaining
Police power
Precedent

Preemption doctrine
Preliminary arraignment
Preliminary hearing
Preponderance of the evidence
Probable cause
Proletariat
Public defenders
Realists
Recross examination
Redirect examination
Referendum
Regulations
Released on one's own
   recognizance
Schools of Jurisprudence
Sequestration
Sociological School
Stare decisis

State and local law enforcement
   officers
Summary offenses
Supremacy Clause
Tort
Tort feasor
Treaty
Trial
Trial by judge
Trial by jury
U.S. Courts of Appeal
U.S. District Courts
U.S. Supreme Court
Verdict
Voir dire
War on Terror
Writ of certiorari
Writ of habeas corpus

CONCEPT REVIEW **QUESTIONS**

1. What is law?
2. What is *stare decisis* and what role does it play in English Common Law?
3. What is jurisprudence?
4. List and explain the major theories of law and schools of jurisprudence.
5. Explain the difference between criminal and civil law.
6. List the three categories of crimes.
7. Explain the federal court system and federalism.
8. Explain the checks and balances between the branches of government in the federal system.
9. What is the Supremacy Clause?
10. What is the Commerce Clause?
11. What is the police power?
12. What are the steps in a criminal trial?
13. List and explain the sources of American law.
14. What are some of the roles that criminal justice professionals fill in the criminal justice system?

CASE **APPLICATIONS**

Building Your Professional Skills

CASE 1

ROPER, SUPERINTENDENT, POTOSI CORRECTIONAL CENTER V. SIMMONS

Certiorari to the Supreme Court of Missouri

This is a landmark Supreme Court decision where the court ruled that it is unconstitutional to execute criminals for a crime committed as a minor. Read the case syllabus and answer the questions at the end.

No. 03-633. Argued October 13, 2004—Decided March 1, 2005

SYLLABUS: At age 17, respondent Simmons planned and committed a capital murder. After he had turned 18, he was sentenced to death. His direct appeal and subsequent petitions for state and federal postconviction relief were rejected. This Court then held, in *Atkins* v. *Virginia,* 536 U.S. 304, that the Eighth Amendment, applicable to the States through the Fourteenth Amendment, prohibits the execution of a mentally retarded person. Simmons filed a new petition for state postconviction relief, arguing that *Atkins'* reasoning established that the Constitution prohibits the execution of a juvenile who was under 18 when he committed his crime. The Missouri Supreme Court agreed and set aside Simmons' death sentence in favor of life imprisonment without eligibility for release. It held that, although *Stanford* v. *Kentucky*, 492 U.S. 361, rejected the proposition that the Constitution bars capital punishment for juvenile offenders younger than 18, a national consensus has developed against the execution of those offenders since *Stanford.*

Held: The Eighth and Fourteenth Amendments forbid imposition of the death penalty on offenders who were under the age of 18 when their crimes were committed.

(a) The Eighth Amendment's prohibition against "cruel and unusual punishments" must be interpreted according to its text, by considering history, tradition, and precedent, and with due regard for its purpose and function in the constitutional design. To implement this framework this Court has established the propriety and affirmed the necessity of referring to "the evolving standards of decency that mark the progress of a maturing society" to determine which punishments are so disproportionate as to be "cruel and unusual." *Trop* v. *Dulles*, 356 U.S. 86, 100–101. In 1988, in *Thompson* v. *Oklahoma*, 487 U.S. 815, 818–838, a plurality determined that national standards of decency did not permit the execution of any offender under age 16 at the time of the crime. The next year, in *Stanford,* a 5-to-4 Court referred to contemporary standards of decency, but concluded the Eighth and Fourteenth Amendments did not proscribe the execution of offenders over 15 but under 18 because 22 of 37 death penalty States permitted that penalty for 16-year-old offenders, and 25 permitted it for 17-year-olds, thereby indicating there was no national consensus. 492 U.S., at 370–371. A plurality also "emphatically reject[ed]" the suggestion that the Court should bring its own judgment to bear on the acceptability of the juvenile death penalty. *Id.,* at 377–378. That same day the Court held, in *Penry* v. *Lynaugh*, 492 U.S. 302, 334, that the Eighth Amendment did not mandate a categorical exemption from the death penalty for mentally retarded persons because only two States had enacted laws banning such executions. Three Terms ago in *Atkins,* however, the Court held that standards of decency had evolved since *Penry* and now demonstrated that the execution of the mentally retarded is cruel and unusual punishment. The *Atkins* Court noted that objective indicia of society's standards, as expressed in pertinent legislative enactments and state practice, demonstrated that such executions had become so truly unusual that it was fair to say that a national consensus has developed against them. 536 U.S., at 314–315. The Court also returned to the rule, established in decisions predating *Stanford,* that the Constitution contemplates that the Court's own judgment be brought to bear on the question of the acceptability of the death penalty. *Id.,* at 312. After observing that mental retardation diminishes personal culpability even if the offender can distinguish right from wrong, *id.,* at 318, and that mentally retarded offenders' impairments make it less defensible to impose the death penalty as retribution for past crimes or as a real deterrent to future crimes, *id.,* at 319–320, the Court ruled that the death penalty constitutes an excessive sanction for the entire category of mentally retarded offenders, and that the Eighth Amendment places a substantive restriction on the State's power to take such an offender's life, *id.,* at 321. Just as the *Atkins* Court reconsidered the issue decided in *Penry*, the Court now reconsiders the issue decided in *Stanford.* Pp. 6–10.

(b) Both objective indicia of consensus, as expressed in particular by the enactments of legislatures that have addressed the question, and the Court's own determination in the exercise of its independent judgment, demonstrate that the death penalty is a disproportionate punishment for juveniles. Pp. 10–21.

(1) As in *Atkins*, the objective indicia of national consensus here—the rejection of the juvenile death penalty in the majority of States; the infrequency of its use even where it remains on the books; and the consistency in the trend toward abolition of the practice—provide sufficient evidence that today society views juveniles, in the words *Atkins* used respecting the mentally retarded, as "categorically less culpable than the average criminal," 536 U.S., at 316. The evidence of such consensus is similar, and in some respects parallel, to the evidence in *Atkins*: 30 States prohibit the juvenile death penalty, including 12 that have rejected it altogether and 18 that maintain it but, by express provision or judicial interpretation, exclude juveniles from its reach. Moreover, even in the 20 States without a formal prohibition, the execution of juveniles is infrequent. Although, by contrast to *Atkins*, the rate of change in reducing the incidence of the juvenile death penalty, or in taking specific steps to abolish it, has been less dramatic, the difference between this case and *Atkins* in that respect is counterbalanced by the consistent direction of the change toward abolition. Indeed, the slower pace here may be explained by the simple fact that the impropriety of executing juveniles between 16 and 18 years old gained wide recognition earlier than the impropriety of executing the mentally retarded. Pp. 10–13.

(2) Rejection of the imposition of the death penalty on juvenile offenders under 18 is required by the Eighth Amendment. Capital punishment must be limited to those offenders who commit "a narrow category of the most serious crimes" and whose extreme culpability makes them "the most deserving of execution." *Atkins*, 536 U.S. at 319. Three general differences between juveniles under 18 and adults demonstrate that juvenile offenders cannot with reliability be classified among the worst offenders. Juveniles' susceptibility to immature and irresponsible behavior means "their irresponsible conduct is not as morally reprehensible as that of an adult." *Thompson* v. *Oklahoma*, 487 U.S. 815, 835. Their own vulnerability and comparative lack of control over their immediate surroundings mean juveniles have a greater claim than adults to be forgiven for failing to escape negative influences in their whole environment. See *Stanford*, *supra*, at 395. The reality that juveniles still struggle to define their identity means it is less supportable to conclude that even a heinous crime committed by a juvenile is evidence of irretrievably depraved character. The *Thompson* plurality recognized the import of these characteristics with respect to juveniles under 16. 487 U.S., at 833–838. The same reasoning applies to all juvenile offenders under 18. Once juveniles' diminished culpability is recognized, it is evident that neither of the two penological justifications for the death penalty—retribution and deterrence of capital crimes by prospective offenders, *e.g., Atkins*, 536 U.S., at 319—provides adequate justification for imposing that penalty on juveniles. Although the Court cannot deny or overlook the brutal crimes too many juvenile offenders have committed, it disagrees with petitioner's contention that, given the Court's own insistence on individualized consideration in capital sentencing, it is arbitrary and unnecessary to adopt a categorical rule barring imposition of the death penalty on an offender under 18. An unacceptable likelihood exists that the brutality or cold-blooded nature of any particular crime would overpower mitigating arguments based on youth as a matter of course, even where the juvenile offender's objective immaturity, vulnerability, and lack of true depravity should require a sentence less severe than death. When a juvenile commits a heinous crime, the State can exact forfeiture of some of the most basic liberties, but the State cannot extinguish his life and his potential to attain a mature understanding of his own humanity. While drawing the line at 18 is subject to the objections always raised against categorical rules, that is the point where society draws the line for many purposes between childhood and adulthood and the age at which the line for death eligibility ought to rest. *Stanford* should be deemed no longer controlling on this issue. Pp. 14–21.

(c) The overwhelming weight of international opinion against the juvenile death penalty is not controlling here, but provides respected and significant confirmation for the Court's determination that the penalty is disproportionate punishment for offenders under 18. See, *e.g., Thompson, supra,* at 830–831, and n. 31. The United States is the only country in the world that continues to give official sanction to the juvenile penalty. It does not lessen fidelity to the Constitution or pride in its origins to acknowledge that the express affirmation of certain fundamental rights by other nations and peoples underscores the centrality of those same rights within our own heritage of freedom. Pp. 21–25.

112 S. W. 3d 397, affirmed.

Kennedy, J., delivered the opinion of the Court, in which *Stevens, Souter, Ginsburg,* and Breyer, JJ., joined. *Stevens, J.,* filed a concurring opinion, in which *Ginsburg, J.,* joined. *O'Connor, J.,* filed a dissenting opinion. *Scalia, J.,* filed a dissenting opinion, in which *Rehnquist, C. J.,* and *Thomas, J.,* joined.

QUESTIONS

1. Did the Supreme Court strictly adhere to the concept of *stare decisis* in this case? What factors influenced the judge's decision?

2. Which school or schools of jurisprudence does this decision represent? Write an essay telling your reasons for the schools of jurisprudential thought represented in this opinion.

CASE 2

HEART OF ATLANTA MOTEL, INC. V. UNITED STATES ET AL. APPEAL FROM THE UNITED STATES DISTRICT COURT FOR THE NORTHERN DISTRICT OF GEORGIA.

379 U.S. 241; 85 S. Ct. 348;

Sometimes Supreme Court Justices rule the same way on a case, but for different reasons. In this landmark case, the Court upheld the constitutionality of the Civil Rights Act of 1964. Read the case syllabus and the portion of Justice Douglas' concurring opinion to understand the arguments for upholding the law's constitutionality.

SYLLABUS: Appellant, the owner of a large motel in Atlanta, Georgia, which restricts its clientele to white persons, three-fourths of whom are transient interstate travelers, sued for declaratory relief and to enjoin enforcement of the Civil Rights Act of 1964, contending that the prohibition of racial discrimination in places of public accommodation affecting commerce exceeded Congress' powers under the Commerce Clause and violated other parts of the Constitution. A three-judge District Court upheld the constitutionality of Title II, §§ 201 (a), (b)(1) and (c)(1), the provisions attacked, and on appellees' counterclaim permanently enjoined appellant from refusing to accommodate Negro guests for racial reasons. Held:

1. Title II of the Civil Rights Act of 1964 is a valid exercise of Congress' power under the Commerce Clause as applied to a place of public accommodation serving interstate travelers. Civil Rights Cases, 109 U.S. 3, distinguished. Pp. 249–262.

   a. The interstate movement of persons is "commerce" which concerns more than one State. Pp. 255–256.

b. The protection of interstate commerce is within the regulatory power of Congress under the Commerce Clause whether or not the transportation of persons between States is "commercial." P. 256.

c. Congress' action in removing the disruptive effect which it found racial discrimination has on interstate travel is not invalidated because Congress was also legislating against what it considered to be moral wrongs. P. 257.

d. Congress had power to enact appropriate legislation with regard to a place of public accommodation such as appellant's motel even if it is assumed to be of a purely "local" character, as Congress' power over interstate commerce extends to the regulation of local incidents thereof which might have a substantial and harmful effect upon that commerce. P. 258.

2. The prohibition in Title II of racial discrimination in public accommodations affecting commerce does not violate the Fifth Amendment as being a deprivation of property or liberty without due process of law. Pp. 258–261.

3. Such prohibition does not violate the Thirteenth Amendment as being "involuntary servitude." P. 261.

Justice Douglas' Concurring Opinion (Abridged)

Though I join the Court's opinions, I am somewhat reluctant here, as I was in *Edwards v. California*, 314 U.S. 160, 177, to rest solely on the Commerce Clause. My reluctance is not due to any conviction that Congress lacks power to regulate commerce in the interests of human rights. It is rather my belief that the right of people to be free of state action that discriminates against them because of race, like the "right of persons to move freely from State to State" (*Edwards v. California*, supra, at 177), "occupies a more protected position in our constitutional system than does the movement of cattle, fruit, steel and coal across state lines." Moreover, when we come to the problem of abatement in *Hamm v. City of Rock Hill*, decided this day, the result reached by the Court is for me much more obvious as a protective measure under the Fourteenth Amendment than under the Commerce Clause. For the former deals with the constitutional status of the individual not with the impact on commerce of local activities or vice versa.

Hence I would prefer to rest on the assertion of legislative power contained in § 5 of the Fourteenth Amendment which states: "The Congress shall have power to enforce, by appropriate legislation, the provisions of this article"—a power which the Court concedes was exercised at least in part in this Act.

A decision based on the Fourteenth Amendment would have a more settling effect, making unnecessary litigation over whether a particular restaurant or inn is within the commerce definitions of the Act or whether a particular customer is an interstate traveler. Under my construction, the Act would apply to all customers in all the enumerated places of public accommodation. And that construction would put an end to all obstructionist strategies and finally close one door on a bitter chapter in American history.

My opinion last Term in *Bell v. Maryland*, 378 U.S. 226, 242, makes clear my position that the right to be free of discriminatory treatment (based on race) in places of public accommodation—whether intrastate or interstate—is a right guaranteed against state action by the Fourteenth Amendment and that state enforcement of the kind of trespass laws which Maryland had in that case was state action within the meaning of the Amendment.

II.

I think the Court is correct in concluding that the Act is not founded on the Commerce Clause to the exclusion of the Enforcement Clause of the Fourteenth Amendment.

In determining the reach of an exertion of legislative power, it is customary to read various granted powers together. See *Veazie Bank v. Fenno*, 8 *Wall.* 533, 548-549; *Edye v. Robertson*, 112 U.S. 580, 595–596; *United States v. Gettysburg Electric R. Co.*, 160 U.S. 668, 683. As stated in *McCulloch v. Maryland*, 4 *Wheat.* 316, 421:

"We admit, as all must admit, that the powers of the government are limited, and that its limits are not to be transcended. But we think the sound construction of the constitution must allow to the national legislature that discretion, with respect to the means by which the powers it confers are to be carried into execution, which will enable that body to perform the high duties assigned to it, in the manner most beneficial to the people. Let the end be legitimate, let it be within the scope of the constitution, and all means which are appropriate, which are plainly adapted to that end, which are not prohibited, but consist with the letter and spirit of the constitution, are constitutional."

The "means" used in the present Act are in my view "appropriate" and "plainly adapted" to the end of enforcing Fourteenth Amendment rights as well as protecting interstate commerce.

Section 201 (a) declares in Fourteenth Amendment language the right of equal access:

"All persons shall be entitled to the full and equal enjoyment of the goods, services, facilities, privileges, advantages, and accommodations of any place of public accommodation, as defined in this section, without discrimination or segregation on the ground of race, color, religion, or national origin."

The rights protected are clearly within the purview of our decisions under the Equal Protection Clause of the Fourteenth Amendment.

"State action"—the key to Fourteenth Amendment guarantees—is defined by § 201 (d) as follows:

"Discrimination or segregation by an establishment is supported by State action within the meaning of this title if such discrimination or segregation (1) is carried on under color of any law, statute, ordinance, or regulation; or (2) is carried on under color of any custom or usage required or enforced by officials of the State or political subdivision thereof; or (3) is required by action of the State or political subdivision thereof."

That definition is within our decision of *Shelley v. Kraemer*, 334 U.S. 1, for the "discrimination" in the present cases is "enforced by officials of the State," i. e., by the state judiciary under the trespass laws, as we wrote in *Shelley v. Kraemer*, supra, 19:

"We have no doubt that there has been state action in these cases in the full and complete sense of the phrase. The undisputed facts disclose that petitioners were willing purchasers of properties upon which they desired to establish homes. The owners of the properties were willing sellers; and contracts of sale were accordingly consummated. It is clear that but for the active intervention of the state courts, supported by the full panoply of state power, petitioners would have been free to occupy the properties in question without restraint.

"These are not cases, as has been suggested, in which the States have merely abstained from action, leaving private individuals free to impose such discriminations as they see fit. Rather, these are cases in which the States have made available to such individuals the full coercive power of government to deny to petitioners, on the grounds of race or color, the enjoyment of property rights in premises which petitioners are willing and financially able to acquire and which the grantors are willing to sell. The difference between judicial enforcement and nonenforcement of the restrictive covenants is the difference to petitioners between being denied rights of property available to other members of the community and being accorded full enjoyment of those rights on an equal footing."

Section 202 declares the right of all persons to be free from certain kinds of state action at any public establishment—not just at the previously enumerated places of public accommodation:

"All persons shall be entitled to be free, at any establishment or place, from discrimination or segregation of any kind on the ground of race, color, religion, or national origin, if such discrimination or segregation is or purports to be required by any law, statute, ordinance, regulation, rule, or order of a State or any agency or political subdivision thereof."

Thus the essence of many of the guarantees embodied in the Act are those contained in the Fourteenth Amendment.

The Commerce Clause, to be sure, enters into some of the definitions of "place of public accommodation" in §§ 201 (b) and (c). Thus a "restaurant" is included, § 201 (b)(2), "if . . . it serves or offers to serve interstate travelers or a substantial portion of the food which it serves . . . has moved in commerce." § 201 (c)(2). But any "motel" is included "which provides lodging to transient guests, other than an establishment located within a building which contains not more than five rooms for rent or hire and which is actually occupied by the proprietor of such establishment as his residence." §§ 201 (b)(1) and (c)(1). Providing lodging "to transient guests" is not strictly Commerce Clause talk, for the phrase aptly describes any guest—local or interstate.

Thus some of the definitions of "place of public accommodation" in § 201 (b) are in Commerce Clause language and some are not. Indeed § 201 (b) is explicitly bifurcated. An establishment "which serves the public is a place of public accommodation," says § 201 (b), under either of two conditions: first, "if its operations affect commerce," or second, "if discrimination or segregation by it is supported by State action."

Thus while I agree with the Court that Congress in fashioning the present Act used the Commerce Clause to regulate racial segregation, it also used (and properly so) some of its power under § 5 of the Fourteenth Amendment.

I repeat what I said earlier, that our decision should be based on the Fourteenth Amendment, thereby putting an end to all obstructionist strategies and allowing every person—whatever his race, creed, or color—to patronize all places of public accommodation without discrimination whether he travels interstate or intrastate.

QUESTIONS

1. As we have read, the Constitution limits each branch of government's power through a series of checks and balances. Also, federalism limits how much the federal government can regulate activities within states. The Civil Rights Act of 1964 expanded federal antidiscrimination protections to all public accommodations. The owner of the Heart of Atlanta Motel, Moreton Rolleston Jr., challenged the law's constitutionality arguing the new law required him to admit guests to his motel whom he did not want there. He viewed that federal mandate as limiting his rights to free association and whom his customers were. Congress could only implement such a sweeping change under a clear grant of authority in the Constitution. Which clause of the Constitution did Justice Clark invoke when defending the law's constitutionality and what was his justification?

2. Justice Douglas agreed the law was constitutional, but cited a different section of the Constitution. Which clause did Justice Douglas cite and why did he feel his argument was a stronger one than the Justice Clark's?

CRITICAL **THINKING EXERCISES**

1. You and five strangers are the only survivors of a plane crash on a desert island. While you hope to be rescued, as time goes on it becomes less likely. The six of you have to decide what rules you will live by. The six of you have widely diverging talents and only four of you speak English and none of you speak the obscure dialect the other two speak. What are your concerns when developing laws to live by?

2. You live in a small Arizona town around 1913. Arizona has just become a state and must adapt territorial decisions to evolving state law. Further, technology is changing and the law may not have caught up. Old man Moneygrubber is the richest man in town. He just bought one of those fancy horseless carriages, the first one in town. One night, Rudy Russler, the town ne'er-do-well, cranks up the contraption and takes a ride over to New Mexico. He's caught and brought back for trial. Clearly, this was a theft, but no specific auto theft statute is on the books. The only precedent is stealing a horse, a capital offense. Considering reliance on *stare decisis*, should Rudy hang?

3. You are a Supreme Court Justice in the future. Several states have completely legalized marijuana despite a federal law, the Controlled Substances Act, ruling that marijuana is a controlled substance. You feel that the states are within their rights to legalize marijuana and the states are bringing a federal lawsuit to have the section of the Controlled Substances Act dealing with marijuana declared unconstitutional. You must convince four fellow justices of your position in order for the states to win. The fellow justices most likely to side with you are Natalie Natural, a natural law proponent; Cathy Critter, a devotee of the Fem-Crit philosophy; Justice Spock of the analytic school; and Karl Marx and Emile Durkheim, who are both living embodiments of their namesakes. Outline what arguments you would use to persuade them to side with you in this decision.

4. You are a police officer investigating a fatal traffic accident. A driver of a car known to have problems with sticking accelerators hit another car at high speed but was not injured himself. What factors will you investigate to determine whether the driver should be charged criminally? Similarly, once all possible criminal charges are adjudicated, what factors will the victim's family assess when mulling a civil lawsuit?

5. Match each crime description to the type of crime:

Crime Description	Type of Crime
A. Refusing to put money in a parking meter during operating hours.	Felony
B. Stealing money from a parking meter.	Summary Offense
C. Using a pipe cutter to cut the head off a parking meter and attempting to pummel a meter maid with it.	Misdemeanor

6. Federal law requires those accused of a crime to have right to counsel, right to a jury trial, and freedom from cruel and unusual punishments, but most criminal trials occur in state courts. Can state courts deny accused criminals these rights? What recourse would a person have if he felt he was denied these basic rights?

7. A small religious sect carries out a terrorist attack on American soil. In response, Congress votes, by just one vote in each house, to imprison all members of the sect in the country indefinitely without trial. What can the president do if he thinks this is a bad law? If the president signs it, what issues can courts expect to see in challenges to the law's constitutionality?

8. Same-sex marriage advocates succeed in amending the Constitution to allow same-sex marriage in the United States. Under this scenario, could states still only recognize opposite-sex marriage?

9. When the 21st Amendment to the Constitution was enacted repealing prohibition, states were given the right to regulate alcohol sales within their borders as an exercise of their police power. But several lawsuits have challenged state practices that essentially make it impossible to purchase some types of alcohol within their borders as an attack on interstate commerce. If you had to make the case for free interstate movement of alcoholic beverages how would you

balance federal government rights under the Commerce Clause with states' rights under their police power?

10. You represent a client accused of burglary. He has posted bail and you accompany him to his preliminary hearing. The arresting officer presents no evidence placing your client at the scene of the crime. What do you do and why?

11. Clearly, an accused may challenge the constitutionality of a law, but what about someone who is accused of violating a regulation written by an executive agency? What must a person prove to have a regulation invalidated?

PORTFOLIO **BUILDING**

EXERCISE 1

Throughout the textbook, you will find several extended exercises designed to help you apply the information you are learning. The scenarios may sound familiar as they are based on events widely reported in the media. You can find a complete list of media sources for the real-life events that form the basis of the extended exercises on the textbook's companion website at http://www.peasonhighered.com/davenport. You will also find some of the underlying court documents reproduced there and in some of the exercises. Similar to the "You Make the Call" exercises presented elsewhere in the textbook, the material is designed to present you with common problems encountered in the criminal justice system by victims, defendants, law enforcement officials, and others and demonstrate the relevance the material has to the day-to-day operation of the criminal justice system.

Scenario: A twenty-seven-year-old female college student, who works as an exotic dancer, is hired to perform at an off-campus party by members of a neighboring university's sports team. The dancer later reported to the police that she had been sexually assaulted by three of the team members at some time during the evening. The female is black, and the accused members of the team are white. Almost immediately, the press descends on the college town and the tabloids print lurid headlines. Not long after, the local district attorney announces that he had no doubt that the dancer was raped and begins a long investigation into the matter. Based on what you have learned so far in this course, answer the following questions about the case:

1. You work as a law clerk for the attorney hired to represent one of the team players. You and she will be meeting with the client to explain what will likely occur if he is charged. What will the two of you tell the client about the process he is about to experience?

EXERCISE 2

As you complete each chapter in your textbook, you will have an opportunity to apply what you have learned in a very practical way. We call this Portfolio Building. By the time you have completed the course and the exercises suggested, you will have a comprehensive and robust collection of materials you can present to a potential employer to show your mastery of the material and demonstrate that you have what it takes to become a valuable member of the legal team.

For your initial portfolio project, you will learn to "brief" cases. Later, you will learn to prepare a legal memorandum applying the cases you have researched and briefed to a set of facts.

The Case Brief

One of the most essential skills for any criminal justice professional is the ability to read and understand case opinions. Recall that the Common Law relies on case precedent. You will be called upon to identify precedents in your jurisdiction. That means you will have to research the case law and summarize the decisions that are relevant precedent. But you cannot simply find the cases, copy them, and dump them on your supervisor's desk. Instead, you will often be asked to prepare a brief of the relevant cases.

A case brief should be just that—brief. You should be able to prepare a one- or two-page brief for all but the most complicated cases. Your case brief should be organized like this:

- The name of the case with the citation
- A summary of the most important and relevant facts
- The procedural history of the case
- The issue or issues before the court
- The court's holding (its decision)
- The court's reasoning (its rationale)

Fortunately, many court opinions are organized in much this way, making your task easier than it might first seem. With time, you should be able to locate, read, and brief cases quickly and efficiently.

Let's take a look at an example, using a real case. First, go to the companion website and read the complete Supreme Court case. Then read the case brief below to see how a brief should look.

Case: *Maryland v. Shatzer,* 559 U.S. ___ (2010)

Facts: While Michael Shatzer, Sr., was incarcerated at the Maryland Correctional Institute–Hagerstown, a detective from the Hagerstown Police Department attempted to interview Shatzer about allegations that he had sexually abused his three-year-old son. The detective read Shatzer his *Miranda* rights and Shatzer said he didn't want to answer questions without an attorney present. The detective ended the interview and Shatzer was released back into the general prison population.

Two years and six months later, another detective attempted to interview Shatzer about the same allegations. Shatzer waived his *Miranda* rights and agreed to take a polygraph test. When Shatzer was asked whether he demanded his son perform oral sex on him, he denied the charge. Shatzer was told he failed the test and then broke down in tears, telling the detective, "I didn't force him, I didn't force him."

Shatzer was convicted of child sexual abuse after his statement was admitted over his attorney's protest that the confession violated his *Miranda* rights because he had initially refused to talk to investigators without an attorney.

Procedural History: Shatzer appealed the denial of his motion to suppress the confession to the Court of Appeals of Maryland. That court ruled that the confession should have been suppressed because Shatzer's initial request for an attorney remained valid. Maryland appealed the decision to the U.S. Supreme Court, which granted *certiorari.*

Issue: If a suspect has been released from custody, does his refusal to speak to police without an attorney present last indefinitely?

Holding: No. Once a suspect has been released from custody and has resumed his life, his invocation of the right to the presence of an attorney terminates after a reasonable period. That time frame is fourteen days.

Reasoning: Suspects who have been released from custody for at least fourteen days are no longer feeling badgered or coerced if a police officer attempts to speak with them again. In this case, more than two years had passed. The court also reasoned that releasing an inmate back into the general prison population after questioning him on an alleged criminal act different from the one for which he was incarcerated already was the equivalent of releasing a suspect from custody after initially questioning him. Therefore, the fourteen-day rule applied.

Now, read the other cases provided on the companion website and create case briefs for your portfolio.

EXERCISE 3

Chances are, if you are taking this course, you aspire to a career in the legal field. This is a good time to begin thinking about your future career. One of the best sources of information on legal careers is the U.S. Department of Labor. You can access the latest *Occupational Outlook Handbook* at http://www.bls.gov/OCO/. Do so now and see what the requirements and prospects are for your chosen profession. Use the information to guide you as you prepare your portfolio.

FOR FURTHER READING

1. Hamilton, J., Madison, J., and Jay, J. *The Federalist Papers.* For the student who wants to develop an understanding of the Constitution as the founding fathers saw it, this classic work is essential reading. Written by Alexander Hamilton, James Madison, and John Jay, the work was originally circulated to argue for the ratification of the Constitution.

2. Young, A. (ed.) (1976). *The American Revolution: Explorations in the History of American Radicalism.* Dekalb, IL: Northern Illinois University Press. This collection of essays by historians explores the ideologies of the men who created the American Revolution.

3. DeTocqueville, A. (1969). *Democracy in America* (rev. ed.). New York: Harper Collins. This classic

study of what makes American democracy unique was first published in the 1800s by a Frenchman who traveled extensively through the new United States. His observations on American democracy are regarded as some of the most insightful ever made.

4. Maier, P. (1997). *American Scripture.* New York: Alfred A. Knopf. This work analyzes the Declaration of Independence and the attitudes that shaped its framers' thoughts.

5. Burger, W. (1995). *It Is So Ordered: A Constitution Unfolds.* New York: William Morrow. Written by former chief justice of the U.S. Supreme Court Warren E. Burger, this book analyzes some of the most important cases to have been decided by the Supreme Court in layperson's terms.

Chapter **two**
WHAT IS A CRIME?

Laws too gentle are seldom obeyed; too severe, seldom executed.

Benjamin Franklin, *Poor Richard's Almanac*

Introduction and Historical Background
What Is a Crime?

A **crime** is a wrong against society or the public interest. It is typically punishable by imprisonment or death and sometimes an additional fine. Generally speaking, criminal law is designed to protect and vindicate public rights. Criminal law seeks to protect society as a whole from the aberrant (as defined by the law) behavior of some members of that society.

Before prosecuting anyone for a crime, the first work of the state is to establish that a crime has been committed. To do so, the state relies on a concept called **corpus delicti,** or the "body of the crime." It is tempting to take this to mean the body of the fallen victim lying outlined in tape on the floor of a crime scene, but *corpus delicti* means something more complex. It requires two things: first, a result or **harm** and second, harm resulting from a criminal act. For example, since we began with a body, imagine an investigator finding a body on the sidewalk in front of a high-rise apartment building, as happened in Harrisburg, Pennsylvania on February 25, 2006. The woman, later identified as twenty-three-year-old Rachel Kozlusky, was dressed in underwear and a sweater and had massive injuries indicating a fall from a great height. Above her, a hole in the skylight of a portico indicated a fall, likely from one of the balconies or windows overhead. The

CHAPTER OBJECTIVES

After studying this chapter, you should be able to:

- Explain what makes an act or omission a crime
- Explain *corpus delicti*
- Explain the role of confessions in crime
- Explain *mens rea*
- List and explain the different types of liability
- Explain how to prove *mens rea*
- List and explain the different types of intent
- Explain *actus reus*
- Explain possession
- Explain omission
- Explain harm
- Explain causation
- Explain conspiracy
- Explain the Uniform Crime Reporting Program
- Explain the difference between direct and circumstantial evidence

Crime
A wrong against society or the public interest.

Corpus delicti
Literally, the body of the crime.

Harm
Injury or damage.

investigator had a dead body and harm aplenty, but no crime. *Corpus delicti* requires a second element: the harm must result from someone's criminal act. The investigator needed evidence to indicate that the woman's fall was more than an accident.

In this case, the state quickly found that evidence in an apartment on the 23rd floor of the building, from which Rachel Kozlusky's boyfriend, Kevin Eckenrode, exited and took the elevator down, "distraught and extremely inebriated." The boyfriend later told authorities that he had taken Kozlusky by the wrists and dangled her over the balcony as a game, and accidentally let go. The incident followed a bout of heavy drinking and partying, ostensibly to celebrate their engagement.

Accident or crime? The state had to establish *corpus delicti.* "Obviously it's an unusual scenario," Dauphin County District Attorney Ed Marsico Jr. told the press shortly after the accident. "Even if [Eckenrode's] version is true, to be holding someone out on a 23rd-story window is beyond ridiculous. It's as reckless an act as I can imagine, if not malicious."[1] The man's actions were not mere accident; they were at the very least criminally reckless. The state had *corpus delicti,* and merely had to move on to prove which crime had occurred—murder or manslaughter. Eckenrode was eventually found guilty of involuntary manslaughter and sentenced to 11 1/2 to 23 months in the county prison after a jury rejected third-degree murder charges. His attorney had argued the whole thing was an unfortunate accident.[2]

Before prosecuting any crime, the state usually must show *corpus delicti* beyond a reasonable doubt. The state does not have to have a suspect or precise explanation of the crime, but it must establish that a crime has taken place. Sometimes, the suspects and circumstances strongly suggest a crime, but prosecution is impossible because *corpus delicti* cannot be confirmed. This would apply to cases for which truly accidental explanations are feasible. Say, for example, that in the Kozlusky case, the boyfriend claimed his girlfriend climbed out on the ledge to rescue their cat. When she began to fall, he grabbed her arms, but lost his grip. In the absence of further evidence, the state might not have been able to establish that a crime had been committed.

Corpus delicti prevents a confession of a crime, unaccompanied by other evidence of either the crime or tying the confessor to the crime, to be used to convict the confessor of the crime he alleges to have committed. The state cannot convict someone of a crime if it cannot show that the crime took place or that the confessor was tied somehow to the criminal act. Otherwise, any person willing to confess could be convicted.

Why would anyone confess to a crime they did not commit? That's a question we'll leave to the psychology experts. However, police officers and others who work in the criminal justice system are familiar with an odd but fairly common occurrence—that of the false confession uttered by someone completely unconnected with the crime being investigated. That's one reason officials often withhold a crucial piece of evidence from the media and the public—a piece of evidence that the real perpetrator would be aware of, but of which a bogus confessor would have no knowledge.

Corpus delicti is often confused with the elements of a crime, which are examined below. While similar, the elements of a crime establish the precise nature

---

I don't think there was any rush to judgment.

Linda Fairstein, best-selling author and former prosecutor on her role in the Central Park Jogger confessions she oversaw

of the crime. *Corpus delicti* merely establishes beyond a reasonable doubt that a crime has taken place. In the Eckenrode case, the body and Eckenrode's confession (which placed him at the scene and showed he was involved in the incident that led to the harm) established the crime, but the elements would determine more specifically whether he should be charged with manslaughter, voluntary or involuntary, or murder.

Sometimes *corpus delicti* determines where a case is tried. In cases where a crime crosses territorial boundaries, the courts will often try the case where the *corpus delicti* was found.

Federal courts and some state courts have moved away from applying *corpus delicti* because some crimes that do not necessarily produce physical evidence, such as conspiracy and fraud, do not fit the requirements well.

YOU MAKE THE CALL

The Duke Rape Case: Was A Crime Committed?

On Saturday night March 13, 2006, the Duke University Lacrosse team held a party. For entertainment, the team had booked a stripper, an African-American student from nearby North Carolina Central University. By the end of the evening, the stripper told police that several Duke team members cornered her in a bathroom, sexually assaulted her, and raped her.

The accusations sent shock waves through the Durham, North Carolina community. The image of privileged white athletes raping a struggling African-American student struck raw nerves, highlighted race and class divisions, politicizing what was at heart a criminal investigation. Newspapers criticized the University for not responding fast enough, insinuating that had the alleged victim been white and the alleged perpetrators black, the school's reaction would have been different. School apologists claimed the university did not know the stripper's race until March 24, eleven days after the incident.[3]

Community tensions were heightened when police alleged that one of the players had written in an e-mail that he wanted to "invite strippers to his dorm room, kill them, and skin them."[4] But the players denied that any sexual activity took place at the party.

The situation was further complicated when District Attorney Richard Nifong chose to handle the case himself instead of delegating it to a subordinate. Many observers felt Nifong wanted to make the case an issue in his November 2006 re-election campaign.

Race, class, sex, politics under intense media scrutiny, the Duke rape case seemed to have it all. Throughout the book, different aspects of the case will be reviewed to show what went right and what went wrong in the pursuit of justice. But the first question is: Was a crime committed here? Based on what you know from this section can you answer that question, or do you think more investigation is needed?

*actus
reus,
mens rea,
harm*

Elements of a Crime

The three main elements of a crime are a wrongful action, or **actus reus,** caused by a wrongful mind, **mens rea,** resulting in damage or harm. Some scholars include **causation,** the requirement that the act must cause the harm, as a separate element. Others substitute concurrence, or the coexistence of *actus reus* and *mens rea,* for causation. Still others have suggested that the **principle of legality,** which says that an action is not a crime unless it is prohibited by law and assigned a punishment by the state, is a separate element.

To successfully prosecute most crimes, a prosecutor usually must prove all the elements of the crime: *mens rea, actus reus,* and resultant harm. There are classes of crime that do not require all three elements, which we will examine below, but most crimes require those three elements.

Mens Rea

Mens rea describes a person's intent while performing a criminal act, and is critical to establishing the nature and degree of a crime. Take the case of a person fatally shooting someone in the chest. If the person is a child playing with a gun, that is not a crime. The child did not intend to harm anyone. If someone picks up a gun, believing it is unloaded, and accidentally fires it, hitting someone in the chest, that is usually not a crime. If a person awakened by an intruder in her room takes a gun from the nightstand in the dark and fires, the action and resulting harm are, again, the same, but the shooter's intent, stopping the intruder, would likely protect the shooter against criminal charges. A person who shoots a convenience store clerk and then empties the cash register, on the other hand, will likely face murder charges, because the shooter fired with the intent to kill.

Since a person's state of mind is not visible, *mens rea* is generally deduced from surrounding circumstances. It is up to the jury or a judge if the defendant elects to be tried without a jury to decide whether the prosecution has proven the element of *mens rea.*

Strict Liability

For some crimes, intent, or *mens rea,* is irrelevant. **Strict liability** crimes require only a wrongful act to occur. Speeding and other traffic violations are an example of strict liability violations—it doesn't matter what is going through the driver's mind or whether the driver knows the speed limit. The only thing that matters is the car's speed. Strict liability imposes a duty on a person, such as a speed limit, and exacts penalties from those who do not uphold that duty, regardless of their intentions.

Generally, crimes **mala prohibita** are strict liability, while **mala in se** crimes require intent. (See Chapter 1 for more on these.)

Vicarious Liability

Another set of crimes that do not require *mens rea* are **vicarious liability** violations in which one person is held responsible for someone else's actions. Under **corporate liability,** for example, employers may be charged with a crime

---

Actus reus
A wrongful action.

Mens rea
A wrongful mind.

Causation
The requirement that the act must cause the harm.

Principle of legality
The theory that an action is not a crime unless it is prohibited by law and assigned a punishment by the state.

It may be true that the law cannot make a man love me, but it can keep him from lynching me, and I think that's pretty important.

Martin Luther King, Jr. (1962)

Strict liability
The legal responsibility for damage or injury, even if you are not at fault or negligent.

Mala prohibita
According to Blackstone, a category of crimes that are crimes because society has decided they are crimes.

Mala in se
According to Blackstone, a category of crimes that are bad in and of themselves.

Men are not hanged for stealing horses, but that horses may not be stolen.

1st Marquess of Halifax (1750)

Vicarious liability
Where one person is held responsible for someone else's actions.

Corporate liability
The legal concept that allows employers to be charged with a crime resulting from their employees' actions while carrying out corporate business.

because of the actions of employees who are carrying out their business. Corporate liability is based on the legal principle of "**respondeat superior,**" or "let the superior reply" borrowed from civil law. The employer does not have to be aware of the employee's actions to be held criminally liable; the liability comes from the employment relationship and the control that it gives the employer, or superior, over the employee.

Respondeat superior
Literally, "let the superior respond," a term indicating liability derived from an agent relationship between the superior and the person committing the crime.

HISTORICAL HIGHLIGHT

Nick Leeson and Barings Bank

Nick Leeson had a problem in early 1995—the Singapore-based investment banker had lost millions of his employer's money in bad trades. So far he had successfully hidden the losses from Barings Bank's administrators. It was only temporary, he thought. He would guess right on one big trade and return all the funds. But when the Japanese stock market tanked, Leeson's hope of making amends went down with it.[5]

Leeson's fall took Barings, a firm that had been in business for 230 years, with him. Barings was bailed out by the Dutch firm ING, which bought Barings for one pound sterling. Although Leeson's guilt was clear,

the company's liability soon came into question. Had the company supervised Leeson closely enough? The Singapore stock exchange was so alarmed by his trades that it hired retired policemen to monitor Barings' trades and end-of-day position. When the stock exchange approached Barings with their concerns, Barings told them the bank had enough in reserve to cover any anticipated shortfall. But Barings was working from Leeson's bogus figures. Some critics argue Barings did not do enough to protect investor's rights. With ING coming to the rescue, Barings eluded some of the more difficult questions. But what should their liability have been?

Another type of vicarious liability is **parental liability,** which holds parents, or adults **in loco parentis,** responsible for their minor children's actions.

Parental liability
The responsibility parents have for the actions of their minor children.

In loco parentis
Acting in the role of parents.

HISTORICAL HIGHLIGHT

Responsibility Follows the Bullet: The Kayla Rolland Murder

Kayla Rolland didn't want to go to school on February 29, 2000. The six-year-old didn't explain why she was kicking and screaming that morning. By that afternoon, her mother was piecing together why Kayla fought so violently.

The day before a boy in her class had tried to kiss her. She slapped him and the two got into an argument. The boy had a history of violent behavior, and Kayla must have sensed the argument wasn't over.

While Kayla was trying to avoid school, the boy was packing his uncle's gun in his backpack. When the

two got to school, the day began normally. But their teacher had to escort two other students to another class. In the few minutes the teacher was gone, the boy pulled the gun and shot Kayla dead.

The courts were now faced with the question of how to punish a six-year-old for an adult crime. The boy was taken from his family and became a ward of the state. The uncle and two other family members were charged on weapon's charges for their negligence in allowing the young boy access to the weapon. Although neither the uncle nor the two other relatives fired the gun, they went to jail for the girl's shooting.[6]

Instead of the criminal offender's intent, which forms the basis of strict liability, vicarious liability generally relies on the standard of what the superior in the relationship, parents or employers, allow or permit the person under their control to do.

Proving *Mens Rea*

Mens rea is the thorniest part of any criminal case because it cannot be measured or proven, but only inferred from circumstances. The convenience store robber cited above may have acted out of fear, may have fired unintentionally, may have felt angry or hostile, or may have made a calculated, cold-blooded decision to terminate a potential witness. Even with a surveillance tape, none of those mental states would be easy to discern. Still, establishing *mens rea* is critical to strict liability cases, which also tend to be the most severe. Model Penal Code § 2.02 defines four levels of intent, or *mens rea*, which determine the **degree** of a crime.

"Purposely" committed crimes are crimes committed with the intent to accomplish a particular result. Purposeful acts, also frequently called wanton or willful acts, are designated **first degree,** and carry the highest penalties. For instance, if a person hires a "hit man" to kill another person, both the person hiring the hit man and the hit man clearly intend to kill the victim. If the hit man is successful, they would both be guilty of first-degree murder.

Next serious are crimes committed "knowingly," which the state defines as knowing a specific conduct will almost certainly bring about a particular result, but without necessarily intending that result. These crimes are **second degree.** For example, the owner of a hunting cabin rigs a gun to shoot in the direction of the front door if someone opens it. A person lost in a snowstorm goes to the cabin seeking shelter, opens the door, and is shot. The cabin owner wanted to wound burglars, not necessarily desperate hikers. But he knew the gun would go off no matter who came in the door.

Following that are crimes committed "recklessly," meaning with knowledge that there is a substantial and unjustifiable risk that the conduct might cause a particular result. Such crimes are **third degree** offenses. The fugitive who leads police on a high-speed chase is behaving recklessly because his driving creates a substantial and unjustifiable risk that others may be harmed.

Finally, crimes committed "negligently" are **fourth-degree** offenses. Negligence means thoughtlessly or carelessly creating a significant unjustifiable risk of harm without realizing the risk has been created, or without intending to create it. For example, someone who stores explosives on his property, but does not post a "No Smoking" sign near them may be negligent if a smoker unknowingly tosses an unextinguished butt into the storage area.

Establishing *mens rea* in second, third, and fourth-degree crimes is particularly challenging because it is based on the notion of "unjustifiable" risk, a term which means something different to every person. One person might not even consider it a risk to go ten miles over the speed limit with a baby in the car, while others might consider that unacceptable. The state tries to define "justifiable" by weighing what the offender's conscious intentions were at the time of the crime, or her **subjective intent,** against what a reasonable person should have known or thought at the time of the event, the legal standard of **objective intent.** It is clear, for example, that a reasonable person would understand that driving 110 miles per hour with a baby in the car puts the child at serious risk of harm; that objective

Degree
A measure of the severity of a crime with first-degree being the most severe.

First-degree offenses
Under the Model Penal Code, crimes that are committed willfully.

Second-degree offenses
Under the Model Penal Code, crimes that are committed knowingly.

Third-degree offenses
Under the Model Penal Code, crimes that are committed recklessly.

Fourth-degree offenses
Under the Model Penal Code, crimes that are committed negligently.

Subjective intent
The offender's conscious intentions at the time of the crime.

Objective intent
What a reasonable person should have known or thought at the time of the event.

standard is imposed on the offender whether the offender had the sense to perceive the risk or not.

The law also distinguishes *mens rea* based on the particular consequences intended by a person committing a crime. If a person does something with intent to cause a specific criminal result, then the person possessed **specific intent.** If a person intended an action only, and not the results of the action, that person possessed **general intent.** For example, say a person sets fire to a building merely intending to burn it down. That person has specific intent to commit arson. If people die as a result of the fire, the state might assign general intent for their deaths to the arsonist. Of course, if the individual set the fire with the specific intent to kill someone inside the building, and succeeds, the crime would be first-degree murder and an example of specific intent. Crimes committed with general intent are generally third or fourth-degree offenses. These classifications overlap with degrees of crime; first-degree crimes are crimes of specific intent, second-degree crimes may be one or the other, and third and fourth are crimes of general intent.

Sometimes to prove specific intent, the state must show that the offender knew a certain fact or understood the law being broken. That requirement is known as **scienter.** For certain crimes, scienter is required. Drug possession is an example of a crime requiring scienter. If a drug runner on the lam slips a stash of drugs into the knapsack of a hapless tourist, the tourist is not guilty of drug possession. Receiving stolen property also requires scienter; the person receiving the goods has to know they're stolen to be guilty of the crime. But that knowledge does not have to be direct—it can be inferred from the circumstances. For example, if you were to purchase a television from a national retailer, and it turned out the set was part of a lot of televisions stolen from a competitor, you would most likely not be aware of that underlying fact—there would be no scienter. On the other hand, if you bought the television in a back alley for $35, scienter probably would be present—since you know new televisions usually are not sold at such a deep discount and certainly not in a dark alley at night. But what if the set was bought at an online auction site like EBay? That would be a murkier matter.

A small group of crimes include a scienter requirement that the people committing them know their actions are illegal. Such laws are the exception that make the oft quoted rule, "Ignorance of the law is no excuse"—in certain, very specialized cases, it is. Scienter requirements protect people from truly innocent errors.

Another type of intent is **transferred intent,** in which a person tries to harm one person and as a result harms someone else. For example, a person might shoot with intent to murder one person and wind up inadvertently killing another. In such cases, the shooter's intention toward the intended victim transfers to the bystander. The shooter did not intend to murder the bystander, but may be charged with murder nonetheless, because the shooter's intentions toward his intended victim transfer to his actual victim.

Some actions are so likely to cause a specific result, the law treats that result as intended whether the person meant to cause it or not. This is known as **constructive intent.** Shooting someone in the chest, for example, is so likely fatal that a person might be charged with murder even if it could be shown that the shooter only meant to injure the victim.

Specific intent
The type of intent where the person commits an act designed to cause a specific criminal result.

General intent
The type of intent where the person intended an action only, and not the results of the action.

Scienter
A necessary element to prove in some crimes where the offender knew a certain fact or understood the law being broken.

Transferred intent
The type of intent where a person tries to harm one person and as a result harms someone else.

Constructive intent
The concept that some actions are so likely to cause a specific result, the law treats that result as intended whether the person meant to cause it or not.

Motive

Motive
The reason a person commits a crime.

Motive is the reason a person commits a crime. *Mens rea* is the intent; motive is the reason behind that intent. For example, a woman who kills her husband's lover has the intent of committing murder. Her motives are jealousy and revenge. Motive is not an element of a crime and therefore does not have to be proven to successfully prosecute a crime, but it often influences the severity of the punishment levied. For example, the true motive behind a crime such as serial killing may not even be clear to the perpetrator, but the killer can be prosecuted regardless. The *mens rea* of a serial killer, however, is an element of the crime: to establish it the prosecution need only show that the killer intended to kill the victims.

Actus Reus

Actus reus is the action that causes the harm. *Actus reus* must be voluntary. It must also be active. Thoughts, for example, cannot be proven and cannot, by themselves, do harm. They cannot be considered a crime until they are acted on. Finally, it must be "wrong," or illegal. Shooting guns, for example, is not a crime. Firing a gun at a target range or in military training does not constitute an *actus reus*. Shooting one in a shopping mall, however, is an *actus reus*.

Voluntary Acts

Voluntary acts
The *actus reus* element of a crime. Crimes must be voluntary acts.

A crime must be a **voluntary act.** Reflex actions, or actions committed under coercion or while unconscious, are generally not crimes. Mere accidents are generally not criminal acts. There are exceptions, however, when people commit involuntary harm, as a result of voluntary decisions. For example, people who drive drunk are held criminally liable for their actions, even though the alcohol impairs their ability to control their actions. A person who suffers seizures and chooses to drive anyway may be similarly held accountable for harm resulting from accidents.

Crimes may be committed involuntarily. For instance, someone encased in a remotely controlled bomb is told to rob a bank or be blown up. Defendants may assert a "duress defense" in these circumstances. (See Chapter 10, Common Law Defenses—*You Make the Call: Criminal or Victim: The Strange Case of Brian Wells.*) It is not always so clear whether a person commits a crime voluntarily. For example, a prostitute forced to exchange sex for money or starve can be said to be under duress, but no single person is forcing her to be a prostitute. But what if she knows her pimp will beat her if she doesn't produce enough money? Is she then committing the crime involuntarily? Of course, the very duress that results in the crime often inhibits testimony against the pimp or person forcing the person to commit the crime.

YOU MAKE THE CALL

Sleep Driving

When Washington, DC police arrived at the scene of an accident in the early morning hours one May day in 2006, they discovered Representative Patrick Kennedy (D-R.I.) at the wheel. The politician claimed he had gone home the evening before and taken prescription medications, including a sleep aid.[7] He claimed to have no memory of getting in his car, although he vaguely reported that he thought he had to get back to the Capitol for an important vote. Later, the Food and Drug Administration issued a warning about certain sleep drugs, which apparently can cause something the FDA dubbed "Sleep-Driving." Victims of the syndrome may get in their automobiles and drive off, all with no awareness that they are doing so. They may even make phone calls and prepare meals while technically asleep.[8]

Assuming a defendant can show he or she was taking one of the sleep medications for which the FDA requires a warning label, what would you argue if the defendant is charged with a crime such as vehicular homicide? What element of a crime would you argue was missing?

Personal status as an act: One's personal status, like one's thoughts, is not an action and generally cannot constitute a crime. This has not always been the case, however. In the past laws prescribed severe criminal penalties for homosexuality, alcoholism, witchcraft, and homelessness. While it may not be a crime, for example, to be homeless, there remain some remnants of status crimes on the books. For example, vagrancy and loitering laws may be used to target the homeless and get them off the streets. But it is not the status as "homeless" that constitutes an element of the crime. Rather, it is an act—such as remaining on a public park bench past the park's stated closing time—that forms the basis of the crime.

Most status crimes have disappeared from the American legal landscape. One notable exception remains—that of the illegal immigrant. He or she committed a crime by entering the country illegally and his or her presence within our borders is also regarded as a criminal act by some. Thus, being an illegal immigrant (status) means that one is also committing a crime (overstaying a visa, or being illegally present in the country).

Possession

Possession is dominion or control over property, although it can be a passive act of failing to get rid of something one shouldn't have. **Actual possession** means physically having the item on one's person, directly under physical control, or within reach. Most jurisdictions divide actual possession into **knowing possession,** which implies that a person possessed and held onto the item on purpose, and **mere possession,** which means the person possesses the item unawares. If a house guest hides cocaine in a spare bedroom, the homeowner might be guilty of mere possession. If the homeowner learns of the illegal items in the house and fails to remove them, the homeowner is guilty of knowing possession or criminal possession. In most jurisdictions, criminal possession implies knowledge of the presence of an illegal item long enough to get rid of it.

Constructive possession extends liability to people who have some control over an item without possessing it. For example, a person may be convicted for possession of drugs found in the trunk of the person's car, or in the person's attic, even though it is never on the defendant's person. A person may be guilty of possession of legal as well as illegal items. In the case of legal items, criminal intention must be shown. For example, a person carrying a box cutter into an airport is

Personal status as an act
Generally current laws do not view personal status as an act, but historically personal status has been seen as a criminal act.

Possession
Dominion or control over property.

Actual possession
Physically having the item on one's person, directly under physical control, or within reach.

Knowing possession
The condition existing when a person possesses and holds onto an item intentionally.

Mere possession
The condition occurring when a person possesses an item unawares.

Constructive possession
The concept that extends liability to people who have some control over an item without possessing it.

carrying something legal. If that person is a postal worker who carries the box cutter routinely, merely possessing it is not a criminal act. If the person intended to do harm with them, however, the person is guilty of criminal possession.

Omission

Omission
The failure to perform a duty.

Duty
An obligation to perform an action.

Duty by statute
A duty imposed by law.

Duty by contract
A duty voluntarily assumed through an agreement.

Sometimes a failure to act is a crime known as an **omission.** An omission can occur only when someone has a **duty** or obligation to do something, which can arise by several means. The law may impose a **duty by statute,** an obligation to perform certain acts imposed by the state. The legal requirement for drivers to stay after an accident and render aid is a common statutory duty. Many states have laws requiring people to report child abuse or other crimes. Filing and paying taxes are duties imposed by statue. Failure to do so is a criminal omission.

Contracts are another means of imposing a duty. A **duty by contract** would require a lifeguard to save a drowning swimmer. A doctor working in a hospital emergency room is legally required to act to save patients; standing by while a patient died could be criminal homicide. On the other hand, a doctor who happens on a crime scene and does not help the victim probably would not be liable for either a crime or a civil wrong. He or she has no duty to render assistance.[9] The exception would be in states that have "good Samaritan" laws that require doctors or others with medical training to render assistance if they see it is needed.

Duty by relationship
A duty expected of certain people, such as parents, by virtue of their connection with the person owed the duty, such as the parents' children.

Duty by volunteering
A duty freely assumed.

Sometimes a duty exists just by virtue of someone's relationship to another. A **duty by relationship** imposes on parents a duty to care for their children. For example, a parent who leaves a child out by the swimming pool unsupervised might be held criminally liable if the child drowns. No contract or specific law is required; the duty arises out of the relationship itself.

People can also assume a legal duty simply by saying they will perform an action. This is known as **duty by volunteering.** A person who offers to watch the neighbor's children assumes the duty of their care, and the liabilities that go along with it. If a group of people is witnessing someone struggling in the water, and one person offers to swim out and save the victim, that person is legally obligated to follow through. If the rescuer decides to instead sit back and watch the victim drown, that person might be held criminally liable, and since his assumption of that duty prevented others from helping.

Duty to render aid to persons placed in peril
A duty assumed when one individual endangers another.

People also assume a **duty to render aid persons they place in peril.** For example, an intoxicated individual who causes an automobile accident cannot walk away without making reasonable efforts to aid those injured by her actions—she must take reasonable steps to mitigate the harm she has caused. Similarly, a person who accidentally started a fire has an obligation to warn others in the building to leave and call the fire department.

Harm

Most crimes result in harm. The seriousness of the harm usually dictates the severity of the punishment. Crime results in five categories of harm: crimes against life, including murder, kidnapping, and battery; crimes against habitation, which include burglary and arson; crimes against property, including theft; crimes against the public order, such as traffic violations; and crimes against public morality, such as prostitution and drug use.

Certain actions are criminal even though they don't harm anyone. Attempted crimes can be prosecuted even though the person never committed the harmful act. For example, if a group of Internet hackers breaks into a bank website and tries to download information, but is caught in the act, the perpetrators will be charged with attempted theft as well as numerous computer law violations, even though they never downloaded or used the information, or harmed their intended victims. Conspiracy and possession are examples of crimes that do not require harm to be successfully prosecuted; the mere act of conspiring to commit a crime is a crime.

To establish an attempted crime, the state must be able to show more than mere preparation. The Model Penal Code requires that a defendant must have completed a "substantial step in the course of conduct planned to culminate in his commission of the crime," § 5.01(1)(c). Courts use various tests to decide whether the steps a defendant has taken are substantial enough to constitute an attempted crime. Some examples of substantial steps are listed in § 5.01 (2)(a–g):

- Lying in wait, seeking or following the victim
- Luring the victim to the contemplated place of the crime
- Reconnoitering the contemplated place of the crime
- Unlawful entry of the contemplated place of the crime
- Possession of materials to commit the crime designed for unlawful use
- Soliciting an agent to participate in the crime

Causation

Causation is the link between the *actus rea* and the harm. The state must be able to show that the criminal conduct, or *actus reus,* directly caused the harm. To do this, the courts rely on the concept of the **"but for" rule**—but for the defendant's actions, the harm would not have occurred. Another name for this is "**sine qua non**," which means "without which, not."

Sine qua non establishes causation. Usually, however, causation is more complex. If there is a clear link between the criminal act and the effect, then the act is the **direct cause** of the harm. A person carjacks an elderly woman. This is a case of direct cause—the carjacking directly caused the harm, which is car theft. But what if the woman suffers a heart attack as the carjacker speeds away, falls to the pavement, and dies? The carjacking is the indirect cause of the woman's death. This is called **proximate cause.** Proximate cause is an act that sets in motion a chain of events leading to the harm. Proximate cause allows the state to hold people responsible for all the damages that result from their crimes.

To establish proximate cause, prosecutors rely on the concept of foreseeable consequences: shooting a gun is an act with clearly foreseeable consequences: bystanders may be shot. If someone hits a pedestrian while leading police on a high-speed chase through busy streets, prosecutors will try to show that injuring pedestrians is a reasonably foreseeable outcome.

But the chain of events following a proximate cause can be interrupted. Other causes of harm occurring after the proximate cause are known as superseding or **intervening causes.** For example, two men get in a fight in a bar room. The police are called and arrest the two men. One of the men is barely conscious, and on the way to jail, the police drop him on the sidewalk. The man later falls over backwards

"But for" rule
The rule that states but for the defendant's actions, the harm would not have occurred.

Sine qua non
Literally, without which, not. The Latin term for the "but for rule."

Direct cause
The case where a clear link between the criminal act and the effect exists.

Proximate cause
An act that sets in motion a chain of events leading to harm.

Intervening causes
Complications that arise between a criminal act and all of its consequences.

at the police station and hits his head on a concrete floor and later dies from the injuries. The other man is charged with involuntary manslaughter with the prosecution arguing the fight was the proximate cause of the man's death because 'but for' the fight, the man would not have died. The defense counters that the police dropping the man on the pavement was an intervening cause that changed the course of events. His fight injuries were not life threatening, and had the police not dropped him, he would have survived. The court ruled that the defendant could not have foreseen the injuries the victim received in police custody and therefore the fall on the sidewalk was a superseding or intervening cause.[10]

Conspiracy

Conspiracy

An agreement by two or more persons to commit a criminal act or series of criminal acts, or to accomplish a legal act by unlawful means. At Common Law, agreement was enough. Under the Model Penal Code and most state laws, the agreement must be followed by an overt act in furtherance of the conspiracy.

Inchoate

A class of crimes known as incomplete crimes, most notably conspiracy.

Birds of a feather flock together.

Old English proverb

Criminal activity is not always a solitary endeavor. Often, it is a group project. When two or more individuals join forces, the overall threat to society may increase. Consider, for example, a network of individuals joined to run a prostitution operation. At the bottom of the enterprise are the individuals who sell sexual favors and at the top are the criminals who "manage" the operation. The operation likely spurs other criminal activity such as drug abuse, theft, and bribery to keep the operation going.

The criminal justice system needs a way to combat such ventures other than merely arresting the individuals selling sexual acts and their customers, who likely will quickly be replaced by others. To get to the heart of the criminal operation, authorities need an effective tool to punish those at the top of the enterprise who reap the biggest benefit. One such tool is the concept of **conspiracy.**

A **conspiracy** is an agreement by two or more persons to commit a criminal act or series of criminal acts, or to accomplish a legal act by unlawful means. It is one of a class of criminal offenses referred to as **inchoate** or incomplete crime. Other inchoate crimes are criminal solicitation and criminal intent. Inchoate crimes like conspiracy are punished as if the crime had been completed. For example, if two people conspire to commit armed robbery, and they are stopped before they can rob the target bank, they can be sentenced as if they actually robbed the bank in most jurisdictions.

The Model Penal Code provides that a person is guilty of conspiracy if he or she agrees to commit an offense, attempts to commit an offense, solicits another to commit an offense, or aids another in the planning or the commission of the offense.

At Common Law, nothing more than the formation of the agreement was necessary for a crime to have taken place. Most states and the Model Penal Code, however, have altered that rule so that an overt act in furtherance of the conspiracy is required. For example, two men decide to steal a Picasso from the Philadelphia Museum of Art and sell it to an art collector. At Common Law, they would already have committed conspiracy the moment they agreed to the caper. However, under the Model Penal Code, one or both of the two would have to take some step toward the commission of the theft before they could be found guilty of conspiracy. What sort of step? It would probably be enough that one of the two went to the museum and got a map showing the painting's location after they agreed to steal it. They would not have to actually break into the building.

Note that there is nothing illegal about walking into the Philadelphia Museum of Art and picking up a map. The act becomes illegal because it is in the furtherance of the conspiracy to commit art theft. Also note that an overt act committed by any of the conspirators means all can be found guilty whether they took an active part or not.

What if one of the conspirators is an undercover police officer sent to infiltrate the art theft world? Does it matter that the undercover police officer is merely pretending to join the conspiracy? At Common Law, it mattered because there had to be a genuine agreement, a meeting of the minds. Without that, there was no *mens rea*. Most states and the Model Penal Code allow prosecution for conspiracy even if there is no genuine consent on the part of one of the conspirators, provided, of course, that there is a subsequent overt act in furtherance of the conspiracy. In our example, that means that if the undercover police officer and his target in the art theft world agree to steal the Picasso and the target obtains the museum map so that they can plan the best approach, the target can be convicted of conspiracy.

Before you begin to think of conspiracies as something hatched around a big table with all the conspirators present, consider that often the individual conspirators may not know each other, but simply know *of* each other. Assume that in our Picasso theft conspiracy example a wealthy art collector agrees with the head of an art theft ring that he will pay the ring $1 million for the Picasso and hands over a down payment. The two have committed an overt act toward achieving the conspiracy goal. Suppose now that the head of the theft ring calls in one of his circle of thieves, and the two agree that this associate will break into the museum and steal the Picasso. This would most likely be considered a second conspiracy. The art collector could possibly be guilty of both conspiracies if he knows that a third party will do the actual stealing.

You will be learning more about the concept of conspiracy in subsequent chapters, including defenses to conspiracy charges and specialized laws created to counter complex conspiracies involving large criminal enterprises. In the next chapter, you will see how the concept of conspiracy can be applied to hold anyone who conspires with another to commit a felony liable for murder if one of the conspirators murders someone during the commission of the agreed-upon felony.

Uniform Crime Report

Throughout this book, you will encounter references to the **Uniform Crime Report.** The FBI runs the Uniform Crime Reporting Program, which produces the Uniform Crime Report based on the voluntary participation of city, county, state, tribal, and federal law enforcement agencies. About 93 percent of the country's population lives in areas where law enforcement agencies participate in the program. The participating agencies submit crime statistics to the FBI. The program is an effort to provide an overview of criminal activity across the country.

As a country, we have been collecting national crime statistics since the 1920s, when the International Association of Chiefs of Police created the Committee on Uniform Crime Records and initiated the voluntary national data collection effort beginning in 1930. Around the same time, Congress gave the FBI legislative authority to run the program. It is important to note that the program tracks arrests, calls for service, complaints, and investigations, and not convictions.

As a paralegal or a criminal justice professional, you may be involved in tracking criminal activity for submission to the FBI in a process called classifying

Uniform Crime Report
An annual tabulation of serious crime in the United States issued by the FBI and based on the voluntary submission of criminal activity information from law enforcement agencies.

and scoring. That is one reason that this textbook follows the Uniform Crime Reporting Program crime classification system when classifying crimes. As you will see, criminal laws vary from state to state and federal law adds yet another dimension to what is a crime. The Uniform Crime Reporting Program provides its own set of definitions for reporting. Each reporting agency is responsible for matching up their unique definitions with the FBI definitions. The process of determining the proper crime category in which to report an offense to the program is referred to as classifying. Scoring is counting the number of offenses after they have been classified and entering the total count on the appropriate reporting form.

The Uniform Crime Reporting Program tracks the following serious crimes:

- Murder and non-negligent manslaughter
- Forcible rape
- Robbery
- Aggravated assault
- Burglary
- Larceny-theft
- Motor vehicle theft
- Arson

Uniform Crime Reporting Handbook
A guide published by the FBI to help law enforcement agencies prepare their annual Uniform Crime Reporting Program report.

The FBI publishes the ***Uniform Crime Reporting Handbook,*** which provides reporting agencies with extensive information on how to classify and score criminal offenses.

The Uniform Crime Reporting Program is not the only collection of crime data for the nation. The U.S. Department of Justice conducts an annual survey called the National Crime Victimization Survey (NCVS). It estimates the number of unreported serious crimes nationwide, including some that are not included in the FBI statistics. The NCVS provides extensive information on crimes and victims.

General Evidence Concepts

Throughout this book, you will learn about specific forms of evidence. As a criminal justice or paralegal professional, you will likely be deeply involved in the evidentiary process, whether interviewing witnesses and preparing them to testify, collecting physical evidence from the scene, or preparing evidentiary exhibits for use at trial. A basic understanding of evidentiary concepts is absolutely crucial. The federal system and many states use the Federal Rules of Evidence and we will use them as our introduction to evidence.

Relevant evidence
Evidence having a tendency to make the existence of any fact that is of consequence to the determination of the action more probable or less probable than it would be without the evidence.

Material evidence
Evidence that is important to the case at hand.

Relevant evidence means evidence having a tendency to make the existence of any fact that is of consequence to the determination of the action more probable or less probable than it would be without the evidence. **Material evidence** is evidence that is important to the case at hand. For example, the presence of the defendant at the scene of a crime is material to a case of alleged rape. If he were not at the scene, he cannot have committed the crime. Relevant evidence that tends to prove a material fact could include the victim's eye witness identification and the presence of the defendant's DNA on the victim. Both pieces of relevant evidence would tend to prove a material fact—that the defendant was present at the scene.

It is then up to the judge or jury to determine if, in fact, the defendant committed the crime.

Only relevant evidence is admissible, but not all relevant will be admitted. For example, the fact that a defendant has a lengthy criminal record may be relevant—that is, the criminal record may make it more probable that he has again committed a crime. However, the criminal record is also highly prejudicial and a judge will exclude the criminal record in all but a few limited circumstances. We will discuss some of those exceptions in the chapter on sexual assault.

Direct evidence is evidence based on first-hand knowledge such as an eyewitness account. For example, if Jane saw Jack rob Jill on top of the hill, Jane's testimony would be direct evidence that Jack robbed Jill. But what if Jane saw Jack run down the hill, but did not actually see Jack rob Jill? Then her testimony would be circumstantial evidence. **Circumstantial evidence** is indirect evidence that requires an inference.

Evidence usually comes in the form of either testimony or as physical evidence backed up by testimony to explain the physical evidence. Before a judge will accept a piece of physical evidence, the party presenting the evidence must show where the evidence came from. This is often referred to as proving the **chain of custody.** Take, for example, DNA test results presented to show that a defendant was at the scene of a crime. The prosecution will have to present a witness who can testify as to how the prosecution came to possess the DNA sample. If a forensic investigator gathered the sample, she will testify about the time, location, and circumstances. Typically, she will examine the sample handed to her while she is on the stand, look at an identifying label, explain how she attached the label, took it to the laboratory, tested it, and placed it in a safe place under lock and key before retrieving it for trial. Another police officer will probably testify that he obtained a warrant for a DNA sample from the defendant, served that warrant, and transported the defendant to a laboratory to obtain the sample. The technician who tested that sample will add his tracking information to the testimony. Finally, the technician who matched the samples will identify the samples and present her expert testimony on whether the samples match. Any breakdown in this process may mean the evidence won't be accepted.

Direct evidence
Evidence based on first-hand knowledge.

Circumstantial evidence
Indirect evidence that requires an inference.

Chain of custody
A process by which a piece of physical evidence is tracked from collection to introduction into evidence. The chain must be unbroken.

CONCEPT **REVIEW AND REINFORCEMENT**

A crime is a wrong against society or the public interest typically punishable by imprisonment or death and sometimes an additional fine. Criminal law is designed to protect and vindicate public rights.

Before prosecuting anyone for a crime, the first work of the state is to establish that a crime has been committed. To do so, the state relies on a concept called *corpus delicti,* or the "body of the crime." The state usually must show *corpus delicti* beyond a reasonable doubt. The state does not have to have a suspect or precise explanation of the crime, but it must establish that a crime has taken place.

Corpus delicti prevents a confession of a crime, unaccompanied by other evidence of either the crime or tying the confessor to the crime, to be used to convict the confessor of the crime he alleges to have committed.

The elements of a crime establish the crime's precise nature. Sometimes *corpus delicti* determines where a case is tried. In cases where a crime crosses territorial boundaries, the courts will often try the case where the *corpus delicti* was found.

Federal courts and some state courts have moved away from applying *corpus delicti* because some crimes that do not necessarily produce physical evidence, such as conspiracy and fraud, do not fit the requirements well.

The three main elements of a crime are a wrongful action, or *actus reus,* caused by a wrongful mind, *mens rea,* resulting in damage or harm. To successfully prosecute most crimes, a prosecutor usually must prove all the elements of the crime: *mens rea*, *actus reus*, and resultant harm.

Mens rea describes a person's intent while performing a criminal act, and is critical to establishing the nature and degree of a crime. Since a person's state of mind is not visible, *mens rea* is generally deduced from surrounding circumstances.

For some crimes, intent, or *mens rea*, is irrelevant. Strict liability crimes require only a wrongful act to occur. Strict liability imposes a duty on a person and exacts penalties from those who do not uphold that duty, regardless of their intentions.

Generally, crimes mala prohibita are strict liability, while *mala in se* crimes require intent. Another set of crimes that do not require *mens rea* are vicarious liability violations, in which one person is held responsible for someone else's actions. Vicarious liability generally relies on the standard of what the superior in the relationship, parents or employers, allow or permit the person under their control to do.

Mens rea is the thorniest part of any criminal case because it cannot be measured or proven, but only inferred from circumstances. The Model Penal Code defines four levels of intent, or *mens rea,* which determine the degree of a crime.

Purposeful acts, also frequently called wanton or willful acts, are designated first degree, and carry the highest penalties. Knowingly committed acts are second-degree crime. Recklessly committed crimes where there is a substantial and unjustifiable risk that the conduct might cause a particular result are third-degree offenses. Negligently committed crimes are fourth-degree offenses. Negligence means thoughtlessly or carelessly creating a significant unjustifiable risk of harm without realizing the risk has been created, or without intending to create it.

Establishing *mens rea* in second, third, and fourth-degree crimes is particularly challenging because it is based on the notion of "unjustifiable" risk, a term which means something different to every person. The state tries to define "justifiable" by weighing what the offender's conscious intentions were at the time of the crime, or her subjective intent, against what a reasonable person

should have known or thought at the time of the event, the legal standard of objective intent.

If a person does something with intent to cause a specific criminal result, then the person possessed specific intent. If a person intended an action only, and not the results of the action, that person possessed general intent.

Sometimes to prove specific intent, the state must show that the offender knew a certain fact or understood the law being broken. That requirement is known as scienter.

Transferred intent is where a person tries to harm one person and as a result harms someone else. Some actions are so likely to cause a specific result, the law treats that result as intended whether the person meant to cause it or not. This is known as constructive intent.

Motive is the reason a person commits a crime. Motive is not an element of a crime and therefore does not have to be proven to successfully prosecute a crime, but it often influences the severity of the punishment levied.

Actus reus is the action that causes the harm. It must be voluntary, active, and illegal. A crime must be voluntary. One's personal status is not an action and generally cannot constitute a crime.

Possession is dominion or control over property. Actual possession means physically having the item on one's person, directly under physical control, or within reach. Most jurisdictions divide actual possession into knowing possession, which implies that a person possessed and held onto the item on purpose, and mere possession, which means the person possesses the item unawares.

Constructive possession extends liability to people who have some control over an item without possessing it. Sometimes a failure to act is a crime known as an omission. An omission can occur only when someone has a duty or obligation to do something. The law may impose a duty by statute. A duty by contract most often occurs when a person's job or skills obligates them to assist individuals in ways people holding different jobs are not.

A duty by relationship imposes on parents a duty to care for their children. No contract or specific law is required; the duty arises out of the relationship itself. Finally, people can assume a legal duty simply by saying they will perform an action.

Crime results in five categories of harm: crimes against life, including murder, kidnapping, and battery; crimes against habitation, which include burglary and arson; crimes against property, including theft; crimes against the public order, such as traffic violations; and crimes against public morality, such as prostitution and drug use.

Certain actions are criminal even though they don't harm anyone. Attempted crimes can be prosecuted even though the person never committed the harmful act. For example, if a group of internet hackers breaks into a bank website and tries to download information, but is caught in the act, the perpetrators will be charged with attempted theft as well as numerous computer law violations, even thought they never downloaded or used the information, or harmed their intended victims. Conspiracy and possession are examples of crimes that do not require harm to be successfully prosecuted. The Model Penal Code requires that a defendant must have completed a "substantial step in the course of conduct planned to culminate in his commission of the crime."

Causation is the link between the *actus rea* and the harm. The state must be able to show that the criminal conduct, or *actus reus,* directly caused the harm. To do this, the courts rely on the concept of the but for rule or sine qua non. If there is a clear link between the criminal act and the effect, then the act is the direct cause of the harm. Proximate cause is an act that sets in motion a chain of events leading to the harm.

A conspiracy is an agreement by two or more persons to commit a criminal act or series of criminal acts, or to accomplish a legal act by unlawful means. Under the Model Penal Code and most state conspiracy statutes, one of the conspirators must take an overt act toward carrying out the conspiracy. Once that has been done, all the persons who were part of the agreement can be held liable for conspiracy.

The Uniform Crime Report is an annual voluntary compilation of crimes reported to law enforcement agencies in the United States. It covers eight categories of serious crime. Reporting law enforcement agencies classify crimes that occurred within their jurisdictions into the categories spelled out in the *Uniform Crime Reporting Handbook* and score (or count) the number of incidents they have classified.

Relevant evidence means evidence having a tendency to make the existence of any fact that is of consequence to the determination of the action more probable or less probable than it would be without the evidence. Material evidence is evidence that is important to the case at hand.

Direct evidence is evidence based on first-hand knowledge such as an eyewitness account. Circumstantial evidence is indirect evidence that requires an inference. Evidence is either testimonial or physical. Physical evidence requires the establishment of the chain of custody through testimony.

KEY **TERMS**

Actual possession
Actus reus
"But for" rule
Causation
Chain of custody
Circumstantial evidence
Conspiracy
Constructive intent
Constructive possession
Corporate liability
Corpus delicti
Crime
Degree
Direct cause
Direct evidence
Duty
Duty by contract
Duty by relationship
Duty by statute

Duty by volunteering
Duty to render aid to persons
    placed in peril
First-degree offenses
Fourth-degree offenses
General intent
Harm
Inchoate
In loco parentis
Intervening causes
Knowing possession
Mala in se
Mala prohibita
Material evidence
Mens rea
Mere possession
Motive
Objective intent
Omission

Parental liability
Personal status as an act
Possession
Principle of legality
Proximate cause
Relevant evidence
Respondeat superior
Scienter
Second-degree offenses
Sine qua non
Specific intent
Strict liability
Subjective intent
Third-degree offenses
Transferred intent
Uniform Crime Report
Uniform Crime Reporting Handbook
Vicarious liability
Voluntary acts

CONCEPT **REVIEW QUESTIONS**

1. Explain *corpus delicti*.
2. Explain what makes an act or omission a crime.
3. Explain the role of confessions in crime.
4. Explain *mens rea*.
5. List and explain the different types of liability.
6. Explain how to prove *mens rea*.
7. List and explain the different types of intent.
8. Explain *actus reus*.
9. Explain possession.
10. Explain omission.
11. Explain harm.
12. Explain causation.
13. Explain conspiracy.
14. Explain the Uniform Crime Reporting Program.
15. Explain direct and circumstantial evidence.
16. Explain the chain of custody.

CASE **APPLICATIONS**

Building Your Professional Skills

CASE 1

Below is an edited narrative taken from court documents from the JonBenet Ramsey murder case when a person later identified as John Mark Karr claimed responsibility for the murder. Read the narrative and answer the question at the end.

1. The People sought the arrest warrant for John Mark Karr after he had been identified as the writer of a series of anonymous e-mails sent to Professor Michael Tracey. The writer at first signed the e-mails as "D" and later as "Daxis." The e-mails were sent through a service that masked the identity and location of the sender.

2. Until April 2006, the anonymous e-mails were not of substantial interest to the District Attorney's Office because they merely demonstrated that the writer had an intense interest in the JonBenet Ramsey case.

3. Starting in April 2006, the writer began to claim more personal knowledge about the death of JonBenet Ramsey and about Mrs. Patsy Ramsey, the victim's mother. Although at first he claimed to know two people who participated in the crime, he later admitted personal responsibility for the death.

4. The anonymous writer described the crime in terms of his love for JonBenet Ramsey. Over time, he provided increasing detail about his "recollection" of the night of the crime. But he refused to provide any detail that he thought might lead to his identification.

5. He did admit to traveling extensively after leaving the United States because he had been investigated in connection with the abduction and/or murder of other young children and that he could not return to the United States because of an active warrant for his arrest.

6. The writer also showed an intense personal desire to communicate with Mrs. Patsy Ramsey and expressed an identification with her through what he perceived to be their common love for JonBenet.

7. The writer expressed great concern and sympathy for Mrs. Ramsey because of her deteriorating condition due to cancer. He wrote a message that he wanted forwarded to Mr. & Mrs. Ramsey in an effort to make contact with them so that he could explain his relationship to their daughter and her death.

8. Mr. Tracey convinced the writer to make telephone contact with the Ramseys. Law enforcement agencies cooperated in an unsuccessful attempt to trace that call.

9. In a further effort to identify and locate the anonymous writer, Mr. Tracey arranged to exchange telephone calls with the writer, who was by then identifying himself as "Daxis." In those calls, Daxis repeated his admissions about his involvement in and responsibility for the death of JonBenet Ramsey, but he continued to refuse to provide information that would help identify him.

10. Daxis took part in eleven phone conversations with Mr. Tracey. In the e-mails and phone conversation he expressed a fascination with not only JonBenet Ramsey but with the sexuality of young girls in general.

11. Daxis revealed that he had taught young girls in various schools and has also tutored, cared for, or otherwise had responsibility for young girls during his travels. He also revealed he was currently teaching young girls.

12. Daxis then began to provide his story in narrative form, which he wanted to be included in a book Mr. Tracey was planning to publish. He provided Tracey with several sections of this manuscript in which he gave descriptions of his own background and development, and his involvement with the death of JonBenet Ramsey.

13. Daxis provided details of his "recollection" of how JonBenet died in a way that supported the conclusion that he firmly believed that he loved JonBenet Ramsey, that he had involved her in sexual activities that included temporarily asphyxiating her, and that he had "accidentally" killed her by becoming so sexually involved that he lost track of time so that the asphyxiation lasted longer than he intended, causing her severe injury and leading him to inflict a severe blow to her head.

14. It was apparent from Daxis' e-mails, his manuscript, and his phone conversations that he believed his narrative of his responsibility for the death of JonBenet.

15. After the death of Mrs. Ramsey, Daxis became more intense about his desire to publish his explanation about himself and his responsibility for the death of JonBenet, but to also keep his identity secret. He began to describe his interest in several girls in much the same terms that he had described his interest in JonBenet Ramsey.

16. The District Attorney's investigators informed authorities of the United States and Thailand about what had been learned and worked with those authorities and others in the effort to locate and identify Daxis.

17. In the course of the numerous phone calls between Daxis and Mr. Tracey and through other means, the authorities were able to trace the calls and to locate him in Thailand. They then were able to identify him as John Mark Karr and ultimately to confirm that he was about to begin to teach young children in the new school he had described.

18. Until Mr. Karr was identified there was no way to try to confirm or disprove his admissions related to causing the death of JonBenet Ramsey. Until he was detained, there was great risk that he might disappear if he became aware that people from his past were being interviewed about his admissions.

19. Because Mr. Karr's description of his sexual involvement with the victim during the events leading to her death included oral sex and tasting her blood after he caused her vagina to bleed, it was apparent that the DNA found in blood spots in her underwear would be crucial to confirming his account of his involvement.

20. Although investigators in Thailand obtained swabs from several items touched by Mr. Karr in an effort to obtain his DNA, our experts who would be responsible for DNA testing, Greggory S. LaBerge, informed us that because of the mixture of DNA involved in the sample from the underwear, it would be necessary to obtain an untainted sample through use of buccal swab from Mr. Karr to provide a definitive comparison.

21. After it was confirmed that Mr. Karr was indeed teaching young children and that the school year had begun, we obtained approval from the Court for an arrest warrant. Thai officials then revoked his work visa and American officials revoked his passport.

22. After he was detained in Thailand, Mr. Karr refused to provide buccal swabs on two occasions. Although he later did consent to submit to such a swab, he did so when investigators were not expecting it and when they did not have the necessary kit available.

23. Once Mr. Karr was detained, investigators from the Boulder District Attorney's office and detectives from the Boulder Police Department made extensive efforts to interview people who might have information about Mr. Karr in an attempt to learn where he was on December 25–26, 1996. Although they could not positively place him anywhere in particular at the time of the crime, Mr. Karr's family provided strong circumstantial support for their firm belief that he was with them in Georgia at the time of the crime.

24. Immediately upon the return of Mr. Karr to Boulder County on August 24, 2006, investigators executed a search warrant to obtain a buccal swab from Mr. Karr. That sample from Mr. Karr was taken to Dr. LaBerge on August 25, 2006. Dr. LaBerge completed the testing and analysis and concluded on August 26, 2006, that Mr. Karr was not the source of the DNA found in the underwear of JonBenet Ramsey.

QUESTION

1. Could prosecutors charge Karr with either sexual assault or murder? Why or why not?

CASE 2

A woman goes for a jog in New York City's Central Park and is brutally attacked and raped. Five black males were interrogated for 40 hours and confessed to the rape and beating, providing graphic details about the event. They were convicted. There was no DNA evidence connecting the teens to the crime. The crime was prosecuted by an aggressive female prosecutor who also happens to have been the best-selling author of police procedurals. Linda Fairstein, author of such bestsellers as Bad Blood, Entombed *and* Cold Hit, *has since been criticized for her handling of the case.*[11] *Below is a summary of the events taken from an after-action review. Answer the questions following the summary.*

On the evening of April 19, 1989, shortly after 9:00 PM, approximately 40 African-American and Hispanic teenagers, mostly between the ages of 14 and 16, entered Central Park at 110th Street and 5th Avenue for the purpose, according to many of them, of assaulting and robbing people. Not all of the individuals in this group knew everyone else. Not every individual was present at each of the events that followed. They proceeded, at times together and at other times splitting up into smaller groups, to terrorize people through a large section of the park for almost an hour. The attacks by the group included:

- Accosting Michael Vigna, a racing biker, who escaped without physical injury;
- Assaulting and robbing Antonio Diaz, who was left on the side of a roadway unconscious;
- Menacing a couple on a tandem bicycle;
- Hurling rocks at and threatening a taxi driver;
- Threatening a male jogger, David Goode, who escaped without physical injury;
- Threatening a male jogger, Robert Garner, who escaped without physical injury;
- Assaulting a male jogger, David Lewis, who sustained physical injuries; and
- Assaulting a male jogger, John Loughlin, who sustained serious injuries from being knocked to the ground, kicked, punched, and beaten with a pipe and a stick.

The most significant event that occurred that evening was the brutal beating and rape of a 29-year-old female jogger, whose bloody and almost lifeless body was found at about 1:30 AM on April 20, 1989. Later investigation showed that she had apparently been accosted and knocked down on a transverse road in the park at about 102nd Street, dragged into the woods where she was assaulted, and then dragged further into the woods, where the major attack upon her occurred. She was found about 200 feet further into the park, near a footpath. Although she survived, the jogger had no memory of any of the events that occurred that evening. This attack was the basis for the most serious charges against the defendants.

Police responded immediately to several 911 calls for help that resulted from the various attacks. Two of the defendants, Raymond Santana and Kevin Richardson, were arrested on the evening of April 19th in the vicinity of Central Park shortly after the attacks. Without being contacted by the police, Antron McCray voluntarily appeared at the precinct, in the company of his mother, and was not held. Because of statements made by the defendants and others implicating them, Kharey Wise and Yusef Salaam, as well as McCray, were contacted by the police the next day, and came to the precinct voluntarily.

Out of the approximately forty teenagers who entered Central Park that night, thirty-seven were interviewed. Ten were arrested and ultimately convicted of charges resulting from their activities. Five of these ten (the defendants) were charged with the assault and rape of the female jogger, the assault of John Loughlin, the assault on David Lewis, and a riot charge. All but Wise were convicted of assault, riot, robbery and rape. Wise was convicted of assault, riot and sexual abuse.

The other individuals who were arrested pled guilty to the assaults on Diaz, Loughlin, or Lewis, but not to the assault of the female jogger. The defendants had implicated these other individuals in the assaults on the victims other than the female jogger.

Matias Reyes, then 18 years of age, was also in the park on the night of April 19, 1989. In 2002, he came forward to reveal that he had raped the female jogger and to claim that he did so alone.[12]

QUESTIONS

1. What arguments would you make if one of the males now says he had nothing to do with the alleged crime, and another man has confessed?
2. Would your answer change if the other man's DNA matched that found at the scene?

CRITICAL **THINKING EXERCISES**

1. A man leaves a bar after drinking enough to raise his blood alcohol level above what is legal in the state. He leaves the parking lot and begins driving down the street at the speed limit. As he approaches a crosswalk filled with pedestrians, he applies the brakes. The pedal goes all the way to the floor indicating a mechanical failure. He slams into a pedestrian, killing her. Which crimes would he be guilty of?
   a. homicide by vehicle
   b. driving while under the influence of alcohol
   c. failure to yield to pedestrians
2. While walking through the woods, you find a partially decomposed human body with what appears to be a gunshot wound in the skull at the front right temple. No gun is in sight. Given this, can you establish *corpus delicti* of a crime?
3. You are a District Attorney. A police officer investigating a series of brutal murders in your jurisdiction tells you a man walked into his office and told him he committed the murders. The man has provided details of the crimes, but nothing that hasn't been in the newspapers. Armed with this information, can you successfully prosecute the man?
4. Two lovers quarrel. The relationship has a history of violence. One person pulls a gun, the other draws one in self-defense. The aggressor's gun jams. The defender fires and kills the aggressor. Did the surviving lover have *mens rea* for

murder? (This scenario is taken from the book *Midnight in the Garden of Good and Evil*.)

If you were the prosecutor, how would you prove *mens rea*? If you were defending the plaintiff, how would you disprove *mens rea*?

5. For each scenario, give the type of liability involved:
   a. A man claiming to be an insurance agent sells you a policy and provides you with a policy. You pay an initial premium. You notice that you have the right to cancel the policy within a few days of buying it if you change your mind. You attempt to contact the company and find that it doesn't exist.
   b. A man claiming to be an insurance agent sells you a policy and provides you with a policy. You pay an initial premium. You notice that you have the right to cancel the policy within a few days of buying it if you change your mind. You contact the company and they verify that the agent does work for them, but tell you they have no record of your policy. Upon investigation, they report the agent pocketed the money.
   c. A child friend of your daughter comes over to play. He brings matches he picked up at his home and begins lighting them, setting your house on fire.

6. Explain what type of intent is associated with the following crimes and identify the *actus reus* in each case:
   a. You burn some trash at the edge of your property. There are no laws against open burning where you live. You leave the fire momentarily. While you are gone, wind gusts carry hot embers onto your neighbor's roof. By the time you return the wind has died down, but soon you hear fire sirens.
   b. You have a property boundary dispute with your neighbor. You believe a corner of his garage is on your property. After months of wrangling, you decide to take matters into your own hands. After making sure no one was inside, you walk to the offending corner of the building and douse it with gasoline and light it on fire.
   c. You have a property boundary dispute with your neighbor. You believe a corner of his garage is on your property. After months of wrangling, you decide to take matters into your own hands. After checking to see no one was inside, you walk to the offending corner of the building and douse it with gasoline and light it on fire. Unbeknownst to you a

homeless person had broken in and was asleep inside the building. He is killed in the fire.
   d. You have a property boundary dispute with your neighbor. You believe a corner of his garage is on your property. After months of wrangling, you decide to take matters into your own hands. You see him walk inside the garage. You walk to the offending corner of the building and douse it with gasoline and light it on fire.

7. Identify the type of possession described in each of the following:
   a. A thief steals a ring from a jewelry store and bolts into the crowded mall. Once he feels safe he tries to blend in by walking at a normal pace. Armed with a description, mall security soon identifies him as the thief. He sees security officers nearing him and slips the ring into another shopper's shopping bag. What type of possession did the thief have and what type did the shopper have?
   b. A teenager grows marijuana in his parents' attic without their knowledge. What type of possession does the teenager have and what type do the clueless parents have?

8. Some friends are clowning around at the deep end of a swimming pool. One person pushes the other into the pool. The dunked person screams between gulps of water, "I can't swim!" What duty does the other friend have to the one in the pool?

9. Identify the type of harm in the following scenarios:
   a. You start a protest against a law you believe to be wrong. You tweet to all your friends to show up on Main Street at rush hour to block traffic. All your friends show up and disrupt traffic.
   b. You start a protest against a law you believe to be wrong. You tweet to all your friends to show up on Main Street at rush hour to block traffic. Your friends show up with guns and begin firing at the police and commuters.
   c. You start a protest against a law you believe to be wrong. You tweet to all your friends to show up on Main Street at rush hour to block traffic. Your friends show up, disrobe, and begin having sex on the hoods of cars.
   d. You start a protest against a law you believe to be wrong. You tweet to all your friends to show up on Main Street at rush hour to block traffic. Your friends show up and start looting stores and breaking into houses along the street.

10. Identify the type of cause for the woman cooking the meals in the following scenarios:
    a. A woman believes her husband is cheating on her. She decides to poison his dinner. But he calls and says he is "working late." Disgusted, she puts the meal in the refrigerator. In the middle of the night, her teenage son wanders downstairs for a midnight snack. He eats the food and dies.
    b. Same scenario as a. except the woman awakes and stops her son after he has eaten just a small portion. She calls an ambulance that takes the son to the hospital where his stomach is pumped and he is held for observation. While he is sleeping, a nurse inadvertently injects the wrong drug into his IV killing him.

11. A businessman is deeply in debt because of some illegal activity. His father-in-law is wealthy, but the businessman cannot reveal his problem. He arranges through intermediaries to have his wife kidnapped and held for ransom. Before the plot is hatched, the businessman changes his mind, but he doesn't communicate with the kidnappers in time. Is the businessman guilty of conspiracy even though he tried to withdraw? Are the kidnappers guilty of conspiracy with the businessman even though they never met him? (Loosely based on the movie *Fargo.*)

12. Could you find the number of conspiracy arrests in the Uniform Crime Report?

13. Which of the following scenarios illustrates direct evidence and which illustrates circumstantial evidence?
    a. A woman sees a man with a gun running through her yard. He disappears from view and hears a gunshot. She sees the same man come running back through the yard and get in a car and drive away. Upon investigation, she finds a neighbor who has been wounded by a gunshot. What type of evidence can she present that the man running through her yard shot her neighbor?
    b. A woman reports a rape. Forensic evidence taken from her provides a DNA profile. Assuming her statements are true, what type of evidence is the DNA?

14. A car with bloodstains on the inside is impounded by the police shortly after what the police suspect is a murder committed by the vehicle's owner. The car is placed on the police lot and locked up prior to forensic examination. Someone breaks into the lot and steals two other cars not related to this crime and leave the gate open when they leave. Can the police demonstrate a clear chain of custody for this vehicle and the evidence it may provide?

PORTFOLIO **BUILDING**

1. After reading this chapter, you should have a pretty good idea of what makes an act or admission a crime. If you are called in your professional life to help in the prosecution or defense of an alleged crime, you should also have a pretty good idea of the traps and pitfalls that can befall either the prosecution or the defense.

   If your role is to assist the prosecution in bringing charges, you now understand that it takes more than an accusation to begin a criminal case. You understand that before charges are brought, a responsible prosecutor will analyze the evidence to assure that the elements of the crime that is alleged to have taken place are present. You may even find it helpful to develop a checklist of what the prosecution needs to show as a way of making sure the case is sound. That checklist may look something like this:

   - What are the elements of the crime charged, and are they all present? (*mens rea, actus rea,* etc.)
   - Has a suspect been identified?
   - Has that suspect confessed or given an account of his/her activities connecting him/her to the alleged crime?
   - Is there some independent evidence actually tying the defendant to the alleged crime, such as DNA or other physical evidence or witness testimony? (*corpus delicti*)

   If you are assisting the defense, you can use a similar list to test the prosecution's case.

2. Review the FBI's *Uniform Crime Reporting Handbook.* You can access a copy at http://www.fbi.gov/ucr/handbook/ucrhandbook04.pdf. You may want to print a copy for reference throughout this course or download a copy to your computer. You work for a police department in your home state. Your supervisor has asked you to handle the next monthly Uniform Crime Reporting Program submission to the FBI. The arrest and investigation records on your desk

include the following case summaries. For each, identify what crime or crimes apply to the fact situation in your state. Then prepare a memo explaining which crimes should be reported and which should not.

a. During the course of an armed robbery at a bank, the perpetrator shoots and kills one teller. The bank manager has a fatal heart attack. How would you classify the bank manager's death?

b. During a domestic dispute, a woman who is in her 39th week of pregnancy (full-term) is hit in the abdomen with a baseball bat. The assailant is her boyfriend. The child is stillborn and the coroner rules that the cause of death was the boyfriend's assault. Is this homicide in your jurisdiction? Do you classify this as a homicide in your Uniform Crime Reporting Program report? Explain.

c. An altar boy at the local Catholic church tells his parents that the Parish priest sodomized him and the parents report the incident to the police. Do you report this incident as a forcible rape in your Uniform Crime Reporting Program report?

d. Another set of parents report that their 16-year-old daughter was forced to have sexual intercourse with her algebra teacher at the local public high school. How do you report this incident in your Uniform Crime Reporting Program report?

e. Someone sets fire to the local public library and three patrons die in the fire. How do you report the deaths and the fire in your Uniform Crime Reporting Program report?

3. You work for a social service agency interested in obtaining grants to help women who are victims of sexual assault. Your boss has asked you to prepare a memo outlining the number of women who were sexually assaulted by their significant other in the United States and in your state. Using the latest available figures from National Crime Victimization Survey, prepare the memo. You can access the statistics at http://bjs.ojp.usdoj.gov/ (look under publications).

FOR FURTHER READING AND VIEWING

1. Forster, E. M. (1924). *A Passage to India.* This classic English novel was also made into a movie starring Alec Guinness and revolves around false rape accusations made by a British tourist visiting colonial India for the first time.

2. Leeson, N. (1996). *Rogue Trader.* Little, Brown. Leeson tells his side of the story, after being released from jail in Singapore and relocating to Galway, Ireland. The book was also made into a movie, *Rogue Trader,* starring Ewan McGregor as Leeson. Leeson has his own Web page and can be booked for dinner speeches. For a look at the new, reformed Leeson, check out www.nickleeson. com. Ironically, two other books written about the scandal are out of print, while Leeson's book is still available in both hardback and paperback. Crime doesn't pay?

3. *Minority Report,* a 2002 Steven Spielberg film starring Tom Cruise in which police are able to prevent crimes by looking into the minds of citizens to determine their intent (mens rea) before they ever take a step toward committing that crime. Citizens are punished for the crime the police determine they will commit. The movie is based on a 1956 short story by Philip Dick.

4. Westervelt, S. (2001). *Wrongly Convicted.* Rutgers University Press. A collection of essays exploring, among other things, why someone would confess to a crime he or she did not commit.

5. Sullivan, T. (1992). *Unequal Verdicts: The Central Park Jogger Trials.* New York: Simon & Schuster. An exploration of the role of coerced confessions in an infamous rape case.

6. Temple-Raston, D. (2002). *A Death in Texas: A Story of Race, Murder, and a Small Town's Struggle for Redemption.* Henry Holt. Recounts the hate crime murder of James Byrd Jr. in Jasper, Texas. The forty-nine-year-old African-American man was tied to a pickup truck by three white men and dragged behind until he died.

Chapter **three**

CRIMES AGAINST THE PERSON: MURDER

And it came about when they were in the field, that Cain rose up against Abel his brother and killed him.

Genesis 4:8

Introduction and Historical Background

The biblical story of Cain and Abel illustrates a second fall of humans from grace following expulsion from the Garden of Eden. Cain was sent to cultivate the ground and be a "vagrant and wanderer on the earth."[1] Cultivating the land is generally regarded as the beginning of modern civilization. Cain's exile at hard labor was both the first punishment for murder and symbolically the start of civilized society's struggle with violence.

As civilized populations increased, so did the number of murders or **homicides.** Traditions arose in each society as to how to treat those who took another's life. Under English Common Law, homicides were divided into three categories: criminal (or felonious), justifiable, and excusable. Attorneys most often deal with **criminal homicide,** which is when a person unlawfully and knowingly, recklessly, or negligently causes the death of another human being.[2] Depending on the circumstances, criminal homicide can be one of several crimes. Most commonly, homicides are categorized as murders, or manslaughter. **Murder** is often defined as the unlawful killing of a human being with malice, but the exact definition will vary by jurisdiction. Murder may be premeditated, or felony murder. Some states have distinctions such as first- or second-degree murder. Check the laws in your state to understand the distinctions. Manslaughter is a lesser crime usually classified as voluntary or involuntary.

CHAPTER OBJECTIVES

After studying this chapter you should be able to:

- Define murder
- Distinguish between degrees of murder
- Define conspiracy
- Explain the felony murder rule as it applies to criminal conspiracies to commit a felony
- Define infanticide
- Distinguish between voluntary and involuntary manslaughter
- Explain when killings are not crimes and when they are
- Explain assisted suicide
- Explain what statements by a murder victim may be admissible

HISTORICAL HIGHLIGHT

Murder in Tribal England

England in the first millennium A.D. was a savage place. Fierce warring tribes competed for dominance during a period punctuated by a series of invasions. Each onslaught brought refinements to the English legal system as the conquerors assimilated into the conquered.

Although tribal customs varied, criminal practices generally followed a fairly set pattern. The victim or his family filed the complaint and often physically brought the accused to court. While this may seem unusual to us in modern times, it is important to bear in mind that these were very close-knit tribal communities. If a person attempted to flee, there simply was nowhere to go. He couldn't lose himself in the anonymity of a large urban area. Each person's ability to make a living and perhaps his entire life was tied up in the tribal community.

A criminal who was convicted of a crime was never imprisoned in tribal England because prisons didn't yet exist. He could be executed for particularly heinous crimes, he could be tortured, or more likely he would simply have to compensate the victims. This compensation fell into three categories: *wergild*, *bot*, and *wite*. **Wergild** was compensation paid to a family group if a member of that family was killed or suffered severe injury. In murder cases, the amount was determined by the victim's social standing. The cause or circumstances of the crime were irrelevant. Bot was compensation paid for minor injuries. **Wite** was a public fine payable to a lord or tribal chieftain. This was then used for the benefit of the entire tribe. If the offender was too poor to pay, the fine would be assessed in livestock.[3]

O, my offence is rank, it smells to heaven; It hath the primal eldest curse upon't, A brother's murder.

Shakespeare, *Hamlet*, Act 3, Scene 3

Homicide
The killing of a human being.

Criminal homicide
A killing that breaks the law, designated as either murder or manslaughter.

Murder
The unlawful killing of a human being with malice, but the exact definition will vary by jurisdiction. See *First-degree murder*.

Wergild
In ancient England, compensation paid to a family group if a member of that family was killed or suffered severe injury.

Bot
In ancient England, compensation paid for minor injuries.

Wite
In ancient England, a public fine payable to a lord or tribal chieftain.

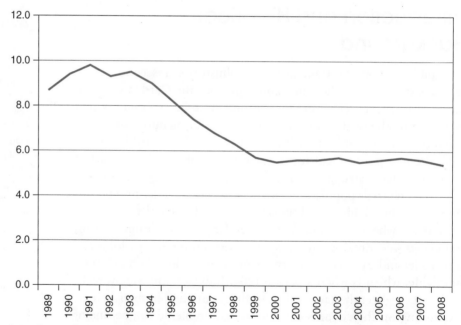

Murder and Nonnegligent Manslaughter Rate per 100,000 Population.
Source: Uniform Crime Report 2009.

Murder

The first job of a prosecutor in a murder case is to prove a crime was committed. Proving a crime is committed is called establishing **corpus delicti**, or the body of the crime. *Corpus delicti* must be established beyond a reasonable doubt. If the state cannot prove a crime was committed, they may not prosecute anyone for its commission. Don't confuse *corpus delicti* with the actual body in a homicide, though. As you will see below, a body may make murder easier to prove, but isn't essential to a successful murder prosecution.

Cases where the victim's body cannot be found present problems for prosecutors. Evidence of violence, witnesses to a struggle, and various pieces of forensic evidence can be pieced together to provide evidence of a crime. Although evidence like this is **circumstantial,** it still may be used as evidence of a crime, if the whole body of evidence, including **direct evidence,** establishes beyond a reasonable doubt that a crime was committed.

Premeditated Murder

The first recorded murder in colonial America was committed by one of the original Pilgrims from the *Mayflower*. Ten years after the Pilgrims landed, John Billington shot his neighbor with a blunderbuss. The punishment for murder was hanging. Billington was convicted and hanged.[4]

At the time, English Common Law made no distinction between the types of murder. But this one-punishment-fits-all approach was soon to change. After the Revolution, state legislatures created various classifications of murders by statute. It probably occurred to them that it wasn't practical to kill every murderer. Clearly, different circumstances dictated different responses.

Premeditated murder is virtually always classified as **first-degree murder.** Second-degree murder is always a lesser charge, but the elements that comprise second-degree murder vary widely from state to state.

By definition, a person committing first-degree murder must form the **intent to kill** his victim. The law requires the person to have "**malice aforethought.**" In other words, the defendant must have an angry mental state toward the victim that allowed him to plan the victim's murder. This malice need not be of long duration. Even if the intent to kill was formed just prior to the act, the person can be convicted of first-degree murder.[5]

Since we cannot read a killer's mind, intent is very hard to prove. However, there are some Common Law doctrines that have traditionally been held to establish intent.

Evidence of the angry state of mind and therefore intent to kill can be developed from the defendant's behavior just before the murder. For example, Idaho's first-degree murder statute lists "the use of poison, or lying in wait, torture, or . . . any other kind of willful, deliberate and premeditated killing"[6] as necessary for a first-degree murder conviction. So the defendant's intent may be clear when evidence shows the murder was planned well in advance. But prosecutors have also obtained first-degree murder convictions when the intent to kill was formed immediately before the killing. In fact, the same Idaho statute says, "There need be no appreciable space of time between the intention to kill and the act of killing."[7]

Many states employ the **deadly weapon doctrine.** Under this doctrine, if the defendant points a loaded gun at the victim and pulls the trigger, he intended to kill the person. In other words, the defendant believed that the natural and probable consequences of his action would occur.

Deadly weapons do not have to be guns or knives. Fists and common items such as scarves, handkerchiefs, and rocks used as weapons have been held to be deadly weapons in murder trials. Juries must determine the presence of a deadly weapon on a case-by-case basis.

Corpus delicti
Literally "the body of the crime," the fact that a crime has been committed.

Circumstantial evidence
Evidence that proves a fact by inference. Circumstantial evidence seldom carries the weight of direct evidence so often many pieces of circumstantial evidence are needed before a judge or jury will find that they add up to proof beyond a reasonable doubt.

Direct evidence
Real, tangible, or clear evidence of a fact or occurrence.

In films, murders are always very clean. I show how difficult it is and what a messy thing it is to kill a man.

Alfred Hitchcock

First-degree murder
Murder committed deliberately with malice aforethought, that is, with premeditation.

Intent to kill
The plan, course, or means a person conceives to take another's life.

Malice aforethought
An intent to kill or injure, or the deliberate commission of a dangerous or deadly act.

Deadly weapon doctrine
Use of a deadly weapon is proof of intent to kill.

Transferred intent
The doctrine that if a defendant who intends to injure one person unintentionally harms another, the intent is transferred to the person who is unintentionally harmed.

Intent can be transferred to a party to whom the defendant bore no malice. **Transferred intent** can occur when the victim is not the one the defendant meant to kill. A person shooting at one person and accidentally hitting another is guilty of both the crime of murder and bad aim. Once the shot is fired with intent to kill and kills someone, the shooter is guilty regardless of who is killed.

When murderers employ less precise weapons, the possibility of harming an unintended victim increases. For example, an angry boyfriend set fire to the apartment building where his ex-girlfriend and her new love were living. They escaped unharmed, but a two-year-old girl living in the same building did not. The hotheaded arsonist was convicted of felony murder. He appealed arguing he never intended to kill the little girl. The case went all the way to the U.S. Supreme Court where the justices sided with the prosecutor citing the doctrine of transferred intent.[8]

Lesser Degrees of Murder

Intent to do serious bodily harm
A defendant's plan to injure another.

Defendants who only intended to "rough someone up," but killed him or her by mistake may lack the intent to kill necessary for first-degree murder. Nevertheless, they are responsible for the person's death. In cases like this, defendants are said to possess an "**intent to do serious bodily harm.**" These murders may result in a conviction of second-degree murder, or even manslaughter depending on the definitions in the state.

Some cases involve people who have no intent to cause bodily harm, but are reckless in their behavior—drunk driving is the most common example. When people behave in a way that endangers others resulting in the death of another person, the person may be charged with a lesser degree of murder or manslaughter depending on the fact situation.

Even sober reckless driving can lead to murder charges. A man who drag-raced at high speed down a winding mountain road was found guilty of Pennsylvania's third-degree murder charge (that state's equivalent of manslaughter) after he hit a car after rounding a blind curve, killing the driver and crippling his ten-year-old son.[9]

Murder begins where self-defense ends.

Georg Buchner

YOU MAKE THE CALL

Should Cultural Defenses Be Permitted in Murder Cases?

Spend enough time in a courtroom and you will hear many far-fetched explanations for crimes. But are they far-fetched or just the product of your cultural prejudice? Foreign-born murder defendants have raised cultural defenses to show that their murderous behavior would have been justified, or at least not as unusual in their native culture. Consider these examples:

- New York, New York, 1987—After Chinese-born Dong Lu Chen's wife admits to having an affair, he beats her to death with a hammer. At trial, a cultural anthropologist explains the deep humiliation and loss of manhood that befalls cuckolds in Chinese culture. Dong is convicted of manslaughter and sentenced to five years probation.

- Chicago, Illinois, 1992—Celerina Galicia, an illegal alien from Mexico, stabs his girlfriend Roberta Martinez forty-four times with a six-inch steak knife. At his murder trial, he explains his belief in *curanderismo*, a Mexican belief in folk healing and spirits. He was convinced that Martinez was a *bruja* or witch who had cast spells on him. When he could not find a healer to perform the ritual cleansing to remove the spells, he saw no option but to kill her.

   The judge in the case allowed some testimony about his beliefs, but refused to let a letter from Galicia's aunt telling him that Martinez was a *bruja* into evidence. Galicia was convicted of first-degree murder and sentenced to 15–50 years in prison.

- Oakland, California, 1993—An Ethiopian man who shot his girlfriend claimed she was witch who was casting spells on him. The charge was reduced from murder to assault.

One of the elements of a crime is intent. Can judges or juries properly ascertain the defendant's state of mind without understanding the defendant's culture? Cultures vary in relevant areas such as trust of the police, attitudes toward women, and comfort with the use of violence to settle disputes.

The late Johnnie Cochran, who defended O.J. Simpson, was a big proponent of cultural defenses. He once told an American Bar Association symposium that when cultural issues are involved, "You are committing malpractice if you do not avail yourself of the appropriate defense."[10]

On the other side of the argument, DePaul Law Professor John F. Decker argues that cultural defenses are just variations on the insanity defense and are "invariably rejected by judges and juries."[11] But the examples above show that may not always be the case.

For instance, an African-born father carried on his culture's custom of celebrating the birth of a son by kissing the newborn's penis. However, a neighbor reported the man for sexual abuse. Is this just a case of cultural misunderstanding or a real crime? What if the father had circumcised his daughter in accordance with African traditions? Would that be a crime? What if someone from a different culture committed the same act? Would that be a crime? You make the call.

Felony Murder

A person can be held responsible for murder even if that person wasn't directly involved in the killing if the killing took place during the commission of a felony under the **felony murder rule.** Generally, the rule applies to those who agree to act with others to commit a criminal act. This agreement creates a conspiracy. Often, defendants accused of felony murder are also charged with conspiracy. If one of the parties to the **criminal conspiracy** commits the murder, all are held to be equally culpable under the felony murder rule. For example, assume two defendants conspire to commit a bank robbery. One defendant drives the getaway car while the other robs the bank and shoots a security guard in the

Felony murder rule
The rule that a death occurring by accident or chance during the course of the commission of a felony is first-degree murder.

Criminal conspiracy
The agreement by two or more people to commit a crime. It requires at least one overt act and is punished as if the parties accomplished the objective of their agreement.

process. The security guard dies. Both can be charged with murder, regardless of who pulled the trigger. In fact, under some circumstances the driver can even be executed.[12]

Felony murder classification varies by state. In Idaho, felony murder is prosecuted as first-degree murder under the assumption that planning to commit the felony constitutes premeditation.[13] Whereas in Pennsylvania, felony murder is a second-degree murder charge.[14] Some states, such as Minnesota, have two degrees of felony murder; first degree where the prosecution proves intent to kill while committing the felony, and second degree where the intent was only to commit the felony.[15] Always check the laws in the state the crime took place to verify felony murder definitions.

"Felony murder is committed when a person, acting alone or in concert with others, commits or attempts to commit one of nine predicate felonies . . . " and "in the furtherance of such crime or of immediate flight therefrom, he, or another participant, if there be any, causes the death of a person other than one of the participants."[16] But, exactly what does "in furtherance of a crime or . . . flight therefrom" mean? Most jurisdictions follow the **Res gestae theory,** that if the "killing was committed in, about or as part of the underlying transaction," all conspirators were guilty of the murder. Some state laws refer to the felony and murder as being part of "a continuous chain of events."[17]

Clearly, the felony murder rule can be very broad in its application. A person who conspires to commit a felony may be charged with felony murder if his accomplice committed the murder. Recall that a conspiracy is an agreement by two or more persons to commit a criminal act or series of criminal acts, or to accomplish a legal act by unlawful means.

One potential pitfall for prosecutors in charging felony murder is that they must obtain a conviction for the underlying felony to prove felony murder. If the defendant is acquitted of the felony, the felony murder charge cannot be sustained.[18] Further, the prosecutor must prove the defendant intended to commit the felony before the murder took place. For example, one defendant had his felony murder conviction overturned because he proved he didn't decide to rob the victim until after the victim died.[19]

Some courts have moved to limit the felony murder rule. For instance, England abolished the felony murder rule in 1957. It is not universally recognized in the United States.[20]

However, in jurisdictions that still have felony murder laws, defendants can possibly face the death penalty. In *Tison v. Arizona*, the Supreme Court ruled that defendants may be executed even if they never "intended to kill the victims nor inflicted the fatal wounds" as long as they "had the culpable mental state of reckless indifference to human life."[21] However, the same set of facts in a jurisdiction lacking a felony murder law will only yield a conviction for the underlying felony.

Many states have limited felony murder laws. Limitations may include one or more of the following:

- The felony that was attempted or committed must be one that is dangerous to life.
- There must be a direct causal connection between the felony and the death that occurred.

Res gestae theory
Literally "the acts of the thing," the acts or words through which an event speaks.

- The act that caused the death must have occurred while the felony was in progress.
- The felony must be *mala in se*.
- The act must be a Common Law felony.

Manslaughter

Manslaughter is a classification of criminal homicide that is less than murder. Manslaughter can either be voluntary or involuntary. The main difference between murder and manslaughter is that often manslaughter is the result of conflict between the defendant and the victim where the victim contributed to the conflict. Manslaughter can also be a "catchall" type of homicide where mitigating circumstances make the defendant's behavior understandable, but not excusable.

Voluntary manslaughter is where the defendant acted willfully, but was somewhat justified in his actions. For instance, a child who kills an abusive parent when he feels no other avenue is open to him would be an example of voluntary manslaughter. Sentences for manslaughter are far less than those for murder.

Manslaughter also comes into play in plea-bargaining arrangements. Defendants may agree to take a manslaughter conviction instead of going to trial and risking a murder conviction.

Murder charges may be reduced to manslaughter charges if the court believes the crime occurred in the **heat of passion** as long as other elements are present. In addition to heat of passion,

- There must be adequate provocation;
- There must have been no opportunity to cool off;
- There must be a causal connection between the provocation, the rage, anger, and the fatal act.

Adequate provocation is weighed on a case-by-case basis, but there are some absolutes. Words and gestures are insufficient provocation to reduce charges from murder to manslaughter.[10] Generally, a person who kills in response to physical attack or fear for the safety of his family will be charged with manslaughter. A person catching a spouse committing adultery will probably get manslaughter, but that rule does not necessarily apply to unmarried partners.

Often the homicide investigation will explore whether the defendant had time to "cool off" between the provocation and the crime. Generally, if there was time to cool off and the defendant killed anyway, the conviction will more likely be for murder than manslaughter.

The killing must be in reaction to the provocation. This deals with both the reason and the time frame of the act. A defendant cannot kill someone for an act that occurred several years ago and argue manslaughter.

Juries must decide heat of passion issues in light of the reasonable person test. How much provocation could a reasonable person withstand without retaliating? The defendant's tolerance threshold is not an issue. If the defendant was less restrained than the jury believes a reasonable person would be, then the verdict will be murder, not manslaughter.

In many manslaughter trials, defendants claim they acted in self-defense. If the jury finds the defendant's actions reasonable in light of the circumstances, the defendant may be acquitted.

Voluntary manslaughter
A homicide committed with the intent to kill, but without deliberation, premeditation, or malice.

Heat of passion
The expression for a mental state on the part of a criminal defendant adequate in law to reduce the crime from murder to manslaughter.

Involuntary manslaughter
The unintentional killing of a human being by a person engaged in doing some unlawful act not amounting to a felony, or in doing some lawful act in a manner tending to cause death or great bodily injury.

Criminal negligence manslaughter
The crime of causing the death of a person by negligent or reckless conduct.

Unlawful act manslaughter
Where the defendant committed a crime that resulted in the death of a person.

Homicide by vehicle
A form of criminal negligence manslaughter reserved for a person operating a motor vehicle.

Euthanasia
The act of causing death to end pain and distress. Also called mercy killing.

Involuntary manslaughter refers to two types of homicides: **criminal negligence manslaughter** and **unlawful act manslaughter.** Criminal negligence manslaughter is the crime of causing the death of a person by negligent or reckless conduct. For instance, the crime of a person who leaves a burning campfire that later consumes a home killing the occupant would be considered criminally negligent manslaughter. Unlawful act manslaughter is where the defendant committed a crime that resulted in the death of a person. Many traffic deaths fall into this category, although some states have a special category of homicide entitled **homicide by vehicle.** Homicides by vehicle are not considered to be premeditated, but often the defendant broke one or more traffic ordinances in the process of causing the fatal accident.

Euthanasia

As a result of medical advances, many terminally ill people are alive today who would not have been decades ago. Therefore, **euthanasia** or mercy killing movement has grown in popularity since the 1970s. Euthanasia advocates claim it gives people the right to end their lives on their own terms, giving the individual death with dignity.

Often, however, seriously ill patients are unable to end their own life. They must be assisted to do so. When someone assists another person to commit suicide, it is sometimes hard to distinguish this act from murder. Many times family members may benefit from the ill person's death and their motives and undue influence come into question.

The debate rages within the medical community as well. Doctors are pledged to provide care as long as there is any hope of recovery. Even when the patient is terminal, doctors are sworn to make the patient as comfortable as possible. Some have argued that patients who request their doctors provide them with drugs to end their life should have their wish granted under certain conditions. Some states have even passed "doctor-assisted suicide" laws.

HISTORICAL HIGHLIGHT

Oregon's Assisted Suicide Law—Death with Dignity or Murder?

In 1997, Oregon's Death with Dignity Act took effect. It allows doctors to provide a terminally ill patient with the means to end his or her life. Under the law, two Oregon doctors must agree that the patient has less than six months to live, has freely chosen to die, and is able to make critical health decisions. The law only applies to Oregon residents.

The law was enacted through a state-wide referendum. Another referendum seeking to repeal the law failed. The question of whether the law is constitutional has never been brought before the Supreme Court; however, the High Court has ruled that bans on assisted suicide on the books in New York and Washington State are constitutional. More to the

point, in each of those cases, the Court ruled that states had the right to decide the issue themselves.

In November 2002, Attorney General John Ashcroft authorized federal drug enforcement agents to revoke the licenses of doctors who assist patients in committing suicide using federally regulated medications under the federal Controlled Substances Act (CSA). However, by April of 2002, U.S. District Judge Robert Jones ruled that states' rights to determine what constitutes legitimate medical practices cannot be overridden by the CSA. The Ninth Circuit Court of Appeals agreed with Oregon, setting up a showdown before the U.S. Supreme Court. The High Court ruled in a 6–3 decision that the Controlled Substances Act did not trump Oregon's right to regulate doctors.[22]

Feelings run strong on both sides of the issue. Pro-life conservatives fear that assisted suicide laws erode legal safeguards protecting life. They see assisted suicide as tied closely to the abortion issue. Pro-choice activists claim to be protecting the right of the individual to choose the time and manner of his or her own death. They view assisted suicide as a reprieve from months of unwanted suffering. Like the abortion issue, assisted suicide is an issue that will be with us for many years to come.

How far can doctors and family members go to assist a suicide? The answer obviously varies from state to state. Generally speaking, without assisted suicide laws in place, it is criminal to aid in someone's suicide.

Doctors also confront the question of how long to leave someone on artificial life support systems. Some patients leave doctors **living wills** that spell out clearly what steps should be taken to revive them and under what circumstances. Living wills should be notarized documents signed freely by an individual of sound mind. Unfortunately, often older people are pressured by family members and doctors to sign documents they might not normally sign. A living will signed under duress is not a valid document.

Living will
A document in which a person sets forth directions regarding medical treatment to be given if she becomes unable to participate in decisions regarding her health care.

YOU MAKE THE CALL

Murder or Mercy: The Terri Schiavo *Case*

Terri Schiavo was a healthy twenty-six-year-old woman in 1990. But one day she collapsed. By the time doctors stabilized her at the hospital, she had suffered irreversible brain damage. Doctors diagnosed her as being in a "persistent vegetative state." No amount of therapy would resurrect any lost brain function. For nine years, Terri's husband, Michael, and her parents, Bob and Mary Schindler, took care of Terri.

Finally, Michael decided it was time to take Terri off the feeding tube. The legal battles soon began. The Schindlers filed for custody to stop Michael arguing he was only withdrawing the tube to collect her life insurance. Michael countered that removing the tube was the humane thing to do in the case.

The Schindlers countered with abuse allegations. The courts consistently sided with Michael. The Schiavo controversy hit the national news just before the 2004 presidential election. Many pro-life voters saw the issue as intricately linked with the abortion debate. Stirred by election fever, Congress passed a law specifically crafted to allow the Schindlers another appeal in court. The Supreme Court refused to hear an appeal, and Terri's feeding tube was removed in early 2005. She died thirteen days later.

The autopsy results fueled both sides of the argument. The medical examiner found no signs of abuse and noted that the brain was completely atrophied. Terri would never have recovered. But they also noted that had she been fed, she could have lived another ten years until infection or other maladies that normally affect the bedridden took their toll.

Some would say Terri Schiavo was murdered, others that she was allowed to die. Michael Schiavo acted under court order when he withdrew her feeding tube, but some feel the law should not have allowed it to happen. What do you think?[23]

Infanticide

Infanticide
The murder of a newborn or very young child.

Infanticide is the murder of a newborn or very young child. Although some cultures condone or at least tacitly permit infanticide, Anglo-American jurisprudence has traditionally held it to be a crime.

Infanticide is different from abortion in that the child has been born. In fact, the live birth of the child is one element the prosecution must prove in an infanticide case. Many infanticides are accomplished by simply abandoning the baby in an area where it would die from exposure and dehydration. Often when children are found still alive, the charge of reckless endangerment or attempted murder is brought against the mother, if she can be located.

Suicide

Western culture has traditionally discouraged suicide. Under English Common Law, suicide was a crime punishable by forfeiture of property to the king. In early America, attempted suicide was a misdemeanor.

Suicide is no longer a crime, but most states interpret suicide attempts as signs of mental illness. Those who survive the attempts are often committed to mental hospitals under civil psychiatric commitment laws in hopes of treating the underlying mental illness.

Killings that are not Crimes

Justifiable homicides
Those killings committed out of duty with no criminal intent.

Sovereign immunity
The protection from lawsuits government agencies enjoy.

Military actions
Actions carried by members of the armed services under the direction of appropriate civilian authorities.

Justifiable homicides are those killings committed out of duty with no criminal intent. When the state executes a person who has been duly convicted, the killing is not a murder. In fact, even if evidence that the person was denied due process comes to light later; the state operates under the color of **sovereign immunity**. Sovereign immunity is a holdover from the English legal system. The king could do no wrong, and to a large extent was above the law.

Military actions are not murders. The need for the state to protect itself supersedes criminal law. For the most part, members of the military on active duty operate under the Uniform Code of Military Justice (UCMJ). The UCMJ prescribes appropriate behavior for active duty personnel. The UCMJ must conform to the Constitution as the military is subject to the civilian authorities.

Of course, innocent civilians caught in a war zone may also be killed during military actions. Their deaths, absent extraordinary circumstances, are also not classified as murder. The intentional killing of civilians, however, may very well be prosecuted as homicide or even as a war crime under the right circumstances.

> To my mind to kill in war is not a whit better than to commit ordinary murder.
>
> Albert Einstein

YOU MAKE THE CALL

Obama Approves Targeted Killing of American Cleric

According to published reports,[24] President Barack Obama has authorized the Central Intelligence Agency (CIA) to kill Anwar al-Awlaki, an American-born U.S. citizen suspected of being a radical cleric and perhaps behind a 2009 attempt to bring down an airliner over the United States. Al-Awlaki is thought to be hiding in Yemen, although the information concerning his activities is secret and no judge or magistrate has examined the evidence against him.

Al-Awlaki is a firebrand cleric who is popular among English-speaking radical Muslims on the Arabic peninsula and is believed to have moved from merely advocating violence against U.S. interests to actively planning attacks.[25] With his name on the CIA kill list, the agency may send in a drone attack should it receive good intelligence on his approximate location.

The State Department's legal adviser, Harold Koh, said in a speech that drone strikes against al Qaeda are lawful under the military action authorized by Congress after September 11, 2001, and that using one of the unmanned airplanes to take out individuals on the CIA kill list is not assassination and therefore doesn't violate earlier presidential orders banning political assassinations.

Al-Awlaki's location away from the battlefields in Iraq and Afghanistan makes his situation unusual. His killing would mark the first time that a U.S. born citizen not located in or near battlefields would be killed at the direction of a U.S. president at least since Gerald Ford signed the order banning political assassinations.

Is it right for the U.S. government to sanction the killing of U.S. citizens who are not enemy combatants on the battlefield? Why or why not? Would your answer be different if the CIA or the president released the intelligence used to decide Al-Awlaki should be on the CIA list?

Discuss

Killings done in self-defense are not murders. For a full discussion of self-defense see Chapter 10, Common Law Defenses.

Murder Evidence Concepts

Dead men may tell no tales, but fortunately science does. When it comes to homicide, the prosecutor's best friend may well be the scientist.

Let's start with the body. The first step is to identify the decedent. Next, we need to know the time of death, the manner of death, and the cause of death. Did the individual die of natural causes, suicide, or by accident? Often, the circumstances make the conclusion obvious. Gunshot or stab wounds make it unlikely death was natural. At other times, determining cause and time of death may take extensive work. An autopsy usually will be conducted, and tissue samples taken to determine whether the victim had drugs, alcohol, or some other substance in the body. In addition, the body will be examined for any physical evidence that may yield a clue to the identity of the murderer. These include DNA from bodily fluids, hair, or skin as well as fiber or other substances. Of course, any obvious wounds will be carefully examined, and any bullets or other foreign objects removed and cataloged.

The physical evidence will then be carefully preserved and tracked to establish an uninterrupted chain of custody. That way, the pathologist performing the postmortem examination and the technician conducting the lab tests on the physical evidence can show the court and the jury that they have the right body and the right physical evidence.

[I]f we believe that murder is wrong and not admissible in our society, then it has to be wrong for everyone, not just individuals but governments as well.

Helen Prejean

Only after the experts are satisfied that they have all the information they need to determine the cause and time of death will the body be released to relatives for burial or cremation.

Dying men may tell tales. It's fairly common for individuals who have been injured to try to tell someone what happened and who hurt them. This is often referred to as a dying declaration. Under the Federal Rules of Evidence, such a statement is an exception to the hearsay rule, which typically does not allow testimony if the other party cannot cross-examine the witness. **Hearsay** is a statement, other than one made while testifying at trial, offered in evidence to prove the truth of the matter asserted.

The Federal Rules of Evidence calls a **dying declaration** a "statement under belief of impending death" and such statements are admissible at trial to prove that the defendant was the killer. Rule 804(b)(2) says that "in a prosecution for homicide . . . a statement made by a declarant while believing that the declarant's death was imminent, concerning the cause and circumstances of what the declarant believed to be impending death" is admissible.

If the dying victim does make a declaration, the individual who heard the statement will be allowed to testify even though he or she can't attest to the truth of the statement. The presumption is that someone facing what he or she believes to be imminent death won't lie about who caused the injuries.

Consider this recent case. When police arrived at a home in New Orleans, they found a chaotic scene. Officers found an eleven-year-old girl and her fifteen-year-old uncle ripped apart from a spray of bullets fired from an AK-47 rifle. The boy, who had been shot in the stomach, survived long enough to tell a friend and two police officers that "Billy shot me" before dying.

A jury convicted Billy Ray Lewis even though none of the survivors could identify him, but after prosecutors put on witnesses who testified that Lewis had told them that the boy needed to "be dealt with" because he was bothering a girl Lewis was seeing.[26]

Of course, in some murder cases there may also be eyewitness accounts.

Thus, murder and other death investigations rely heavily on scientific evidence, eyewitness accounts, and any statements made by the victim before death. Other circumstantial evidence will also play a role, such as fingerprints, possession of the murder weapon, alibis, and perceived motivation.

Dead men tell no tales.

Attributed to pirate lore

Hearsay
A statement, other than one made while testifying at trial, offered in evidence to prove the truth of the matter asserted. It is not admissible.

Dying declaration
A statement made by an individual who believed death is imminent to explain the circumstances of his condition. Such statements may be admissible as an exception to the hearsay rule.

HISTORICAL HIGHLIGHT

Chandra Levy's Murder Illustrates Limits of Physical Evidence in Homicide Investigations

May 1, 2001, was a beautiful day in Washington, DC, and Chandra Levy prepared for a jog in the District's Rock Creek Park. Levy, a twenty-four-year-old intern at the Federal Bureau of Prisons, was spending her last few days in Washington before a scheduled return to her parents' home in California for an anticipated May 11 graduation from the University of Southern California. Shortly before noon, she logged on to her laptop computer, checked the weather, clicked on the map of Rock Creek Park, and strolled out of her apartment in Washington's tony DuPont Circle neighborhood and never returned.[27]

In the weeks and months that followed, the nation's capital was awash in rumors and tabloid headlines. Attention quickly focused on Gary Condit, a married congressman from California with whom Chandra was allegedly having an affair. Meanwhile,

Ingmar Guandique, a Salvadoran immigrant, was charged in two other park assaults that occurred in the weeks round Chandra's disappearance and was sent to prison.

It would be more than a year until Chandra Levy's remains were found. By then, Washington's hot, humid summer and nature had taken their toll. On May 22, 2002, a man walking his dog in the park spotted what he thought at first was a turtle shell. It turned out to be Chandra's skull. She was identified through dental records. In the ensuing days and weeks, forensic investigators found scattered bits of Chandra's body in the ravine where her skull was first found. An autopsy—if it could be called that given that so little remained—revealed little except that a bone in her neck had been damaged, leading to speculation that she might have been strangled.[28]

Unfortunately, because her body was left in the elements for over a year and her bones were scattered by wildlife, there was little or no physical evidence to tie anyone to the murder. DNA testing of clothing found in the area did reveal the presence of male DNA.[29]

It would be almost eight years after Chandra's disappearance and seven years after her remains were discovered that Ingmar Guandique, then still serving time for the other attacks, was charged with first-degree murder. The case will turn on his alleged confession and reports that he bragged to fellow inmates about his possible involvement in Chandra's murder. When DC detectives interviewed him in prison, they took a DNA sample and bluffed, telling him that they expected the DNA would match DNA collected at the scene. According to the detectives, Guandique responded, "So what if I touched her?" Prosecutors are planning to introduce the statement and testimony from other inmates who allege Guandique confessed to raping and killing Chandra as she walked in Rock Creek Park on that bright spring day in 2001. Their case is a circumstantial one. They have the body—the *corpus delicti*. They know she was murdered. They have placed Guandique in the park in the days surrounding Chandra's disappearance. They have his one-line statement and testimony from fellow inmates. A jury will decide if that's enough.

CONCEPT **REVIEW AND REINFORCEMENT**

Prosecutors in murder cases must prove that a crime was committed or establish a *corpus delicti* beyond a reasonable doubt. Where investigators cannot produce a body, circumstantial evidence such as evidence of violence, witnesses to a struggle, and various pieces of forensic evidence can be pieced together to provide evidence of a crime.

A person committing first-degree murder must form the intent to kill his victim. The law requires the person to have "malice aforethought." The deadly weapon doctrine is used to establish intent to kill. If the defendant uses a deadly weapon to kill a person, it is assumed the requisite intent was present. Transferred intent can occur when the victim is not the one the defendant meant to kill.

Defendants who possess an "intent to do serious bodily harm" are frequently convicted of second-degree murder. Cases involving people who have no intent to cause bodily harm, but are reckless in their behavior, generally result in manslaughter charges.

The felony murder rule states "Felony murder is committed when a person, acting alone or in concert with others, commits or attempts to commit one of nine predicate felonies, . . . " and

"in the furtherance of such crime or of immediate flight therefrom, he or another participant, if there be any, causes the death of a person other than one of the participants." In jurisdictions that still have felony murder laws, defendants can possibly face the death penalty if they "had the culpable mental state of reckless indifference to human life."

Manslaughter is a classification of criminal homicide that is less than murder. Manslaughter can either be voluntary or involuntary. Voluntary manslaughter is where the defendant acted willfully, but was somewhat justified in his actions. Sentences for manslaughter are far less than those for murder.

Murder charges may be reduced to manslaughter charges if the court believes the crime occurred in the heat of passion as long as other elements are present.

Involuntary manslaughter refers to two types of homicides—criminal negligence manslaughter, which is the crime of causing the death of a person by negligent or reckless conduct; and unlawful act manslaughter, which is when the defendant committed a crime that resulted in the death of a person.

Euthanasia is mercy killing. When someone assists another person to commit suicide, it is sometimes hard to distinguish this act from murder. Some states have even passed "doctor-assisted suicide" laws.

Infanticide is the murder of a newborn or very young child. Prosecutors must establish that the child was born alive to prosecute an infanticide case. Suicide is no longer a crime, but may lead to civil commitment.

Justifiable homicides are those killings committed out of duty with no criminal intent.

Executions are killings that are not murders, as are military actions. Killings done in self-defense are not murders.

Murder and other death investigations rely heavily on scientific evidence, eyewitness accounts, and any statements made by the victim before death. Other circumstantial evidence will also play a role, such as fingerprints, possession of the murder weapon, alibis, and perceived motivation.

KEY **TERMS**

Bot
Circumstantial evidence
Corpus delicti
Criminal conspiracy
Criminal homicide
Criminal negligence manslaughter
Deadly weapon doctrine
Direct evidence
Dying declaration
Euthanasia
Felony murder rule

First-degree murder
Hearsay
Heat of passion
Homicide
Homicide by vehicle
Infanticide
Intent to do serious
    bodily harm
Intent to kill
Involuntary manslaughter
Justifiable homicides

Living will
Malice aforethought
Military actions
Murder
Res gestae theory
Sovereign immunity
Transferred intent
Unlawful act manslaughter
Voluntary manslaughter
Wergild
Wite

CONCEPT **REVIEW QUESTIONS**

1. Define murder.
2. Distinguish between degrees of murder.
3. Define conspiracy.
4. Explain the felony murder rule as it applies to criminal conspiracies to commit a felony.
5. Define infanticide.
6. Distinguish between voluntary and involuntary manslaughter.

7. Explain when killings are not crimes and when they are.
8. Explain assisted suicide.
9. Explain what statements by a murder victim may be admissible.

CASE **APPLICATIONS**

Building your Professional Skills

CASE 1

KIRK NOBLE BLOODSWORTH V. STATE OF MARYLAND
No. 1376, September Term, 1987
Court of Special Appeals of Maryland
76 Md. App. 23; 543 A.2d 382; 1988 Md. App. LEXIS 158
July 8, 1988

Opinion

A jury in the Circuit Court for Baltimore County convicted Kirk Noble Bloodsworth, appellant, of first degree murder, felony murder and first degree sexual offense under MD.ANN.CODE Art. 27, §§ 407, 410 and 462, respectively. For the first degree murder conviction and for the first degree rape conviction, the trial court sentenced Bloodsworth to consecutive life terms. Bloodsworth asks whether:

I. There was sufficient evidence.

II. The trial court erred in admitting as rebuttal evidence appellant's testimony from his first trial.

III. The State withheld exculpatory evidence.

IV. The trial court abused its discretion in denying appellant a new trial.

V. The trial court erred in admitting "other crimes" evidence.

VI. The trial court erred in admitting certain hearsay evidence.

VII. The trial court erred in excluding certain evidence of a composite sketch.

VIII. The trial court erred in refusing to call a witness as a court's witness.

IX. The trial court erred in admitting photographic evidence of the pattern of the sole of Richard Gray's shoe.

X. The trial court erred in admitting evidence that appellant became a suspect as a result of a "tip."

XI. The State made an improper closing argument.

Note: The Court of Appeals reversed Bloodsworth's initial convictions for first degree murder, first degree rape and first degree sexual offense and awarded him a new trial in *Bloodsworth v. State*, 307 Md. 164, 512 A.2d 1056 (1986). The present appeal stems from the second trial.

Sufficiency

Bloodsworth challenges the sufficiency of the evidence to convict, just as he did in *Bloodsworth v. State*. As the Court of Appeals stated in Bloodsworth. "we first address that issue because if there were insufficient evidence to convict there could be no new trial. The applicable standard is whether after viewing the evidence in the light most favorable to the prosecution any rational trier of fact could have found the essential elements of the crime beyond a reasonable doubt."

On July 25, 1984, police discovered the partially nude body of nine year old Dawn Hamilton in a wooded area near Golden Ring Mall in eastern Baltimore County. The victim was found lying on her stomach with an eight inch stick protruding from her vagina. Near the victim's head was found a large piece of concrete with a possible blood stain. The victim's skull was "fractured" and "depressed" and her scalp had "two tears" with a "very rough edge." The victim's neck had a "patterned abrasion." The opinion of the medical examiner, Dr. Dennis Smyth was that the death was a homicide and "was a result of blunt trauma to the head and strangulation."

On the morning of the murder, ten year old Christian Shipley and seven year old Jackie Poling were fishing at a pond near the scene. Christian testified that after a few hours, a man came by and Jackie showed him a turtle he had caught. Shortly thereafter, Dawn came by and asked the two boys to help her look for her cousin Lisa. The boys refused and resumed their fishing. The man, however, agreed to help Dawn and the two walked off together.

After Dawn's body was found, Christian assisted police in the production of a composite likeness of the man. Christian also picked Bloodsworth from a photographic array as the man he saw walk off with Dawn. Christian testified that at a police line-up, held on August 13, 1984, he recognized the man in the sixth position as the man who went into the woods with Dawn, but was afraid to tell the police. He made no identification at that time. Nonetheless, one of the investigating police officers, Detective Robert Capel, testified that immediately after the lineup, Christian told him that he "knew all the time that it was number six but he didn't want the man to hear his voice because the man could tell it was him because it was a little kid's voice." Christian also made an in-court identification of Bloodsworth.

Although he could not remember the exact day or year, Jackie Poling testified that he remembered going fishing with Christian Shipley on a day when he caught a turtle and that a man stopped to talk with him about the turtle. Jackie testified that Dawn came by and asked for help in finding her cousin and that, after he and Christian refused to help her, the man told Dawn he would help her look for her cousin and the two "walked off into the woods." He was unable to make an in-court identification of the man he saw at the pond.

When Jackie attended a line-up on August 13, 1984, he identified the man in the third position, not the appellant who was in the sixth position. After the line-up, Jackie, Christian and their mothers were taken to their homes in a police car. There is conflicting testimony regarding when Jackie informed his mother that the man he saw walk off with Dawn was "number six." Jackie's mother, Denise Poling, testified that he told her it was number six after the line-up but before they left the Towson police station. She acknowledged, however, that she did not inform any of the police officers at the station that Jackie had recanted his earlier identification and was now claiming that the man who walked off with Dawn had been number six. She testified further that although on the way home from the police station she discussed with Christian's mother the fact that Jackie had told her he had been scared and had identified the wrong man in the line-up, she did not mention that fact to the police officer who was driving the patrol car. Jackie, on the other hand, testified that he did not tell his mother about his misidentification until after they had been returned home from the line-up. It is undisputed, however, that Mrs. Poling did not tell the police what Jackie had told her until September 4, 1984, almost three weeks after the line-up. Upon receiving this information from Mrs. Poling, an officer went to the Poling home that evening and took a statement from Jackie which contained the above information.

Donna Ferguson testified that she saw the victim talking with a man near the woods at approximately 10:30 a.m. on the day of the murder. At a police line-up, Ms. Ferguson identified Bloodsworth as the man she saw with the victim. Ms. Ferguson also made an in-court identification of Bloodsworth.

James Keller testified that he was driving down Fontana Lane, near the scene of the murder, at approximately 6:30 a.m. when he saw a man standing by the side of the road. From both a photo array and a police line-up, Keller identified Bloodsworth as the man he saw that day.

Soon after the murder, Bloodsworth's wife, Wanda, filed a missing person's report concerning Bloodsworth. Based on information obtained from that report, Detective Capel interviewed Bloodsworth in Cambridge on August 8, 1984, concerning his activities on the day of the murder. Detective Capel testified that Bloodsworth "had a hard time remembering his exact whereabouts," but that Bloodsworth said he had never been to the area near the murder scene. The detective testified that Bloodsworth told him that after picking up his paycheck, he left Baltimore on August 3, 1984, and took a bus to Cambridge. Prior to concluding the interview, Detective Capel took two photographs of Bloodsworth.

Detective Capel testified that he placed Bloodsworth's photograph in a photo array and showed the array to Jackie Poling and Christian Shipley. Christian Shipley identified Bloodsworth, but Jackie Poling was unable to make a positive identification. Based upon Christian's positive identification, Detective Capel obtained an arrest warrant for Bloodsworth, returned to Cambridge on August 9, 1984, arrested Bloodsworth and interviewed him a second time. The detective testified that he once again asked Bloodsworth about his activities on the day of the murder, July 25, 1984. He testified that Bloodsworth was unsure of his precise whereabouts, but that he was sure he had never been to the area where the victim was murdered. Detective Capel testified that he "asked the defendant why he was going around telling people in Cambridge about a bloody rock when only a few policemen and the killer knew about a bloody rock and he said that he didn't know why. He denied it at first and then stated he just didn't know why he did it. And at that point he said that I didn't kill that child, only somebody sick would hurt a child."

Tina Christopher testified that she had a conversation with Bloodsworth in Cambridge, "He was talking about this little girl. I thought it was his daughter, so I didn't really pay too much attention to him, but he described what this little girl was supposed to have been wearing and things that went on, and he said that him and that other guy was on this beach and this girl come up to him and asked him to help her, and this other guy was supposed to took her off somewheres [sic]."

Tina Furbush testified that in August of 1984, she had a conversation with Bloodsworth in Cambridge in which Bloodsworth said, "he was a suspect in the rape and the murder of the little girl in Baltimore." Ms. Furbush testified that Bloodsworth also "talked about this guy that, you know, raped this little girl and the things that, something about some bloody rock and some underwear that was down at the police station that was supposed to scare him." Ms. Furbush also testified that Bloodsworth told her the little girl was "in some wooded area by some water" and that "the little girl had asked to find, for him to help to find the friend, her friend, and I guess that's where he went and helped her find her friend." Ms. Furbush added further that Bloodsworth "didn't say he heard it from the police."

Rose Carson testified that in August of 1984, Bloodsworth came to Cambridge and asked if he could spend the night in her home. Bloodsworth said that on the next day "he would go admit himself to the State Hospital." Ms. Carson testified that Bloodsworth told her, "I have done something really terrible. I am afraid that me and my wife won't get back together because of it . . . ." Ms. Carson also testified that Bloodsworth said he was a suspect in the rape and murder of a little girl. This conversation took place on a Sunday.

Donna Hollywood testified that she owned a company called "Harbor to Harbor" in Baltimore County, near Essex. In July, 1984, Bloodsworth worked at Harbor to Harbor for "about four weeks." Ms. Hollywood testified that on August 3, 1984, Bloodsworth "was due to be at work at ten o'clock that day and he came in around maybe 10:30, quarter of eleven, into my office. And he said he was very ill and he looked very ill. He, I mean, very, he was very, very sick looking and he was sweating and white. And he said that he had the flu and that he wanted to know if I would give him his paycheck because he wanted to go, he had to meet his father downtown to go to a doctor because he was that sick. And so I went into the other office, and I gave him his paycheck and I told him that he looked so sick that he shouldn't go downtown."

In challenging the sufficiency of the evidence Bloodsworth argues that "although it is clear that the victim was murdered, it is also clear that Appellant's convictions are founded upon nothing but exceedingly suspect identification evidence of him as a person seen with the child four hours before her body was discovered. This evidence cannot form the basis for a rational finding of guilt beyond a reasonable doubt."

It is settled, however, that it is the province of the jury as fact finder, not the trial judge or an appellate court, to weigh the credibility of testimony and determine the issue of guilt or innocence." We hold that the evidence reported above was sufficient for a rational fact finder to have found Bloodsworth guilty beyond a reasonable doubt of the crimes for which he was convicted.

Admission of Testimony from First Trial

Bloodsworth argues that it was improper for the court to admit testimony from his first trial, because it was not proper rebuttal evidence and because it was irrelevant. In *Henze v. State*, the Court said "The admissibility of the evidence given at a former trial depends upon the question whether or not it was voluntary. To be admissible it must be voluntary, and where there is no evidence to the contrary, it will be presumed that the evidence so given was voluntary. The defendant at the former trial went upon the stand of his own volition, and the evidence there given is, we think, admissible in this case."

Bloodsworth does not argue, and the record does not indicate, that he testified at his first trial involuntarily. Accordingly, the State was free to use his former testimony in the later proceeding.

Rose Carson had testified that Bloodsworth told her, "I have done something really terrible." On cross-examination, Ms. Carson testified that she had "assumed" that in that statement Bloodsworth referred to certain marital problems with his wife. Douglas Orr, a defense witness, testified that he and Bloodsworth had a conversation, in Baltimore, on a Friday in early August, 1984, approximately one week after Dawn Hamilton's murder. Bloodsworth, who looked "sick" and "depressed," told Orr that the "terrible thing" Bloodsworth had done was that "he left his wife and quit his job."

Suppression of Exculpatory Evidence and Denial of Motion for New Trial

Bloodsworth argues that the State violated his right to a fair trial by suppressing exculpatory evidence and that the trial court erred in failing to grant him a new trial. The same evidence forms the basis for both of these contentions.

On March 28, 1985, several days after Bloodsworth had been tried, convicted and sentenced to death in Bloodsworth I, Judge Hinkel, the trial judge, received a telephone call from a psychiatrist, Dr. Gene Ostrom, who is the Director of the Eastern Regional Mental Health Center. Judge Hinkel promptly notified the Baltimore County Police Department of the call. It was not until March 12, 1987, almost two years later, that the State notified Bloodsworth of the existence and substance of Dr. Ostrom's call to Judge Hinkel. The following is the relevant portion of the State's letter to counsel for Bloodsworth:

> This is also to inform you that after trial on March 28, 1985 Judge Hinkel received a phone call from a Gene F. Ostrom, Director of the Eastern Regional Mental Health Center, who told Judge Hinkel that on the same day as the murder David M. Rehill, d.o.b. 11/16/55, 1013 Cherlyn Road, 21221, came into the office at 3:30 p.m. and said he had done a terrible thing. Dr. Ostrom believed Rehill looked like the composite made in this case. According to Dr. Ostrom, Rehill had committed prior acts of violence and had a history of alcohol and drug abuse. Rehill had been known to the clinic for seven (7) years. Dr. Ostrom felt he was capable of this crime.

The State included in its letter to counsel a photostated copy of a picture of Rehill and a copy of the police interview with Rehill. The following is the relevant portions of the police interview:

On March 24, 1987, two weeks after the notification, Bloodsworth's trial began. Bloodsworth concedes that he waited "until after trial to investigate Rehill . . . ." On April 22, 1987, after Bloodsworth had been tried and convicted but not yet sentenced, he moved for a new trial but he did not base his motion on the Rehill issue. The trial court denied the motion. It was not until June 12, 1987, the date set for sentencing, that Bloodsworth moved for a new trial based on "newly discovered evidence"; the Rehill evidence he had been supplied with before trial. At this second hearing, David Rehill testified that he had previously received treatment at the Eastern Regional Medical Center. Based on Rehill's assertion of a privileged communication between himself and his psychiatrist, the trial court upheld his refusal to answer questions with reference to his activities on July 25, 1984, the date of the murder.

Dr. Ostrom testified that Rehill made an unscheduled visit to the health center on July 25, 1984 between 12:30 and 1:30 p.m. After waiting several hours, social worker Frances Marks saw Rehill. Ms. Marks testified that Rehill was "calm" and "oriented" and that he had come to talk about "a personal relationship" he had with a "little girl." Ms. Marks did not recall seeing any scratches or blood on Rehill that day. Beverly Raymond, a secretary at the health center, remembered seeing Rehill on the day of the murder and she remembered that he had fresh scratches on the right side of his face. The next day, Ms. Raymond told Ms. Marks that a composite of the suspect which she saw on a newscast "looked like Mr. Rehill." Sally Lysakoski, another secretary at the health center, testified that she saw Rehill on the day of the murder and that he appeared "calm and quiet" and she did not notice any scratches on his face. (The health center was approximately four to six blocks from the murder scene.)

The trial court offered the following comment on the manner in which the Rehill matter was handled by the State:

> We are not talking about every blond man in Baltimore County. We are talking about a blond man who, according to information from a Doctor Ostrom, came into the medical clinic, which is approximately ten minutes from the location of this horrible crime, on the day of the crime, without an appointment, according to a proffer of the witnesses' testimony, with scratches on his face and arms. Someone who is, as I look at him, fitting the general description of the man who was last seen with the victim in this case, and whom the police investigate, never even put in a lineup according to what I have before me, because they concluded that he didn't fit the general description given by the two boys who last saw the little girl before she disappeared. Now, I look at that man and I look at that defendant, and to conclude conclusively that they do not look alike, sufficiently to at least put him in a lineup, is surprising if not more than surprising to this judge. I remember the eyes testified to by the little boy. I look at the defendant and I look at Mr. Rehill. I look at the size testified. The blond hair testified. Quite frankly, Mr. Pulver [Assistant State's Attorney, it gives me pause. For the police to conclude on their own that this information did not even warrant a lineup is shocking to me.]

Nevertheless, the trial court denied Bloodsworth's motion for a new trial on the basis that the evidence presented was not "newly discovered" and because Bloodsworth had failed in pursuing the David Rehill issue with "due diligence."

Suppression Under Brady

Bloodsworth argues that the State's "belated disclosure" of the information regarding David Rehill constituted a "suppression of material evidence exculpatory to an accused and is a violation of due process." Bloodsworth argues that "the delay in disclosing the material is so egregious as to give this Court grounds for dismissing the charges against appellant and barring the State from further prosecution of the case against him." Bloodsworth also argues that the State violated Rule 4-263(e) in failing to disclose the information concerning Rehill in a timely fashion.

In response, the State argues that the issue of the timeliness of the State's disclosure under Rule 4-263(e) was not argued to the trial court and was not preserved for our review under Rule 1085. We agree. We can find no indication that the timeliness issue was either argued or decided by the trial court. We hold that the issue was not preserved for our review under Rule 1085.

"Newly Discovered Evidence"

Bloodsworth makes a three pronged attack on the trial court's denial of his second motion for a new trial. First, Bloodsworth argues that the trial court failed to "recognize, much less exercise, the discretion vested in the trial court to grant a motion for new trial" under Rule 4-331. Second, he argues that the trial court erred in finding a lack of due diligence and that the evidence was not newly discovered. Lastly, Bloodsworth argues that the trial court erred in failing to consider the State's lack of diligence in disclosing the Rehill matter.

The State responds that Bloodsworth failed to argue to the trial court any basis for a new trial other than "newly discovered evidence" and therefore the other issues raised are not preserved for our review. Our review of the record confirms the State's argument. Bloodsworth's new trial motion proceeded solely upon the basis of "newly discovered evidence" under Rule 4-331(c), and our review is limited to that issue. Rule 1085.

In his disposition of the motion the trial judge said:

> As a result, I only reach the first two prongs of the newly discovered evidence test. That is that it in fact is newly discovered and that due diligence in pursuing it was made on behalf of the movant, and I find that is not the case here. I find that what has been presented to this court is not newly discovered, and the motion for new trial will consequently be denied.

In [this case], the fact that the State disclosed the evidence prior to trial is dispositive. The evidence was not "newly discovered" because that definition requires that the evidence be discovered since the trial. Furthermore, the fact that Bloodsworth chose not to seek a postponement, given the circumstances and the gravity of his case, demonstrates a lack of "due diligence." There was no error in denying the motion for a new trial.

Other Crimes

Bloodsworth argues that the trial court admitted, on two separate occasions, inadmissible evidence that he had bought "drugs" and smoked "marijuana." Bloodsworth bases his inadmissibility argument on the fact that the "other crimes" evidence had no recognizable exception, and that it was irrelevant to the issues in the case.

The State responds that in both instances the trial judge gave an appropriate curative instruction sufficient to correct the error. By so arguing the State concedes that the evidence was generally inadmissible. In *Wilhelm v. State*, the Court of Appeals said:

> When in the first instance the remarks of the State's Attorney do appear to have been prejudicial, a significant factor in determining whether the jury were actually misled or were likely to have been misled or influenced to the prejudice of the accused is whether or not the trial court took any appropriate action, as the exigencies of the situation may have appeared to require, to overcome the likelihood of prejudice, such as informing the jury that the remark was improper, striking the remark and admonishing the jury to disregard it. When such action has been taken by the trial court and found to have been sufficient by the reviewing court, judgments have not been reversed.

The logic of Wilhelm applies equally to [this case]. The curative instructions given by the trial court with respect to the inadmissible evidence was sufficient to attenuate adequately any prejudice that Bloodsworth may have suffered.

Hearsay

Bloodsworth argues that the State was permitted, through the testimony of Detective Capel, to introduce inadmissible hearsay evidence about the identifications made by Christian Shipley and Jackie Poling. Bloodsworth argues that Detective Capel impermissibly testified that Christian said: (1) that he was dissatisfied with the composite sketch of Bloodsworth he had helped to create because Bloodsworth's hair was "bushier" and his "eyes were weird", two qualities the composite sketch did not contain; (2) that Bloodsworth's hair in a photograph "looked redder than he saw. He said it was sandier when he saw it"; and (3) that Christian initially described the man he saw at the pond as six feet, five inches tall.

Bloodsworth's hearsay argument also includes the following testimony of Detective Capel about Jackie Poling's statement which dealt with his misidentification during the police line-up of the man he saw at the pond:

Q. Now, Detective, if you would read what Jackie said to you at that time?

A. Yes. Jackie, how old are you? And Jackie's answer was 8. Did you attend a lineup at Baltimore County Police Headquarters on August 13, 1984? Yes. Who was with you in the lineup room? My Mom. Did you make an identification at the lineup? And Jackie answered, yes, number three. Question, was that the right person you saw at the pond with Chris who went with Dawn? Answer, no. I picked the wrong person because I was afraid. But I told my Mom later that night when we got home that it was really number 6. Question, did anyone tell you it was number 6 prior to you getting home? His answer was no. Question, you knew number 6 was the man you saw at the pond and the man you saw take Dawn in the woods? Yes. Do you wish to add anything to this statement? No. And then Jackie signed it and Detective Ramsey and I signed it as witnesses.

In [this case], all of the disputed testimony relates directly to the identification of Bloodsworth and all of the witnesses "were present and subject to cross-examination." We hold there was no error in admitting the evidence.

Limitation of Evidence of the Second Composite Sketch

Bloodsworth argues that the trial court erred in preventing Detective Capel from being cross-examined on the circumstances surrounding the creation and disposition of a second composite picture of the suspect made with the assistance of Faye McCullough.

At trial, on cross-examination, Detective Capel was asked whether there was another composite made of the suspected killer. The detective replied in the affirmative. The trial court sustained the State's objection and refused to allow Bloodsworth to ask the detective what had become of the second composite. Bloodsworth proffered that Ms. McCullough, who had not then testified, would say that Detective Capel "became angry that her composite didn't match the composite that Shipley has given, so he said to her we are going with the little boys and threw her composite away." The trial court, however, reserved its ruling on whether it would allow Bloodsworth to recall Detective Capel for cross-examination until after Ms. McCullough had testified.

Faye McCullough testified on behalf of Bloodsworth that on the day of the murder, at approximately 6:15 a.m., when she was driving down Fontana Lane, near the murder scene, she noticed a "guy," matching the suspect's general description, "standing out in the middle of nowhere." Later that night, when Detective Capel and another officer visited Ms. McCullough in her home, she helped to create a composite. Ms. McCullough testified, however, that once the sketch was finished she told the police, "it didn't look like the man that I saw." Bloodsworth did not ask the trial court to recall Detective Capel.

The State contends that under these circumstances, Bloodsworth's right of cross-examination was not improperly curtailed. We agree.

Richard Gray as Court's Witness

Bloodsworth argues that the trial court erred in denying his request that the court call Richard Gray as a "court's" witness and in requiring him to call Gray as a hostile witness. From our review of the record it appears that what the court did was to create a "hybrid" of sorts since it told Bloodsworth to call Gray "as a hostile witness, without the necessity of laying any testimonial foundation for his hostility, with the right to lead, cross-examine, impeach and no vouching for the veracity of the witness." Without commenting on the propriety of the trial court's novel procedure, we note that Bloodsworth said, "I have no problem with that at all, sir." Given Bloodsworth's consent, he cannot now be heard to argue that it was error.

Photographic Evidence of Gray's Shoe

On the basis of relevance, Bloodsworth claims that the trial court erred in admitting, during the rebuttal portion of the State's case, a photograph of the sole of one shoe worn by Richard Gray on the day of the murder. The purpose was so that the jury could compare the pattern of that sole with one which the medical examiner previously found on the victim's neck and which he compared with that on "running type shoes" and on "some car mats." The State replies that the photograph was relevant to rebut Bloodsworth's implication that Gray was the killer. Bloodsworth concedes that his strategy was "to try to convince the jury that Mr. Gray was more likely the killer than appellant."

In [this case], the disputed evidence had a natural tendency to rebut Bloodsworth's strategy that Gray was the killer because the pattern on Gray's shoe did not match the pattern on the victim's neck. In this context, the evidence was relevant. The fact that the evidence could not conclusively absolve Gray does not detract from its relevancy.

The "Tip"

Bloodsworth argues that the trial court erred in admitting, over his objection, the following testimony from Detective Capel:

> Q. Now, what did you tell the defendant when he, when you first interviewed him, why you were there?
>   A. We told him we were investigating the murder of Dawn Hamilton and that through a tip he came up as a suspect.

Hearsay is defined as "testimony in court, or written evidence, of a statement made out of court, the statement being offered as an assertion to show the truth of matters asserted therein, and thus resting for its value upon the credibility of the out-of-court asserter." In *Purvis v. State*, we quoted with approval the following:

> "In criminal cases, the arresting or investigating officer will often explain his going to the scene of the crime or his interview with the defendant, or a search or seizure, by stating that he did so 'upon information received' and this of course will not be objectionable as hearsay, but if he becomes more specific by repeating definite complaints of a particular crime by the accused, this is so likely to be misused by the jury as evidence of the fact asserted that it should be excluded as hearsay."

In the [this case], Detective Capel never revealed what the substance of the "tip" was. The detective's testimony was not inadmissible hearsay. The court did not err in admitting the evidence.

Improper Closing Argument

Finally, Bloodsworth claims that the following closing argument by the State constituted improper comment on his failure to testify:

> So, let's look at what that evidence is. First of all, the State has brought before you all five eyewitnesses who placed the defendant at Fontana Village on July 25, 1984. Now, why is that significant? Well, it is significant because the defendant denies ever having been there. Now, these five people—

The State argues that it is proper to comment on "the question in issue and the evidence relating thereto adduced at the trial and such inferences, deductions, and analogies as can be reasonably and properly drawn therefrom . . . ." The State contends that its comments were based on facts already in evidence, i.e., the testimony of the eyewitnesses who placed Bloodsworth at the scene and Bloodsworth's statement to police that he had never been to the place of the murder. We agree.

In Wilhelm, the Court said:

> In considering whether, in the first instance, any of the remarks attributed to the prosecutor had the effect of unfairly creating prejudice against the defendant, recognition must be given to the fact that the trial judge, who presides in the arena where the forensic adversaries are engaged, is in the best position to evaluate and asses—in the context in which the remarks are made and their relationship to other factors in the trial—whether they were in fact prejudicial.

We do not construe the prosecutor's comments as an attack on Bloodsworth's failure to testify (prosecution in criminal case is not permitted to comment on accused's failure to testify). We hold that there was no error in allowing the State's argument.

QUESTIONS

1. Because appeals courts are often loath to address issues defense attorneys did not object to at trial, having competent defense attorneys is very important. List the items this Appeals Court states Bloodsworth lost his right to challenge because they were not addressed during the trial.

2. By all accounts, Bloodsworth was somewhat of an odd duck. How did his erratic behavior provide fodder for the prosecution?

3. The aptly named Bloodsworth became the first person released from death row because of the innocence project. Despite all the circumstantial evidence against him, DNA evidence from blood at the crime scene excluded him as a suspect. Read his story at http://www.innocenceproject.org.

CRITICAL **THINKING EXERCISES**

1. Tell which degree of murder would be appropriate for each of the following scenarios:
   a. Two men decide to rob an elderly lady's home. They think she is asleep. One man drives the other to the home. The driver waits in the car while the other breaks in the back door. He finds some valuables, but the lady is awake and tries to stop him. In the heat of the moment, he hits her and kills her. Which degree of murder is appropriate for the killer?
   b. In Scenario a. which degree of murder is appropriate for the driver?
   c. A man decides to kill his wife and hires a hit man to perform the job. The hit man is in fact an undercover policeman. The man is arrested. No harm befalls the wife. What degree of murder, if any, is appropriate for the man?
   d. Same scenario as above, but the hit man is a real hit man. He kills the wife, collects his bounty, and both men are arrested. What degree of murder is appropriate for the husband?
   e. What degree of murder is appropriate for the hit man in Scenario d.?
   f. A woman wants to see how fast she can drive her car over a particular stretch of road. She speeds down the road and as she rounds a curve, she hits a car stalled in the road, killing the driver. What degree of murder is appropriate for her?

2. Apply what you know about conspiracy to the following scenarios:
   a. Two gang members are drinking one night and discuss murdering the gang's leader. They never take the action. Are they guilty of conspiracy?
   b. Two wealthy businessmen discuss murdering their boss over martinis. One of them contacts someone they believe to be a hit man. They never carry out the murder. Are they guilty of conspiracy?
   c. A CIA operative discusses killing an American-born radical Islamic cleric living in the Middle East with another agent. Although there is no evidence the cleric has participated in any terrorist plots, he advocates jihad against the United States. The two agents obtain weapons and start tracking the cleric's movements. Are they guilty of conspiracy?

3. Two men decide to rob a convenience store. One will drive the getaway car and one will steal the

money. The "inside man" goes into the store, steals the money, but the clerk goes for a gun behind the counter. The robber shoots the clerk dead and leaves. The robber does not tell the driver the clerk was murdered. They drive off into the night and split the money. Can the driver be charged with felony murder?

4. A woman is in her third trimester of pregnancy, past the stage where she can obtain a legal abortion in her state. She decides she does not want the child, and arranges to have the child aborted illegally. Has she committed infanticide?

5. Explain which manslaughter charge is appropriate (voluntary or involuntary) in each of the following scenarios:

   a. A man has been shaking down elderly couples in a neighborhood for money. He has told them that he has "friends on the police force" who will protect him if they report his activity. One man gets sick of the situation and buys a gun. When the robber shows up, the elderly man pulls the gun and tells the robber to leave. When the robber moves toward him, he shoots and kills the robber.

   b. A man is cleaning his gun when a neighbor walks in. The gun is loaded, but the owner does not know it. The gun accidentally discharges killing the neighbor.

6. A woman is on the phone when her ex-husband climbs in her window screaming, "You ruined my life!" He grabs her around the throat and begins choking her. She grabs a kitchen knife and stabs him in the heart. Is his killing a crime?

7. A man suffering from ALS or Lou Gehrig's disease has decided to end his life. His condition dictates that someone must assist him to do so. He contacts a doctor who is willing to prescribe drugs that will end his life.

   a. If the doctor assists him in ending his life, has he committed murder?

   b. Does it matter what state the man and doctor live in?

   c. If both actors in this scenario live in Oregon, what steps must the doctor take before administering the fatal drugs?

8. A woman is found dead in her bed, with a gunshot wound to the head. Her sister tells police that she believed the woman's husband must have shot her. She then gives the police investigator a sealed letter postmarked a year earlier that she received from her sister with instructions to open only if "something happens to me." The investigator opens the letter, and reads that the dead woman believed her husband was planning to kill her and had threatened to shoot her while she slept.

   a. Can the letter be admitted into evidence?

   b. If you represent the husband, what argument will you make to keep the letter out of evidence?

PORTFOLIO **BUILDING**

1. The consequences for those convicted of murder or any of the related offenses are so serious that these cases deserve great attention, regardless of what side of the case you are working for. Capital cases in particular have been in the spotlight and will continue to receive media and academic attention. Sloppy handling of these cases can result in grave injustices and destroyed careers, and contribute to the potential breakdown of the justice system. Representation of a capital defendant should not be taken lightly. It is an awesome responsibility, whether you are part of the prosecution team or the defense.

   There are resources available today that were not available a few years ago. Visit each of the following sites and gather basic information about each, paying particular attention to how each may be helpful in prosecuting or defending a murder or other type of homicide case. Then begin creating a resource guide in your portfolio that you can use later.

   - National Association of Legal Investigators at www.nali.com
   - The National Legal Aid and Defender Association at www.nlada.org
   - The National District Attorneys' Association at www.ndaa.org
   - The National Association of Attorneys General at www.naag.org
   - The National Association of Criminal Defense Lawyers at www.criminaljustice.org
   - The American Bar Association's Criminal Justice Section at www.abanet.org/crimjust
   - The National Criminal Justice Reference Service at www.ncjrs.org

2. There are a number of universities with criminal justice or journalism programs that run legal clinics or investigative programs designed to help those facing charges or who believe they are deserving of exoneration. Investigate whether any such programs are available in your area and prepare a resource list for your portfolio. Here are a few resources to get you going:

   - The Exoneration Project at the University of Chicago Law School. http://www.law.uchicago.edu/clinics/exoneration

   - The Exoneration Initiative. http://exonerationinitiative.org/
   - Medill Innocence Project. http://www.medillinnocenceproject.org/
   - Criminal law clinics located at law schools in New York City. http://pages.prodigy.net/kipsively/plc.html
   - Stanford University legal clinics for prosecution and defense. http://www.law.stanford.edu/program/ clinics/

FOR FURTHER READING

1. Scottoline, L. (2001). *The Vendetta Defense.* HarperCollins. This legal thriller by a former Philadelphia attorney explores a very delayed vendetta as defense to a murder committed by a senior citizen for wrongs long ago.
2. Berendt, J. (1994). *Midnight in the Garden of Good and Evil.* Random House. Nonfiction account of a Savannah, Georgia, murder trial; later made into a movie starring Kevin Spacey.
3. Capote, T. (1994 ed.). *In Cold Blood: A True Account of Multiple Murder and Its Consequences.* Vintage Books. Classic true crime nonfiction, made into an award-winning movie.

Chapter **four**

CRIMES AGAINST THE PERSON: SEX CRIMES

CHAPTER OBJECTIVES

After studying this chapter, you should be able to:

- Define Common Law rape and explain how modern rape statutes differ from the Common Law definition
- Define forcible rape
- Understand rape shield laws and the type of evidence they exclude and allow
- Understand the consent defense
- Define forcible sodomy
- Define sexual assault with an object
- Define forcible fondling
- Define incest
- Define statutory rape
- Understand key sex crime evidence concepts

Women have got to make the world safe for men since men have made it so darned unsafe for women.

Lady Nancy Astor

Introduction

Sex crimes are perhaps the most underreported crimes. Even though crime reports show falling numbers of offenses, it is difficult to know how much faith to place in those numbers. Law enforcement personnel, paralegals, and attorneys all must tread carefully when accusing perpetrators and questioning victims. Sex crime victims often are reluctant to report the crime out of guilt feelings or fear they won't be believed and their personal life will be dissected in an attempt to turn any past indiscretion against them.

Further complicating rape and sexual assault charges is the fact that most perpetrators are someone the victim knows. According to the 2007 Crime Victimization Survey, 63.5 percent of attempted rapes were carried out by nonstrangers, for sexual assault the figure is 60.1 percent.[1] Logically, victims would be more likely to report attacks by strangers than people they knew. So many criminal justice experts believe the overall percentage of acquaintance rape and sexual assault is actually much higher.

This chapter discusses sex crimes as defined in the FBI's Uniform Crime Report. Those crimes are divided into forcible and nonforcible crimes. Forcible crimes include **forcible rape, forcible sodomy, sexual assault with an object,** and **forcible fondling.** Nonforcible crimes include **incest** and **statutory rape.** Prostitution and child molestation will be discussed in Chapter 7, Social Crimes.

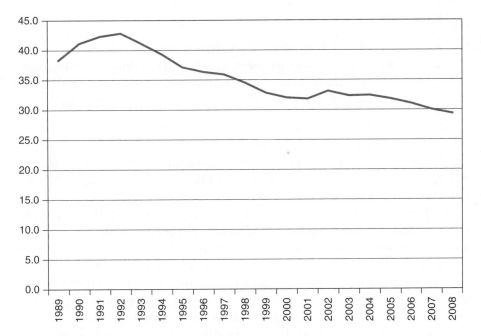

Forcible Rape Rate per 100,000 People.
Source: FBI's Preliminary Uniform Crime Report 2009.

Forcible Rape

Rape was traditionally defined as forced sexual intercourse with a woman, not one's wife. Rape was a serious offense at Common Law, often punished harshly if the victim were high-born. Remedies included payment of wergild (see Chapter 3) to the family of the victim, presumably because the victim's value on the marriage market was decreased by the loss of her virtue.

Today, every state has amended its rape laws to reflect that both males and females can be victims of rape. Most have also amended the law to allow at least limited claims of **marital rape.** For example, a woman in Virginia, one of thirty-two states to exempt spouses from rape prosecution, could only have her husband charged with rape if the two were not living together or if she was physically harmed. However, in 2002 the Virginia legislature changed the law to now allow prosecution for rape regardless of whether the couple was cohabitating or the victim suffered physical harm.[2]

Rape usually tops the sex crime hierarchy in each state's crime code. The Model Penal Code defines rape as a male having intercourse with a female other than his wife if:

a. He compels her to submit by force or by threat of imminent death, serious bodily injury, extreme pain, or kidnapping, to be inflicted on anyone; or

b. He has substantially impaired her power to appraise or control her conduct by administering or employing without her knowledge drugs, intoxicants, or other means for the purpose of preventing resistance; or

c. The female is unconscious; or

d. The female is less than ten years old.

Forcible rape
The carnal knowledge of a person against that person's will.

Forcible sodomy
Oral or anal intercourse with another person against that person's will.

Sexual assault with an object
The use of an object or instrument unlawfully to penetrate, however slightly, the genital or anal opening of another person's body against that person's will or nonforcibly when that person is unable to give consent.

Forcible fondling
The involuntary touching of another person's private body parts for the purpose of sexual gratification.

Incest
Sexual activity between relatives within a prescribed degree of sanguinity or affinity.

Statutory rape
Sexual intercourse with a victim below the age of consent or unable to consent due to a physical or mental impairment. The crime is commonly referred to as statutory rape because it is the statute that defines what may otherwise seem to be a consensual act as a crime. The legislative presumption is that some persons cannot give meaningful consent.

Rape
Traditionally defined as forced sexual intercourse with a woman, not one's wife. Modern rape definitions don't distinguish between male or female victims and have expanded the types of sexual contact that are included in the definition. Most states also allow at least a limited right to bring rape charges against a spouse and no longer require the use of direct force or physical harm.

Marital rape
The rape of one's wife.

Indecent assault or indecent touching
An attack on a person in which there is groping or other offensive touching, but no sexual act is performed or attempted.

If the male:

- "inflicts serious bodily injury upon anyone"; or
- "was not a voluntary social companion" of the victim on the occasion of the crime and she had not permitted him earlier sexual liberties; then the rape is a first-degree felony. Otherwise, it is a second-degree felony.[3]

One criticism of the Model Penal Code is that it has not been updated since 1988. Evolving concepts of sexual behavior may render some of the terms obsolete. Clearly, the abovementioned laws never contemplated marital rape, male rape victims, or female rapists. Yet, male rape victims clearly exist and females have been implicated in rape cases.

Other sex crimes include sexual assault short of rape (cases in which there is no penetration), **indecent assault or indecent touching** (in which there is groping or other offensive touching, but no sexual act is performed or attempted), incest (sexual activity between relatives within a prescribed degree of sanguinity or affinity), statutory rape (rape of a victim below the age of consent or otherwise defined by the statute as incapable of consenting due to physical or mental incapacity), and offenses such as public exposure. Because each state has a different set of sexual offenses on its books, practitioners must review the offenses in their jurisdiction. The elements the prosecution must prove vary greatly from state to state, as do the specific definitions of sexual acts covered.

Most rape statutes require prosecutors to prove three elements:

- **Proof that a sex act took place, as defined in the particular statute.** Generally, the sex act that constitutes rape is vaginal intercourse, but it can also include anal intercourse for both male and female victims as well as oral sex acts. Many state statutes require proof that there was penetration of the vagina or anus by the defendant's penis. Ejaculation is not required to prove rape.
- **Proof that the charged sex act took place by force or threat of force.** Most modern rape statutes don't require that there be physical evidence of force. The victim's testimony that he or she was forced or was afraid is enough. The victim need not risk physical harm by fighting back.
- **Proof that the sex act performed by force or threat of force was without consent or under circumstances that made consent either invalid or impossible to get.**

Defense to Rape

Consent
Voluntary agreement by a competent person to another person's proposition.

The most common defense to a rape charge is that the victim consented to sexual activity. **Consent** is a valid defense in most forcible rape cases, but not against statutory rape charges. (Statutory rape is discussed later in this chapter.)

In a rape case, the prosecution must prove as an essential element of the crime that a sexual act took place and that the victim did not consent. Sexual activity and lack of consent can be proven directly by the victim's testimony and indirectly through evidence such as bruises, medical damage, ripped clothing, and other signs of a struggle or that physical force had been used. The defense may question the victim about the physical aspects of the attack and ask her if she consented.

Once the prosecution has rested its case, the defense may again raise consent by having the defendant testify. He can also present circumstantial evidence to bolster his claim, such as evidence that the victim freely entered his apartment or bedroom or that the two had sexual relations in the past. This tactic is very likely when the victim and the defendant have known each other for a time.

If the rape case involves a stranger and there was no biological evidence obtained from the victim (as could happen if there is a delay in reporting the crime, or the assailant used a condom, or the act was not completed, or the victim showered before reporting the crime), a common tactic is to claim the victim has misidentified her assailant. This defense typically involves casting doubt on the victim's state of mind and ability to make a positive identification. Given the trauma associated with an attack and that most attacks aren't witnessed, a claim of mistaken identity can be an effective defense.

YOU MAKE THE CALL

Kobe Bryant: Mining the Victim's Past

Basketball star Kobe Bryant visited Vail, Colorado, on June 30, 2003, in preparation for knee surgery. After checking in, Bryant met a nineteen-year-old college student who worked at the hotel. What happened next is a matter of conjecture, but evidence shows the two had sex. She claimed Bryant raped her and reported the assault to the police. Bryant was later charged with sexual assault and bound over for trial. In a TV appearance, Kobe tearfully admitted to adultery, but not rape.

At a pretrial hearing, Bryant's lawyer, Pamela Mackey, mentioned the accuser's name, thus putting it in the court record. After being warned by the judge, she mentioned it five more times.[4] In fact concealing the alleged victim's identity was a problem in the run-up to the trial. Several websites published the woman's name, picture, and address. An LA disk jockey broadcast her name, and one website offered her likeness on a tee shirt with the caption "lying bitch" under it.

Bryant's legal team sought to have the woman's mental health and sexual history brought in as evidence.[5] Ultimately, both sides worked out a deal.

Bryant made a statement in court that he may have not understood the young woman was saying no. The Eagle County District Attorney dropped the charges. Bryant later paid his accuser an undisclosed sum.

If you had been the judge in the case, and the case had gone to trial, would you have let the defense bring in the accuser's mental health history? Victim advocates say doing so puts the accuser on trial, and virtually strips anyone with a mental health history of legal protection against rape. The defense argued revealing her mental health history would help the jury decide on her credibility. You make the call.

Rape Shield Laws

Before rape shield laws were enacted, defendants frequently attempted to show their victims were less than chaste by presenting evidence the victims were sexually experienced. The tactic effectively discouraged many victims from coming forward. As a result, many rapes went unreported or unprosecuted.

Rape shield law
Codified rule of evidence that provides for the exclusion of a rape victim's sexual history unless it is directly relevant to his or her consent or other evidence in the case.

In response to pressure for fair treatment in sexual assault cases, states began passing rape shield laws. **Rape shield laws** are codified rules of evidence that exclude a rape victim's sexual history unless it is directly relevant to evidence in the case. The laws are based on the premise that evidence of past sexual conduct with others simply aren't relevant to the question of whether the victim consented to sex with the defendant in this case.

A typical rape shield law from Virginia provides that:

> evidence of the complaining witness's unchaste character or prior sexual conduct shall not be admitted. Unless the complaining witness voluntarily agrees otherwise, evidence of specific instances of his or her prior sexual conduct shall be admitted only if it is relevant and is . . . [e]vidence offered to provide an alternative explanation for physical evidence of the offense charged which is introduced by the prosecution, limited to evidence designed to explain the presence of semen, pregnancy, disease, or physical injury to the complaining witness's intimate parts.[6]

Some evidence can still be admitted. Evidence that the victim had consensual sex with the defendant before is admissible if the court finds it relevant to the question of whether the victim consented this time. If there is evidence the victim engaged in sexual activity, then evidence that the victim had sex with someone else in the hours or days preceding the alleged rape (such as evidence of injury, but no biological evidence tying the victim to the defendant) would be admissible. In that case, prior sexual contact that could have caused the injury is relevant to showing that it was someone else other than the defendant who did the damage.

Evidence that the victim discussed wishing to have a sexual relationship with the defendant before the alleged rape, even if that evidence reveals prior sex acts with others, may also be admissible. In general, rape shield laws only exclude evidence of unchaste character. A prostitute's sexual history would be excluded in most cases, although evidence that she had sex for money with the defendant before may be admitted to show that she consented this time also.

HISTORICAL HIGHLIGHT

Rape Shield Law Can't Exclude Victim's Sexually Explicit E-Mail Addressed to Alleged Assailant

It began with a dinner date in November 1996. Oliver Jovanovic was a Columbia University doctoral student close to completing a PhD in molecular biology when he arranged a dinner date with a Barnard College coed he had met in an Internet chat room. The two had exchanged a series of steamy e-mail messages where the coed identified herself as a submissive partner dating a sadomasochist.

After dinner the two went to Jovanovic's apartment. What happened next is unclear. The Barnard student claimed that Jovanovic tied her up, bit her, molested her with a baton, dripped hot wax on her, and held her captive for twenty hours, all against her will. Jovanovic claimed the activities were consensual.[7] At the

ensuing trial, the defense sought to introduce the e-mail messages from the alleged victim and to question her about any prior sadomasochistic sexual activity. The trial judge ruled the evidence inadmissible under New York State's rape shield laws, and a jury convicted him. He was sentenced to at least fifteen years.[8]

Jovanovic appealed and the conviction was overturned. The appeals court ruled that New York's Rape Shield Law wasn't meant to exclude evidence of the victim's interest in sadomasochistic sexual activity when her consent to such activity was at the heart of the case. The e-mail can be used to show the victim's state of mind about consent as well as the defendant's reasonable belief about the victim's intentions. The case was scheduled for a second trial, but was dismissed when the victim declined to testify a second time.[9]

Forcible Sodomy

The FBI's *Uniform Crime Report Handbook* defines forcible sodomy as "Oral or anal sexual intercourse with another person forcibly and/or against that person's will; or not forcibly against the person's will where the victim is incapable of giving consent because of his/her youth or because of his/her temporary or permanent mental or physical incapacity."[10]

The forcible sodomy definition mirrors the definition of rape. Forcible sodomy differs from rape in that the physical act is oral or anal sex rather than vaginal intercourse. Forcible sodomy often is associated with child sexual abuse, which will be discussed in greater detail in Chapter 7. However, a growing area of concern is when teens or young adults are charged with forcible sodomy with a partner who is significantly younger than the defendant.

Studies suggest that current teenagers view oral sex very differently than previous generations. In fact many view it as 'safe sex' because there is no chance of pregnancy and low probability of venereal disease transmission.[11] The Centers for Disease Control and Prevention reports that more than half of fifteen- to nineteen-year-olds are having oral sex.[12] States have faced the conundrum of crafting laws that protect children from predatory adults while not criminalizing teen sex.

Each state has established an age of consent ranging from fourteen to eighteen. The law considers a person younger than the age of consent to lack the capacity to give consent. On the other hand, the power relationship between an adult and a teen may also impact the teen's capacity to say no. Recognizing this, many states have built an age gap provision into their forcible sodomy law. The gap is often two to four years. For example, a fifteen-year-old girl is dating an eighteen-year-old boy in a state where the age of consent is fourteen and the gap is four years. If they become sexually active, no crime is committed. Under the same scenario in a state where the age of consent is sixteen, the eighteen-year-old is guilty of a crime. If the age gap is still three years, the crime is often a misdemeanor and the eighteen-year-old is not forced to register as a sex offender as sex offender registration is usually reserved for felony sex crime convictions.

When the victim is under the **age of consent,** and the perpetrator is older than the state's age gap, forcible sodomy is a strict liability crime meaning the prosecutor need only prove that the sex act occurred to obtain a conviction. Since the law views the victim as unable to grant consent, the defendant can offer no consent defense and the power relationship based on the age difference is assumed to be sufficient to have forced the victim to perform the act.

Age of consent
The age at which the individual may consent to sexual activity. Ages of consent vary from state to state.

Sexual Assualt with an Object

The FBI's *Uniform Crime Reporting Handbook* defines sexual assault with an object as "The use of an object or instrument unlawfully to penetrate, however slightly, the genital or anal opening of the body of another person, forcibly and/or against that person's will or non forcibly or against the person's will where the victim is incapable of giving consent because of his/her youth or because of his/her temporary or permanent mental or physical incapacity."[13]

Like rape and forcible sodomy, the consent defense is available if the person possessed the capacity to give consent at the time the act occurred. A person who is inebriated, unconscious, under the age of consent, or who is physically or mentally disabled is generally considered to be unable to give consent to having an object inserted in his or her genital or anal opening if the condition is so debilitating that they can't understand what is happening or are unable to communicate effectively with the person wielding the object.

One particularly egregious example of sexual assault with an object occurred in Brooklyn, New York, in 1997 when police were called to a brawl involving Haitian immigrants. The officers arrested several of the combatants including a young Haitian named Abner Louima. After being booked for assault, Louima was led to a restroom where an officer held him down while Officer Justin Volpe repeatedly rammed a broomstick in Louima's anus. Volpe later confessed that he was getting even because he mistakenly believed Louima had punched him during the arrest. Volpe was convicted and is serving thirty years for the crime. Another officer, Charles Schwarz, was convicted of holding Louima down while the attack took place and is serving a fifteen-year sentence.[14]

Forcible Fondling

The *Uniform Crime Reporting Handbook* defines forcible fondling as "The touching of the private body parts of another person for the purpose of sexual gratification, forcibly and/or against the person's will, or not forcibly or against the person's will where the victim is incapable of giving consent because of his/her youth or because of his/her temporary or permanent mental incapacity."[15]

For example, a grandfather who videotaped himself massaging his two-year-old grandson's penis in a way that simulated masturbation was convicted of creating child pornography. Although the prosecutor in the case did not bring a forcible fondling charge, the Appeals Court's opinion related to the case made it clear the action constituted forcible fondling.[16]

Teens and adults often encounter forcible fondling in the form of workplace sexual harassment. The practice became so prevalent among teenage employees that the Equal Employment Opportunity Commission launched its Youth@Work initiative to let teenage workers and their parents know their rights to a harassment-free workplace.[17]

Nonforcible Sex Crimes

Incest

Incest is defined as "Sexual intercourse between persons who are related to each other within the degrees wherein marriage is prohibited by law."[18] Marriage laws vary from state to state. Generally, two people who could not legally marry one another because they are too closely related may not have sexual relations with one another. For example, Alaska's incest statute bars sexual relations between any two people "related, either legitimately or illegitimately, as an ancestor or descendant of the whole or half blood; a brother or sister of the whole or half blood; or an uncle, aunt, nephew, or niece by blood."[19] Other states have even broader restrictions. Delaware bars sex between people related through marriage such as "A male and his father's wife; a male and his wife's child; or a female and the child of her husband's son or daughter."[20] The difference can be important. For example, a man and his stepdaughter having consensual sex is a crime in Delaware, but not in Alaska.

When incest is not consensual, the state may bring both sexual assault and incest charges against the defendant without running afoul of double jeopardy laws.[21] In fact, consent is not a defense to incest. In cases where consent was freely given, both parties could be criminally liable.

YOU MAKE THE CALL

Incest or Love?

Woody Allen and Mia Farrow, both well-known Hollywood movie stars, had a long-term romantic relationship from 1980 to 1992. They had one biological child together and adopted two other children while together. They never lived in the same household or married, but Allen had a close relationship with their children and several other children from Ms. Farrow's previous relationships. One of those children was South Korean–born Soon-Yi Previn.

In 1992, Farrow discovered that Allen was having a relationship with twenty-one-year-old Soon-Yi. Both Allen and Previn denied that Allen was—technically at least—her stepfather. Had he been (i.e., had Farrow and Allen been legally married) the relationship would have been illegal in many states as incest based on legal affinity. No criminal charges were ever brought, and Previn married Allen in 1997.[22]

You make the call—should the relationship between Allen and Previn be classified as an incestuous one?

Statutory Rape

Defendants are charged with statutory rape when the victim was incapable of consenting because of age or because consent was obtained through trickery or coercion. Statutory rape charges are entirely dependent on the victim's age. Persons under the age of consent are unable to legally consent to sex. In many states, statutory rape is a strict liability crime, meaning the prosecution need only prove the act occurred and the victim was underage or the age gap was greater than allowed under state law.

However, some states have recognized a **mistake of age defense** where the defendant may argue that the victim lied about her age. If successful, this defense could result in a lesser charge or no charge depending on the circumstances.

For example, let's assume the state's age of consent is sixteen and the state's age gap is three years. An eighteen-year-old male dates a fifteen-year-old girl, but she tells him she is sixteen. If her parents bring statutory rape charges against him, he may argue the mistake of age defense if the state permits that defense. Since the actual age difference is three years or less, prosecutors may not charge him with a lesser sexual assault charge. If he demonstrates he did not know her true age, he has committed no crime.

Some states stratify their rape crimes based on the victim's age. For example, Tennessee has a statutory rape statute barring sex with a minor age thirteen to eighteen and a more serious rape charge for victims under thirteen. A man who

Mistake of age defense
A defense to statutory rape where the perpetrator believed the victim to be older than she actually was.

had sex with an eleven-year-old girl was charged with the more serious charge based on her age. He argued the girl told him she was sixteen. Using the mistake of age defense, he was convicted of the less serious statutory rape charge. In effect, the jury believed his intent was to break the statutory rape law, not the more serious statute.[23]

Sex Crimes Evidence Concepts

Physical evidence plays a major role in rape cases. In particular, the presence of semen and saliva can be powerful evidence that, at the very least, sexual activity took place. With the advances made in DNA analysis, identifying whose semen or saliva is present on the victim has become a routine matter. Experts can now state with virtual certainty what individual left biological material at the scene or on the victim.

But that perceived certainty presents a challenge to legal defense teams. Defense lawyers may lack the expertise to intelligently cross-examine experts. Lawyers who fail to challenge expert testimony during a trial risk losing the chance to ever do so.[24] Some defendants have cited their attorney's failure to adequately cross-examine experts as evidence they were ineffective counsel. Courts are divided on the issue and the Supreme Court has refused to address the issue.

Defense attorneys and their defendants face another hurdle. If they fail to get physical evidence tested prior to a verdict, they may never be able to. The Supreme Court has ruled that defendants lose their right to test DNA samples from crime scenes once they are convicted unless a specific state law exists giving them that right.[25] To date, forty-eight states have passed such a law.[26]

But the courts are far from one-sided on DNA evidence. The Supreme Court has ruled that the actual forensic technicians who performed DNA tests must testify in court in order to provide the accused with their Constitutional right to confront their accuser.[27] This poses problems and additional cost for prosecutors. Prior to this ruling, prosecutors often entered reports in the form of an affidavit into the record rather than demanding in-person testimony. Because trials sometimes occur years after crime scene tests, the technician perform who perform the test may be retired or even dead by the time the case comes to trial.

Prosecutors face other headaches as well. Sometimes they have DNA evidence, but no suspect. Once a crime is committed, police and prosecutors are running a race to match their DNA profile with a person before the statute of limitations expires for that crime. One creative approach has been to pass a law allowing prosecutors to bring charges against a DNA profile. In many states, prosecution begins when the prosecutor files an indictment. If the prosecutor is permitted to file charges against the DNA profile, the clock stops running on the statute of limitations and law enforcement may continue the prosecution whenever they find the person matching the profile regardless of when it occurs.[28]

In a sexual assault case, it's crucial that evidence be promptly gathered and preserved. Unfortunately, far too few rape victims report the crime immediately. Many feel angry and upset or are in a state of shock after the attack. However, prompt reporting and immediate medical attention are vital to a successful prosecution. Today, most police departments have available specially trained counselors who can work with rape victims and help gather the necessary evidence as soon as possible. Special rape kits are generally used to gather evidence and assure that the appropriate chain of custody for the evidence is followed. Most local governments also have a victim assistance program to help victims through the many stages of a criminal prosecution.

Of course, there are also cases in which the victim is unaware that an assault has occurred. For example, children may delay reporting a sexual assault or attempted assault for months or even years. And victims who have been incapacitated before the attack may not recall exactly what happened, or even they were attacked. Such cases are more difficult to prosecute than other cases, but certainly not impossible.

CONCEPT REVIEW AND REINFORCEMENT

Rape was traditionally defined as forced sexual intercourse with a woman, not one's wife. Every state has amended its rape laws to reflect that both males and females can be victims of rape. Most have also amended the law to allow at least limited claims of marital rape. The Model Penal Code defines rape as a male having intercourse with a female other than his wife if:

a. He compels her to submit by force or by threat of imminent death, serious bodily injury, extreme pain or kidnapping, to be inflicted on anyone; or

b. He has substantially impaired her power to appraise or control her conduct by administering or employing without her knowledge drugs, intoxicants, or other means for the purpose of preventing resistance; or

c. The female is unconscious; or

d. The female is less than 10 years old.

If the male:

- "inflicts serious bodily injury upon anyone"; or
- "was not a voluntary social companion" of the victim on the occasion of the crime and she had not permitted him earlier sexual liberties, then the rape is a first-degree felony. Otherwise, it is a second-degree felony.

Other sex crimes include sexual assault short of rape (cases in which there is no penetration), indecent assault or indecent touching (in which there is groping or other offensive touching, but no sexual act is performed or attempted), incest (sexual activity between relatives within a prescribed degree of sanguinity or affinity), statutory rape (rape of a victim below the age of consent or otherwise defined by the statute as incapable of consenting due to physical or mental incapacity), and offenses such as public exposure.

Most rape statutes require prosecutors to prove three elements:

- Proof that a sex act took place, as defined in the particular statute.
- Proof that the charged sex act took place by force or threat of force.
- Proof that the sex act performed by force or threat of force was without consent or under circumstances that made consent either invalid or impossible to get.

The most common defense to a rape charge is that the victim consented to sexual activity. Consent is a valid defense in most forcible rape cases, but not against statutory rape charges. Sexual activity and lack of consent can be proven directly by the victim's testimony and indirectly through evidence such as bruises, medical damage, ripped clothing, and other signs of a struggle or that physical force had been used. The defense may question the victim about the physical aspects of the attack and ask her if she consented. If the rape case involves a stranger and there was no biological evidence obtained from the victim (as could happen if there is a delay in reporting the crime, or the assailant used a condom, or the act was not completed, or the victim showered before reporting the crime), a common tactic is to claim the victim has misidentified her assailant. This defense typically involves casting doubt on the victim's state of mind and ability to make a positive identification. Rape shield laws are codified rules of evidence that exclude a rape victim's sexual history unless it is directly relevant to evidence in the case.

Physical evidence that may show the accused is not guilty may be admitted without violating rape shield laws. Evidence that the victim discussed wishing to have a sexual relationship with the defendant before the alleged rape, even if that evidence reveals prior sex acts with others, may also be admissible. In general, rape shield laws only exclude evidence of unchaste character.

Forcible sodomy is "Oral or anal sexual intercourse with another person forcibly and/or against that person's will; or not forcibly against the person's will where the victim is incapable of giving consent because of his/her youth or because of his/her temporary or permanent mental or physical incapacity."

Forcible sodomy differs from rape in that the physical act is oral or anal sex rather than vaginal intercourse. Each state has established an age of consent ranging from fourteen to eighteen. The law considers a person younger than the age of consent to lack the capacity to give consent. Many states have built an age gap provision into their forcible sodomy law. The gap is often two to four years.

When the victim is under the age of consent, and the perpetrator is older than the state's age gap, forcible sodomy is a strict liability crime, meaning the prosecutor need only prove that the sex act occurred between the two to obtain a conviction.

Sexual assault with an object is "The use of an object or instrument unlawfully to penetrate, however slightly, the genital or anal opening of the body of another person, forcibly and/or against that person's will or nonforcibly or against the person's will where the victim is incapable of giving consent because of his/her youth or because of his/her temporary or permanent mental or physical incapacity."

Forcible fondling is "The touching of the private body parts of another person for the purpose of sexual gratification, forcibly and/or against the person's will, or not forcibly or against the person's will where the victim is incapable of giving consent because of his/her youth or because of his/her temporary or permanent mental incapacity."

Incest is defined as "Sexual intercourse between persons who are related to each other within the degrees wherein marriage is prohibited by law." Generally, two people who could not legally marry one another because they are too closely related may not have sexual relations with one another.

When incest is not consensual, the state may bring both sexual assault and incest charges against the defendant without running afoul of double jeopardy laws. Defendants are charged with statutory rape when the victim was incapable of consenting because of age or because consent was obtained through trickery or coercion. Statutory rape charges are entirely dependent on the victim's age. Persons under the age of consent are unable to legally consent to sex. Some states have recognized a mistake of age defense where the defendant may argue that the victim lied about her age.

Physical evidence plays a major role in rape cases. In particular, the presence of semen and saliva can be powerful evidence that, at the very least, sexual activity took place. With the advances made in DNA analysis, identifying whose semen or saliva is present on the victim has become a routine matter. Experts can now state with virtual certainty what individual left biological material at the scene or on the victim.

Lawyers who fail to challenge expert testimony during a trial risk losing the chance to ever do so. In fact, the Supreme Court has ruled that defendants lose their right to test DNA samples from crime scenes once they are convicted unless a specific state law exists giving them that right. On the other hand, the Supreme Court has ruled that the actual forensic technicians who performed DNA tests must testify in court in order to provide the accused with their constitutional right to confront their accuser.

In a sexual assault case, it's crucial that evidence be promptly gathered and preserved. Most police departments have available specially trained counselors who can work with rape victims and help gather the necessary evidence as soon as possible.

KEY **TERMS**

Age of consent	Incest	Rape
Consent	Indecent assault or indecent	Rape shield law
Forcible fondling	touching	Sexual assault with
Forcible rape	Marital rape	an object
Forcible sodomy	Mistake of age defense	Statutory rape

CONCEPT **REVIEW QUESTIONS**

1. Define common law rape and explain how modern rape statutes differ from the Common Law definition.
2. Define forcible rape.
3. Explain rape shield laws and the type of evidence they exclude and allow.
4. Explain the consent defense.
5. Define forcible sodomy.
6. Define sexual assault with an object.
7. Define forcible fondling.
8. Define incest.
9. Define statutory rape.
10. Explain key sex crime evidence concepts.

CASE **APPLICATIONS**

Building Your Professional Skills

The following is an account of a horrific crime, a mistaken identification, and an innocent man's quest for release from a prison sentence.

It was a June night in 1998, and a little six-year-old girl was sleeping over at her grandmother's house. After falling asleep, she awoke to her grandmother's screams and ran into the kitchen to see what was going on. Her grandmother was struggling with a man, who then followed the child as she ran back to the bedroom where she had been sleeping. The man, who had killed her grandmother, then sexually assaulted the young child. When police arrived, the child told them that the man who had hurt her and her grandmother looked like her uncle, Clarence Elkins.

The police collected biological evidence, including hairs, from the crime scene and from the victims' bodies. Mitochondrial DNA testing was conducted before trial on pubic hairs found on the body of each victim. These tests excluded Elkins as the possible contributor of the hairs.

The only direct evidence presented to the jury at trial was the testimony of Elkins' niece, who had seen her attacker for a short time in poor lighting and was, after all, a young child. The prosecution admitted there was no physical evidence connecting Elkins to the crime. Elkins even had an alibi. He said he had been out drinking at several bars and then came home and took a walk with his wife.

Elkins was convicted of murder, attempted murder, and rape and sentenced to life in prison. Elkins' wife immediately went to work to prove her husband not guilty.

In 2002, Elkins' niece recanted her testimony. Elkins then paid for Y-STR testing on evidence from the crime. Y-STR is a relatively new form of testing that isolates certain characteristics of the male chromosome suitable for comparison. In 2004, Elkins' lawyers at the Ohio Innocence Project cooperated with the prosecutor's office to send evidence to nationally recognized forensic lab, Orchid Cellmar.

The testing results excluded any possibility that Elkins committed the rapes and murder. But even with two tests showing no match between crime scene evidence and Elkins, the court denied Elkins' motion for a new trial.

Mrs. Elkins didn't stop. She hired an investigator who discovered that a serial sex offender had lived close by at the time of the crimes and was serving time. Then, by coincidence, the man, Earn Mann, happened to be transferred to the Elkin's cell block. Elkins somehow managed to get a cigarette butt Mann dropped and mailed it to his wife for DNA testing. It was a match for the crime scene DNA. Elkins not only proved his own innocence, but also proved who in fact committed the horrific crime that had torn his family apart. He finally walked out of prison on December 15, 2005, after serving $6^{1}/_{2}$ years in prison.

Mann pled guilty to aggravated murder, attempted murder, aggravated burglary, and rape in 2008.[29]

QUESTIONS

1. While Elkins' attorneys supplied an alibi for him, the jury apparently didn't believe him. Remember that the public's, meaning the jury's, understanding of DNA evidence would have been limited. In fact, his attorneys may not have understood it either. Do you think the outcome would have been different if his attorneys had told the jury or elicited in testimony the fact that the DNA profile generated by the police absolutely cleared Elkins?

2. Questioning minors, especially ones who have been traumatized, is a tricky business. Attorneys who are too harsh or push too hard to get the child to change her story can be seen as ruthless or mean by a jury. No doubt Elkins' attorneys faced this conundrum. Given this, do you think Elkins would have fared better with a bench trial instead of one before a jury? If you were on his defense team, which path would you choose and why?

CRITICAL **THINKING EXERCISES**

1. A man and a woman go out on a date. They return to her apartment and get into bed. She offers him a drink and he accepts. Without his knowledge or consent, she has placed a drug in the drink that renders him unconscious. She handcuffs him to the bed, drips hot wax on him, and sodomizes him with a stick. When he wakes up in the morning, she tells him how great their night of passion was. He has her release him and goes to the hospital to tend to his injuries. Was this a rape at Common Law? Was this a rape under most modern rape statutes? Would this be reported as a rape in the Uniform Crime Report?

2. A man and a woman meet at a party. They begin making out. When he begins to get too intimate, she asks him to stop. He does not, but she keeps saying no, but takes no physical action to push him away. Is this a forcible rape under modern rape laws?

3. You are a judge in a rape case. The defense wants to introduce evidence that the victim was promiscuous. You must rule whether each item is admissible under your state's rape shield law. The items are:

   a. The fact that the victim was molested as a child.

   b. The fact that the victim went through a period of promiscuity several years ago before getting counseling.

   c. The fact that the victim and the defendant had been intimate before.

4. Using the scenario in Question 2, could the man use the consent defense to avoid conviction?

5. Again using the scenario in Question 2 except that when the woman says no, the man forces her to perform oral sex on him. She fears his reaction if she says no, so she agrees to perform the act. Is this forcible sodomy?

6. A man hits a woman with a baseball bat, knocking her unconscious and then rapes her. Is this sexual assault with an object?

7. A man and a woman are dancing at a party. He runs his hands over her breasts and grinds his hips against her during the dance. She does not object, but she does not dance with him anymore. Was this forcible fondling?

8. A seventy-year-old widower with grown children from his first marriage marries a thirty-year-old woman. His twenty-year-old son and the new wife become intimate. Is this incest? Does it make a difference if the widower becomes disabled? Does the situation change after the older man's death?

9. A twenty-year-old man has sex with a woman he believes to be eighteen. She is in fact fourteen. The state in which they reside has a consent age of sixteen and a maximum age difference of four years. Is he guilty of statutory rape? What defense could he use?

10. A woman claiming to have been raped delays reporting the rape for two days. What implications does her delay have for the gathering of evidence?

PORTFOLIO **BUILDING**

1. As a criminal justice or paralegal professional, you may spend considerable time working with victims or perpetrators of sexual assaults. The victims you encounter may belong to some of the most vulnerable segments of society. For that matter, it is also likely that some of the perpetrators you will encounter were themselves victimized earlier in their lives. Your work will require sensitivity, patience, compassion, and a healthy amount of fortitude.

Fortunately, there are resources available from a variety of sources that you can call on—many in your own community. One of the best resources is the National Sexual Violence Resource Center (NSVRC):

National Sexual Violence Resource Center
123 North Enola Drive
Enola, PA 17025
www.nsvrc.org
717.909.0710

The NSVRC collects and disseminates a wide range of resources on sexual violence including statistics, research, position statements, statutes, training curricula, prevention initiatives, and program information. Among other things, the NSVRC publishes a newsletter and coordinates National Sexual Assault Awareness Month programming and lists numerous grant opportunities for other organizations working in the field of sexual assault. Gather information from the NSVRC and add the information to the reference section in your portfolio.

2. Where would a sexual assault victim turn at your school? Research what resources are available on campus or in the immediate community. Then prepare a memo outlining those local resources. You can find additional useful information in the National Institute of Justice's study, *The Sexual Victimization of College Women*, 2000, at http://www.ojp.usdoj.gov/nij/pubs-sum/182369.htm

3. A twenty-seven-year-old female college student, who works as an exotic dancer, is hired to perform at an off-campus party by members of a neighboring university's sports team. The dancer later reported to the police that she had been sexually assaulted by three of the team members at some time during the evening. The female is black, and the accused members of the team are white.

Police and the attorneys representing the team members review twenty-three pages of medical reports, including the statement made by the sexual assault nurse who first spoke with the victim. The nurse described swelling of the victim's vaginal area and said the woman had undergone a traumatic experience.

Interviews with the victim reveal that she claimed none of the assailants used a condom during the assault.

Meanwhile, an article in a nationally known magazine reports that the victim's parents said the victim had reported another alleged gang rape ten years earlier. At that time, she is reported to have told police that three young men beat and raped her three years earlier, when she was just fourteen years old.

Based on what you have learned in this chapter, prepare a memorandum addressing the following questions:

a. If you represent the team members who have been accused of rape, what arguments will you make after reviewing the medical reports and reading the magazine article? What additional investigation will you do? If you get independent confirmation of the earlier rape allegations, what will you do with that information? What do you think the chances are you will be able to tell the jury that will hear the case about the victim's occupation? Sexual history? Past allegations? Sexual behavior in the days leading up to the party in question?

b. If you represent the victim, what arguments will you make about the medical reports? About the admissibility of the victim's prior accusations? About her recent sexual contacts?

4. As you can see, the use of DNA evidence is crucial in sexual assault cases. Locate and read the Department of Justice Office of Victims of Crime publication *Understanding DNA Evidence: A Guide for Victim Service Providers*, available at http://www.ojp.usdoj.gov/ovc/publications/bulletins/dna_4_2001/welcome.html

5. Research your state's rape and sexual assault laws. In your portfolio, outline the elements of your state's statutory rape and marital rape laws. Then describe the evidence you would need in order to secure a conviction. Then outline the elements of your state's rape law and describe what evidence you would have to present to defend against a charge of rape.

6. Locate your state's rape shield law. What evidence of the victim's past sexual history does it allow into evidence and under what circumstances?

FOR FURTHER READING

1. Brownmiller, S. (1975). *Aginst Our Will: Men, Women, and Rape.* Simon & Schuster. Classic study of rape, its origins, and its effect on women.

2. Farrow, M. (1997). *What Falls Away.* Doubleday. Mia Farrow's memoir, including her account of her relationship with Allen and adopted daughter Previn.

3. Groth, N. (2006). *Men Who Rape: The Psychology of the Offender.* Basic Books. A comprehensive clinical profile of sexual offenders with extensive information on counseling, prevention, and psychiatric treatment.

4. Kobe Bryant material online. For a look at some of the court documents in the case, visit Findlaw's document archive at http://news.findlaw.com/legalnews/documents/archive_b.html

Chapter **five**

CRIMES AGAINST THE PERSON: OTHER VIOLENT CRIMES

It is but reasonable that, among crimes of different natures, those should be most severely punished which are the most destructive of the public safety and happiness.

Blackstone, *Commentaries on the Laws of England*

Introduction

In this chapter, we look at crimes against the person other than murder and sex crimes. Robbery, assault, violent arson, and abduction and kidnapping are the traditional crimes against the person that the Common Law has dealt with for centuries. Modern technology and evolving views of proper behavior have created new laws and therefore new crimes. Cyber solicitation, online threats, and furtherance of terrorism are the personal side of the Internet's criminal legacy.

Legislatures have recognized the societal cost of prejudice and social division when they approved enhanced sentencing for hate crimes. As a result, many acts that would have simply been crimes, or not prosecuted at all in the past, now carry hefty jail sentences. Ultimately, citizens establish governments to protect themselves, their property, and their rights. Laws against violent crimes are at the heart of the social contract.

CHAPTER OBJECTIVES

After studying this chapter, you should be able to:

- Define robbery
- Explain the difference between robbery and theft
- Explain the Common Law concepts of assault and battery
- Explain the modern criminal law concept of assault and list some common variations of assault
- Define violent arson
- Define cyber solicitation
- Describe how hate groups use the Internet to recruit and incite terrorism
- Define hate crime and explain the Supreme Court's major hate crime decisions
- Define kidnapping and abduction
- Define trafficking in persons
- Describe how video surveillance is used to combat robberies
- Identify the federal agencies engaged in the fight against cyber crime

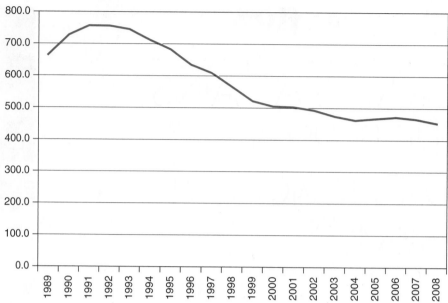

Violent Crime Rate per 100,000.

Source: FBI Uniform Crime Report 2008.

Robbery

Robbery
A theft made by force or threat of force.

Robbery is the taking of personal property from the person of another against his will, by either force or threat of force.[1] It is forcible stealing. To convict a defendant of robbery, the prosecution must prove that there was:

- A taking and carrying away of the property of another
- The intent to steal that property
- Property taken from the person or in the presence of the person
- The use of force or threat of the use of imminent force

Common acts of robbery include stopping someone and demanding his wallet when the demand is accompanied by the threat, either actual or implied, that the robber will harm the victim if he doesn't acquiesce, and demanding a teller in a bank to hand over cash. What distinguishes robbery from other forms of theft is the element of threat to the person.

Simple robbery
A theft made by force or threat of force where no weapon is used.

Armed robbery
A theft committed by force or threat of force by a person or persons carrying a weapon.

Generally, states have two categories of robbery—**simple robbery** and **armed robbery.** Simple robbery is accomplished without weapons, while armed robbery is accomplished with the use of some sort of weapon such as a knife, gun, or other dangerous instrument. Armed robbery is punished more severely than simple robbery. In fact, many states mandate long prison terms for those who commit armed robbery.

Caution: Federal Law Differs from Common Law

There are also federal criminal laws prohibiting robbery. In some cases, federal laws do not parallel the Common Law of robbery. For example, if a banking institution is federally chartered, federal law defines a bank robber as:

> Whoever by force and violence, or by intimidation, takes, or attempts to take, from the person or presence of another, or obtains or attempts to obtain by

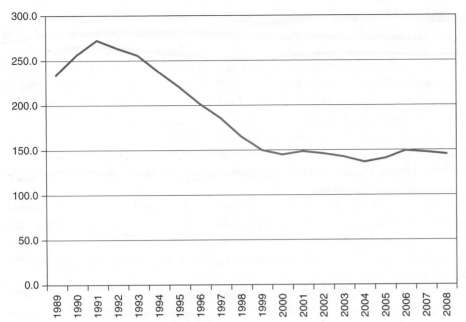

Robbery Rate per 100,000 Population.
Source: FBI Uniform Crime Report 2008.

extortion any property or money or any other thing of value belonging to, or in the care, custody, control, management, or possession of, any bank, credit union, or any savings and loan association.[2]

The Supreme Court has ruled that prosecutors seeking bank robbery convictions under this statute do not have to prove that the robber took or carried away the valuables he attempted to take.[3]

We now turn to the elements of the crime of robbery that differ from those of theft. Remember that under most state statutes, the elements of the crime of theft must also be satisfied. You will learn about theft in the next chapter.

From the Person or in the Presence of the Person

Robbery does not occur if force is neither threatened nor used. For example, if you have a party at your house, and a guest picks up a ring you left by the sink, pockets it, and leaves, she has not committed robbery even if you saw her take the ring. However, if she pockets the ring while grabbing a steak knife and brandishes it threateningly toward you while she makes her exit, then she has committed robbery. The difference is in the fear she has inflicted on you. In the first example, she has committed theft, whereas in the second, she has committed robbery. In each instance, you are out the ring, but society punishes robbery as a more serious crime because of the additional risk to the victim inherent in the use of a weapon.

By the Use of Force or Threat of the Use of Imminent Force

Robbery must be committed with the aid of the use of force or the threat of the imminent use of force. A robbery can be committed when a defendant makes a threatening move toward the victim, if it seems to the victim that the defendant is capable of inflicting harm. A demand for "Your money or your life" from an octogenarian weighing 100 pounds would probably not be robbery, but the same demand from a burly twenty-five-year-old weight lifter probably would be.

Generally, if a weapon is displayed in the presence of a victim when a theft is attempted or takes place, the crime committed is armed robbery. A typical statute defines armed robbery as: "the crime of robbery while armed with a pistol, dirk, slingshot, metal knuckles, razor, or other deadly weapon. . . . "[4]

There is an interesting line of cases in which toy weapons were used. In most cases, the fact that a toy gun appears real is enough to sustain a charge of armed robbery. However, when the victim realizes the weapon used is fake, the crime committed is simple robbery.

Two Tampa, Florida men were arrested and charged with multiple felonies for trying to rob a cab driver with a plastic gun. After arriving at their destination just after midnight, the men pulled the toy gun on the cabbie and demanded his van and all his property. The cab driver struggled with the men, drawing the attention of passing police, who arrested them.

Both men were charged with felony armed carjacking and felony attempted armed robbery. A sheriff's office spokeswoman said it didn't matter that the gun was plastic, because it looked real and was used to commit a crime. The cab driver said he "feared for his life" during the robbery.[5]

What if the defendant keeps a toy gun hidden during a robbery but it is discovered on him after the arrest? At least under federal law, that would not be armed robbery.[6]

What if the gun used in a bank robbery isn't loaded? Is that still the use of a dangerous weapon during the robbery of a federally chartered bank, qualifying the defendant for a longer sentence than if no weapon was used? According to the Supreme Court, the answer is "yes." The case involved two men who, both wearing stocking masks and gloves, entered a bank in Baltimore. One displayed a dark handgun and ordered everyone in the bank to put their hands up and not to move. While he remained in the lobby area holding the gun, his partner jumped over the counter and put $3,400 in a brown paper bag. The two were apprehended by a police officer as they left the bank. The officers discovered that the gun was unloaded. One defendant was convicted of using a dangerous weapon during a robbery. In a unanimous opinion, the Supreme Court reasoned that " . . . the display of a gun instills fear in the average citizen; as a consequence, it creates an immediate danger that a violent response will ensue. Finally, a gun can cause harm when used as a bludgeon."[7]

Bank tellers robbed by a seventy-six-year-old woman in West Mifflin, Pennsylvania, in March 2006, would agree. Marilyn Devine pointed an unloaded black 9 mm handgun at tellers in the National City Bank and gathered $5,960 in cash, stuffing it into a white trash bag. She was arrested after a low-speed chase. Devine was sentenced to twenty-three months of house arrest.[8]

Devine offered several explanations for the robbery, including that her son was suicidal over financial troubles, and she wanted to help him. The tellers she robbed, however, testified that they were harmed when Devine pointed her pistol at their faces. One of the tellers said she suffered nightmares. "You don't remember my face, but I'm haunted by yours," she said in court. In addition to the trauma Devine inflicted on her, the teller said she was upset by "the ridicule of people laughing that I got robbed by a grandmother."[9]

how does this square w/the concept of proving mens rea?

Discharging a Weapon during a Robbery

Individuals who discharge a weapon during a robbery face stiffer prison sentences than those who merely carry weapons while robbing. Federal law requires that defendants convicted of carrying a weapon "in relation to any violent or drug trafficking crime or possessing a firearm in furtherance of such a crime" face a five-year mandatory minimum sentence in addition to the sentence for the robbery. The minimum increases to seven years "if the firearm is brandished" and ten years "if the firearm is discharged."[10]

So what happens if the gun goes off accidentally? That's what happened to Christopher Dean when he was robbing a bank. After entering a bank, yelling for everyone to get down, he started emptying the teller's drawers. As he gathered cash with his left hand, he held the gun with his right. When the gun went off and blew a hole in a partition between teller stations, he cursed and ran out of the bank. Witnesses testified he seemed surprised by the gun firing.

Once he was convicted of robbery, he argued he should not get the ten-year minimum sentence because he did not intend for the gun to go off. His argument was "no intent, no crime." The Supreme Court ruled against Dean stating that the law in this case does not require separate proof of intent. For lack of putting on the gun's safety, Mr. Dean will serve a ten-year firearm discharge minimum sentence instead of a seven-year brandishing sentence.[11]

Assault

Aggravated Assault

Assault is an act of force or threat of force intended to inflict harm upon a person or to put the person in fear that harm is imminent. At Common Law, assault did not involve the infliction of physical harm. Rather, it was an act by the perpetrator that placed the victim in fear that bodily harm was imminent. Battery was the actual physical harm. Today, most crime codes combine the two into the crime of assault. States often create categories of assault, grading the crime in accordance with its seriousness. Possible criminal charges stemming from a bar brawl, for example, could include simple assault, aggravated assault, assault with a deadly weapon (if one is used), or assault with intent to kill, depending on the seriousness of the harm inflicted.

The FBI's *Uniform Crime Reporting Handbook* distinguishes between aggravated assault and simple assault. **Aggravated assault** is defined as "An unlawful attack by one person upon another for the purposes of inflicting severe or aggravated bodily injury." This type of assault usually is accompanied by the use of a weapon or by means likely to produce death or great bodily harm. (It is not necessary that injury result from aggravated assault when a gun, knife, or other weapon is used and probably would result in serious personal injury if the crime were successfully completed.)[12] The *UCR Handbook* defines **simple assault** as "An unlawful physical attack by one person upon another where neither the offender displays a weapon nor the victim suffers obvious severe or aggravated bodily injury involving apparent broken bones, loss of teeth, possible internal injury, severe laceration, or loss of consciousness."[13]

Other modern offenses more akin to the Common Law concept of assault as an act placing the victim in fear of imminent harm include ethnic intimidation, making terroristic threats, harassment, stalking, and making bomb threats. Each has its own set of unique elements that the prosecution must prove beyond a

Assault
An act of force or threat of force intended to inflict harm upon a person or to put the person in fear that such harm is imminent.

Aggravated assault
An unlawful attack by one person upon another for the purposes of inflicting severe or aggravated bodily injury. This type of assault usually is accompanied by the use of a weapon or by means likely to produce death or great bodily harm.

Simple assault
An unlawful physical attack by one person upon another where neither the offender displays a weapon nor the victims suffers obvious severe or aggravated bodily injury involving apparent broken bones, loss of teeth, possible internal injury, severe laceration, or loss of consciousness.

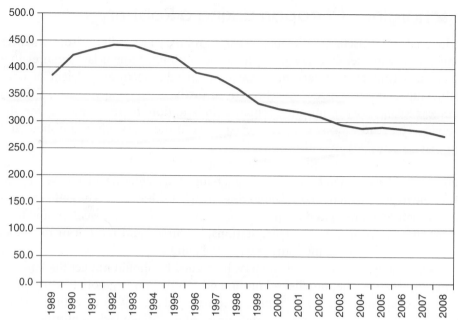

Aggravated Assault Rate per 100,000 Population.
Source: FBI Uniform Crime Report 2008.

reasonable doubt. For example, in Pennsylvania the Commonwealth must prove that someone it charges with stalking engaged in " . . . . a course of conduct or repeatedly commits acts toward another person, including following the person without proper authority, under circumstances which demonstrate . . . an intent to place the person in reasonable fear of bodily injury or an intent to cause substantial emotional distress to the person."[14] Always check the law in your jurisdiction for guidance on the specific elements required to be proven in a particular case.

Essential Elements of Assault

As you have seen in the previous discussion, each type of assault has its own specific proof requirements. It is impossible to provide a general list of elements of assault that would cover the wide variety of crimes that fall under the umbrella of "assault." However, the following example of a state assault statute serves as a starting point for analyzing the essential elements of assault:

> *The defendant commits assault if he or she:*
>
> - attempts to cause or knowingly, recklessly, or intentionally causes bodily injury to another; or
> - negligently causes bodily injury to another with a deadly weapon; or
> - attempts by physical menace to place another in fear of imminent serious bodily injury.[15]

The statute defines bodily injury as "impairment of physical condition or substantial pain" and serious bodily injury as "Bodily injury which creates a substantial risk of death or which causes serious, permanent disfigurement, or protracted loss or impairment of the function of any bodily member or organ." Deadly weapon is defined as "Any firearm, whether loaded or unloaded, or any device designed as a weapon and capable of producing death or serious bodily injury, or any other device or instrumentality which, in the manner in which it is used or intended to be used, is calculated or likely to produce death or serious bodily injury."[16]

As you can see, the simple assault statute above allows room for charging a defendant with assault for a number of acts, including injuring someone in an automobile accident, leaving a gun unlocked and unattended leading to an injury, or threatening people in such a way that they fear for their life. Depending on which subsection the defendant is charged with, the prosecution must prove there was bodily injury or serious bodily injury as that term is defined in the statute. Because so many acts may constitute assault and so many definitions to consider, proving assault can be challenging. Many prosecutors use a simple checklist during the presentation to make sure each element has been proven.

Generally, aggravated assault can be charged if the state can prove that the defendant attempted to cause or caused serious bodily injury to the victim under circumstances manifesting extreme indifference to the value of human life. In some jurisdictions, simple assault is charged as aggravated assault if the victim belongs to a class of specially protected persons such as police, firefighting personnel, teachers, and public officials.[17] Simple assault is often graded as a misdemeanor, while aggravated assault is generally graded as a felony of the first or second degree.

Violent Arson

Arson is the malicious, intentional burning of a building, vehicle, or some other property. When arson is committed with the intent to kill or injure a person it is **violent arson.** Violent arson differs from property arson in the intent of the arsonist. An arsonist who sets fire to a house with his ex-girlfriend and her new boyfriend in it in an attempt to kill them is very different from someone burning down their house to collect the insurance money.

States generally differentiate the crimes accordingly. For example, the Pennsylvania Consolidated Statutes list "Arson Endangering Persons" as a first-degree felony. "Arson Endangering Property" is a second-degree felony, and "Reckless Burning or Exploding" is a third-degree felony.[18] This chapter discusses violent arson. Arson against property will be discussed more thoroughly in Chapter 6.

At Common Law, explosions were not arson unless the building burned in the aftermath. The Model Penal Code and most state statutes consider someone who causes an explosion to have committed arson. The Model Penal Code cites the *mens rea* for arson is that the act is purposeful and reckless.[19] As a result, any intentional and reckless burning or explosion is arson even if the targeted building never ignites or explodes.

For example, a person sets a fire at the corner of a house. Before the building catches fire, a rainstorm douses the flames. The fire starter is still guilty of arson. If the act was done with the intent of killing or harming a person or persons, he may face other charges such as attempted murder. Similarly, a planted bomb that malfunctions and does not explode would still be arson because of the intent.

Hate Crimes

In recent years there has been an increase in the number of state and local governments that have enacted laws defining certain crimes as **hate crimes.** The U.S. Department of Justice defines hate or bias-motivated crimes as "offenses

Arson
Any willful or malicious burning or attempt to burn, with or without intent to defraud, a dwelling house, public building, motor vehicle, or aircraft, or personal property of another.

Violent arson
Arson committed with the intent to endanger a person or persons.

Hate crimes
Offenses motivated by hatred against a victim based on his or her race, religion, sexual orientation, handicap, ethnicity, or national origin.

motivated by hatred against a victim based on his or her race, religion, sexual orientation, handicap, ethnicity or national origin."[20]

Generally, hate crimes consist of enhanced punishment for crimes that are motivated by hate or bias against a group, ethnicity, or religion. The Department of Justice, in accordance with a federal law requiring collecting data nationwide on the prevalence of hate crimes, publishes hate crime statistics each year. The agency identified 7,783 hate crime incidents during 2008. Most of those, 4,490 were crimes against people, the remainder were crimes against property.

Today, there is hate crime legislation covering a wide range of bias, including:

- Race, ethnicity, and religion
- Sexual orientation
- Gender
- Institutional vandalism and interference with religious practices
- Mental and physical disability
- Age
- Political affiliation

The first model hate crime statute was developed by the Anti-Defamation League. The model language provides that: "A person commits a Bias-Motivated Crime if, by reason of the actual or perceived race, color, religion, national origin, sexual orientation or gender of another individual or group of individuals . . . " he violated the state's criminal laws such as murder, assault, battery, or the like. The model provision calls for bias-motivated crimes to be punished at least one degree greater than the underlying offense.

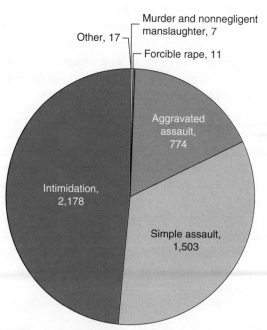

Hate Crimes: Incidents, Offenses, Victims, and Known Offenders by Offense Type, 2008.
Source: FBI Uniform Crime Report 2008.

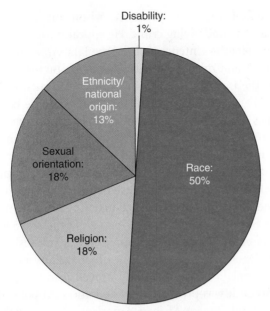

Hate Crime Incidents by Bias Motivation, 2008.

Source: FBI Uniform Crime Report 2008.

Essential Elements of a Hate Crime

To obtain a conviction for a hate crime, the prosecution must prove the underlying criminal offense such as murder, rape, assault, battery, or harassment and also prove that the defendant was motivated to commit the crime by bias against a group or category covered by the specific hate crime law in the jurisdiction. That bias is an additional essential element of the offense. The Supreme Court has upheld enhanced penalties for hate crimes in face of a challenge that such laws violate the First Amendment because they punish speech in the form of intent to commit a crime based on prejudice, and not just the underlying crime.

Proving bias may be difficult in some cases. For example, belonging to a hate group or espousing racist or religiously bigoted views are generally considered free speech and free association privileges protected by the First Amendment. But even though expression of unpopular views may be protected, acting on those views is not. Thus, if a prosecutor has evidence that a defendant declared his intent to commit a crime against a member of a class protected by a hate law, and then took action, that is not protected. If those statements occur a short time before the crime, the more likely they can be introduced as evidence of intent.

In *Wisconsin v. Mitchell*, 508 U.S. 476 (1993), the Supreme Court considered Wisconsin's hate crime statute. The case involved a young black defendant who was convicted of selecting a white youth as target for a beating. A group of young black men had gathered at an apartment complex and talk turned to a scene in the film *Mississippi Burning* in which a white youth beat a black youth praying. Mitchell suggested the group beat a white youth, stating "There goes a white boy; go get him." The group chased the white boy down and beat him so severely he spent four days in a coma.

After a jury trial, Mitchell was found guilty beyond a reasonable doubt. The same jury concluded that Mitchell had been motivated by racial bias. As a result,

Mitchell was sentenced to seven years in prison rather than the maximum two-year sentence for the underlying crime. He appealed arguing that the hate crime statute that led to his lengthy sentence violated the First Amendment. The Wisconsin Supreme Court agreed, and ruled that the law effectively punished offensive thoughts.

On appeal to the U.S. Supreme Court, the state argued that the statute only punished offensive conduct, not thought (i.e., the offensive conduct of selecting a victim on the basis of race rather than the offensive thought of wanting to select a victim because of his race). The Court concluded that the use of speech as evidence of intent in a criminal prosecution does not violate the Constitution.

However, if the state statute doesn't require that the prosecution prove beyond a reasonable doubt as part of its case in chief that bias was the motivating factor for the crime, the enhanced sentence may not be constitutional. That's the issue that faced the Supreme Court in *Apprendi v. New Jersey*, 530 U.S. 466 (2000). In 1994, a few days before Christmas, Apprendi, a white resident of the suburb of Vineland, New Jersey, shot several .22-caliber bullets into the home of an African-American family who had recently moved into the previously all-white neighborhood. Apprendi was promptly arrested and told police he had fired into the home because he didn't want African-Americans in the neighborhood. He was charged under New Jersey law with various offenses, none of which laid out a bias motivation. Apprendi plead guilty to one weapon charge, and the plea was accepted on condition that at sentencing the state could argue for an enhanced sentence due to the alleged racial motivation for the shooting. Apprendi agreed on condition he could raise the constitutionality of the enhanced sentence on appeal.

At the sentencing hearing, the prosecution presented evidence of bias, and the judge found by a preponderance of the evidence that racial bias was the motive for the shooting. The judge then enhanced the sentence as New Jersey's hate crime legislation allowed. He appealed, arguing that the due process clause of the Constitution required that a jury, not a judge, decide whether bias was the motive for the crime, and that the appropriate standard of proof was beyond a reasonable doubt. When the case reached the Supreme Court, a majority of the justices agreed. The Court held that "The Constitution requires that any fact that increases the penalty for a crime beyond the prescribed statutory maximum, other than the fact of a prior conviction, must be submitted to a jury and proved beyond a reasonable doubt."[21]

The Court ruled in 2003 that states can make it a crime to burn a cross. Virginia's legislature had passed a law that created a presumption that burning a cross was racially motivated and made it a crime to do so. The Supreme Court struck the presumption, but ruled that the state can charge and convict citizens who burn crosses with the intent to intimidate. Criminalizing cross burning does not violate the First Amendment.[22]

For those working in law enforcement investigating and prosecuting hate crimes, the Anti-Defamation League collects data on hate crime legislation, available at its website, http://www.adl.org/.

Cyber Crimes—Solicitation, Hate Speech, and Inciting Terrorism

The computer and, more specifically, the Internet have created massive opportunities for business and criminals. Internet communications can be accomplished anonymously or operate under the privacy protections provided by Internet service providers (ISPs), many of whom operate overseas far from the reach of U.S. law enforcement. Additionally, the sheer volume of Internet traffic makes finding any particular message difficult.

Law enforcement officials may have been slow to realize the threat posed by cyber criminals, but now computer-based crimes occupy a significant portion of law enforcement efforts. A **cyber crime** is a criminal act performed with the aid of a computer. Most cyber crimes are property based, where the perpetrator is trying to steal an unwitting person's money, identity, or other property. But the computer can be an entrée into violent crime when it becomes the medium to:

Cyber crime
Criminal act performed with the aid of a computer.

- solicit others to commit violent acts;
- agitate for racial, religious, or gender-based violence; or
- facilitate acts of terror.

Law enforcement officials thus far have been reluctant to name computer-based crimes differently from the same crime committed without a computer. They fear tying any legal definition to a specific technology when technology changes so quickly.

Solicitation

Criminal solicitation under Common Law occurs when one person requests or encourages another to perform a criminal act. The charge is the same whether the solicitation occurs in person, through the mail, on the phone, or over the Internet. But Internet solicitation is particularly harmful because it can reach large numbers of people easily, and is more likely to involve minors.

Criminal solicitation
Under Common Law, a crime which occurs when one person requests or encourages another to perform a criminal act.

Some studies have suggested that one in five children receives an unwanted sexual solicitation online each year, and that 50,000 sexual predators prowl the Internet for child victims at any given time.[23]

In any solicitation scenario, the crime is committed when the perpetrator makes an offer or suggestion that the other person or persons commit a crime. Whether the person to whom the suggestion is made commits the crime is irrelevant. To convict a person of solicitation, the prosecutor must prove that the solicitation was made and that the person soliciting the crime sought to induce the person hearing the solicitation to commit the crime.

The soliciting individual need only attempt to communicate with the person he hopes to induce to commit a crime. In cyberspace, that means that a person soliciting a child to have sex with him is guilty of the crime even if the child's e-mail filter moves the e-mail message to the trash bin.

Hate Speech

Threatening e-mails directed at particular people because of their race, religion, or sexual orientation may run afoul of state hate speech laws. Hate speech laws make it a crime to "under . . . threat of force, willfully injure, intimidate, interfere with, oppress, or threaten any other person in the free exercise or enjoyment of any right or privilege secured to him or her by the Constitution or laws . . . of the United States because of the other person's race, color, religion, ancestry, national origin, disability, gender, or sexual orientation."[24]

Hate speech
The crime of using the threat of force to willfully injure, intimidate, interfere with, oppress, or threaten any other person in the free exercise or enjoyment of any right or privilege secured to him or her by the Constitution or law of the United States because of the other person's race, color, religion, ancestry, national origin, disability, gender, or sexual orientation.

Like other hate crime laws, hate speech, if proven, is used to increase the sentence given to the person convicted of the crime. E-mailed threats of violence would probably bring a charge of "making terroristic threats," but if the e-mail indicated the motivating reason for the threat was the recipient's race, color, religion, ancestry, national origin, disability, gender, or sexual orientation, then the crime could be considered a hate crime warranting a longer sentence.

Terrorism

In addition to providing an outlet for pedophiles and racists, the Internet has created safe forms of communication for terrorists residing in different countries around the world. Some communications between some of the 9/11 hijackers consisted of computer code embedded in an image on a website. A Canadian woman of Iranian descent testified that she was part of a group who jointly accessed an e-mail account. Each member would write a message and save it as a draft of an e-mail. No e-mail was actually transmitted across the Internet. Group members could access the site and communicate by reading and writing drafts.

Currently, Internet service providers are not required to preserve e-mails for any specific period of time. However, law enforcement officials may ask ISPs to preserve e-mails they may find relevant to a criminal investigation and must hold such electronic communications for ninety days pending the issuance of a subpoena.

Abduction and Kidnapping

Perhaps no crime sends more chills down a parent's back than the thought of a child being abducted. Yet children disappear at an alarming rate every year. For example, according to the National Center for Missing and Exploited Children, "800,000 children are reported missing every year in the U.S. or 2,000 every day. Of that number, an estimated 200,000 are abducted by family members; 58,000 by nonfamily members, the primary motive for which is sexual;[25] and 115 represent the most serious cases in which the child is abducted by a stranger and killed, held for ransom, or taken with the intention to keep."[26]

All fifty states as well as the federal government have laws in place criminalizing abduction, whether the victim is a child or an adult. In addition, removing a child from a custodial parent or guardian's care outside the parameters of a visitation order is a crime. Transporting a child across state lines in conjunction with a parental or other abduction violates federal law, as is transporting an abducted adult. But for a long time, there was very little coordination of efforts to recover missing children or adults since so many jurisdictions were involved. That all changed after several well-publicized cases involving the abduction and murder of children, including the abduction and murder of Adam Walsh and Polly Klaas. Adam was snatched from a store in Florida in 1981, and Polly was abducted from a slumber party in her California home in 1993 and later found murdered.

Kidnapping
The crime of taking and detaining a person against his will by force, intimidation, or fraud. Holding the victim for ransom is not required.

Abduction
The illegal carrying away of a person by force or coercion, generally with the intent to do harm to the victim. Today, the same criminal statute generally covers kidnapping and abduction.

State Statutes

Kidnapping is generally defined as the crime of taking and detaining a person against his will by force, intimidation, or fraud. **Abduction** is generally defined as the illegal carrying away, by force or deception, of a person. Kidnapping can occur when the person is held even momentarily, whereas abduction requires that the victim be moved from one place to another. Both crimes may involve the demand for a ransom, and may be punished more severely when ransom is demanded.

Many states combine kidnapping and abduction into one offense and then create other offenses to cover situations outside the definition. A typical state kidnapping and abduction statute is Pennsylvania's. It provides that:

> A person is guilty of kidnapping if he unlawfully removes another a substantial distance under the circumstances from the place where he is found, or if he unlawfully confines another for a substantial period of time in a place of isolation, with any of the following intentions:
>
> - To hold for ransom or reward, or as a shield or hostage;
> - To facilitate the commission of a felony or flight thereafter;
> - To inflict bodily injury on or to terrorize the victim or another;
> - To interfere with the performance by public officials of any governmental or public function.

The Pennsylvania statute goes on to define confinement or removal as unlawful if " . . . it is accomplished by force, threat or deception, or, in the case of a person who is under the age of 14 years or an incapacitated person, if it is accomplished without the consent of a parent, guardian or other person responsible for general supervision of his welfare."[27]

Pennsylvania also prohibits unlawful restraint,[28] false imprisonment,[29] interfering with custody of children,[30] interfering with custody of committed persons,[31] concealment of whereabouts of child,[32] and luring a child into a motor vehicle.[33] Each crime has its own elements and its own penalty. For example, the crime of luring a child into a motor vehicle does not require proof of the intent to harm that child, only proof that the child was persuaded or threatened and that there was no permission given by a guardian.[34]

HISTORICAL HIGHLIGHT

The Lindbergh Baby Abduction

The first federal kidnapping law was known as the Lindbergh Law, and required that the victim be transported over a state line for federal jurisdiction to attach. Charles Lindbergh was the first man to fly a plane solo across the Atlantic, piloting the *Spirit of St. Louis* across the ocean on May 21, 1927. He would again attract national attention when his son was kidnapped and murdered.

The Lindbergh kidnapping began on March 1, 1932, when Charles Lindbergh's twenty-month-old son disappeared from his crib at the family's Princeton, New Jersey, home.[35] A note left by the kidnappers demanded a ransom of $50,000. A baby believed to be the abducted child was found dead after the ransom was paid, and his suspected kidnapper was tried and executed. The FBI, which had no jurisdiction over kidnapping at the time, became involved because the ransom was paid in gold certificates, over which it did have jurisdiction. Its investigation eventually led to the suspect, Bruno Hauptmann, a carpenter who quit his job on the day the ransom was paid and began playing the stock market.

At the time, the trial was referred to as the Trial of the Century.[36] When the Lindbergh baby was kidnapped, it was not yet a federal offense to take and hold a person for ransom, but almost immediately such a law was proposed.[37] The current federal kidnapping statute was originally named the Lindbergh Act. It greatly expanded the influence of the Federal Bureau of Investigations, which used the law to crack down on a nationwide rash of abductions for ransom.[38]

Essential Elements of Kidnapping and Abduction

To prove kidnapping, the government must show that the victim was taken or detained against his or her will. If the victim is competent to testify and survives and can testify, her testimony can establish that the defendant took or detained her against her will. Of course, witnesses to the event can also testify as to what they observed. In the case of a young victim who cannot be qualified to testify due to his tender years, a witness or circumstantial evidence can be used. For example, the elements can be established by showing that the child was recovered from the defendant's presence or custody and the defendant lacked the legal guardian's permission to take the child. Prosecutors can also present circumstantial evidence in cases where the victim doesn't survive.

Kidnapping doesn't require that the perpetrator demand a ransom. Since state laws differ, always check the specific statute in your jurisdiction for the essential elements the prosecutor must prove.

Federal Statutes

Federal law defines a kidnapper as someone who "unlawfully seizes, confines, inveigles, decoys, kidnaps, abducts, or carries away and holds for ransom or reward or otherwise any person . . . " and transports that person " . . . in interstate or foreign commerce, regardless of whether the person was alive when transported across a State boundary if the person was alive when the transportation began."[39] Kidnapping those under the age of eighteen carries the potential for a longer sentence than if the victim is an adult. Likewise, if the young victim is subjected to life-threatening treatment or sexual or physical abuse, the penalty may be increased when the defendant's sentence is calculated under the federal Sentencing Guidelines.[40]

Trafficking in Persons

The Justice Department refers to trafficking in persons as a "form of modern day slavery." Specifically, the Trafficking Victims Protection Act identifies two forms of trafficking in persons: sex and labor. **Sex trafficking** is an enterprise "in which a commercial sex act is induced by force, fraud, or coercion, or in which the person induced to perform such act has not attained 18 years of age." Trafficking also supplies what are colloquially known as "sweat shops" with cheap or free labor. **Labor trafficking** is defined as "the recruitment, harboring, transportation, provision, or obtaining of a person for labor or services, through the use of force, fraud, or coercion for the purpose of subjection to involuntary servitude, peonage, debt bondage, or slavery."[41]

The crime is tied heavily to illegal immigration and both the Justice Department and the Department of Homeland Security enforce laws against human trafficking. Even though victims are often foreign nationals, trafficking victim protection is available to U.S. citizens as well. Because human trafficking victims are often in the country illegally and/or are sending money home to their families, they are often reluctant to report their situation to authorities.

In response, the government, operating under a presidential executive order, grants many victims of human trafficking refugee status. In some circumstances, minors may receive refugee status as well.[42]

Sex trafficking
An enterprise "in which a commercial sex act is induced by force, fraud, or coercion, or in which the person induced to perform such act has not attained 18 years of age."

Labor trafficking
The recruitment, harboring, transportation, provision, or obtaining of a person for labor or services, through the use of force, fraud, or coercion for the purpose of subjection to involuntary servitude, peonage, debt bondage, or slavery.

When caught, human traffickers are often charged with a variety of crimes including kidnapping, prostitution, assault, immigration violations, and wage and hour violations.

HISTORICAL HIGHLIGHT

The Doctor's Maid

Wealthy Filipinos traditionally have maids to help with housework and child rearing. So when Jefferson and Elnora Calimlim needed help, they recruited Erma Martinez, a poor farmer's daughter, to travel from the Philippines to their home in Milwaukee, Wisconsin. The Calimlims were both doctors and had three children.[43]

Ms. Calimlim's father brought Erma to the United States on a tourist visa. He gave his daughter her passport to keep. Erma lived in the basement of the Calimlim's 8,000 square feet house, where she was hidden from all those outside the family. Erma believed she was only going to work for the Calimlims for five years, but she ended up in what amounted to modern slavery for almost two decades.

Erma cleaned, painted, washed laundry, and made grocery lists for the family. She was never allowed outside of the house and did not have a driver's license. The Calimlims paid her $150 per month for the first ten years she worked for them, and $400 per month after

that. Erma sent money home to her family, providing money for clothes and education for her siblings.

In letters, her family pressed her for more money. Faced with demands from the Calimlims and her family, she kept working.

Only after the oldest Calimlim child divorced his wife did the scheme unravel. The scorned ex-wife phoned the Justice Department with an anonymous tip. FBI and Immigration and Customs Enforcement agents raided the Calimlim home and found Erma hiding in her closet, scared she would be deported.

Erma testified at the Calimlim trial. Both Drs. Calimlim were sentenced to four years in prison after being convicted of forcing Erma to work as their domestic servant, harboring an illegal alien for nineteen years, and using threats of serious harm and physical restraint against her. The oldest Calimlim son received a sentence of 120 days' home confinement, three years' supervised release, and a $5,000 fine.

Erma is also suing for back wages, which have been estimated at $704,635.[44]

Evidence in Violent Crimes Against the Person

We turn now to evidence. Some of the concepts you learned in earlier chapters apply to the crimes you have studied in this chapter, too. This section is not meant to be exhaustive, as an entire course can easily be devoted to evidentiary issues, but is meant to alert you to evidentiary issues. If you can identify potential evidentiary problems, you will know when to get expert help.

We start with robbery—a crime in which eyewitness accounts and videotaped evidence play key roles. No doubt you have seen many examples of armed robbery videotapes on television, perhaps on the local daily newscast. Often, the tapes are used as a way for police to request for anyone who recognizes the suspect caught in the act on camera to call and identify him or her. Frequently, suspects identified on film will plead guilty after having been caught red-handed. Of course, prosecutors have to be ready to follow standard rules of evidence should they have to take the case to trial. They will have to explain how the camera works and authenticate the image. They will also have to explain how the defendant was identified.

If the defendant is nabbed at the scene or close by, perhaps with cash, or in the case of a jewelry store heist, with expensive jewelry, then an eyewitness identification is likely. That's in addition to having the owner identify the goods. In the case of a bank robbery, that may mean providing a list of serial numbers from the cash taken and matching it against the cash in the defendant's possession. If the robbery involved jewelry, the store owner would identify the jewelry as his.

Video equipment is everywhere these days and can greatly help efforts to identify suspects or track their movements. Some jurisdictions even have cameras mounted at strategic locations that can be remotely activated when needed. For example, in the District of Columbia, the Metropolitan Police Department has a secure, wireless network of nineteen permanently installed cameras at strategic locations. Other cameras can be added as needed. The system is not always in operation, but can and has been operated during major events like large-scale demonstrations, the 2009 presidential inauguration event, and during major investigations or when the terror alert is raised. The cameras are in addition to numerous traffic cameras in constant operation at strategic intersections. These can be viewed in real time by anyone with an Internet connection.

Arson investigations will naturally focus on the cause of the fire. An accidental fire is not a criminal act, while an intentional one may very well be. Determining the cause of the fire is therefore of primary concern for prosecutors and the defense. This requires the assistance of experts who can often determine whether there was an accelerant used to start and intensify the fire—a key finding to support the hypothesis that the fire was not accidental. When the alleged arson involves loss of human life, investigators will also look for other circumstantial evidence to establish motive such as the relationship between the suspect and the victim.

HISTORICAL HIGHLIGHT

Barbie Bandits Identified on Video

When two attractive blonde teens in big, bold sunglasses walked into a Bank of America branch on February 27, 2007, no one except the teller they approached had any inkling that the bank was about to be robbed. But the women, Ashley Miller and Heather Johnston, approached the teller station and handed over a note to Benny Allen III, who was in on the deal. He gave the women $11,000 in cash.[45]

The women then took the money, bought designer clothes, and had their hair done. Meanwhile, their laughing and giggling faces barely concealed behind the dark glasses were broadcast on the local news channels and on the Internet. Soon, tips poured in. The women were identified by viewers and arrested just two days after the video began circulating.

Johnston cooperated with authorities and received a lengthy probation sentence while Miller received a ten-year sentence, of which she will have to serve two years before being placed on parole.

With the explosion of cyber crimes worldwide, law enforcement and the legal system are fighting to keep up. Local law enforcement departments seldom have the expertise to track down the perpetrators of cyber crimes and have to rely on expertise from other agencies. Sometimes, though, cyber crime is local and surprisingly easy to track. New technology simply creates alternative ways to commit the same old crimes. Consider the recent arrest of a Pennsylvania man for allegedly setting up a fake MySpace page using a woman's name and identity and then posting under her name. After the Pennsylvania State Police tracked him down, presumably by identifying the computer service from which the postings were made and subpoenaing that company for their customer's name and address, they charged him with stalking, identity theft, and harassment.[46]

The Department of Justice has assumed a lead role in cyber crime evidence. The agency has created a manual, *Searching and Seizing Computers and Seizing*

Electronic Evidence in Criminal Investigations, which helps law enforcement agencies tackle cyber crime effectively. The agency maintains a Web page devoted to cyber crime at www.cybercrime.gov. The Web page provides information for local law enforcement agencies on where to turn for help when they suspect a cyber crime has hit within their jurisdiction.

The primary federal law enforcement agencies that investigate domestic crime on the Internet include the Federal Bureau of Investigation (FBI), the U.S. Secret Service, the U.S. Immigration and Customs Enforcement (ICE), the U.S. Postal Inspection Service, and the Bureau of Alcohol, Tobacco and Firearms (ATF).

Each law enforcement agency has a headquarters in Washington, D.C., and has specialists available to handle cyber crime. ICE, the FBI, and the Department of Justice also provide assistance for cases involving kidnapping and trafficking in persons.

CONCEPT **REVIEW AND REINFORCEMENT**

Robbery is the taking of personal property from the person of another against his will, by either force or threat of force. To convict a defendant of robbery, the prosecution must prove that there was:

- A taking and carrying away of the property of another
- The intent to steal that property
- Property taken from the person or in the presence of the person
- The use of force or threat of the use of imminent force

What distinguishes robbery from other forms of theft is the element of threat to the person. Simple robbery is accomplished without weapons, while armed robbery is accomplished with the use of some sort of weapon such as a knife, a gun, or other dangerous instrument. Armed robbery is punished more severely than simple robbery.

Under most state robbery statutes, the elements of the crime of theft must also be satisfied.

Robbery must be committed with the aid of the use of force or the threat of the imminent use of force. Generally, if a weapon is displayed in the presence of a victim when a theft is attempted or takes place, the crime committed is armed robbery. Individuals who discharge a weapon during a robbery face stiffer prison sentences than those who merely carry weapons while robbing.

Assault is an act of force or threat of force intended to inflict harm upon a person or to put the person in fear that harm is imminent. Today, most crime codes combine assault and battery into the crime of assault. States often create categories of assault, grading the crime in accordance with its seriousness.

Aggravated assault is defined as "An unlawful attack by one person upon another for the purposes of inflicting severe or aggravated bodily injury. This type of assault usually is accompanied by the use of a weapon or by means likely to produce death or great bodily harm." The *UCR Handbook* defines simple assault as "An unlawful physical attack by one person upon another where neither the offender displays a weapon nor the victim suffers obvious severe or aggravated bodily injury involving apparent broken bones, loss of teeth, possible internal injury, severe laceration, or loss of consciousness."

Each type of assault has its own specific proof requirements. *The defendant commits assault if he or she*:

- attempts to cause or knowingly, recklessly, or intentionally causes bodily injury to another; or
- negligently causes bodily injury to another with a deadly weapon; or
- attempts by physical menace to place another in fear of imminent serious bodily injury.[47]

The statute defines bodily injury as "impairment of physical condition or substantial pain" and serious bodily injury as "Bodily injury which creates a substantial risk of death or which causes serious, permanent disfigurement, or protracted loss or impairment of the function of any bodily member or organ." Deadly weapon is defined as "Any firearm, whether loaded or unloaded, or any device designed as a weapon and capable of producing death or serious bodily injury, or any other device or instrumentality which, in the manner in which it is used or intended to be used, is calculated or likely to produce death or serious bodily injury."

Generally, aggravated assault can be charged if the state can prove that the defendant attempted to cause or caused serious bodily injury to the victim under circumstances manifesting extreme indifference to the value of human life. In some jurisdictions, simple assault is charged as aggravated assault if the victim belongs to a class of specially protected persons such as police, firefighting personnel, teachers, and public officials. Simple assault is often graded as a misdemeanor, while aggravated assault is generally graded as a felony of the first or second degree.

Robbery and related crimes are often solved with the assistance of video filmed during the commission of the event and eyewitness identification.

Arson is the malicious, intentional burning of a building, vehicle, or some other property. When arson is committed with the intent to kill or injure a person it is violent arson.

At Common Law, explosions were not arson unless the building burned in the aftermath. The Model Penal Code and most state statutes consider someone who causes an explosion to have committed arson. The Model Penal Code cites the *mens rea* for arson is that the act is purposeful and reckless. As a result, any intentional and reckless burning or explosion is arson even if the targeted building never ignites or explodes. Proof of arson often requires expert testimony on the origin of the fire and whether it was likely intentionally set or accidental.

The U.S. Department of Justice defines hate or bias-motivated crimes as "offenses motivated by hatred against a victim based on his or her race, religion, sexual orientation, handicap, ethnicity, or national origin." Generally, defendants convicted of hate crimes receive enhanced punishment because the crime was motivated by hate or bias against a group, ethnicity, or religion.

Model hate crime language provides that: "A person commits a Bias-Motivated Crime if, by reason of the actual or perceived race, color, religion, national origin, sexual orientation or gender of another individual or group of individuals . . . " he violated the state's criminal laws such as murder, assault, battery, or the like. The model provision calls for bias-motivated crimes to be punished at least one degree greater than the underlying offense.

To obtain a conviction for a hate crime, the prosecution must prove the underlying criminal offense such as murder, rape, assault, battery, or harassment and also prove that the defendant was motivated to commit the crime by bias against a group or category covered by the specific hate crime law in the jurisdiction. That bias is an additional essential element of the offense.

Proving bias may be difficult in some cases. For example, belonging to a hate group or espousing racist or religiously bigoted views are generally considered free speech and free association privileges protected by the First Amendment. But even though expression of unpopular views may be protected, acting on those views is not. Prosecutors must prove the defendant's bias beyond a reasonable doubt to obtain the enhanced sentence.

Computer-based crimes occupy a significant portion of law enforcement efforts. Most cyber crimes are property based, where the perpetrator is trying to steal an unwitting person's money, identity, or other property. But the computer can be an entrée into violent crime when it becomes the medium to:

- solicit others to commit violent acts;
- agitate for racial, religious, or gender-based violence; or
- facilitate acts of terror.

Criminal solicitation under Common Law occurs when one person requests or encourages another to perform a criminal act. Whether the person to whom the suggestion is made commits the crime is irrelevant. To convict a person of solicitation, the prosecutor must prove that the solicitation was made and that the person soliciting the crime sought to induce the person hearing the solicitation to commit the crime.

The soliciting individual need only attempt to communicate with the person he hopes to induce to commit a crime. In cyberspace, that means that a person soliciting a child to have sex with him is guilty of the crime even if the child's e-mail filter moves the e-mail message to the trash bin.

Threatening e-mails directed at particular people because of their race, religion, or sexual orientation may run afoul of state hate speech laws. Hate speech laws make it a crime to "under . . . threat of force, willfully injure, intimidate, interfere with, oppress, or threaten any other person in the free exercise or enjoyment of any right or privilege secured to him or her by the

Constitution or laws . . . of the United States because of the other person's race, color, religion, ancestry, national origin, disability, gender, or sexual orientation."

Several federal agencies have taken the lead in cyber crimes and have experts on hand who can help local law enforcement who encounter a suspected crime committed with the assistance of a computer or related technology. These agencies include the Federal Bureau of Investigation (FBI), the U.S. Secret Service, the U.S. Immigration and Customs Enforcement (ICE), the U.S. Postal Inspection Service and the Bureau of Alcohol, Tobacco and Firearms (ATF).

Kidnapping is the crime of taking and detaining a person against his will by force, intimidation, or fraud. Abduction is the illegal carrying away, by force or deception, of a person. Kidnapping can occur when the person is held even momentarily. Abduction requires that the victim be moved from one place to another.

To prove kidnapping, the government must show that the victim was taken or detained against his or her will. If the victim is competent to testify and survives and can testify, her testimony can establish that the defendant took or detained her against her will. Of course, witnesses to the event can also testify as to what they observed. In the case of a young victim who cannot be qualified to testify due to his tender years, a witness or circumstantial evidence can be used.

Federal law defines a kidnapper as someone who "unlawfully seizes, confines, inveigles, decoys, kidnaps, abducts, or carries away and holds for ransom or reward or otherwise any person . . ." and transports that person " . . . in interstate or foreign commerce, regardless of whether the person was alive when transported across a State boundary if the person was alive when the transportation began." Kidnapping those under the age of eighteen carries the potential for a longer sentence than if the victim is an adult. Likewise, if the young victim is subjected to life-threatening treatment or sexual or physical abuse, the penalty may be increased when the defendant's sentence is calculated under the federal Sentencing Guidelines.

The Trafficking Victims Protection Act identifies two forms of trafficking in persons: sex and labor. Sex trafficking is an enterprise "in which a commercial sex act is induced by force, fraud, or coercion, or in which the person induced to perform such act has not attained 18 years of age." Trafficking also supplies what are colloquially known as "sweat shops" with cheap or free labor. Labor trafficking is defined as "the recruitment, harboring, transportation, provision, or obtaining of a person for labor or services, through the use of force, fraud, or coercion for the purpose of subjection to involuntary servitude, peonage, debt bondage, or slavery."

KEY **TERMS**

Abduction
Aggravated assault
Armed robbery
Arson
Assault
Criminal solicitation

Cyber crime
Hate crimes
Hate speech
Kidnapping
Labor trafficking
Robbery

Sex trafficking
Simple assault
Simple robbery
Violent arson

CONCEPT **REVIEW QUESTIONS**

1. What is robbery?
2. What is the difference between robbery and theft?
3. What are the Common Law concepts of assault and battery?
4. What is the modern criminal law concept of assault? List some common variations of assault.
5. What is violent arson?
6. What is cyber solicitation?

7. How do hate groups use the Internet to recruit and incite terrorism?

8. What is a hate crime? Why did the Supreme Court rule that hate crime legislation is constitutional?

9. What are kidnapping and abduction?

10. What is trafficking in persons?

11. How is video surveillance is used to combat robberies?

12. Which federal agencies have taken the lead role in the fight against cyber crime?

CASE **APPLICATIONS**

Building Your Professional Skills

READ THE FOLLOWING ABRIDGED CASE AND ANSWER THE QUESTIONS THAT FOLLOW.

Scott Sornberger and Theresa Sornberger, et al., v. City of Knoxville, Illinois, et al., 434 F. 3d 1006 (2006)

On January 12, 2000, First Bank was robbed by a perpetrator wearing a baseball cap. Only two First Bank employees got a firsthand look at the robber, and only Tracy Clevenger, the teller who handed money to the robber, caught a glimpse of the robber's face. Clevenger described the perpetrator as male, 5′9″, approximately 160 pounds, dark complected, with dark eyes and hair, clean-shaven, and in his thirties. Knoxville, Illinois, Chief of Police Rick Pesci was the first law enforcement official to arrive at the scene. He took the robber's description from Clevenger and called the FBI to assist in the investigation.

Initially, neither eyewitness nor any other First Bank employee was able to identify the robber. Shortly after the robbery, however, as three First Bank employees began reviewing bank surveillance video, Brent Dugan, a First Bank employee, remarked that the robber "looked like" Scott Sornberger, who was an acquaintance of Dugan and a former customer of First Bank. First Bank employees Diane Carter and Roger Schultz agreed that the perpetrator captured on video bore some likeness to Scott. After watching the same footage from a different angle, however, Dugan remarked that he was less sure of the likeness. Chief Pesci, who was present intermittently while the employees viewed the surveillance tapes, heard at least one of these comments on the resemblance of the robber to Scott.

Acting on this information, Chief Pesci proceeded to question the First Bank employees about Scott Sornberger. Chief Pesci learned that Scott and Teresa had been customers of First Bank, but that their account had been closed because of a zero or negative account balance. That evening, Chief Pesci sent Knoxville police officers to Scott's workplace to bring him to the police station for questioning. When the police found Scott, he stood 5′11″, had blond hair, blue eyes, a fair complexion, and a mustache. Despite the discrepancies between Scott's appearance and the description of the bank robber, the police proceeded to question Scott at the station house. They learned that the Sornbergers had experienced recent financial difficulties. Scott also told the officers that he had placed a call to Consumer Credit Counseling earlier in the day. The same evening, Knoxville officers brought Teresa to the police station for questioning. They interviewed her outside of Scott's presence. In the course of questioning, both Sornbergers offered consistent alibis: They were together at Scott's parents' home, using his parents' computer when the robbery occurred.

To assist in the robbery investigation, Chief Pesci obtained the services of City of Galesburg police officers Dennis Sheppard, Anthony Riley, and David Clauge. The day after the robbery, Officer Clauge brought still photographs from the bank's surveillance cameras along with digital photos of Scott to show Illinois State's Attorney Paul Mangieri. Mangieri declined to seek an arrest warrant for Scott, but successfully obtained a search warrant for the computer in Scott's parents' house to allow Officer Clauge to confirm Scott's alibi. Later that day, Officer Clauge met again with Mangieri, this time accompanied by Chief Pesci and FBI agent Jeff Jackson. Officer Clauge expressed to Mangieri his belief that the pictures of Scott presented a close match to the ones taken of the robber by the bank surveillance cameras. At the same meeting, Chief Pesci told Mangieri about the Sornbergers' financial problems and their closed account at First Bank. On the information provided by Clauge and Pesci, Mangieri told the officers that they had probable cause to arrest Scott for armed robbery. The officers decided to make the arrest during the execution of the search warrant for Scott's parents' computer. The officers also decided that Officers Sheppard and Riley would reinterview Teresa if she could be found at Scott's parents' home.

The day after the robbery, when Chief Pesci and Officers Clauge, Riley, and Sheppard arrived at Scott's parents' house to execute the search warrant, only Teresa was present. The parties dispute whether the officers requested or instructed Teresa to accompany them to the Galesburg police station for questioning. In either case, she complied and was transported to Galesburg in the front seat of a police car, unrestrained by handcuffs. Chief Pesci stayed behind at Scott's parents' home and arrested Scott when he returned.

After Officers Sheppard and Riley arrived at the Galesburg Public Safety Building with Teresa, they conducted her to an interview room and began to question her. This interview resulted in a verbal and eventually a written confession from Teresa in which she admitted that she had assisted her husband in robbing First Bank. According to Teresa, she was told immediately after arriving in Galesburg that she was a suspect in the robbery. Teresa claims that she was then psychologically coerced into confessing by Officer Sheppard who allegedly falsely informed her that witnesses placed her at the scene of the robbery; repeatedly told her to think about her kids, yelled at her and accused her of lying, promised her that, if she implicated her husband, she would not be charged with any crime, threatened to call the Department of Children and Family Services (DCFS) to take her children away if she continued to maintain her innocence, and refused to honor her request to speak with an attorney.

The officers, however, claimed that they told Teresa that they believed that Scott had committed the robbery, asked Teresa about a witness who had seen Teresa at the bank on the day of the robbery, and implored Teresa to tell the truth and to think of her children rather than protecting Scott. They also maintain that Officer Sheppard advised Teresa of her *Miranda* rights before she orally confessed to the robbery.

After hearing Teresa confess, Officer Sheppard brought Chief Pesci into the interrogation room and asked Teresa to repeat her statement. She resisted, and the officers again suggested that she think of her children; this time, they admittedly made threats to call DCFS. The officers then presented Teresa with a transcribed version of her confession and asked her to sign it. Teresa complied.

Criminal proceedings were instituted against the Sornbergers for bank robbery by the State of Illinois.

While the Sornbergers were imprisoned awaiting trial, a man named Philip Pitcher committed a string of bank robberies in Illinois and Indiana. Pitcher resembled Scott Sornberger, prompting State's Attorney Mangieri to ask the FBI to conduct a more detailed comparison of Scott's facial features to the images taken by First Bank's surveillance equipment. The FBI compared Scott's ear to that of the perpetrator as pictured in the bank's surveillance photographs. The FBI comparison turned up physical differences between Scott and the bank robber that eliminated Scott as a suspect. Charges against the Sornbergers were dropped, and they were released from jail.

QUESTIONS

1. What evidence did the police have to justify the arrest of the Sornbergers?
2. Create a chart of the evidence, listing evidence tending to implicate the couple on one side and evidence that could potentially exculpate them on the other. Write a memo justifying the arrest and one arguing against the arrest based on the evidence.
3. Look up the case and read the court's opinion. What do you think of the result?

CRITICAL **THINKING EXERCISES**

1. Consider these two scenarios and determine which, if either, describe a robbery.
   a. A large stranger, dressed in ripped blue jeans and a torn sweat shirt, approaches you and says, "Hey, give me five dollars!" You give him the money because you fear he will hurt you.
   b. A well-dressed man in a blue suit, with shined shoes and perfectly coiffed hair approaches you and says, "I'd be ever so grateful if you gave me five dollars." You give him the money out of the kindness of your heart, not because you were afraid of him.

   Neither man displayed a weapon or made an explicit threat of violence, yet their appearance and demeanour produced a different emotional reaction from you. Was either, both, or neither a robbery?

2. You are walking down a crowded street continually being jostled by passersby when you realize your wallet is missing. You yell "I've been robbed!" Assuming someone has pickpocketed you, is your statement correct? In other words, is pickpocketing robbery or theft?

3. A person approaches you, sticks his finger in your face and says, "You worthless scumbag, I should rip your heart out and feed it to the dogs." Using Common Law definitions, what crime has the irate person committed?

4. Using the same scenario as Question 3, except that the irate person actually grabs you and starts trying to rip your heart out, what crime has the person committed at Common Law? At

what point did he commit assault or assault and battery under modern law?

5. Which of the following scenarios constitutes violent arson:
   a. A man sets his house on fire to collect the insurance money.
   b. A man throws a tire around his neighbor and lights it on fire.
   c. Knowing that her ex-boyfriend and his new love are making mad passionate love in his apartment, a woman sets fire to the building with the intent of making their date hotter than they anticipated.

6. You receive an e-mail stating that numerous lonely women are available in your area. All you need do is supply your credit card number and more pleasure than you ever dreamed of will be available in the surrounding community. What crime have the pleasure purveyors seeking your credit card number committed?

7. Which of the following are examples of terror cells using the Internet to recruit?
   a. You receive an e-mail from Jihad Joan telling you how the United States is the Great Satan and the only way to make things right is for you to convert to Islam and take up jihad against the infidels.
   b. You receive an e-mail from the Modern Militia telling you how Washington politicians have taken the United States too far from the land the Founding Fathers dreamed of two centuries ago and the only way to make things right is to don your khakis, buy automatic

weapons at the next completely legal gun show, and help them "take back America."

c. A group concerned about the Palestinian's plight in occupied Israel is raising money to build schools and build badly needed infrastructure in the West Bank.

8. All of your neighbors are of European ancestry. An Asian Indian family purchases a home across the street. You are upset. You throw a brick through the front window. When the police show up you are still ranting about the Indian family. The police charge you with a hate crime. You claim the First Amendment protects your right to complain about the new neighbors. Based on Supreme Court precedent, do you think will get additional jail time because the crime is a hate crime? Assuming you get a jury trial, who must decide whether your crime was a hate crime and consequently whether you receive an enhanced sentence?

9. Sometimes it is not clear whether a kidnapping has taken place. For example, a couple leaves their children with a trusted, elderly neighbor while they go out of town. While they are gone, the neighbor receives news of a death in her family in another state. She calls the traveling parents and explains she is taking the children with her to the funeral and she will be out of town with them when the parents return. She also requests additional money to cover their expenses. The parents deny her permission to take the children. They call the police explaining their children have been kidnapped. By the time the police arrive, the neighbor and children have left the state. The neighbor is arrested upon arrival at the funeral and the children are returned to the parents when they return from their trip. Was this a kidnapping or just a series of misunderstandings and overreactions?

10. Is someone who assists illegal aliens to get into the United States for a fee, but does not have any contact with them after they arrive, guilty of trafficking in persons?

11. After committing a robbery, you are arrested. Because you already got rid of the items you stole, the police can find nothing in your possession tying you to the crime. They claim, however, that they have a surveillance tape of you committing the robbery. Can you argue that the camera violated your right to privacy and have the tape dismissed? What other tactics can your attorney use to keep the tape from being admitted to evidence?

12. You suspect your neighbor is trafficking in persons. You could report the incident to the local police, but they would probably just pass it along to a federal agency. If you wanted to report it directly to an appropriate federal agency, which agency or agencies would you contact?

PORTFOLIO **BUILDING**

1. Research your state's assault statutes and discuss how assault offenses in your state differ from those illustrated in this chapter. Select one assault offense in your jurisdiction and outline the elements of the offense. Then draft a memo to your supervisor describing the evidence you would need to present in order to secure a conviction.

2. The U.S. Department of Justice, Bureau of Justice Statistics collects an enormous amount of data on crimes and crime victims. Its data collection is a rich source of information for anyone concerned about crime and its consequences. Visit the Bureau of Justice Statistics Web page at http://www.ojp.usdoj.gov/bjs/abstract/cvusst.htm and answer the following questions:

a. What type of crimes are you most likely to become victimized by? What about your parents? Your grandparents?

b. Would the answer change if you were a member of the opposite sex? If your ethnicity was different? If your household income doubled? If you moved to another setting—that is, from the city to the suburbs or a rural area?

c. Did your answers surprise you? Why or why not?

3. Download the latest version of the *Searching and Seizing Computers and Seizing Electronic Evidence in Criminal Investigations* manual from the Department of Justice at http://www.cybercrime.gov/ssmanual/01ssma.html. It is available as a PDF document and you will refer to it in additional chapters. Then answer the following questions in a memo to your supervisor:

a. Explain the basics of the Stored Communications Act (Chapter 3 of the manual).

b. Describe how you would authenticate records stored on a computer (Chapter 5 of the manual).

FOR FURTHER READING

1. Walsh, J. (1998). *Tears of Rage: From Grieving Father to Crusader for Justice.* Pocket Books. This book tells the story of Adam Walsh's kidnapping and murder through his father's perspective and chronicles John Walsh's efforts to make recovering lost and abducted children easier.

2. Those interested in historical materials from the FBI archives, which have been released to the public through the Freedom of Information Act, can visit the agency's Freedom of Information Act Electronic Reading Room. The archives include documents on the Lindbergh kidnapping and other high-profile cases. The website is http://foia.fbi.gov/. The Department of Justice maintains a similar virtual reading room at http://www.usdoj.gov/04foia/index.html.

Chapter **six**

CRIMES AGAINST PROPERTY

. . . nor shall any State deprive any person of life, liberty, or property without due process of law.

U.S. Constitution, Amendment 14, Section 1

Introduction

In order to have a true appreciation for crimes involving property, you must first understand what **property** is and is not. Implicit in any discussion of property is the premise that individuals can actually hold property. Some societies simply don't accept that premise. Under the Common Law tradition, the individual's right to own property is a bedrock concept underlying virtually every aspect of the rules governing society. In England and the United States, one of the most important rights accorded citizens is the protection of his or her right to property, both real and personal.

In the American Common Law tradition, property consists of a bundle of rights, including the right to possess, use and enjoy, and dispose of something. It is not a material object itself, but a person's right to do what he or she wishes with that object, subject to limitations provided in the law.[1] Thus, the "owner" of a book has the right to possess it (perhaps put it on her bookshelf or nightstand), the right to use it (perhaps to read it and make notes in the margins), and the right to dispose of it (perhaps by selling it or even to burn it).

Understanding property law basics is essential to understanding crimes such as theft, burglary, forgery, and criminal trespass. Each of these crimes involves interference with another's property rights, and requires that the prosecution prove ownership as well as interference with that ownership to convict the accused.

CHAPTER OBJECTIVES

After studying this chapter, you should be able to:

- Understand what property is and the bundles of rights that accompany each type of property
- Explain the terms *fee simple, joint tenants with right of survivorship, tenancy by the entireties,* and *tenant in common*
- Define *theft* and name the different classifications of theft
- List the essential elements required to prove theft
- Differentiate embezzlement from other forms of theft
- Define *burglary* and describe its Common Law origins
- Define *arson* and explain why so few cases are cleared
- Explain the most common methods of check fraud and forgery
- Explain what the Brady Act requires before the purchase of a handgun
- Explain laws aimed at defacing property
- Explain where graffiti fits as a property crime
- Define identity theft
- Explain how cyber crime fits into traditional concepts of crimes against property
- Describe how prosecutors go about proving ownership in a theft case
- Explain forensic accounting

Property
A bundle of rights, including the right to possess, use and enjoy, and dispose of something. It is not a material object itself, but a person's right to do what he or she wishes with that object, subject to limitations provided in the law.

Real property
Consists of land and everything permanently attached to it. It includes land, subsurface rights, air rights, timbering and harvesting rights, and any buildings and structures permanently attached to the land.

Personal property
All property other than real property.

Chattel
Personal property.

Eminent domain
The state's power to take private property for a public use or public purpose without the owner's consent. The U.S. Constitution requires that property can only be taken after due process of law.

Fee simple
The legal term for ownership of the entire bundle of rights that go with a piece of property.

Leasehold rights
The rights a tenant in real property possesses through agreement with the property owner.

Property comes in two varieties. **Real property** is land and everything permanently attached to it. Land rights include the land itself, subsurface rights (i.e., the right to mine the land), air rights, timbering and harvesting rights (i.e., the right to farm, harvest, or log the land), and any buildings or structures permanently attached to the land (i.e., house, barn, silo, garage, and the like). Real property can be either private or public. Private property is property owned by a private individual, while public property is held by a state government or the federal government on behalf of us all. Examples of public real property are the national seashore and other national parks.

Personal property is everything else the law grants ownership rights to. It is also known as **chattel.**[2] Personal property can be tangible, with a physical presence. For example, a car or a book is personal property. Personal property can also be intangible, without a physical presence. Examples include patents and copyrights. Personal property also includes domestic animals and livestock as well as wild animals that have either been domesticated or placed under control.

Property rights are not without limit. Real property, for example, is subject to seizure by governmental entities as part of the state's power of **eminent domain.** Eminent domain is the state's power to take private property for a public use or public purpose without the owner's consent.[3] A controversial 2005 Supreme Court decision allows governments to use eminent domain to condemn land and turn it over to a private developer under a state devised economic development plan that provided more than "incidental or pretextual public benefits."[4]

Under the Constitution, any such taking must be after due process of law. Private property can't just be seized; some kind of a hearing is required. For example, when a criminal's ill-gotten gains from a criminal enterprise are seized in a drug raid, the state must still afford the defendant a hearing on that seizure before it becomes permanent. Typically, the state must show the court that there was some minimum nexus between the criminal activity and the acquisition of the property by the defendant.

Property can be owned outright. If it is, the owner is said to hold the property in **fee simple.** Fee simple is a legal term for ownership of the entire bundle of rights that go with a piece of property.[5] For example, you may own your house in fee simple. If you do, you have the right to use, possess, or dispose of the property during your lifetime and to pass it on to your heirs. You can dispose of some of your bundle of rights and keep the rest if you desire. For example, if you own a beach house in fee simple, you may periodically transfer your right to possess and enjoy the property to someone else by renting out the house to vacationers. While they rent the house, it is they who have the right to enjoy and possess it. These rights are considered **leasehold rights.**

By contrast, condominium owners have a form of ownership with fewer rights than fee simple title holders but more than leasehold rights. In a condominium someone else owns the land the condominium sits on and the building the condominium is in. Generally, condominium owners own from the wall in, everything else belongs to the condominium association which is made up of all the owners in the building or a developer. The condominium owner may have a vote in how the building, land, or other amenities owned by the association is managed, but does not exercise complete control. Condominium owners often pay a fee to support the building and common areas. The owners cannot be evicted for not paying the fee like a renter could. The association can place a **lien** against the property and initiate a lawsuit to collect. The owner would have to pay the fees to remove the lien or pay the lien before he or she could convey a clear title to a new owner.

Ownership is not restricted to one person; many persons can own the same property together. For example, husbands and wives often own property as **tenants by the entireties.** Tenancy by the entirety is a legal joint ownership in which both spouses own an undivided interest in the whole property and in which neither spouse can sell his or her interest without the consent of the other.[6] Gay marriage advocates point to tenants by the entireties as a type of ownership that excludes gay couples. Gay couples also more likely to face inheritance tax when one of them dies because they cannot marry.

Other forms of joint ownership are **tenancy in common** and **joint tenancy with right of survivorship.**[7] Tenants in common each own an undivided interest in the whole property. Neither tenant in common can exclude the other from the property, but any of the tenants can sell or will the property to another without the consent of the other tenants. If the owners hold property as joint tenants with right of survivorship, the surviving tenants receive the property upon the death of a tenant. However, if one joint tenant sells or gives away his interest before he dies, the property would no longer pass to the other joint tenant. Instead, the new owner would become a tenant in common. Both tenancy in common and joint tenancy with right of survivorship are ownership forms that can accommodate two or more people. Tenants by the entireties, because it is restricted to married couples, only involves two owners.

Title to property can be acquired in several ways. Property rights can be bought for a price, inherited, acquired as a gift, or acquired by mere possession. Property rights are most commonly transferred through purchase or inheritance. Purchase of property is done by contract and involves the exchange of something of value. For example, if you purchase a book for $20, you have bought title to that book. Acquiring property by gift or inheritance requires three things. First, the owner must intend to give the property away. Second, the gift must be delivered to the recipient. Third, the recipient must accept the gift. Property can also be acquired by possession. For example, a hunter who shoots a deer passing over his land becomes the owner of the deer when he takes possession of it. Before it was shot, the deer belonged to no one; after, it belongs to the hunter. Abandoned property can also be acquired by possession. For example, if a jogger spots a treasure sitting on the curb for garbage collection, she can take possession of it and becomes its owner.

In criminal law, ownership is important for several reasons. For example, a thief can only steal that which does not belong to him; he cannot steal his own property. Nor can he trespass against his own property. Thus, an estranged husband who breaks into the house he still owns jointly with his wife cannot be charged with criminal trespass, nor can he be charged with burglary if he removes personal articles that belong to the couple. Theft also requires that the prosecution prove beyond a reasonable doubt that the defendant intended to permanently deprive the owner of the property taken.

Lien
A creditor's claim against a particular property as collateral for a debt.

Private property is held sacred in all good governments, and particularly in our own.
Andrew Jackson, 1815

Tenancy by the entirety
The legal joint ownership in which both spouses own an undivided interest in the whole property and in which neither spouse can sell his or her interest without the consent of the other.

Tenants in common
Form of joint ownership in which each owns an undivided interest in the whole property.

Joint tenants with right of survivorship
Form of ownership in which the joint tenant receives the property should the other die. Either may sell their share before death and the new owners then become tenants in common.

In no other country in the world is the love of property keener or more alert than in the United States, and nowhere else does the majority display less inclination toward doctrines which in any way threaten the way property is owned.
Alexis de Tocqueville, *Democracy in America* 1840

HISTORICAL HIGHLIGHT

Who Owns the Rights to Sunken Treasure?

On September 11, 1857, the steamship *Central America* was making the last leg of its journey from Panama to New York when it encountered a hurricane off the coast of South Carolina. The ship developed a leak that became worse as the storm went on. Eventually water flooded the steam boilers, extinguishing the fire and leaving the ship at the mercy of the storm. A few passengers were set afloat in life boats and were safely picked up by another ship. The other 336 people onboard perished when the ship went down.

The *Central America* was a wooden-hulled luxury liner. Most of its passengers had found gold in California, and were carrying it home to families on the East Coast. They had sailed from San Francisco to Panama, crossed the isthmus by train, and boarded the steamer on the Atlantic side. The ship was carrying gold for various companies as cargo, and many of the passengers had large personal amounts of gold. The newspaper reports of the day estimated the ship to be carrying $2 million of gold in 1857 dollars. Estimates of its modern-day equivalent ran as high as $1 billion.

As news of the sinking reached the United States, insurers paid the various claims for the lost gold. Because the ship sank in more than 2,000 feet of water, the insurers held no hope they would ever salvage the cargo.

In the late 1970s, ocean research scientist Thomas Thompson began studying newspaper accounts of the *Central America* sinking. He became convinced that modern ocean mapping and deep-sea exploration technology could make recovering the *Central America*'s treasure possible. Thompson began putting an investor syndicate together to fund the massive undertaking.

By 1987, Thompson had put together his syndicate, now called the Columbus-America Discovery Group, and began salvage operations. The group recovered one ton of gold bars and coins from the wreck. Insurance companies challenged Columbus-America's right to the treasure, claiming they had paid for the gold after the shipwreck in 1857. This claim would have been valid if the property were lost property.

However, Thompson and his group argued that it was abandoned property. In court, they showed that even after papers telling of the *Central America*'s location were published, insurers mounted no effort to salvage the gold. Further, no documentation existed from the 1857 claims.

Columbus-America won in federal district court where the judge ruled that conventional property laws applied, and the property was abandoned and could be given to the first group to recover it. The Appeals Court saw things somewhat differently. Since the shipwreck was in international waters, maritime law applied. It sent the case back to the district court with instructions to apply maritime law.

Maritime laws date from the ancient city of Rhodes. The inhabitants of Rhodes instituted the first maritime code sometime around 900 B.C. When the Romans conquered Rhodes, they preserved the maritime code, and it came down through Anglo-American legal tradition. Maritime law has always held that salvors (those who salvage ships) are entitled to very liberal awards.

In this case, the district judge applied the maritime law and awarded the salvagers 90 percent of the market value of the treasure. Those few insurers whose claims survived would get the remainder. But dividing the spoils proved problematic. Columbus-America wanted to keep the treasure's full value and contents secret to increase its market value. The value of each item in the treasure was dependent on the value and contents of the entire find. Ultimately a federal judge ordered Columbus-America to submit a full inventory and parcel out the insurers' shares. On June 17, 1998, after nearly a decade of legal wrangling, representatives from both sides met in a Brinks armored warehouse in Chesapeake, Virginia, where Columbus-America divided the treasure into ninety lots of equal value. Attorneys for each side took turn picking lots until the insurers had their share.

Thompson and his syndicate are still battling in court over claims to the treasure. In 2006, ten technicians from the recovery crew, including sonar operators and search-and-recovery experts, filed suit for their promised share of the booty. The group persuaded judges on the east and west coasts to allow them to seize $11.8 million in assets. Federal marshals, using a court order from U.S. District Court in Los Angeles, took six gold bars weighing a total of 115 pounds and a gold coin, which is being held by an armored-truck company while the lawsuit is tried. More than 161 partners who helped finance the expedition have divided into factions and filed suit over the treasure. Estimates of the treasure's full value run as high as $400 million.

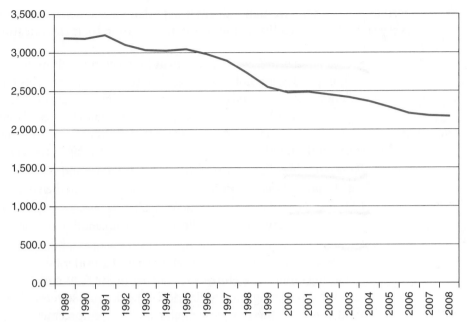

Larceny-Theft Rate per 100,000 Population.
Source: FBI Uniform Crime Report 2008.

HISTORICAL HIGHLIGHT

Telepossession: Laying Claim to Property in Outer Space?

In deciding the fate of sunken treasure recovered from the *Central America*, the courts relied on the legal concept *pedis possessio*, Latin for "foothold," literally, "to walk on is to establish ownership."[8] According to this principle, the salvors of the Columbus-America Discovery Group gained possession of the sunken treasure by establishing a live video link with the wreck site using telerobotic equipment. Richard Westfall, of Galactic Mining Industries, Inc., along with Declan O'Donnell PC, of United Societies in Space, Inc., and Gary Rodriguez, of sysRAND Corporation, all of Colorado, are trying to use that principle to establish title to asteroids, comets, moons, minerals, and even gravity wells and orbits. Relying on the *Central America* case, the group argues that "the telepresence of a research group can have legal

standing to establish a priori domain over a property, and establish a form of legal possession." The group calls this remote-control claim on property "telepossession."[9]

The group proposes laying claim to objects in space using telerobotic probes, which can perform tasks such as assaying composition of the object, manipulating materials and relaying information to Earth. The group also proposes planting RADAR transponders on them, which would transmit signals back to Earth. It might seem like a flight of fancy, but consider the case of an abandoned satellite orbiting Earth. Remote technological links with the satellite could be used to establish salvage rights to it, just as Columbus-America claimed the wreckage of the *Central America*. Could the same logic be applied to real estate on the moon? Might the future colonization of space rely on the legal precedent set by the *Central America*?

Theft or Larceny

The terms *theft* and *larceny* are interchangeable. Some jurisdictions call the crime theft, while others refer to it as larceny. We will use the term **theft** to refer to the crime. At Common Law, theft was defined as the taking and carrying away of another's personal property with the intent to deprive him or her of it

Theft

The taking and carrying away of another's personal property with the intent to deprive him or her of it permanently.

permanently. There are many distinct acts that fit the definition of theft, and every state has its own list. Below are some common theft classifications.

Shoplifting or retail theft: More than $13 billion worth of goods, over $35 million per day, are stolen from U.S. retailers every year.[10] This form of theft includes concealing goods in stores to avoid paying for them or altering the price on an item in order to pay a lower price. Many states have escalating penalties for retail theft. The penalty varies according to the value of the merchandise stolen or the number of prior convictions the defendant has on record.

Purse snatching: This form of theft involves a quick and usually observed taking of a purse, briefcase, or the like in a public place and then fleeing the scene.

Pickpocketing: This form of theft usually involves a secretive snatching of personal property such as a wallet or cash from another person's possession.

Looting: Looting is taking property from or near a building damaged or destroyed by a fire, riot, or natural disasters. Consider two recent examples of looting. Following Hurricane Katrina in 2005, looters floated garbage cans full of clothing and jewelry down the flooded streets of New Orleans. With much of the city underwater and law enforcement organizations paralyzed, the city fell into chaos. A crowd of looters in a drug store near the French Quarter was interrupted by police, who came to seize drugs and water for sick residents of a nearby hotel. The police told the waiting crowd they would be out of their way as soon as they got the things they needed. In another incident a man, arms loaded with clothes, reportedly asked a policeman if he could borrow his car.[11]

One of the most famous examples of looting in recent history is the ransacking of Baghdad's Iraq Museum following the end of Saddam Hussein's regime in 2003. More than 15,000 objects, some more than 1,000 years old, were stolen or destroyed in a matter of days in the wake of the city's fall.

Library theft: This type of theft is generally defined as theft of a circulating library item such as a book or record that is kept beyond its return date, and after notification that the item must be returned. Library theft can also cover the concealing and taking of rare manuscripts from a library. A recent example of library theft involved a rare map dealer, Edward Forbes Smiley III, who pled guilty in July 2006 to stealing a circa 1578 Flemish map of the world, valued at about $150,000, from Yale's Beinecke Rare Book and Manuscript Library. As part of his plea agreement, Smiley confessed to removing an additional ninety-six maps from the Boston Public Library, the New York Public Library, and other institutions. The total value of the maps he stole is estimated between $1.8 million and $3 million.[12]

Theft by deception: When a person commits theft by deception, he or she steals through surreptitious means such as fraud.

HISTORICAL HIGHLIGHT

Woman Faked Cancer, Stole Donations

In March 2001, Jeffrey Clark, special agent for the U.S. Drug Enforcement Agency (DEA) requested a medical-hardship transfer from Houston, Texas, to Utah so his wife, Tania, could undergo chemotherapy at the Huntsman Cancer Institute in Salt Lake City. "Over the past year and a half, I have had to exhaust my sick leave to care for Tania and my two sons during her ongoing illness," Clark wrote in his transfer request. "This has created a tremendous emotional and physical strain for me during these time periods." Clark included a letter from a Dr. Robert Bates at the University of Texas M.D. Anderson Cancer Center. He also included a letter from his wife, which said "Our family has been crying, hugging, laughing and healing since all this started."[13]

The DEA granted his request, and paid nearly $48,000 to transfer the Clark family to Utah.

After moving to Utah, where Tania Clark's family lived, the couple told family, friends, neighbors, and other members of the community that she needed $62,000 for a bone marrow transplant. Members of her sons' hockey league, the Timpanogos Amateur Hockey Association, donated $1,000. Students at Oakcrest Elementary School held a "Coins for Caring" drive, collecting more than $6,000 to help her. Neighbors gave the Clarks more than $5,000, and some offered to donate their bone marrow. The donations totaled more than $16,000.[14]

After an article about the Clarks' plight appeared in the *South Valley Journal*, Clark's sister e-mailed the newspaper saying her sister was not trustworthy. An investigation showed that Tania Clark had never been

a patient at M.D. Anderson Cancer Center in Houston or the Huntsman Cancer Institute. No Robert Bates had ever practiced medicine at Anderson.[15] On February 16, 2005, Tania Clark confessed to a West Jordan detective that she had never had cancer.

Tania Clark was sentenced by Third District Judge Paul Maughan in 2005 to thirty days in jail. He ordered prison sentences of one to fifteen years for theft by deception and up to five years for attempted theft by deception, but suspended the sentences. He placed Clark on three years' probation instead, and ordered her to perform 200 hours of community service and pay $5,378 in restitution. She also pleaded guilty to felony theft in neighboring Utah County, where she received probation and community service, and was ordered to pay $5,800 in restitution.

Jeffrey Clark was also charged with theft by deception and forgery, but the charges were later dropped for lack of evidence that Mr. Clark knew of the scheme. He left his job under undisclosed circumstances. The DEA later filed suit against the couple, seeking restitution for the agency's moving expenses. In June 2007, the couple settled the lawsuit, agreeing to pay $60,000 to the DEA.[16]

Theft of services: This form of theft is committed when someone obtains services such as cable television or other utilities by tapping into the source of those utilities with the intention not to pay for those services. Theft of services can also occur when someone uses false information to receive utility services.

Theft by bailee or trustee: This form of theft occurs when someone other than the true owner of property has custody of that property. For example, a jeweler who is going to repair a ring has temporary custody of the property. The owner of the ring has temporarily turned over the property for repair and safekeeping. If the jeweler keeps or sells the ring, she has committed theft. In some jurisdictions, this crime may be known as theft by failure to make required disposition of funds received. A Lexington, Kentucky lawyer and his secretary were indicted for taking $500,000 from a title company escrow account used for holding money during home sales and refinancing. The pair faced four counts of theft by failure to make a required disposition of property for failing to forward the funds to mortgage companies and other lenders.[17]

The types of theft previously outlined are examples. Many jurisdictions have created other crimes of theft, and will continue to do so as the need arises. For example, fifty years ago there was no need to define theft to include offenses like stealing someone's credit profile and identity in order to apply for fraudulent credit cards. But all these crimes have the basic elements of theft in common. It is to these elements that we now turn.

Taking and Carrying Away

The first element of the crime of theft is "taking and carrying away." The prosecution must prove that the defendant took possession of the object of the theft and carried it away. As you have seen in the discussion of specific types of theft, the taking can include keeping possession of something placed in the defendant's custody. But the essence of any theft is that the defendant takes personal property belonging to another and places it under his own control. For example, a customer who tries on a dress in a department store, and then walks out with the dress on, has taken and carried it away (and committed the crime of retail theft). The degree of carrying away can be slight. She would be guilty of retail theft even if she were caught before she got out of the store because she had taken possession of the dress and had begun to take it out of the store.

Personal Property

Under the Common Law, the only type of property that could be stolen was tangible personal property. Real estate could not be stolen, nor could other intangible things like copyrights, stocks, or bonds. Now all jurisdictions have revised their theft statutes to include intangible personal property under their definitions of theft. That personal property can include such things as electric and cable service, and intangible computer files. In addition, someone who forges a deed to real estate can also be charged with theft (by deception).

Of Another

The property stolen must belong to someone other than the defendant. The prosecution must therefore prove ownership of the property. Prosecutors need the cooperation of property owners in order to secure theft convictions. In order to constitute theft, the defendant must take the property without the consent of the owner. It would not be theft, for example, to take your friend's ring if she gave it to you. But the prosecutor would have to put your friend on the stand to testify that she both owned the ring and did not give it to you in order for you to be convicted of theft.

Another very real problem is proving that the property the police found the defendant in possession of is actually the victim's property. For example, if the victim claims the defendant stole her diamond ring, she will have to identify the diamond as hers. If the ring is engraved, the victim can identify it. But what if the diamond has been removed from its setting (a common tactic used by gem thieves)? How will she identify the diamond as hers? Unless she has had the diamond marked, mapped, and registered (a service available for rare and high-end gems), she will be unable to tell her diamond from another and the thief will walk away with the gem.

Because stolen property must be positively identified as belonging to the owner, it is crucial that owners keep careful track of serial numbers and other identifying characteristics of their property in case of theft. Without positive proof, the thief may very well walk away with his ill-gotten lot.

With the Intent to Permanently Deprive the Owner of the Property

The final element of the crime of theft involves intent. It is not enough that the defendant took possession of property belonging to another. He must also intend to permanently deprive the owner of the property. Intent may be proven with indirect or circumstantial evidence. Thus, a thief's actions may speak of his intent. For example, an art thief who steals a gallery's Monet painting and then displays it in his private study will likely find that a jury can be convinced that his actions indicate he intended to permanently deprive the gallery of the use and enjoyment of the painting. But what about a neighbor who takes a gas grill from down the block and is caught red-handed rolling the grill toward his house? Did he intend to permanently deprive the owner of the grill or did he just borrow it?[18] Other cases where intent is less than clear are cases where absent-minded shoppers claim to have inadvertently placed merchandise in their pockets or bags, and never intended to leave the store without paying. In such cases, credibility plays a major factor.

Embezzlement occurs when someone who has legal possession of property of another uses, converts, or retains that property for his own use or the use of someone other than the owner. It differs from other forms of theft because it does not require proof that the perpetrator took and carried away property of another. That's because the embezzler already lawfully possesses the property, albeit on behalf of the other. Many cases of embezzlement involve a trusted insider stealing from an employer.

> **Embezzlement**
> Theft committed by someone who has legal possession of property of another when the thief uses, converts, or retains that property for his or her own use or the use of someone other than the owner.

Embezzlement tends to be a crime of opportunity, and can often be avoided with proper oversight and financial controls. Take the case of a former Prothonotary and Clerk of Court for Mifflin County, Pennsylvania. Sue Ellen Saxton controlled thousands of dollars submitted to the court in fines, penalties, and other funds. Over the years she managed to divert over $800,000 of funds in her possession and control to her personal use. The funds were allegedly used to fund gambling expeditions to Las Vegas and Atlantic City. The embezzlement was accomplished by marking funds actually diverted to her personal account as having been returned to criminal defendants. She pled guilty to one count of conspiracy under federal law.[19]

In some cases, embezzlement can be a very subtle case of using resources inappropriately. For example, a retired professor at the University of North Texas pled guilty to embezzlement after an investigation revealed he had habitually used university staff, computers and telephone systems to support a side business, Public Management Associates, while working at the university. From 1993 to 2006, the university estimated he used $463,000 in university resources to support his own business.[20]

HISTORICAL HIGHLIGHT

Bookkeeper Hid Her Double Life

When Angela Buckborough Platt first came to work as a temporary bookkeeper for J&J Materials of Rehboth, Massachusetts, a landscaping and masonry supplier, owner John Ferreira was so impressed with her work that he paid a fee to the temp agency to hire her full-time. "Why isn't everybody like Angela?" Ferreira would ask others in the office. "She never leaves her office. She doesn't hang out at the copy machine and talk. She just works all day long."

Platt lived in an unassuming split level home in Cumberland, Rhode Island. Her only extravagance was a wild Halloween display, which grew so lavish after she joined the company that Ferreira's sister asked about the cost.

By 2004, the general manager of J&J's Nantucket Pavers plant became suspicious of the profit-and-loss reports Platt gave him every year. The company was not profiting as much as it should have been. In 2006, the manager brought in a second accountant, telling her, "We need to watch everything, 'cause we're getting robbed." The new bookkeeper was immediately suspicious, and called vendors to verify three checks written out to them totaling about $74,000. None of the vendors had received the checks.

Ferreira sent his vice president to the bank to examine the checks, who called shortly after to say, "I'm looking at a check here for $44,000, and it's made out to Angela Buckborough."

Ferreira called Angela into his office that afternoon, where two Rehoboth police officers were waiting. He slid the $44,000 check across the table and asked if she knew anything about it. Angela replied, "Yes. I've been stealing money." When Ferreira asked how much, she said about $200,000. Ferreira asked Angela to get as much cash as she had in the bank, $60,000, and return it to him the following Tuesday, after a holiday weekend.

On Tuesday morning, Angela walked back into the conference room and told Ferreira and his lawyer, "I did some figuring over the weekend and it was a little more than I thought." She slid a piece of paper over to Ferreira. It read "$1,530,000," followed by a list of purchases.

When it was all said and done, her total take came to $6.9 million. "What, was she embezzling from the mob?" Ferreira asked. "That can't all be my money."[21]

Platt had been leading a double life. She owned a 104-acre ranch in West Haven, Vermont with a heated saltwater swimming pool and two barns, one full of show horses, the other housing a commercial-caliber arcade. She owned timeshares in Florida and the Bahamas. She had assembled a fleet of motor vehicles, many vintage or unusual custom cars, including a 1937 Chevy panel car with a Bonnie and Clyde mural, faux bullet holes and a portrait of Platt's husband dressed as a gangster on the rear tire compartment, and a 1920s-era beer truck custom made from a toy model at a cost of $100,000. Platt had also purchased an unusual assortment of celebrity and cinema memorabilia, including six talking trees from the Wizard of Oz at $3,000 each, a twenty-foot smoke-breathing dragon called "The Slayer," and a life-size ceramic statue of Al Capone, seated and smoking a cigar. She had hired Burt Bacharach to perform at her brother's wedding, and planned a lavish party complete with $19,000 in fireworks.

She and her husband were known for going out to eat near their home in Vermont, picking up the tab for everyone in the restaurants, and giving $300 tips to the waitresses. When anyone asked where they got their money, the couple said they were CEOs of seven companies, or that they had won the lottery.

Platt pleaded guilty to embezzling and was sentenced to four years in prison. She was also ordered to pay $4.48 million plus interest in restitution.[22]

How could Platt siphon off $6.9 million, seemingly right under her employer's nose? That's exactly how embezzlement happens. It's a crime committed in broad daylight, by a person entrusted with a position of power. Ferreira trusted Platt so much he put her in charge of a fortune, and never looked over her shoulder. Many companies rely on the same people who write checks to audit the company's finances and do taxes and other accounting. This opens them up to abuse, as John Ferreira found out too late.

Motor Vehicle Theft

Auto theft: One of the most costly property crimes in the United States is auto theft. The crime is costly because nearly every auto owner is insured for theft, so that most car thefts result in payment of the value of the car by an insurer. A car is stolen in the United States every thirty-three seconds, making the odds of a vehicle being stolen 1 in 210.[23]

Motor vehicle theft, or auto theft, as the chart indicates has steadily fallen over the last several years because of two key factors: driver education and enhanced antitheft systems on the cars themselves. Drivers have been taught through public service campaigns not to leave their keys in cars, park in well-lit areas, and always lock the car when leaving it. Vehicle manufacturers have made autos more theft-resistant as well by installing car alarms, satellite tracking devices, and remote control systems that can disable a vehicle if it is stolen.

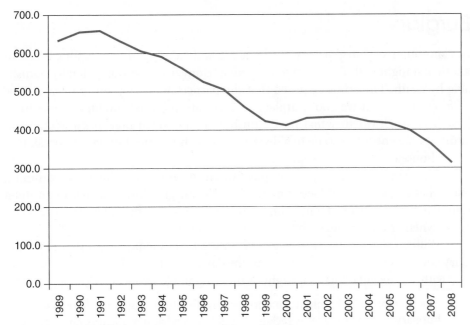

Motor Vehicle Theft Rate per 100,000 Population.

Early public service announcements focused on the teenage "joy rider" who saw a hot car with the keys in it and took it for a ride, abandoning it somewhere. But most auto theft is less romantic and more economically driven. Auto theft rings steal specific models of cars for their parts that can be resold to auto repair shops on the black market. The stolen vehicles are taken to "chop shops" where skilled workers disassemble the car within a very short period of time, making recovery almost impossible. Auto manufacturers have attempted to combat this practice by placing the car's serial number in various locations throughout the car in the hope that the various parts can eventually be tracked back to the original stolen vehicle.

Law enforcement officials are using better technology to track stolen vehicles. Some Canadian and American police departments have adopted police cruiser mounted cameras that use photo radar technology to read every license plate the camera sees. The numbers are automatically checked against license plate numbers from stolen vehicles. The patrolman is then alerted to the stolen vehicle in real time.[24]

Sadly, auto theft continues because thieves very often get away with the crime. Only 12.6 percent of auto thefts result in an arrest.[25] Carjacking, the forcible taking of a vehicle while the driver is in the car, accounts for only 3 percent of all auto thefts.[26] Stolen vehicles are also commonly used in crimes so that they cannot be traced to the perpetrators.

Like other thefts, the prosecution must prove the defendant took the car, did not own the car, and intended to permanently deprive the owner of the use of the car. Theft or larceny statutes generally divide theft into two classes based on the value of the goods or services stolen: petit and grand. For example, Virginia's statutes define petit larceny as stealing any item worth more than $5 and less than $200.[27] Because virtually all autos are worth more than $200, they are usually prosecuted as grand larceny. Petit larceny is generally a misdemeanor while grand larceny is a felony.

Burglary

Burglary
At Common Law, the breaking
and entering of the dwelling
house of another at night with
the intent to commit a felony
inside. Today, burglary is the
forcible entry into a structure
with the intent to commit a
felony once inside.

At Common Law, **burglary** was the breaking and entering of the dwelling house of another at night with the intent to commit a felony inside. It was generally punishable by death. The crime required that the perpetrator secure entry by some use of force. That is, it was not burglary to enter an unlocked dwelling. Force must have been used, whether that meant pushing in a door or breaking a window. In addition, the entry had to be to a dwelling house. It was not burglary to break into a warehouse or other storage place.

The crime of burglary is complete when the entry with intent to commit a felony has taken place. It doesn't matter that the burglar doesn't actually commit a crime once inside. In fact, any crime committed once inside will be charged separately whether that crime is an assault, murder, or theft.

William Blackstone, the great English legal commentator, insisted that burglary could only occur at those times of the day when it was too dark to see a man's face without the aid of artificial light or moonlight. He wrote:

> The time must be by night, and not by day: for in the day time there is no burglary . . . . As to what is reckoned night, and what day, for this purpose: anciently the day was accounted to begin only at sun-rising, and to end immediately upon sun-set; but the better opinion seems to be, that if there be daylight or crepusculum enough, begun or left, to discern a man's face withal, it is no burglary. But this does not extend to moonlight; for then many midnight burglaries would go unpunished: and besides, the malignity of the offence does not so properly arise from its being done in the dark, as at the dead of night; when all the creation, except beasts of prey, are at rest; when sleep has disarmed the owner, and rendered his castle defenceless.[30]

Today, states have expanded the definition of burglary to cover just about any unauthorized entry into a structure, at any time of day or night. Some states simply retain the nighttime provision in their statutes and have added other sections to their crimes codes that also punish daytime break-ins. They distinguish between nighttime and daytime break-ins by punishing night activity more severely than the same crime committed in broad daytime. The most common definition today is that burglary is the unlawful entry of a structure to commit a felony or theft. For example, the criminal law of Pennsylvania provides that:

HISTORICAL HIGHLIGHT

Armed Robbery of LSAT Proves Costly

Law school may be a dream for many, but if you want to go, you have to have good grades and a good score on the Law School Admissions Test (LSAT). Taking the standardized test is a required ritual for all law school hopefuls. Some students are apparently so intent on getting a good score that they will resort to armed robbery.

During the February 8, 1997, exam, a student using fake identification to take the test at the University of California at Los Angeles walked out about fifteen minutes into the test. When the proctor followed him onto the street and demanded the test back, the student pulled a switchblade knife, got in a car, and left. Shortly after, Danny Khatchaturian and Dikran Iskendarian, two students taking the test in Hawaii, began receiving the answers on their pagers. The time difference between Hawaii and California meant there was a two-hour delay in the test.[28] In January 2001, the two were sentenced to one-year home detention and five years' probation as well as to pay $97,000 in restitution to the LSAT.[29]

A person is guilty of burglary if he enters a building or occupied structure, or separately secured or occupied portion thereof, with intent to commit a crime therein, unless the premises are at the time open to the public or the actor is licensed or privileged to enter.[31]

Pennsylvania grades the offense on the basis of how the building or occupied structure is used. If the building isn't set up for overnight accommodations (i.e., it isn't a residence or a hotel or inn) and no one is present during the burglary, the offense carries a lesser penalty than if the building is a home. A burglar who enters a jewelry store to steal the merchandise is subject to a lesser penalty than if the same burglar broke into a private home. However, if the same burglar broke into the jewelry store, and the night watchman was there, he would face the higher penalty.

Unlawful Entry into Premises

What does it mean to unlawfully enter premises? Does the burglar have to physically enter the premises with his whole body or is it enough that he breaks a window and reaches in to help himself to another's belongings? Most states hold that reaching in is enough to constitute burglary. Most states still require that there must be at least some form of unauthorized entry into the premises. That's because the crime of burglary is based in part on the concept of the tort of trespass. Trespass is the unlawful and unprivileged entry or intrusion onto the property of another. If the building entered is normally open to the public, and the defendant is legally present in the building, it is not burglary just as his presence would not constitute the tort of trespass.

Dwelling House of Another

The Common Law definition required that to constitute burglary, the unlawful entry must have been to a dwelling house of another. At Common Law, a dwelling house was a structure in which people lived and slept. States no longer limit burglary to dwelling houses, and include just about any structure, occupied or unoccupied, in their definitions. Some states have expanded the definition to include unoccupied automobiles and even telephone booths. For example, California defines "burglary" so broadly as to include shoplifting and theft of goods from a "locked" but unoccupied automobile.[32]

The requirement that the building entered by a would-be burglar be "of another" is another reflection that the genesis of the crime of burglary is in the tort of trespass. Just as you cannot trespass on your own property, neither can you burglarize your own home. Although this may seem obvious, it is a fairly common problem, and courts must sometimes determine what is meant by "of another." For example, assume a husband and wife have separated, but the husband still is an owner of the marital home in which the wife continues to live. If the husband breaks the window and enters the house with the intent to steal property belonging to his wife, he cannot be charged with burglary. He has not entered the property of another. He could still be charged with theft, of course, if he successfully made off with his wife's property.

In addition to proving that the defendant entered the dwelling house (or other building, depending on the definition used in your state's burglary statute), the prosecution must show that the defendant didn't have permission to be present in the structure. Clearly, a person present in a public place during normal business hours when the facility is open to the public has implied permission to be there. He was invited and therefore isn't trespassing. The prosecution typically puts the property owner or a manager on the stand during trial to testify that the defendant didn't have permission to enter the building.

With Intent to Commit a Felony

A defendant's entry into another's structure, no matter how violent or destructive that entry was, isn't burglary unless the defendant can be shown to have intended to commit a felony while inside. Many states have made proof even easier, as they have specified that the intent that must be shown is merely the intent to commit a crime once inside. That crime does not have to be theft related. It would still be burglary to break into a home with the intent to kill or rape someone inside. In many cases, there will be direct evidence of intent—as happens when a defendant is caught leaving the site of the burglary with stolen goods.

Sometimes it's not clear whether the defendant formed the intent to commit a felony or other crime once inside. For example, a homeless person who seeks shelter in what appears to be an empty house but runs into the owner during his visit and then injures that owner may not be guilty of burglary. He may be guilty of a lesser offense like unlawful entry or criminal trespass. He would also likely be guilty of assault, but not burglary.

Proving intent is generally not difficult in burglary cases even if the defendant isn't "caught in the act." Juries and judges rely on circumstantial evidence and common sense to prove intent. The fact that the defendant broke into a building containing personal property and was caught often leads to an inference that he intended to steal some of that property once inside. Unless the defendant testifies and comes up with a plausible explanation for his presence, judge or jury likely will consider his presence and the circumstances surrounding it as proof of intent.

Property Arson

Arson

The intentional and malicious burning of a structure. At Common Law, it was the malicious burning of the dwelling house of another.

At Common Law, **arson** was the malicious burning of the dwelling house of another. The building burned had to be the dwelling of another, so that burning down a stable or other outbuilding was not arson. Nor was it a crime to burn down one's own building. In order to curtail insurance fraud (as might happen if an insured homeowner burned down his property and collected the insurance) and so-called spite arson (as might happen when an angry spouse burned down the home previously shared with a spouse and still jointly owned), most states expanded their definition of arson. In both of those cases, the arsonist damages a property interest of another, either the insurance company or the spouse. Today, most states have changed their laws to define arson as the willful and malicious burning of a structure or building.

By setting the standard of intent as willful and malicious burning, arson statutes cover all the common motives for committing the crime. Possible motives for committing arson include:

- *Arson for profit:* Arson committed in order to collect on insurance carried on the structure burned or by an owner who cannot sell the property and wants to move on. The latter can be a major problem in decaying urban areas with a large concentration of abandoned and boarded-up warehouses and businesses.
- *Arson for revenge:* Arson committed as payback for a failed love affair or marriage or in retaliation for an adverse employment decision. As discussed

in Chapter 5, arson committed with the intent to kill or harm an individual is considered violent arson.

- **Evidence destruction:** Arson committed to cover up another crime or destroy evidence, such as evidence that a victim in the structure was killed by fire rather than other means, or as a means of eliminating documents sought in a criminal investigation.

- **Political act:** Arson to make a political statement, such as the fire-bombing of abortion clinics by antiabortion extremists.

- **Arson for thrill:** Some cases of arson are the work of thrill seekers who are frequently juveniles. These cases represent a high proportion of arson cases in which there is an arrest. Other fires may be set by perpetrators plagued by mental illness. Pyromaniacs may start fires as part of a quest for sexual or other excitement.[33]

Arson is a serious crime in the United States. Federal Bureau of Investigation data show that 62,807 arson offenses were reported in 2008, causing just under $1 billion in damages. Unfortunately, the clearance rate for arson was only around 18 percent. A crime is defined as "cleared" in the FBI crime reports when a suspect is arrested and charged with the crime. That means a great many incidents of arson go unpunished every year.[34]

When arson is politically motivated, the arsonist is sometimes also charged under federal law. For example, Suzanne Nicole Savoie was sentenced under a federal terrorism law for her part in two Oregon arsons. Savoie, a member of "The Family," a secretive cell of the Environmental Liberation Front (ELF), pled guilty to serving as a lookout during an arson at Superior Lumber Co. in Glendale, which caused $1 million in damage. She also pled guilty to helping to plan and commit an arson that caused $994,000 in damage to Jefferson Poplar Farm in Clatskanie. U.S. District Judge Ann Aiken sentenced Savoie to four years and three months in prison. Judge Aiken ruled the tree farm arson a crime of terrorism because the conspirators' communications about the arsons ridiculed proposed legislation aimed at such crimes, making the government a target of the acts.[35]

Essential Elements of Arson

The essential elements that the government must prove beyond a reasonable doubt in an arson case are:

- The fire was willfully and maliciously set by the defendant or someone else on his orders. Carelessness isn't enough.
- The fire set by the defendant caused damage. Merely scorching a building is not enough (although the offense charged might instead be attempted arson or criminal trespass and criminal mischief).

Arson cases are not easy to prove. First, the fire itself, if successful, destroys much of the evidence. Second, there are many fires that are accidental and not the result of intentional wrongdoing. Cigarettes left to smolder, careless cooking, faulty electrical systems, and lightning are frequent causes of fires. In addition, getting the appropriate evidence may sometimes be difficult. Fire officials who

How the FBI Began Collecting Crime Data

Early in the twentieth century it became apparent to law enforcement officials that tracking the type and frequency of criminal activity was important to its containment. At the time, individual states seldom shared information about criminal activity within their borders with others in the union. In addition, each state had a unique set of criminal laws, and there were as many definitions of specific crimes as there were states.

In the late 1920s the International Association of Chiefs of Police suggested the creation of a national database of crime and criminal activity. Voluntary data collection began in 1930, with information coming from state, county, and city law enforcement agencies. The information is now gathered at the Federal Bureau of Investigation. Law enforcement agencies use uniform definitions when deciding which crimes to report to help overcome differences in state laws. There are eight classifications of crimes reported to the FBI. These are:

1. Murder and nonnegligent manslaughter
2. Forcible rape
3. Robbery
4. Aggravated assault
5. Burglary
6. Larceny-theft
7. Motor vehicle theft
8. Arson

The FBI publishes an annual report of crime in America, which is available at the FBI website www.fbi.gov.

arrive on the scene can make a preliminary decision whether the fire was intentionally set or not, and can seize any evidence in plain sight.

The Supreme Court has ruled that once a blaze has been extinguished and the firefighters have left the premises, a warrant is required to reenter the premises. The Fourth Amendment protects the owner of the premises from intrusion without probable cause that the fire was deliberately set. In order to get a warrant, a government official must show more than that a fire occurred. However, the firefighters who initially respond may seize evidence that is in plain view and investigate the cause of the fire as part of their efforts to contain it and make the area safe. That evidence can then be used to support an application for a warrant if it reached the level of probable cause. The case *Michigan v. Tyler*[36] involved a fire at a furniture store. When the fire chief arrived, the fire was still smoldering. Discovered in the embers were several plastic containers of flammable liquid, which aroused suspicion. Over the next few weeks, police and fire officials returned several times to gather evidence, all without a warrant. The testimony of fire experts and evidence obtained from the visits were introduced into evidence and the store owners were convicted of arson. The Supreme Court reversed the convictions and ordered any evidence seized after the immediate exigency was over without a warrant be excluded in any retrial.

Defacing Property and Graffiti

Malicious mischief
Also known as criminal mischief, it is defined as the criminal offense of intentionally destroying another person's property.

Defacing property by damaging or writing on it, commonly known as graffiti, often falls under the catchall term, *criminal* or **malicious mischief.** Generally, malicious mischief is a lesser crime than arson, but also results in the destruction of property. Primarily, malicious mischief involves a threat to property only; arson has the potential to injure or kill people.

To prove malicious mischief, a prosecutor must prove that the defendant intended to destroy or harm property in a way that diminishes the property's value

or dignity. Graffiti often involves diminishing the dignity of a piece of property. For example, spray painting satanic symbols on a church would be a crime even though the paint could probably be cleaned off. Plus, doing so might also be classified as a hate crime if the intent is to intimidate the worshippers.

Often malicious mischief involves cleanup costs for the property owner even if the property is not permanently damaged. For instance, pranksters putting soap into a public fountain in hopes the circulating water would create bubbles are guilty of malicious mischief. Usually, the amount of property damage determines whether the charge is a felony or misdemeanor. For instance, swinging a hammer to break a window is probably a misdemeanor, swinging a hammer to damage a Renaissance-era sculpture is most likely a felony.

Firearm offenses

The Second Amendment to the U.S. Constitution provides that "A well regulated militia, being necessary to the security of a free State, the right of the people to keep and bear arms, shall not be infringed." In the past few years, the meaning of this cumbersomely worded sentence has taken on increasing importance.

When the crime rate was rising, many states and the federal government engaged in legislative efforts to restrict the purchase, use, and possession of various firearms. Nowhere was the ban on guns stricter than in Washington, D.C. The nation's capital had banned the possession of virtually every type of gun in an effort to reduce the amount of violent crime in the city.

Then the Supreme Court took up the first Second Amendment rights case it had been asked to hear in over seventy years. In *District of Columbia v. Heller,* No. 07-290, 2008, the Supreme Court ruled that the Second Amendment grants rights to citizens and not just to state-controlled militias (i.e., National Guard units), to own and carry guns. The case involved three District of Columbia firearms ordinances: the first generally barred the registration of handguns, the second prohibited carrying a pistol without a license, and the third required that all lawfully owned firearms be kept unloaded and either disassembled or trigger locked.

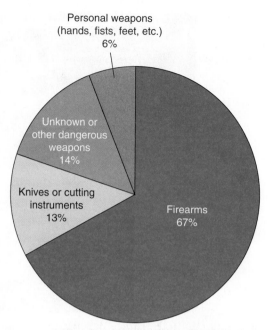

Type of Weapons Used in Homicides.
Source: FBI Uniform Crime Report 2008.

Dick Heller, who was a D.C. special police officer entitled to carry a gun while working as a guard at the Federal Judicial Center, sued after he was denied the right to register his gun to keep at home. Several other plaintiffs joined in the lawsuit seeking to either register handguns to use for self-defense in their homes or to keep legally owned and registered rifles loaded and ready to use at home.

The majority of the justices ruled that "the Constitution leaves the District of Columbia a variety of tools for [combating gun violence], including some measures regulating handguns. But the enshrinement of constitutional rights necessarily takes certain policy choices off the table. These include the absolute prohibition of handguns held and used for self-defense in the home." It pointedly concluded that the Second Amendment does, indeed, protect the right of individual citizens to bear arms and that the federal government went too far when it passed the three ordinances.

The court also wrote, "nothing in our opinion should be taken to cast doubt on longstanding prohibitions on the possession of firearms by felons and the mentally ill, or laws forbidding the carrying of firearms in sensitive places such as schools and government buildings."

A day after the Supreme Court ruled in *District of Columbia v. Heller*, the National Rifle Association sued the city of Chicago and its suburb of Oak Park, Illinois, to overturn an ordinance banning handguns and automatic weapons within city limits. This time, the issue was whether states or cities can, in effect, ban handguns and assault rifles. That case, *McDonald v. City of Chicago*, No. 08-1521, is still pending.

Currently, the state of the law on weapons like assault rifles is in flux. While such weapons were banned under the Public Safety and Recreational Firearms Use Protection Act, more commonly referred to as the Assault Weapons Ban, the law expired in 2004. President Obama has said he supports the reinstatement of the ban.

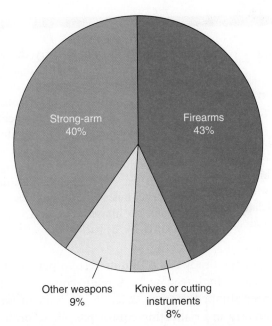

Type of Weapons Used in Armed Robberies.
Source: FBI Uniform Crime Report 2008.

At present, the federal gun restriction law is the **Brady Handgun Violence Prevention Act** (18 U.S.C. Sections 921–922), which requires background checks before the sale of most handguns in the United States. If there are no additional state restrictions, a firearm may be transferred to an individual upon approval by the National Instant Criminal Background Check System (NICS) maintained by the FBI. In some states, proof of a previous background check can be used to bypass the NICS check. For example, a state-issued concealed carry permit usually includes a background check equivalent to the one required by the Act. Other alternatives to the NICS check include state-issued handgun purchase permits or mandatory state or local background checks.

Brady Handgun Violence Prevention Act
A federal law which requires a background check before the purchase of certain guns and prohibits some individuals from owning purchasing those guns.

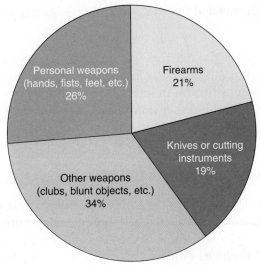

Type of Weapons Used in Aggravated Assaults.
Source: FBI Uniform Crime Report 2008.

Gun Carrying Soccer Mom Draws Attention to Open-Carry Laws

"The way people look at me sometimes when I am out running errands, I feel as if I am wearing a scarlet letter, and really it's a Glock 26." That's how Meleanie Hain, thirty-one, of Lebanon, Pennsylvania, described the attention she received in the aftermath of winning the right to carry her gun holstered on her hip.[37]

It all started on September 11, 2008, when Hain decided to carry the gun to her five-year-old daughter's soccer game in a public park. First, the local sheriff revoked her permit to carry the weapon concealed. Then a local judge reversed that decision, reinstated her permit, and suggested that she carry the weapon concealed at games to avoid frightening children. She refused, carrying the weapon openly, arguing that it was her Second Amendment right to do so.

Her case garnered national attention, and she was soon the poster child for the right to carry movement. Then, while she was chatting online with a friend, her husband shot and killed her before turning the gun on himself. Her gun was tucked away in a backpack by the back door.

Section 922(g) of the Brady Act prohibits certain persons from shipping or transporting any firearm in interstate or foreign commerce, or receiving any firearm which has been shipped or transported in interstate or foreign commerce, or possessing any firearm in or affecting commerce. These prohibitions apply to any person who:

1. Has been convicted in any court of a crime punishable by imprisonment for a term exceeding one year;
2. Is a fugitive from justice;
3. Is an unlawful user of or addicted to any controlled substance;
4. Has been adjudicated as a mental defective or committed to a mental institution;
5. Is an alien illegally or unlawfully in the United States;
6. Has been discharged from the Armed Forces under dishonorable conditions;
7. Having been a citizen of the United States, has renounced U.S. citizenship;
8. Is subject to a court order that restrains the person from harassing, stalking, or threatening an intimate partner or child of such intimate partner, or;
9. Has been convicted in any court of a misdemeanor crime of domestic violence.

Section 922(n) of the Act makes it unlawful for any person who is under indictment for a crime punishable by imprisonment for a term exceeding one year to ship or transport any firearm in interstate or foreign commerce, or receive any firearm which has been shipped or transported in interstate or foreign commerce.

Forgery and Check Fraud

Forgery
The fraudulent making or altering of any writing in a way that alters the legal rights and liabilities of another.

The number of checks written in the United States every year is staggering. Many of these checks are stolen and altered or counterfeited, resulting in a loss of more than $20 billion per year, according to the Payments Fraud and Control Survey of the Association of Financial Professionals.[38] **Forgery** is the fraudulent making or altering of any writing in a way that alters the legal rights and liabilities of another. Although many types of documents can be forged, checks are the most common targets. Check fraud includes forgery and other forms of theft accomplished through the misuse of checks or the check processing system.

Check fraud and forgery can be committed in a number of creative ways. The most common forms of check fraud are:

- *Forged signatures:* Forged signature checks are legitimate checks with a forged signature. A thief may steal a checkbook from the owner or intercept an order of checks arriving in the mail and fill out the checks, supplying his signature for that of the account holder.
- *Forged endorsement:* In this form of check fraud, a thief steals an already-made-out check and forges the endorsement signature on the back and cashes or deposits the funds.
- *Altered checks:* In this form of check fraud, a thief alters a check to make it appear the check is made out to someone other than the intended payee or the amount to be drawn against the drawer's account is altered.
- *Check kiting:* In this form of check fraud, criminals deposit a check into one account, which is drawn on another bank's account, and then draws on the deposit knowing that the deposited check is no good.
- *Counterfeit checks:* This form of check fraud involves the creation of fake checks. Today, with the rapid development of computer technology and software, forging checks is easy. All a thief needs is a computer, a checking account number and bank routing number (found on every check), check writing software, and a printer. Software intended to be used by consumers to print their own legitimate checks can churn out checks that look and seem indistinguishable from the real thing.

All states have criminal laws punishing check fraud and forgery, although the language varies from state to state. For example, in Minnesota, a person

. . . is guilty of check forgery . . . if the person, with intent to defraud, does any of the following:

1. falsely makes or alters a check so that it purports to have been made by another or by the maker under an assumed or fictitious name, or at another time, or with different provisions, or by the authority of one who did not give authority; or
2. falsely endorses or alters a check so that it purports to have been endorsed by another.[39]

In addition, the United States Code has many provisions dealing with forged and counterfeited securities and other commercial documents.[40] Note also that the Uniform Commercial Code, which all states have adopted with some variation, has extensive provisions that govern liability of financial institutions and account holders when a check is forged or altered.

Most states also have laws that criminalize writing checks when there are insufficient funds in the account to cover the checks. Generally, these statutes provide that the maker of the check must be notified that the check has been dishonored and be given an opportunity to make the check good if the account was open. If he or she doesn't, criminal charges can be filed. For example, Pennsylvania provides that the drawer be notified that the check was dishonored within thirty days of presentment, and that the drawer must make the check good within ten days of notification. If he or she does not, the Commonwealth can rely on the presumption that the maker's intent was fraudulent.[41]

Identity Theft

> But he that filches from me my good name/Robs me of that which not enriches him/And makes me poor indeed.
>
> Shakespeare, *Othello, Act iii, Scene 3.*

Phishing
The attempt to obtain personal identifying information by posing as a bank or financial institution in an e-mail communication.

Identity theft is a computer-era crime where the criminal uses another person's name, Social Security number, or other identifying information to represent that person for personal gain. Identity theft wreaks tremendous havoc on its victims and law enforcement agencies are devoting increasingly more time to solving identity theft and similar cybercrimes.

Of course, identity theft can also be accomplished without the aid of computers. For example, thieves may go through garbage cans looking for discarded bills, tax returns and other documents with identification information. Armed with Social Security numbers, names, and addresses, they can apply for credit, order goods, or—as is becoming increasingly common—sell the information on the identity theft black market to the highest bidder.

HISTORICAL HIGHLIGHT

The Black Market for Stolen Data

Analysts say the nature of computer crime has changed over the past decade. Web-wide attacks by ingenious hackers have given way to targeted thefts by organized groups. "We're seeing rapid growth in cooperative attacks, where an insider works in concert with some sort of external source to make a financial gain," says Brian Contos, chief security officer at ArcSight and author of *Enemy at the Water Cooler*, a book analyzing computer crime trends. "It's not just hackers looking randomly for easy points of entry—these are attacks on specific companies."

Most companies today rely heavily on automated systems. Even small companies use computers to store data, and most use the World Wide Web. Access to corporate data is also more widespread than ever before, with a large share of employees in many companies working on personal computers. What once might have occupied a filing cabinet now fits in a tiny zip drive, smaller than a credit card, and can be broadcast at the touch of a button. In such an environment, it can be very difficult to keep data secure.

And while access has increased, the black market for data has exploded. Social Security numbers, bank account information, mailing lists, customer lists, and even corporate secrets are readily bought and sold by individuals and organized groups. "There is a growing interest from organizations, like the Russian or Italian mafias, which basically just see stolen data as another revenue stream, like drugs or prostitution," says Chris Pierson, founder of the cybersecurity and cyberliability practice at Lewis and Roca LLP, a Phoenix law firm.

Thieves also use the Web to directly solicit information from unwary users. Phishers pose as banks or other financial concerns to try to get personal data directly from their customers. "You can buy a rootkit for $75 that will give you all of the advice, logos, and templates you need to execute a **phishing** attack," says Michael Rothschild, Director of Marketing at CounterStorm, maker of data security tools. The data goes pretty cheap. "You can get a hacked credit card on the Web for as little as $10," Rothschild says.[42]

Even Alcatel-Lucent, which helped develop data protection technology with Bell Labs and provides data protection services through its Security division, suffered a serious security breach when a disk mailed to an insurer went missing in Somerset County, New Jersey, in April 2007. The disk contained names, addresses, Social Security numbers, salaries, and other personal information for all Lucent employees in the United States. Hewitt Associates in Bridgewater, which handles Lucent's health and pension benefits, prepared the disk and mailed it to insurer Aon Corporation on April 5. Aon reportedly received an empty envelope. Employees were dismayed to discover the data hadn't been encrypted.

The company hired a firm to provide free identity protection and credit monitoring for one year to the more than 200,000 affected employees, and turned the case over to the Secret Service.[43]

Identity theft is a crime of intent. Simply finding out someone's Social Security number is not a crime if you don't use it for personal gain. The Washington state code defines identity theft as follows:

1. No person may knowingly obtain, possess, use, or transfer a means of identification or financial information of another person, living or dead, with the intent to commit, or to aid or abet, any crime.

2. Violation of this section when the accused or an accomplice uses the victim's means of identification or financial information and obtains an aggregate total of credit, money, goods, services or anything else of value in excess of one thousand five hundred dollars in value shall constitute identity theft in the first degree. Identity theft in the first degree is class B felony.

3. Violation of this section when the accused or an accomplice uses the victim's means of identification or financial information and obtains an aggregate total of credit, money goods services, or anything else of value that is less than one thousand five hundred dollars in value, or when no credit, money goods, services, or anything of value is obtained shall constitute identity theft in the second degree. Identity theft in the second degree is a class C felony.

4. A person who violates this section is liable for civil damages of one thousand dollars or actual damages, whichever is greater, including costs to repair the victim's credit record, and reasonable attorneys' fees as determined by the court.

5. In a proceeding under this section, the crime will be considered to have been committed in any locality where the person whose means of identification or financial information was appropriated resides, or in which any part of the offense took place, regardless of whether the defendant was ever actually in that locality.

6. The provisions of this section do not apply to any person who obtains another person's driver's license or other form of identification for the sole purpose of misrepresenting his or her age.

7. In a proceeding under this section in which a person's means of identification or financial information was used without that person's authorization, and when there has been a conviction, the sentencing court may issue such orders as are necessary to correct a public record that contains false information resulting from a violation of this section.[44]

Because so much identity theft occurs via the computer, the perpetrator does not have to be near the victim. The Washington State statute above gives prosecutors wide geographic latitude in prosecuting identity thieves wherever they may be. Of course, there is only so long a reach. It's almost impossible to track down and prosecute some identity thieves, who may operate out of Internet cafes in Third World or other foreign countries.

Identity theft also comes into play when illegal immigrants attempt to provide false identification to obtain employment. Because the I-9 form employers use to determine whether employees may legally work in the United States is a federal form issued by the Immigration and Customs Enforcement, identity theft to obtain a job is a federal crime.

Federal identity theft law attempts to cast a wide net looking to combat government fraud, terrorism and illegal immigration. When an individual is convicted of "theft of government property, fraud, or engaging in various unlawful activities related to passports, visas and immigration," an individual is guilty of aggravated identity theft. Those convicted of aggravated identity theft face an additional two years of imprisonment in addition to the sentence for the underlying crime if he or she "knowingly transfers, possesses, or uses, without legal authority, a means of identification of another person."[45]

In one case, a Mexican immigrant used a Social Security Card and Alien Registration Card with his name on it, but wrong account numbers. He was convicted of illegal immigration and the government sought to increase his sentence by charging him with aggravated identity theft. His lawyers moved to have the charge dismissed because the government could not prove the man knew the cards were "a means of identification of another person." For example, if the account numbers did not match anyone, they would not be "identification of another person" and even if the numbers did match the government would still have to prove the man knew that to establish the *mens rea* of the crime. The trial court dismissed the defense's argument, as did the Court of Appeals, but the U.S. Supreme Court ruled that the plain language of the statute supported the defense's position. The aggravated identity theft charge was dismissed.[46]

Cyber Crimes—Theft, Deception

Identity theft is not the only crime committed in cyberspace. The following were the eight most prevalent types of Internet fraud committed in 2009, according to Federal Bureau of Investigation statistics:

Advance fee fraud: Scams where the consumer is asked to pay a fee up front for a benefit that never materializes totaled 9.8 percent of cybercrime complaints. The median loss for these complaints was $1,500.

Auction fraud: The number of auction fraud cases has fallen over the years, as more people have become familiar with eBay and other online auction sites. Still auction fraud complaints comprised 10.3 percent of all cyber-complaints lodged with law enforcement.

Nondelivery: Merchandise and services not delivered as promised accounted for 19.9 percent of cases.

Credit and debit/card fraud: 10.4 percent of fraud cases involved bankcard abuses.

Computer fraud: Sometimes hackers merely want to get into people's computer to steal identities or use the machines as "zombies" to spread computer viruses to other computers in hopes of netting valuable information. Sometimes, they just want to damage a computer. It's the cyber equivalent of malicious mischief. Computer fraud constituted 7.9 percent of complaints.

Identity theft: Identity theft comprised 8.2 percent of fraud cases.

Investment fraud: Even in the post-Bernie Madoff era, people are still falling for phony investments and pyramid schemes. The median loss was $3,200.

Overpayment fraud: The consumer is given money in the form of a payment instrument, such as a check, that is greater than the amount agreed upon. The consumer writes a check or issues a refund for the difference, but later finds out that the original payment was bogus (i.e., a bad check). Overpayment fraud constituted 7.3 percent of Internet crimes reported to the FBI with a median loss of $2,500.[47]

Prosecuting cyber crimes is difficult because the perpetrators could be anywhere in the world. Cyber scammers prey on people's fears and greed. One new scam, dubbed "The Hitman Scam," works this way. The target receives an e-mail from a person claiming to be a member of an international gang. He says a contract has been put out on your life and he must kill you and your family for some wrong perpetrated by some distant relative of yours. However, another gang member knows your family and has interceded on your behalf. In exchange for a sum of money wired to a location in the United Kingdom, your life will be spared. Another popular scam was spawned by the 2009 government stimulus bill. Some people received recorded messages from someone sounding very much like President Obama directing them to websites where, for a processing fee of $28, they could find out if they qualified for federal stimulus money.

Lest you think only the uneducated or unsophisticated get snared in these scams, consider this: at least two major law firms lost funds in overpayment fraud scams in 2009. See, lawyers aren't always as smart as they should be.

Property Crime Evidence Concepts

With property crimes, the primary evidentiary challenge is proving ownership. Fortunately, in most cases proving ownership is not difficult in most cases. For example, to prove ownership during a theft trial, the prosecution simply puts the owner on the stand and he or she identifies the stolen item as his or her own. Often, there will be a serial number, a title, or some other way to identify the property in addition to the owner's personal testimony.

In a case involving real estate, public records can be used to prove ownership as well as the type of ownership.

In a case of arson (i.e., when law enforcement and fire officials have concluded that the fire was deliberately set), suspicion often falls on the owner. That's especially true if the owner was having financial difficulties and had an insurance policy in place. An entire subfield of forensics has emerged to tackle the problem. **Forensic accounting,** for example, is a specialty field in which accountants look for evidence of fraud in financial documents or for evidence that a business was undergoing financial distress serious enough to serve as a motive for torching the property. Heavy debt and a failing or underperforming business may be perceived as motivation for arson, but can be countered with evidence that business was on the upswing or that alternative financing was in the works.

Forensic accounting
An accounting subspecialty using auditing to prove fraud or other financial wrongdoing.

Forensic accounting also plays a major role in sophisticated fraud cases.

Forgery and check fraud cases often depend heavily on expert testimony about the authenticity of a signature. Both the prosecution and the defense are likely to employ experts in document examination. When identifying an expert in arson or document examination, keep these guidelines in place:

- Examine each potential expert's resume and experience carefully. Note membership in relevant professional organizations and publications in juried or peer-reviewed journals. If the expert is affiliated with a major university or other well-respected organization, so much the better.

- Experts who only testify for the prosecution or only testify for the defense are suspect. At best, they appear less credible than those whose testimony has been more evenly spread. At worst, the expert will appear to be a hired gun or in the prosecutor's pocket.

- Check credentials carefully. In recent years there has been a rash of cases involving erroneous or intentionally false testimony by forensic experts. Nothing will sink an expert's testimony faster than evidence that he or she faces professional negligence or even criminal charges arising out of testimony in other cases. This is an area where defense counsel have recently become more proactive, seeking out evidence that a particular laboratory or expert has lied or misled in other cases.

- When preparing the case, note any special rules in your jurisdiction about the exchange of expert testimony or notice of the intended use of an expert's opinion at trial.

CONCEPT **REVIEW AND REINFORCEMENT**

In the American Common Law tradition, property consists of a bundle of rights, including the right to possess, use and enjoy, and dispose of something. It is not a material object itself, but a person's right to do what he or she wishes with that object, subject to limitations provided in the law.

Property comes in two varieties. Real property is land and everything permanently attached to it. Land rights include the land itself and any buildings or structures permanently attached to the land. Real property can be either private or public. Private property is property owned by a private individual, while public property is held by a state government or the federal government on behalf of us all.

Personal property is everything else the law grants ownership rights to. Personal property can be tangible, with a physical presence. Personal property can also be intangible such as patents and copyrights. Personal property also includes domestic animals and livestock, as well as wild animals that have either been domesticated or placed under control.

Real property is subject to seizure by governmental entities as part of the state's power of eminent domain. Under the Constitution, any such taking must be after due process of law.

Property can be owned outright. If it is, the owner is said to hold the property in fee simple. *Fee simple* is a legal term for ownership of the entire

bundle of rights that go with a piece of property. When someone rents property, he or she has the right to enjoy and possess it. These rights are considered leasehold rights.

Condominium owners have a form of ownership with fewer rights than fee simple title holders but more than leasehold rights. Generally, condominium owners own from the wall in, everything else belongs to the condominium association which is made up of all the owners in the building or a developer. The association can place a lien against the property and initiate a lawsuit to collect unpaid fees. The owner would have to pay the fees to remove the lien or pay the lien before he or she could convey a clear title to a new owner.

Ownership is not restricted to one person; many persons can own the same property together. For example, husbands and wives often own property as tenants by the entireties. Tenancy by the entirety is a legal joint ownership in which both spouses own an undivided interest in the whole property and in which neither spouse can sell his or her interest without the consent of the other. Other forms of joint ownership are tenancy in common and joint tenancy with right of survivorship.

Property rights can be bought for a price, inherited, acquired as a gift, or acquired by mere possession. Purchase of property is done by contract and involves the exchange of something of value. Acquiring property by gift or inheritance requires three things. First, the owner must intend to give the property away. Second, the gift must be delivered to the recipient. Third, the recipient must accept the gift. Property can also be acquired by possession. Abandoned property can also be acquired by possession.

A thief can only steal that which does not belong to him; he cannot steal his own property. Nor can he trespass against his own property. Theft also requires that the prosecution prove beyond a reasonable doubt that the defendant intended to permanently deprive the owner of the property taken.

At Common Law, theft was defined as the taking and carrying away of another's personal property with the intent to deprive him or her of it permanently. There are many distinct acts that fit the definition of theft, and every state has its own list.

The first element of the crime of theft is "taking and carrying away." The prosecution must prove that the defendant took possession of the object of the theft and carried it away.

Under the Common Law, the only type of property that could be stolen was tangible personal property. Now all jurisdictions have revised their theft statutes to include intangible personal property under their definitions of theft.

The property stolen must belong to someone other than the defendant. The prosecution must therefore prove ownership of the property. Prosecutors need the cooperation of property owners in order to secure theft convictions. In order to constitute theft, the defendant must take the property without the consent of the owner.

Because stolen property must be positively identified as belonging to the owner, it is crucial that owners keep careful track of serial numbers and other identifying characteristics of their property in case of theft.

The final element of the crime of theft involves intent. It is not enough that the defendant took possession of property belonging to another. He must also intend to permanently deprive the owner of the property. Intent may be proven with indirect or circumstantial evidence. Thus, a thief's actions may speak of his intent.

Embezzlement occurs when someone who has legal possession of property of another uses, converts, or retains that property for his own use or the use of someone other than the owner. It differs from other forms of theft because it does not require proof that the perpetrator took and carried away property of another.

One of the most costly property crimes in the United States is auto theft. Auto theft rings steal specific models of cars for their parts that can be resold to auto repair shops on the black market. Like other thefts, the prosecution must prove the defendant took the car, did not own the car, and intended to permanently deprive the owner of the use of the car. Theft or larceny statutes generally divide theft into two classes based on the value of the goods or services stolen: petit and grand. Petit larceny is generally a misdemeanor while grand larceny is a felony.

At Common Law, burglary was the breaking and entering of the dwelling house of another at night with the intent to commit a felony inside. The crime required that the perpetrator secure entry by some use of force. That is, it was not burglary to enter an unlocked dwelling. Force must have been used, whether that meant pushing in a door or breaking a window. In addition, the entry had to be to a dwelling house. It was not burglary to break into a warehouse or other storage place.

The crime of burglary is complete when the entry with intent to commit a felony has taken place. Any crime committed once inside will be charged separately whether that crime is an assault, murder, or theft.

Today, states have expanded the definition of burglary to cover just about any unauthorized entry into a structure, at any time of day or night. Some states simply retain the nighttime provision in their statutes and have added other sections to their crimes codes that also punish daytime break-ins. They distinguish between nighttime and daytime break-ins by punishing night activity more severely than the same crime committed in broad daytime.

Most states hold that reaching in is enough to constitute burglary. Most states still require that there must be at least some form of unauthorized entry into the premises. That's because the crime of burglary is based in part on the concept of the tort of trespass. Trespass is the unlawful and unprivileged entry or intrusion onto the property of another.

The Common Law definition required that to constitute burglary, the unlawful entry must have been to a dwelling house of another. At Common Law, a dwelling house was a structure in which people lived and slept. States no longer limit burglary to dwelling houses, and include just about any structure, occupied or unoccupied, in their definitions. Some states have expanded the definition to include unoccupied automobiles and even telephone booths.

The prosecution must show that the defendant lacked permission to be present in the structure. A defendant's entry into another's structure, no matter how violent or destructive that entry was, isn't burglary unless the defendant can be shown to have intended to commit a felony while inside.

Proving intent is generally not difficult in burglary cases even if the defendant isn't "caught in the act." The fact that the defendant broke into a building containing personal property and was caught often leads to an inference that he intended to steal some of that property once inside.

At Common Law, arson was the malicious burning of the dwelling house of another. The building burned had to be the dwelling of another, so that burning down a stable or other outbuilding was not arson. In order to curtail insurance fraud and so-called spite arson, most states expanded their definition of arson.

By setting the standard of intent as willful and malicious burning, arson statutes cover all the common motives for committing the crime. Possible motives for committing arson include arson for profit, arson for revenge, evidence destruction, political act, and arson for thrill.

When arson is politically motivated, the arsonist is sometimes also charged under federal law.

The essential elements that the government must prove beyond a reasonable doubt in an arson case are: the fire was willfully and maliciously set by the defendant or someone else on his orders; and the fire set by the defendant caused damage.

Defacing property by damaging or writing on it, commonly known as graffiti, often falls under the catchall term criminal or malicious mischief. Malicious mischief involves a threat to property only.

To prove malicious mischief, a prosecutor must prove that the defendant intended to destroy or harm property in a way that diminishes the property's value or dignity. Often malicious mischief involves cleanup costs for the property owner even if the property is not permanently damaged.

Forgery is the fraudulent making or altering of any writing in a way that alters the legal rights and liabilities of another. Although many types of documents can be forged, checks are the most common targets. The most common forms of check fraud are forged signatures, forged endorsements, altered checks, check kiting, and counterfeit checks.

In addition, the U.S. Code has many provisions dealing with forged and counterfeited securities and other commercial documents. Most states also have laws that criminalize writing checks when there are insufficient funds in the account to cover the checks. Generally, these statutes provide that the maker of the check must be notified that the check has been dishonored and be given an opportunity to make the check good if the account was open.

Identity theft is a computer-era crime where the criminal uses another person's name, Social Security number, or other identifying information to represent that person for personal gain. Armed with Social Security numbers, names, and addresses, identity thieves can apply for credit, order goods, or—as is becoming increasingly common—sell the information on the identity theft black market to the highest bidder.

Identity theft is a crime of intent. Simply finding out someone's Social Security is not a crime if you don't use it for personal gain. Because so much identity theft occurs via the computer, the perpetrator does not have to be near the victim.

Other types of Internet-based crimes include advance fee fraud, auction fraud, nondelivery, credit and debit card fraud, computer fraud, identity theft, investment fraud, and overpayment fraud.

KEY **TERMS**

Arson
Brady Handgun Violence Prevention Act
Burglary
Chattel
Embezzlement
Eminent domain
Fee simple

Forensic accounting
Forgery
Joint tenants with right of survivorship
Leasehold rights
Lien
Malicious mischief

Personal property
Phishing
Property
Real property
Tenancy by the entirety
Tenants in common
Theft

CONCEPT **REVIEW QUESTIONS**

1. Explain what property is and the bundles of rights that accompany each type of property.

2. Explain the following terms:
   a. fee simple
   b. joint tenants with right of survivorship
   c. tenancy by the entireties
   d. tenants in common.

3. Define *theft* and name the different classifications of theft.

4. List the essential elements required to prove theft.

5. Differentiate embezzlement from other forms of theft.

6. Define *burglary* and describe its Common Law origins.

7. Define *arson* and explain why so few cases are cleared.

8. Explain the most common methods of check fraud and forgery.

9. Explain what the Brady Handgun Violence Prevention Act requires before the purchase of a gun.

10. Explain laws aimed at defacing property.

11. Explain where graffiti fits as a property crime.

12. Define identity theft.

13. Explain how cyber crime fits into traditional concepts of crimes against property.

14. Describe how prosecutors go about proving ownership in a theft case.

15. Explain how forensic accounting is used in fraud or arson cases.

CASE **APPLICATION**

Building Your Professional Skills

1. READ THE FOLLOWING PRESS RELEASE FROM THE FBI AND ANSWER THE QUESTIONS WHICH FOLLOW.

Department of Justice Press Release

For Immediate Release
May 28, 2010

United States Attorney's Office
District of Maryland
Contact: (410) 209-4800

Vice President of A&B Check Cashing Sentenced to Three Years in Prison in $12.4 Million Check Kiting Scheme

One of the Largest Fraud Schemes Ever Perpetrated in Maryland

BALTIMORE—U.S. District Judge Benson E. Legg, Jr. sentenced Brian I. Satisky, age 56, of Pikesville, Maryland, today to three years in prison, followed by four years of supervised release, for bank fraud in connection with a check kiting scheme in which his check cashing service business withdrew money based upon inflated balances in its business accounts. Judge Legg also ordered Satisky to pay restitution totaling $12.4 million to the victim banks.

The sentence was announced by United States Attorney for the District of Maryland Rod J. Rosenstein and Special Agent in Charge Richard A. McFeely of the Federal Bureau of Investigation.

"Mr. Satisky did not use a weapon, but his specialty was stealing money from banks," said U.S. Attorney Rod J. Rosenstein. "This was essentially a bank robbery scheme carried out by con artists who caused one of the largest fraud losses ever prosecuted in Maryland, resulting in actual losses of more than $12 million to local banks."

Brian Satisky became the President of the Maryland Association of Financial Service Centers, Inc., a trade group. He served on the board of directors of Financial Service Centers of America (FiSCA) which is a national trade group representing more than 5,000 money service businesses. In June 2003, Satisky testified before Congress on behalf of FiSCA. According to the plea agreement, the check kite fraud scheme described below began in June 2003.

According to Satisky's plea agreement, Brian Satisky and his brother Alec owned and operated Colleen, Inc., which their parents began as a family shoe store in the Hollingswood Shopping Center. The shoe store became their secondary business and their primary business became A&B Check Cashing, a money services company operating from 21 locations in the Baltimore metropolitan area. For a fee, A&B Check Cashing: cashed checks; sold money orders, transit passes, prepaid phone and calling card products and lottery tickets; transferred money; and provided bill payer services for Verizon and BGE. Many of its customers were "unbanked" individuals who did not have access to traditional forms of banking, credit, or traditional loans.

In 2001, the business was sued in a class action law suit alleging that one of its products constituted a payday loan in violation of Maryland law. Brian Satisky and his brother settled the law suit in 2003, agreeing that they would not collect some $1.6 million in customers' checks which had been received to repay the alleged payday loans. This caused a significant and immediate shortfall for the business.

In an effort to stay ahead of the business's debt, the brothers began to "kite" checks between two of the business's bank accounts. Each day, checks were drawn on two of the business's bank accounts when the brothers knew A&B Check Cashing had insufficient funds to cover the checks. The checks, when cross-deposited into the two bank accounts, artificially inflated the balances of the accounts and enabled the brothers to write checks to the operating account and to third party vendors and creditors in excess of the amounts of cash their business actually had.

The scheme required that either Alec or Brian write fraudulently inflated checks every day to cross deposit into the business's bank accounts. Whomever was to write the checks that day calculated the amount needed for the kited checks by examining the day's legitimate deposits, the online bank balance and outstanding checks for the account at Carrollton Bank. A telephone call would then be made to the Baltimore County Savings Bank (BCSB) to obtain a telephonic message of the bank balance and outstanding checks there. Eighty percent of the checks were written by Alec, with Brian writing checks on days when Alec had his regularly scheduled day off or was on vacation. While Alec was on vacation from October 18–26, 2005, Brian wrote in excess of $10 million of kited checks daily to keep the kite going. The kited amounts gradually increased as A&B Check Cashing used kited funds to cover business expenses, including paying their own salaries and the costs of opening new locations.

The kite continued until it collapsed in June 2006. At that time, Alec Satisky committed suicide. A&B Check Cashing is no longer in business. BCSB lost $10.6 million and Carrollton Bank lost $1.8 million.

United States Attorney Rod J. Rosenstein thanked Assistant United States Attorney Joyce K. McDonald, who prosecuted the case.

QUESTIONS

1. How do you think the prosecution would have gone about proving their case? List the elements of the crime and what the defendant did that met each element.

2. Why do you think it took so long for the victim banks to discover the fraud?

2. Jose Lara was confused. An Arlington County, Virginia, bank sent him a check for almost $2,800 claiming it an overpayment on his second mortgage. Jose was confused because he didn't have a second mortgage.

Jose did remember losing his wallet a few months before. He had reported his credit cards missing, but his wallet contained his Social Security card and other identifying information. The person who found it was Elizabeth Cabrera-Rivera. Elizabeth used Jose's information to obtain a mortgage from a predatory lender who never checked tax returns or income. Elizabeth bought a $419,000 townhouse in the Washington, D.C., suburb of Springfield, Virginia.

Unlike many identity thieves she did not abscond with money. Instead, she refinanced the mortgage with a local bank, and proceeded to make every payment. Things got dicey for Mr. Lara, though, when he went to refinance his own mortgage and was turned down because of the other outstanding loans in his name.

QUESTIONS

1. Did Elizabeth commit a crime? If so, what crime(s)?
2. Research the case and determine what happened to the parties (Tip—search newspapers).

CRITICAL **THINKING EXERCISES**

1. You own several acres of land. You own all rights to the land. Unbeknownst to you, a mining company owns an adjacent property and begins digging horizontal shafts under your property and begins mining valuable minerals. What crime is the mining company guilty of? Theft? Burglary? Trespass? Robbery?

2. Match the description on the left with the type of ownership that it best describes on the right.

A married couple owns a home.	joint tenants with right of survivorship
Three friends own a hunting camp. When one of them dies, the other two inherit the property.	tenancy by the entireties
Four people buy a house together. One of them dies and his children inherit his interest in the property based on his will. The children continue to own a partial interest with the other three parties.	tenant in common

3. Match the description on the left with the theft classification on the right.

A man borrows a rare book from a library and fails to return it.	Shoplifting or retail theft
A woman takes several blouses to a dressing room in a store to try on. She dons one under the clothes she wore into the store and leaves the store without paying for it.	Purse snatching
A salesman persuades a person to invest in a company that does not exist.	Pickpocketing
A fire breaks out at an appliance store. People on the street take out merchandise and leave the scene before the police and fire departments arrive.	Looting

You are on a crowded subway, a group of young men crowd around you and begin jostling you. As you leave the train you see one of the men putting your wallet in his coat.	Library theft
An elderly lady is walking down the street. A man speeds by on a moped and grabs her purse and continues on up the road.	Theft by deception

4. A community has enacted a law that requires residents to separate their garbage into recyclables and nonrecyclables. The recyclable items are placed in plastic containers marked "Property of the City of Ecology." The city collects the contents of the containers and sells it to a recycling facility, boosting the city budget by several hundred thousand dollars per year. Joe, a homeless man, makes the rounds on garbage collection day and selects metal cans from the recycling bins, which he crushes and sells to a recycling facility. He is arrested and charged with theft of city property. You have been asked to analyze the case on behalf of the public defender representing Joe. What is Joe's best defense to the theft charges?

5. A bookkeeper devises an elaborate scheme. She pays a contractor for work he doesn't perform in return for the contractor paying her a kickback. Is she guilty of embezzlement or theft? What about the contractor? What element distinguishes the two crimes?

6. A twenty-five-year-old six feet seven inch tall man weighing 250 pounds encounters an eighty-year-old five foot tall ninety pound woman on a bus. He towers over her, looks at her and says, "You don't mind if I take a few bills from your wallet, do you?" She stammers, "Uh, No." He takes $100 in cash. Has a robbery been committed? What if the man were her son instead of a total stranger?

7. Jerry is separated from his wife and still owns a house jointly with her. She has changed the keys to the house, and Jerry breaks a window to enter the house and retrieve personal belongings. He is charged with burglary. How do you defend him? Is your answer different if he takes his wife's possessions rather than his own?

8. Mary has been thinking about remodeling her kitchen. She has contacted several contractors, and has received several estimates. She has also applied for a home equity loan to finance the project, but has been turned down because she does not have enough equity in the home to qualify. Saturday night she fries some chicken and leaves the deep fryer full of oil on in the kitchen. She leaves for a walk. When she returns, she finds the firefighters dowsing a fire in her kitchen. Although the rest of the structure is saved, the kitchen is a total loss. Insurance covers the rebuilding. If you are the local prosecutor, how would you go about putting together a case against Mary? What evidence would you seek, and how would you obtain it?

9. What form of check fraud has occurred in each of the following factual scenarios?
   a. Carla receives a birthday check from her grandmother and adds a "1" in front of the $10 and writes "One Hundred" in front of the Ten Dollars and no cents on the check.
   b. Sarah buys a copy of "Easy Check" software for her computer and uses the account number and bank routing number from her roommate's checks to print checks, which she then uses to pay her tuition bill.
   c. Jack finds a purse at a bus stop, and takes a check from the checkbook he finds inside. He makes the check out to "cash" and signs the check with the account holder's name.
   d. Smitty maintains two checking accounts at two banks. He will be paid on Friday and has no funds in either account on Wednesday. Wednesday he writes a check for $100 to himself on account number one and deposits it in account number two. He then withdraws $100 from account number two. On Friday he deposits his paycheck in account number one to cover the check.

10. Joe was dishonorably discharged from the Army and has a Protection From Abuse Order against him. He has his eyes on a shiny new Glock at the local gun show. Will he be able to purchase the weapon?

11. You own a building that needs some repair. In fact the paint is peeling. A teenager in your neighborhood scrapes off the loose paint in one spot and spray paints graffiti there. You see him and report it to the police. When the police arrest him, he claims he was just beautifying a building in the neighborhood. What would you have to prove to press charges?

12. Which of the following are examples of identity theft?
    a. Your older brother and you look very much alike. You are eighteen years old and would like to go drinking at a local bar. You ask your twenty-one-year-old brother for his driver's license. He gives it to you, and tells you to have a good time. You use his license to prove you are of age to drink, and get served.
    b. You hack into a computer and obtain credit card information, but never use it for any purpose.

    c. You are a terrorist whose name is on a no-fly list. You alter your identification to show a different spelling of your name.

13. You are a prosecutor examining a case where Harry Hacker allegedly sent an e-mail to Larry Lonely promising to find him a Russian wife. All Larry had to do was pay a finder's fee of $200. Larry paid using his credit card. Harry proceeded to charge the $200, and then kept adding fees while promising Larry great sex with an outrageously beautiful woman. Larry eventually tired of the cash drain and lack of sex. He cancelled his credit card, called the police, and they tracked down Harry and arrested him. What elements do you have to prove to convict Harry? How would the case have been different if Harry had contacted Larry through the U.S. mail? How would the case have been different if Harry had contacted Larry in person?

PORTFOLIO **BUILDING**

1. As with most criminal laws covered in this textbook, they are just guidelines and a starting point for research. Research theft statutes in your jurisdiction and summarize them for your portfolio.

2. You work for the local police department. The department has just received a complaint from several senior citizens who say that a nice young man came to their door, explained that he had just finished resurfacing a neighbor's driveway and has extra materials that must be used or will go to waste. For $500 cash, he offers to refinish their driveways. Several agreed and the man applied a coat of a black substance to their driveways and then left. A rainstorm washed the coating away. Using your research on theft offenses in your jurisdiction, prepare a memo to

the police chief outlining possible charges (assuming the young man is nabbed in another neighborhood).

3. Research arson statutes in your jurisdiction and summarize them for your portfolio.

4. You work for a law firm that has just been hired by a business owner whose warehouse burned to the ground. The owner was facing financial problems, but had insurance coverage on the warehouse and its contents. The local fire chief just announced that the fire appeared to have been set and the owner fears he will be charged. Prepare a memo to the attorney who will be handling the case, outlining what the prosecution in your jurisdiction will have to prove to charge the owner with arson.

FOR FURTHER READING

1. Morris, J. (1995). *DSM IV Made Easy*. The Guilford Press. This handbook helps demystify psychiatric diagnosis and is especially helpful for legal professionals working with psychiatric experts.

2. Faith, N. (2000). *Blaze: The Forensics of Fire*. St. Martin's Press. This book describes historic fires and the techniques used to determine their cause.

3. Bouquard, T. (2004). *Arson Investigation: The step-by-step procedure*, 2nd ed. Charles C. Thomas

Publisher. A guidebook for fire and arson investigators.

4. Shover, N. (1996). *Great Pretenders, Pursuits and Careers of Persistent Thieves.* Westview Press. This book looks at the career criminal who resumes a life of crime despite efforts to "go straight."

5. Cromwell, P. (ed.) (1998). *In Their Own Words: Criminals on Crime.* Roxbury. An anthology in which criminals explain their life of crime.

6. Berendt, J. (2005). *The City of Falling Angels.* Penguin Books. A story of the Venice Opera House arson in Venice, Italy, set among a rich cast of real-life characters.

7. Crichton, M. (2004). *State of Fear.* Harper Collins. A thriller involving eco-terrorism.

Chapter **seven**
SOCIAL CRIMES

Of all tyrannies a tyranny sincerely exercised for the good of its victims may be the most oppressive. It may be better to live under robber barons than under omnipotent moral busybodies. The robber baron's cruelty may sometimes sleep, his cupidity may at some point be satiated; but those who torment us for our own good will torment us without end for they do so with the approval of their own conscience.

James Madison, *The Federalist No. 51*

Introduction

Every society has generally accepted rules of conduct for its members. Those rules vary from place to place and time to time. In some societies, the rules are strict and plentiful, while in others they are few and far between. Conduct rules often have their roots in religious doctrines, but sometimes have more practical origins. For example, the prohibition against prostitution has its origin in religion, but some counties in the United States allow prostitutes to operate in licensed brothels where presumably regular health checks help prevent the spread of disease that might flourish in an unsupervised setting.

Most rules of conduct in modern societies don't carry criminal penalties, but instead rely on self-censorship or public ostracism for enforcement. Some violations carry criminal sanctions, and it is those we now turn our attention to. The list of social offenses that have at one time or another been considered crimes include:

- Adultery and fornication
- Bestiality and buggery (sodomy)
- Miscegenation (mixed-race marriage)
- Seduction and alienation of affections

CHAPTER OBJECTIVES

After studying this chapter, you should be able to:

- Define prostitution and explain the elements required to be proven in a prosecution
- Define what a controlled substance is
- Understand the problem of drug abuse and law enforcement efforts to curtail the use and trafficking in illegal drugs
- Describe some of the laws that regulate gambling
- Understand the special laws designed to combat child pornography production
- Define what domestic violence is and how it affects its victims
- Understand what constitutes child molestation
- Understand what constitutes child abuse
- Understand what constitutes elder abuse
- List the factors that contribute to teenage runaways
- List the two laws that govern drunk driving
- List the two key areas where the state regulates alcoholic beverages
- Understand what constitutes disorderly conduct and the defenses to the charge
- Understand what constitutes public indecency
- Understand what constitutes vagrancy and defenses to the charge
- Understand what constitutes polygamy and associated religious freedom issues
- Understand the laws concerning abortion
- Understand the laws concerning consensual sodomy

Prostitution and Commercialized vice

Prostitution
Engaging in sexual intercourse or other sexual activity for pay.

Prostitution is generally defined as engaging in sexual intercourse or other sexual activity for pay. It can be engaged in by either sex, although most prostitutes are women. It was widespread across the ancient world in Greece, Egypt, and Rome, and is sometimes referred to as the world's oldest profession. For some practitioners, selling sex acts supports a drug habit. Others who may have few job or social skills turn to prostitution for economic reasons. Still others are runaway teens who find themselves on the streets with no money or shelter and few support systems available. Prostitutes are also frequent targets for criminal acts, including murder. In fact, some of the most notorious serial killers in our history specifically targeted prostitutes.

Sex workers
A term preferred by some working in the sex industry such as prostitutes, porn actresses or actors, exotic dancers, and the like.

Most states outlaw sex for money and make it a crime for both parties involved. It has long been a federal crime to transport someone over state lines for immoral purposes,[1] as the original language of the Mann Act stated. The law now defines "immoral purposes" with precision, and provides that:

HISTORICAL HIGHLIGHT

Sex Workers Try to Dispel Stereotypes about Prostitution

Not everyone involved in prostitution and related activities do so out of desperation or the need to feed an addiction. Some claim to have chosen their profession freely and have formed organizations aimed at improving working conditions and gaining respect and legal protection for members. Many of these participants in prostitution and related acts, such as acting in pornographic films, working in massage parlors, and dancing in strip clubs, prefer to be called **sex workers.**

The North American Task Force on Prostitution is a network of sex workers and sex workers' rights organizations, and individuals and organizations that support the rights of sex workers to ply their trades without interference from law enforcement, and with the ability to organize into what amounts to trade unions or guilds. There are member organizations in many large cities offering education, health screening, and even legal assistance to sex workers.

Other groups operate on a model designed less to make prostitution a legitimate business, and more to assure that sex workers are safe and healthy and able to receive medical treatment or drug counseling if desired. For example, in the nation's capital, HIPS (Helping Individual Prostitutes Survive) runs an outreach van nightly to assist sex workers. HIPS also operates a toll-free national hotline.

Whoever knowingly transports any individual in interstate or foreign commerce, or in any Territory or Possession of the United States, with intent that such individual engage in prostitution, or in any sexual activity for which any person can be charged with a criminal offense, or attempts to do so, shall be fined under this title or imprisoned not more than 10 years, or both.

At one point, the U.S. Supreme Court went as far as to say that a man who "transported a woman in interstate commerce so that she should become his mistress or concubine" was transporting her with an "immoral purpose" within the meaning of the Mann Act.[2] Over the years, the Act was also used to convict a Mormon practitioner of polygamy from bringing his brides home across state lines.[3] Eventually, the language was changed to its present wording to assure that only those transported over state lines to engage in the sale of sex for money would run afoul of the law.

State criminal laws outlawing prostitution generally outlaw two distinct behaviors: soliciting someone to engage in sex for money in a public place and working in a brothel or other private setting selling sex for money. For example, in Pennsylvania a person is guilty of prostitution if he or she:

> is an inmate of a house of prostitution or otherwise engages in sexual activity as a business; or loiters in or within view of any public place for the purpose of being hired to engage in sexual activity.[4]

Many states have graduated penalties for engaging in prostitution, with each additional conviction resulting in a longer prison term and fine. Many states, in recognition that prostitution can be a factor in the spread of sexually transmitted diseases, make selling sexual favors by those who know they are infected with the human immunodeficiency virus (HIV) a felony offense.

Those who hire prostitutes also commit a criminal offense in most states. In addition, anyone who works to procure clients for a prostitute (the definition of a **pimp**) can also be prosecuted. Although it was not always so, most states now punish pimps, prostitutes, and their clients equally. In addition, those who patronize prostitutes are sometimes subject to publicity. For example, in Pennsylvania, the second conviction for soliciting a prostitute carries with it a requirement that the conviction shall be published in a local newspaper (at the defendant's expense).[5]

There is only one state in the United States in which prostitution is legal. Since 1971, counties in Nevada have been able to elect to allow brothels within their borders.[6] The state requires that counties with brothels license their prostitutes and also requires that all clients wear condoms. It is still illegal to sell sex outside of brothels and in Las Vegas itself.

Pimp
One who works to procure clients for a prostitute.

YOU MAKE THE CALL: THE DUKE RAPE CASE

Does Stripping Contribute to Prostitution or Sexual Violence?

When three Duke Lacrosse players were accused of raping a stripper they had hired for a party, it set off a storm of controversy. The stripper claimed she was stripping to support herself and her child while she attended school.

When the story first broke, civil rights leaders such as the Rev. Jesse Jackson decried a society where a woman would have to resort to stripping to get through college. He even offered to pay for her college education so that she would not have to strip.

The issue raised points to the very role of women, particularly young attractive women, in our society. Is stripping just innocent fun? After all, male strippers often perform for women. Or is stripping sexually exploitive in itself, and does it contribute to viewing women as sex objects? If so, as sex objects are they more vulnerable to sexual violence? Should more restrictive laws governing the hiring of strippers be enacted? You make the call.

Drug Production and Use

Drug use in the United States is a considerable problem. According to the federal agency responsible for developing a national drug policy, the Office of National Drug Control Policy, in 2008, 8 percent of Americans age twelve or older had used illegal drugs in the last month. Other statistics include:

- 7.6 percent of teens between the ages of twelve and seventeen needed treatment for drug abuse in 2008.
- Children who smoke "pot" at an early age are less likely to finish school and more likely to commit crimes than those who don't.[7]
- More than 1.84 million Americans were arrested for drug-law violations in 2005.[8]

Clearly, illicit drug use and abuse is a serious problem for law enforcement. Today, the "war on drugs" has taken on a new urgency as it has become clear that terrorist organizations abroad have a hand in the production and distribution of illicit drugs in the United States. The profits from these operations in turn may be providing valuable cash for terrorist organizations across the globe.

Those who use illicit drugs violate a variety of state and federal criminal laws, and those who produce, import, and sell those drugs face the harshest penalties. We will focus on federal drug laws, but every state has similar laws on its books. A few states have experimented with decriminalizing the usage, possession, and sale of some controlled substances, primarily marijuana.

A **controlled substance** is defined as a drug considered dangerous under the law because of its effects, including intoxication, stupor, or addictive potential.[9] That is, the drug is listed on either a state or federal directory of controlled substances, and may in some cases be available by prescription to treat medical conditions. Examples include many commonly prescribed pharmaceuticals like Dilantin and Ritalin. Some controlled substances, such as cocaine or heroin, are so dangerous that they are not legally available at all.

> It's so important for Americans to know that the traffic in drugs finances the work of terror, sustaining terrorists, that terrorists use drug profits to fund their cells to commit acts of murder. If you quit drugs, you join the fight against terror in America.
>
> George W. Bush, President of the United States (December 14, 2001)

Controlled substance
A drug considered dangerous under the law because of its effects, including intoxication, stupor, or addictive potential.

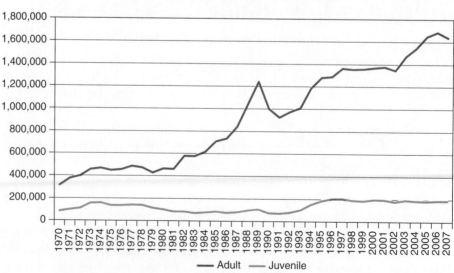

Estimated Drug Arrests by Age 1970–2007.
Source: FBI Uniform Crime Report 2008.

Penalties

Most criminal cases brought against drug abusers are state violations. As a practical matter, federal law enforcement officials handle cases involving trafficking of controlled substances across our borders and across state lines while local law enforcement handles individual drug use and local drug distribution and dealing. However, agents from federal agencies like the Drug Enforcement Agency (DEA) and the FBI work closely with state attorneys general and local police departments to coordinate the war on drugs. For example, in areas designated as High Intensity Drug Trafficking Areas (HIDTAs), the federal government takes a lead role in coordinating federal, state, and local law enforcement efforts. There are thirty-one such areas in the United States.[10]

Arrests for drug use are quite common. In 2008, there were over 1.8 million arrests by state and local law enforcement agencies.[11] More than four-fifths of drug law violation arrests are for possession violations, and drug abuse violations in 2008 accounted for 13.1 percent of all arrests. The most frequent drug possessed by the defendants was marijuana, followed by heroin and cocaine. Marijuana and heroin are Schedule I drugs (see the following list) while cocaine is a Schedule II drug. Approximately 92 percent of drug defendants handled by the court system during 2004 were convicted.[12]

There are five schedules of controlled substances cataloged by the federal drug laws and additions are made when new drugs surface or a previously unscheduled drug is determined to belong on the list. Almost every state has adopted the same schedules. The penalty for possession of a substance on the list depends on which schedule the substance is on, and how much of the substance with which the defendant was caught. The schedules can be found at 21 U.S.C. § 811 and at the DEA website, www.dea.gov. The major categories are:

Schedule I.	(A)	The drug or other substance has a high potential for abuse.
	(B)	The drug or other substance has no currently accepted medical use in treatment in the United States.
	(C)	There is a lack of accepted safety for use of the drug or other substance under medical supervision.
Schedule II.	(A)	The drug or other substance has a high potential for abuse.
	(B)	The drug or other substance has a currently accepted medical use in treatment in the United States or a currently accepted medical use with severe restrictions.
	(C)	Abuse of the drug or other substances may lead to severe psychological or physical dependence.
Schedule III.	(A)	The drug or other substance has a potential for abuse less than the drugs or other substances in Schedules I and II.
	(B)	The drug or other substance has a currently accepted medical use in treatment in the United States.
	(C)	Abuse of the drug or other substance may lead to moderate or low physical dependence or high psychological dependence.
Schedule IV.	(A)	The drug or other substance has a low potential for abuse relative to the drugs or other substances in Schedule III.

	(B)	The drug or other substance has a currently accepted medical use in treatment in the United States.
	(C)	Abuse of the drug or other substance may lead to limited physical dependence or psychological dependence relative to the drugs or other substances in Schedule III.
Schedule V.	(A)	The drug or other substance has a low potential for abuse relative to the drugs or other substances in Schedule IV.
	(B)	The drug or other substance has a currently accepted medical use in treatment in the United States.
	(C)	Abuse of the drug or other substance may lead to limited physical dependence or psychological dependence relative to the drugs or other substances in Schedule IV.

The statute then delineates the chemical name for each substance classified on the list. The penalties are found in 21 U.S.C. § 841 through 863. For example, the penalty for simple possession of some controlled substance ranges from up to a year in prison for the first offense to a minimum of five years in prison for the possession of more than five grams of cocaine. For those engaged in trafficking in drugs, the penalties include life in prison. If the quantities are very high, or if the defendant attempted to kill another to evade detection or arrest, the law authorizes the imposition of the penalty of death.[13] The average sentence in 2006 for drug trafficking was fifty-seven months in prison.[14]

Crack versus Powder Cocaine

Crack cocaine is the slang term for powder cocaine that has been cooked into a crystalline form that can be smoked. Crack cocaine is generally cheaper than powder cocaine. When crack came on the scene in the 1980s, its low price made it a drug of choice for poorer drug abusers. To combat what was perceived to be a "crack epidemic," Congress passed the Anti-Drug Abuse Act of 1986. The Act created a "two-tiered scheme of five- and ten-year mandatory minimum sentences for drug manufacturing and distribution offenses."[15] The law made possession of crack cocaine the only possession crime that carried a mandatory minimum five-year sentence even if the defendant had no prior criminal history.

Most drug sentences are based on the weight of the drug found in the defendant's possession at arrest. But the 1986 Act required judges to use a 100:1 ratio for crack to powder cocaine when calculating jail time. As a result, those caught with crack cocaine received longer sentences than those arrested with powder cocaine.

Critics of the scheme pointed out that penalizing crack possession more harshly than powder cocaine possession disproportionately punished poor and African-American defendants. Further, they noted that street-level users received harsher sentences than the drug lords who brought the drug into the country. This is because generally the drug enters the country as powder and is cooked into crack at the street level and then sold. In effect, the critics claimed, the law did little to stop large-scale drug trafficking, but decimated poor and African-American communities. The lengthy crack sentences also gave fodder to those who claim that law enforcement tends to prosecute drug charges against African-Americans more zealously. In fact, the U.S. Sentencing Commission stated in its 2006 report that African-Americans constituted 82 percent of those sentenced for crack cocaine violations as opposed to 8.8 percent whites. By contrast, the Substance Abuse and Mental Health Services Administration claims that 65 percent of crack users are white.[16]

Faced with this inequity, and emerging science showing that crack and powder cocaine "have the same physiological and psychotropic effects,"[17] the U.S. Sentencing Commission dropped the 100:1 ratio in 2007. Previously, the Supreme Court ruled that sentencing guidelines other than mandatory minimum sentences were only advisory.[18] Finally, a case dealing squarely with the crack versus powder cocaine issue came before the Court in 2007. Derrick Kimbrough was caught with both crack and powder cocaine that he planned to distribute. He pled guilty to conspiracy to distribute crack and powder cocaine, possession with intent to distribute more than fifty grams of crack, possession of powder cocaine with intent to distribute, and possession of a firearm in furtherance of drug trafficking. The minimum sentence would have given Kimbrough fifteen years to life in jail. But the sentencing guidelines called for a range of 19–22.5 years. However, had he only possessed powder cocaine, the sentencing guidelines would have only called for just over eight years to just under ten. The judge ruled that the fifteen-year minimum was sufficient. The government appealed seeking the higher sentence. The Supreme Court ruled that the judge did not abuse his discretion in sentencing Kimbrough to fifteen years.[19]

In 2010, Congress passed the Fair Sentencing Act of 2010 that eliminated most sentencing differences between crack and powder crack cocaine.

Gambling

Gambling and games of chance have been with us for most of history. Gambling is generally defined as the act of taking a monetary risk on the chance of receiving a monetary gain. Gambling therefore involves chance, rather than skill.[20] It is the taking of a chance as opposed to the use of skill that distinguishes gambling from a game of skill or a contest. For example, suppose you wanted to sell your house in a hurry. If you held a raffle, and charged every entrant $200, could you award the house to the lucky holder of the winning ticket? Probably not, because a game of chance, such as your raffle, would be gambling under most state laws (and as you will see later, might be a federal crime if you used the Internet to sell your raffle tickets).

But what if you held a contest with a $200 entry fee and awarded the house to the person who wrote the best essay? Would that qualify as a skill contest rather than a game of chance? The answer is unclear. At best the contest would have to comply with state sweepstake and contest laws. But the owners would still risk having their raffle declared an illegal lottery or numbers game.

Today, most states[21] run their own gambling operations in the form of lotteries or otherwise permit limited legal gambling while churches run bingo games and Monte Carlo nights regularly to raise funds. Some states have funded entire new social programs with lottery proceeds. For example, Pennsylvania's lottery provided nearly $1.3 billion in funding to programs that benefit older citizens in 2009, after taking in almost $3.08 billion in ticket sales. The programs funded include prescription drug discounts, transportation, and property tax breaks for senior citizens that might otherwise be funded with tax dollars. Gamblers buying tickets won back $1.8 billion in prizes.[22]

Gambling
The act of taking a monetary risk on the chance of receiving a monetary gain.

Gambling also takes place at racetracks, on Indian reservations that have established casinos, and in states that have legalized casinos and riverboat gambling. But legal gambling isn't the only form of gambling taking place. Many billions of dollars are spent every year on illegal games of chance, including Internet gambling.

What is the impact of gambling? In 1996, Congress wanted answers to that question and authorized the creation of the National Gambling Impact Study Commission. The commission released its study in June 1999, and made a number of findings and recommendations. These included:

- A recommendation that there be a moratorium on the expansion of gambling until a more complete assessment of the social harm that may result from expansion can be studied.
- A recommendation that federal law be considered to regulate the new area of Internet gambling, but that states, local authorities, and tribal leaders can best determine what restrictions should be placed on gambling within their jurisdictions.

In response, Congress tacked an Internet gambling ban on the SAFE Port Act of 2006. The ban allows courts and the Treasury department to block credit card usage for online gambling. Some estimates show the law has had little effect. One estimate of Internet gambling wagers puts the figure at $106 billion per year.[23]

The law's ineffectiveness, along with the search for more government revenues, has led some in Congress to advocate legalizing and taxing Internet gambling.[24] How legal Internet gambling would impact proposed and existing state-run casinos is unclear.

States that have legalized some forms of gambling nonetheless regulate it carefully. Bingo and other small games of chance are generally allowed. Tempting as it might be to assume that legal, state-run, or state-supervised gambling would end criminal involvement in gambling, that does not appear to be the case. A significant amount of illegal gambling takes place as sports gambling, or gambling on the outcome of sporting events. Illegal gambling also takes the form of "numbers" games.[25] These illegal operations work much like the legal state-sponsored ones, except that the winnings aren't taxed, nor are the profits taxed or returned to the community in the form of social program funding or additions to the general funds. In areas where legal casinos and legal lotteries exist, there is also a thriving illegal business in loan sharking, as gamblers seek ready access to cash.

Illegal gambling operations can be prosecuted under federal law if they meet the following criteria:

- The gambling operation violates state law where it is operated.
- It involves five or more persons who conduct, finance, manage, supervise, direct, or own all or part of the business.
- It has been or remains in substantially continuous operation for a period in excess of thirty days or has a gross revenue of $2,000 in any single day.[26]

The types of gambling operations covered by the law include lotteries, slot machines, pool selling, bookmaking, roulette wheels, and dice tables. The law also explicitly excludes bingo games and other similar gambling devices operated by organizations recognized as a tax-exempt organization by the Internal Revenue Service.

Another section of the U.S. Code has recently been used to prosecute those involved in Internet gambling. 18 U.S.C. § 1084 provides that:

> Whoever being engaged in the business of betting or wagering knowingly uses a wire communication facility for the transmission in interstate or foreign commerce of bets or wagers or information assisting in the placing of bets or wagers on any sporting event or contest, or for the transmission of a wire communication which entitles the recipient to receive money or credit as a result of bets or wagers, or for information assisting in the placing of bets or wagers, shall be fined under this title or imprisoned not more than two years, or both.

Other federal laws that attempt to control illegal interstate gambling include 18 U.S.C. § 1952, which prohibits interstate or foreign travel to further gambling or other illegitimate business dealings, and 18 U.S.C. § 1953, which outlaws the interstate transportation of gambling paraphernalia.

Offenses Against the Family

Pornography Including Child Porn Distribution and Possession

For decades, pornography sat on the front lines of the culture wars. Government's attempts to regulate pornography often led to litigation filed by free speech advocates concerned that government restrictions were censoring art and strangling free expression. The problem lay in the definition of pornography. At one time, Justice Byron White is said to have remarked that he "knew it when he saw it." But that standard was hardly helpful to lower courts when they ruled on specific cases.

The matter was largely settled when the Supreme Court handed down its ruling in *Miller v. California*. The Court gave three criteria to identify pornography that have come to be known as the *Miller* test:

1. Whether the average person, applying "contemporary community standards" would find that the work, taken as a whole, appeals to prurient interest.
2. Whether the work displays or describes, in a patently offensive way, sexual contact specifically defined by a state statute.
3. Whether the work, again taken as a whole, lacks serious literary, artistic, political, or scientific value.[27]

The *Miller* test raises many questions, but clarifies some aspects of the debate. First, obscenity can only involve sexual activity. Violence absent sexual content cannot be legally obscene. The law does not define "community" or "community standards."

Child Porn Production

At the time *Miller* was decided (1973), child pornography was relatively virtually legislated out of existence. But the birth of the Internet allowed pornographic images to move around the world freely. With the burgeoning online market for pornography, many suppliers got into the act. Most operate overseas where American laws cannot touch them.

The *Miller* test is irrelevant to child pornography. All states have enacted laws against producing, possessing, or distributing child pornography. Child pornography has been defined in the *United States v. Dost* where the Supreme Court said child pornography is a "visual depiction . . . of explicit sexual conduct" through "lascivious exhibition of the genitals or pubic area" where the:

- focal point of the visual depiction is on the child's genitalia or pubic area;
- setting of the visual depiction is sexually suggestive (i.e., in a place or pose generally associated with sexual activity);
- child is depicted in an unnatural pose, or in inappropriate attire, considering the age of the child;
- child is partially clothed or nude;
- visual depiction suggests sexual coyness or a willingness to engage in sexual activity; or
- visual depiction is intended or designed to elicit a sexual response in the viewer.[28]

The difference between adult and child pornography goes to the issue of consent. Children simply lack the legal capacity to consent to sexual acts, simulated sexual acts, or sexual exposure. Courts have consistently recognized the state's interest in protecting children by aggressively attacking both the supply and demand for child pornography.

While the law's intent is clear, the definition of child pornography isn't always. In 1998, anti-abortion activist Randall Terry launched a campaign against two books he described as child pornography—Jock Stuges' *Radiant Identities* and David Hamilton's *The Age of Innocence*. Rather than attack the artists directly, Terry went after bookselling giant Barnes & Noble. At one point he discussed going into stores and ripping up the books. The publicity resulted in two lawsuits, one in Tennessee and one in Alabama. The Tennessee case was settled when Barnes & Noble stores in that state agreed to keep the books on higher shelves with opaque covers so that children would not see them. The Alabama case was eventually dismissed on a technicality.[29]

When veteran National Public Radio reporter Lawrence Matthews was arrested for child pornography possession, he claimed he had downloaded the images as part of an investigative series on child pornographers. He moved to have the charges dismissed on First Amendment grounds. Both the trial court and appeals court dismissed his argument saying that no First Amendment protection exists for child pornography "when the production and dissemination of the child pornography picture caused overwhelming harm to the children involved."[30]

Sexting
The sending of nude pictures over cell phones.

Most recently the practice of **sexting,** where teens transmit nude pictures of themselves to friends via their cell phones, has challenged conventional definitions of child pornography. Can a minor who takes pictures of herself be said to be an unwilling participant? If the recipient never asked for the picture, is he guilty of child pornography trafficking?

The definitions of child pornography are critical in these cases because the consequences are quite severe. First, any conviction of creating or trafficking in child pornography places the defendant on his state's sex offender register, often for the rest of his life. Second, a provision of the Adam Walsh Child Protection and Safety Act of 2006 allows the U.S. Attorney General to involuntarily commit sex offenders after they have served their full sentence if the government can prove by "**clear and convincing evidence,**" a lower standard than "beyond a reasonable doubt," that the individual (1) had previously "engaged or attempted to engage in sexually violent conduct or child molestation," (2) currently suffers from a mental illness, abnormality or disorder, and (3) as a result of that mental illness, abnormality, or disorder is "sexually dangerous to others," in that "he would have serious difficulty refraining from sexually violent conduct or child molestation if released."[31] The case challenging this law's constitutionality was brought by five North Carolina inmates, three of whom had been convicted only of possessing child pornography. In several cases, the attorney general certified them as sexually dangerous just days before the end of their sentences. The Supreme Court ruled the law constitutional by a 7–2 vote.

Clear and convincing evidence
A standard of proof normally used in civil cases higher than "preponderance of the evidence," but lower than "beyond a reasonable doubt."

Domestic Violence

Domestic violence in this country is overwhelmingly directed at women by men. According to the Department of Justice, 85 percent of all domestic violence incidents involve men directing violence at women.[32] The death toll is high. In 2008, more than 55 percent of all female murder victims in the United States were killed by their husbands or boyfriends.[33] For the twenty-year period from 1976 to 1996, the total toll of women murdered by their husbands or boyfriends stood at over 31,000 women.[34]

Domestic violence
A person's actions designed to hurt or dominate a domestic partner.

Most states do not make domestic violence a specific crime. Rather, battery, assault, aggravated assault, harassment, stalking, and other crimes involving physical or mental injury to a victim when perpetrated by the victim's partner are characterized as domestic violence. The best way to look at domestic violence may be to view it as a syndrome, consisting of a series of criminal acts perpetrated against a spouse or paramour rather than as a specific crime.

Until recently, enforcement of criminal laws when the victim was the perpetrator's partner was spotty. Many in law enforcement viewed cases of domestic violence as nuisance cases, and sometimes even refused to respond to calls or arrest the perpetrator. In cases where law enforcement did respond, often the matter was dropped when the victim refused to press charges or to cooperate with police.

It has only been in the last few decades that the psychological forces at play in domestic violence have begun to be understood. A victim with no or few economic resources, no place to go, and fear of the perpetrator often saw no way out but to reconcile and drop the charges. Psychologists have an explanation for abused spouses' behavior in these cases. Dubbed the "**Battered Wife Syndrome,**" the theory holds that wives both fear retribution and hope their spouses or partners will not become violent again. Some, in an attempt to excuse the abuser's behavior, will claim they are actually at fault and the abuser's reaction was a reasonable response to her bad behavior. Women who suffer from Battered Wife Syndrome have what psychiatrists call "learned helplessness" where all attempts to stand up for their rights bring violence or alienation. As a result they are unlikely to report abuse, or will often recant their charges if they do.

Battered Wife Syndrome
The condition where abused spouses refuse to leave abusive partners in the belief either that they deserve the abuse or that it will stop eventually.

One key tool law enforcement officers have to combat domestic violence is the **Protection From Abuse Order** commonly called a PFA. Once filed, the alleged abuser may not come near the complaining spouse. Violation of the PFA is grounds for immediate arrest. Domestic abuse victims who change their mind will

Protection from abuse order
An order requiring a spouse accused of abuse to not contact the person filing the complaint.

often move to have the PFA revoked or invite the abusive spouse back without notifying law enforcement officials or the court. Usually, without psychological intervention, the violence recurs.

With the advent of more shelters for victims and their families, the availability of educational and job opportunities, and the increasing recognition that acts of violence, no matter who the victim is, should be punished, more victims are cooperating with law enforcement. As a result, today there are far more successful prosecutions than in decades past.

HISTORICAL HIGHLIGHT

Victims of Domestic Violence Win Right to New Identity

One of the most pressing concerns victims of domestic violence may have when leaving their abusers is that the abuser will simply follow them. Moving to another address, finding a new job, and starting a new life are difficult for anyone, especially someone fleeing physical danger. Disappearing isn't easy, especially in a time when access to public and private databases has become relatively easy and inexpensive.

Consider how easy it would be to track a victim's whereabouts with just one piece of information—the victim's Social Security number. If the victim was married to her abuser, he certainly had access to her Social Security number since it appears on their joint tax return. Social Security numbers, because they are unique to each holder, are commonly used on credit reports, and on medical, insurance, and school records.

Today, anyone who can provide basic information such as a Social Security number and a credit card account number can get a credit report online in minutes. That credit report contains current addresses, phone numbers, and name of employer. Although it is a violation of federal law to access credit information for someone else without that person's permission, that's unlikely to stop an abuser who is intent on locating the victim.

To help domestic abuse victims establish new identities and avoid being tracked, the Social Security Administration now will issue new Social Security numbers to victims of domestic abuse and harassment. The policy went into effect in 1998, and allows victims to start new lives in relative anonymity. The Social Security Administration will cross-reference the numbers on earnings records to assure that victims later receive the retirement or disability payments to which they are entitled.

Federal Efforts to Combat Domestic Violence

Recent years have seen an increase in federal involvement in domestic violence issues. Because it saw domestic violence as a problem affecting not just families and communities, but the economy as a whole, Congress passed the Violence Against Women Act (**VAWA**) in 1994, and declared "all persons within the United States shall have the right to be free from crimes of violence motivated by gender."[35]

Violence Against Women Act
The primary attempt by the federal government to address domestic violence.

VAWA was enacted under the authority of the Commerce Clause of the U.S. Constitution, and sought to end the cycle of violence and draw more women into the workplace and economy by strengthening state efforts to control domestic violence and by enacting federal crimes related to domestic violence.

One provision that received widespread attention was Section 13981(c), which declared that:

A person (including a person who acts under color of any statute, ordinance, regulation, custom, or usage of any State) who commits a crime of violence motivated by gender and thus deprives another of the right declared in subsection (b) of this section [to be free of crimes of violence motivated by gender] shall be liable to the party injured, in an action for the recovery of compensatory and punitive damages, injunctive and declaratory relief, and such other relief as a court may deem appropriate.

Essentially, VAWA gave victims of domestic or sexual violence a federal private right of action against the assailant for damages. The first test of the statute came when a student at Virginia Tech claimed she had been forcibly raped by two members of the varsity football team. She was unsatisfied with the administrative punishments meted out by the university, and sued the university and the students in federal court for damages, as provided for in VAWA. The defendants raised the Constitution as a bar to the lawsuit, claiming that Congress exceeded its authority under the Commerce Clause when it enacted the law. The U.S. Supreme Court heard the case, *United States v. Morrison*, and concluded Congress didn't have the authority to " . . . regulate non-economic, violent criminal conduct based solely on that conduct's aggregate effect on interstate commerce."[36]

The Supreme Court decision has wider implications for congressional efforts to enact civil and criminal penalties for crimes that occur within state boundaries, and most likely will mean Congress will not set up a parallel federal criminal and tort law system.

In response to the *Morrison* decision, VAWA was amended in 2000. Rather than relying on the economic impact domestic and sexual violence had on women, Congress focused on providing criminal penalties that punish behavior that crosses state lines, a traditional authority used to enact federal criminal laws. The major criminal provisions that existed in the original VAWA and were added in VAWA II are:

- *18 U.S.C. § 2261 (a): Interstate Domestic Violence:* Makes it a federal crime for anyone to cross a state line with the intent to injure, harass, or intimidate an intimate partner if, in the course of or as a result of such travel, the perpetrator intentionally commits a violent crime that causes bodily harm to his or her partner.

- *18 U.S.C. § 2261 (a) (2): Coercing Across State Lines:* Makes it a federal crime to cause an intimate partner to cross a state line by force, coercion, duress, or fraud and, in the course or as a result of that conduct, intentionally committing a crime of violence and thereby causes bodily injury to the intimate partner.

- *18 U.S.C. § 2262 (a) (1) and (2): Interstate Violation of a Protective Order:* Makes it a federal crime for anyone to cross a state line or force an intimate partner to cross a state line with the intent to engage in conduct that violates a state protection from abuse order already in place.

- *18 U.S.C. § 2261A: Interstate Stalking:* Makes it a federal crime to cross a state line intending to injure or harass another person and then placing that person in reasonable fear of death or serious bodily injury or reasonable fear of death or serious bodily injury to his or her immediate family.

- *18 U.S.C. § 922 (g) (1), (8), and (9): Possession of Firearm:* Makes it a federal crime for anyone who is subject to a state protection from abuse order, or has been convicted of a misdemeanor crime of domestic violence, or who has been convicted of a crime punishable by a year or more in prison to possess, transport, or receive a firearm or ammunition that has been in interstate or foreign commerce.

Child Molestation

Child molestation or sexual abuse
The engaging of a child in sexual activities that the child cannot comprehend, for which the child is developmentally unprepared and cannot give informed consent, and/or that violate the social and legal taboos of society.

Child molestation or child sexual abuse is broadly defined as "the engaging of a child in sexual activities that the child cannot comprehend, for which the child is developmentally unprepared and cannot give informed consent, and/or that violate the social and legal taboos of society. The sexual activity may include all forms of oral genital, genital, or anal contact by or to the child, or non-touching abuses, such as exhibitionism, voyeurism, or using the child in the production of pornography. . . . "[37]

HISTORICAL HIGHLIGHT

Child's Abduction and Murder Gives Birth to America's Most Wanted Television Program

On July 27, 1981, six-year-old Adam Walsh was abducted and murdered. His head was found floating in a Florida river, but his body was never found. During the frantic search for Adam, his father, John Walsh, discovered there was little coordination between police departments when a child is reported missing, and no centralized agency to coordinate the search. As the result of his lobbying, Congress passed the Missing Children Act of 1982 and the Missing Children's Assistance Act of 1984. Those laws led to the creation of the *National Center for Missing and Exploited Children*. The center maintains a toll-free line to report missing children or the sighting of one. John Walsh also went on to host the television show *America's Most Wanted*, which introduces the nation to unsolved crimes and serves as a clearinghouse for tips. Leads garnered through the program have resulted in the capture of over 1,606 suspects as of May 2010.

Although most child sexual abuse cases are prosecuted on the state level, there are several federal statutes that may impact a particular case and lead to a federal rather than state prosecution. For example, it is a federal offense to cross state lines with the intent to engage in a sexual act with a child under twelve or to transport a child across state lines in order to engage in criminal sexual activity with that child.[38]

HISTORICAL HIGHLIGHT

AMBER Alert System Helps Recover Abducted Children

The first few hours following a child's abduction are crucial for the safe return of the child. The more time that passes, the less likely the child will return home safely. According to the Department of Justice, 74 percent of children who are kidnapped and later found murdered are killed within three hours of being abducted.[39] The AMBER (America's Missing Broadcast Emergency Response) Alert system was created to shorten response time in child abductions.

According to the National AMBER Alert website, http://www.amberalert.gov, as of January 2010, the AMBER Alert system has helped rescue more than 495 children nationwide. The AMBER Alert system began in 1996 in Texas and is named for Amber Hagerman, a young child who was abducted while riding her bike and brutally murdered. Since then, AMBER Alert has evolved into a program that includes news flashes and broadcasting information along electronic signs on the nation's highways. In 2002, the system went national, with many states coordinating their systems. In addition, AMBER Alerts are now available online and via pagers, cell phones, and other wireless devices.

Child Abuse and Neglect

The King's Chancellor is the general guardian of all infants, idiots, and lunatics.

Blackstone, *Commentaries on the Laws of England*

When children are concerned, government plays an important role. Since Elizabethan days, government (whether king or state or federal jurisdiction) has served in the role of **parens patriae.** That role has required government to protect the interests of those who cannot protect themselves. As early as 1890, the

U.S. Supreme Court held that the *parens patriae* theory was inherent in the power of the state to regulate the treatment of children.[40] In addition, states have rights under their general police powers to regulate the "treatment of children within their jurisdictions."

On the other end of the spectrum are parents' rights to regulate family life in accordance with their personal, religious, and ethical belief systems. These constitutionally derived rights sometimes conflict with the government's *parens patriae* and police powers. For example, the state may intervene when a religious belief may harm children. Parents cannot in most cases deny life-saving treatment to their children on the basis of religious belief in the power of prayer to heal without risking criminal child endangerment charges. Likewise, harsh punishments meted out on the religious theory that sparing the rod spoils the child may result in criminal charges of assault. Should death result, the parent may be charged with manslaughter or murder.

The border between parental rights and the state's *parens patriae* role is not always clear. Some parents have been charged with child endangerment when they tattooed their underage children. In one California case, a father administered a gang tattoo to his seven-year-old son. He was convicted of child endangerment. At his trial, he argued the tattoo is no different than piercing or circumcision.[41] Of course, those are seldom performed at home. A Georgia couple were arrested for tattooing small crosses on their children. Georgia law forbids all tattooing by unlicensed artists and all tattooing of anyone under eighteen.[42]

Corporal Punishment and Child Abuse

Corporal punishment is another area where criminal law and parental authority conflict. Were an adult to slap another adult across the face, there would be no doubt that the act could be prosecuted as an assault. But if the same adult slaps his child, that may be seen as appropriate punishment in some jurisdictions, but as child abuse in another. Most state criminal assault statutes provide a defense for acts of reasonable corporal punishment. For example, Pennsylvania provides that the use of force on another person is justifiable if:

1. The actor is the parent or guardian or other person similarly responsible for the general care and supervision of a minor or a person acting at the request of such parent, guardian, or other responsible person and:
2. The force is used for the purpose of safeguarding or promoting the welfare of the minor, including the prevention or punishment of his misconduct; and
3. The force used is not designed to cause or known to create a substantial risk of causing death, serious bodily injury, disfigurement, extreme pain or mental distress or gross degradation.[43]

Slapping a child on the rear as you stop him from running into the street is probably allowable under this statute, while slapping the child until he bruises probably is not. But the reality is that with corporal punishment as a defense, few children on whom the rod is not spared will find their parents prosecuted. The defense allows for a considerable amount of leeway for parents.

Generally, if the parent or guardian's conduct goes beyond the corporal punishment defense, he or she can be charged with assault. Of course, a stranger committing the same act as a parent or guardian may be privileged to commit

cannot use the defense. Many states apply ordinary criminal prohibitions against physical harm done to children and provide for a greater sentence when the victim is a child.

Other Defenses

Because child abuse and neglect laws must balance the state's interest in protecting children and parents' rights to raise their offspring as they see fit, child abuse laws are often written in a way that opens them to a varying interpretations. As a result, those charged under the statutes can sometimes successfully claim that the law is so vague as to be unconstitutional. The Supreme Court has ruled on a number of occasions that a criminal law must "define the criminal offense with sufficient definiteness that ordinary people can understand what it prohibits and in a manner that does not encourage arbitrary and discriminatory enforcement."[44] The challenge can be that the statute overall is so vague or overbroad that it has no validity in any case. Defense counsel can also allege that as applied to the conduct a particular defendant is charged with, the statute is arbitrary and vague.

Elder Abuse

Elder abuse is the physical and mental abuse of an elderly person by someone responsible for his or her care. Law enforcement officials encounter many of the same problems addressing elder abuse crimes as they do with child or spousal abuse. First of all, the crime is severely underreported because elderly victims are often afraid to complain fearing retribution by their abuser. Second, elderly victims may lack the mobility or mental acuity to contact law enforcement. And even if they did, those with mental health issues may not be credible witnesses.

Elder abuse usually occurs in one of two settings: at home or in an institution. Elderly people, whose caregiver is a family member or friend, often receive that care in their own home or the caregiver's home. If the caregiver is abusive, the elderly person becomes trapped in the home, unable to report the crime, or the victim may feel he or she has nowhere else to go and must accept the abuse.

Elder Abuse Syndrome
The condition elderly victims of abuse sometimes exhibit characterized by "learned help-lessness" and the feeling they can do nothing to stop the abuse.

Psychiatrists have labeled this syndrome as "**Elder Abuse Syndrome.**" The syndrome incorporates the learned helplessness concept of Battered Wife Syndrome and applies it to the elder abuse scenario. In both cases, the sufferer will be reluctant or unwilling to report the abuse to authorities.

Institutional elderly abuse is where paid caregivers abuse an elderly person in a nursing home or other similar institution. If the abuser is a licensed medical professional in the state, the abuse is also medical malpractice. In these cases, the abused victim could pursue civil damages from the abuser's malpractice insurance policy.

As a practical matter, insurance companies and other civil defendants opposing an elderly plaintiff may delay settling as long as possible with the cynical attitude that the victim will die before proceedings end. Although elder abuse is another example of how society must protect its weakest citizens, the good news is that elderly Americans as a group are victimized less than the population as a whole (see chart below).[45]

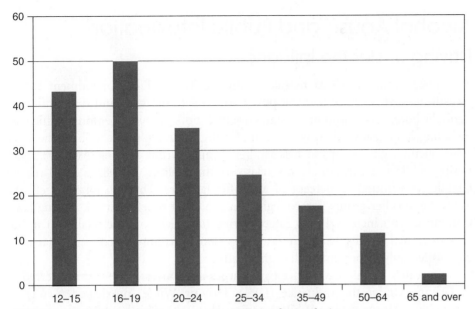

Violent Crime Victimization Rates per 1,000 of Population.
Source: U.S. Department of Justice, Bureau of Justice Statistics, 2007 Crime Victimization Study.

Runaways

At the other end of the spectrum, teens sixteen to nineteen years of age are the most victimized age group. Contributing to that victimization rate is the problem of runaway or sometimes thrown-away children. As a result, runaway children pose unique challenges for law enforcement professionals. When a runaway is reported, there are several possibilities. First, the child could have left voluntarily and is in no immediate danger, but still a source of concern for the family. Unless the child left a note or somehow communicated his or her whereabouts, the family and law enforcement personnel must take seriously the possibility of abduction at which point every second counts. Further complicating the situation are "throw-away" children who are children the caretakers in the house no longer want.

To sift through the probabilities, law enforcement personnel have developed profiles that help determine, but cannot definitively state, what has occurred when a teenager is missing. Most runaway/throwaway teens are fifteen to seventeen years of age and have had some sort of conflict with their caretakers. Generally, children younger than fifteen years of age are assumed to have been abducted.

The problem is not insignificant. One in seven children will run away at some point between ages ten and eighteen. At any given time, there are between one million and three million runaways or homeless teenagers living on American streets.

Lacking job and life skills, these teenagers are often exploited by criminals or turn to criminal activities such as selling drugs or prostitution to support themselves. The leading cause of teens running away is to escape from physical or sexual abuse at home. Runaways have higher incidents of drug use than other children their age.

Caretakers for runaway/throwaway children only contact law enforcement approximately one-third of the time. While law enforcement may not be involved when the teens disappear, they almost certainly will later in the teen's life when the teen turns to criminal activity to survive.

Alcohol Abuse and Public Intoxication

Driving under the Influence

Ever since prohibition was repealed with the Twenty-First Amendment to the Constitution, states have had the power to regulate the sales and distribution of alcoholic beverages. Additionally, states use their police power to enforce traffic laws including laws against driving while under the influence of alcohol. In the early 1980s, victim rights groups such as Mothers Against Drunk Driving (MADD) began raising public awareness of alcohol-related traffic fatalities. In 1982, alcohol-related fatalities constituted 52 percent of all traffic fatalities. Through lobbying efforts, MADD and other groups forced legislatures to enact tougher drunk driving laws. Combined with increased auto safety during this period, traffic fatalities fell, but alcohol-related deaths fell even faster. By 2008, alcohol-related traffic fatalities constituted only 37 percent of all traffic deaths.

In reality, drunk drivers face two charges upon arrest.. The first is referred to as Driving Under the Influence (DUI), Driving While Intoxicated (DWI) or Operating a Motor Vehicle While Intoxicated (OWI). This is where the arresting officer determines, based on observable behavior such as the driver weaving in and out of traffic, slurred speech, or inability to walk a straight line, that the driver is too intoxicated to operate the vehicle safely. Under this charge, the defendant can present evidence to counter the police officer's testimony.

The second charge is "illegal driving *per se*." This charge is filed when the driver's blood alcohol levels exceed the state minimum. These minimums vary from 0.08 to 0.10 blood alcohol levels. The defendant may not present any evidence to counter the blood alcohol level reading. Drivers who refuse to provide

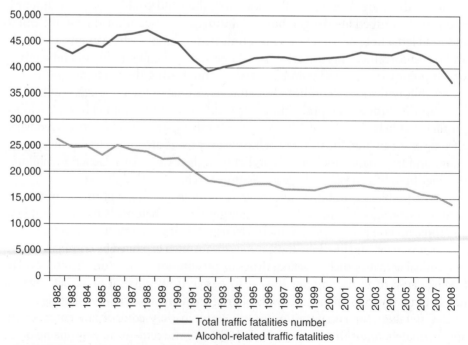

Alcohol-Related Traffic Deaths.
Source: National Highway Traffic Safety Administration.

a breath or blood sample are presumed to be guilty. In exchange for the privilege of driving, drivers give **implied consent** to provide breath or blood samples when requested by law enforcement personnel.

Most states treat first offenses relatively lightly, with a license suspension, alcohol counseling, and defensive driving classes. Repeat offenders face increased suspensions, fines, and even imprisonment. Some states use ignition interlock devices that require the driver to blow into a tube that measure alcohol content before the car will start. If the device detects any alcohol, the vehicle will not start.

Implied consent
The consent given as a condition of obtaining a driver's license to provide proof of sobriety when legitimately requested by a law enforcement officer.

Liquor Laws

As stated above, states have the power to regulate alcohol consumption. States set the minimum age that its citizens may purchase or consume alcoholic beverages. Many states lowered their drinking age to eighteen in the 1970s after the voting age was lowered to eighteen. But the number of alcohol-related accidents and fatalities involving younger drivers was alarming. Congress made raising the drinking age to twenty-one a condition of receiving federal highway funds. The states quickly came into compliance. Bars and liquor stores risk losing their liquor licenses if they fail to check identification and sell alcohol to underage individuals.

Most municipalities have laws against public drunkenness. Public drunkenness is usually a misdemeanor resulting in a small fine.

Disorderly Conduct

Disorderly conduct, also called disturbing the peace, is a crime against public order. Disorderly conduct ordinances are intentionally broad and vague to allow law enforcement officer discretion in enforcing them. As a result, many ordinances have been challenged as unconstitutional violations of First Amendment rights of free speech.

Of course, the First Amendment is not absolute. Words that might incite a riot are not protected, for example. The old saying about "yelling 'fire' in a crowded theater" (assuming there is no fire) illustrates the limits of free speech. The Supreme Court has also carved out an exception for "**fighting words**" defined as "words that inflict injury, tend to incite an immediate breach of the peace, or by their nature will cause a violent reaction by a person who hears them."[46]

Fighting words
Words that inflict injury, tend to incite an immediate breach of the peace, or by their nature will cause a violent reaction by a person who hears them.

Disorderly conduct charges are flexible tools allowing law enforcement officials to keep the peace in a variety of unpredictable situations. This very flexibility sometimes leaves police open to charges of selective enforcement or prosecution. For example, in the Jim Crow South, African-Americans used this argument when they entered segregated facilities to show that the laws, that often never mentioned race, were only enforced against African-Americans.[47]

Public Indecency or Lewdness

All states have laws that criminalize behavior that constitutes **public indecency** or lewdness. Public indecency is generally defined as lewd or lascivious conduct that is open to public view.[48] Typical actions punished under these types of statutes include nude dancing, performing sex acts in a public place (where there is no reasonable expectation of privacy), and exposing one's genitals in a public place.

Public indecency
Lewd or lascivious conduct that is open to public view.

Public indecency charges typically don't result in long sentences or large fines and tend to be viewed as catchall provisions of penal codes unless the defendant has been arrested on several occasions for the same conduct, or appears to be threatening or dangerous. For example, a male suspect who makes it a habit to expose his genitalia to young children may have a greater likelihood of prosecution and punishment than a first-time offender caught masturbating in a dirty movie theater or engaging in sexual behavior in a parked car.

Perhaps the public lewdness case that has garnered the most publicity in recent history is that of children's program creator Pee Wee Herman, or Paul Reubens. In 1991, he was caught in an adult theater while allegedly exposing his genitals and masturbating. He later pleaded no contest to a charge of indecent exposure and was sentenced to perform seventy-five hours of community service and to pay a fine.[49] The episode lost him his television show and made him a social outcast for nearly a decade.

Vagrancy

Vagrancy in medieval England was the act of being a vagabond, or a homeless person with no job or means of support. In nineteenth-century America, antivagrancy statutes were broadly drawn to allow the police to disperse any person they found objectionable. Usually, this meant moving panhandlers and the homeless from public areas. Because the laws often targeted the offender's personal status and not a behavior, they faced legal challenges. States and cities narrowed their laws to target specific behaviors such as "wandering." This practice ended in 1972 when the Supreme Court ruled that behaviors such as walking around or frequenting liquor stores were "too precarious for a rule of law" and violated both the Constitution's Due Process and Cruel and Unusual Punishment Clauses.[50]

Modern vagrancy ordinances often include a *mens rea* element forcing the state to prove the defendant was loitering with the intent of panhandling, gambling, or some other clearly defined activity.

Fornication, Adultery, and Polygamy/Polyandry

Both **fornication** and **adultery** were originally crimes in all states. Fornication is defined as voluntary sexual intercourse between two unmarried persons.[51] Adultery is sexual intercourse by a married person with someone not his or her spouse.[52]

Today, statutes criminalizing adultery and fornication are generally limited to situations where the acts take place between people who otherwise cannot marry and in cases where there is independent verification of the offense. For example, in Mississippi it is a crime punishable by up to ten years in prison to commit even one act of adultery or fornication with someone you could not marry because he or she was too close of a blood relative.[53] North Carolina outlaws fornication and adultery but does not allow the testimony of either of the participants against the other.[54] Those in the military can still face a court-martial for committing adultery under a section of the Uniform Code of Military Justice that prohibits conduct "prejudicial to good order and discipline."

Polygamy, or having several wives, and polyandry, or having several husbands, are practices that exist today in some parts of the world, but that have

---

Vagrancy
Under modern laws, loitering with the intent of committing an illegal act.

Fornication
Voluntary sexual intercourse between two unmarried persons.

Adultery
Sexual intercourse by a married person with someone not his or her spouse.

been outlawed in all states. The term **bigamy** is used to describe the criminal act of marrying when one already has a spouse, and applies to both polygamists and polyandrists. In the United States, it was officially practiced by Mormons until the Church of Jesus Christ of Latter-Day Saints prohibited it in 1890.[55] Outlawing polygamy was made a condition of joining the United States when western territories that had accepted the practice sought entry, as was the case for Utah's admission to the Union in 1896.

Some states even criminalize the teaching of bigamy. For example, in Mississippi, you may be fined up to $500 and imprisoned up to six months if you:

> teach another the doctrines, principles, or tenets, or any of them, of polygamy; or shall endeavor so to do; or shall induce or persuade another by words or acts, or otherwise, to embrace or adopt polygamy, or to emigrate to any other state, territory, district, or country for the purpose of embracing, adopting, or practicing polygamy . . . .[56]

Anyone charged under this act could likely defend by arguing that this statute is contrary to the First Amendment prohibition against curtailing free speech and religious freedom of thought, even though practicing bigamy may be punished. The Supreme Court early on upheld the right of a state to outlaw polygamy and bigamy even if they were practiced as part of a sincerely held religious belief.[57]

Abortion

Perhaps no issue divides America as does the legalization of **abortion.** Abortion is the termination of pregnancy by something other than birth (i.e., when something goes spontaneously wrong or by intervention). During most of the late nineteenth and early- to mid-twentieth century, states held that those who performed abortions were guilty of murder. These rigid rules have not historically been in place, however. Greek and Roman women practiced abortion without fear of retribution or punishment. However, the Hippocratic Oath, which has long been the source of medical ethics rules, does warn physicians not to induce abortions.

Nonetheless, abortion was not considered a violation of the Common Law in England. At Common Law, an abortion performed before "quickening" was not an indictable offense.[58] It wasn't until the mid-1800s that abortion became a crime, and then only after "quickening." Quickening was generally believed to occur around the fifteenth to eighteenth week of pregnancy, and was the time a woman first felt her child move. But by the 1950s virtually every state had enacted abortion laws outlawing all abortions that weren't performed to save the life of the mother. It is against this backdrop that the controversial Supreme Court abortion decisions were made.

Until the 1973 Supreme Court decision in *Roe v. Wade*,[59] every state but four had on its books laws that criminalized abortion. In *Roe*, the plaintiff was a pregnant woman who sought an abortion, but could not get one in her home state of Texas because it was a criminal offense to procure an abortion if the mother's life was not in danger. She sued, arguing that the state law that would let her face possible criminal sanctions were she to procure an abortion in Texas violated her constitutional right to privacy.

The Supreme Court concluded that a woman's right to privacy and personal liberty encompassed allowing her to make the determination of whether she

Bigamy
The criminal act of marrying when one already has a spouse.

Laws are made for the government of actions, and while they cannot interfere with mere religious belief and opinions, they may with practices.

Chief Justice Waite in *Reynolds v. United States*, 98 U.S. 145 (1878)

Abortion
The termination of pregnancy by something other than birth.

I will neither give a deadly drug to anybody if asked for it, nor will I make a suggestion to this effect. Similarly, I will not give to a woman an abortive remedy.

Hippocratic Oath

desires children. That right, however, was balanced against the state's right to protect her life and that of the fetus she carries by regulating the conditions under which she can seek an abortion. The Court came up with a three-prong decision, summarized as follows:

1. During the first trimester of pregnancy, the decision to have an abortion rests with the woman and her physician.
2. During the second trimester, the state can regulate the procedure in ways consistent with protecting maternal health.
3. During the final trimester, the state may prohibit abortions except to save the life of the mother.

The Court's decision in *Roe* has been one of the most controversial. In the nearly three decades since the initial decision, the Court has heard related cases many times and settled some questions left open. The Court has on several occasions refused to overrule itself. Since then, the Court has decided that a state cannot require notification to a husband as a condition for an abortion, but allowed to stand laws that require a short waiting period, parental notification with an alternative judicial petition in some cases, preabortion counseling and informed consent, and strict recordkeeping requirements.[60] It also removed the strict trimester approach, and instead stated that abortion laws can't "unduly burden" a woman's right to choose. The Supreme Court also struck down a Nebraska law criminalizing so-called "partial-birth" abortions.[61] In response, Congress passed the Partial-Birth Abortion Ban Act of 2003, which specifically defined partial birth abortion and provided exceptions to the ban for the mother's health. The law's constitutionality was almost immediately challenged, but the U.S. Supreme Court pointed to the law's specificity and safeguards for the mother's health when upholding the law in 2007.[62]

Consensual Sodomy

Sodomy
Sexual relations between members of the same sex, sexual conduct *per anus* or *per os* between unmarried persons of the opposite sex, and sexual intercourse with animals.

Chapter 4 discussed forcible sodomy. In this chapter we address consensual sodomy. **Sodomy** is generally defined as sexual relations between members of the same sex, sexual conduct *per anus* or *per os* between unmarried persons of the opposite sex, and sexual intercourse with animals.[63] Historically, sodomy laws played a large role in controlling homosexual behaviors. The proscription of sodomy goes back at least as far as Roman times, where it was a capital offense.[64] In England, sodomy was an offense handled by the Catholic Church until the time of the Reformation when Henry VIII transferred all ecclesiastic offenses over to the King's Court.[65] All thirteen states made sodomy a crime at the time the Bill of Rights became the law of the land.[66] Many state laws criminalizing sodomy have been challenged on the basis that they interfere with the constitutional right to privacy.

A crime not fit to be named.

William Blackstone on the subject of sodomy

The Supreme Court heard one such challenge in *Bowers v. Hardwick*.[67] In that case, Hardwick, the defendant, was charged with engaging in sodomy with another male in the privacy of his bedroom. Sodomy was against the law in Georgia. After his preliminary hearing on the charges, at which the district attorney announced he would not prosecute the case unless more evidence surfaced, Hardwick sued. He asserted that he was a practicing homosexual, and that the Georgia sodomy statute placed him in imminent danger of arrest. He argued that the Constitution granted him a right to privacy in his bedroom, and that the state had no business charging him with committing a sex act with another consenting adult. The Court, in a 5–4 vote, concluded that homosexuals did not have a constitutional right to violate state sodomy laws, and that states were free to criminalize such behavior if they saw fit to.

In the years following the *Hardwick* decision, many states repealed their sodomy laws, making any kind of sexual contact (other than prostitution) between consenting adults of any sex legal. In 2003, the Supreme Court made an abrupt about-face on the question of criminalized sodomy. In a 6–3 decision, the Court overturned its decision in *Hardwick* and concluded that community standards have changed. They cited the states that had since decriminalized sodomy and found that remaining laws were unconstitutional as a denial of due process and violation of privacy. The case is *Lawrence v. Texas*, 539 U.S. 558 (2003). The decision is viewed by many as a milestone in the Court's long journey to recognize of an inherent right to privacy.

Social Crimes Evidence Concepts

Some of the major evidentiary issues that arise with social crimes are covered in subsequent chapters. For example, in child abuse or sexual exploitation, conviction often depends on the physical evidence and testimony from the victim, which is covered in the sections on the right to confront one's accuser. In driving under the influence, blood alcohol levels are often the determinative factor and the accuracy of the tests is dependent on expert testimony and the eyewitness account of the arresting officer. In disorderly conduct, prostitution, and many other social crimes, it is that arresting officer's testimony that often serves as the only evidence against the accused.

CONCEPT **REVIEW AND REINFORCEMENT**

Prostitution is generally defined as engaging in sexual intercourse or other sexual activity for pay. Prostitutes are also frequent targets for criminal acts, including murder. Most states outlaw sex for money and make it a crime for both parties involved. It has long been a federal crime to transport someone over state lines for immoral purposes. State criminal laws outlawing prostitution generally outlaw two distinct behaviors: soliciting someone to engage in sex for money in a public place, and working in a brothel or other private setting selling sex for money. Many states, in recognition that prostitution can be a factor in the spread of sexually transmitted diseases, make selling sexual favors by those who know they are infected with the human immunodeficiency virus (HIV) a felony offense.

Drug use in the United States is a considerable problem. A **controlled substance** is defined as a drug considered dangerous under the law because of its effects, including intoxication, stupor, or addictive potential. Some controlled substances are so dangerous that they are not legally available at all.

Most criminal cases brought against drug abusers are state violations. Federal law enforcement officials handle cases involving trafficking of controlled substances across our borders and across state lines while local law enforcement handles individual drug use and local drug distribution and dealing. Agents from federal agencies work closely with state attorneys general and local police departments to coordinate the "war on drugs."

There are five schedules of controlled substances cataloged by the federal drug laws and additions are made when new drugs surface or a previously unscheduled drug is determined to belong on the list. The penalty for possession of a substance on the list depends on which schedule the substance appears and the amount in the defendant's possession. For those engaged in trafficking in drugs, the penalties include life in prison. Defendants carrying large quantities of drugs or who attempt to kill another while evading detection or arrest face the possibility of the death penalty.

The Anti-Drug Abuse Act of 1986 made possession of crack cocaine the only possession crime that carried a mandatory minimum five-year sentence even if the defendant had no prior criminal history. Also those caught with crack cocaine received longer sentences than those arrested with powder cocaine. Court decisions and pending legislation may equalize crack and powder cocaine possession penalties.

Gambling is generally defined as the act of taking a monetary risk on the chance of receiving a monetary gain. Today, most states run their own gambling operations. Congress banned Internet gambling in 2006, but large-scale Internet gambling continues. In areas where legal casinos and legal lotteries exist, there is also a thriving illegal business in loan sharking, as gamblers seek ready access to cash.Illegal gambling operations such as lotteries, slot machines, pool selling, bookmaking, roulette wheels, and dice tables can be prosecuted under federal law.

For decades, government's attempts to regulate pornography often led to litigation filed by free speech advocates concerned that government restrictions were censoring art and strangling free expression.

In *Miller v. California*, the court gave three criteria to identify pornography that have come to be known as the *Miller* test. Obscenity can only involve sexual activity.

All states have enacted laws against producing, possessing, or distributing child pornography. Children simply lack the legal capacity to consent to sexual acts, simulated sexual acts, or sexual exposure. Courts have consistently recognized the state's interest in protecting children by aggressively attacking both the supply and demand for child pornography. Sexting, where teens transmit nude pictures of themselves to friends via their cell phones, has challenged conventional definitions of child pornography.

Any conviction of creating or trafficking in child pornography places the defendant on his state's sex offender register, often for the rest of his life. Federal law allows the U.S. Attorney General to involuntarily commit sex offenders after they have served their full sentence.

Domestic violence in this country is overwhelmingly directed at women by men.

Psychologists have an explanation for abused spouses' behavior called the "Battered Wife Syndrome" where wives both fear retribution and hope their spouses or partners will not become violent again. Improvement in support services for abused spouses has led to more successful prosecutions. Abused spouses may request a protection from abuse order which requires the accused abuser to avoid contact with the accuser.

Congress passed the Violence Against Women Act (VAWA) in 1994 which gave victims of domestic or sexual violence a federal private right of action against the assailant for damages. Congress amended VAWA in 2000 focusing on providing criminal penalties that punish behavior that crosses state lines.

Child molestation is broadly defined as "the engaging of a child in sexual activities that the child cannot comprehend, for which the child is developmentally unprepared and cannot give informed consent, and/or that violate the social and legal taboos of society."

Government has served in the role of *parens patriae* to protect the interests of those who cannot protect themselves. States have rights under their general police powers to regulate the treatment of children within their jurisdictions.

Elder abuse is the physical and mental abuse of an elderly person by someone responsible for his or her care. Law enforcement officials encounter many of the same problems addressing elder abuse crimes as they do with child or spousal abuse. The crime is severely underreported.

Older abuse victims may develop a condition similar to Battered Wife Syndrome known as "Elder Abuse Syndrome."

Institutional elderly abuse is where paid caregivers abuse an elderly person in a nursing home or other similar institution. If the abuser is a licensed medical professional in the state, the abuse is also medical malpractice and the abused victim may pursue civil damages from the abuser's malpractice insurance policy.

Runaway and throwaway children pose unique challenges for law enforcement personnel. When first reported, it is difficult to determine whether the child left voluntarily or was abducted. Children fifteen to nineteen years of age are the most victimized age group. The leading cause of teens running away is the escape from physical or sexual abuse at home. Runaways have higher incidents of drug use than other children their age.

States use their police power to enforce traffic laws including laws against driving while under the influence of alcohol. Drunk drivers face charges of Driving Under the Influence (DUI), Driving While Intoxicated (DWI) or Operating a Motor Vehicle While Intoxicated (OWI) and "illegal driving *per se*."

Bars and liquor stores risk losing their liquor licenses if they fail to check identification and sell alcohol to underage individuals. Public drunkenness is usually a misdemeanor resulting in a small fine.

Disorderly conduct ordinances are intentionally broad and vague to allow law enforcement officer discretion in enforcing them. Words that might incite a riot and "fighting words" are not protected by the First Amendment.

All states have laws that criminalize behavior that constitutes public indecency defined as lewd or lascivious conduct that is open to public view. Public indecency charges typically don't result in long sentences or large fines.

Modern vagrancy ordinances often include a *mens rea* element forcing the state to prove the defendant was loitering with the intent of panhandling, gambling, or some other clearly defined activity.

Fornication is defined as voluntary sexual intercourse between two unmarried persons. Adultery is sexual intercourse by a married person with someone not his or her spouse. Today, statutes criminalizing adultery and fornication are generally limited to situations where the acts take place between people who otherwise cannot marry and in cases where there is independent verification of the offense.

Polygamy, or having several wives, and polyandry, or having several husbands, are practices that exist today in some parts of the world, but that have been outlawed in all states.

Abortion is the termination of pregnancy by something other than birth (i.e., when something goes spontaneously wrong or by intervention).

The Supreme Court concluded in *Roe v. Wade* that a woman's right to privacy and personal liberty encompassed allowing her to make the determination of whether she desires children. That right, however, was balanced against the state's right to protect her life and that of the fetus she carries.

Sodomy is generally defined as sexual relations between members of the same sex, sexual conduct *per anus* or *per os* between unmarried persons of the opposite sex, and sexual intercourse with animals. In 2003, the Supreme Court concluded that community standards have changed. They cited the states that had since decriminalized sodomy and found that remaining laws were unconstitutional as a denial of due process and violation of privacy.

KEY **TERMS**

Abortion	Elder Abuse Syndrome	Protection from abuse order
Adultery	Fighting words	Public indecency
Battered Wife Syndrome	Fornication	Sex workers
Bigamy	Gambling	Sexting
Child molestation or sexual abuse	Implied consent	Sodomy
Clear and convincing evidence	*Parens patriae*	Vagrancy
Controlled substance	Pimp	Violence Against Women Act
Domestic violence	Prostitution	

CONCEPT **REVIEW QUESTIONS**

1. Define prostitution and explain the elements required to be proven in a prosecution.
2. Define what a controlled substance is.
3. List the ways that law enforcement seeks to curtail the use and trafficking in illegal drugs.
4. Describe some of the laws that regulate gambling.
5. What laws combat child pornography production?
6. What is domestic violence and how does it affect its victims?
7. What constitutes child molestation?
8. What constitutes child abuse?
9. What constitutes elder abuse?

10. List the factors that contribute to teenage runaways.

11. List the two laws that govern drunk driving.

12. List the two key areas where the state regulates alcoholic beverages.

13. What constitutes disorderly conduct and what defenses may defendants raise to the charge?

14. What constitutes public indecency?

15. What constitutes vagrancy and what defenses may defendants raise to the charge?

16. What constitutes polygamy?

17. What are the laws regulating abortion?

18. What are the laws concerning consensual sodomy?

CASE **APPLICATIONS**

Building Your Professional Skills

1. Some religions claim that a part of their religious practice requires the use of substances that otherwise would be illegal under federal and state controlled substances laws. Such was the case of the practitioners of a South American religion—who are, in the words of Chief Justice Roberts:

"A religious sect with origins in the Amazon Rainforest receives communion by drinking a sacramental tea, brewed from plants unique to the region that contains a hallucinogen regulated under the Controlled Substances Act by the Federal Government."

When their "tea" was seized by authorities, members of the church challenged the right of the federal government to confiscate what they claimed was sacramental materials. They cited the Religious Freedom Restoration Act, a 1993 law which prohibits the federal government from "unduly burdening" the exercise of religion. Of course, the United States raised the Controlled Substances Act as legal authority.

An edited version of the decision appears below. Read it and then answer the questions that follow.

ALBERTO R. GONZALES, ATTORNEY GENERAL, ET AL., PETITIONERS V. O CENTRO ESPIRITA BENEFICENTE UNIAO DO VEGETAL ET AL.

No. 04-1084

SUPREME COURT OF THE UNITED STATES

November 1, 2005, Argued
February 21, 2006, Decided

DISPOSITION: Affirmed and remanded.

CHIEF JUSTICE ROBERTS delivered the opinion of the Court.

A religious sect with origins in the **Amazon Rainforest** receives communion by drinking a sacramental tea, brewed from plants unique to the region, that contains a hallucinogen regulated under the Controlled Substances Act by the Federal Government. The Government concedes that this practice is a sincere exercise of religion, but nonetheless sought to prohibit the small American branch of the sect from engaging in the practice, on the ground that the Controlled Substances Act bars all use of the hallucinogen. The sect sued to block enforcement against it of the ban on the sacramental tea, and moved for a preliminary injunction.

It relied on the Religious Freedom Restoration Act of 1993, which prohibits the Federal Government from substantially burdening a person's exercise of religion, unless the Government "demonstrates that application of the burden to the person" represents the least restrictive means of advancing a compelling interest. 42 U.S.C. § 2000bb-1(b). The District Court granted the preliminary injunction, and the Court of Appeals affirmed. We granted the Government's petition for certiorari. Before this Court, the Government's central submission is that it has a compelling interest in the *uniform* application of the Controlled Substances Act, such that no exception to the ban on use of the hallucinogen can be made to accommodate the sect's sincere religious practice. We conclude that the Government has not carried the burden expressly placed on it by Congress in the Religious Freedom Restoration Act, and affirm the grant of the preliminary injunction.

. . . Under RFRA [The Religious Freedom Restoration Act], the Federal Government may not, as a statutory matter, substantially burden a person's exercise of religion, " . . .

The Controlled Substances Act, 84 Stat. 1242, as amended, 21 U.S.C. § 801 *et seq.* (2000 ed. and Supp. I), regulates the importation, manufacture, distribution, and use of psychotropic substances. The Act classifies substances into five schedules based on their potential for abuse, the extent to which they have an accepted medical use, and their safety. See § 812(b) (2000 ed.). Substances listed in Schedule I of the Act are subject to the most comprehensive restrictions, including an outright ban on all importation and use, except pursuant to strictly regulated research projects. See §§ 823, 960(a)(1). The Act authorizes the imposition of a criminal sentence for simple possession of Schedule I substances, see § 844(a), and mandates the imposition of a criminal sentence for possession "with intent to manufacture, distribute, or dispense" such substances, see §§ 841(a), (b).

O Centro Espirita Beneficente Uniao do Vegetal (UDV) is a Christian Spiritist sect based in Brazil, with an American branch of approximately 130 individuals. Central to the UDV's faith is receiving communion through *hoasca* (pronounced "wass-ca"), a sacramental tea made from two plants unique to the Amazon region. One of the plants, *psychotria viridis*, contains dimethyltryptamine (DMT), a hallucinogen whose effects are enhanced by alkaloids from the other plant, *banisteriopsis caapi*. DMT, as well as "any material, compound, mixture, or preparation, which contains any quantity of [DMT]," is listed in Schedule I of the Controlled Substances Act. § 812(c), Schedule I(c).

In 1999, United States Customs inspectors intercepted a shipment to the American UDV containing three drums of *hoasca*. A subsequent investigation revealed that the UDV had received 14 prior shipments of *hoasca*. The inspectors seized the intercepted shipment and threatened the UDV with prosecution.

The UDV filed suit against the Attorney General and other federal law enforcement officials, seeking declaratory and injunctive relief. The complaint alleged, *inter alia*, that applying the Controlled Substances Act to the UDV's sacramental use of *hoasca* violates RFRA. Prior to trial, the UDV moved for a preliminary injunction, so that it could continue to practice its faith pending trial on the merits.

At a hearing on the preliminary injunction, the Government conceded that the challenged application of the Controlled Substances Act would substantially burden a sincere exercise of religion by the UDV . . . . The Government argued, however, that this burden did not violate RFRA, because applying the Controlled Substances Act in this case was the least restrictive means of advancing three compelling governmental interests: protecting the health and safety of UDV members, preventing the diversion of *hoasca* from the church to recreational users, and complying with the 1971 United Nations Convention on Psychotropic Substances, a treaty signed by the United States . . .

The District Court heard evidence from both parties on the health risks of *hoasca* and the potential for diversion from the church. The Government presented evidence to the effect that use of *hoasca*, or DMT more generally, can cause psychotic reactions, cardiac irregularities, and adverse drug interactions. The UDV countered by citing studies documenting the safety of its sacramental use of *hoasca* and presenting evidence that minimized the likelihood of the health risks raised by the Government. With respect to diversion, the Government pointed to a general rise in the illicit use of hallucinogens, and cited interest in the illegal use of DMT and *hoasca* in particular; the UDV emphasized the thinness of any market for *hoasca*, the relatively small amounts of the substance imported by the church, and the absence of any diversion problem in the past.

The District Court concluded that the evidence on health risks was "in equipoise," and similarly that the evidence on diversion was "virtually balanced." In the face of such an even showing, the court reasoned that the Government had failed to demonstrate a compelling interest justifying what it acknowledged was a substantial burden on the UDV's sincere religious exercise. The court also rejected the asserted interest in complying with the 1971 Convention on Psychotropic Substances, holding that the Convention does not apply to *hoasca*.

The court entered a preliminary injunction prohibiting the Government from enforcing the Controlled Substances Act with respect to the UDV's importation and use of *hoasca*. The injunction requires the church to import the tea pursuant to federal permits, to restrict control over the tea to persons of church authority, and to warn particularly susceptible UDV members of the dangers of *hoasca* . . . .

The Government appealed the preliminary injunction and a panel of the Court of Appeals for the Tenth Circuit affirmed . . . We granted certiorari.

. . . .

iii

The Government's second line of argument rests on the Controlled Substances Act itself. The Government contends that the Act's description of Schedule I substances as having "a high potential for abuse," "no currently accepted medical use in treatment in the United States," and "a lack of accepted safety for use . . . under medical supervision," by itself precludes any consideration of individualized exceptions such as that sought by the UDV. The Government goes on to argue that the regulatory regime established by the Act—a "closed" system that prohibits all use of controlled substances except as authorized by the Act itself . . . "cannot function with its necessary rigor and comprehensiveness if subjected to judicial exemptions." . . . Under the Government's view, there is no need to assess the particulars of the UDV's use or weigh the impact of an exemption for that specific use, because the Controlled Substances Act serves a compelling purpose and simply admits of no exceptions.

RFRA, and the strict scrutiny test it adopted, contemplate an inquiry more focused than the Government's categorical approach. RFRA requires the Government to demonstrate that the compelling interest test is satisfied through application of the challenged law "to the person"—the particular claimant whose sincere exercise of religion is being substantially burdened . . . . In *Yoder*, for example, we permitted an exemption for Amish children from a compulsory school attendance law . . . .

Under the more focused inquiry required by RFRA and the compelling interest test, the Government's mere invocation of the general characteristics of Schedule I substances, as set forth in the Controlled Substances Act, cannot carry the day. It is true, of course, that

Schedule I substances such as DMT are exceptionally dangerous . . . . Nevertheless, there is no indication that Congress, in classifying DMT, considered the harms posed by the particular use at issue here—the circumscribed, sacramental use of *hoasca* by the UDV . . . . But Congress' determination that DMT should be listed under Schedule I simply does not provide a categorical answer that relieves the Government of the obligation to shoulder its burden under RFRA.

This conclusion is reinforced by the Controlled Substances Act itself. The Act contains a provision authorizing the Attorney General to "waive the requirement for registration of certain manufacturers, distributors, or dispensers if he finds it consistent with the public health and safety." 21 U.S.C. § 822(d). The fact that the Act itself contemplates that exempting certain people from its requirements would be "consistent with the public health and safety" indicates that congressional findings with respect to Schedule I substances should not carry the determinative weight, for RFRA purposes, that the Government would ascribe to them.

And in fact an exception has been made to the Schedule I ban for religious use. For the past 35 years, there has been a regulatory exemption for use of peyote—a Schedule I substance—by the Native American Church. In 1994, Congress extended that exemption to all members of every recognized Indian Tribe. Everything the Government says about the DMT in *hoasca*—that, as a Schedule I substance, Congress has determined that it "has a high potential for abuse," "has no currently accepted medical use," and has "a lack of accepted safety for use . . . under medical supervision,"—applies in equal measure to the mescaline in peyote, yet both the Executive and Congress itself have decreed an exception from the Controlled Substances Act for Native American religious use of peyote. If such use is permitted in the face of the congressional findings in § 812(b)(1) for hundreds of thousands of Native Americans practicing their faith, it is difficult to see how those same findings alone can preclude any consideration of a similar exception for the 130 or so American members of the UDV who want to practice theirs . . . .

Before the District Court, the Government also asserted an interest in compliance with the 1971 United Nations Convention on Psychotropic Substances, Feb. 21, 1971, [1979–1980] 32 U.S. T. 543, T. I. A. S. No. 9725. The Convention, signed by the United States and implemented by the Controlled Substances Act, calls on signatories to prohibit the use of hallucinogens, including DMT. The Government argues that it has a compelling interest in meeting its international obligations by complying with the Convention.

The fact that *hoasca* is covered by the Convention, however, does not automatically mean that the Government has demonstrated a compelling interest in applying the Controlled Substances Act, which implements the Convention, to the UDV's sacramental use of the tea. . . .

We have no cause to pretend that the task assigned by Congress to the courts under RFRA is an easy one. Indeed, the very sort of difficulties highlighted by the Government here were cited by this Court in deciding that the approach later mandated by Congress under RFRA was not required as a matter of constitutional law under the Free Exercise Clause. . . . But Congress has determined that courts should strike sensible balances, pursuant to a compelling interest test that requires the Government to address the particular practice at issue. Applying that test, we conclude that the courts below did not err in determining that the Government failed to demonstrate, at the preliminary injunction stage, a compelling interest in barring the UDV's sacramental use of *hoasca*.

The judgment of the United States Court of Appeals for the Tenth Circuit is affirmed, and the case is remanded for further proceedings consistent with this opinion.

It is so ordered.

QUESTIONS

1. What laws are in apparent conflict?

2. How did the court come to the conclusion that the church members should be allowed to drink their hallucinogenic tea?

3. How do you think the court would have ruled had the case involved the sale and distribution of tea bags at a tea shop or "on the street"?

CRITICAL **THINKING EXERCISES**

1. You are a woman in a bar. You have had a few drinks, but want another one. The man you're talking with, whom you just met that night, says with a mischievous smile, "So, will you sleep with me tonight?" In the same tone, you reply, "Sure, if you buy me another drink?" He then reveals himself to be an undercover policeman and arrests you for prostitution. What would be your defense?

2. You live in a state where medical marijuana is legal. You suffer from glaucoma and are an organic gardener. You decide to cut out the middleman and grow your own marijuana. You neither sell it nor give it to anyone else to use. One day, federal law enforcement officials arrest you for violating the Controlled Substances Act. What is your defense?

3. You are a city policeman in a small town. You have made several arrests for heroin possession, all of which appear to come from the same source. None of the suspects have revealed the supplier, but you think it is coming from outside your jurisdiction. What resources are available to you to find the drugs' source?

4. Which of the following gambling activities are legal?
   a. Purchasing a lottery ticket from an authorized vendor at a local convenience store.
   b. Betting money with a bookie in a local numbers game.
   c. Playing blackjack at a state-licensed casino.
   d. Playing penny-ante poker in your basement with your friends.
   e. Betting $5 on the outcome of a football game.

5. You post a picture of your one-year-old daughter in the bathtub smiling and playing with the bubbles on your Facebook page. A law enforcement officer arrests you for distributing child pornography. What is your defense?

6. Can a husband obtain a protection from abuse order against his wife?

7. You are a prosecutor handling a complaint of child molestation filed by the mother of a small girl against the girl's father. The two parents are in the midst of a custody battle. What elements would you have to allege to take the case to trial?

8. A teacher reports a child who was in visible discomfort at school. When questioned, the child said his bottom hurt because his father paddled him with a wooden stick. The school nurse examined the child and noticed redness, but no bruising. You are a prosecutor reading this report. Is this sufficient evidence to charge the father with child abuse?

9. An elderly woman lives with her grown married daughter and the daughter's husband. The elderly woman is hard of hearing, has poor veins and circulatory problems. Neighbors have reported sounds of loud shouting and have noticed bruising on the elderly woman. You are a policeman receiving this report. Do you investigate? If so, if you find no other evidence than what the neighbor reported, would you file charges?

10. You are a police officer investigating a report of a sixteen-year-old male who has disappeared from his parents' home. When you go to the home, what questions will you ask the parents?

11. You have condition that sometimes causes you to slur your speech. You work late on a Friday night and are driving home. A little anxious to get there, you drive ten miles over the speed limit. A policeman pulls you over and asks if you have been drinking. You deny drinking, but your words are slurred because of your condition. You are charged with DUI. What defense, if any, can you bring against the charge?

12. You are of legal drinking age. On an out-of-state trip, you purchase a bottle of wine

at what you think is a great price. Driving back home, you are pulled over for speeding. The policeman notices the bottle on the seat and asks where you bought it. You tell him and he writes you an additional ticket for violating the state's liquor laws because by purchasing the bottle out of state you evaded state excise taxes on alcohol. Is this regulation of alcoholic transportation between states a power given to state governments?

13. Your local city council has voted to raise taxes. You lead a march in protest. When speaking to the assembled marchers, you reference the Boston Tea Party. The crowd takes the cue and charges the council room yelling "Time for a new tea party" and begin destroying furniture. Both you and the "tea partiers" are arrested. You claim your actions were legal under the First Amendment. What doctrine would the prosecution use?

14. You suffer from frequent urination. While walking through a town, you seek a bathroom, but can't find any. In desperation, you duck around the corner of an industrial building to do your business. After exposing yourself, you look up to see a policewoman. She charges you with public indecency. What defenses are available to you?

15. You feel like stretching your legs and take a walk around town. You need a rest and sit down in the town's bus station and fall asleep. Soon, a policeman wakes you and tells you he's issuing a vagrancy citation. What defense would you use?

16. You have an abortion performed by a licensed physician in the second trimester of pregnancy. A zealous prosecutor charges you with having an illegal abortion. What would you have to prove to avoid conviction?

17. Can states outlaw consensual sodomy?

PORTFOLIO **BUILDING**

1. BetonSports.com was once advertised as "the largest online wagering service in the world," and allegedly allowed gamblers worldwide to place bets on professional and college sports. Now, the company founder finds himself serving a federal prison sentence.

As you can see in the press release below, he pled guilty to various gambling and wire transfer violations. As part of the plea, he wired over $43 million from a Swiss bank account to the U.S. District Court for the Eastern District of Missouri. Read the press release.

UNITED STATES ATTORNEY'S OFFICE
EASTERN DISTRICT OF MISSOURI

MICHAEL W. REAP

Acting United States Attorney

NEWS RELEASE

For further information call (314) 539-2200

November 2, 2009

BETONSPORTS FOUNDER SENTENCED ON FEDERAL RACKETEERING CHARGES—AGREES TO THE FORFEITURE OF OVER $43 MILLION

St. Louis, MO: Gary Stephen Kaplan, founder of BetonSports, a large illegal offshore sports wagering business, was sentenced to 51 months in prison on multiple federal charges, Acting United States Attorney Michael W. Reap announced today.

Pursuant to a complex plea agreement, on August 14, 2009, Gary Stephen Kaplan, entered pleas of guilty to charges of conspiracy to violate the RICO statute, conspiring to violate the Wire Wager Act and violating the Wire Wager Act. He appeared today for sentencing before United States District Judge Carol E. Jackson, in St. Louis, Missouri.

As part of the plea, Kaplan has forfeited to the United States $43,650,000 in criminal proceeds. An additional amount of approximately $7 million has been forfeited in related proceedings, bringing the total forfeiture in this case to over $50 million.

Kaplan admitted that beginning in the mid to late 1990s, he set up business entities offshore in Aruba, Antigua and eventually Costa Rica to provide sportsbook services to U.S. residents through Internet websites and toll-free telephone numbers. He founded, operated and controlled, with other co-conspirators, the enterprise known as "BetOnSports." BetOnSports advertised heavily in the U.S. to solicit U.S. residents to place sports wagers by telephone and over the Internet. BetOnSports-related entities controlled toll free numbers and domain names advertised by BetOnSports. Technologically, Kaplan's toll-free telephone lines terminated in Houston, Texas or Miami, Florida and then were forwarded to Costa Rica by satellite transmitter or fiber-optic cable. Some of Kaplan's web servers were located in Miami and were remotely controlled from Costa Rica. U.S. residents became customers of BetOnSports by depositing funds on account and placing wagers over U.S. toll-free telephone lines and via the Internet using the deposited funds. Funds were sent from the U.S. customers to BoS operations outside the U.S. and BoS sent winnings from outside the U.S. to its U.S. customers.

BetOnSports was highly successful and attracted a large number of U.S. customers. By 2004, the BETONSPORTS organization's principal base of operations in Costa Rica employed approximately 1,700 people. During the year ended January 31, 2004, BetOnSports had close to 1 million registered customers, accepted over 10 million sports bets in a cumulative gross amount that exceeded one billion dollars. In mid-2004, Kaplan made a successful public offering of the stock of BetOnSports on the London Alternative Investment Market that netted him over $100,000,000. Those funds eventually found their way into various Isle of Jersey trusts which invested the funds in Swiss bank accounts.

Reap stated, "Kaplan was unique in the scope and scale of his illegal operation. Despite his immense profits, he is living in federal custody. This case should serve as a warning to others who might choose to defy the laws of the United States on such a grand scale." Reap also noted that "Kaplan's business model itself was built on a wager that the U.S. could not and would not enforce its anti-sports book laws to reach Kaplan. Today, Kaplan lost that wager."

"In addition to a lengthy prison sentence, Mr. Kaplan forfeited over $43 million to the United States government," said Toni Weir.

1. One of your firm's long-time clients has come in for advice on setting up an online gaming company and your boss has asked you to prepare a memo explaining the law and highlighting any risks. Prepare the memo, using BetOnSports as a cautionary tale.

FOR FURTHER READING AND VIEWING

1. Albert, A. (2001). *Brothel: Mustang Ranch and Its Women*. Random House. This book provides an inside look at what went on at the Mustang Ranch in Nevada until it closed. "Love Ranch," a 2010 movie starring Joe Pesci and Helen Mirren tells a fictionalized version of the Mustang Ranch.

2. Solinger, R. (2001). *Abortion Wars: A Half Century of Struggle, 1950–2000*. University of California Press. A collection of essays on abortion by writers who are pro-choice. Includes extensive discussion of *Roe v. Wade* and *Planned Parenthood v. Casey*.

3. Hull, N. E., and Hoffer, P. C. (2001). *Roe v. Wade: The Abortion Rights Controversy in American History.* University Press of Kansas. An overview of the abortion rights controversy.

4. Gordon, S. B. (2001). *The Mormon Question: Polygamy and Constitutional Conflict in Nineteenth-Century America.* University of North Carolina Press. A look at the history of polygamy in the West.

5. Goldstein, A. (2001). *Addiction: From Biology to Drug Policy.* Oxford University Press. Explores the nature of addiction to categories of drugs and the laws and policies needed to fight addiction.

6. Schlosser, E. (2003). *Reefer Madness: Sex, Drugs and Cheap Labor in the American Black Market.* Houghton Mifflin. An inside look at the illegal drug and adult entertainment industries and how demand has spurred a black market economy in sin.

7. Krakauer, J. (2003). *Under the Banner of Heaven: A Story of Violent Faith.* Doubleday. Expose of religious fanaticism in the United States, especially in Utah.

8. *September Dawn* (2007). Film featuring John Voight about the September 11, 1857, massacre of a wagon train by Mormon activists in Utah.

Chapter **eight**

TREASON, TERRORISM, AND WARTIME CRIMINAL JUSTICE

They that can give up essential liberty to obtain a little temporary safety deserve neither liberty nor safety.

Benjamin Franklin

The Congress shall have the power . . . to declare war, grant letters of marque and reprisal, and make rules concerning captures on land and water.

U.S. Constitution, Article I, Section 8

Treason against the United States, shall consist only in levying war against them, or in adhering to their enemies, giving them aid and comfort. No person shall be convicted of treason unless on the testimony of two witnesses to the same overt act, or on confession in open court.

U.S. Constitution, Article III, Section 3

Introduction and Historical Background

Our history is full of contradictions when it comes to judging loyalty and putting out the welcome mat. On one hand, we are a country made up of a large population of immigrants. With the exception of those among us who can trace our ancestry to members of Native American tribes, we all descend from immigrants. The Statue of Liberty asks the world to "Bring me your tired, your poor, your huddled masses yearning to breathe free."[1] On the other hand, as a nation we have been quick to judge and sometimes misjudge the loyalty of new arrivals, particularly in times of war or domestic turmoil.

Treason and sedition are crimes that punish the disloyalty of a country's citizens and resident aliens. All who reside in a country are assumed to owe it a duty of loyalty. Loyalty to one's nation is such an ingrained value that governments punish disloyalty reflexively. Similarly, espionage, whether for economic or ideological reasons, constitutes a breach of trust on both a personal and national level. Our discussion of treason, terrorism, and wartime criminal justice necessarily begins with a discussion of history. As you will see, what was done in the past is often prologue to the present. For example, when President George W. Bush issued an Executive Order on November 13, 2001, calling for secret military tribunals to try suspected terrorists, his supporters pointed to the trial of suspected WWII saboteurs by a military court as precedent for the order. At the time (early fall 2001) their story had all but been relegated to the dustbin of history. Their story, resurrected in support of the War on Terror, is now well known.

One of the earliest examples of restrictions borne of doubts about loyalty was the Alien and Sedition Acts of 1798 signed into law by President John Adams. At the time, international tensions with France were high, and the president feared war was imminent. In particular, he eyed the many newly arrived French immigrants suspiciously. Their sheer number—an estimated 25,000 French immigrants lived in Philadelphia alone—looked like fertile recruiting ground for French spies. Additionally, newly arrived Irish refugees from the Irish Rebellion of 1798 represented another large Catholic population in the still largely Protestant country.

The Alien Act increased the time needed to qualify for citizenship from five to fourteen years and gave the president the power to expel any foreigner he considered dangerous. The Sedition Act made it a crime to either make "[f]alse, scandalous, and malicious" writings against the government or to stir up sedition among otherwise loyal Americans. The law was subsequently used to quiet troublesome newspaper editors.[2] Both laws remained in force for only a few years. In contrast, we are now nearly a decade post-9/11, and most of the restrictions put into place shortly after the attacks are still in force.

Wartime Power

As you have learned, the Constitution sets forth the framework for the American system of justice. The arrangement relies heavily on all three branches of government having a say in running the country. Each branch has powers that serve as a check on the other branches lest any one branch become too powerful. The Constitution's framers wanted to avoid any possibility that a monarch or head of state could assume dictatorial powers.

The framers foresaw that there would inevitably be times when the country would face enemies, internal and external, as well as times of peace. To assure that our form of government would survive the inevitable challenges ahead, the Constitution provides for the **power to declare war.** Among the checks and balances found in the Constitution are power-sharing provisions for just such times. For example, the Constitution grants to Congress "the power . . . to declare war, grant letters of marque and reprisal, and make rules concerning captures on land and water."[3]

Letters of marque and reprisal are letters from a government formerly used to grant a private person the power to seize the subjects of a foreign state. The same clause of the Constitution also gives Congress the power:

Power to declare war
The power reserved by Congress in the Constitution. Congress can declare war on a belligerent, and then the Executive Branch conducts the war.

Letters of marque and reprisal
A letter from a government formerly used to grant a private person the power to seize the subjects of a foreign state.

- To raise and support armies

- To provide and maintain a navy

- To make rules for the government and regulation of the land and naval forces

- To call up the militia to execute the laws of the Union and suppress insurrections and repel invasions.

The president also plays a role in wartime. The Constitution provides that:

The President shall be the Commander in Chief of the Army and Navy of the United States, and of the Militia of the several states when called into the actual Service of the United States.[4]

As you can see, it is Congress that has the power to declare war and the president who is in charge of planning, organizing, and executing that war. The limitation of the president's power in time of war has been tested several times, with the deciding vote coming from the Judicial Branch of government. Since 1973, the power to commit troops overseas had also been governed by the War Powers Resolution, passed by Congress. The legislation provides that the president may commit troops when Congress has declared war, when Congress has specifically authorized troops to be deployed, or when the United States has been attacked.

> I venture to say no war can be long carried on against the will of the people.
>
> Edmund Burke

HISTORICAL HIGHLIGHT

Laws Restricting Freedom in Times of War or National Emergency

In times of war and national emergency, the federal government has historically enacted special legislation designed to protect the people from real or perceived danger. The most infamous of laws was the Executive Order authorizing the federal government to inter Japanese Americans in camps during World War II. Other examples include:

- *The Alien and Sedition Acts of 1798.* These laws gave the president the authority to exclude any alien he thought was dangerous and made it illegal to make false accusations against the government or to incite citizens to sedition.

- *The Habeas Corpus Act of 1863.* During the Civil War, Congress passed a law suspending *habeas corpus* for security purposes. The law effectively legalized steps President Lincoln had already taken.

- *The Sedition Act of 1918.* This law made it illegal to criticize the United States' role in the war effort during World War I.

- *The Smith Act of 1940.* This law made it a crime to "knowingly or willfully advocate, abet, advise, or teach the duty, necessity, desirability, or propriety of overthrowing any government in the U.S. by force or violence or to print, publish, edit, issue, circulate, sell, distribute, or publicly display any written or printed matter advocating, advising, or teaching the duty, necessity, desirability, or propriety of overthrowing governments."

- *The McCarran Act of 1950.* Also known as the Internal Security Act, this federal law allowed for the establishment of internment camps for use in national emergencies.

- *The McCarran–Walter Act of 1952.* This law, also known as the Immigration and Nationality Act, tightened restrictions on aliens and reduced immigration from nonwhite countries. It also legalized stripping naturalized citizens who were judged "subversive" of their citizenship and deporting them. In addition, the law allowed deportation of resident aliens engaged in political activity.

Both Congressional power and presidential power have been fine-tuned with the assistance of the Supreme Court. In times of turmoil, presidents sometimes issue orders citing as authority the inherent power of the president as commander in chief. That was the case during the Korean Conflict. Starting in 1950, North Korea, with the support of the People's Republic of China and the Soviet Union, waged war against South Korea. It was a conflict widely viewed as an attempt by Communist forces to expand their influence. President Harry Truman bypassed Congress, and did not ask for a declaration of war. Instead, he called the conflict a "police action" and worked with the United Nations in defending South Korea.

By 1952, the conflict in Korea was in full force, and at home steel workers were talking about going on strike. President Truman saw the steel industry as essential to a successful police action in Korea, and to avoid a shutdown, took decisive action. He issued an Executive Order that authorized the secretary of commerce to "take possession of all such plants, facilities, and other property . . . as he may deem necessary in the interests of national defense."[5]

Within hours, the owners of the steel plants seized sought help from federal courts. The case came to the Supreme Court within weeks. The president argued that he had the power as commander in chief to take immediate action in an emergency. The Supreme Court disagreed. Justice Black concluded that "the founders of this Nation entrusted the lawmaking power to the Congress alone in both good and bad times" so that if the president wanted to nationalize an industry he had better get Congress to pass legislation doing so.[6]

At times when Congress has declared war, the Supreme Court has been less reluctant to second-guess presidential Executive Orders. For example, after the Japanese bombed Pearl Harbor in a sneak attack and Congress declared war on Japan, people on the West Coast became concerned about the prospect of either a direct invasion by the Japanese or acts of internal sabotage by Japanese aliens and immigrants and even their American-born children. One of the first to call for the internment of Japanese Americans was the Republican congressman from Santa Monica, Leland M. Ford. Congressman Ford insisted that "all Japanese, whether citizens or not, be placed in inland concentration camps." His voice was joined by others, and soon the delegations from California, Oregon, and Washington were calling for internment.

Earl Warren was the California attorney general at the time. He ordered his staff to prepare maps detailing the location of all Japanese and Japanese American landowners in California. These maps revealed that people of Japanese ancestry owned land located near or around what could be considered strategic targets for sabotage, such as beaches, air and oil fields, and water reservoirs.

On February 19, 1942, President Roosevelt signed Executive Order 9066. The order authorized the military to clear sensitive areas of any and all persons and to restrict movement into and out of such areas. Excluded from many areas, the presence of Japanese Americans in communities could, according to Warren, " . . . bring about race riots and prejudice and hysteria and excesses of all kinds." The solution was, allegedly for their own safety, that the displaced should be confined. By March 2, the military designated the western half of California, Oregon, and Washington as a military area and ordered those of Japanese heritage removed.[7]

Recently, the U.S. Census Bureau revealed that it provided the Justice Department and other federal agencies with the names and addresses of Japanese Americans. Individual information is confidential under normal circumstances, but the Second War Powers Act allowed federal agencies to share information.

Hardships are part of war, and war is an aggregation of hardship.

Justice Black in *Korematsu v. United States*

Similar information sharing was authorized under the USA PATRIOT Act. The Census Bureau provided numbers of Arab-Americans by ZIP Code to the Justice Department, but claims not to have turned over individual information.[8]

All in all, over 110,000 people were confined to internment camps during World War II. The Supreme Court went on to uphold the evacuation and internment in *Korematsu v. United States*.[9] Many of the internees, most of whom were U.S. citizens, lost their homes and businesses. Although the internment of Japanese-Americans is probably best known, the United States also interned Italian and German-Americans and resident aliens from Italy, Germany, and Japan. Congress apologized decades later, and President Ronald Reagan signed the Civil Liberties Act of 1988. The Act was passed by Congress to provide a presidential apology and symbolic payment of $20,000 to the internees, evacuees, and persons of Japanese ancestry who lost liberty or property due to the forced internments. Earl Warren, who played such a pivotal role as California attorney general, went on to become chief justice of the Supreme Court. His decisions were to be known as some of the most liberal ever, and included *Brown v. Board of Education* and *Miranda v. Arizona*, which integrated the nation's schools.

> We'd be in a bad way if we won the war and lost our civil liberties.
>
> Earl Warren, on the dismissal of all Japanese Americans for civil service positions after Pearl Harbor

Habeas Corpus in Wartime and the Question of Military Tribunals

Habeas corpus
The "Great Writ," which orders another authority to bring a person held to the court. It was originally used to prevent kings from simply making enemies disappear.

You may recall that **habeas corpus** is a legal term that literally means "have the body." When a court exercises the writ of *habeas corpus*, or the "Great Writ," it literally orders another authority to bring a person held to the court. It was originally used to prevent kings from simply making enemies disappear. Today, *habeas corpus* petitions are commonly filed by prisoners in state systems who want a federal court to review whether the justice they are receiving at the hand of the state meets minimum constitutional standards. Thus, a state prisoner who believes the conditions in his prison cell amount to cruel and unusual punishment can have access to a federal court to hear that complaint by filing a *habeas corpus* petition.

The right of *habeas corpus* is an important one in both English and American jurisprudence. It is seen as a pivotal right. For example, the great English legal scholar Blackstone thought the right of *habeas corpus* as "the bulwark of the British Constitution." He wrote that the right to *habeas corpus* was even more important than the right to be free from the loss of property without due process of law because "confinement of the person, by secretly hurrying him to jail, where his sufferings are unknown or forgotten is a less public, a less striking, and therefore a more dangerous engine of arbitrary government."[10]

The Constitution provides that "The privilege of the Writ of Habeas Corpus shall not be suspended, unless when in cases of rebellion or invasion the public safety may require it."[11] The standard, then, is a tough one. The presumption is that every person held under the control of an agent or unit of government is entitled to some means of judicial review of his confinement, conviction, or sentence. Even during World War II when the federal government tried suspected German saboteurs in a military tribunal, the prisoners had the right to have their case reviewed by courts.

Military tribunal
A military court convened in times of emergency to try those accused of war-related crimes, such as terrorism, espionage, or treason.

The federal government has employed the use of **military tribunals** during time of war. For example, President Lincoln used a military court to try Lambdin P. Milligan during the Civil War. He was sentenced to hanging by a military tribunal for planning to form a secret military faction to free captured Confederate soldiers, rearm them, and invade Indiana. The case came before the Court on a petition for *habeas corpus* even though President Lincoln had suspended *habeas corpus*. The Supreme Court wrote that only Congress had the authority to set up military tribunals, and then only in time of war. As long as the country's courts are open, concluded the Court, they were the proper venue for trial and reversed the conviction.[12] Congress later passed the Habeas Corpus Act of 1863 to give legal cover to Lincoln's actions.

Military Tribunals Today

In the aftermath of the terrorist attacks on September 11, 2001, President George W. Bush signed an Executive Order authorizing the detention and trial of noncitizens by military tribunals. This order cites as authority by Congress for Authorization for Use of Military Force. That authorization declared:

> That the President is authorized to use all necessary and appropriate force against those nations, organizations, or persons he determines planned, authorized, committed, or aided the terrorist attacks that occurred on September 11, 2001, or harbored such organizations or persons, in order to prevent any future acts of international terrorism against the United States by such nations, organizations or persons.

HISTORICAL HIGHLIGHT

Habeas Corpus Lends Helping Hand to Imprisoned Student after September 11th Attacks

Imagine that you are a twenty-one-year-old student from Jordan who is being questioned after the attacks on America on September 11th. You are being asked hundreds of questions while strapped to a lie-detector machine. Imagine further that, although you did not commit any crime and are not being charged with any crime, you might know a few things about what happened, making you a material witness. Would you be nervous or scared?

Osama Awadallah, a student at Grossmont College in El Cajon, California, was in just this situation. After being questioned by the FBI and being identified as a possible material witness for a grand jury, Awadallah

was in maximum security prisons for the next three weeks, transported from Southern California, to Oklahoma, and then to Manhattan. During this time, he was shackled, strip-searched, and sometimes kept in solitary confinement. But Osama Awadallah had not been arrested for any crime, he was being held to testify before a grand jury.

Thanks to *habeas corpus*, Shira A. Scheindlin, a judge for the U.S. District Court for the Southern District of New York, was able to find that Awadallah was unlawfully detained and that "since 1789, no Congress has granted the government the authority to imprison an innocent person in order to guarantee that he will testify before a grand jury conducting a criminal investigation." Osama Awadallah was released and his testimony to the grand jury was suppressed.[13]

President Bush's order calls for some suspected terrorists to be tried by military tribunals, and announced that the rules of evidence ordinarily applied to criminal cases tried in federal court would not be followed. The order covers noncitizens designated personally by the president for military tribunal trial after he concludes any of the following:

- If they are or were al-Qaeda members.
- If they engaged in, aided or abetted, or conspired to commit acts of international terrorism.
- If they have harbored such individuals.

The order also says the president can designate noncitizens for military trials if "it is in the best interest of the United States that such individual be subject to this order."

Those designated by the president for military trial will be tried either in the United States or abroad under the following conditions:

- The military commission sits as trier of fact and law; roles usually split between the jury and judge.
- The presiding officer can admit any evidence that has "probative value to a reasonable person."
- The secretary of defense designates the prosecutor, and the defendant may have an attorney.
- Conviction need not be unanimous, but can be by vote of two-thirds of the commission, and sentencing agreed upon by two-thirds of the commission.
- Any appeal goes to the president or the secretary of defense, and their decision is final. The order specifies that those tried by military tribunal can't appeal to any court in the United States, foreign country, or any international tribunal.

HISTORICAL HIGHLIGHT

FBI Rushes World War II Would-Be Saboteurs to Electric Chair

In 1942, after the United States declared war on Germany, eight would-be Nazi saboteurs left German-occupied France for America. Submarines dropped the two groups off along the Long Island, New York, beach and Ponte Vedra Beach in Florida. Seven were German citizens, but the eighth was a U.S. citizen. One declared to his partner that he intended to turn himself in rather than commit acts of sabotage. He did so, and was questioned for eight days by the FBI. He told the FBI that the Germans were intent on landing others and engaging in a war of terror by leaving bombs in public places and blowing up vital industrial plants.[14]

The FBI arrested all eight men and turned them over to a military commission. They were tried under the Articles of War (military laws authorized by Congress earlier), convicted, and sentenced to death.

While the trial was still underway, they filed a request for *habeas corpus* with the Supreme Court, relying on *Ex parte Milligan* to claim that the military tribunal had no jurisdiction and that state or federal courts should handle the case.

The Court agreed to hear the case. The Articles of Law previously enacted by Congress allowed a military commission to try those not ordinarily tried by court-martial. Therefore, this time the Court upheld the military tribunal's convictions of spying, conspiracy, and violating the laws of war. It held that those who are unlawful combatants such as these men who entered the country secretly and did not wear uniforms or carry identification weren't prisoners of war and could be tried by a military commission when Congress has provided for such commissions in legislation. Within a month, all eight men were sentenced and six of them were executed by electrocution in a D.C. jail.[15]

One problem with the president's order is that it may well interfere with efforts to extradite to the United States or otherwise put suspected terrorists in the hands of U.S. military tribunals. For example, the idea of secret hearings, few rights for the accused, and military officers serving as both judge and jury may violate treaties in force such as the 1950 European Convention on Human Rights.

In addition, the European Union (EU) countries have all banned capital punishment, and may refuse to extradite suspects without promises that they would not be executed if convicted. Even if an EU country did agree to extradite a suspect, he or she would have the right to appeal to the European Court of Human Rights, whose decision is binding on all EU member countries.

Some members of Congress as well as civil rights organizations were questioning whether President Bush had the authority to call for tribunals without the express consent of Congress and whether any president or Congress had the authority to suspend the right of *habeas corpus* under the circumstances and in the manner the order purports to.

Now that several years have passed since the events of 9/11, the legal community has begun looking more closely at the need for special tribunals and especially at the idea that "enemy combatants" can be detained indefinitely without charges being filed or their cases being adjudicated. In fact, the U.S. Supreme Court decided two so-called enemy combatant cases during 2004. Both involve American citizens being held by the military as suspected terrorists.

The first case involves Yasir Esam Hamdi, a Saudi national who was born in Louisiana while his parents worked for an oil company. As a result, he is an American citizen. Hamdi was captured on a battlefield in Afghanistan and eventually moved to the detention center in Guantanamo, Cuba. When the U.S. military discovered he was a citizen, it transferred him to a naval brig in Virginia.

His parents filed a lawsuit, alleging that as a citizen he could not be held indefinitely. The Fourth Circuit Court of Appeals concluded that because he was caught on the battleground as an enemy, he could be held without charges.[16] His parents appealed, and the Supreme Court agreed to decide whether Hamdi was being legally held as an enemy combatant. The Department of Defense argued that Hamdi had been caught on the battlefield, that he was armed and ready to fight other American citizens, and that he had been interrogated by our military. That interrogation gave him the opportunity to challenge his detention, the government argued.

The High Court ruled that any American citizen held as an enemy combatant without charges must be given a meaningful opportunity to challenge that designation before an independent and neutral decision maker. The Court wrote, "An interrogation by one's captor, however, effective as an intelligence-gathering tool, hardly constitutes a constitutionally adequate fact-finding before a neutral decision-maker." The Court did not specify the mechanics of that review, but instead sent the case back to the federal trial court.[17] The Court left open the possibility that a military tribunal like that authorized by the president shortly after 9/11 might be adequate, but reiterated that any decision could be challenged in federal courts.

The government released Hamdi on October 11, 2004, and sent him home to Saudi Arabia. He agreed to renounce his U.S. citizenship, as the government was apparently not prepared to try him.

The second case involves Jose Padilla, a U.S. citizen from Chicago who was arrested in 2001 after returning on a flight from the Middle East. He was alleged to have been involved with al Qaeda plans to detonate a "dirty bomb" (a bomb capable of dispersing radiological material over a large area, but without a nuclear explosion) in the United States. Rather than charging him with any specific crime, President Bush designated him an "enemy combatant" and had him moved to the naval brig in Charleston, South Carolina.

An attorney eventually contacted to represent Padilla filed a petition to have him released or charged. On December 18, 2003, the Second Circuit Court of Appeals ordered that he be charged or released within 30 days. Solicitor General Theodore Olson (who lost his wife on 9/11—she was a passenger on the plane that hit the Pentagon) filed an appeal to the Supreme Court in order to halt Padilla's release. The Supreme Court sent it back to the trial court on the premise that Padilla had filed his case in the wrong federal circuit.[18] Padilla then refiled in the correct circuit and the federal district court ruled he should be charged or released. The government appealed the decision, and it was overturned. Padilla appealed to the Supreme Court, but while the appeal was pending, the government transferred him to federal prison and filed charges.[19]

A jury found Padilla guilty of far lesser charges than those originally made. Based on a fingerprint found on an alleged "al Qaeda application" retrieved by the CIA in Afghanistan, he was convicted of "providing material support for terrorists," and two other related charges. The jury did not hear that he had been held in a military brig for more than three years, or that he had originally been accused of plotting to detonate dirty bombs in U.S. cities. Padilla was sentenced to seventeen years in jail. He has filed an appeal alleging "outrageous government action" during his imprisonment.[20]

The Supreme Court also took up the case of several noncitizens who challenged their internment at Guantanamo Bay, Cuba. They challenged the Bush administration's indefinite detention. The government argued that the facility they are held in is in Cuba and therefore outside federal court jurisdiction. The Court disagreed and ordered their cases to be heard by a federal district judge without expressing an opinion on whether they are entitled to a trial or can be held indefinitely.[21]

In response, President Bush asked Congress to pass legislation removing the detainees from federal jurisdiction. Congress enacted and the president signed the Detainee Treatment Act of 2005 which provides:

"no court, justice, or judge" may exercise jurisdiction over

1. "an application for a writ of habeas corpus filed by or on behalf of an alien detained by the Department of Defense at Guantanamo Bay, Cuba; or

2. any other action against the United States or its agents relating to any aspect of the detention by the Department of Defense of an alien at Guantanamo Bay, Cuba, who

   (A) is currently in military custody; or

   (B) has been determined by the United States Court of Appeals for the District of Columbia Circuit . . . to have been properly detained as an enemy combatant."[22]

The detainees' lawyers challenged the law in court. Ultimately, the Supreme Court ruled that the Detainee Treatment Act did not apply to detainees whose cases were already in the federal courts at the time the law was passed.[23] Congress then passed the Military Commissions Act of 2006 barring any federal judge from reviewing any case involving the detainees.[24] In 2008, the Supreme Court ruled that the detainees at Guantanamo fall within federal court jurisdiction effectively nullifying the section of the Military Commissions Act keeping Guantanamo detainees out of the federal courts.[25]

After President Obama assumed office, Congress passed the Military Commissions Act of 2009 in an attempt to balance the government's need to obtain intelligence from detainees and the detainees' right to a fair trial. The attorney general can make the determination which detainees will be tried in civilian courts and which will face military tribunals.

The new law largely keeps the existing military tribunal structure. The prosecution may only introduce evidence obtained from detainees who were tortured under tightly regulated rules determined by the secretary of defense. (See Evidence Concepts Section at end of chapter.) Detainees may attend their trials and can only be removed if they become disruptive. The Military Tribunals have jurisdiction over thirty-two offenses including conspiracy and providing material support for terrorism.[26]

Defining Treason and Sedition

Treason is the only crime that is specifically defined in the Constitution. The Constitution provides that "Treason against the United States, shall consist only in levying war against them, or in adhering to their enemies, giving them aid and comfort."[27]

The Constitution also specifically singles out treason as a crime that requires the government to produce more evidence against the accused than any other crime. It provides that "No person shall be convicted of treason unless on the testimony of two witnesses to the same overt act, or on confession in open court."[28] Thus, treason requires very solid evidence or a confession in the courtroom before a conviction can be obtained. Why did the framers of the Constitution see fit to accord extraordinary protection to those charged with treason? Perhaps because they saw charges of treason as so serious that a wrongful conviction must be guarded against. Perhaps they feared that unless a confession was repeated in open court, it was susceptible to being obtained fraudulently or through the use of torture. Perhaps the framers simply wanted to avoid the possibility that government officials might prosecute political disagreements as treason without concrete evidence of disloyalty. Whatever the reason, treason was singled out for special attention.

The crime of treason is defined in the U.S. Code as a person "owing allegiance to the United States, levies war against them or adheres to their enemies, giving them aid and comfort within the United States or elsewhere."[29] Traditionally, treason has been viewed as the most serious crime.[30]

Treason is a breach of allegiance to the United States; therefore, only those who the law defines as owing allegiance to the United States can be prosecuted for treason.[31] Allegiance can be either temporary or permanent. U.S. citizens, whether natural-born or naturalized, are viewed as having permanent allegiance to the United States, but aliens residing in the United States are perceived to have only temporary allegiance.[32]

Treason
Levying war against the United States, or in adhering to their enemies, giving them aid and comfort. Treason must be proven by the testimony of two witnesses to the same overt act, or the defendant's confession in open court.

Money is this man's god, and to get enough of it he would sacrifice his country.

Quote in a leaflet attacking Benedict Arnold

I would love to say that I did what I did out of some moral outrage over our country's acts of imperialism, or as a political statement or out of anger toward the CIA or even a love for the Soviet Union. But the sad truth is that I did what I did because of money . . .

Aldrich Ames, a CIA agent who spied for the Soviet Union

Elements   There are two elements to the crime of treason:

- Adherence to the enemy
- Rendering the enemy aid and comfort

Adherence to the Enemy   Enemies of the United States are defined as any "party who was [a] subject of foreign power in state of open hostility with [the] United States." Adherence to the enemy can take the form of:

- Selling goods to an agent of an enemy of the United States[33]
- Statements praising the enemy[34]

- Residing in an enemy country[35]
- Delivery of prisoners to the enemy, unless under a death threat that was likely to be carried out[36]

Rendering the Enemy Aid and Comfort   Examples of rendering aid and comfort to the enemy are:

- A person who acted as an interpreter at a Japanese mine during World War II where American soldiers were beaten in order to increase production[37]
- Any act that strengthens the enemy or weakens the United States[38]
- Concealing a spy's identity, or supplying him with funds and assistance[39]

In order to commit treason, a person must have not only the intent to commit the overt act in question, but also to betray the country by that act.[40] A person who commits no overt act, but still sides with the enemy, is not guilty of treason. A person who commits an overt act, but without treasonous intent, is also not guilty of treason.[41]

Defenses   Various defenses are available to a person charged with treason. Some of them are:

- Duress
- First Amendment privilege
- Immunity from prosecution

Duress   In order for this defense to succeed, the defendant must demonstrate that he or she was in immediate danger of loss of life or severe bodily harm.[42] Of course, any assertion of duress must be substantiated by facts.[43]

First Amendment Privilege   The First Amendment's guarantee of free speech does not apply to treasonous speech. The First Amendment defense was tried by a man who made short-wave radio broadcasts for the enemy during World War II. The Court ruled that this type of speech fell outside the protection of the First Amendment.[44] A similar fate awaited a man who made anti-American broadcasts on German radio during World War II.[45]

Immunity from Prosecution   If the defendant can demonstrate that he or she is part of a class of people who have been granted immunity, he or she can avoid prosecution. The most notable case of this happening was the blanket amnesty given Confederate soldiers after the Civil War.[46]

Very few treason trials have actually taken place in the United States. One of the most significant treason trials in our history is that of Aaron Burr. Aaron Burr served as vice president under Thomas Jefferson. During Jefferson's second term (and after Burr was no longer vice president), President Jefferson charged Burr with treason.[47] Burr faced the prospect of being put to the gallows or a firing squad for activities allegedly involving seeking foreign support for a new country in the western part of the American continent. Burr was caught with a flotilla of armed men and was accused of treason by Jefferson. During the trial, Jefferson was ordered to turn over private papers concerning his communications with the general who investigated the charges. It was the first time in our history that a president had been ordered to produce documents or appear in court. Justice Marshall, who heard the case, told the jurors that "levying war" meant more than making plans to go to war; it meant "the actual assembling of men for the treasonable purpose." In the end, the jury did not convict Burr, since there was no confession in court, nor evidence presented by two witnesses to the same act.[48]

More recently, the Department of Justice debated whether it should charge John Walker Lindh, the alleged "American Taliban" picked up in Afghanistan with other Taliban fighters, with treason. In the end, it elected not to charge him, most likely because Lindh probably would never confess in open court to acts of treason. In addition, it seems unlikely that two witnesses can be found willing to testify that he committed an act of treason. Instead, the "American Taliban" was charged with violating federal antiterrorism laws and pled guilty in a plea agreement.

HISTORICAL HIGHLIGHT

The Clash between Church and State: Henry II and Thomas Becket

Thomas Becket was the Paris-educated son of a former sheriff of London. Becket was admired for his administrative abilities. He was politically astute, well connected, and universally admired and respected. When introduced to King Henry II, the attraction was immediate. Henry recognized Becket's political skill and strong intellect. Henry would eventually appoint Becket to the position of chancellor.

Henry relied on Becket's advice and considered him an ally in his ongoing power struggle with the Church. When archbishop of Canterbury Theobald died in 1161, Henry appointed Becket to the post. Henry was sure that with Becket in the archbishop's chair, the Church would be subservient to him.

Becket, however, underwent something of a religious conversion after assuming office. He saw his loyalty to the Church in religious terms. He could not, in good conscience, put his allegiance to Henry before his allegiance to God.

The Church in those days would try any clerics accused of wrongdoing in the ecclesiastical courts. Henry was determined that they should be tried in the king's court. The disagreement came to a head when a canon was accused of murder in 1163. The ecclesiastical court acquitted the cleric and the public demanded justice. The king insisted on trying the cleric, but Becket protested. Henry relented in this particular case, but proposed the Constitutions of Clarendon that would extend the king's jurisdiction over the clerics. Becket reluctantly agreed.

Henry began to see Becket as unreliable and disloyal. Henry summoned Becket to his castle at Northampton and demanded to know what he had done with the large sums of money he had handled when he was chancellor. Becket saw the trap set for him and fled to France. His exile lasted six years.

Even in exile, Becket agitated against the king. He excommunicated all clerics who supported the king. In 1170, Henry met with Becket in France, and it appeared the rift was healed. Becket returned to his post in Canterbury. Henry requested that Becket reinstate the excommunicated clerics, but Becket refused. Henry, while still in France, is said to have flown into a rage, shouting: "What sluggards, what cowards have I brought up in my court, who care nothing for their allegiance to their lord. Who will rid me of this meddlesome priest?"

Four of the king's knights sailed to England, and confronted Becket in Canterbury Cathedral. When Becket still refused to reinstate the excommunicated clerics, they drew their swords and struck his head repeatedly until the altar was splattered with his brains and blood. Allegedly the stains are still visible today. Henry was despondent when he heard the news. His momentary rage had led to the martyrdom of his nemesis.

Becket's reputation grew in death far beyond what it was in life. Miracles were said to have occurred at his tomb. Henry was forced to do penance four years later. He wore sackcloth in a procession to Becket's tomb while being flogged by eighty monks. He then spent the night at the tomb. Becket remained a cult figure for centuries. The pilgrimages made by the faithful to his tomb were immortalized in Chaucer's *Canterbury Tales*.

Percent of Terror Referrals Prosecuted.
Source: Transactional Records Access Clearinghouse.

Sedition
A conspiracy "to overthrow, put down, or to destroy by force the Government of the United States, or levy war against them, or to oppose the authority thereof, or by force to prevent, hinder, or delay the execution of any law of the United States, or by force to seize, take, or possess any property of the United States contrary to the authority thereof."

Sedition is a conspiracy "to overthrow, put down, or to destroy by force the Government of the United States, or levy war against them, or to oppose the authority thereof, or by force to prevent, hinder, or delay the execution of any law of the United States, or by force to seize, take, or possess any property of the United States contrary to the authority thereof."[49]

Elements The elements of sedition are:

- Conspiracy
- Overthrow of the United States
- Oppose by force the authority of the United States
- Prevent, hinder, or delay execution of law
- Use of force

Conspiracy A conspiracy is an agreement between two or more persons to engage in a criminal act.[50] For purposes of sedition, the conspirators must agree among themselves to commit an act of sedition.[51]

Overthrow of the United States Any group who state that their goal is the overthrow of the government of the United States by unconstitutional means would possess this element. The Communist Party met this requirement in a 1922 case.[52]

Oppose by Force the Authority of the United States This element is satisfied if a person or persons attempt by force to prevent actual exercise of federal authority. Merely disobeying a law is not sufficient to satisfy this element.[53]

Prevent, Hinder, or Delay Execution of Law To satisfy this element the person or persons involved must forcibly resist the government's execution of the law. As an example, when Chinese immigrants became the target of violence in the American West in the 1880s, the U.S. government entered into two treaties with China that obligated the U.S. government to protect Chinese citizens residing in the United States. Those who opposed the U.S. government's efforts to protect Chinese immigrants were charged with sedition. However, their actions were taken against the Chinese, but not in actual defiance of the civil authority; therefore, their actions did not constitute sedition.[54]

During World War I, draft resistors were prosecuted under the sedition statute.[55]

Use of Force   Any seditious conspiracy must contemplate the use of force.[56] However, no overt act must necessarily take place for a sedition prosecution, merely the planning of one.

Defining Terrorism

Because treason is a crime singled out for special protection, and can be hard to prove given the Constitution's restrictions, Congress has enacted other laws designed to punish activities that serve the same purpose as treasonous behavior, but fall short of fitting the definition of treason. Espionage, terrorism, and other subversive activities may amount to treason, but are separate crimes. Here are some samples of acts that are federal crimes:

- **Espionage** includes "[w]hoever knowingly and willfully communicates, furnishes, transmits, or otherwise makes available to an unauthorized person, or publishes, or uses in any manner prejudicial to the safety or interest of the United States or for the benefit of any foreign government to the detriment of the United States any classified information."[57]

- **Rebellion or insurrection** includes "Whoever incites, sets on foot, assists, or engages in any rebellion or insurrection against the authority of the United States or the laws thereof, or gives aid or comfort thereto. . . ."[58]

- **Advocating overthrow of government** includes "Whoever knowingly or willfully advocates, abets, advises, or teaches the duty, necessity, desirability, or propriety of overthrowing or destroying the government of the United States or the government of any State, Territory, District or Possession thereof, or the government of any political subdivision therein, by force or violence, or by the assassination of any officer of any such government. . . ."[59]

Espionage
Knowingly and willfully communicating, furnishing, transmitting, or otherwise making available to an unauthorized person, or publishing, or using in any manner prejudicial to the safety or interest of the United States, or for the benefit of any foreign government to the detriment of the United States, any classified information.

What took you so long?

Robert Hanssen, after his arrest

HISTORICAL HIGHLIGHT

Hanssen Betrays His Country

On July 6, 2001, former FBI agent Robert Hanssen pled guilty in federal court to fifteen counts of espionage and conspiracy. He did so pursuant to a plea agreement with prosecutors that saved him from a potential death sentence. Hanssen, who worked for the FBI for fifteen years, admitted to spying for the former Soviet Union and later for Russia between 1979 and 1999. Prosecutors alleged that the father of six and long-time FBI agent was paid about $1.4 million in cash and diamonds in exchange for intelligence information. The information included identities of American spies, classified information about eavesdropping technology, and nuclear secrets. Hanssen was accused of compromising dozens of Soviet spies who were working for the United States, some of whom were executed.

Hanssen was caught after leaving a package under a wooden footbridge in a Virginia park when the United States had been given the tip-off by an informant in Russian intelligence that the FBI had a double agent.

The plea agreement provided that in exchange for a guilty plea, Hanssen would receive a life sentence with no possibility of parole and would be required to cooperate with both the FBI and the CIA. He is currently serving his sentence in the Supermax federal prison in Florence, Colorado. His wife will receive part of the pension he would have earned had he retired.

Terrorism
The unlawful use or threat of violence, especially against the state or the public, as a politically motivated means of attack or coercion.

There are also federal laws against acts of **terrorism,** generally defined as the unlawful use or threat of violence especially against the state or the public as a politically motivated means of attack or coercion, which we examine next. We will examine both international and domestic terrorism, as those terms are defined in federal criminal laws.

Terrorism is not a new problem for the United States. In fact, terrorist acts have been the focus of law enforcement with some frequency in the last century and appear likely to continue to be well into the new century.

For example, during the years 1919 and 1920, the nation found itself facing an internal security threat: anarchists who sought to destroy the American government and a modern capitalist world. The most outward sign of this revolutionary fervor was a series of attempted bomb attacks on American institutions and government officials. Beginning in the spring of 1919, government officials like Supreme Court Justice Oliver Wendell Holmes and Attorney General A. Mitchell Palmer received bombs (which did not injure either man). A post office clerk discovered over thirty bombs awaiting delivery in the system in New York. Later the next year, a bomb did go off in the New York City financial district. It had been left in a horse-drawn wagon between a U.S. Treasury office and J.P. Morgan & Company office.

Attorney General Palmer's response was to crack down on those perceived to be radicals. Recent immigrants from southern and eastern Europe were deported, and over 6,000 people were arrested in a roundup Attorney General Palmer alleged would prevent a large-scale terror attack. When no new terror attacks emerged, the crisis ended.[60]

Until the 9/11 attacks, the deadliest terror attack on the United States happened in Oklahoma City, Oklahoma. Timothy McVeigh, a disaffected former soldier who claimed to engage in terror as retaliation for alleged FBI wrongdoing, blew up the Alfred P. Murrah Federal Courthouse with a homemade fertilizer bomb. The explosion killed 168 people, including 19 children, and injured hundreds. McVeigh was tried under federal law and executed by lethal injection on June 11, 2001. He became the first federal prisoner executed since 1963.

Following the 9/11 attacks, Congress passed tough new amendments to the Antiterrorism and Effective Death Penalty Act of 1996. The amendments are commonly referred to as the USA PATRIOT Act of 2001. The Act provides that:

International terrorism
Activities that occur primarily outside U.S. jurisdiction, and involve criminal acts dangerous to human life, including acts of mass destruction, intended to influence the policy of a government by intimidation or coercion or to affect the conduct of a government by assassination or kidnapping.

Domestic terrorism
Activities that occur primarily within U.S. jurisdiction, that involve criminal acts dangerous to human life, and that appear to be intended to intimidate or coerce a civilian population, to influence government policy by intimidation or coercion, or to affect government conduct by mass destruction, assassination, or kidnapping.

- Wiretaps can be obtained to follow the persons whose conversations are sought, rather than being linked to a specific phone. This provision allows investigators to track the conversations of a suspect whether he is using his own phone, a cell phone, or another phone.
- Law enforcement officers, armed with a subpoena, are allowed to seize voice mail and other electronic communication and to obtain information about the means of payment and account numbers.
- Aliens may be detained for seven days without charges being filed.
- The federal criminal code is amended to: (1) revise the definition of **international terrorism** to include activities that appear to be intended to affect the conduct of government by mass destruction; and (2) define **domestic terrorism** as activities that occur primarily within U.S. jurisdiction, that involve criminal acts dangerous to human life, and that appear to be intended to intimidate or coerce a civilian population, to influence

government policy by intimidation or coercion, or to affect government conduct by mass destruction, assassination, or kidnapping.

- Harboring any person knowing or having reasonable grounds to believe that such person has committed or is about to commit a terrorism offense is prohibited.
- There is no statute of limitations for terrorist offenses.

The federal penal code provisions dealing with terrorism are extensive and reach out beyond our borders. In most cases, criminal acts that involve the use of bombs or chemical, biological, or nuclear weapons against Americans abroad or in the United States and that kill those targets are punishable by death. The specific provisions and definitions are found in Title 18, Part I, Chapter 113B of the U.S. Code.

The PATRIOT Act also attempts to limit funding of terrorist organizations. But the law criminalizes providing "material support or resources" to terrorist organizations. This part of the law has been challenged as being too vague because it prevents humanitarian agencies from providing training to entities listed as terrorist groups such as Hamas. Specifically, the Humanitarian Law Project works with Hamas to help build civil government and provide dispute resolution training in the Gaza Strip. They fear this may run them afoul of the law and have sued the government claiming this provision of the Act is so vague as to be unconstitutional. The Supreme Court upheld the law's constitutionality.[61]

Terror Prosecutions

Terror prosecutions would appear to be incident driven. In the aftermath of the September 11 attacks, prosecutors brought charges in approximately two-thirds of the cases referred to them by investigators. As time moved on, however, prosecutors attempted fewer prosecutions. Individuals being investigated for terrorism charges now face only about a one-in-five chance of being prosecuted. Of course, that could change at any time.

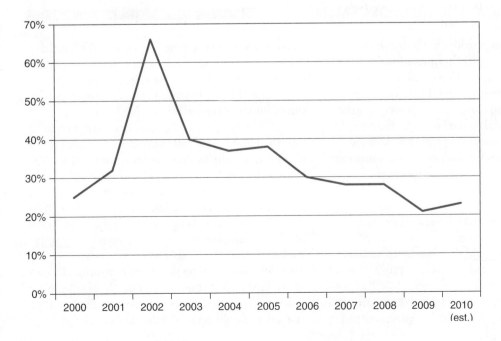

Treason and Terrorism Evidence Concepts

The Constitution clearly requires the government to produce two witnesses to the same overt act or a confession in open court to obtain a treason conviction. The defense may attack the witness' credibility or try to show that their testimony does not actually describe the same overt act.

More troublesome are evidence in terrorism trials. Debate has raged over whether terror suspects are entitled to hear their *Miranda* rights informing them that they have the right to remain silent. Reading *Miranda* not only diminishes the chance of receiving worthwhile intelligence from the suspect, but it also creates a presumption that the suspect will be tried in civilian court. Often, that determination has not been made at the time the suspect is first questioned.

Suspects tried in civilian courts would be tried by federal rules of evidence. Because many key terror suspects have been interrogated without the benefit of counsel and have been subjected to sleep deprivation, water boarding and what many would call torture, confessions or testimony against other terror suspects would not be admissible in civilian courts.

To address this situation, Congress passed the Military Commissions Act of 2009, which creates a presumption against admitting testimony obtained through torture. The Act directs the secretary of defense to develop rules for introducing evidence from interrogations into military tribunals. Those rules were due ninety days after the law was signed in October 2009. However, that deadline has come and gone without even a draft of the document submitted for public comment. The rules developed under the Military Commissions Act of 2006 are available at www.loc.gov/rr/frd/Military_Law/pdf/manual-mil-commissions.pdf.[62]

CONCEPT **REVIEW AND REINFORCEMENT**

The U.S. Constitution provides the framework for much of the law that applies in times of war or domestic turmoil. First, the Constitution sets forth the power of both Congress and the president in time of war. It gives to Congress the power to make declarations of war and to the president the role of commander in chief. Once Congress has declared war, the president exercises his power as commander in chief to set, execute, and achieve war goals.

The power to conduct war has led presidents to order groups suspected of disloyalty into internment camps and suspected saboteurs tried by military commissions. In each of these two examples, the Supreme Court upheld the presidents' actions by finding that the procedures were authorized by Congressional legislation.

The Constitution also defines treason and sets strict standards required to find someone guilty of treason. Treason is levying war against the United States, or in adhering to their enemies, giving them aid and comfort. Treason must be proven by the testimony of two witnesses to the same overt act, or the defendant's confession in open court.

Congress has passed other laws designed to punish activities that fall short of treason, but that harm the security of the country or its citizens. Examples include criminal laws punishing the disclosure of classified information to unauthorized persons or foreign countries.

Congress has also passed federal criminal laws outlawing activities that may be crimes under state law but the commission of which has as an intention undermining governmental authority or intimidating the population. Thus, the bombing of abortion clinics by domestic terrorists, the leveling of a federal building in Oklahoma City, or the destruction of U.S. embassies overseas have been labeled as terrorist acts and prosecuted accordingly.

The September 11 attacks and subsequent capture of terror suspects in Afghanistan have created challenges as the government tries to balance the need to obtain intelligence to defeat the terrorists and prevent future attacks against the rights of detainees. President Bush created the term *enemy combatant* to categorize those who fought against the United States in Afghanistan,

but did not do so under the flag of another nation. The term also applies to terror suspects associated with al-Qaeda captured throughout the world. Through a series of laws and court decisions, detainees have obtained the right to challenge their designation as enemy combatants and to seek to have their trial moved to civilian courts. The Military Commissions Act of 2009 sought to clarify which trials went before military tribunals and which did not.

KEY **TERMS**

Domestic terrorism
Espionage
Habeas corpus
International terrorism

Letters of marque and reprisal
Military tribunal
Power to declare war
Sedition

Terrorism
Treason

CONCEPT **REVIEW** **QUESTIONS**

1. List wartime criminal laws through history.
2. List and explain the provisions in the U.S. Constitution that govern the powers of Congress and the president in time of war.
3. Define treason and list and explain the provisions in the U.S. Constitution that apply to treason.
4. List the elements of treason and sedition.

5. List two federal laws that define and punish terrorist acts.
6. List the major provisions of the PATRIOT Act of 2001.
7. List key presidential orders for military tribunals in time of war or armed conflict.

CASE **APPLICATIONS**

Building Your Professional Skills

1. Consider the following case: Lynne Stewart is a former attorney (having been automatically disbarred following the conviction that is the subject of this exercise) who once represented Sheikh Omar Abdel-Rahman. The Sheikh is the so-called "blind cleric" who is imprisoned for his involvement in the first World Trade Center bombing. He is also reportedly the mastermind behind the 1997 murder of 58 tourists in Luxor, Egypt.

As a condition of her representation of the Sheikh, Stewart agreed to not pass any information or comments made by her client to the press. Apparently, the government feared that her client could direct further terror attacks from his cell and suspected that he might attempt to send coded messages through the media.

Unbeknownst to Stewart, all her conversations with her client, which were conducted with the help of a translator, were recorded. Stewart and the translator were charged with giving material support to terrorists, based in part on a press release by Stewart that purportedly stated the Sheikh had withdrawn his support for a ceasefire in his home country of Egypt. This statement the government later said amounted to

Stewart's passing on of a "fatwa" or religious order to commit terror acts against Americans and others.

A federal jury convicted Stewart of the charges, after they listened to hundreds of hours of taped conversations between Stewart and her client. Stewart was convicted of conspiracy to provide and conceal material support to the conspiracy to murder persons in a foreign country (18 U.S.C. sec. 2339A and 18 U.S.C. sec. 2), conspiring to provide and conceal such support (18 U.S.C. sec. 371), and knowingly and willfully making false statements (18 U.S.C. sec. 1001). The judge sentenced her to 28 months in prison, but allowed her to remain free pending appeal. The Second Circuit Court of Appeals then denied her appeal and ordered her to jail and ordered the trial judge to review the sentence for possible enhancement. At least one of the judges called the 28-month sentence "shockingly" light.

QUESTIONS

1. Do you think attorneys should be allowed to speak freely with their clients without the fear that their conversations will be recorded?
2. Is releasing a statement by a client to the press a criminal act?
3. Would your answer change if Stewart had promised, as a condition of representing the cleric, that she would not pass any messages to the outside?

2. Until recently, it seemed unlikely that those working in the criminal justice system would have to work with terrorism statutes to bring alleged terrorists to justice or to defend them. That recently changed when Attorney General Eric Holder announced that some of the Guantanamo detainees would be transferred to the federal court system in order to face trial. His announcement follows. Read it and answer the questions that follow.

> Good morning. Just over eight years ago, on a morning our nation will never forget, nineteen hijackers working with a network of Al Qaeda conspirators around the world launched the deadliest terrorist attacks our country has ever seen. Nearly 3,000 people lost their lives in those attacks, and in the years since, our nation has had no higher priority than bringing those who planned and plotted the attacks to justice.
>
> One year before, in October 2000, a terrorist attack on the USS Cole killed seventeen American sailors.
>
> Today we announce a step forward in bringing those we believe were responsible for the 9/11 attacks and the attack on the USS Cole to justice.
>
> Five detainees at Guantanamo have been charged before military commissions with participation in the 9/11 plot: Khalid Sheikh Mohammed, Walid Muhammed Salih Mubarak Bin Attash, Ramzi Bin Al Shibh, Ali Abdul-Aziz Ali, and Mustafa Ahmed Al Hawsawi. Those proceedings have been stayed since February, as have the proceedings pending in military commissions against four other detainees accused of different crimes. A case in military commissions against the alleged mastermind of the Cole bombing, Abd al-Rahim al-Nashiri, was withdrawn in February.
>
> For the past several months, prosecutors at the Department of Justice have been working diligently with prosecutors from the Pentagon's Office of Military Commissions to review the case of each detainee at Guantanamo who has been referred for prosecution. Over the past few weeks, I have personally reviewed these cases, and in consultation with the Secretary of Defense, have made determinations about the prosecution of ten detainees now held at Guantanamo, including those charged in the 9/11 plot and the alleged mastermind of the Cole bombing.
>
> Today, I am announcing that the Department of Justice will pursue prosecution in federal court of the five individuals accused of conspiring to commit the 9/11 attacks. Further, I have decided to refer back to the Department of Defense five defendants to face military commission trials, including the detainee who was previously charged in the USS Cole bombing.
>
> The 9/11 cases that will be pursued in federal court have been jointly assigned to prosecutors from the Southern District of New York and the Eastern District of

Virginia and will be brought in Manhattan in the Southern District of New York. After eight years of delay, those allegedly responsible for the attacks of September the 11th will finally face justice. They will be brought to New York—to New York—to answer for their alleged crimes in a courthouse just blocks from where the twin towers once stood.

I am confident in the ability of our courts to provide these defendants a fair trial, just as they have for over 200 years. The alleged 9/11 conspirators will stand trial in our justice system before an impartial jury under long-established rules and procedures.

I also want to assure the American people that we will prosecute these cases vigorously, and we will pursue the maximum punishment available. These were extraordinary crimes and so we will seek maximum penalties. Federal rules allow us to seek the death penalty for capital offenses, and while we will review the evidence and circumstances following established protocols, I fully expect to direct prosecutors to seek the death penalty against each of the alleged 9/11 conspirators.

In his speech at the National Archives in May, the President called for the reform of military commissions to ensure that they are a lawful, fair, and effective prosecutorial forum. The reforms Congress recently adopted to the Military Commissions Act ensure that military commission trials will be fair and that convictions obtained will be secure.

I know that the Department of Defense is absolutely committed to ensuring that military commission trials will be consistent with our highest standards as a nation, and our civilian prosecutors will continue to work closely with military prosecutors to support them in that effort.

In each case, my decision as to whether to proceed in federal courts or military commissions was based on a protocol that the Departments of Justice and Defense developed and that was announced in July. Because many cases could be prosecuted in either federal courts or military commissions, that protocol sets forth a number of factors—including the nature of the offense, the location in which the offense occurred, the identity of the victims, and the manner in which the case was investigated—that must be considered. In consultation again with the Secretary of Defense, I looked at all the relevant factors and made case by case decisions for each detainee.

It is important that we be able to use every forum possible to hold terrorists accountable for their actions. Just as a sustained campaign against terrorism requires a combination of intelligence, law enforcement and military operations, so must our legal efforts to bring terrorists to justice involve both federal courts and reformed military commissions. I want to thank the members of Congress, including Senators Lindsay Graham, Carl Levin and John McCain who worked so hard to strengthen our national security by helping us pass legislation to reform the military commission system.

We will continue to draw on the Pentagon's support as we bring cases against the alleged 9-11 conspirators in federal court. The Justice Department has a long and a successful history of prosecuting terrorists for their crimes against our nation, particularly in New York. Although these cases can often be complex and challenging, federal prosecutors have successfully met these challenges and have convicted a number of terrorists who are now serving lengthy sentences in our prisons. And although the security issues presented by terrorism cases should never be minimized, our marshals, our court security officers, and our prison officials have extensive experience and training dealing with dangerous defendants, and I am quite confident they can meet the security challenges posed by this case.

These detainees will not be transferred to the United States for prosecution until all legal requirements are satisfied, including those in recent legislation requiring a 45 day notice and report to the Congress. I have already spoken this morning to Governor Paterson and Mayor Bloomberg and am committed to working closely with them to ensure that all security and related concerns are properly addressed. I have every confidence that we can safely hold these trials in New York, as we have so many previous terrorism trials.

For the many Americans who lost friends and relatives in the attacks of September 11, 2001 and on the USS Cole, nothing can bring back those loved ones back. But they deserve the opportunity to see the alleged plotters of those attacks held accountable in open court, an opportunity that has been too long delayed. Today's announcements mark a significant step forward in our efforts to close Guantanamo and to bring to justice those individuals who have conspired to attack our nation and our interests abroad.

For over two hundred years, our nation has relied on a faithful adherence to the rule of law to bring criminals to justice and provide accountability to victims. Once again we will ask our legal system, in two venues, to rise to that challenge. I am confident it will answer the call with fairness and justice."

QUESTIONS

1. Based on what you have learned so far in this chapter and in earlier chapters, what do you think are some of the likely charges that may be brought against the individuals Mr. Holder has said will be tried in federal court?

2. If you were working for the defense, what concerns, practical and legal, might you have about participating in the case?

CRITICAL **THINKING EXERCISES**

1. A political commentator criticizes the current administration and vows to "take the country back" and displays the faces of senators facing re-election with gun-sight crosshairs over their faces. A prosecutor claims these are statements of sedition. You are retained as the defense attorney. How do you defend the commentator?

2. Same set of facts as Question 1, except this time the prosecutor is charging treason. How do you defend the commentator?

3. You are an attorney. A client comes to you who has been accused of "providing material support and resources" to a terrorist group. She claims she gave money to an Islamic charity fighting poverty in the West Bank. How do you defend her?

4. You are investigating a terrorist cell. You wish to monitor all phone calls that a person of interest in the case makes. What power does the PATRIOT Act give you to do this?

PORTFOLIO **BUILDING**

1. Typically, investigative agencies such as the FBI take the lead in building terrorism cases that do not involve individuals caught on the battlefield and then refer those cases to the Department of Justice for possible prosecution. Syracuse University tracks such referrals and subsequent prosecutions. Examine their statistics and write a memo tracing the number of referrals and prosecutions in the years since 2001 (http://trac.syr.edu/tracreports/index.html).

2. Those who work at defending suspects accused of planning or committing terror acts or of aiding and abetting such acts may want to seek information or assistance from several groups interested in the larger issues raised by new enforcement realities like the PATRIOT Act and the prospect of military tribunals. Visit the websites for the following organizations and summarize in your portfolio what each organization does:

- Center for Constitutional Rights, a New York group initially organized to defend civil rights protesters in the 1960s, at http://ccrjustice.org/
- The Cato Institute, a group known for championing "conservative" causes, at www.cato.org
- People for the American Way, a Washington area group known for championing "liberal" causes, at www.pfaw.org
- The American Civil Liberties Union, at www.aclu.org
- National Association of Criminal Defense Lawyers, at www.nacdl.org

FOR FURTHER READING

BOOKS

1. Chapin, B. (1971). *American Law of Treason: Revolutionary and Early National Origins.* University of Washington Press.
2. Hurst, J. W. (1971). *The Law of Treason in the United States: Collected Essays (Contributions in American History, No. 12).* Greenwood Publishing.
3. Vise, D. (2001). "The Bureau and the Mole: The Unmasking of Robert Philip Hanssen, the Most Dangerous Double Agent in FBI History." *Atlantic Monthly.*
4. Vidal, G. (2000). *Burr.* Vintage Books. Fictional account of the Burr affair.
5. Goldenberg, E. (1993). *The Spy Who Knew Too Much: The Government Plot to Silence Jonathan Pollard.* SPI Book. Another true spy-catching story.
6. Scottoline, L. (2004). *Killer Smile.* Harper Collins. Legal thriller set in 2004, but exploring what happened to an Italian immigrant interned during WWII. Ms. Scottoline's parents were required to register as alien enemies during WWII even though they had made their home in Philadelphia for decades.
7. Dobbs, M. (2004). *Saboteurs: The Nazi Raid on America.* Alfred A. Knopf. This recent account of the Nazis tried by military tribunals during WWII includes recently unearthed material from the National Archives.
8. Otsuka, J. (2004). *When the Emperor Was Divine.* Penguin Books. This short novel tells the story of a Japanese American family sent to the camps during WWII.

FILMS

1. *The Wind and the Lion,* a 1975 film telling the story of an American woman and her children who were kidnapped by a Berber tribe in 1904 and rescued by the application of Teddy Roosevelt's Big Stick policy; stars Candice Bergen, Brian Keith, and Sean Connery.
2. *The Spy Who Came in From the Cold,* a 1965 classic Cold War thriller based on John LeCarre's book of the same name; stars Richard Burton.
3. *Black Sunday,* a 1976 thriller in which Palestinian terrorists try to wipe out the crowd at the Super Bowl; stars Robert Shaw and Bruce Dern.
4. *The Day of the Jackal,* a 1973 thriller, deals with an attempted assassination of Charles de Gaulle and is a chilling look at the cool composure of someone capable of terrorist acts.
5. *The Eye of the Needle* stars Donald Sunderland as a Nazi spy in England who must deliver information about Britain's military capacity directly to Hitler. This 1981 thriller has a surprise ending.
6. *The Year of Living Dangerously* is a 1983 Mel Gibson, Linda Hunt, and Sigourney Weaver film set in 1965 Jakarta during the political upheavals that were threatening to collapse the unstable government of President Sukarno.
7. *The Ugly American,* featuring Marlon Brando, is the film adaptation of Eugene Burdick's Cold War thriller based loosely on Vietnam.
8. *The Little Drummer Girl* stars Diane Keaton as a left-wing pro-Palestinian actress recruited to spy for Israel.
9. *Breach,* starring Chris Cooper as FBI-turned-Soviet mole Robert Hanssen.
10. *The Good Shepherd* starring Matt Damon and Angelina Jolie in a fictionalized account of the founding of the Central Intelligence Agency and its early years.

Chapter **nine**

CRIMES AGAINST THE STATE

CHAPTER OBJECTIVES

After studying this chapter, you should be able to:

- Understand the significance of perjury
- Explain the essential elements of obstruction of justice
- Understand the different types of contempt
- Understand how escape affects sentencing
- Know what constitutes bribery
- Explain the ways that the government seeks to control corrupt organizations
- Explain the steps in the impeachment process
- Explain what constitutes tax evasion
- Explain what constitutes mail fraud

A single witness shall not rise up against a man on account of any iniquity or any sin he has committed; on the evidence of two or three witnesses a matter shall be confirmed.

Deuteronomy 19:15

Introduction

Every system of government must establish laws that protect its own integrity. The American system drew heavily on its English heritage to enact laws that preserve the public's trust in its institutions. Crimes like perjury, obstruction of justice, and contempt are committed by those who seek to thwart our judicial system's proper operation. The system simply could not function if no steps were taken to counter these crimes. Simply put, our legal system cannot function if the people do not trust that it delivers fair and impartial judgments most of the time.

The natural law tradition that governments exist by the consent of the governed demands that political officials have a duty to the people. Bribery, the selling of an office, constitutes a betrayal of that duty. In addition, much of the proper functioning of government relies on the integrity of the people who work within it. When corrupt officials lack that integrity and refuse to leave office voluntarily, government must use its impeachment power to remove them and restore integrity to the system.

Corrupt organizations also pose a threat to government, often by seeking to usurp government's role. Organized crime operations may, for example, offer "protection" for businesses in exchange for a "contribution." Legitimate government's battle with organized crime has been a long and arduous one. We will examine some of the laws crafted to disrupt the operations of corrupt organizations and punish the operators.

Unfortunately, the very guarantees that undergird a free society sometimes create a refuge for criminals. When writing laws governing crimes against the state, the battle has always been to structure laws that prevent corruption and preserve liberty. As you will see, that means that those engaged in sophisticated criminal activities are sometimes difficult to catch and punish.

Perjury

Perjury is defined as "giving false testimony in a judicial proceeding or an administrative proceeding, lying under oath as to a material fact, swearing to the truth of anything one knows or believes to be false."[1] Obviously, telling the truth is vital to the judicial system's integrity. Judges and juries often base decisions on witness testimony, and false testimony may mean unjust conviction. False convictions impair the integrity of the justice system, and injure us all. Therefore, perjury is a very serious crime against the state.

Under federal law there are three types of perjury. The first type, often referred to as section 1621 perjury (for the section of the U.S. code describing it— 18 U.S.C. § 1621), is a general giving of false testimony. Section 1621 perjury is the broadest of the three types of perjury. It applies to all material statements or information provided under oath "to a competent tribunal, officer, or person, in any case in which a law of the United States authorizes an oath to be administered." It is not limited to testimony in court, but includes any sworn statement to a government official or representative. Students seeking federal financial aid, for example, may commit perjury if they provide false or misleading information on the Free Application for Federal Student Aid (FAFSA).

The second type of perjury is section 1623 perjury (18 U.S.C. § 1623). Section 1623 perjury is false testimony given in court or before a grand jury. Unlike the general giving of false testimony, this type is limited to court and grand jury testimony.

The third type is subornation of perjury (18 U.S.C. § 1622). **Subornation of perjury** is defined as convincing or seeking to convince another person to commit perjury. In order to be convicted of subornation of perjury, a person must convince another to commit perjury, and that person must then actually perjure himself or herself.

Every state has its own set of criminal laws punishing perjury and other forms of dishonest testimony or representation. For example, Pennsylvania has a criminal offense called "Unsworn Falsification to Authorities," which provides that a

> person commits a misdemeanor of the second degree if, with intent to mislead a public servant in performing his official function, he . . . makes any written false statement which he does not believe to be true.[2]

Differences between Section 1621 and Section 1623 Perjury

The Two-Witness Rule   Section 1621 perjury has its origins in Common Law concepts of perjury. Under Common Law, a person could not be convicted of perjury unless two people testified that the alleged perjurer's statements were not true. This is called the **two-witness rule.** The 1621 section carries on this Common Law tradition, but with some modifications. For example, physical evidence that corroborates

---

But who is to guard the guard themselves?

Juvenal, in *Satires*

Perjury
Giving false testimony in a judicial or administrative proceeding; lying under oath as to a material fact; swearing to the truth of anything one knows or believes to be false.

Subornation of perjury
Convincing or seeking to convince another person to commit perjury.

Two-witness rule
The Common Law rule that requires two witnesses to testify to another's perjury in order for a conviction to take place.

testimony satisfies the two-witness rule. That is, if the prosecution presents one witness who testifies that the defendant lied and an additional piece of physical evidence that corroborated the testimony, the rule is satisfied.

Section 1623 requires that "proof beyond a reasonable doubt . . . is sufficient for conviction."[3] In other words, the proof may take any form—physical evidence, testimony, or any other type of proof. The standard of proof is thus lower than for section 1621 perjury. Stated another way, proving section 1621 perjury requires a stricter standard than is required for most other crimes. The two-witness rule specifically does not apply to section 1623 cases. You may recall from the last chapter that there is another crime that requires this higher level of proof for conviction—treason.

Recantation
The retraction of testimony.

Another key difference between section 1621 and section 1623 is what occurs when a witness recants his or her testimony. **Recantation** is the retraction of testimony. Under section 1621, even if a witness recants his or her testimony, he or she can still be prosecuted for perjury.[4] However, under section 1623, a witness can recant testimony during the same proceeding as long as that testimony has not "substantially affected the proceeding."[5]

Another important difference comes into play when a witness contradicts himself or herself on the stand. Under section 1621, the government must prove which of the contradictory statements is false. However, section 1623 places no such burden on the prosecution. Contradictory statements are sufficient for conviction in and of themselves.[6]

Elements of Perjury   The elements of perjury are:

- An oath
- Intent
- Falsity
- Materiality

An Oath   Perjury can only occur if a false statement is made under oath to speak truthfully. There is no standard wording for the oath, but a legally authorized person must administer the oath. The authority for administering the oath can be derived from law, rules, or regulation. Rules and regulations often govern administrative proceedings, but the oath is just as valid in these cases as it would be in a courtroom. Consequently, sworn false statements in administrative hearings can be prosecuted under perjury statutes.

Intent   Under both sections 1621 and 1623, the person giving the false testimony must be aware that what he or she is saying is false and must intend to mislead by giving the false testimony.

Falsity   In any perjury or subornation of perjury case, the falsity of the statement in question must be proved beyond a reasonable doubt in order to secure a conviction.

Materiality   In order to qualify as perjury, a statement must be material to a case. Lying about something of no consequence is not a crime. A statement is material if it is likely that the case or matter in which the falsehood was presented was influenced by it. In other words, if the statement had the possibility of influencing the outcome of a proceeding, it is material. A witness who tells the court that he had scrambled eggs for breakfast when he had pancakes is not guilty of perjury unless what he had for breakfast is relevant to the case.

Defenses to Perjury   The defenses to perjury are:

- Recantation
- Assistance of counsel
- Double jeopardy
- The "perjury trap"
- Fifth Amendment

Recantation   Recantation, as noted earlier, is the retraction of earlier testimony. Recantation traditionally has not done well as a defense, but is most effective when the defendant uses recantation to demonstrate that there was no criminal intent in testifying falsely. In other words, recantation is used to clarify statements later discovered to have been misleading or in error. A defendant, in effect, explains away his or her earlier statements by "clarifying" them.

Assistance of Counsel   Sometimes witnesses called to testify don't consult with an attorney before testifying, and thus may never know that being less than truthful can be a crime. There is no requirement, however, that a witness be told he or she can consult with an attorney. However, a witness can assert that he or she testified on the advice of counsel. In this case, the defendant eliminates the element of intent if he or she can prove the testimony was given in good faith on bad advice.

Double Jeopardy   The double jeopardy defense can be raised when the defendant's acquittal in a criminal trial was based on the jury believing his or her untrue testimony.[7] Prosecutions for perjury after an acquittal sometimes give the appearance of being a vindictive prosecution. There is no blanket prohibition against prosecuting someone for perjury in a case where he or she was the defendant. As a practical matter, it seldom happens.

HISTORICAL HIGHLIGHT

The Anglo-Saxon Way to the Truth: Oath-Helpers and Trial by Ordeal

In the tribal society of Anglo-Saxon England, two very important things were a man's reputation and the perceived "will of God." A person's reputation was measured by the number of "oath-helpers" he could find to speak on his behalf when accused of a crime.

If a person was accused of a crime and maintained his innocence, he could bring in oath-helpers. They would take an oath swearing that the accused was telling the truth. The oath read: "In the name of Almighty God, so I stand here in true witness, unbidden and unbought, as I saw with my eyes and heard with my ears that which I pronounce with him." The oath-helper was not required to testify or present evidence; he merely stated that he believed the accused. In most cases, this was enough for charges to be dropped.

However, if the court still had reason to doubt the accused's innocence, it could employ trial by ordeal. The Church administered the trial by ordeal. It was seen as a way of determining the will of God. The trial began with three days of fasting and a mass. The accused had the opportunity to confess if he chose. If he insisted he was innocent, he was offered the choice between the water or iron ordeal.

The water ordeal came in two varieties, hot and cold. The cold water ordeal involved the accused drinking holy water, and then being thrown into a river. If he floated, he was guilty. If he was innocent, he sank. With any luck, the innocent were fished out before they drowned.

The hot water ordeal involved the accused reaching into boiling water to retrieve a stone. In the iron ordeal, the accused had to carry a red-hot iron bar nine feet. In both cases the accused's hands were bandaged, and if the wounds did not fester in three days, he was pronounced innocent. Contrary to popular belief, the trial by ordeal was not used to force confessions, but rather as a good faith attempt to ascertain divine truth. All in all, it was probably a good idea to avoid being accused of a crime in the first place.[8]

Trial by ordeal has fortunately disappeared from criminal courts, but the use of "oath helpers" survives in the form of character witnesses.

Perjury trap
A situation where a grand jury subpoenas a witness for the sole purpose of obtaining perjured testimony.

Witness tampering
An illegal attempt to influence a witness' sworn testimony.

The Perjury Trap   Grand juries often serve an investigative function. They can call witnesses and seek out evidence in a case in order to decide whether there are grounds to charge someone with a crime. Zealous prosecutors may sometimes use the grand jury's power to attempt to force a witness to provide testimony contradicting what he or she told investigators. The witness is then caught in the **perjury trap.** If the witness tells the truth this time, it is the same as admitting the earlier testimony was a lie. If the witness lies again, the prosecutor may file additional charges. If the witness can prove that the prosecutor's main purpose in subpoenaing the witness was to force the witness into the perjury trap, the witness may be able to defend against any subsequent perjury prosecution.

Fifth Amendment   As you learned earlier, the Fifth Amendment to the Constitution protects an accused person from self-incrimination. A witness may invoke Fifth Amendment immunity ("Taking the Fifth") if testifying leaves the witness with the choice of committing perjury or proving the witness committed perjury earlier.

When an individual asks or coerces another person into committing perjury it is subornation of perjury. If you ask someone to perjure themselves and they do not you have not suborned perjury. You may be guilty of **witness tampering** or attempting to obstruct justice though. If the person commits perjury at your behest, you are guilty of suborning perjury and that individual is guilty of perjury. That individual may assert the Common Law defense of duress, arguing that you threatened that individual with some consequences unless he or she committed perjury (see Chapter 10, Common Law Defenses).

When we think of subornation of perjury, we generally think of mobsters threatening to do someone bodily harm if they don't lie on the stand. But what happens when officers of the court or even the police coerce someone into lying in court? In a case in Iowa, two men, Terry Harrington and Curtis W. McGhee Jr., were convicted for killing a security guard at an auto dealership largely on the testimony of a sixteen-year-old auto thief who faced significant legal troubles of his own. The men went to prison, but continued to profess their innocence. Harrington told his story to prison employee Anne Danaher, who began her own independent investigation. She found that the auto thief had changed his story many times before telling the one police wanted him to tell. He had been promised a $5,000 reward if he helped solve the crime. She also found that the murder victim had noted in his security log from the night before his death that a man with a shotgun and a dog had approached the dealership and the guard had told him to leave. The guard was killed by a shotgun blast the next night. Witnesses identified the man with the gun and the dog to police and prosecutors, but they never revealed this to Harrington and McGhee's defense teams. The Iowa Supreme Court eventually freed the two men. They sued the prosecutors and police for defamation and denial of civil rights. All defendants asserted sovereign immunity, but the court ultimately allowed charges against the prosecutors to go forward finding that violating "a person's substantive due process rights by obtaining, manufacturing, coercing and fabricating evidence . . . was not a prosecutorial function" and was therefore outside the scope of their employment for the county.[9]

Obstruction of Justice

Closely related to perjury is **obstruction of justice.** Obstruction of justice is defined as "the crime of impeding or hindering the administration of justice in any way." *Obstruction of justice* is a broad term that may apply to many different types of activities. Witness tampering or intimidation, jury tampering, or even suborning perjury can be forms of obstruction of justice. At the heart of the crime is interfering with the full and fair administration of justice. For example, prosecutors or police officers who hide, tamper with, or destroy evidence can be charged with obstruction of justice, as can defendants who threaten or bribe witnesses.

> **Obstruction of justice**
> The crime of impeding or hindering the administration of justice in any way.

Elements   In order to prove the crime of obstruction of justice, the following elements must be satisfied:

- There is a pending judicial proceeding.
- The defendant knew of the proceeding.
- The defendant acted corruptly with the specific intent to obstruct or interfere with the proceeding or due administration of justice.[10]

Pending Proceedings   A proceeding must be pending in order to charge obstruction of justice. A person believing that an investigation may begin can be convicted of obstruction of justice if he or she takes action that may destroy evidence. Consider this example. A police department is running out of space to keep evidence collected over the years, including evidence used in prior cases that have concluded and the final appeal completed. If the department decided to dispose of old evidence, they may do so. However, if the department has reason to believe the evidence in a particular case is tainted, has been tampered with, or will be needed in a pending appeal, it would be obstruction of justice to destroy it.

In recent years, there has been a dramatic improvement in the use of scientific evaluation of evidence. There have been cases in which new scientific tests on old evidence have either confirmed to a high degree of probability that the convicted individual was guilty or proven that he was innocent. These new tests have been performed on evidence that in some cases had been in storage for decades. Because of this, some legislatures have proposed extending the time that those holding evidence must store and maintain it.

Knowledge   Very simply, the defendant must have known a judicial proceeding was pending in order to form the intent to obstruct justice—no knowledge, no intent, no crime.

Acting Corruptly with Intent to Obstruct Justice   The defendant must intentionally commit an act designed to disrupt a judicial proceeding. The act must occur in a time frame that is consistent with that purpose. In order to act "corruptly," the act must be done with the intent of obstructing justice. The term *corruptly* means acting with an improper purpose, personally or by influencing another, including making a false or misleading statement, or withholding, concealing, altering, or destroying a document or other information.[11]

The defendant need not succeed in obstructing justice, but only in attempting to. He or she must "endeavor" to obstruct justice.[12] Endeavor is loosely defined to mean any effort carried out with the intent of obstructing justice. It is not limited to any one or group of activities, but applies generally to any attempt to obstruct justice.[13]

Types of Obstruction   Obstruction of justice can take many forms, but the actions generally prosecuted under the federal statute fall into three groups. The first group involves hiding, changing, or destroying relevant documents such as court records, the second is encouraging or giving false testimony, and the third group is comprised of offenses involving intimidation, threats, or other harm to witnesses, jurors, judges, or others involved in legal proceedings or investigations in an attempt to prevent or shape their testimony or judgment. Examples of obstruction under federal law include:

> 18 U.S.C. § 1503. Influencing or Injuring Officer or Juror Generally
>
> 18 U.S.C. § 1504. Influencing Juror by Writing
>
> 18 U.S.C. § 1505. Obstruction of Proceedings Before Departments, Agencies
>
> 18 U.S.C. § 1506. Theft or Alteration of Record or Process
>
> 18 U.S.C. § 1509. Obstruction of Court Orders
>
> 18 U.S.C. § 1510. Obstruction of Criminal Investigations
>
> 18 U.S.C. § 1511. Obstruction of State or Local Law Enforcement
>
> 18 U.S.C. § 1512. Tampering with a Witness, Victim, or an Informant
>
> 18 U.S.C. § 1513. Retaliating Against a Witness, Victim, or an Informant
>
> 18 U.S.C. § 1516. Obstruction of Federal Audit
>
> 18 U.S.C. § 1517. Obstructing Examination of Financial Institution
>
> 18 U.S.C. § 1518. Obstruction of Criminal Investigations of Health Care Offenses

States have similar statutes in place that apply to state investigations and legal proceedings.

HISTORICAL HIGHLIGHT

Did Chemists Obstruct Justice?

The legal system depends on the integrity of the participants. This is especially true of those who are called to testify as experts about scientific evidence. In many criminal cases, the outcome of the case depends on the scientific analysis of bits of evidence found at the scene of the crime implicating the defendant. Take DNA evidence. Scientific analysis of hair, body fluids, and other organic matter can exclude or implicate the defendant. What happens if the presumably neutral scientists, who perform the tests and inform the jury of their conclusions, do sloppy and unreliable work or even worse? What if they actually lie?

Take, for example, the work of serologist Fred Zain. Mr. Zain has twice been tried by the state of West Virginia for defrauding the state and lying under oath in dozens of criminal cases. He headed up the serology unit of the West Virginia State Police crime lab. So far, no jury has convicted him. Both times, the jury was hung six–six on all charges. However, five men have had their convictions overturned because of errors in the tests Zain performed on evidence used to convict them. Many others are asking for new DNA testing of the evidence used to convict them.[14]

Then there is the mess in which Oklahoma had found itself. There, chemist Joyce Gilchrist is alleged to have falsified evidence reports in perhaps hundreds of cases before she was fired in September 2001. Reexamination of her work has freed a convicted rapist, a death row inmate, overturned another death sentence, and may call into question the guilt of one man who was executed. Malcolm Johnson was executed in January 2000 for the rape and murder of an Oklahoma City woman. He claimed that he was innocent, but Gilchrist had testified that semen found at the scene was consistent with Johnson's blood type. Later examination of the slides Gilchrist reviewed showed no semen present.[15]

Finally, there are the numerous cases handled by Pennsylvania State Police chemist Janice Roadcap.[16] In 1987, she testified at the trail of Barry Laughman, who was accused of raping and murdering an elderly distant relative who lived nearby. Roadcap testified that the semen on the victim's body matched Laughman's blood type. When police claimed that Laughman, a mildly retarded man, confessed to the crime it seemed like an open and shut case. In 1994, after DNA evidence gained credibility, Laughman's court-appointed attorney sent the semen sample to a Penn State professor for analysis. The professor asked for a comparative sample, but the court-appointed attorney never responded. Had he responded, the tests would have cleared Laughman and shown Roadcap's testimony to be wrong.

But Janice Roadcap had other skeletons in her laboratory. John Eddie Mitchell was thirteen in 1970 when he was brutally murdered inside a garage belonging to Steven Crawford's family in Harrisburg, Pennsylvania. The garage was open and many neighborhood children played there. Four years after the murder, the State Police charged Crawford, who was a year older than Mitchell at the time of the murder, with bludgeoning the boy and stealing the $32 he had collected on his paper route.

The key prosecution theory was the blood splattered on handprints on a car in the garage. Everyone agreed the handprints belonged to Crawford. According to Roadcap's testimony, because the blood was only on the ridges of the palm prints, the blood must have been on Crawford's hands when he touched the car. This evidence was used to convict Crawford three times—in 1974, 1977, and 1978.

Chief investigator Walton Simpson kept Roadcap's notes even after he retired. Simpson died in 1994, and the notes became part of his estate. Two youths found the documents in 2001, and turned them over to Dauphin County prosecutors. The notes show that Roadcap had found blood in the valleys of Crawford's handprints but testified otherwise at his trial. Crawford was released in 2002, and in 2006 Roadcap and the Pennsylvania Attorney General's office settled a federal lawsuit filed by Crawford.[17]

Because juries these days, fed on a steady diet of *CSI* and *Court TV*, put particular stock in forensic evidence, the reliability of that evidence is crucial to a fair trial. Tampering with, lying about, or otherwise misstating what forensic evidence means is a serious matter.

YOU MAKE THE CALL: THE DUKE RAPE CASE

Did the Duke Prosecutor Obstruct Justice?

District Attorney Richard Nifong used the alleged rape victim's eyewitness testimony to pursue three members of the Duke University Lacrosse team. According to the African-American exotic dancer, the three white players—Reade Seligmann, Collin Finerty, and David Evans—cornered her in a bathroom after she had danced for the entire group and gang-raped her.

But her story changed repeatedly in subsequent interviews. As the racially charged case moved toward prosecution, Nifong needed physical evidence to back his waffling witness' account. But Nifong had a problem: the DNA recovered in the rape kit didn't match any of the three Lacrosse players.

Nifong made the contract technician agree not to disclose this fact to the Lacrosse players' attorneys. Only under cross-examination in court did the technician reveal that no DNA linked the players to the alleged rape. The charges were dropped on December 22, 2006, eight months after Nifong knew of the DNA results.

YOU MAKE THE CALL: Did Nifong's refusal to turn over exculpatory evidence to the lacrosse players' attorneys constitute obstruction of justice? See some of the documents for this chapter on the companion website to help you decide.

Civil Disobedience, Trespass, and Protest

The Bill of Rights prohibits government from limiting American citizens' freedom of speech. Originally viewed as an individual right, large-scale political movements took legal cover under the First Amendment to produce mass demonstrations. Adherents of the Indian ascetic Mahatma Gandhi such as the Reverend Doctor Martin Luther King Jr. used nonviolent protests to focus national and international attention on the plight of African Americans.

Gandhi and King advocated a protest form popular among nineteenth-century American transcendentalists known as civil disobedience. Civil disobedience was used to show that a particular law or practice was unconscionable and should be repealed. For instance, in 1957 buses in Montgomery, Alabama, were segregated by race. Black leaders arranged for Rosa Parks, an African-American woman, to refuse to give up her seat for a white rider as required by Alabama law. Ms. Parks was arrested and Dr. King helped to arrange a boycott of Montgomery buses until the law was changed. Eventually, the Supreme Court ruled segregation on public transportation was illegal. Similar protests took place to highlight discriminatory laws that limited African-Americans' rights to vote, obtain housing, and jobs.

Civil disobedience has not always remained civil. Protesters challenging President Nixon's invasion of Cambodia in 1970 burned the campus ROTC building at Kent State University. Ohio's governor called in the National Guard and when students began protesting the next day, the guardsmen opened fire killing four and wounding nine.

Civil disobedience often becomes criminal behavior by design. At a minimum civil disobedience often involves trespass. In the 1960s, antiwar protesters would simply sit down and refuse to leave various public buildings in what became known as sit-ins. These protesters were intentionally trespassing to occupy the buildings to generate publicity for their cause. In some cases, protesters damaged the property they were occupying leaving them open to charges of vandalism.

Protest using civil disobedience tactics always attempts to portray law enforcement in a bad light. The more extreme law enforcement's reaction, the more sympathy the protesters generate for their cause when the videotape is played on the evening news. After arrest, the protesters can also seek to generate publicity from their trial. For a textbook example of putting the system on trial by provoking police, see the Historical Highlight in the Contempt section.

Contempt
Conduct that brings the authority and administration of the law into disrespect or that embarrasses or obstructs the court's discharge of its duties.

Contempt

Contempt is defined as "Conduct that brings the authority and administration of the law into disrespect or that embarrasses or obstructs the court's discharge of its duties."[18] Contempt is descended from English Common Law where disobedience

Police Confront antiwar protesters in front of U.S. Capital, January 2007

to a writ under the king's seal was considered contempt. The federal rule on contempt states that:

> A court of the United States shall have power to punish by fine or imprisonment, at its discretion, such contempt of its authority, and none other, as—
>
> 1. Misbehavior of any person in its presence or so near thereto as to obstruct the administration of justice;
> 2. Misbehavior of any of its officers in their official transactions;
> 3. Disobedience or resistance to its lawful writ, process, order, rule, decree, or command.[19]

There are two forms of contempt—civil and criminal. Civil contempt findings can be issued on the spot by judges. In most cases, civil contempt cases involve a finding by the presiding judge that an individual is in contempt of court, and an order for the payment of a fine. The proof required is simple: The individual knew there was a court order directing him to do something, and he did not comply. For example, a witness who was served with a subpoena for records and does not bring those records can be held in contempt. Sometimes judges issue civil contempt orders to attorneys involved in a case who do not behave appropriately in the courtroom in accordance with the standards of decorum the judge has set. In those cases, the punishment is typically a fine.

Civil contempt orders can also order an individual to comply with a court order and impose incarceration until the person held in contempt complies with the order or demand. He or she can be jailed until he or she complies. In essence, civil contempt proceedings are remedial in nature, meant to force compliance with the court's will. The incarcerated individual holds the "keys to the jailhouse."

Persons charged with and convicted of criminal contempt, however, cannot purge themselves of that contempt by later complying. That is, criminal contempt is a separate crime for which the individual is being punished, rather than a mechanism to force someone to comply. Criminal contempt can be either a summary offense or a felony. Criminal contempt requires both a contemptuous act and a wrongful state of mind.[20]

Criminal contempt is reserved for obstinance and does not cover a good faith disagreement.[21] Judges can impose summary criminal contempt with no due process for charges of misconduct in open court in the presence of the judge which disturbs the court's business. Recall that the right to a jury trial in criminal cases does not apply in every case, only in those where the punishment includes a substantial prison term. Felony contempt would require a trial by jury and finding of guilt beyond a reasonable doubt since it could be punished by a substantial jail term.

Defenses   Some of the more popular defenses against contempt are:

- Absence of warning by court
- Attorney–client privilege
- Double jeopardy
- Reporter's privilege

Absence of Warning by Court   While a warning by the court that certain behavior will result in a contempt citing is not absolutely necessary, the absence of a warning has been successfully used as a defense. The defense has worked on at least one occasion when the defendant claimed to have no idea the behavior in question would result in contempt.[22]

HISTORICAL HIGHLIGHT

The Chicago Eight Minus One: The Story of Bobby Seale

It was the last week of August in 1968. America was weary of the Vietnam War. The Democrats gathered in Chicago to nominate their candidate for president. Chicago was at the crossroads of epochs. The era of big-city boss politics was about to end, and the quintessential big-city boss, Richard Daley, was hosting the convention. He fully expected to have his man, Vice-President Hubert Humphrey, nominated.

Outside the convention, a well-organized antiwar protest was taking place in Chicago's Grant Park. When the protesters attempted to leave the park and march to the convention center, the Chicago police reacted with reckless violence. They began beating the protesters with clubs, often attacking innocent bystanders and members of the press.

Despite the fact that a national study labeled the event a "police riot," eight demonstration organizers were charged with violating antiriot statutes. The eight were long-time liberal activist David Dellinger; two of the founders of the Students for a Democratic Society, Rennie Davis and Tom Hayden; the cofounders of the Youth International Party or Yippies, Abbie Hoffman and Jerry Rubin; student Lee Weiner; Professor John Froines; and Black Panther activist Bobby Seale.

In court, seven of the defendants were represented by activist attorney William Kunstler. Bobby Seale had retained the services of California attorney Charles Garry. But Garry had to have gallbladder surgery, and asked for a six-week continuance. Judge Julius Hoffman denied the motion despite the fact that local attorneys had put in appearances for Seale with the understanding they were only to help with the pretrial preparation. Judge Hoffman replied "There was no such thing as a limited appearance in a criminal case."[23]

Hoffman's gruff demeanor and no-nonsense, old school attitude appeared right out of central casting, and the Chicago Eight decided to treat the trial like theater. In fact, they referred to their strategy as "guerilla theater," a confrontational style pioneered by defendant Jerry Rubin. Rubin had used it successfully when the House Un-American Activities Committee subpoenaed him. Rubin showed up to testify dressed in eighteenth-century colonial costume. The hearing adjourned and Rubin's subpoena was forgotten.

The eight viewed the trial as an attempt by the Nixon administration to intimidate them. Their suspicion had some basis in fact. As the investigation of the Chicago riots concluded in the waning days of the Johnson administration, Attorney General Ramsey Clark felt that the eight should not be prosecuted. Clark, however, left the decision to the new administration. Nixon's Attorney General John Mitchell wanted to prosecute.[24] He even went so far as to have the FBI monitor communications between the defendants and their lawyers.

At the trial, Seale repeatedly protested his not being allowed to have the counsel of his choice. Seale attempted to represent himself. The exchanges between Seale and Hoffman grew more heated. Seale, noting that all the white defendants had the counsel of their choice, called Hoffman a racist, fascist pig. Finally, Hoffman ordered Seale to be gagged and chained to his chair.

Eventually, Hoffman severed Seale's case from the others. When he severed the case, he cited Seale for sixteen counts of contempt for which he was to serve three months each.

The Court of Appeals ruled Hoffman's actions were abuses of power. Under the law at that time, a judge could not impose a contempt sentence for longer than six months without a jury trial. In the eyes of the appeals court, Hoffman was trying to circumvent the law. Seale's case was remanded for a jury trial, but by then news of the FBI's monitoring of the attorney–client communications was public. The government elected to drop the charges rather than reveal the contents of the taped conversations.

Attorney–Client Privilege   An attorney cannot be forced to reveal privileged information communicated to him or her by a client. In other words, an attorney can't be charged with contempt for refusing to disclose information she received while discussing a case with a client. However, for this defense to work, an attorney must provide independent evidence that the communications in question are attorney–client communications. The attorney's mere assertion that they are is not enough.[25]

Double Jeopardy   Double jeopardy defenses for contempt seldom prevail. The defense has been raised when the same conduct resulted in both civil and criminal contempt charges, but was unsuccessful.[26] Courts are free to charge each incident of contemptuous behavior as a separate count of contempt.[27] Even acts that are punishable by other crimes can also be cited as contempt. For example, a defendant who assaulted the prosecutor in court was successfully charged with both assault on a federal officer and contempt.[28]

Reporter's Privilege   Over the years, journalists seeking to protect sources have sometimes asserted that they cannot be forced to testify about those sources. Sometimes courts have held them in contempt for refusing to provide the information. For example, a *Los Angeles Herald-Examiner* reporter who refused to disclose his source of material related to the Charles Manson trial was jailed for forty-six days in 1972.

In a federal criminal case or grand jury proceeding, the U.S. attorney general is required to review each subpoena for a journalist's testimony before it is sought. The regulations require that the Department of Justice, when reviewing the request, "strike the proper balance between the public's interest in the free dissemination of ideas and information and the public's interest in effective law enforcement and the fair administration of justice."[29]

HISTORICAL HIGHLIGHT

New York Times Reporter Does 85 Days for Contempt

Judith Miller knew all the players. The *New York Times* reporter met regularly with high-ranking Bush administration officials in the run-up to the Iraq war. Miller had the reputation of keeping confidential sources confidential. She would learn the price of such professionalism.

The Bush administration thought it had information tying Saddam Hussein to the 9/11 attacks. The intelligence never quite panned out. Then a report surfaced indicating Hussein was trying to buy "yellowcake" uranium from the African nation of Niger. The CIA wanted to verify the claim and asked its Weapons Intelligence, Non-Proliferation, and Arms Control (WINPAC) unit to check into it.

WINPAC operative Valerie Plame Wilson told her superiors that her husband, Joseph C. Wilson IV, was a former ambassador to Niger and knew the country well. The CIA sent Wilson to investigate. Wilson reported back that he could find no evidence that anyone had contacted Niger attempting to purchase uranium.[30]

CIA Director George Tenet convinced the White House to remove any reference to Niger and uranium from an upcoming presidential speech in October 2002.[31] But someone in the White House got the announcement back into a presidential speech, specifically the State of the Union speech where the president said, "The British government has learned that Saddam Hussein recently sought significant quantities of uranium from Africa."

The president used this information to urge Congress to back an invasion of Iraq. Even though the United Nations labeled the documents supporting Hussein–Niger connection as bogus, Congress gave the president the authority to invade. In July, Wilson criticized the administration in an op-ed piece for its rush to war using faulty intelligence.

Administration operatives allegedly started looking for ways to get even with Ambassador Wilson. After some investigation, I. "Scooter" Libby, who worked in the vice president's office, found that Valerie Plame was Wilson's wife. He leaked her name to Miller, and *Time* magazine's Matthew Cooper.

When Plame's name was broadcast by CNN's Robert Novak, the CIA asked the Justice Department to investigate. By the end of the year, a special prosecutor had been appointed and a grand jury convened. Miller and Cooper were subpoenaed, and both the *New York Times* and *Time* tried to quash the subpoenas.

When those efforts failed, both reporters were held in contempt. Libby released Cooper from his vow of confidentiality and Cooper testified before the grand jury. But Libby didn't release Miller, even though she never used the information he gave her in an article. Miller refused to testify and was sent to jail.

Eighty-five days later after her source "voluntarily and personally released [her] from [her] promise of confidentiality," Miller was released to testify before the grand jury. Libby was indicted for obstruction of justice and two counts each of making false statements and perjury.

Libby was later convicted on four of the five counts and sentence to two and one-half years in jail. His sentence was commuted to time served by President Bush in June 2007.

Escape

A person in custody has an obligation to remain in custody until the state releases him. A person who intentionally leaves custody is guilty of escape. If the escapee uses force, the charge is "prison break" or "breach of prison." The prisoner must intend to escape. For instance, a prisoner on work release who falls asleep in a truck that is driven to a private home may be a bad employee, but not an escapee. He would, however, be wise to turn himself in at the earliest possible moment.

Similarly, a prisoner chained to another prisoner who attempts an escape could argue he had no intention of escaping. If the other prisoner threatened him, he could argue he was forced to escape under duress. Some jurisdictions allow escapees to use the duress defense also if they can demonstrate they would have been murdered, assaulted, or subject to bodily harm had they stayed in prison.

Those convicted of escape face penalties based on the offense for which they were incarcerated originally. For example, misdemeanor convicts face misdemeanor escape charges. Felony convicts face felony escape charges. Many states have increased penalties for sex offenders who escape. Anyone who assists a prisoner to escape will be guilty of aiding escape.

Bribery

Bribery is defined as "the crime of giving something of value with the intention of influencing the action of a public official."[32]

Elements   The elements of bribery are:

- The recipient or target of the bribe must be a governmental official.
- A bribe in the form of money, goods, favors, or something of value was offered or given.
- The bribe was meant to induce an action or inaction.

A Recipient of the Bribe   A bribe recipient can be any government official ranging from a congressman to a clerk issuing permits or licenses. For example, after the September 11 terror attacks, investigators discovered that a number of men of Middle Eastern heritage had received special permits allowing them to transport hazardous material via truck across the nation's highways. The licensees had not taken the special test required of applicants. Eventually, a clerk working in the Pennsylvania Department of Transportation was charged with accepting bribes in exchange for issuing the licenses without examinations. Though a low-level clerk, he held a government position and was in a position to take official action. In this case, he could issue or deny a license to applicants.

A Bribe   The bribe itself is money or something of value that is given to the recipient in return for certain action or, in some cases, inaction. The crime of bribery is complete when the "offeror" expresses ability and desire to pay, assuming he intends the proffered payment will lead to a favorable decision by the "offeree."[33] Therefore, the bribe doesn't have to be given directly to the government official. It can be given to someone else, if that's what the recipient wants. The bribe itself can be anything of value such as cash, paid vacations, jewelry, or anything else other than a fee charged to all. In fact, some states even regulate the type and value of gifts that can be given to government officials such as holiday and appreciation gifts. The U.S. Postal Service prohibits gifts to carriers and others that are worth more than $20.

Action Meant to Result from the Bribe   The action meant to result from the bribe need not be illegal in and of itself. The government must merely show that the receipt of the bribe influenced the decision. For example, it would still be bribery to offer a passport clerk a $500 "bonus" if he or she issues you a passport today instead of tomorrow.

Bribery can also be prosecuted despite the fact that the recipient lacks the authority to accomplish the action desired by the offeror. It also doesn't matter if the recipient of the bribe never delivers what he or she promises to do for the bribe.

State of Mind   The person offering the bribe must intend that his or her offer will result in favorable action on the part of the recipient. So long as the bribe was intended as *quid pro quo* for a favor, the intent requirement has been met.

Moral principle is a looser bond than pecuniary interest.

Abraham Lincoln

Bribery
The crime of giving something of value with the intention of influencing the action of a public official.

The whole art of government consists in the art of being honest.

Thomas Jefferson

Defenses

Entrapment   Entrapment can be claimed as a defense where it can be proven that the government agent initiated the bribery scheme, and forced the defendant into a course of action he or she normally would not have taken. An entrapment defense has two elements: government inducement and the defendant's lack of predisposition to commit the crime.[34] Keep in mind that proving entrapment in any case is difficult; the defendant must prove that he or she wasn't predisposed to paying a bribe or was unaware that the requested payment was a bribe rather than the customary fee for a government service. Even in cases where a government official demands payment before carrying out official duties, the person from whom the bribe is being extorted has other avenues for recourse. He or she can, for example, file a mandamus action, which is a lawsuit seeking to compel government to do something they are required to do. The target can also report the attempted extortion to police or other law enforcement.

What happens if a defendant pays money as a bribe, and then raises entrapment as a defense? Does he get his money back? In at least one case, the answer was no even though there was no bribery conviction.[35]

Corrupt Organizations

RICO
Racketeering Influenced and Corrupt Organizations Act is legislation that enables the government to prosecute individuals and organizations for a pattern of criminal activity; originally meant to target organized crime.

For many years government has sought to control and eliminate corrupt organizations. One of the most comprehensive pieces of legislation in this battle is the Organized Crime Control Act. Part of this act is the Racketeering Influenced and Corrupt Organizations Act or **RICO,** which was passed in 1970.[36] RICO was originally intended to prosecute organized crime, but was drafted very broadly. The original intention was to provide a way to prosecute organized crime activities run through both illegitimate business enterprises and through legitimate-appearing businesses. Sometimes legitimate businesses serve as a shield for illegitimate activities or a way to funnel earnings from crime to make the profits appear legitimate. However, in recent years RICO has been applied to business activities far removed from organized crime syndicates.

Under RICO, it is a federal crime to acquire or maintain an interest in, use income from, or conduct or participate in the affairs of an "enterprise" through a pattern of "racketeering activity."

An enterprise can be:

- A corporation
- A partnership
- A sole proprietorship
- Any business or organization
- The government

In fact, a recent Supreme Court ruling stated that enterprises do not need any ascertainable structure other than its racketeering activity.[37]

Racketeering activity includes many crimes and activities such as:

- Bribery
- Embezzlement

- Gambling
- Arson
- Counterfeiting money, recordings, copyrighted materials, and computer programs
- Trafficking in contraband cigarettes
- Harboring illegal aliens

At least two acts must be committed by the organization being charged with racketeering within a ten-year period. In addition to fines and imprisonment, persons or organizations convicted under RICO are subject to seizure of property obtained with illegally acquired funds. For example, a partnership that used a pizza shop as a front for dealing in cigarettes on which the partnership hasn't paid cigarette taxes may find that the pizza shop will be seized and sold, with the proceeds going to the government.

Because RICO is so broadly written, it has invited unique legal approaches to address problems far from what its authors envisioned. The U.S. Supreme Court recently ruled that pro-life protesters at abortion clinics do not violate RICO.[38] A Wyoming rancher alleged the U.S. government violated RICO through a pattern of harassment, but the Court decided the man had other avenues available to address individual government actions that he had not pursued and dismissed the case.[39] A New York retailer tried to take a competitor to court because the store did not charge New York State sales tax. The court ruled the charging retailer lacked standing to file a RICO suit, but it is likely New York State revenue agents will be checking the no-tax retailer's books very closely.[40]

One RICO case that may break new ground involves illegal immigration. Four North Georgia employees have filed suit against the Mohawk Carpet Company alleging the company conspired with a temporary service company to bring in illegal aliens who will work for low wages. Mohawk had attempted to have the case dismissed and the Eleventh Circuit Court of Appeals refused. Mohawk appealed to the Supreme Court, who was looking at the New York State RICO case at the time. The Court sent the case back to the Eleventh Circuit to decide in light of the New York decision. The Eleventh Circuit concluded the case could go to trial under the guiding Supreme Court opinion.[41]

Impeachment

Impeachment is an indictment of a federal official charging him or her with "treason, bribery, and high crimes and misdemeanors."[42] Once an official is impeached, he or she is tried and, if found guilty, removed from office.

The form of impeachment outlined in the U.S. Constitution owes much to its English predecessor. Although impeachment is no longer used in the United Kingdom (all officials now serve at the pleasure of Parliament), in the days of a strong executive, in the form of a king, it was necessary to have a mechanism to remove corrupt royal appointees.

Impeachment articles are voted upon by the House of Representatives (House of Commons in England), and then a trial is held in the Senate (House of Lords in England). In order to be removed from office the Senate must vote to convict by a two-thirds supermajority.

Impeachment
An indictment of a public official that leads to a trial to determine whether he or she should be removed from office.

Impeachment was intended to be a seldom-used remedy. The standard of "high crimes and misdemeanors," while vague, does imply that the framers intended it to be a remedy for very serious infractions by public officials. The widened context of "treason, bribery, high crimes and misdemeanors" leads to the conclusion that the founding fathers were concerned about officials selling their office or betraying the citizens to whom they must ultimately answer.

One reason there have been few impeachment cases in our history is that in many cases public officials have simply been voted out when their term expired. There is one group of officials for whom impeachment is the only avenue for removal, absent death or voluntary retirement. Recall that federal judges are appointed for life. Thus, a federal judge can only be forced out of office by impeachment.

The most high-profile impeachment cases are those of presidents. Two U.S. presidents, Andrew Johnson and Bill Clinton, have been impeached, but neither was removed from office. A third president, Richard Nixon, lost an impeachment vote in the U.S. House of Representatives Judiciary Committee, where the process begins, but resigned before the matter came before the full House of Representatives.

Procedures

The procedures in an impeachment are not spelled out in the U.S. Constitution or U.S. Code. Congress can decide on procedures on an ad hoc basis. In modern times, Congress has initiated two presidential impeachment proceedings, against Presidents Nixon and Clinton.

When proceedings began against President Nixon, Congress found that the Constitution offered little guidance. The House Judiciary Committee developed rules of evidence and procedures for the impeachment proceedings. However, those rules only bound Congress for the duration of the Nixon impeachment process.

> The greater the power, the more dangerous the abuse.
>
> Edmund Burke

HISTORICAL HIGHLIGHT

Impeachment after Acquittal: The Story of Alcee Hastings

Alcee Hastings was a pioneer for African-Americans. He was the first black to be named U.S. District Judge for the Southern District of Florida. Unfortunately, he also became the first black federal official ever to be impeached. He was also the first federal official of any race to be impeached and removed from office after being acquitted in federal court on the same charges.

How this strange turn of events came to be owes much to Hastings's magnetic personality. He is a bright, articulate, persuasive speaker. At his trial he spoke convincingly in his own behalf and the jury did not convict. The Senate trial was different.

A judicial inquiry had produced voluminous evidence that Hastings had solicited a $150,000 bribe from two racketeers. He had allegedly solicited it through an intermediary to maintain deniability, but an undercover agent impersonated one of the racketeers.

Balancing this damning information was the acquittal in court. The U.S. House of Representatives was faced with a dilemma. African-American Congressman John Conyers of Michigan was chosen to head the House's investigation. He gravely weighed the evidence and came to the conclusion that Hastings was guilty. Conyers addressed Congress and said: "We did not wage (the) civil rights struggle merely to replace one form of judicial corruption for another . . . . The principle of equality requires that a black public official be held to the same standard that other public officials are held to." The House voted 413–3 for impeachment.

Hastings' supporters were optimistic about the Senate vote. The Senate is required to vote for impeachment by a two-thirds majority before an official can be removed from office. The consensus was that Hastings could charm, cajole, and convince the requisite number of Senators to assure an acquittal.

The Senate, however, had to view the facts. The undercover agent testified that he asked the contact to demonstrate that he could get Hastings to do what he wanted; the contact arranged for Hastings to have dinner at a Miami hotel, and appear in the lobby at a specific time. Hastings did just as the agent requested. When the money was paid, Hastings made his law clerk stay late to finish the paperwork releasing seized property belonging to the man the agent was impersonating.

In the end, despite the acquittal in court, the Senate voted to convict on October 20, 1989.[43] A visibly shaken Hastings left the chamber in tears. However, within a few years, he was elected to the House of Representatives from his south Florida district. Hastings now belongs to the body that voted for his impeachment.

When Congress began impeachment proceedings against President Clinton, it did not immediately establish its procedures. It did so only after receiving the report of Special Prosecutor Kenneth Starr. Congressional critics charged that Congress appeared to be shaping the procedures to the evidence, instead of designing them to impartially evaluate the evidence.

Impeachment in Congress is no guarantee that the elected official will not have to face charges in state or federal court. During President Nixon's impeachment ordeal, he faced a parallel prosecution in federal court. In fact, it was his loss before the U.S. Supreme Court that forced him to reveal the most damaging evidence against him, the Oval Office tapes. Had Mr. Nixon not resigned, those tapes would have been used against him in his Senate trial.

In the same vein, President Clinton was forced to relinquish his law license as part of the settlement of the perjury charges against him. President Clinton was accused of lying under oath concerning his affair with Monica Lewinsky during testimony in a civil suit brought against him for sexual harassment by Paula Jones.

Ambiguities

Unlike criminal proceedings where the burden of proof is "guilt beyond a reasonable doubt," or civil actions where the "preponderance of evidence" standard applies, the burden of proof is not codified in impeachment proceedings. Congress has never specified what standard is to be used, but has left it up to the individual senator when voting to convict.

Additionally, the definition of "high crimes and misdemeanors" is nebulous. President Clinton's supporters argued that perjury in a civil case did not rise to the level of "high crimes and misdemeanors" as intended in the Constitution. They apparently convinced enough of the Senate to prevent conviction.

President Clinton's impeachment also raised another question: Can a president or federal judge be impeached for activities not related to the duties of his or her office? President Clinton's questionable conduct was carried out as a private citizen. None of the impeachment articles alleged that he abused the privileges of his office. Almost all previous impeachments were prosecuted against office holders who acted illegally in the execution of their office.

Conclusion

Impeachment was designed to be a seldom-used tool. Despite having the form of a legal proceeding, it is in reality a political exercise. The Founding Fathers recognized this and put the safeguard of requiring a two-thirds majority to convict. Even though this section has focused on federal impeachment proceedings, the states each have impeachment proceedings.

Some states also use a process known as a recall vote. A recall vote is where the citizens choose to remove or recall an official through a referendum. Usually it is necessary to get a certain number of signatures on a petition to get the issue on the ballot. If a majority of the citizens vote to recall the individual, he or she must leave office.

Impeachment is a process fraught with ambiguity. It can be open to political manipulation. In fact, no president has been impeached when his own party controlled Congress. Some historians have noted that when impeachment is abused, the public loses its appetite for it for years afterward.[44] House Minority Leader Richard Gephart referred to the Clinton impeachment as part of "the politics of personal destruction." Despite its possible misuse, impeachment is a process deeply ingrained in American jurisprudence.

Tax Evasion

Tax evasion
An attempt to defeat or avoid paying a tax.

Tax evasion occurs when someone attempts to "evade or defeat" a legitimate tax.[45] Tax fraud occurs when someone knowingly provides fraudulent or false statements with the intent of evading taxes.[46] Failure to file a tax return is also a violation. This may apply to individuals as well as businesses. Because criminal enterprises generally do not wish to reveal their income, prosecutors can use tax evasion as a way to obtain financial data from and prosecute organized crime figures. This is the reason tax forms ask for income from illegal activities.

Mail Fraud

Mail fraud
Using the U.S. Postal Service in furtherance of a fraudulent scheme.

Mail fraud in its original intent was to protect consumers from fraudulent offers received in the mail. The statute is quite broad reading:

> Whoever, having devised or intending to devise any scheme or artifice to defraud, or for obtaining money or property by means of false or fraudulent pretenses, representations, or promises, or to sell, dispose of, loan, exchange, alter, give away, distribute, supply, or furnish or procure for unlawful use any counterfeit or spurious coin, obligation, security, or other article, or anything represented to be or intimated or held out to be such counterfeit or spurious article, for the purpose of executing such scheme or artifice or attempting so to do, places in any post office or authorized depository for mail matter, any matter or thing whatever to be sent or delivered by the Postal Service, or deposits or causes to be deposited any matter or thing whatever to be sent or delivered by any private or commercial interstate carrier, or takes or receives therefrom, any such matter or thing, or knowingly causes to be delivered by mail or such carrier according to the direction thereon, or at the place at which it is directed to be delivered by the person to whom it is addressed, any such matter or thing, shall be fined under this title or imprisoned not more than 20 years, or both. If the violation occurs in relation to, or involving any benefit authorized, transported, transmitted, transferred, disbursed, or paid in connection with, a presidentially declared major disaster or emergency (as those terms are defined in section 102 of the Robert T. Stafford Disaster Relief and Emergency Assistance Act (42 U.S.C. 5122)), or affects a financial institution, such person shall be fined not more than $ 1,000,000 or imprisoned not more than 30 years, or both.[47]

Prosecutors can use mail fraud as leverage when prosecuting other crimes. For instance, Alaska state legislator Bruce Weyhrauch is alleged to have acted on legislation related to an oil field services company while sending them a résumé in hopes they would hire him after he left the legislature. Prosecutors tacked the mail fraud charge onto the other allegations because he mailed the résumé.

CONCEPT **REVIEW AND REINFORCEMENT**

Perjury is defined as "giving false testimony in a judicial proceeding or an administrative proceeding, lying under oath as to a material fact, swearing to the truth of anything one knows or believes to be false." Under federal law there are three types of perjury. The first type, often referred to as section 1621 perjury (for the section of the U.S. code describing it—18 U.S.C. § 1621), is a general giving of false testimony. It applies to all material statements or information provided under oath and is not limited to testimony in court, but includes any sworn statement to a government official or representative. Section 1623 perjury is limited to court and grand jury testimony.

Subornation of perjury is defined as convincing or seeking to convince another person to commit perjury. In order to be convicted of subornation of perjury, a person must convince another to commit perjury, and that person must then actually perjure himself or herself. Under Common Law, a person could not be convicted of perjury unless two people testified that the alleged perjurer's statements were not true. This is called the two-witness rule. Physical evidence that corroborates testimony satisfies the two-witness rule.

Section 1623 requires that "proof beyond a reasonable doubt . . . is sufficient for conviction." The proof may take any form—physical evidence, testimony, or any other type of proof. The standard of proof is thus lower than for section 1621 perjury. The two-witness rule specifically does not apply to section 1623 cases.

Recantation is the retraction of testimony. Under section 1621, even if a witness recants his or her testimony, he or she can still be prosecuted for perjury. However, under section 1623, a witness can recant testimony during the same proceeding as long as that testimony has not "substantially affected the proceeding."

Under section 1621, the government must prove which of the contradictory statements is false. However, under section 1623 contradictory statements are sufficient for conviction in and of themselves.

The elements of perjury are: an oath, intent, falsity, and materiality. The defenses to perjury are: recantation, assistance of counsel, double jeopardy, the "perjury trap," and the Fifth Amendment.

When an individual asks or coerces another person into committing perjury it is subornation of perjury.

Obstruction of justice is defined as "the crime of impeding or hindering the administration of justice in any way." Witness tampering or intimidation, jury tampering, or even suborning perjury can be forms of obstruction of justice. The elements of the crime of obstruction of justice are: there is a pending judicial proceeding, the defendant knew of the proceeding, and the defendant acted corruptly with the specific intent to obstruct or interfere with the proceeding or due administration of justice.

Obstruction of justice can take many forms, but the actions generally prosecuted under the federal statute fall into three groups. The first group involves hiding, changing, or destroying relevant documents such as court records, the second is encouraging or giving false testimony, and the third group is comprised of offenses involving intimidation, threats, or other harm to witnesses, jurors, judges, or others involved in legal proceedings or investigations in an attempt to prevent or shape their testimony or judgment.

At a minimum civil disobedience often involves trespass. Protest using civil disobedience tactics always attempts to portray law enforcement in a bad light. The more extreme law enforcement's reaction, the more sympathy the protesters generate for their cause when the videotape is played on the evening news. After arrest, the protesters can also seek to generate publicity from their trial.

Contempt is defined as "Conduct that brings the authority and administration of the law into disrespect or that embarrasses or obstructs the court's discharge of its duties." The federal rule on contempt states that: A court of the United States shall have power to punish by fine or imprisonment, at its discretion, such contempt of its authority, and none other, as: (1) Misbehavior of any person in its presence or so near thereto as to obstruct the administration of justice; (2) Misbehavior of any of its officers in their official transactions; (3) Disobedience or resistance to its lawful writ, process, order, rule, decree, or command.

There are two forms of contempt—civil and criminal. Civil contempt findings can be issued on the spot by judges. In most cases, civil contempt cases involve a finding by the presiding judge that an individual is in contempt of court, and an order for the payment of a fine. The proof required is that the individual knew there was a court order directing him to do something, and he did not comply.

Civil contempt orders can also order an individual to comply with a court order and impose incarceration until the person held in contempt complies with the order or demand.

Persons charged with and convicted of criminal contempt, however, cannot purge themselves of that contempt by later complying. Criminal contempt requires both a contemptuous act and a wrongful state of mind.

Criminal contempt is reserved for obstinance and does not cover a good faith disagreement. Judges can impose summary criminal contempt with no due process for charges of misconduct in open court in the presence of the judge which disturbs the court's business.

Some of the more popular defenses against contempt are: absence of warning by court, attorney–client privilege, double jeopardy, reporter's privilege.

A person who intentionally leaves custody is guilty of escape. If the escapee uses force, the charge is "prison break" or "breach of prison." The prisoner must intend to escape.

Those convicted of escape face penalties based on the offense for which they were incarcerated originally. Anyone who assists a prisoner to escape will be guilty of aiding escape.

Bribery is defined as "the crime of giving something of value with the intention of influencing the action of a public official." The elements of bribery are: the recipient or target of the bribe must be a governmental official; a bribe in the form of money, goods, favors, or something of value was offered or given; and the bribe was meant to induce an action or inaction. The main defense to bribery is entrapment.

The Racketeering Influenced and Corrupt Organizations Act (RICO) was originally intended to provide a way to prosecute organized crime activities run through both illegitimate business enterprises and through legitimate-appearing businesses. Under RICO, it is a federal crime to acquire or maintain an interest in, use income from, or conduct or participate in the affairs of an "enterprise" through a pattern of "racketeering activity."

An enterprise can be: a corporation, a partnership, a sole proprietorship, any business or organization, or the government. Racketeering activity includes many crimes and activities such as: bribery; embezzlement; gambling; arson; counterfeiting money, recordings, copyrighted materials, and computer programs; trafficking in contraband cigarettes; or harboring illegal aliens.

At least two acts must be committed by the organization being charged with racketeering within a ten-year period. In addition to fines and imprisonment, persons or organizations convicted under RICO are subject to seizure of property obtained with illegally acquired funds. Because RICO is so broadly written, it has invited unique legal approaches to address problems far from what its authors envisioned.

Impeachment is an indictment of a federal official charging him or her with "treason, bribery, and high crimes and misdemeanors." Once an official is impeached, he or she is tried and, if found guilty, removed from office.

Impeachment articles are voted upon by the House of Representatives, and then a trial is held in the Senate. In order to be removed from office the Senate must vote to convict by a two-thirds supermajority.

Tax evasion occurs when someone attempts to "evade or defeat" a legitimate tax. Tax fraud occurs when someone knowingly provides fraudulent or false statements with the intent of evading taxes. Failure to file a tax return is also a violation.

Mail fraud in its original intent was to protect consumers from fraudulent offers received in the mail. Prosecutors can use mail fraud as leverage when prosecuting other crimes.

KEY **TERMS**

Bribery	Perjury	Subornation of perjury
Contempt	Perjury trap	Tax evasion
Impeachment	Recantation	Two-witness rule
Mail fraud	RICO	Witness tampering
Obstruction of justice		

CONCEPT **REVIEW QUESTIONS**

1. Why is perjury significant to the legal system's integrity?

2. What are the essential elements of obstruction of justice?

3. What are the different types of contempt?

4. What are the elements of crime of escape?

5. What constitutes bribery?

6. How does the government seek to control corrupt organizations?

7. Explain the steps in the impeachment process.

8. What constitutes tax evasion?

9. What constitutes mail fraud?

CASE **APPLICATIONS**

Building Your Professional Skills

In this chapter, you learned about Alcee Hastings, his impeachment and removal from the federal bench, and his subsequent election to the House of Representatives. Mr. Hastings tried unsuccessfully to appeal his impeachment to the federal courts. He lost that appeal because the Supreme Court ruled in another impeachment case while his case was pending. An edited version of that decision appears below. Read it and answer the questions that follow.

NIXON *v.* UNITED STATES ET AL.

CERTIORARI TO THE UNITED STATES COURT OF APPEALS FOR THE DISTRICT OF COLUMBIA CIRCUIT

No. 91-740. Argued October 14, 1992

Decided January 13, 1993

When the petitioner Nixon, the Chief Judge of a Federal District Court, was convicted of federal crimes and sentenced to prison, the House of Representatives adopted articles of impeachment against him and presented them to the Senate. Following proceedings pursuant to Senate Rule XI, which allows a committee of Senators to hear evidence against an impeached individual and to report that evidence to the full Senate, the Senate voted to convict Nixon, and the presiding officer entered judgment removing him from his judgeship. He then commenced the present suit for a declaratory judgment and reinstatement of his judicial salary and privileges, arguing that, because Senate Rule XI prohibits the whole Senate from taking part in the evidentiary hearings, it violates the first sentence of the Constitution's Impeachment Trial Clause, Art. I, § 3, cl. 6, which provides that the "Senate shall have the sole Power to try all Impeachments." The District Court held that his claim was nonjusticiable, i. *e.,* involved a political question that could not be resolved by the courts. The Court of Appeals affirmed.

Held: Nixon's claim that Senate Rule XI violates the Impeachment Trial Clause is nonjusticiable.

A controversy is nonjusticiable where there is "a textually demonstrable constitutional commitment of the issue to a coordinate political department; or a lack of judicially discoverable and manageable standards for resolving it. . . . " *Baker* v. *Carr*, 369 U. S. 186, 217. These two concepts are not completely separate; the lack of judicially manageable standards may strengthen the conclusion that there is a textually demonstrable commitment to a coordinate branch.

The language and structure of Art. I, § 3, cl. 6, demonstrate a textual commitment of impeachment to the Senate. Nixon's argument that the use of the word "try" in the Clause's first sentence impliedly requires a judicial-style trial by the full Senate that is subject to judicial review is rejected. The conclusion that "try" lacks sufficient precision to afford any judicially manageable standard of review is compelled by older and modern dictionary definitions, and is fortified by the existence of the three very specific requirements that the Clause's second and third sentences do impose—that the Senate's Members must be under oath or affirmation, that a two-thirds vote is required to convict, and that the Chief Justice presides when the President is tried—the precise nature of which suggests that the Framers did not intend to impose additional limitations on the form of the Senate proceedings. The Clause's first sentence must instead be read as a grant of authority to the Senate to determine whether an individual should be acquitted or convicted, and the common sense and dictionary meanings of the word "sole" indicate that this authority is reposed in the Senate alone. Nixon's attempts to negate the significance of "sole" are unavailing, while his alternative reading of the word as requiring impeachment only by the full Senate is unnatural and would impose on the Senate additional procedural requirements that would be inconsistent with the three express limitations that the Clause sets out. A review of the Constitutional Convention's history and the contemporary commentary supports a reading of the constitutional language as deliberately placing the impeachment power in the Legislature, with no judicial involvement, even for the limited purpose of judicial review.

Justiciability is also refuted by (1) the lack of finality inherent in exposing the country's political life—particularly if the President were impeached—to months, or perhaps years, of chaos during judicial review of Senate impeachment proceedings, or during any retrial that a differently constituted Senate might conduct if its first judgment of conviction were invalidated, and by (2) the difficulty of fashioning judicial relief other than simply setting aside the Senate's judgment of conviction. . . .

Affirmed.

QUESTIONS

1. What did the Supreme Court decide?
2. Who has the final say on whether a judge loses his judgeship via impeachment? Why?

CRITICAL **THINKING EXERCISES**

1. Match the following descriptions with the type of perjury they describe:

Action	Perjury Type
You are filling out a questionnaire designed to determine who is entitled to a property tax rebate targeted at people 65 and older. You list your age as 66 when you are actually 47.	A. 1621
When testifying before a grand jury, you knowingly identify the wrong person as fleeing the scene of a crime.	B. 1622
You committed a robbery and ran back to your house. Your neighbor saw you. You tell him to tell the police you didn't get a good look at the person running that night. He does so.	C. 1623

2. You find your son, along with a friend, has stolen money. You tell your son's friend that if he tells anyone about the situation, you will harm him in some way. At this point, the investigation is just beginning, but no hearings or trial has been scheduled. Are you guilty of obstruction of justice?

3. You are an attorney representing a person charged with a crime. The accused has provided you with certain incriminating evidence. That client later fires you and hires another attorney. The prosecutor in the case subpoenas you to testify about conversations you had with the accused. You refuse citing attorney–client privilege. Can you be held in contempt?

4. You are a prisoner on a work-release program. The conditions of the program require you to return to

the prison at 5:00 PM each workday. While working at a restaurant, you are inadvertently locked in the walk-in freezer. By the time you are rescued, it is 5:30 PM. Are you guilty of escape?

5. Which of the following is an example of bribery?

a. You make a large campaign contribution to a judge who will hear a case involving a lawsuit against your company. You never discuss the case with the judge, but you do make sure he knows you made the contribution.

b. You need a permit from the city to continue a development project. You pay the city official responsible for permitting a bribe, but the permit is still denied.

c. A police officer pulls you over for speeding. You hand him a $100 bill when he asks for your license. He hands you back the license and tells you to have a good day.

6. You and your brother make contact with three people you've never met before and plan and execute several bank robberies. You are arrested and the prosecutor claims the five of you are a criminal enterprise under RICO. Is the prosecutor correct?

7. Which of the following presidents, if any, were impeached?

a. Andrew Johnson

b. Richard Nixon

c. Bill Clinton

8. You are a drug kingpin making millions of dollars from illegal drug sales. You report all that income as income from an import–export business. Are you guilty of tax evasion? Tax fraud?

9. You have an auto repair shop that uses e-mail to send out bills to customers. You overcharge a customer and e-mail him his bill. Have you committed mail fraud?

PORTFOLIO **BUILDING**

1. Legal professionals in paralegal or investigative positions who work for attorneys representing business owners, partnerships, and corporations will find themselves working on cases involving possible criminal charges typically considered "white-collar crimes." These clients pose special challenges since they are generally educated and understand how the legal system works. Many seek representation while the case is still under investigation or even before. Representation often involves cooperation with investigations and plea-bargaining negotiation. These are processes in which members of the professional support staff often play a significant role.

Clients often want to know how likely it is that they could face charges. The U.S. Department of Justice has issued guidelines. They are available at http://www.justice.gov/usao/eousa/foia_reading_room/usam/title9/28mcrm.htm

Review the information and summarize the considerations that go into the decision to charge or not charge for your portfolio. You can then use the summary as a starting point for those tough conversations with clients facing potential charges.

2. In the event federal charges are filed against a client, the odds of conviction after trial are high, often over 90 percent. If the case goes to trial, significant time and resources will be spent preparing documents and testimony to support efforts to reduce the sentence to be served. You may be actively involved, for example, in seeking out mitigating factors that support an argument for deviation from the federal sentencing guidelines. This preparation may mean the difference between a prison sentence or supervised release and house detention. Review the federal sentencing guidelines at http://www.ussc.gov/GUIDELIN.HTM.

QUESTIONS

1. What factors play into sentencing?

2. What steps can a defendant take before conviction or a guilty plea to minimize his or her sentence?

FOR FURTHER READING

1. Mass, P. (1997). *Underboss: Sammy the Bull Gravano's Story of Life in the Mafia.* Harper Collins.
2. Jackson, D. D. (1973). *Judges: An Inside View of the Agonies and Excesses of an American Elite.* Antheneum.
3. Black, C. L. (1998). *Impeachment: A Handbook.* Yale University Press.
4. Caplan, G. M. (1983). *ABSCAM Ethics: Moral Issues and Deception in Law Enforcement.* HarperInformation.
5. Noonan, J. T. (1984). *Bribes.* Macmillan.
6. Wilson, J. C. (2004). *The Politics of Truth: Inside the Lies that Led to War and Betrayed My Wife's CIA Identity.* New York: Carroll & Graf.
7. *And Justice for All* (1979). This is the classic Al Pacino film about corruption in the legal system.
8. *The Firm* (1993). Tom Cruise and Gene Hackman star in this adaptation of the John Grisham novel, centering on corrupt lawyers, blackmail, and racketeering, with a satisfying and ironic ending.

Chapter **ten**

COMMON LAW DEFENSES

(The intoxicated) shall have no privilege by this voluntarily contracted madness, but shall have the same judgment as if he were in his right senses.

M. Hale

Introduction

In every criminal trial the prosecution has the burden of proof and must prove the case against the defendant beyond a reasonable doubt. The defendant isn't required to answer the charges except to plead not guilty or guilty.

As we have seen, every crime can be broken down into its essential elements, and the government is required to prove each element beyond a reasonable doubt. We have already examined the elements of many crimes. A prosecutor who proves these elements will generally get a conviction unless the defendant raises a defense to the crime. The law provides legitimate defenses that, if proven, dictate an acquittal.

Depending on the crime, a number of defenses may be available to defendants. Defenses take their legitimacy from Common Law, constitutional law, and statutory law. For instance, the insanity defense, known as the M'Naghten Rule, takes its name from the defendant in a nineteenth-century English case that established the precedent. The defense became codified into law in the United States and has been altered by statute in some states. The *ex post facto* defense is written plainly in the Constitution. Anglo-American law has a rich tradition of limiting the power of the state, protecting the rights of the accused, and recognizing a defendant's right to use specific defenses to crimes.

CHAPTER OBJECTIVES

After studying this chapter, you should be able to:

- Know the Common Law defenses, and their essential elements
- Understand the concept of self-defense and be able to explain when non-deadly and deadly force can be used
- Explain under what circumstances consent is a defense
- Explain when mistake of law and mistake of fact are defenses
- Explain entrapment and legal traps law enforcement officials use
- Differentiate between the consequences of voluntary and involuntary intoxication
- Explain the different standards for the insanity defense and how each operates

Justification Defenses and castle laws

Justification defenses
A legal excuse for committing an act that otherwise would be a tort or a crime.

Self-defense
The use of force to protect oneself from death or imminent bodily harm at the hands of an aggressor.

Castle Laws
Laws passed by states that allow homeowners (and renters) the right to defend their property and persons within that property from intruders, including through the use of deadly force.

Go ahead, make my day.

Clint Eastwood playing Harry Callahan in the movie *Sudden Impact*

Justification defenses can be used where the commission of the proscribed act is justified and, therefore, not appropriate for criminal sanctions. In other words, the person accused of the crime had a legitimate reason for committing the act and was therefore justified in committing an act that would otherwise be a crime. The justification defense most people are familiar with is **self-defense** in what would otherwise be a murder case. It is far from the only justification defense available.

Individuals have the right to defend themselves, innocent people, and their property from harm from others. Citizens trying to prevent a crime from occurring may also have a defense if their actions otherwise violate the law. Each case's circumstances dictate whether a justification defense protects the accused. There are no hard and fast rules; justification defenses are fact-driven affairs requiring the jury to decide whether the defendant's actions were reasonable under the circumstances.

Over the last decade or so, there has been an increase in so-called **Castle Laws**. Based on the Common Law concept that a man's (or woman's) home is his (or her) castle, the doctrine allows the defense of home against intruders. All in all, thirty states have Castle Laws on the books and some go beyond the Common Law defense concepts discussed below. For example, some states have added a "stand your ground" addition to their Castle Laws, which essentially says a homeowner does *not* have to back off even if the intruder turns and tries to leave.

HISTORICAL HIGHLIGHT

Do Good Fences Make Good Neighbors?

Sarah Palin, the former governor of Alaska and former vice presidential candidate, lives in Wasilla, Alaska. Her colorful personality and controversies over her political beliefs have spurred writer Joe McGinniss to write a book on Palin. McGinniss is best known for his true crime books such as *Blind Faith* and *Fatal Vision*, and is working on *Sarah Palin's Year of Living Dangerously*, due out in the fall of 2011.

McGinniss rented a house in Wasilla, ostensibly to spend time in the town as he researches his book.

The rental is right next to the Palin family home, which prompted Palin to post this question on her Facebook page:

"Wonder what kind of material he'll gather while overlooking Piper's bedroom, my little garden, and the family's swimming hole?"

The Palins are building a fence. And an editorial in the local paper included a note on Alaska's Castle Laws. The editors wrote:

> Finally, those who are fond of Joe McGinnis might remind him (if he doesn't already know) that Alaska has a law that allows the use of deadly force in protection of life and property.[1]

Non-deadly force
Force used to subdue a criminal or prevent a crime without risking death.

A person may always use **non-deadly force** to prevent an attacker from committing a crime against him or her. The person may use a reasonable amount of force to restrain or render harmless the attacker. Persons using non-deadly force are not required to retreat at any time during the use of force. Consider this example. A woman walking down a busy street feels someone brush by her. She then feels her handbag's shoulder strap tighten and realizes the youth who brushed by her is trying to steal her purse. She can hit him over the head with her purse to subdue him, tie him to the nearest lamppost with her belt, and wait for the police to arrive. She has used non-deadly force to subdue and hold him and will be able to defend her actions if criminal assault and kidnapping charges are filed against her.

However, the use of **deadly force** is much more tightly controlled. A person may only use deadly force in self-defense when it reasonably appears necessary to prevent immediate death or serious injury or prevent the commission of a serious felony involving risk to human life. Deadly force may only be used against an attacker who has initiated the aggression using unlawful force. Consider the following example. You are on a flight over the Atlantic when you notice that the man in the next seat is attempting to light his shoes. On closer observation, you notice that the shoelace resembles a fuse. You call attention to his behavior by summoning the cabin crew. Together, you and other passengers attempt to subdue the passenger, but he struggles to light the shoe. You hit him over the head with a wine bottle and kill him. It turns out his shoes were loaded with plastic explosives. Your actions involved the use of deadly force, but you were justified because it appears he was attempting to blow up the plane. You used deadly force to prevent death and destruction. However, if the first blow knocked the passenger out, and the rest of the crew tied him to a chair and removed his shoes, you cannot continue to hit him over the head until he is dead.

Often in deadly force situations, there is a question of whether a person could have or should have retreated from the situation when the opportunity arose. A **retreat rule** has grown out of Common Law decisions through the years. The rule has two parts:

- A person must retreat rather than use deadly force unless the person is at his or her home or business.
- Most states have adopted the rule that there is no duty to retreat unless the retreat can be made in complete safety.

Consider the shoe bomb case again. You were under no duty to retreat since to do so would be impossible. You can't get off the plane.

Oddly enough, aggressors can avail themselves of the self-defense argument under certain circumstances. Aggressors can regain the right to self-defense if theys remove themselves from the fight. This is referred to as **withdrawal**.

Consider the following scenario. An armed gunman enters a store with the intent of robbing it. He pulls his gun and demands cash. The owner of the store instead pulls his gun. Shots are exchanged, but no one is hit. The gunman flees and throws his gun in a nearby dumpster. The storeowner pursues the gunman and begins firing at him. At this point, the gunman has regained his right to self-defense. The storeowner is now the aggressor.

Similarly, initial aggressors are protected under the doctrine of **sudden escalation**. If a fight that was not life threatening suddenly becomes life threatening, the initial aggressor can take whatever action is necessary to protect himself. For example, one teenager approaches another and picks a fight. The second teenager at first defends himself in like fashion. However, at some point, the attacked teenager becomes enraged, picks up a sharp object lying nearby, and attacks the aggressor. The aggressor now has the right to take whatever steps necessary to defend himself. If the attacked teenager is now using deadly force, the initial aggressor may use deadly force to stop the attack.

Another Common Law defense is the **defense of others.** A defendant can use the defense of others defense when he acts in the belief the intended victim had a legal right to act in his or her own defense. No special relationship need exist between the

Deadly force
Force intended to cause death or likely to result in death.

Retreat rule
The rule governing when a person must retreat rather than use deadly force.

Withdrawal
The act of removing oneself from a conflict.

Sudden escalation
The concept that a conflict that was not life threatening escalates to the point that it is.

Defense of others
The defense used when otherwise criminal activities are done to save other people from harm.

defendant and the intended victim. In this case, the defendant does not have to retreat unless he is sure the victim is safe.

This could be played out as follows. A man is walking down the street and sees a perpetrator attacking a woman. The man can use appropriate force to stop the attack. If the attacker is using deadly force, the man can use deadly force to stop him. However, if his initial interference is enough to drive off the attacker, and the intended victim is now safe, the man may not pursue the attacker with the intent of doing him bodily harm.

The law delineates between what force may be used to defend people and what may be used to defend property. For instance, it is not permissible to kill an unarmed purse-snatcher. It is legal to try to catch him and hold him for police. Deadly force may only be used in property crimes where the aggressor is placing people in imminent danger.

Deadly force is permissible in the act of crime prevention if the crime is a serious felony that may endanger human life. For other less dangerous crimes, non-deadly force is appropriate. You cannot, for example, rig a deadly trap to prevent break-ins to your home or hunting camp. For example, in the classic case, *Katko v. Briney*, 183 N.W.2d 657 (1971), the Iowa Supreme Court let stand a jury verdict for actual and punitive damages against the owner of an abandoned farmhouse who had rigged a rifle to go off if an intruder entered. An intruder did, and sued successfully when he was injured.

Sometimes breaking the law is necessary to protect human life or property. For instance, a person may trespass on a property to save a person from imminent danger. In order for the **necessity defense** to work, the defendant must reasonably believe his or her action was necessary to avoid harm to society, which is greater than any harm caused to the property. The necessity defense may never be used to justify a death to protect property. In any use of the necessity defense, the defendant must be without fault. For example, a co-conspirator to burn down a house cannot break into a neighbor's house to phone the fire department.

Bear in mind that Common Law defenses may have been modified in your jurisdiction. Always check local laws before using or advising the use of deadly force to protect either people or property. There is also a growing trend, perhaps fueled by well-publicized mass killings such as those that occurred at Virginia Tech in 2007, to legalize the carrying and use of weapons in public places and to allow aggressive action in the defense of people and property, even in situations where there is the possibility of retreat.

YOU MAKE THE CALL

Doctor Euthanizes Patients as Hurricane Rages

Dr. Anna Pou was working at the Memorial Medical Center in New Orleans on August 29, 2005, as Hurricane Katrina hit the city. As the waters rose, hospital staff evacuated the lower floors. Eventually the wind and water knocked out the hospital's power.

Nurses had nowhere to empty bedpans, and operated respirators manually. The temperature rose to 110 degrees inside the building. Despite pleas for help in evacuating patients, none had been moved by the morning of September 1. The situation was getting desperate.

Rose Savoie, age ninety, Ireatha Watson, age eighty-nine, and Holis Alford, age sixty-six, were among the suffering patients too sick to get out of bed. Emmett Everett Sr., age sixty-one, presented particular challenges to the doctors. He weighed 380 pounds and was paralyzed. Evacuation efforts began at 11 a.m. on September 1. According to the Orleans Parish prosecutor, all four patients were alive at that time. By five o'clock that afternoon when the hospital had been completely evacuated they were dead.

The prosecutor asserted Dr. Pou and two nurses administered the four and possibly others a "lethal cocktail"[2] of morphine and midazolam hydrochloride. The four victims had never been prescribed these drugs, but they were found in their systems during their autopsy. After Dr. Pou was arrested in July 2006, the New Orleans medical community held protests claiming the charges were politically motivated, noting that Louisiana Attorney General Charles Foti, who ran the investigation, was seeking re-election.

Foti turned the case over to Orleans Parish prosecutor Eddie Jordon to handle. But Jordon wasn't as sure of the case. Even the Orleans Parish coroner said the evidence was inclusive to tell whether the four were murdered, died accidentally, or by natural causes. Jordon empaneled a grand jury to decide whether to indict the doctor and two nurses. The two nurses testified in return for immunity and charges against them were dropped.

The grand jury ultimately decided not to charge Dr. Pou with anything. Attorney General Foti blamed Jordon for not presenting all the evidence including the conclusions of five forensic experts that not only these four patients, but also five others were murdered.[3]

Did Dr. Pou and the two nurses get away with murder? On the one hand, testimony from other doctors seemed to indicate Pou said she was willing to euthanize the suffering patients. Another doctor saw nurses with syringes in their hands. But no one saw Dr. Pou or the nurses inject the patients. Prosecutors point out that someone obviously did. Did the New Orleans jury just want the city to move on with rebuilding? Did some medical professional make an error of judgment while under extreme duress? Or did Dr. Pou get away with murder? You make the call.

Duress Defenses

Defendants sometimes commit acts under duress and can then use the **duress defense**. Duress is a defense if the defendant committed the crime out of a well-grounded fear of death or serious bodily harm. For instance, it would be illegal for a bank teller to hand a bag of cash to her best friend, but not to a robber with a gun in his hand. The difference is that the teller hands the money to the robber under duress. In these cases, the defendant is arguing that she is the victim of the crime, not the perpetrator. Hostages who are made to commit crimes such as bank robberies while under the control of their captors can also use the defense.

Duress defense
The defense that a person acted under threat of bodily harm to themselves or a family member. It may not be used to justify killing. The crime committed must be less serious than the harm threatened.

The following conditions must be met for the duress defense to apply:

- The actor was wrongfully threatened by another to perform an act that he or she otherwise would not have performed.
- The threat was of serious bodily harm or death to the person or an immediate family member.
- The threat was immediate and there was no way for the threatened person to escape or avoid the threatened action.
- The harm threatened was greater than the harm from the crime committed.
- The threatened person wasn't intentionally involved in the situation.

Cases like these are seldom prosecuted if the police and prosecutors are convinced that the hostage acted out of fear and the threat was real. The person in question must be under threat of death to herself or a family member. The threat must be immediate and real. The duress defense is generally not a defense to murder. That's because the crime committed under duress (murder) isn't greater than the harm threatened (death if the threatened person doesn't kill as ordered). In other words, you can't kill to avoid being killed, but you can rob to avoid being killed. Duress may be a defense to felony murder, if the person was under duress to commit the underlying felony. (See Chapter 3 for a discussion of the felony murder rule.)

The U.S. Supreme Court recently clarified the burden of proof for defendants using the duress defense. Keshia Dixon purchased firearms at gun shows using a false identity and address to conceal the fact that she was under a felony indictment at the time. She was caught and charged with illegally attempting to purchase a firearm. At trial, she claimed her purchases were made under duress because her boyfriend promised to hurt her children if she did not buy the guns. Her lawyer asked the judge to instruct the jury that unless the prosecutor had proved her claim was a lie beyond a reasonable doubt, then they had to acquit. The judge disagreed and instead told the jury that the defendant had to prove her duress story to be true by a preponderance of the evidence. Dixon appealed. Ultimately, the Supreme Court backed the judge. Defendants have the burden of proof in the duress defense, but they must only prove their story by a preponderance of the evidence.[4]

YOU MAKE THE CALL

Criminal or Victim? The Strange Case of Brian Wells

Brian Wells was a forty-six-year-old pizza delivery man in Erie, Pennsylvania on August 28, 2003. An order for two large sausage and pepperoni pizzas came into Mama Mia's Pizza during the lunchtime rush. Brian took the order and went to deliver the pies a little over a mile down the road. When he didn't return right away, shop owner Tony Ditmo became concerned. Brian was one of his most reliable workers.

Ditmo's concern turned to bewilderment at two o'clock as he watched Brian on television pleading with the state trooper pointing the gun at him to get some help. According to the news reports, Brian had robbed a bank and had some sort of device around his neck that Brian claimed was a bomb that was going to go off. After asking the policeman, "Why is it nobody's trying to come get this thing off me? I don't have a lot of time," Brian pulled a pin out of the device, starting a timer. "It's gonna go off. I'm not lying. Did you call my boss?" Then came the explosion. Brian fell backward and died as confused police looked on.

Subsequent investigation has shed some light on that afternoon's events, but whether Brian Wells was a betrayed accomplice or innocent victim is still a debatable issue. Investigators have found this string of facts. A caller ordered the pizza from a pay phone at a gas station and asked that it be delivered to an address of a nearby TV station satellite dish. Investigators believe the man who called was sixty-year-old William Rothstein, a shop teacher and engineer who lived near both the gas station and pizza delivery site.

Police would come to know Rothstein better after he called them on September 21, 2003, to tell them about the murder victim stored in his freezer. Rothstein told them that the victim was James Roden, who had the bad fortune to have been the boyfriend of Marjorie Diehl-Armstrong. Diehl-Armstrong had been engaged to Rothstein twice in the thirty-five years they had known each other. The broken engagements appear to be the only reason Rothstein was still alive.

Diehl-Armstrong shot an ex-boyfriend, but at her trial claimed she was a victim of domestic abuse. The jury acquitted her. Her first husband hung himself. Her second died from head injuries after a fall at home. Rothstein told the police that Diehl-Armstrong shot Roden with a shotgun in bed in her home, and asked him to dispose of the body, paying him $2,000 for his efforts. Rothstein measured the body and bought the appropriate size freezer for storage. But when Diehl-Armstrong insisted he run the body through an ice grinder to dispose of it, Rothstein balked.

In exchange for immunity, he testified against Diehl-Armstrong. She is currently serving a twenty-year sentence. But police still believed Rothstein and Diehl-Armstrong were connected to Brian Wells' death and the botched bank robbery. One reason for their suspicion was that the FBI profiler assigned to the case believed that more than one person was behind the plan. The team would need someone sadistic and controlling and a mechanical genius who could build the complicated device and provide the twelve pages of complex directions Brian was to follow. Investigators could only find circumstantial evidence tying Wells to Rothstein and Diehl-Armstrong; the last message on Wells answering machine was from a prostitute who knew a drug dealer named Kenneth Barnes who had gone fishing with Diehl-Armstrong.[5] Were the elaborate directions just a ruse allowing Brian to claim innocence? Could Rothstein and Diehl-Armstrong been on the way to get the money from Brian when the police caught him? Investigators theorize that the two masterminds intended to intercept Wells, disarm the collar bomb and split the money, but the police arrested Wells before that happened. At least one eyewitness describes a car carrying both Diehl-Armstrong and Rothstein going the wrong way down a highway on that day. Rothstein has since died, so his story will never be told. Barnes eventually testified that Wells was part of the conspiracy, but Barnes testified against Diehl-Armstrong in return for a reduced sentence. Diehl-Armstrong was deemed to mentally ill to stand trial.[6] Brian Wells will never get to tell his story. The question remains: how much did Brian Wells know as he sat there pleading for help? Was he a criminal or a victim?

Other Common Law Defenses

Mistake of fact
A defense used when a defendant honestly believes something to be true that isn't.

The **mistake of fact** defense can be used when a defendant honestly believes something to be true that isn't. For instance, a person retrieving a piece of luggage at an airport that looks exactly like his or hers may be guilty of not checking the claim check, but not of stealing someone's luggage. The mistake of fact defense applies to different crimes differently. For instance, for general intent crimes the mistake must be a reasonable mistake. But for specific intent crimes, any mistake of fact may be used as a defense. You could not form the specific intent to commit a crime if you are mistaken about the facts. For example, in a hypothetical jurisdiction it is a specific intent crime to have sexual contact with a brother or sister. You and your twin brother were separated at birth and placed in different foster homes. Thirty years later, you meet but do not know you are related. You fall in love and have sexual relations. The fact that you don't realize you are related is a defense to criminal charges of incest. Once you find out you are sister and brother, however, the defense is no longer available. The mistake of fact defense may not be used for strict liability crimes.

Mistake of law
A defense used when a person in good faith relied on an interpretation of law from a person charged with administering the law.

The **mistake of law** defense can generally be used when a person in good faith relied on an interpretation of law from a person charged with administering the law. For instance, an IRS official tells you that the cost of your "Home of the Whopper" boxer shorts is a legitimate entertainment deduction. You take the deduction, but it is later disallowed. You could use the mistake of law defense to avoid any criminal penalty. Most likely though you will have to pay the tax due.

The mistake of law defense can also be used if an interpretation of the law changed. For instance, in the above scenario the IRS agent was accurate at the time he gave you the interpretation, but the interpretation changes the following year to only allow deductions for Elvis "Hunka Hunka Burning Love" boxers. If this were the case, you could avoid criminal liability for deducting the "Whopper" boxers. The mistaken interpretation of law may not come from an attorney. They deal in briefs, not boxers.

Consent defense
Usually used in rape cases; argues the defendant had the "victim's" consent to perform the acts.

A defendant may use the victim's **consent** as a defense in some circumstances. For instance, a defendant accused of rape is not guilty if the sex was consensual. The consent defense is unavailable for statutory rape. A victim's consent is not valid if:

- The victim is a minor
- The victim has a mental disease or defect
- The victim is intoxicated to the point he or she is unable to make a reasonable judgment
- Consent is obtained by force or duress
- Consent is obtained by fraudulent or deceptive means
- The victim has been judged to be legally incompetent
- The law in question precluded the consent defense

Generally consent is not a defense to crimes involving grievous bodily harm or death. For example, it isn't a defense to murder that the victim wanted to die, or a defense to assault that the victim wanted to be beaten or disfigured. These acts would be crimes whether the victim wanted the acts to take place or not, unlike rape, which wouldn't be a crime if the other party consented.

Entrapment and Legal Traps

Entrapment is a defense used when law enforcement officials lure a person into committing a crime. Most frequently, this occurs in bribery cases. To work, the entrapment defense must pass a two-prong test. First, the criminal design must have originated with law enforcement. Second, the defendant must not be predisposed to commit the crime.

Depending on the case law in your jurisdiction, one of two tests for predisposition is used. Most jurisdictions use the **subjective standard**, also known as the **majority rule**. The subjective standard revolves around the answer to one question, "Was the defendant predisposed to commit the crime?" Other jurisdictions use the **objective standard** or the **minority rule**. The objective standard focuses on the government's inducement and asks the question, "Would an innocent person be induced to commit the crime by the officer's acts?"

The Supreme Court answered that question in a case involving the receipt of child pornography. It ruled that the entrapment defense prohibited prosecution of a defendant who ordered child pornography after a twenty-six-month mail campaign by the government to induce him to order a catalog. The campaign included personal letters from a postal inspector posing as another male interested in seeing nude teenage boys, solicitations to join associations dedicated to freedom of the press, and requests that he purchase magazines depicting boys. When his order from the sting operation arrived, he was arrested. A search of his house turned up nothing but the materials the government had sent him. The Supreme Court ruled that the government's campaign to get him to order was entrapment.[7]

It is important to understand the difference between entrapment and **legal traps**. Legal traps are techniques used by law enforcement to catch individuals involved in criminal activity that don't rise to the level of entrapment. For example, it is a fairly common practice for vice squads to send an attractive police officer disguised as a prostitute to catch those who may be on the lookout to engage in an illegal sex trade. While many of those "caught" when they approach the officer and make an offer may believe this is entrapment, it is merely a legal trap.

Capacity Defenses

Capacity defenses may be used when the defendant lacks the capacity or ability to control his or her actions or understand that the act was criminal in nature. Age, mental disabilities, intoxication, and insanity can affect the ability to understand the law and control one's actions. Capacity defenses shield from liability those who can't understand right from wrong or control their actions.

Infancy Defense

Debate rages about how to try minors who commit violent crimes. Under the Common Law, children of tender age could not be held liable for criminal acts under the presumption that they lacked the capacity to tell right from wrong.

Entrapment
A defense used when law enforcement officials lure a person into committing a crime.

Government agents may not originate a criminal design, implant in an innocent person's mind the disposition to commit a criminal act, and then induce commission of the crime so that the Government may prosecute.

Justice White in *Jacobson v. United States,* 503 U.S. 540 (1992)

Subjective standard (majority rule) for entrapment
Asks the question, "Was the defendant predisposed to commit the crime?"

Objective standard (minority rule) for entrapment
Asks the question, "Would an innocent person be induced to commit the crime by the officer's acts?"

Legal traps
Techniques used by law enforcement to catch criminal activity that fall short of entrapment.

Infancy defense
The defense that a child is too young to either be prosecuted, or stand trial as an adult.

Although some states have sought to modify the standard by statute, the Common Law standard for the **infancy defense** is as follows:

- Children under seven years of age are conclusively presumed to be incapable of knowing the wrongfulness of their crimes.
- Children seven to fourteen years of age have a rebuttable presumption of incapacity. The burden of proof is on the prosecutor to prove beyond a reasonable doubt that the defendant appreciated the quality and nature of his or her actions.
- Children over fourteen were treated as adults and presumed to fully appreciate the difference between right and wrong.

Keep in mind that capacity is only part of the story. Children who have the capacity to commit crimes can be tried in the state's juvenile court system or in the adult system. Before a child is tried in adult court, a hearing is held. That hearing may include a discussion of the child's capacity as well as an examination of the charges and any prior record. Some states have recently enacted legislation that allows more children to be charged as adults in response to demands by the public that "doing adult crime ought to mean doing adult time." A full discussion of the treatment of juveniles as adults is beyond the scope of this text.

Intoxication Defense

Involuntary intoxication
The condition of a person who unknowingly ingests an intoxicating substance. Generally treated like insanity.

Voluntary intoxication
The condition where a person knowingly ingests an intoxicating substance. Not a defense to murder or most crimes.

The intoxication defense is most successfully used in cases of **involuntary intoxication**. This happens when a person unknowingly ingests an intoxicating substance. Date-rape drugs are an example of this. This defense may be made to both specific and general intent crimes. Persons who are involuntarily intoxicated are treated the same as insane defendants. They must meet whatever test the jurisdiction uses for insanity. (See the next section in this chapter.)

Voluntary intoxication is quite another matter. It may never be used as a defense to a general intent crime. It also cannot be used as an excuse or justification of a crime of homicide. It cannot be used as a defense to crimes involving negligence, recklessness, or strict liability. Voluntary intoxication has been used as a defense to specific intent crimes where the intoxication prevents the defendant from formulating the requisite intent. If successful, this can reduce a charge of first-degree murder to second-degree murder.

Insanity

Insanity defense
States that the defendant lacked the mental state to understand the nature and consequences of the crime.

Courts have long wrestled with the concept of trying the mentally ill or handicapped. Just as young children do not understand the nature of their actions, mentally ill or handicapped people may not either. Over the years, courts have recognized several defenses based on the defendant's inability to distinguish right from wrong when committing a crime.

The most common of these defenses is the **insanity defense**. In essence, a defendant using the insanity defense is claiming he or she lacked the mental state to understand the nature and consequences of the crime. Federal law requires defendants to show by clear and convincing evidence that they were insane at the time of the crime.[8] The insanity defense is often used when the evidence against the defendant is overwhelming. Under these circumstances, the defendant cannot deny committing the crime, but can argue insanity. If the defendant were successful, he or she would be committed to a mental hospital rather than prison. The defendant would remain there until the state determined the person to be sane.

HISTORICAL HIGHLIGHT

The Move Away from Capital Punishment for the Mentally Retarded

In 2002, Virginia became the eighteenth state to outlaw execution of the mentally retarded. Under Virginia law, convicts with an IQ below seventy may not be executed. Twelve other states have no capital punishment. Virginia's decision may have tipped the scales for the Supreme Court. Later the same year, the Court ruled that applying the death penalty to mentally retarded persons was cruel and unusual punishment in violation of the Eighth Amendment. The case was *Atkins v. Virginia*, 536 U.S. 304 (2002). States who still have the death penalty will now have to come up with standards to determine who is mentally retarded and who is not.

Several high-profile executions of prisoners with very low IQs brought the capacity question to the fore of the debate over capital punishment. Since people with very low IQs never develop the equivalent of "adult minds," the question of whether they can form intent or understand the consequences of their actions cannot be answered clearly. Some even argue that trying and convicting these people amounts to trying a child in an adult court.

Additionally, the "deterrent" aspects of capital punishment may very well be lost on a person who neither understands what he is doing or its consequences. Nor is there a general deterrent effect that would likely dissuade other mentally retarded persons to refrain from criminal acts, given diminished capacity to understand the connection between the criminal act and the consequences. Persons with low IQs may also lack the ability to aid their own defense at trial, resulting in false convictions. Given the permanent nature of the death penalty, life imprisonment would seem a better alternative.[9] The Supreme Court seems to agree. For a fuller discussion of the death penalty, see Chapter 14.

HISTORICAL HIGHLIGHT

Guns and Alcohol: The James Allen Egelhoff Story

James Allen Egelhoff was camping and picking mushrooms in northwestern Montana when he met Roberta Pavlova and John Christenson. They sold their mushrooms and went to a bar for some drinks. After drinking at the bar, they proceeded to a private party where more drinking occurred. Sometime during the evening Egelhoff gave his gun to Pavlova to store in the car's glove compartment.

That night around midnight Montana state troopers were called to the scene of a car that had gone off the road into a ditch. In the front seat were Pavlova and Christenson. Each had been shot in the head once and killed. In the back seat was Egelhoff, yelling obscenities and behaving wildly. His gun lay on the floor at his feet with two discharged rounds.

The policemen arrested Egelhoff. His hands tested positive for gunshot residue, and his blood alcohol level an hour after his arrest was 0.36, over four times the legal intoxication level.

Egelhoff was charged with two counts of deliberate homicide. However, he had no memory of committing the crimes. Under Montana law, a person is guilty of deliberate homicide if he purposely or knowingly causes the death of another human being.

At trial, Egelhoff maintained that he was so drunk he could not have committed the crimes. He argued that some fourth person must have pulled the trigger, and he was too intoxicated to remember the incident. In the charge to the jury, the judge informed them that they could not take Egelhoff's intoxication into account when "determining the existence of a mental state which is an element of the offense." The jury convicted him of both homicides and sentenced him to eighty-four years in prison.

Egelhoff appealed to the Montana Supreme Court. He argued that his intoxication was relevant to his ability to form intent. If he could not form intent, he was not guilty of deliberate homicide, but some lesser offense such as manslaughter. The Montana Supreme Court agreed and reversed the conviction. The case was appealed to the U.S. Supreme Court.

This case proved to be a very divisive one for the justices. At issue was whether excluding the intoxication evidence from consideration as it affected his ability to form intent was a denial of due process. By a 5–4 margin, the Court ruled that the trial judge had not erred in instructing the jury to determine Egelhoff's intent without taking his intoxication into account. In other words, his voluntary intoxication could never be an excuse for committing homicide.[10]

The insanity defense was first used successfully in 1843. The defendant in that case was named Daniel M'Naghten. Hence, future insanity cases would be governed by the **M'Naghten rule.** If a defendant at the time of the crime was "laboring under such a defect of reason, from diseases of the mind, as not to know the nature and quality of the act he was doing, or, if he did know it, that he did not know that what he was doing was wrong," no conviction is warranted. The burden of proof for the insanity defense is as follows:

> Every man is presumed to be sane and to possess a sufficient degree of reason to be responsible for his crimes, until the contrary be proved to (the jury's) satisfaction; and that to establish a defense on the ground of insanity, it must be clearly proved.[11]

M'Naghten rule
Holds that a defendant "is presumed to be sane and to possess a sufficient degree of reason to be responsible for his crimes, until the contrary be proved to (the jury's) satisfaction" beyond a reasonable doubt.

Beyond M'Naghten

Some American states have modified the M'Naghten rule. In 1886, Alabama adopted the more liberal "irresistible impulse" test. In effect, this created a "temporary insanity" for people who committed "crimes of passion."[12]

HISTORICAL HIGHLIGHT

The M'Naghten Case

Sir Robert Peel was the British Home Secretary in the mid-1840s. Mr. Peel was a crusader in the fight against crime. In fact, he is generally considered to be the father of the British police—hence, the nickname "Bobbies."

Of course, not everyone appreciated Sir Robert's passion. One individual in particular did not take kindly to the war on crime. His name was Daniel M'Naghten, and he believed that Sir Robert Peel was the head of a conspiracy to kill him. In his paranoid rage he shot and killed Edward Drummond, Peel's private secretary. M'Naghten mistook Drummond for Peel.

At trial, his attorney argued that M'Naghten was insane at the time he shot Drummond, and should be hospitalized, not imprisoned. The jury agreed, and M'Naghten was found "not guilty by reason of insanity."

Durham test
Test of insanity that only requires a "substantial lack of capacity" on the part of the defendant.

M'Naghten was expanded even further in the 1954 *Durham v. United States* case. In this case, the District of Columbia Appeals Court ruled, "an accused is not criminally responsible if his unlawful act was the product of mental disease or defect."[13] Where M'Naghten required a complete lack of capacity, the **Durham test** only required a "substantial lack of capacity." The "substantial lack of capacity" test is part of the Model Penal Code, but has not been adopted by all states.

Guilty, But Mentally Ill

The insanity defense debate has paralleled the capital punishment debate in the United States for most of its history. Very shortly after the Supreme Court outlawed the death penalty as it was practiced in 1972, states began working on new death penalty laws, and tighter restrictions on the insanity defense.

Illinois enacted a "**guilty, but mentally ill**" statute in the wake of the acquittal of a defendant by reason of insanity and subsequent repeat murders. But the national spotlight shone on the subject after the 1980 assassination of John Lennon by a deranged fan, and the 1981 attempt on President Reagan's life by the delusional John Hinckley. The thought of releasing either Hinckley or Lennon's assassin, Mark David Chapman, was more than many could bear. In response, several states enacted "guilty, but mentally ill" statutes.

Under "guilty, but mentally ill" laws, defendants who do not meet the M'Naghten standard of a complete lack of capacity, but fall under the substantial lack of capacity standard, are convicted and sent to a mental hospital. If they recover, they are sent to prison for the rest of their term.

Guilty, but mentally ill
Defendants who do not meet the complete lack of capacity standard but fall under the substantial lack of capacity standard are convicted and sent to a mental hospital. If they recover, they are sent to prison for the rest of their term.

Competency to Stand Trial

A variation on the insanity defense is to claim that the defendant is **incompetent to stand trial**. Common Law has long held that a person must be able to understand the proceedings against him and be able to interact with his attorneys in order to have a fair trial. However, a defendant who is incompetent today may be competent tomorrow. Can the state hold someone indefinitely until they can stand trial?

This question came before the Supreme Court in 1972. In that case, *Jackson v. Indiana*, the High Court ruled that defendants could only be held for a reasonable amount of time. Subsequent decisions have generally held that defendants cannot be held more than the lesser of eighteen months or the maximum sentence for the crime they are charged with. At that point, the state must:

Incompetent to stand trial
A person unable to understand the proceedings against him and be able to interact with his attorneys.

Where does the violet tint end and the orange tint begin? Distinctly we see the difference of the colors, but where exactly does the one first blending enter into the other. So with sanity and insanity.

Herman Melville

- Try the defendant, if he or she is competent to stand trial,
- Dismiss the charges, or
- Commence civil proceedings to have the defendant committed to a mental institution.[14]

The standard for competency in many jurisdictions comes from Justice Thurgood Marshall's dissent in *White v. Estelle*, where he stated: "This Court has approved a test of incompetence which seeks to determine whether the defendant 'has sufficient present ability to consult with his lawyer with a reasonable degree of rational understanding—and whether he has a rational as well as factual understanding of the proceedings against him'".[15]

In recent years, older defendants have avoided trial temporarily or permanently due to their health condition. Often this is a combination of senility, or overall health condition. This concept is recognized in international law as well. In 2000, former Chilean dictator Augusto Pinochet was arrested in England for crimes committed during his reign. A Spanish court had issued the indictment. An English judge ruled that the man was in too ill health to stand trial, and released him.

In the United States, the cases of Thomas E. Blanton Jr. and Bobby Frank Cherry, accused of bombing the 16th St. Baptist Church in Birmingham, Alabama, in 1963, were delayed because of the defendant's age. Blanton was not convicted until 2001, and Cherry's trial was delayed when he was at first ruled incompetent to stand trial, and later ruled competent.

HISTORICAL HIGHLIGHT

Bombingham: The Death Throes of Segregation

It was April 1963. Dr. Martin Luther King Jr. set his sights on Birmingham, Alabama, the last bastion of southern segregation. Almost nine years after the famous *Brown v. Board of Education* decision, Birmingham's schools were still segregated. Neither the city nor downtown merchants employed African-Americans. In addition to segregated drinking fountains, restrooms, and dressing rooms, local ordinances required separate taxi cabs, ambulances, hospitals, cemeteries, elevators, eating places, hotels, and theaters. Marriage between the races was a felony.

Dr. King's arrival was designed to help the city's already growing civil rights movement headed by local minister, the Rev. Fred Shuttlesworth. At the time, local officials and members of the Ku Klux Klan were terrorizing the African-American community. Black homes were frequently bombed, leading to the city's nickname "Bombingham." King's plan was to train large groups of protesters to protest nonviolently and be arrested in large numbers. The mass arrests would overwhelm local law enforcement and focus national attention on segregation.

Shuttlesworth's church, the 16th Street Baptist Church, was the epicenter of the movement. After Dr. King was arrested for illegally demonstrating, teenagers left the church in waves of fifty only to be arrested. As each group was arrested, another took their place. Eventually, the city had to turn fire hoses and dogs on the protesters because they had no place to incarcerate them. When it happened, the TV cameras were rolling.

City merchants, fearing the city's reputation would be forever sullied, relented. They met with Dr. King and ended the protests, as well as the accompanying black boycott of the stores. But the segregationists were not finished. That September, Klansmen set off a bomb in the basement of the 16th Street Baptist Church, killing four young girls.

Law enforcement officials suspected four men—Robert "Dynamite Bob" Chambliss, Herman Cash, Thomas Blanton Jr., and Bobby Frank Cherry. Chambliss was the first to go to trial, and was convicted in 1977. Herman Cash was never charged and died in 1994. The case seemed dead until the FBI received new evidence in 1997. Charges were eventually brought against Blanton and Cherry. Blanton was convicted in 2001 and sentenced to life in prison. Cherry was charged based partly on evidence provided by his son, who claimed Cherry was not home the night before the bombing as he had told police.[16]

Cherry, however, was now old and in poor health. Initially, Cherry was found incompetent to stand trial. After receiving medical treatment, his condition improved. Cherry's case went to trial in 2002. He was found guilty and sentenced to life in prison. He died in prison in 2004. The story of Cherry's relationship with his son is told in the television movie *Sins of the Father*.

In addition to poor physical health, defendants may have mental health problems that prevent them from fully participating in their defense. People with schizophrenia or psychosis may experience hallucinations or hear voices making their perception of the proceedings unreliable. In one case, Charles Thomas Sell, a federal defendant with a long history of mental illness, was found to be competent for trial when taking his medication, but not at other times. Sell, however, was less than religious in taking his medication.

Sell was held at a mental hospital until he could be deemed competent to stand trial. He refused his medication. His psychiatrist asked for a hearing in order to obtain permission to provide involuntary medication to Sell, arguing that Sell was a danger to himself and others. Sell's attorney appealed, and the district magistrate found that Sell was not dangerous, but that medicating him was appropriate to make him competent to stand trial. The Appeals Court agreed. The case was appealed to the U.S. Supreme Court who ruled that it was appropriate to medicate federal prisoners involuntarily to render them competent to stand trial. However, hearings must be held focusing on the competency issue to make that determination.[17]

Incapacity and Punishment

In cases where the death penalty has already been imposed, convicts can postpone execution by claiming **insanity just prior to execution**. The Common Law basis for this defense also goes back to England. The legal scholar Blackstone opined that this safeguard was necessary because the condemned prisoner may be able to produce some valid reason that execution should be stayed. In the United States, the Supreme Court upheld this standard in 1958.[18]

Prisons tend to have a damaging effect on a person's sanity. Consequently, prisoners may become insane during their prison term. Should **insanity during incarceration** occur, prisoners are moved to a psychiatric hospital for the remainder of their term. Should they still be insane at the end of their term, they may be committed to a mental hospital until they recover.

Insanity just prior to execution
Most jurisdictions will not execute an insane person. Persons whose sanity returns are rewarded with death.

Insanity during incarceration
Prisoners who become insane are generally removed to mental hospitals. If they are still insane at the conclusion of their prison term, they are generally committed.

CONCEPT **REVIEW AND REINFORCEMENT**

Common Law has carved out several defenses for defendants who would otherwise be found guilty. Justification defenses can be used where the person accused of the crime had a legitimate reason for committing the act. The most common justification defense in murder cases is the self-defense justification. Individuals have the right to defend themselves, innocent people, and their property. Individuals also have some protection when they are attempting to prevent a criminal act from occurring. A person may use non-deadly force to prevent an attacker from committing a crime against him or her.

A person may only use deadly force in self-defense when it reasonably appears necessary to prevent immediate death or serious injury or prevent the commission of a serious felony involving risk to human life. Many states have Castle Laws on the books that allow homeowners the right to defend themselves against intrusions. The retreat rule defines criminal behavior when the option of using deadly force or retreating exists The rule has two parts:

1. A person must retreat rather than use deadly force unless the person is at his or her home or business.

2. Most states have adopted the rule that there is no duty to retreat unless the retreat can be made in complete safety.

Aggressors who withdraw from a fight may defend themselves from subsequent charges by showing they backed down. Aggressors may also protect themselves from the sudden escalation of a fight. The defense-of-others defense allows defendants to protect innocent citizens from criminal attack.

Deadly force may only be used in property crimes where the aggressor is placing people in imminent danger. Deadly force is permissible in the act of crime prevention if the crime is a serious felony that may endanger human life. A person may use the necessity defense when the crime was committed in the process of saving human life or property.

Defendants may use the duress defense if someone is threatening to kill the person or a family member if the crime is not committed.

The mistake-of-fact defense can be used when a defendant honestly believes something to be true that isn't. The mistake-of-fact defense may not be used for strict liability crimes. Similarly, the mistake-of-law defense can generally be used when a person in good faith relied on an interpretation of law from a person charged with administering the law. The mistaken interpretation of law may not come from an attorney.

Entrapment is a defense used when law enforcement officials lure a person into committing a crime. The entrapment defense must pass a two-prong test. First, the criminal design must have originated with law enforcement. Second, the defendant was not predisposed to commit the crime. Legal traps are techniques used by law enforcement to catch those who are predisposed to commit the crime.

A defendant may use the victim's consent as a defense in some circumstances. For instance, a defendant accused of rape is not guilty if the sex was consensual. The consent defense is unavailable for statutory rape and crimes involving death or serious bodily injury.

Capacity defenses may be used when the defendant lacks the capacity or ability to control his or her actions or understand that the act was criminal in nature. The Common Law standard for the infancy defense says that children under seven years of age may not be tried, and children seven to fourteen years of age have a rebuttable presumption of incapacity. The prosecutor must prove beyond a reasonable doubt the defendant appreciated the quality and nature of his or her actions. Children over fourteen are treated as adults for purposes of capacity. Juvenile courts may authorize trying the defendant as an adult.

Involuntary intoxication occurs when a person unknowingly ingests an intoxicating substance. This defense may be made to both specific and general intent crimes. Persons who are involuntarily intoxicated are treated the same as insane defendants. They must meet whatever test the jurisdiction uses for insanity.

Voluntary intoxication may never be used as a defense to a general intent crime. It cannot be used as an excuse or justification of a specific intent crime such as murder. It cannot be used as a defense to crimes involving negligence, recklessness, or strict liability.

Under the insanity defense, a defendant claims he or she lacked the mental state to understand the nature and consequences of the crime. The Common Law insanity defense derives from the M'Naghten case. The M'Naghten rule states that a defendant "is presumed to be sane and to possess a sufficient degree of reason to be responsible for his crimes, until the contrary be proved to (the jury's) satisfaction" beyond a reasonable doubt.

Some American states have modified the M'Naghten rule employing "irresistible impulse" or "temporary insanity" defense for people who committed "crimes of passion." More liberal interpretations include the Durham test, which is the "substantial lack of capacity" test.

Some states have a "guilty, but mentally ill" statute where defendants who do not meet the M'Naghten standard of a complete lack of capacity, but fall under the substantial lack of capacity standard, are convicted and sent to a mental hospital. If they recover, they are sent to prison for the rest of their term.

Some defendants are judged to be incompetent to stand trial. Generally, defendants cannot be held more than the lesser of eighteen months or the maximum sentence for the crime they are charged with. At that point, the state must try the defendant, if he or she is competent to stand trial, dismiss the charges, or commence civil proceedings to have the defendant committed to a mental institution.

The standard for competency in many jurisdictions is whether the defendant "has sufficient present ability to consult with his lawyer with a reasonable degree of rational understanding—and whether he has a rational as well as factual understanding of the proceedings against him."

Older defendants may not be competent for trial due to their overall health condition. They have the same rights as other defendants judged to be incompetent to stand trial.

In cases where the death penalty has already been imposed, convicts can postpone execution by claiming "insanity just prior to execution." Prisoners who become insane during their prison term are moved to a psychiatric hospital for the remainder of their term. Should they still be insane at the end of their term, they may be committed to a mental hospital until they recover.

KEY TERMS

Castle Laws
Consent defense
Deadly force
Defense of others
Duress defense
Durham test
Entrapment
Guilty, but mentally ill
Incompetent to stand trial
Infancy defense

Insanity defense
Insanity during incarceration
Insanity just prior to execution
Involuntary intoxication
Justification defenses
Legal traps
Mistake of fact
Mistake of law
M'Naghten rule
Non-deadly force

Objective standard (minority rule) for entrapment
Retreat rule
Self-defense
Subjective standard (majority rule) for entrapment
Sudden escalation
Voluntary intoxication
Withdrawal

CONCEPT **REVIEW QUESTIONS**

1. What are the Common Law defenses, and their essential elements?
2. When can non-deadly and deadly force be used in self-defense?
3. Explain under what circumstances consent is a defense.
4. Explain when mistake of law and mistake of fact are defenses.
5. Explain entrapment and legal traps law enforcement officials use.
6. Differentiate between the consequences of voluntary and involuntary intoxication.
7. Explain the different standards for the insanity defense and how each operates.

CASE **APPLICATIONS**

Building Your Professional Skills

1. Read the following edited Supreme Court decisions and answer the questions that follow.

Patterson v. New York, 432 U.S. 197 (1977)

No. 75-1861
Argued March 1, 1977
Decided June 17, 1977
432 U.S. 197
APPEAL FROM THE COURT OF APPEALS OF NEW YORK

MR. JUSTICE WHITE delivered the opinion of the Court.

The question here is the constitutionality under the Fourteenth Amendment's Due Process Clause of burdening the defendant in a New York State murder trial with proving the affirmative defense of extreme emotional disturbance as defined by New York law.

I

After a brief and unstable marriage, the appellant, Gordon Patterson, Jr., became estranged from his wife, Roberta. Roberta resumed an association with John Northrup, a neighbor to whom she had been engaged prior to her marriage to appellant. On December 27, 1970, Patterson borrowed a rifle from an acquaintance and went to the residence of his father-in-law. There, he observed his wife through a window in a state of semiundress in the presence of John Northrup. He entered the house and killed Northrup by shooting him twice in the head.

Patterson was charged with second-degree murder. In New York, there are two elements of this crime: (1) "intent to cause the death of another person"; and (2) "caus[ing] the death of such person or of a third person." . . . Malice aforethought is not an element of the crime. In addition, the State permits a person accused of murder to raise an affirmative defense that he "acted under the influence of extreme emotional disturbance for which there was a reasonable explanation or excuse."

New York also recognizes the crime of manslaughter. A person is guilty of manslaughter if he intentionally kills another person "under circumstances which do not constitute murder because he acts under the influence of extreme emotional disturbance." Appellant confessed before trial to killing Northrup, but at trial he raised the defense of extreme emotional disturbance.

The jury was instructed as to the elements of the crime of murder. Focusing on the element of intent, the trial court charged:

"Before you, considering all of the evidence, can convict this defendant or anyone of murder, you must believe and decide that the People have established beyond a reasonable doubt that he intended, in firing the gun, to kill either the victim himself or some other human being. . . ."

"Always remember that you must not expect or require the defendant to prove to your satisfaction that his acts were done without the intent to kill. Whatever proof he may have attempted, however far he may have gone in an effort to convince you of his innocence or guiltlessness, he is not obliged, he is not obligated to prove anything. It is always the People's burden to prove his guilt, and to prove that he intended to kill in this instance beyond a reasonable doubt."

The jury was further instructed, consistently with New York law, that the defendant had the burden of proving his affirmative defense by a preponderance of the evidence. The jury was told that, if it found beyond a reasonable doubt that appellant had intentionally killed Northrup but that appellant had demonstrated by a preponderance of the evidence that he had acted under the influence of extreme emotional disturbance, it had to find appellant guilty of manslaughter, instead of murder.

The jury found appellant guilty of murder. Judgment was entered on the verdict, and the Appellate Division affirmed. . .

II

It goes without saying that preventing and dealing with crime is much more the business of the States than it is of the Federal Government . . .

In determining whether New York's allocation to the defendant of proving the mitigating circumstances of severe emotional disturbance is consistent with due process, it is therefore relevant to note that this defense is a considerably expanded version of the common law defense of heat of passion on sudden provocation, and that, at common law, the burden of proving the latter, as well as other affirmative defenses—indeed, "all . . . circumstances of justification, excuse or alleviation"—rested on the defendant. . . .

III

We cannot conclude that Patterson's conviction under the New York law deprived him of due process of law. The crime of murder is defined by the statute, which represents a recent revision of the state criminal code, as causing the death of another person with intent to do so. The death, the intent to kill, and causation are the facts that the State is required to prove beyond a reasonable doubt if a person is to be convicted of murder. No further facts are either presumed or inferred in order to constitute the crime.

The statute does provide an affirmative defense—that the defendant acted under the influence of extreme emotional disturbance for which there was a reasonable explanation—which, if proved by a preponderance of the evidence, would reduce the crime to manslaughter, an offense defined in a separate section of the statute. It is plain enough that, if the intentional killing is shown, the State intends to deal with the defendant as a murderer unless he demonstrates the mitigating circumstances. . . .

It is said that the common law rule permits a State to punish one as a murderer when it is as likely as not that he acted in the heat of passion or under severe emotional distress and when, if he did, he is guilty only of manslaughter. But this has always been the case in those jurisdictions adhering to the traditional rule. It is also very likely true that fewer convictions of murder would occur if New York were required to negative the affirmative defense at issue here. But in each instance of a murder conviction under the present law, New York will have proved beyond a reasonable doubt that the defendant has intentionally killed another person, an act which it is not disputed the State may constitutionally criminalize and punish. If the State nevertheless chooses to recognize a factor that mitigates the degree of criminality or punishment, we think the State may assure itself that the fact has been established with reasonable certainty. To recognize at all a mitigating circumstance does not require the State to prove its nonexistence in each case in which the fact is put in issue, if, in its judgment, this would be too cumbersome, too expensive, and too inaccurate.

We thus decline to adopt as a constitutional imperative, operative countrywide, that a State must disprove beyond a reasonable doubt every fact constituting any and all affirmative defenses related to the culpability of an accused.

As we have explained, nothing was presumed or implied against Patterson; and his conviction is not invalid under any of our prior cases. The judgment of the New York Court of Appeals is

Affirmed.

> **Martin v. Ohio, 480 U.S. 228 (1987)**
> **No. 85-6461**
> **Decided February 25, 1987**
> **480 U.S. 228**

CERTIORARI TO THE SUPREME COURT OF OHIO

Under the Ohio Revised Code (Code), the burden of proving the elements of a criminal offense is upon the prosecution, but, for an affirmative defense, the burden of proof by a preponderance of the evidence is placed on the accused. Self-defense is an affirmative defense under Ohio law, and therefore must be proved by the defendant. Petitioner was charged by Ohio with aggravated murder, which is defined as "purposely, and with prior calculation and design, causing the death of another." She pleaded self-defense, and testified that she had shot and killed her husband when he came at her following an argument during which he had struck her.

As to the crime itself, the jury was instructed (1) that, to convict, it must find, in light of all the evidence, that each of the elements of aggravated murder was proved by the State beyond reasonable doubt, and that the burden of proof with respect to those elements did not shift; and (2) that, to find guilt, it must be convinced that none of the evidence, whether offered by the State or by petitioner in connection with her self-defense plea, raised a reasonable doubt that she had killed her husband, that she had the specific purpose and intent to cause his death, or that she had done so with prior calculation and design.

However, as to self-defense, the jury was instructed that it could acquit if it found by a preponderance of the evidence that petitioner had proved (1) that she had not precipitated the confrontation with her husband; (2) that she honestly believed she was in imminent danger of death or great bodily harm and that her only means of escape was to use force; and (3) that she had satisfied any duty to retreat or avoid danger.

The jury found her guilty, and both the Ohio Court of Appeals and Supreme Court affirmed the conviction, rejecting petitioner's Due Process Clause challenge, which was based on the charge's placing on her the self-defense burden of proof. In reaching its decision, the State Supreme Court relied on *Patterson v. New York*, 432 U. S. 197.

Held:

1. Neither Ohio law nor the above instructions violate the Due Process Clause of the Fourteenth Amendment by shifting to petitioner the State's burden of proving the elements of the crime. The instructions, when read as a whole, do not improperly suggest that self-defense evidence could not be considered in determining whether there was reasonable doubt about the sufficiency of the State's proof of the crime's elements.

Furthermore, simply because evidence offered to support self-defense might negate a purposeful killing by prior calculation and design does not mean that elements of the crime and self-defense impermissibly overlap, since evidence creating a reasonable doubt about any fact necessary for a finding of guilt could easily fall far short of proving self-defense by a preponderance of the evidence, but, on the other hand, a killing will be excused if self-defense is satisfactorily established even if there is no reasonable doubt in the jury's mind that the defendant is guilty.

2. It is not a violation of the Due Process Clause for Ohio to place the burden of proving self-defense on a defendant charged with committing aggravated murder. There is no merit to petitioner's argument that it is necessary under Ohio law for the State to disprove self-defense, since both unlawfulness and criminal intent are elements of serious offenses, while self-defense renders lawful that which would otherwise be a crime, and negates a showing of criminal intent. The Court will follow Ohio courts that have rejected this argument, holding that unlawfulness in such cases is the conduct satisfying the elements of aggravated murder, and that the necessary mental state for this crime is the specific purpose to take life pursuant to prior calculation and design. Furthermore, the mere fact that all but two States have abandoned the common law rule that affirmative defenses, including self-defense, must be proved by the defendant does not render that rule unconstitutional. The Court will follow *Patterson* and other of its decisions which allowed States to fashion their own affirmative defense burden of proof rules.

21 Ohio St.3d 91, 488 N.E.2d 166, affirmed.

QUESTIONS

1. In each case, what was the main issue?
2. Compare how New York and Ohio handle justification defenses.

CRITICAL **THINKING EXERCISES**

1. You are a former governor with a penchant for hunting moose. Unbeknownst to you, someone gets your neighbor very drunk, ties moose antlers to his head, and places him on your property. It is dark; you see antlers and think, DINNER! You fire wounding the man before you realize your prey is not quite as tasty as you thought. What defense could you use?

2. You own a store. A robber enters the store, draws a gun and demands cash. He looks away for a moment. You pull your gun out from under the counter. Would you be justified in shooting him now?
   a. If instead of shooting him at that point you tell him to drop his weapon and he makes a move that you interpret as preparing to fire, would you be justified in shooting him now?
   b. If instead of him making a move to shoot, he turns to run out the door, would you be justified in shooting him now?

3. You ask a co-worker to borrow his truck to move some items on the weekend. You have never been to his house. He says he will call and give you all the details. He leaves a message on your answering machine with directions, the address, and says the keys will be under the floor mat. Unfortunately, the message with the return phone number and the address are slightly garbled. You persevere. You go to the address you think is correct, go in the garage, and find a truck. It is unlocked, the keys are under the floor mat, and off you go. A few minutes later, a policeman pulls you over and charges you with auto theft. What defense could you use?

4. This chapter briefly described how consent may be a defense to some criminal charges, such as an allegation of rape. But in the United States, there are very few instances in which the victim's request to become a victim (i.e., consent to be harmed) will operate as a valid defense. Consider the following example and determine whether you believe consent *should* be a valid defense: An individual responds to an online invitation to be killed, dismembered, and cannibalized. The gruesome event is videotaped so that authorities have a clear record of both the consent and the specific acts. Should consent be a defense to charges of murder?[19]

5. You find out your girlfriend is pregnant. Embarrassed, you both agree to keep it secret, give birth, abandon the baby, but call the police so it can be adopted. She gives birth in a hotel room. You follow the plan and call the police. By the time the police arrive the baby is dead. They track you both down, separate you, and begin questioning you. You are distraught and tell the whole story. After a break, a policeman comes in and says your partner has accused you of murdering the child. But the policeman says, he thinks, she really did it and if you testify against her, he can get the judge to go easy on you. Meanwhile, your girlfriend has heard a story that is the mirror image. Have the police entrapped either of you?

6. You wake up one morning with a dead body next to you and blood all over the place. You had been drinking the night before, but didn't think you had that much. Since you don't remember murdering anyone, could you use the intoxication defense? What if you found out someone slipped a drug into your drink during the evening, what type of intoxication defense would you use then?

7. You are an attorney who has a client accused of killing his wife's lover after catching them in the act. The prosecution has presented no evidence of premeditation or that your client knew of the relationship prior to the day of the killing. What capacity defense can you use?

PORTFOLIO **BUILDING**

1. Research self-defense and Castle Laws in your jurisdiction and summarize them for your portfolio. Then prepare a memo for your supervisor explaining the law in your jurisdiction.

2. Research your state's insanity rule and summarize it for your portfolio. Prepare a memo for your supervisor explaining the law in your jurisdiction.

3. Does your jurisdiction require notification to the prosecution if you plan on using a defense like entrapment or insanity? If so, how and when do you provide that notice?

4. Create a checklist for your portfolio that provides a space for examining each charge against a defendant and outlining the elements needed to prove the charge. Provide space for an assessment of the evidence against the accused and to list potential defenses such as self-defense, entrapment, and mental impairment.

FOR FURTHER READING

1. Smith, R. (1981). *Trial by Medicine: The Insanity Defense in Victorian England.* Edinburgh University Press. Discusses the advances in the jurisprudence of insanity in Victorian England.

2. Moran, R. (1981). *Knowing Right from Wrong: The Insanity Defense of Daniel M'Naghten.* Free Press. Recounts the story of the insanity defense.

3. Bonnie, R. (1986). *Trial of John W. Hinckley, Jr.: A Case Study in the Insanity Defense.* Foundation Press.

Chapter **eleven**

CONSTITUTIONAL RIGHTS BEFORE ARREST

CHAPTER OBJECTIVES

After studying this chapter, you should be able to:

- Explain the constitutional protection against unreasonable searches and seizures
- Give examples of searches that violate the Fourth Amendment
- Explain what proof law enforcement must have before a search warrant will be issued
- Explain the steps that law enforcement officers must take in order to get a search warrant issued
- List areas that can be searched without a warrant
- Explain probable cause
- Explain the use of informants
- Explain the exclusionary rule
- Explain the right to remain silent
- Explain double jeopardy
- Define and explain *ex post facto* laws and bills of attainder

The poorest man may in his cottage bid defiance to all the forces of the Crown. It may be frail, its roof may shake, the wind may blow through it, the storm may enter, the rain may enter, but the King of England cannot enter! All his forces dare not cross the threshold of the ruined tenement.

William Pitt the Elder, Lord Chatham,
English statesman in a speech (1763)

The right of the people to be secure in their persons, houses, papers, and effects, against unreasonable searches and seizures, shall not be violated, and no Warrants shall issue, but upon probable cause, supported by Oath or Affirmation, and particularly describing the place to be searched, and the persons or things to be seized.

U.S. Constitution, Fourth Amendment (1791)

The protection guaranteed by the [Fourth and Fifth] Amendments is much broader in scope. The makers of our Constitution undertook to secure conditions favorable to the pursuit of happiness. They recognized the significance of man's spiritual nature, of his feelings and of his intellect. They knew that only a part of the pain, pleasure and satisfactions of life are to be found in material things. They sought to protect Americans in their beliefs, their thoughts, their emotions and their sensations. They conferred, as against the Government, the right to be let alone—the most comprehensive of rights and the right most valued by civilized men.

Justice Louis Brandeis from his dissent
in *Olmstead v. United States* (1928)

Introduction and Historical Background

The U.S. Constitution is more than just a framework for government. It is in fact a series of limitations on governmental power. Like many documents, the Constitution was a product of its time. When the constitutional convention convened in 1787, British abuses of power were still fresh in the founding fathers' memories. But they also understood that a weak central government invited foreign attack and domestic instability. The constitutional framers set out to balance these two concerns.

When it came to protecting individual rights, the framers thought specifically of abuses suffered under British rule. In the 1760s, it was common practice for British agents to enter American buildings and homes searching for goods on which customs taxes hadn't been paid. These searches took place without the British having to state a reason for suspecting that they would find contraband in the house.

The American colonists resented the expanding British control over numerous aspects of American life ranging from religious practices to where and how the colonists were tried if charged with a crime. Put in its simplest terms, the colonists wanted to be left alone. Once they freed themselves from Britain's yoke, they were reluctant to replace the harness with a new one. One reflection of the American spirit of independence is the Constitution's guarantee that the government can't conduct "**unreasonable searches and seizures,**" or arrest citizens except "upon **probable cause.**"

So strong is the populace's resistance to governmental intrusions that evidence obtained in violation of the prohibition against unreasonable searches and seizures generally can't be admitted into evidence, no matter how incriminating the evidence turns out to be. If the police don't follow the law, the consequence may well be that a guilty man or woman goes free.

The Constitution also protects citizens from being tried repeatedly for the same crime after being acquitted—**double jeopardy.** In the United States, citizens also can't be tried for acts committed before the behavior was made a criminal offense; the government is prohibited from making *ex post facto* **laws.** Nor can governments pass **bills of attainder.** Bills of attainder are criminal laws that apply only to named individuals or specific, identified groups. These three constitutional protections help assure that citizens aren't harassed or oppressed by their government through the use of the criminal process and assure that the laws are applied uniformly and fairly.

The Constitution also protects persons charged with crimes from having to incriminate himself or herself through oral testimony or a confession. The right against **self-incrimination** is an important safeguard that prevents, for example, the use of torture to extract confessions. Persons charged with crimes are also entitled to effective assistance of counsel and a reasonable opportunity to post **bail** so that he or she can assist in the preparation for trial.

As you study this chapter, think about the liberties accorded to all citizens and ask yourself whether the great legal scholar William Blackstone was right when he said, "It is better that ten guilty persons escape than that one innocent suffer." Is that the price we all must pay in order to live in a free society? Does the price become too high in time of war?

A right is not what someone gives you; it's what no one can take from you

Ramsey Clark, former U.S. attorney general, *New York Times* (October 2, 1977)

Unreasonable searches and seizures
The rule, based on the Fourth Amendment, that police must obtain a warrant before searching a home or arresting a suspect. The rule has numerous exceptions.

Double jeopardy
The rule, based on the Fifth Amendment, that a person can only be tried once for the same offense. The rule has several exceptions.

Bill of attainder
A law passed that singles out a person or persons as the only individuals affected by a criminal law. Originally, a bill of attainder singled out an individual for capital punishment without benefit of a trial.

Ex post facto **law**
The rule that a person cannot be charged with a crime that became a crime after he committed the act made illegal.

Bail
Money or other guarantee posted to assure a defendant who is released from custody pending trial or appeal will appear when called or forfeit the security posted.

Self-incrimination
The act of giving testimony against one's penal interest. Generally, persons have a right to withhold information that may incriminate and to refuse to answer questions that incriminate. The right does not generally extend to giving DNA samples or submitting to blood-alcohol testing or withholding other physical evidence.

For my part I think it less evil that some criminals should escape, than that the government should play some ignoble part.

Oliver Wendell Holmes Jr., in
Olmstead v. United States (1928)

The right to be let alone is indeed the beginning of all freedoms.

William O. Douglas (1952)

What is an Unreasonable Search?

The Fourth Amendment to the Constitution provides that "The right of the people to be secure in their persons, houses, papers, and effects, against unreasonable searches and seizures, shall not be violated." This right has evolved over the years to protect citizens from overzealous law enforcement officers and judges eager to secure criminal convictions. One of the key words in the Fourth Amendment is "unreasonable." *Reasonable* searches and seizures are allowed; it's only unreasonable ones that are unconstitutional.

Expectation of Privacy

Searches are unreasonable if they unduly interfere with the people's expectations of privacy. Thus, it can be said that people, not places, are protected from unreasonable searches. That is, if a person has a reasonable expectation of privacy in a place, the place may not be searched without a warrant. However, if he or she does not have a reasonable expectation of privacy in a place, the area can be searched without a warrant.

Courts have long held that people have an expectation of privacy in their homes. Police must either get permission to search a home, be in hot pursuit of someone, or obtain a warrant. The Supreme Court has held that " . . . except in certain carefully defined classes of cases, a search of private property without proper consent is 'unreasonable' unless it has been authorized by a valid search warrant."[1] (For an explanation of the requirements for obtaining a warrant, see the discussion on probable cause later in this chapter.) Simply put, unless an officer gets permission to enter, is acting in an exigent situation, or gets a search warrant, it's illegal for him or her to enter someone's home or apartment.

HISTORICAL HIGHLIGHT

The Right to Privacy

The word *privacy* does not appear in the Constitution. So where does the "right to privacy" come from? It is a legal construct based on various amendments to the Constitution. The "right to be let alone" was first noted by Justice Louis Brandeis in a 1928 case challenging the government's right to tap phones.[2]

Brandeis's "right to be let alone" wasn't applied to sexual or reproductive matters. Brandeis specifically refused to invoke it in a case deciding whether the state could forcibly sterilize a "promiscuous" girl. Brandeis concurred in the majority opinion allowing sterilization, apparently with no qualms about its effect on the "right to be let alone."[3]

However, the seed was planted. When the state of Oklahoma wanted to sterilize a career criminal (whose last conviction was for chicken theft) Justice

William O. Douglas ruled that the right to have children was a "basic liberty."[4]

In 1961, the Court was faced with a challenge to a Connecticut law that forbade doctors to distribute contraceptives. Noted conservative jurist John Harlan cited the Oklahoma case when he wrote that the due process clause in the Fourteenth Amendment protected the "privacy of the home." When the same doctor challenged the Connecticut law four years later, Justice Douglas wrote that the state could not violate the "zone of privacy" surrounding the marital bedroom.[5]

This right to privacy was further enlarged in the case of *Roe v. Wade*, when it was expanded to include a woman's right to have an abortion under certain circumstances.[6]

There have been limits placed on this right to privacy. Subsequent decisions have failed to expand the right. Other types of sexual activity have been ruled to not be covered by the "right to privacy" until recently.

In 1986, a homosexual male sought unsuccessfully to have Georgia's sodomy law overturned. The plaintiff had been arrested for engaging in oral sex with another man in his own apartment. If convicted under Georgia's 1816 anti-sodomy law, he would have faced up to twenty years in prison. The district attorney dropped the charges, but the plaintiff sought to have the law declared unconstitutional. The Supreme Court ruled against him on a 5–4 vote, arguing that moral concerns outweighed the "right to privacy" in this case. In effect, the Supreme Court ruled that it was a matter left to the states to regulate.[7]

Recently, the Supreme Court revisited the matter and overturned its earlier ruling in a 6–3 decision. The Court concluded that the right to privacy includes what consenting adults do in the privacy of their own home and due process protects them from criminal prosecution for that conduct, however offensive it may be to other members of the community.[8] The case is seen by some as a major step forward for the gay rights movement.

The law gets more complicated, however, when the area to be searched isn't the suspect's own home or apartment. For example, when can police search a car? Can they search your desk at work? What about listening in on the calls you make from a public phone booth? Can they read your e-mail? What if you're a guest at someone's home? What about your backyard? Your luggage? The Supreme Court has considered these and other cases on a case-by-case basis.

For example, what happens if a wife calls the police to report her husband's illegal drug use? The police show up and the wife invites the police in to show them evidence of her husband's drug use. The husband refuses to consent to the search. Can the police go in? The Supreme Court addressed this situation and determined that when police encountered this situation and entered the property and eventually charged the man with cocaine possession, they acted illegally. The Court ruled the husband's refusal barred the police from entering unless they had a warrant.[9]

Essentially, the higher the reasonable expectation of privacy, the greater the likelihood that the police can't invade that privacy. For example, a conversation overheard by an off-duty police officer at a restaurant in which the dining companions discuss a murder-for-hire scheme wouldn't be protected, but the same conversation in the privacy of the conspirators' home would be. In the first, the diners have no reasonable expectation that their conversation is private since they are in public. In the last, the speakers can reasonably expect that their conversations aren't being monitored. It is the cases that fall between these extremes that have called for judicial interpretation.

For example, in *Mancusi v. De Forte*[10] the Supreme Court held that a union official had an expectation of privacy in an office he shared with other workers. The warrantless search of his office space was a violation of the Fourth Amendment. For the search to have been valid, the police officers needed to get a warrant *or* the consent of the employer. They had done neither. However, the Supreme Court recently refused to review an Alaska case in which a worker complained that a secret video camera was aimed at her desk. The college where she worked suspected she was stealing money from the college theater, and local police crawled through the vents in the ceiling and installed a video camera aimed at her desk, all without a warrant. She was caught on tape taking money from an office moneybag and putting it in her purse. She asked the Court to suppress the evidence, but the Alaska Supreme Court concluded she had no expectation of privacy in her desk, since it was in an area accessible to other workers.[11]

YOU MAKE THE CALL:

The Duke Rape Case—Warrantless Search Of Student Dorms

According to one news report, police investigating the Duke University rape case entered a campus dormitory where several of the lacrosse players lived without a warrant. For security reasons, anyone entering the building had to swipe a Duke ID card through an electronically locked door to gain access. Police allegedly waited until a student opened the door and then followed the student in. The police spoke with several lacrosse players and entered at least one player's dorm room.[12]

Did the police violate the dormitory residents' civil rights? If so, at what point? Do dormitory residents in a building, where a key card is necessary for entry, have an expectation of privacy? Are dormitory halls public or private space? Should the police need a warrant to enter them uninvited? At the time, many of the lacrosse players had retained legal counsel. Should the police have contacted the attorneys to speak with the players? Was this just a case of police intimidation of young men who feared their lack of cooperation would make them look guilty?

Consider all of these questions and you make the call.

In another case, *Minnesota v. Olson*,[13] a suspected driver of the getaway car used in a murder took refuge in an apartment rented by two female friends. The police surrounded the apartment and called the occupants. When one of the women answered, police heard a male voice say "tell them I left." Although they had the apartment surrounded, the officers stormed the apartment and arrested Olson. He challenged his arrest, arguing that the officers should have obtained a warrant or permission from the women before entering. The Supreme Court agreed. Olson, as an overnight guest, had a reasonable expectation of privacy. The Court wrote:

> To hold that an overnight guest has a legitimate expectation of privacy in his host's home merely recognizes the everyday expectations of privacy that we all share. Staying overnight in another's home is a longstanding social custom that serves functions recognized as valuable by society. We stay in others' homes when we travel to a strange city for business or pleasure, when we visit our parents, children, or more distant relatives out of town, when we are in between jobs or homes, or when we housesit for a friend. We will all be hosts and we will all be guests many times in our lives. From either perspective, we think that society recognizes that a houseguest has a legitimate expectation of privacy in his host's home.

Minnesota v. Olson, 495 U.S. 91, 99 (1990)

Persons who use a pay phone and close the door behind them to make a call have a reasonable expectation of privacy. Their conversation can't be intercepted by police officers without a warrant.[14] But no one has a reasonable expectation of privacy in things that are in plain view. For example, if an officer walking down the street sees a marijuana plant growing next to the petunias in your flowerbed, he can use the plants as evidence without a warrant. But he can't knock your door down and seize the plants you were also growing in the basement.

Nor can police use a heat-sensing device to sniff out energy use as a way to get probable cause to search for marijuana plants. That's what the Supreme Court ruled in a 5–4 decision in *Kyllo v. United States*.[15] In that case, the Court concluded that the warrantless use of a thermal-imaging device aimed at a private home from a public street to detect relative amounts of heat within a home was an unlawful search within meaning of the Constitution's Fourth Amendment. Justice Scalia, who wrote the Court's opinion, concluded that a device that could tell "at what hour each night the lady of the house takes her daily sauna and bath" surely violated the right to privacy in one's home.

As you can see, each case is evaluated on its own merits. Because the standard of "reasonable expectation" is subjective, search-and-seizure questions are frequently raised in criminal cases. Many of these have reached the Supreme Court. Consider that from 1969 through 1986 the Supreme Court under Chief Justice Warren Burger decided 130 search-and-seizure cases.

Probable Cause

How exactly does a police officer go about getting a search warrant? The details of the procedure vary from jurisdiction to jurisdiction, but the generally the officer must present enough evidence to a magistrate to show there is **probable cause** to make an arrest or search the premises for evidence of criminal wrongdoing. While open to interpretation, "probable cause" generally means enough evidence to conclude that it is more likely than not that a crime was committed or that the place to be searched is connected with a crime. It is more than a suspicion, but less than that needed for a conviction.[16]

Exceptions to the Rule

There are several exceptions to the rule that a search requires a warrant. The most obvious exception is consent. If the person whose home or possessions were searched gave his permission for the search, then the search does not violate the Fourth Amendment. Unsophisticated defendants who are politely asked if the officers can "look around" have waived any right to later object. The police are not required to educate you that you have the right to refuse a search or a stop and frisk if they come without a warrant. It is expected that any reasonable person would know that he or she has the right to refuse the search.[17]

The same holds true if the owner of the premises you are visiting, or someone else in charge such as an employer, gives permission. It may even be the case when a police informant or undercover officer gains entry to a home. This is the so-called **consent once removed** doctrine, which several circuit courts of appeal have ruled is an exception to the warrant rule. Consent once removed posits that when someone in control of entrance to the home invited in an undercover agent or informant, the consent works for the police department, too, even though they are "once removed" from the original decision to grant entry. The U.S. Supreme Court recently considered such a case, but did not rule one way or another.[18]

But landlords generally can't give consent to the search of a renter's apartment.[19] Three other exceptions we will consider are the automobile exception, the **exigent circumstances** exception, and the **stop and frisk** exception.

Probable cause
The amount of proof required before an officer can obtain a search warrant, stop a suspect, or make an arrest. Enough evidence from which a reasonable person could conclude that the facts alleged are probably true.

Consent once removed
An exception to the warrant to search requirement which says that consent to enter given to an undercover police officer or informant transfers to others in the police force who may then enter without a warrant.

Exigent circumstances
Situations that require urgent action, sufficient to excuse delay to get a warrant issued.

Stop and frisk
Police officers may briefly stop, identify, and frisk persons reasonably believed to have committed a crime during the course of an investigation.

Automobiles are by their nature mobile. And with a few exceptions, such as large travel trailers, automobiles are generally not homes. There is therefore a reduced expectation of privacy associated with cars and other motorized vehicles. As a result, courts considering whether automobiles could be searched early on concluded that a lower standard was appropriate. Although a man's home may be his castle, his car is only a means of transportation.

The first Supreme Court case to consider a search of an automobile was decided in 1925.[20] The case, *Carroll v. Illinois*, held that if the officer conducting the search had "probable cause" to have a warrant issued, but didn't ask for one, the search was still valid. The chief reason was the mobility of automobiles. By the time the officer could have gotten a warrant, the car, unlike a house, would be long gone.

Over the years, the Supreme Court has continued to allow warrantless searches of automobiles, trunks, and glove compartments on the premise that the car is mobile *and* that there is a reduced expectation of privacy. This is true even if the car has been impounded and the owner jailed. As the Court wrote in *United States v. Ross:*[21]

> In many cases, however, the police will, prior to searching the car, have cause to arrest the occupants and bring them to the station for booking. In this situation, the police can ordinarily seize the automobile and bring it to the station. Because the vehicle is now in the exclusive control of the authorities, any subsequent search cannot be justified by the mobility of the car. Rather, an immediate warrantless search of the vehicle is permitted because of the second major justification for the automobile exception: the diminished expectation of privacy in an automobile.

Under the law, the police seize the driver of a car they pull over for purposes of searching it. The Fourth Amendment protects the driver from unreasonable searches, but what about passengers? In one case, police pulled over a California man to "check his registration." The police recognized a passenger in the car as a parole violator. They used his parole status as justification to search the car where they found drugs and drug paraphernalia. At his trial, the passenger argued the police lacked probable cause to pull the car over and all evidence found in the search should be suppressed. But the government argued they only pulled over the driver, in effect seizing him within the meaning of the Fourth Amendment. The passenger was not seized and could have left at any time. In other words, by remaining in the car, he agreed to be searched. The Supreme Court disagreed. They ruled the man was seized by the police because no reasonable person would believe the police would allow him to leave the scene. As a result, he could challenge whether the search was legal.[22]

But what if the police are waiting at a suspect's house with an arrest warrant and he pulls into the driveway and gets out of his car before he notices the police officers at his door? Can the police arrest him and search the car he just got out of? According to the Supreme Court, no. That's because once the suspect has voluntarily left the car, he can no longer reach for a weapon, drive off, or remove evidence. The situation is not exigent and there is plenty of time for the officers to get a warrant for a car search.[23]

Another issue that arises with some frequency is the question of whether a roadblock set up by police to stop motorists is a legitimate practice or violates the Fourth Amendment. In 2000, the Supreme Court ruled 6–3 in *Indianapolis v. Edmond*[24] that many such police checkpoints violate the Fourth Amendment. In that case, the Indianapolis police created a roadblock program that was designed to interdict illegal drug activity. The police set up six roadblocks between August and November 1998 on city roads. All told, they stopped 1,161 vehicles and made 104 arrests—55 for drug-related offenses and the remainder for other crimes. Edmond challenged the roadblocks as warrantless and without probable cause. The Supreme Court agreed, writing

> The Fourth Amendment requires that searches and seizures be reasonable. A search or seizure is ordinarily unreasonable in the absence of individualized suspicion of wrongdoing . . . . We have never approved a checkpoint program whose primary purpose was to detect evidence of ordinary criminal wrongdoing. Rather, our checkpoint cases have recognized only limited exceptions to the general rule that a seizure must be accompanied by some measure of individualized suspicion.

The Supreme Court decided another roadblock case in early 2004. The question posed was whether the police can set up a roadblock at the site of an earlier accident in order to attempt to find a motorist who might have witnessed an earlier fatal accident. The case, *Illinois v. Lidster*, involved a motorist who was arrested for drunk driving after he stopped at the roadblock. This time, a unanimous Court sided with the police. It distinguished earlier cases by pointing out that the police weren't searching for a *suspect* in the earlier crime, but were simply asking if anyone had information about the crime. It was more akin to police officers asking people in a crowd what they may have observed.[25] Similarly, police may stop vehicles in emergency situations such as stopping vehicles when a flood has washed out a bridge. Stops at border crossings or for regulatory purposes such as emissions testing are permissible without warrants.

Because nearly 100 cases involving the Fourth Amendment and the search of automobiles have been decided by the Supreme Court since 1925, any questions about the legality of automobile searches and seizures should be carefully researched before concluding that the search was or wasn't legal.

Exigent circumstances sometimes justify a search and seizure without a warrant. Generally speaking, exigent circumstances are those situations in which the law enforcement officer believes that getting a warrant will create the risk of injury or death or result in the destruction of evidence. One example is blood alcohol testing following an accident or arrest, since the level of alcohol in the blood may fall by the time a warrant can be obtained. Blood alcohol levels are considered **evanescent evidence** meaning they are evidence that will change or evaporate in a manner that will destroy its evidentiary value. You will learn more about blood testing and breath analysis in Chapter 12.

Evanescent evidence
Evidence that will change or evaporate in a manner that will destroy its evidentiary value.

The Supreme Court recently addressed a case where police entered a home to prevent bodily harm to an individual and ended up arresting those in the home. The situation began with a 3 A.M. call from a neighbor complaining about a loud party in the neighborhood. Police from the Brigham City, Utah, Police Department arrived to investigate. The police saw two underage individuals drinking beer in the backyard. The police entered the yard and looked in the house where they saw four adults and one juvenile arguing. When the juvenile hit one of the adults in the face hard enough to force the victim to spit blood into the sink, the police moved in announcing their presence. Ultimately they arrested three of the adults and charged them with contributing to the delinquency of a minor, disorderly conduct, and intoxication.

At trial, the accused moved to have all evidence seized during the search of the home suppressed because the police lacked warrants or any viable reason to enter the house. The Utah State Supreme Court agreed, noting that the police could not have been there to assist the injured adult because they provided him no aid, therefore entered the house without either warrant or probable cause. The city appealed to the Supreme Court, who ruled the officers acted within the law because they "had an objectively reasonable basis for believing that an occupant was seriously injured or imminently threatened with such an injury."[26]

The most obvious situation that qualifies as exigent is when a police officer is in hot pursuit of a defendant, either on foot or in an automobile. Obviously, the suspect will get away if the officer had to first get a warrant from a magistrate! However, the circumstance must truly be an emergency or involve the destruction of evidence. Like other search-and-seizure cases, exigent circumstances cases are fact driven; that is, each case is decided on its unique facts. For example, the Supreme Court recently concluded that there is no bright line between conducting a warrantless search of a car with the driver still in the car or outside it. In *Thornton v. United States*,[27] the defendant parked his car before a police officer had a chance to stop him. The defendant got out of the car and was stopped by the officer. Because the defendant had drugs in his pocket, the officer arrested him and then searched the parked car. The officer found a handgun and added a firearms charge.

Thornton asked the Court to suppress the gun evidence on the premise that a warrantless search of a parked car was illegal. The Court disagreed and ruled 7–2 that officers can search a parked car when the occupant recently left the car. Would the result be the same if the driver had parked in his own driveway and had entered his house before the officer pulled up? It's hard to say. The Supreme Court seems to decide a case on the limits of exigent automobile cases every year.

What happens if the car you are riding in is pulled over by police for speeding and during the course of the stop, an officer finds illegal drugs? Can the officer arrest all passengers and wait for one to confess? That's the question the Supreme Court tackled in *Maryland v. Pringle*.[28] In that case, police became suspicious when the driver reached into the glove compartment for his registration information, revealing a wad of cash. He asked the driver if he could look around and was given permission. The officer found cocaine under the back seat armrest. Pringle, who was seated in the front passenger seat, was arrested along with the driver and another passenger. Pringle finally confessed that the drugs were his and was eventually convicted and sentenced to ten years in prison. He then alleged that the officer had no probable cause to arrest all three and did so only to coerce a confession. The Supreme Court decided the case in late December 2003, again unanimously. It was reasonable, wrote the Court, to arrest all three in the car on the premise that they were engaged in a common criminal enterprise. That the others were released after Pringle confessed was immaterial.[29]

Police officers can also stop and frisk suspicious individuals.[30] In *Terry v. Ohio*, a police officer noticed two African-American men in downtown Cleveland in the late afternoon in 1963. The officer later said that they " . . . didn't look right to me." After observing the men looking in windows and pacing back and forth many times, he stopped them and frisked one man. In the man's coat he found a gun. The defendant argued that he had been searched in violation of the Fourth

Amendment. The Supreme Court disagreed and upheld the stop and frisk as constitutional.

Since then, the right to stop and frisk has been limited. Officers must have more than a suspicion about an individual; they must describe specific suspicious actions or be faced with what they perceive as a dangerous situation. And police can't stop individuals because of their race or appearance unless they match the description of individuals wanted by the police or seen leaving the scene of a crime.[31] On the other hand, the Supreme Court recently ruled that an individual stopped for a minor traffic violation could be frisked if the officer has an "articulable" basis to believe the passenger might be armed and dangerous. Tucson police officer Maria Trevizo pulled over a car for minor traffic violations and decided to search passenger Lemon Johnson because he was wearing "gang colors" and she thought he appeared dangerous. She found a gun and marijuana on Johnson and arrested him. He appealed his subsequent conviction, alleging Trevizo had no right to search him since it did not appear that he was committing any crime. The Supreme Court ruled that the pat down was legal because Trevizo had articulated a reasonable suspicion that Johnson was dangerous.[32]

However, the Supreme Court recently explained that citizens are not free to refuse to give police their identity. If an officer conducts a *Terry* stop, the citizen stopped must provide his or her name and faces criminal penalties if uncooperative. The case, *Hiibel v. Nevada*,[33] involved a police officer responding to a report that a woman was being assaulted in a car. The officer responded to the reported location and stopped Hiibel outside a car with a woman inside. The officer asked Hiibel his name and arrested Hiibel when he refused to identify himself. Hiibel's attorney argued that his client's Fourth Amendment rights included the right to refuse to give his name when he believed he wasn't engaging in criminal conduct. The Supreme Court disagreed and ruled that states can charge uncooperative persons criminally if they refuse to disclose their name. As long as the stop meets *Terry* standards for reasonableness, the suspect is required to identify himself.

One area of stop and frisk that has recently expanded is that of airport searches. This is partly in response to increased terrorist attacks and partly as a result of increased drug smuggling. Generally, persons entering the country can be frisked, and even strip-searched, based upon nothing more than their appearance and point of origin.[34]

Infiltration

Law enforcement agencies sometimes have to rely on infiltration and informants to investigate and fight criminal activities. Sometimes, this means using an undercover officer to infiltrate criminal enterprises. Other times, this requires finding someone already on the inside to pass information or provide proof of criminal activity. Both investigative methods are risky. Undercover work is obviously dangerous for the officer, while using an informant immediately raises questions about reliability and loyalty. Plus, when it is time for the informant to testify, he or she will inevitably be grilled about criminal involvement, whether the police struck a deal for testimony and whether anything coming from the informant can be trusted as the truth.

Generally, police try to use collaborative evidence whenever relying on an informant. For example, if what an informant claims is used as the basis for a search or arrest warrant, the magistrate responsible for approving or rejecting the warrant will want to know whether the police have used the informant in the past and found him reliable or information to collaborate what the informant claims, such as the police officer's direct observation. For example, in *Illinois v. Gates*,[35] an informant's tip led the police to observe what appeared to be a lot of movement at the home of Lance and Susan Gates. In addition, Susan was observed taking trips to Florida for no apparent reason. The original tip came anonymously in a note which said:

> "This letter is to inform you that you have a couple in your town who live on Greenway, off Bloomingdale Rd. in the condominiums. Most of their buys are done in Florida. Sue, his wife, drives their car to Florida, where she leaves it to be loaded up with drugs, then Lance flies down and drives it back. Sue flies back after she drops the car off in Florida. May 3 she is driving down there again and the car back he has the trunk loaded with over $100,000.00 in drugs. Presently they have over $100,000.00 worth of drugs in their basement. They brag about the fact they never have to work and make their entire living on pushers. I guarantee, if you watch them carefully you will make a big catch. They are friends with some big drug dealers who visit their house often."

The Supreme Court concluded that under the totality of the circumstances, there was probable cause for the issuance of a search warrant. The court wrote:

> " . . . [T]he task of the issuing magistrate is simply to make a practical, common sense decision whether, given all the circumstances set forth in the affidavit before him, including the veracity and basis of knowledge of persons supplying hearsay information, there is a fair probability that contraband or evidence of a crime will be found in a particular place."

The practice of using informants isn't going to go away, even as their reliability has come under increasing pressure. According to the Center on Wrongful Convictions, there were fifty-one individuals convicted of murder and sent to death row based in whole or in part on the testimony of informants who have been exonerated as of 2005.[36]

Executing Search Warrants

Once officers have a warrant in hand, they are supposed to "knock and announce" their presence. That is, the right to privacy includes the right to not be surprised by officers who knock down your door and storm in. A case recently decided by the Supreme Court tested the limits of the "knock and announce" requirement. During an afternoon, North Las Vegas police officers in SWAT uniforms raided the apartment of Lashawn Banks, whom they suspected was a drug dealer. Warrant in hand, they knocked and waited about fifteen seconds before using a battering ram to gain entrance. Banks, who was showering, heard the loud noise and ran into the living room. There he was ordered to the floor by police officers wearing hoods. He claimed that their actions violated his right to privacy and that the evidence the officers found should be suppressed.

The Ninth Circuit sided with Banks, and the police appealed. A unanimous Supreme Court ruled in late 2003 that under the circumstances, the police were justified in breaking the door down. Given that the officers were executing on a warrant for possession of cocaine, they could reasonably have suspected that the defendant's brief delay in answering the door was due to his efforts to dispose of the evidence.[37]

Police frequently work with informants and others whose reputations for honesty and integrity are suspect. So police may be on shaky ground when seeking a warrant based on the word of an informant. When weighing whether to issue the warrant, the court uses a totality of the circumstances test as discussed earlier in this chapter.

To meet constitutional standards, a search warrant must describe specifically "the place to be searched and the persons or things to be seized."[38]

The Exclusionary Rule

To discourage the abuse of the rules against unreasonable searches and seizures, the Supreme Court adopted the **exclusionary rule.** The rule makes any evidence seized in violation of the Fourth Amendment inadmissible in court. The Court, in *Mapp v. Ohio*, 367 U.S. 643 (1961), ruled that such evidence is like the "fruit of a poisonous tree," and can't be used against the defendant. The rule has since been modified so that evidence obtained through search warrants obtained in good faith, but which are invalidated for technical reasons, can be used at trial.[39]

What happens if police officers make a mistake in executing an arrest warrant? Should they be barred from using any evidence they find while executing that warrant? That depends. The U.S. Supreme Court has recently ruled that evidence does not have to be suppressed if the officers relied in good faith on faulty information. Bennie Herring was pulled over after an employee in a neighboring jurisdiction told officers that there was an outstanding warrant for his arrest. Police found methamphetamine in his pocket and a gun under the front seat and charged him with drug and gun offenses. It turned out that the warrant was no longer valid and had been withdrawn over five months earlier, but an employee had failed to update the records. Herring wanted the evidence suppressed, but the Supreme Court said that an innocent error such as this one did not taint the subsequent search and conviction.[40]

> **Exclusionary rule**
> The "fruit of the poisonous tree" doctrine that prohibits the admission of evidence obtained illegally at a defendant's criminal trial. The rule does allow the use of evidence obtained with a technically defective warrant, but in good faith.

HISTORICAL HIGHLIGHT

Police Can Search Indian Reservation with Warrant

Native American members of the Paiute-Shoshone tribe run the Paiute Palace Casino in Bishop, California, on tribal lands. The casino has 300 slot machines and seven game tables and provides much-needed jobs to tribe members. Police in Inyo County became suspicious that some tribe members were collecting welfare benefits while working at the casino and obtained a warrant to search the premises for evidence of welfare fraud. The casino had previously refused to turn over records, citing confidentiality.

The police officers raided the casino offices and seized employment records. No evidence of fraud was discovered, but the police threatened to enter tribal lands again. That's when tribal leaders sued in federal court, alleging that the police were violating the tribe's sovereign immunity. The tribe won in the Ninth Circuit, but lost in the Supreme Court, 9–0. Police can, using a warrant, enter and search tribal lands. The case is *Inyo County v. Paiute-Shoshone Indians*, 538 U.S. 701 (2003).

Technology and Searches

Only one of the founding fathers had any real experience with electricity. But Ben Franklin's kite flying is as removed from modern electronic communications as the caveman's wheel is from the space shuttle. The founding fathers' concept of searches consisted largely of broken-in doors and ransacked homes. Modern electronics provide far more information with less violence.

Wiretaps

Law enforcement officers recognized early on that listening in on phone conversations could yield valuable evidence. No law existed governing phone taps in the 1920s and most jurisdictions treated phone taps like any other search. When a Seattle police shut down the operation of a bootlegger named Olmstead using evidence from wiretaps, Olmstead challenged the wiretaps' legality. The prosecutor in the case argued that since government officials did not access the phone calls, no law was broken. The case eventually landed in the Supreme Court, where the Court said that no law forbade law enforcement officials from using information obtained by nongovernment actors even if obtained illegally. (Seattle police hired a lineman to tap the phones by accessing lines running through publicly accessible areas to skirt the Fourth Amendment. However, Washington state law at the time made it a misdemeanor to listen in on someone else's phone conversation.) The opinion practically begged Congress and state legislatures to pass laws to guide law enforcement officers.[41]

In response, Congress passed the Federal Communications Act of 1934, which prohibited wiretapping without a court order.[42] Rules for how to obtain such a court order were left to the states. New York State's law required law enforcement officers to provide a state judge (not just any old magistrate) with the target's name and the reason why the wiretap was needed. Unless renewed, wiretaps expired in 60 days.[43]

The law was challenged as unconstitutional, and the challenge eventually reached the U.S. Supreme Court, who struck it down as too vague.[44] Congress then passed the Omnibus Crime Control and Safe Streets Wiretap Act of 1968. Title III of the Act regulates the interception of all oral and wire communications. To obtain authorization for a wiretap under Title III:

1. The law enforcement officer must show that normal investigative procedures have been tried and failed, are unlikely to succeed, or are dangerous;[45]

2. The surveillance must be conducted in a way that minimizes the interception of irrelevant information;[46]

3. There must be probable cause to believe the interception will reveal evidence of one of a list of specific predicate crimes;[47]

4. The order must be authorized by a high-level Justice Department official and signed by a federal judge;[48] and

5. The order is time-limited to thirty days (the government can request an extension).[49]

Federal courts later brought warrant requests for video surveillance under Title III requirements as well.[50] In 1986, Congress passed the Electronics Communications Privacy Act, which extended Title III to cover e-mails and other electronic messages.[51]

Following the terror attacks of September 11, 2001, Congress passed the Uniting and Strengthening America by Providing Appropriate Tools Required to Intercept and Obstruct Terrorism Act of 2001. Commonly known as the PATRIOT Act, the law supersedes Title III in many ways including:

- Expanding federal law enforcement authority to monitor e-mail and other electronic communications by treating stored voicemail messages like e-mail instead of telephone conversations. No warrant is necessary to access stored voice or e-mail.

- Federal courts can issue pen register and trap orders (devices that catalogue the phone numbers or e-mail addresses contacted by a particular person) throughout the nation.

- Law enforcement officials can now catalog the Web addresses visited by a computer without a warrant if they can show the information is "relevant to an ongoing investigation."

- Roving wiretaps, where multiple phones used by the same person may be tapped, eliminating the need to get a new court order each time a person of interest obtained a new cell phone.

- The PATRIOT Act created several new crimes including money laundering in support of terrorism or cyber crime, overseas use of fraudulent U.S. credit cards, terrorist attacks on mass transit, and harboring terrorists.

- The Act also increased penalties for counterfeiting.

- Law enforcement agencies are now permitted to share grand jury testimony and wiretap information with intelligence agencies if it meets the definition of "foreign intelligence."

One of the more controversial PATRIOT Act provisions allows federal agents to enter a home without a warrant to "look around" and then seek a warrant if they find any evidence. This "sneak-a-peek" provision became a central theme in the Brandon Mayfield saga (see Historical Highlight).

> Those who would give up essential liberty to purchase a little temporary safety deserve neither safety nor liberty.
>
> Benjamin Franklin

HISTORICAL HIGHLIGHT

"Sneak-a-Peek" Gone Awry: The Brandon Mayfield Saga

Spanish police found a fingerprint in the aftermath of the 2004 Madrid train bombing they believed belonged to one of the terrorists. They shared the fingerprint with the FBI. After running it through the national fingerprint database, the FBI thought they had a match. They sent the matching fingerprint back to Spanish authorities. But the Spanish weren't so sure and concluded there was no match.

Undeterred, the FBI checked out the owner of their "matching" fingerprint. He was Portland, Oregon, attorney Brandon Mayfield. The FBI also learned the attorney was a convert to Islam. How did the FBI come to have Mayfield's fingerprint? Mayfield had served in the military and the fingerprint was in the database from his time in the U.S. Army.

Since leaving the military, Mayfield met an Egyptian woman, converted to Islam, married, had two children, and opened a small law office. Through his local mosque, Mayfield met several Arab-Americans, some of whom he represented in family court matters.

To the FBI, the matching fingerprint, the conversion to Islam, and identifying one of Mayfield's clients as being on a terror watch list added up to a likely participant in the Madrid bombing. Under the PATRIOT Act, the FBI did a sneak-a-peek investigation of Mayfield's home, took over 300 pictures, and planted listening devices.

The Mayfields began to find clues someone had been in their house. The deadbolt they never locked would be locked when they returned home at the end of the day. Even though they never wore shoes in the house, muddy shoe prints appeared in one of their children's bedrooms.[52]

On May 6, 2004, the FBI arrested Mayfield. Almost immediately the FBI was unable to answer obvious questions. Mayfield's passport showed he had not left the country. The FBI maintained he must have done so using someone else's passport. The FBI produced papers with words written in Spanish seized from the Mayfield's home. It turned out to be one of the Mayfield children's Spanish homework. (Imagine telling your teacher the FBI seized your homework.) The Spanish authorities again told the FBI the fingerprint did not match.

By the time Mayfield was released, he had been held in jail for two weeks. He claimed he was subject to "lockdowns, strip searches, sleep deprivation, unsanitary living conditions, shackles and chains, threats, physical pain, and humiliation." Mayfield sued the attorney general and the Justice Department settled the case for $2 million. Mayfield retained his right to challenge the constitutionality of the PATRIOT Act.[53]

The FBI's misidentification of the fingerprint arose from the image being flipped when faxed to the United States. They were looking at a mirror image. The agency has apologized.

The Department of Justice conducted an investigation into the botched investigation. You can review the report at http://www.usdoj.gov/oig/special/s0601/Chapter1.pdf.

Double Jeopardy

The Fifth Amendment to the U.S. Constitution provides that no person shall "be subject for the same offense to be twice put in jeopardy of life or limb. . . . " Its roots can be traced to Roman times, when the Emperor Justinian declared, "The governor should not permit the same person to be again accused of crime of which he has been acquitted."[54] This constitutional provision assures that no one can be put on trial a second time for the same offense after a court or jury has decided that the government was unable to prove its case beyond a reasonable doubt. In other words, it doesn't matter if the defendant, after being acquitted, takes out a full-page ad in the local paper declaring that he "did it." He can't be tried again after the jury has spoken.

Prosecutors only have one opportunity to present the case to a jury; if the case is botched or if evidence is uncovered later, the opportunity has been lost. As a practical matter, this means that the government must bring all possible charges arising out of one incident against an individual at one time. The government can't, for example, first try a defendant for murder and later try him for possession of a firearm during the robbery in which the murder took place. If it fails to convict on the murder charge, it can't retry on the weapons charge. "All the charges against a defendant that grow out of a single criminal act, occurrence, episode, or transaction" must be tried together.[55]

The guarantee, however, has several well-established exceptions. These include the government's:

- Right to retry a suspect if the jury is deadlocked, or "hung"
- Right to retry a suspect when an appellate court has ordered a retrial because of some error in an earlier trial
- Right to try a suspect in federal court on federal criminal charges if a state court acquitted on state charges and vice versa or to try and convict an individual in both state and federal court if the same act violated both state and federal law
- Right on retrial to ask for and get the death penalty if the defendant was originally sentenced to life in prison but appealed the conviction and won a new trial. Each of these exceptions is discussed below.

Retrial after Hung Jury

When a jury is unable to reach a verdict of guilty or not guilty, the defendant may be, and often is, retried. There is no violation of the double jeopardy clause because both the defendant and the government are entitled to a jury's decision on the case. The Supreme Court explained the issue this way:

> The double-jeopardy provision of the Fifth Amendment, however, does not mean that every time a defendant is put to trial before a competent tribunal he is entitled to go free if the trial fails to end in a final judgment. Such a rule would create an insuperable obstacle to the administration of justice in many cases in which there is no semblance of the type of oppressive practices at which the double-jeopardy prohibition is aimed. There may be unforeseeable circumstances that arise during a trial making its completion impossible, such as the failure of a jury to agree on a verdict. In such event the purpose of law to protect society from those guilty of crimes frequently would be frustrated by denying courts power to put the defendant to trial again.
>
> *Wade v. Hunter*, 336 U.S. 684 (1949)

In one recent case involving a former Enron executive, the Supreme Court said he could not be retried after being acquitted on some counts, while other related counts resulted in a hung jury. The court said that the fact the executive had already been acquitted on some counts weighted in favor of no additional charges. That was especially true since the charges were based on the same set of facts. Had there been a hung jury on all the related charges, there would have been no problem with prosecuting him again.[56]

Retrial after Reversal on Appeal

When a judge or jury finds a criminal defendant guilty of a crime, the defendant may appeal the decision to an appellate court if he or she believes an error occurred during the trial. Errors include incorrect rulings on the admissibility of testimony, ineffective assistance of counsel, violation of a constitutional right, and the like. Only the criminal defendant can appeal a conviction; the government can't appeal an acquittal.[57]

The remedy ordered by the appellate court is typically a new trial. That new trial allows the defendant to exclude the erroneously admitted evidence the second time around, to have the assistance of effective counsel, to have evidence admitted, or the like. In other words, the new trial gives the defendant another opportunity for acquittal. Only in rare circumstances will an appellate court find that the errors in the first trial are so egregious that a second trial would be double jeopardy (see Historical Highlight: *Commonwealth v. Smith*).

Trial in Both State and Federal Court for the Same Act   Another exception to the rule against double jeopardy is a second trial in the event a defendant violates the laws of two or more jurisdictions by one act. The double jeopardy clause doesn't prevent both state and federal courts from prosecuting, convicting, and sentencing the same defendant for committing one act that is both a federal and a state crime. For example, if a defendant makes moonshine that violates both a state law against home-brewing and federal laws against producing moonshine for transportation across state lines, he or she can be punished under both laws. That's because each jurisdiction has the right to enforce its criminal laws.[58] If he or she was acquitted of state charges, he or she can still be convicted on the federal charges.

Before going to prison I believed that criticism of the criminal justice system for its treatment of the poor was so much liberal bleating and bunk. I was wrong.

G. Gordon Liddy (1977)

HISTORICAL HIGHLIGHT

Commonwealth v. Smith, *Suppressed Evidence Taken with a Grain of Sand*

Susan Reinert had reason to be happy in the summer of 1979. She was engaged to a fellow teacher, William Bradfield, and was to be married that summer. She also had reason to be afraid. Bradfield and Jay Smith, the assistant principal of the school where Reinert and Bradfield taught, may have planned to murder her and her children. The possible reason was the $730,000 of insurance Bradfield had persuaded her to purchase, naming him as the beneficiary.

Ms. Reinert and her two children left their home on the evening of June 22, and were not seen alive again. Reinert's nude and beaten body was discovered in the trunk of a car parked in a hotel parking lot 100 miles away from her home. Her children's bodies were never found.

According to the prosecution, Bradfield and Smith had planned to kill Reinert and her children for the insurance money. The prosecution also showed that the two had engaged in a criminal conspiracy before. In 1977 Smith had been accused of theft, but Bradfield had provided an alibi for him. Despite Bradfield's testimony, Smith had been convicted. Smith was due to start his sentence on June 26, 1979, the day after Reinert's body was discovered.

The prosecution theorized that it was a double-cross. Bradfield was to kill Reinert, and Smith was to dispose of the children. The bodies were not supposed to be found, and after the seven-year waiting period, the two would share in the insurance money. Smith would have the alibi of being incarcerated at the time of the "disappearance." Perhaps, the prosecution argued, Bradfield realized that Smith would be in jail, and if Reinert's body was discovered, he could collect the money right away and be long gone by the time Smith finished his sentence.

Both men were eventually charged with the murders and they were tried separately. Bradfield was convicted and sentenced to three life terms. He died in prison in 1998. Smith was convicted and sentenced to death.

However, the prosecution had suppressed a piece of evidence at Smith's trial. The State Police had lifted grains of sand from Reinert's feet. Smith had maintained as his defense that Bradfield had taken Reinert to the New Jersey shore and killed her there. Despite the fact that several other key pieces of physical evidence tied Smith to Reinert's death, the Pennsylvania Supreme Court ruled that the suppression of evidence was prosecutorial misconduct. Normally, this would mean a new trial, but the high court went further. They ruled that the conduct was so egregious that to try Smith again would violate the constitutional prohibition against double jeopardy. The conviction was overturned and Smith was set free.

In 1998, Smith sued prosecutors, policemen, and author Joseph Wambaugh, who wrote a best-seller about the case, *Echoes in the Darkness*, alleging they violated his civil rights. Smith claimed Wambaugh had offered to pay a Pennsylvania State police officer if his book was a success. Attorneys for the prosecutors and policemen argued in the civil trial that the "grains of sand" were quartz that could have come from anywhere. Thus, they were not deemed important at the time of trial. The jury apparently was convinced by this argument, but was skeptical of Smith's explanation of how one of his combs was found under Reinert's body, and how pieces of her clothing were discovered in his car.

Smith remained free until his death in 2009.[59] This case shows that even in cases where there is strong evidence pointing to a person's guilt, the constitutional protection against double jeopardy can prevent the state from trying that person again.

A number of crimes have both state and federal consequences. For example, both the federal government and the individual states have laws against the sale and distribution of controlled substances. In most cases, the state laws are virtually identical to the federal law. A defendant who sells heroin violates two criminal laws with each sale and can be prosecuted in both state and federal court. As a practical matter, though, most defendants are prosecuted under either state or local laws, not under both. This is due in part to the Petite policy, a policy developed by the Department of Justice that essentially prohibits federal prosecutors from prosecuting a defendant on state charges if the federal law violated is substantially similar to a state one and the state has prosecuted the defendant on the state charges.

Only in cases that would create a manifest injustice if the defendant were allowed to go free does the federal government prosecute an individual who has already been tried and convicted or acquitted of an act that is a state crime and also a federal crime. For example, the Los Angeles police officers who were acquitted of beating Rodney King were later tried and convicted in federal court for violating Mr. King's civil rights. The unique fact situations of the Rodney King beatings and the riots that followed the acquittal of the police officers caught on camera was such a circumstance warranting another prosecution.

Right on Retrial to Ask for and Get the Death Penalty If the Defendant was Originally Sentenced to Life in Prison but Appealed the Conviction and Won a New Trial   What happens if a murder defendant is convicted and sentenced to life in prison, but receives a new trial? Can the prosecution seek the death penalty? The answer was until recently "No." The Supreme Court had ruled that to do so would be double jeopardy.[60] But in 2003, a divided Court concluded the opposite. The case involved a Pennsylvania defendant who was convicted of murder by a jury for killing a restaurant worker during a robbery. The jury was unable to agree on whether the defendant should receive death or life in prison. Because it was deadlocked, Pennsylvania law dictated he be sentenced to life. He appealed and was granted a new trial based on other defects in the trial. The prosecution again sought death, and this time the jury was willing to order it. The Supreme Court ruled that there was no double jeopardy in this case, but left open the possibility that had the first jury voted for life rather than being unable to agree, the prosecution would be barred from seeking death.[61] When the case was remanded to state court, the court let the death sentence stand.[62]

Ex Post Facto Laws and Bills of Attainder

Two rights granted by the Constitution that are rarely the subject of controversy in criminal law deserve at least a brief mention, if only to illustrate the mind-set of the founding fathers and the tyranny from which they sought to protect the citizens of their new nation. These two concepts are the prohibition against the passage of *ex post facto* laws and *bills of attainder*. *Ex post facto* laws are laws that criminalize behavior after the behavior has already taken place. Bills of attainder are criminal statutes passed that make behavior a crime for only some persons and not others.

Ex Post Facto Laws

The Constitution outlaws *ex post facto* laws. That is, neither the federal government nor a state or local government can pass a law that makes an act a crime that was not a crime when the defendant committed the act. Nor can a legislature pass laws that increase the penalty for a crime that was committed before the law was passed. "The Constitution forbids the application of any new punitive measure to a crime already consummated, to the detriment or material disadvantage of the wrongdoer."[63]

The reason for the prohibition is rooted in the criminal law concept that holds crimes are intentional acts in disobedience of the law. A person can't disobey a law that does not yet exist. And it would be patently unfair for the justice system to punish people after the fact. There is an exception, though. So-called "three times, you're out" recidivism statutes aren't *ex post facto* even if the first two crimes were committed before the passage of the recidivism law went into effect, as long as the third strike happened after the recidivism law went into effect. In other words, a defendant must be on notice that another conviction will mean a longer sentence than the third conviction ordinarily would carry but for his or her prior record.

What about a prisoner sentenced to a lengthy term who would have had a parole hearing every year until the law changed the interval between hearings? The Supreme Court has ruled that since the change doesn't affect the original sentence, only his potential early release, the change wasn't an *ex post facto* law.[64]

A recent Supreme Court opinion clarified how far the legislature can go to punish behavior that occurred a long time ago. The case involved a seventy-year-old grandfather who was charged with sexual offenses against minors—something that happened more than fifty years earlier. In response to complaints that the state's statute of limitations for sex crimes for minors was too short (it had been three years for some time), the California legislature authorized prosecutors to charge defendants up to one year from the time they were notified by a victim that the assault had taken place. The law was passed in part to help victims of childhood sexual abuse who may have feared coming forward for years.

The Supreme Court ruled that the law violated the prohibition against *ex post facto* laws and threw out the conviction by a 5–4 vote.[65] The decision put in question the arrest and conviction of a number of priests accused of abusing young boys in their charge. In states that have changed their statute of limitations since the abuse occurred, no prosecution seems likely.[66]

On the other hand, if conduct becomes illegal and the defendant continues to engage in the conduct, he or she may be charged and the jury may hear testimony that includes reference to some of the conduct that occurred before it was illegal. Such was the case involving the so-called "S&M Svengali," a man who ran a website dedicated to sadistic and masochistic sex. A woman featured on his website claimed she had been kept a virtual slave against her will. Glenn Marcus, aka Svengali, was charged under the 2000 Trafficking Victims Protection Act, but testimony included sex and other acts that had occurred before Congress passed the law. He was convicted and appealed, arguing that his conviction violated the *ex post facto* clause. The Supreme Court upheld the conviction, reasoning that it wasn't based on conduct entirely outside the effective date of the law.[67]

HISTORICAL HIGHLIGHT

Ex Post Facto and Sex Offender Registration

Perhaps no crime strikes greater fear in the community than violent offenses against children. Children who are victims of rape or other forms of sexual abuse are understandably sympathetic victims. Likewise, their assailants are almost universally reviled, even among other criminal offenders. So deep does the prohibition against harming defenseless children go that prisons almost always separate child abusers from the rest of the inmate population to protect the abusers from harm.

It should come as no surprise, then, that laws designed to identify criminals who prey on children are popular in many communities. So-called sexual predator laws typically require those convicted of sexual offenses involving children to register their addresses. Usually referred to as *Megan's Laws*, because they were inspired by the tragic death of Megan Kanka at the hands of a sexual predator who lived in her neighborhood, the laws require community notification when a sex offender moves into a neighborhood. Presumably, parents and other adults will be more vigilant when they know their neighbor has a history of violent sexual crimes.

Sexual predator registration laws have been challenged by offenders who argue that having to register as predators is additional punishment inflicted after they have served their sentences, especially for those who committed their crimes before the laws were passed. *Megan's Laws*, they argue, amount to *ex post facto* laws and violate the Constitution.

When Alaska passed a version of *Megan's Law*, two former sex offenders sued. They argued that registering after they had served their sentences was additional punishment for a crime they had committed long before the law was passed. The Alaska Sex Offender Registration Act required that the former offender's name, address, place of employment, conviction and sentence, driver's license information, and photograph be published on the Internet. One offender had been convicted of sexually abusing his daughter from age nine through eleven and the other had pled no contest to charges he had sexually abused a fourteen-year-old teen.

The Supreme Court, in a 6–3 decision, upheld the legislation. Although registering might subject the offenders to shame, that was not punishment as contemplated by the *ex post facto* clause, reasoned the majority. The Court wrote that:

> The purpose and the principal effect of notification are to inform the public for its own safety, not to humiliate the offender. Widespread public access is necessary for the efficacy of the scheme, and the attendant humiliation is but a collateral consequence of a valid regulation.
>
> The purpose and the principal effect of notification are to inform the public for its own safety, not to humiliate the offender. Widespread public access is necessary for the efficacy of the scheme, and the attendant humiliation is but a collateral consequence of a valid regulation.

Smith v. Doe, 538 U.S. 1009 (2003)

Bills of Attainder

Bills of attainder are criminal laws passed that only apply to a specific person or specific group of persons. In England, bills of attainder originally singled out individuals for capital punishment without benefit of a trial. The term now refers to any law that targets a specific individual or group for criminal punishment. For example, assume a local city government passed an ordinance that made it a crime for John Smith to smoke in public. Since the law names an individual, it is a bill of attainder. Everyone else can smoke in public, except John Smith. Laws also can't designate an identifiable group as the subject. For example, a law banning all Communist Party members from holding union offices unfairly singled out a specific group for special treatment and was ruled a bill of attainder.[68] In short, a law is a bill of attainder if it singles out either a specific person or a group of persons for prosecution or other punishment.

Right to Remain Silent

The Fifth Amendment provides that no person "shall be compelled in any criminal case to be a witness against himself." The right against self-incrimination, or the **right to remain silent,** is fundamental to the American system of justice. It reflects the fundamental belief of the founding fathers that it's the government that has the burden of proof in criminal cases and that the accused can't be forced to do the prosecutor's job. Simply put, a defendant cannot be compelled to confess to a crime or to provide testimony against himself. He may, of course, do so voluntarily.

Police have an obligation to inform suspects in custody or under arrest of the right to remain silent, among other rights. Since the Supreme Court's decision in *Miranda v. Arizona*,[69] law enforcement officers routinely read suspects their rights. This has become known as "mirandizing" a suspect. *Miranda's* effect after arrest is discussed in the next chapter.

Right to remain silent
The right of all persons not to testify against their own interests when suspected of or charged with a crime. The right to remain silent is rooted in the belief that it is the government's obligation to prove guilt.

There are several exceptions to the rule, however. Volunteered statements defendants make when not under interrogation are not covered by *Miranda*. The courts do not require investigators to interrupt a defendant's confession to read him his rights. It would be both rude and poor law enforcement technique.

The courts also do not recognize routine questions, such as requests for name, address, and age, as interrogation requiring the police to *Mirandize* the person being questioned. Police interrogations at routine traffic stops do not trigger *Miranda*. So you can refuse to answer when the police officer asks, "Did you see that stop sign?" if you think it will help.

Police can also ask questions in the interest of public safety without reading the person his rights. For example, police at a fire do not need to *Mirandize* the captured arsonist before asking if anyone is inside the building.

Similarly, "undercover" officers do not have to read anyone their rights. Obviously, doing so would blow their cover and shorten their career. Courts do not consider undercover situations covered by *Miranda* because no one is in custody and they do not take place in a "police-dominated atmosphere"[70] However, once someone is in custody, the police may not use undercover agents to elicit information.

Presumption of Innocence

Each person is presumed to be innocent until proven guilty of the charges against him or her in court. The presumption of innocence is therefore a **rebuttable presumption,** meaning that the prosecution can present evidence showing that presumption is false, and if the evidence proves guilt beyond a reasonable doubt, then the defendant is no longer presumed innocent.

Some presumptions are **irrebuttable.** For instance, it is presumed a child under seven cannot commit a felony because the child lacks *mens rea*. No evidence the prosecution presents can prove the child committed the felony.

The presumption of innocence stays with the defendant after arrest and throughout the trial. As a result, the prosecution must prove all elements of the crime to secure a conviction. Savvy defendants often refuse to speak with investigators out of fear they will provide evidence that may overcome their presumption of innocence.

Prearrest Interrogation
The Role of the Polygraph

Polygraphs or lie detectors are machines that measure heart, respiration, and perspiration rates based on the theory that people will display stress reactions when they lie. Most polygraph results are inadmissible in court because of their unreliability. Defense attorneys often use polygraph results to bolster the defendant's credibility.

A professionally performed polygraph test will start with some routine questions that both the interrogator and the person being questioned know the answers to, such as name, address, and date and place of birth. This provides the interrogator with baseline readings when the subject is relating truthful answers. Significant deviations from these readings are assumed to be false answers or some tests may be ruled inconclusive. Defense attorneys whose tests indicate their clients may be lying often report the results as "inconclusive."[71]

Rebuttable presumption
A presumption that can be overcome by presenting evidence to the contrary.

Irrebuttable presumption
A presumption that cannot be disproved regardless of the amount or quality of evidence to the contrary.

Even an attorney of moderate talent can postpone doomsday year after year, for the system of appeals that pervades American jurisprudence amounts to a legalistic wheel of fortune, a game of chance, somewhat fixed in the favor of the criminal, that the participants play interminably.

Truman Capote, *In Cold Blood* (1965)

Because polygraph results are inadmissible, defense attorneys seldom let police or prosecutors conduct them on their clients. Polygraph tests can be subject to abuse. In her days as a prosecutor, the author heard the story of police running some wires from a kitchen colander to a copy machine and telling a suspect the contraption was a lie detector. They placed the colander on his head and interrogated him. When he gave what they thought to be an untruthful answer, they would press the copy button that always printed a sheet that said "LIE" on it. The author never actually saw this ploy in action and hopes the police officers were making it all up. She did tell them that this method should not be used.

In recent years voice stress tests have gained some acceptance. Like polygraphs, voice stress tests operate on the premise that stress will show up in measurable form when someone lies. Interrogations are recorded and experts examine the recording to detect stress. Voice tests are also generally inadmissible in court.[72]

Confessions

Because no one can be compelled to testify against himself, the state must prove that the defendant gave the **confession** voluntarily. If the defense can prove otherwise, the confession can be excluded. Courts have a specific procedure for evaluating whether confessions are to be entered into evidence.

Before a defendant's confession can be entered into evidence, the court will hold a **Jackson-Denno hearing.** The hearings take their name from a landmark Supreme Court case, *Jackson v. Denno,*[73] where the issue was first addressed.

At Jackson-Denno hearings, the state must prove the confession was offered voluntarily. Usually, the policemen who obtained the confession will testify about the events leading to the confession, noting exactly where in the sequence the defendant acknowledged understanding the *Miranda* rights, whether the defendant asked for an attorney, and when the confession began.

Because many cases hinge on the admissibility of confessions, many jurisdictions have taken to recording confessions with either audio or video equipment. In fact, European Union (EU) countries are required to allow arrested defendants to have eight hours of sleep and a meal before they are interrogated. All interrogations in the EU are videotaped with an attorney present.[74] Increasingly, federal judges have looked to the EU to judge the American criminal justice system's fairness.

In addition to fairness issues, prosecutors and police have found that recordings of interrogations provide strong evidence that confessions were voluntary. The audio or videotapes can bolster police testimony in Jackson-Denno hearings.

Confession
The act of admitting guilt or complicity to the commission of a crime.

Jackson-Denno Hearing
A hearing preparatory to admitting a confession into evidence where the prosecutor must prove that the confession was voluntary.

Warrant
A document issued by a magistrate or judge authorizing the search of a place or the arrest of a person.

CONCEPT **REVIEW AND REINFORCEMENT**

Americans enjoy a long list of protections from police and governmental interference in their lives. These protections naturally extend to persons suspected of criminal activities. Working from the presumption that all persons are innocent until proven guilty, law enforcement officials must go about the task of solving crimes by assembling the evidence to prove beyond a reasonable doubt that a defendant is guilty without interfering with the people's right to liberty.

All persons are accorded the right to be free from unreasonable searches and seizures. The Constitution protects the public's reasonable expectation of privacy, whether at home, at work, or in a closed phone booth along the interstate. Police can only search private places with either consent or a search **warrant.** A search warrant requires that police officers obtain one from a neutral magistrate or judge after presenting probable cause that the place to be searched will yield evidence of a crime or the person to be detained has committed a crime.

Officers can detain, search, and arrest individuals without a warrant, but with probable cause, if certain circumstances mitigate against obtaining a search warrant from a magistrate or judge. These include the searching of an automobile stopped for reasons that amount to probable cause, exigent circumstances like the pursuit of a suspect on foot or in a car, and the temporary detainment, identification, and search of an individual in a stop and frisk.

If a defendant can show that the police violated his or her right to be free of unreasonable searches and seizures, the remedy may be that the evidence obtained cannot be used in court. This is the exclusionary rule.

In the American system of justice, the government has only one opportunity to try a suspect; if a jury acquits him, he is free to go even if later he shouts his guilt from the highest rooftop. Double jeopardy protects him, and all others, from repeated attempts at conviction for the same offense. It does not mean that a defendant who wins an appeal can't be retried. Nor does it prevent another trial if the jury is unable to reach a verdict. Defendants can also be tried in both state or federal court for activities that violate both state and federal laws.

The rule against *ex post facto* laws prevents the government from punishing persons who committed acts that were legal at the time but were made illegal later. The rules against bills of attainder prevent the government from passing laws that apply only to certain individuals or specific groups of people.

Finally, defendants and suspects have the right to legal counsel to represent them at most stages of a criminal prosecution and the right to remain silent throughout the process.

KEY **TERMS**

Bail	*Ex post facto* law	Rebuttable presumption
Bill of attainder	Exclusionary rule	Right to remain silent
Confession	Exigent circumstances	Self-incrimination
Consent once removed	Irrebuttable presumption	Stop and frisk
Double jeopardy	Jackson-Denno Hearing	Unreasonable searches and seizures
Evanescent evidence	Probable cause	Warrant

CONCEPT REVIEW **QUESTIONS**

1. What constitutional protections exist against unreasonable searches and seizures?
2. What are some examples of searches that violate the Fourth Amendment?
3. What proof must law enforcement have before a search warrant will be issued?
4. What steps must law enforcement officers take in order to get a search warrant issued?
5. What areas can be searched without a warrant?
6. What is probable cause?
7. How are informants used?
8. What is the exclusionary rule?
9. What is the right to remain silent?
10. What is double jeopardy?
11. What is an *ex post facto* law? A bill of attainder?

CASE **APPLICATIONS**

Building Your Professional Skills

1. Do you carry a cell phone? Most students do. If you want to be absolutely sure no one is listening in on your conversation—or anyone else's conversation in the room—remove the battery. That's right. Your trusty communications device may be a bug. That's what the

world learned when a federal judge considering a criminal case against a purported member of the Genovese crime family ruled that the FBI was free to reprogram cell phones as roving electronic eavesdropping bugs. Here's how it supposedly works: Technology is available in software form that switched on the microphone in recent model cell phones even when the phone is powered off. This allows persons sitting in, for example, an FBI cubicle in Washington, D.C., to listen in on live conversations anywhere in the world. Nextel, Samsung, and Motorola Razr phones are reportedly the easiest to "tap" this way. The only way to defeat the "bug" is to remove the battery from the handset. Some phones, like Apple's iPhone, have batteries that cannot be removed at all.

Read the following edited opinion and answer the questions that follow.

United States of America
v.
John Tomero et al., Defendants.
United States District Court, S.D. New York.

Memorandum Opinion

KAPLAN, District Judge.

Thirty-four defendants are charged with various criminal acts associated with the operations of the Genovese organized crime family. Ten move to suppress conversations intercepted by listening devices, colloquially known as "roving bugs," installed in cellular telephones . . . The indictment stems from a three-year investigation into the criminal activity of members and associates of the Genovese organized crime family.

The investigation initially focused on the crew of John Ardito, a high-ranking member of the family. The FBI learned from cooperating witnesses that Ardito's crew met regularly at a restaurant called Brunello Trattoria in New Rochelle, New York, to conduct family business. In December 2002, the Honorable Barbara S. Jones of this Court authorized the interception of oral communications of Ardito and other subjects at this location.

The intercepted conversations revealed that Ardito and his crew met at three additional restaurants, in part because they were suspicious of law enforcement surveillance. The government applied for, and Judge Jones authorized, the interception of conversations at these three restaurants as well as continued interception at Brunello Trattoria. In July 2003, however, Ardito's crew found the listening devices in three of the restaurants and became even more wary of surveillance whenever they returned to their usual meeting places.

Based on physical surveillance and the conversations previously intercepted, the FBI learned that Ardito's crew no longer conducted meetings exclusively at the four restaurants, but met also in twelve additional restaurants, automobiles, Ardito's home, an auto store, an insurance office, a jewelry store, a doctor's office, a boat, and public streets.

The government applied for a "roving bug," that is, the interception of Ardito's conversations at locations that were "not practical" to specify, as authorized by 18 U.S.C. § 2518(11)(a). Judge Jones granted the application, authorizing continued interception at the four restaurants and the installation of a listening device in Ardito's cellular telephone. The device functioned whether the phone was powered on or off, intercepting conversations within its range wherever it happened to be. . . .

By February 2004, the government had learned that Peter Peluso, an attorney and close associate of Ardito, was relaying messages to and from high-ranking family members who were wary of government listening devices and who used Peluso as a messenger to avoid meeting together directly. In a renewal application dated February 6, 2004, the government sought, and Judge Jones in due course granted, authority to install a roving bug in Peluso's cellular telephone. This order was renewed several times throughout 2004, as the government continued to identify locations where Peluso and Ardito discussed family matters and learned that the subjects were growing increasingly cautious of government surveillance. . . .

By the conclusion of the investigation, the government had intercepted hundreds of hours of Ardito's and Peluso's conversations . . .

Defendants now seek suppression of the conversations intercepted by the listening devices. . . .

The essence of the motion to suppress is that the statute unconstitutionally permits interception in the absence of any specification of the place where communications are to be intercepted. In *Bianco*, the Second Circuit rejected precisely this argument. The fact that the unspecified location in *Bianco* happened to be in a building had nothing to do with the holding.

Furthermore, while a mobile device makes interception easier and less costly to accomplish than a stationary one, this does not mean that it implicates new or different privacy concerns. It simply dispenses with the need for repeated installations and surreptitious entries into buildings. It does not invade zones of privacy that the government could not reach by more conventional means . . .

QUESTIONS

1. Knowing what you know, do you think it would be a good idea to have clients, investigators, and attorneys who meet to discuss a case remove the batteries from their cell phones?

2. What are the implications of a roving bug on attorney–client privilege and the right to an attorney?

CRITICAL **THINKING EXERCISES**

1. You have been stopped by a police officer because your brake light is out. Your brother, whom you suspect has a drug problem, throws something under your seat. The officer asks if he can look around. What do you do?

2. A police surveillance team is monitoring your house because it believes you are growing marijuana in your attic. The team wants to use infrared cameras to locate heat sources in your house. Do they need a warrant? What if they suspected you of growing drugs to fund terrorist organizations, do they need a warrant then?

3. Assume the same facts in the first part of the question above, and that the police believed they needed a warrant to use infrared cameras on your house. What standard of proof would the officers need to convince the judge to issue the warrant?

4. A rape occurred in your apartment building. The police go door-to-door to gather information. When they knock on your door, they do not announce that they are the police and you open the door without asking who is on the other side. You're kind of buzzed and forget that your marijuana is sitting in plain view on your coffee table that is visible from the door. You tell the police investigator that you know nothing about the rape, but the investigator clearly saw the pot on your table. If the police investigator chooses to pursue the matter, is a warrant necessary?

5. You are wearing clothing that identifies you as a member of a street gang. Based on your dress, do the police have probable cause to arrest you?

6. You are an attorney representing a client currently serving a sentence for burglary.

Another inmate has come forward claiming your client confessed to a murder during one of their conversations. To challenge the informant's credibility, what arguments do you put forward?

7. You are at home one evening when the police break down your door telling you they have a search warrant to search your property. You are handcuffed and forced on the floor while the police ransack your house. All they find is an unregistered handgun that violates local ordinances. When you finally get to see the search warrant you point out that the name on it is not yours and the address is incorrect. Can the police use the evidence from this search to prosecute you on weapons charges?

8. A policeman pulls you over for a moving violation. You provide him with your driver's license and registration. He notices a bundle covered by a tarp in your backseat. He asks you what is under the tarp. Do you have to answer him?

9. You are an attorney and your client was tried and acquitted for the murder of his wife. The police, armed with new evidence, charge the man with assaulting his wife immediately prior to her death. Can you use the double jeopardy defense?

10. A trend in recent years has been for state legislatures to pass laws that require sex offenders who have served their sentences to register their address with the police and for the government to notify communities that a convicted sex offender is now their neighbor. What arguments would you make on behalf of a sex offender who committed the offense before the passage of the registration law?

11. You are an attorney and your client has been taken into custody. The police inform you he is a material witness in an ongoing investigation and they wish to hold him indefinitely. What steps must you take to get him released?

PORTFOLIO **BUILDING**

1. Research the pending U.S. Supreme Court cases dealing with constitutional rights before arrest. Prepare a brief summary for your portfolio of each pending case, including the specific question the Supreme Court agreed to consider when it granted cert. A good place to start is with On The Docket at http://otd.oyez.org/.

2. Pick one of the pending cases, locate the underlying opinion, and prepare a brief for your portfolio. Then predict the Supreme Court's decision based on what you read.

FOR FURTHER READING AND VIEWING

1. Alderman, E., and Kennedy, C. (1997). *The Right to Privacy.* Vintage Books. Examines the origin of the right to privacy and its application in civil and criminal law through case studies such as the story of the routine strip-searching performed on women arrested for minor traffic violations.

2. Alderman, E., and Kennedy, C. (1992). *In Our Defense: The Bill of Rights in Action.* Avon Books. Explores the origin and history of the Bill of Rights using case examples.

3. Amar, A., and Hirsch, A. (1998). *For the People: What the Constitution Really Says About Your Rights.* Free Press. Provides an alternative interpretation of the history of the Constitution and the Bill of Rights that focuses on the rights of the collective "we the people" rather than on the rights of the individual.

4. Katz, L., and Shepard, T. (1994). *Know Your Rights.* Banks-Baldwin. This practical legal guide answers questions like what to do when stopped by a police officer on the road or arrested.

5. Moore, W. (1996). *Constitutional Rights and Powers of the People.* Princeton University Press. This book examines how the social and political climate of the time affects the interpretation of the Constitution.

6. *The Bourne Ultimatum* (2007). Action thriller staring Matt Damon as Jason Bourne based on the novel by Robert Ludlum. The film features lots of real time cell phone tracing and bugging as the CIA tries to track Bourne across the world.

7. *The Star Chamber* (1983). This film stars Michael Douglas and centers on a secret justice system that "tries" defendants released on a technicality in the real justice system.

8. *Cape Fear* (1991). Nick Nolte stars as a former defense attorney who allowed evidence he should have moved to exclude go forward, resulting in the conviction of the character played by Robert Deniro. Deniro seeks revenge for the legal malpractice and stalks the attorney's family. A Martin Scorsese remake of the 1962 film starring Gregory Peck and Robert Mitchum, both of whom appear in cameo roles in this version.

Chapter **twelve**

CONSTITUTIONAL RIGHTS AFTER ARREST

Every society gets the kind of criminal it deserves. What is equally true is that every community gets the kind of law enforcement it insists on.

Robert Kennedy, *The Pursuit of Justice*

If one really wishes to know how justice is administered in a country, one does not question the policemen, the lawyers, the judges, or the protected members of the middle class. One goes to the unprotected, those, precisely, who need the law's protection most! And listen to their testimony.

James Baldwin, *The Price of the Ticket* (1972)

CHAPTER OBJECTIVES

After studying this chapter, you should be able to:

- Explain the *Miranda* warning
- Explain when a criminal defendant has a right to counsel
- Explain the rights of indigent defendants to a public defender
- Explain the right against self-incrimination
- List and explain the circumstances under which a person can be compelled to testify against himself
- Explain the attorney–client privilege, husband–wife privilege, and priest–penitent privilege
- Explain when physical evidence can be compelled from defendants without violating the right against self-incrimination
- Explain the right to a speedy trial
- Distinguish statutes of limitations from the constitutional right to a speedy trial

Introduction and Historical Background

As you have learned in the last few chapters, many of the rights we accord persons charged with crimes stem from abuses suffered by the colonists at the hand of the British crown. The Constitution and the Bill of Rights serve as reminders that our forefathers vowed that never again would they be subjected to the whims of a monarch, but that the right to a prompt, fair, public trial and adequate legal representation would be sacrosanct. In this chapter, we will explore the defendants' rights in the crucial time between arrest and trial.

Most importantly, defendants have the right to an attorney who will represent their interests as the case winds its way through the court system. Since many defendants lack financial resources, the right to counsel includes the right to a court-appointed attorney for poor defendants.

Defendants also have the right to remain silent; that is, the right to compel the government to prove the case against him or her. As we will see, that right is limited to testimonial silence. In some circumstances, defendants can also prevent others from providing testimony.

The right to remain silent is not absolute. The government can compel the production of some forms of physical evidence. Similarly, a person can also be compelled to testify if he or she has received immunity from prosecution or the statute of limitations has expired.

Arrest

Arrest
The official taking of a person to answer criminal charges.

In the last chapter, you learned that law enforcement officers must establish probable cause to obtain a search warrant from the court. Similarly, officers must also have probable cause to believe an individual committed a crime before making an **arrest.** An arrest is the official taking of a person to answer criminal charges. The person is detained and is not free to perform his or her normal daily duties. Usually, the person is handcuffed or otherwise restrained.

Police officers or other law enforcement personnel carry out most arrests. An officer need not be in uniform or on duty to make an arrest. Some states even authorize citizens to make arrests in certain circumstances. Often states have different sets of rules governing citizens' arrest depending on whether the crime was a felony or misdemeanor. Generally, citizens may arrest anyone they witness committing a crime. However, if the citizen only hears of a crime being committed, most states will not allow him to arrest the person if the crime is a misdemeanor. Citizens are always free to arrest someone to prevent a felony, but not always a misdemeanor. Check the laws in your state and always be ready to dial 911.

Custody
The state of being detained by law enforcement officers. A person is in custody when that person is not free to leave.

Custody   Courts consider a person to be in custody when he or she is not free to leave. Defendants can be in custody even if they are not in jail. In one case, the Supreme Court ruled a defendant was in custody when being questioned in his own bedroom.[1] Courts look at the totality of circumstances in each case. As soon as the defendant was not free to leave, police must read the defendant the *Miranda* rights and affirm that the defendant understands the rights. Any statements made by the defendant between being placed in custody and acknowledging understanding the rights are not admissible.

Postarrest Interrogation

Once a defendant has been arrested and read his or her rights, police may begin interrogation. Again, under *Miranda* the defendant has the right to remain silent and the right to have an attorney present during questioning. Once the defendant acknowledges that he or she understands the *Miranda* rights, any statement made is presumed to be voluntary.

HISTORICAL HIGHLIGHT

The Christian Burial Speech

Skilled interrogators will often use tricks or bring psychological pressure to bear to get the defendant to make voluntary statements. But courts place limits on what interrogators can do.

An example of both skilled interrogation technique and violating a prisoner's rights is the "Christian Burial" case. In this Iowa case, recently released mental patient Robert Williams was suspected

of abducting and killing ten-year-old Pamela Powers on Christmas Eve, 1968. The abduction occurred in Des Moines and Williams' abandoned car was found 160 miles east in Davenport. Based on eyewitness accounts linking Williams and his car to the abduction, police issued a warrant for his arrest.

Williams contacted Des Moines attorney, Henry McKnight, who advised him to turn himself in to the Davenport police. Williams turned himself in, and the

Davenport police spoke with the attorney by phone and agreed not to interrogate Williams until he was returned to Des Moines where the attorney could be present. A Davenport attorney reiterated the agreement to the policemen transporting Williams.

Despite these warnings, the police tried to engage Williams in a conversation about the girl. Each time, he rebuffed them stating, "When I get to Des Moines and see Mr. McKnight, I am going to tell you the whole story." Finally, one of the detectives started talking about other issues including religion. When he ascertained that Williams was a religious man, he gave what came to be known as the "Christian Burial" speech, where he asked Williams to observe the worsening weather conditions of sleet and freezing rain and that several inches of snow were forecast for the evening. He told Williams that since he was the only person who knew where the body was, he should tell them now so they could find it before the snow piled up. He concluded by saying, "I feel that we could stop and locate the body, that the parents of this little girl should be entitled to a Christian burial for the little girl who was snatched away from them on Christmas Eve and murdered." Williams agreed to show them the body's location.

Prior to his trial, his attorney moved to have all evidence of the car ride conversation suppressed, but the motion was denied. Williams was convicted of first-degree murder. On appeal, the court ruled Williams waived his right to remain silent by volunteering the information. The Iowa Supreme Court affirmed, but the U.S. Supreme Court saw it differently.

The High Court ruled that questioning Williams without counsel present after he had repeatedly asked for it violated both his Sixth and Fourteenth Amendment right to counsel.[2]

The Interrogator's Tools: Trickery and Deceit   Police are free to trick defendants into confessing within limits. Anyone who watches police shows on television knows some of the more familiar tricks such as telling a defendant someone else is blaming him for the crime when that is not true. Police tricks often provoke court scrutiny and skirt the borders of legality.

For instance, telling a defendant his statements are "off the record" is not allowed. Obviously, threats of or actual torture to obtain a confession or testimony are illegal and will result in the evidence being excluded. Similarly, depriving a defendant of sleep, food, drink, or other necessities of life in order to obtain a confession is illegal.

> The quality of a nation's civilization can be largely measured by the methods it uses in the enforcement of its criminal law.
>
> Harvard Professor Schaefer

> Pain forces even the innocent to lie.
>
> Publilius Syrus, first century B.C.

The Right Against Self-Incrimination

Throughout the criminal investigation process, police, investigators, or even the grand jury can interrogate a defendant. Defendants do not have to answer questions that may incriminate them. The right against self-incrimination is enshrined in the Fifth Amendment to the Constitution as, "No person . . . shall be compelled in any criminal case to be a witness against himself." A person who refuses to answer questions about alleged criminal activities is said to "plead the Fifth." No right is fundamentally more representative of the American way of justice. It is always the government's prosecutor and police officers who must prove a person guilty of a crime, not the person's responsibility to prove himself innocent. All men and women are indeed innocent until proven guilty. To protect that fundamental right, no person can be compelled to help the government by being forced to give evidence against him or herself.

Confessions can only be used against a defendant if the prosecution can show that they followed the procedures laid out in *Miranda* and that they did not coerce or otherwise extract a confession from the defendant. All confessions must be voluntary and have been given after notification of the right to remain silent. You may recall from Chapter 1 a recent Supreme Court case, *Maryland v. Shatzer*. In that

Confession
A voluntary statement by a person that he or she is guilty of a crime or any admission of wrongdoing.

case, the Supreme Court concluded that a prisoner who had refused to speak with police officers without his attorney present could be questioned if at least fourteen days had passed since he invoked the right to remain silent. In other words, invoked *Miranda* rights don't last forever, but have to be renewed.[3] Shatzer made an incriminating statement when questioned again about two years after he initially demanded his right to an attorney and that statement was used to convict him.

The right to remain silent is not without limits. In some circumstances, there is no risk associated with speaking. In that case, prosecutors and others can compel testimony. That's because the right to remain silent is the **right against self-incrimination.** That is, in order for the right to apply, the act of speaking must be related to the possibility of criminal prosecution. If that possibility doesn't exist, there is no potential self-incrimination. For example, if the statute of limitations has expired, there is no restriction on what can be asked. There is also nothing to prevent police or others from demanding sworn testimony under oath when the defendant's criminal trial has already ended and he or she has been sentenced or acquitted. That's because he or she no longer faces the possibility of the testimony being used against him or her. In addition, if a defendant has been given immunity, testimony can be compelled. Immunity is explored later in this chapter.

Right against self-incrimination
The right embodied in the Fifth Amendment that allows an accused person to remain silent. Its corollary is "innocent until proven guilty."

Bail

Initial appearance
A court proceeding shortly after a suspect's arrest where the suspect is informed of specific rights.

The first legal proceeding after a person is arrested is the **initial appearance,** where the accused is informed of the seriousness of the charge, the consequences of the initial appearance and future hearings, and his or her right to have a counsel represent him or her. If the defendant cannot afford an attorney, he or she can request one at this initial appearance. The practice varies from jurisdiction to jurisdiction, but attorneys can be appointed for defendants before or at the initial hearing.

Shortly after the initial appearance, the court holds a bail or bond hearing. Judges often weigh the seriousness of the charge and the chance the defendant will flee rather than face charges in court, when setting bail. In very serious cases or when the judge feels the flight risk is very high, the magistrate can refuse to set bail, and the defendant must remain in custody until trial. Often the time served counts toward fulfilling the defendant's sentence if convicted.

The Constitution offers specific prohibitions against setting excessive bail. Consequently, the defendant can challenge an extremely high bail.

Most defendants do not have enough cash on hand to post bail. Bail bondsmen often step in to fill this gap. Most bail bondsmen take a 10 percent nonrefundable deposit to post a defendant's bail. If the defendant doesn't show for trial, the bail bondsman forfeits the full amount of the bond until the defendant is brought in. As a result, bail bondsmen are highly motivated to find fugitive defendants. Judges have sole discretion over whether bail is forfeited and often allow bail bondsmen to get their bond back once the fugitive is brought in.

Some jurisdictions limit the types of cases that certain courts can set bail. Often bail for murder and other serious crimes is set by higher court judges.

Another fundamental right enjoyed by Americans is the Eighth Amendment guarantee against excessive bail. Though not without limits, defendants are generally entitled to bail pending trial. Release from prison before trial serves several purposes. First, it serves as an incentive for the government to bring cases to closure. If defendants could be indefinitely detained in prison pending trial, there would be little incentive to moving the case forward. Second, the **right to bail** allows the defendant to fully participate in his or her defense, something difficult to do from the inside of a prison cell. Coupled with the right to a speedy trial (discussed in the next chapter), the right to bail helps grease the wheels of justice.

The amount of bail set is intended as a guarantee that the defendant will show up for trial. Bail generally is set in an amount that will guarantee that the defendant doesn't skip town. Since 1987, however, bail can be denied altogether if the defendant poses a danger to the community. Bail can be denied in capital cases, in cases where the defendant may intimidate witnesses, or in cases where the public's safety is at stake. A hearing is required before bail can be denied and the government must show that the defendant poses a public threat that no conditions of release can change.[4]

Right to bail
The limited right to be released from prison pending trial after posting enough security to assure appearance at the time of trial. The right is subject to limitation in cases of murder or where release has been shown to pose a threat to the public.

The Constitutional Right to Counsel In Criminal Cases

The Sixth Amendment states that: "In all criminal prosecutions, the accused shall enjoy the right . . . to have the Assistance of Counsel for his defense." Given the complexity of the legal system and the high stakes for a defendant, very few persons accused of a crime elect to represent themselves. Most prefer to have a trained attorney at their side. But the right to assistance of counsel wasn't widespread until this century, at least in "minor" criminal cases.

For many years, the right to be represented by a member of the bar was limited to capital cases (cases where the death penalty was sought by the prosecution). In 1932, the Supreme Court wrote that a layman:

> lacks both the skill and knowledge adequately to prepare his defense, even though he has a perfect one. He requires the guiding hand of counsel at every step . . . without it, though he is innocent, he faces the danger of conviction because he does not know how to establish his innocence.[5]

By 1938, the right was extended to all federal felony cases. By 1963, defendants charged with any felony, state or federal, were entitled to counsel regardless of their ability to pay for one.[6] And by 1964, the Supreme Court had ruled that confessions obtained after police didn't tell the defendant he was entitled to counsel or refused to let him talk to his attorney are not admissible.[7]

The right to counsel isn't limited to having an attorney to represent you at trial. A defendant has a right to counsel at his or her arraignment, preliminary hearing, during most police questioning, during a lineup, at trial, and at sentencing. In addition, he or she has a right to counsel for his or her first appeal.

The right to counsel means little if the defendant is ignorant of his right to counsel. Therefore, the Supreme Court decided in the *Miranda* case that police have an obligation to inform a suspect of his rights under the Constitution.

Police must inform any person put under arrest or held in a custodial interrogation, such as at a police station, that he has the following rights before questioning begins:

1. That he has the right to remain silent,
2. That anything he says can and will be used against him,

3. That he has the right to an attorney during questioning,

4. That if he can't afford one, one will be appointed at no charge before questioning, and

5. That at any time during the questioning, he can stop and the interrogation will end.

HISTORICAL HIGHLIGHT

The Scottsboro Boys: The Right to Counsel

On March 31, 1931, a train was rolling through the Alabama countryside. As was often the case during the Depression, many drifters were riding in the train's boxcars. This train had a group of young black boys, ages twelve to nineteen, and a group of white boys along with two white girls. A fight broke out among the boys and all the white boys except for one were thrown from the train. They immediately alerted the authorities and at the next stop the blacks were arrested after the girls accused them of rape.

As a group, these boys had little or no education. All were illiterate and not one of them was an Alabama native. By the time they were in custody, word had spread of the incident and a large angry crowd awaited them at Scottsboro. The local sheriff called for the state militia to help protect the boys.

The trial was set for a week after the indictment. The local judge appointed all members of the local bar to assist in the boys' defense, but charged no one attorney in particular to represent them. A Tennessee attorney was contacted by the families of one of the defendants and appeared at the first day of trial offering to assist the court-appointed attorney. Although some members of the local bar had spoken with the defendants, none were prepared to conduct their defense. The Tennessee attorney was given the opportunity to represent them by himself, but explained that he wasn't prepared for trial and was unfamiliar with court practices in Alabama. Eventually, one of the local attorneys was appointed and the Tennessee attorney assisted him.

The defendants were tried as three groups, and with the exception of the twelve-year-old defendant, separately sentenced to death. The trials lasted one day each. The convictions were upheld by the appeals court and the Alabama Supreme Court, and only Chief Justice Anderson dissented, stating he did not feel the boys received a fair trial.

The International Labor Defense, a Communist organization, represented the boys when the case was appealed to the U.S. Supreme Court. The case was appealed on three grounds: (1) they were not given a fair, impartial, and deliberate trial; (2) they were denied the right of counsel with the accustomed incidents of consultation and opportunity of preparation of trial; and (3) they were tried before juries from which qualified members of their own race were systematically excluded.[8]

The Supreme Court dealt only with the second charge, the denial of right to counsel. The High Court, citing the Sixth Amendment, reaffirmed the right to counsel for all citizens accused of a crime, and described the type of defense afforded the Scottsboro boys as "rather pro forma than zealous and active."[9] The Court noted the lack of time for the defense to prepare for trial, and the lack of time for the defendants, all of whom lived out of state, to secure counsel of their own choice as sufficient to invalidate their defense. The Court reversed the convictions and sent the cases back to be retried with adequate counsel.

At the second trial, the boys were convicted, but the judge found the testimony of the girls unbelievable and set aside the verdict and ordered a new trial. He was defeated in the next election.[10]

The Scottsboro boys' saga dragged on for many years. None of them were ever executed, but all spent time in prison. The last one, Clarence Norris, was finally pardoned by Governor George Wallace in 1976.[11]

Miranda is discussed more fully in the Historical Highlight: *How Mirandizing Became a Verb*. In 1968, Congress passed a law that essentially intended to gut the *Miranda* decision. This law (18 U.S.C.S. § 3501) provided that as long as the defendant's confession was voluntary, it needn't be preceded by the *Miranda* warning. In 2000, the Supreme Court had an opportunity to consider *Miranda* again. In that case the defendant had been indicted for a bank robbery. He confessed to the crime when asked by the FBI and then moved to strike his confession because he gave it without being warned as required by *Miranda*. The government argued that under 18 U.S.C.S. § 3501, it wasn't required to warn him.

The trial judge suppressed the confession, but the Fourth Circuit Court of Appeals reversed. The defendant appealed to the Supreme Court. The Court, in a strongly worded opinion, ruled that it meant what it said in *Miranda* and ordered the confession suppressed. The Court found the warning to be a fundamental constitutional right.[12]

What happens if a police officer deliberately doesn't read a suspect her *Miranda* rights, gets her to confess, then *Mirandizes* her, and gets the confession the second time? That was the issue before the Court in a 2004 case involving a mother who allegedly conspired to commit arson to cover up a child's natural death. Unfortunately, the cover-up arson went badly and killed another youth. The officer who questioned her claimed to have learned the double confession trick at a training seminar. The Court ruled 5–4 that the tactic was illegal and the second confession was invalid.[13]

The Supreme Court recently heard another case involving double confessions. In that case, the officers came to the defendant's house and asked him if he had been involved in illegal drug use after telling him he had been indicted. He confessed and was taken to the police station, where he was read his *Miranda* rights and again confessed. On appeal, he argued both confessions should be thrown out because he had not been read his rights. A unanimous Supreme Court sent the case back to the lower court, stating that the real question was whether the defendant's Sixth Amendment rights to counsel had been violated in that he had not been offered the opportunity to have his lawyer present.[14]

The issue is one that doesn't seem to want to go away. On the same day it concluded that the arson-setting mother's confession was illegal, the Court also decided that a gun found after a defendant admitted he had one can be used as evidence even though the admission came after the police failed to read the suspect his *Miranda* rights. The case involved a defendant, who, when arrested, stopped the officer from reading the *Miranda* warning because he claimed to know it already. The confession he made was suppressed, but the gun the police seized was allowed into evidence. The Court, in another 5–4 decision, upheld the use of physical evidence found as a result of information gleaned from an illegal confession.[15]

Then, in 2010, the Supreme Court went further to limit the impact of *Miranda*. In *Berghuis v. Thompkins*,[16] an inmate who did not specifically say that he wanted to remain silent was not able to challenge the statements he made to police. Van Chester Thompkins was read his rights by two police officers interrogating him about a shooting in which one of the victims died. Thompkins didn't say that he wanted to remain silent, although he said very little during the three-hour interrogation that followed the reading of his rights. Finally, one of the officers asked Thompkins whether he prayed to God to forgive him for the shooting, to which he replied, "Yes." He was convicted of first-degree murder and sentenced to life in prison without parole. Thompkins appealed, arguing that his silence after being read his rights indicated he wanted to invoke the right to remain silent.

The Supreme Court disagreed. It wrote that "Thompkins' silence during the interrogation did not invoke his right to remain silent. A suspect's *Miranda* right to counsel must be invoked "unambiguously." If the accused makes an "ambiguous or equivocal" statement or no statement, the police are not required to end the interrogation, or ask questions to clarify the accused's intent." Had Thompkins said he wanted to remain silent and wanted counsel present, the interrogation would have stopped, at least until his attorney showed up.

What would happen if a defendant is arrested, arraigned, and the district justice rules that he is entitled to counsel and orders one, but the police then take the defendant aside, read him his *Miranda* rights again, and he agrees to take the police to the weapon he used in a crime? And while on the ride, the defendant writes a letter to the widow apologizing for killing her husband. They return to the courthouse, where the appointed counsel is ready to talk with the defendant. Should the letter be suppressed because the defendant hadn't yet spoken with appointed counsel? That's the question recently answered in another Supreme Court decision.

The Supreme Court concluded that because this defendant, like Thompkins, did not state that he wanted to talk with his newly appointed lawyer, he, too, had not invoked the rights read him in the *Miranda* warning. If he wanted to speak with his counsel, he should have spoken up, the court reasoned.[17]

The Poor and the Right to Counsel

A criminal defendant is entitled to more than just an attorney to represent him or her. The defendant has the right to "effective" assistance of counsel. Effective counsel is competent counsel.[18]

Obviously, the right to counsel would mean very little if a defendant doesn't have the means to retain an attorney. After all, the government expends a vast amount of money on its police force, district attorneys, judges, and other court personnel. As the Supreme Court pointed out in *Gideon v. Wainwright*, the fact that "[t]he government hires lawyers to prosecute and defendants who have the money hire lawyers to defend are the strongest indications of a widespread belief that lawyers in criminal courts are necessities, not luxuries."[19]

Indigent defendants have the right to court-appointed counsel at no charge. Since 1964, when the Criminal Justice Act of 1964 was passed into law, defendants charged with federal crimes are entitled to a federal public defender. The states have passed similar legislation to assure experienced criminal law attorneys are have available professional investigators who can assist in preparing cases for trial.

> The need for counsel in order to protect the privilege [against self-incrimination] exists for the indigent as well as the affluent.
>
> Chief Justice Earl Warren, *Miranda v. Arizona* (1969)

HISTORICAL HIGHLIGHT

How Mirandizing *Became a Verb*

Watch any police show on television or in a movie theater and invariably at some point in the plot line, a police officer will read a defendant or suspect his rights. You can probably recite the warning verbatim yourself, so often have you heard it. "You have the right to remain silent and the right to consult an attorney. Anything you say can and will be used against you in a court of law . . . ."

The warning has almost become a police officer's mantra. In fact, almost every police officer carries a copy of the *Miranda* warning with him or her. That's not because he or she is likely to "forget" to inform a defendant of a right. Rather, it reflects an easy way for officers to testify later. Sometime in the future, the officer will be asked whether he or she read the defendant his rights. The officer is unlikely to remember the exact details of an arrest or interrogation that happened months, even years, earlier. Instead, the officer will testify that he did read the suspect his rights, by pulling out the card, and reading it to him word for word. The officer will tell the court how he *Mirandized* the defendant.

Just how did *Mirandizing* become a verb? The term, of course, is derived from the 1966 Supreme Court decision in *Miranda v. Arizona*. The case actually involved not just Ernesto Miranda, the Arizona defendant who lent his name to the legal warning. In the same decision, the Court also decided that Michael Vignera, a New Yorker, Carl Calvin Westover of Kansas City, and Roy Allen Stewart of Los Angeles had confessed without knowing their constitutional rights.

Together, their cases served to highlight just how common the police practice of extracting quick confessions from suspects unfamiliar with their rights was. All gave confessions after lengthy interrogations. At least one confession declared that the statement was made "with full knowledge of my rights." Another confessed after a series of interrogations that spanned five days. Together, their cases convinced the Court that something as simple as a warning was needed to curb the widespread denial of suspects' right to remain silent. Ever since, police officers *Mirandize* suspects.

Judges sometimes appoint and the government pays for experienced private attorneys in complex or serious cases where the local public defender office is short staffed or lacks an attorney with specific expertise. Court-appointed private counsel is generally reserved for high-profile capital cases such as the Oklahoma City bombing cases. The right to counsel continues after trial through the post-trial appeals and any direct appellate appeals.

Arraignment

Once a grand jury has issued a felony **indictment**, the defendant must then attend an **arraignment**. At the arraignment, the court reads the charges against the defendant and the defendant pleads guilty or not guilty to the charges. If the defendant is still without representation at this point, he or she can request the court appoint an attorney.

The right to an arraignment includes the right to a prompt arraignment after arrest. Otherwise, defendants could be held indefinitely without knowing what crimes they have been charged with committing, while under the control of the police. Arraignment is with a member of the judiciary, another branch of government, and this separation of power helps maintain a fair and balanced legal system in which defendants aren't simply charged and then disappear. For example, the Supreme Court has ruled that a defendant must be arraigned promptly or any confession made while he or she is in custody waiting to be arraigned is invalid. In that case, Johnnie Corley was arrested and charged with conspiracy to commit armed bank robbery and other charges and held for thirty hours before being arraigned and informed of the charges against him. In the interim, he made several statements that were used against him. The Supreme Court suppressed those statements.[20]

Defendants are usually notified of their arraignment date when they post bail, or through certified mail from the prosecutor. Defendants who fail to appear for their arraignment may be required to forfeit their bail. In that case, the judge will issue a **bench warrant** giving the police the power to arrest the defendant. Once the defendant is arrested, he will sit in jail until the next scheduled arraignment.

Depending on the jurisdiction, the arraignment gives defendants and their attorneys a glimpse of the prosecution's case. At minimum, the prosecution

Indictment
A written accusation claiming that a specific person committed a specific crime or crimes. Prosecutors present indictments to grand juries so the jury can vote on whether the indictment is a true bill.

Arraignment
A judicial proceeding where an accused hears the charges against him and enters a plea of guilty or not guilty to the charges.

Bench warrant
A warrant issued by a judge ordering law enforcement officers to arrest a specific person.

must provide the indictment and a list of state witnesses who will be called to testify. Some states require one or both sides to serve discovery documents at the arraignment.

Preliminary Hearings

Preliminary hearings are held within a short time of the defendant's arrest. Some jurisdictions have specific time limits prosecutors must meet. Preliminary hearings are held to determine whether the state has probable cause for the defendant's arrest. The state must show by a preponderance of the evidence that the defendant committed the crime.

This standard is different than the beyond-a-reasonable-doubt standard necessary to convict the defendant at trial. As a result, prosecutors will often only present enough evidence to show that it is more likely than not that the defendant committed the crime.

Defendants can waive a preliminary hearing if they so choose. Often, this is a matter of negotiation between the defendant's attorney and the prosecutor. The prosecutor may agree to a lower bail request in return for waiving the preliminary hearing.

The preliminary hearing is less formal than a full trial. Similarly, evidentiary rules are more lax. Hearsay testimony is acceptable at a preliminary hearing, but would not be at trial. The hearing is before a judge, not a jury. The judge will make the decision whether to bind the case over for trial.

Binding
An order moving jurisdiction from court where the preliminary hearing took place to the trial court.

If the judge believes the prosecution has made its case, it will issue a **binding**, transferring the case to another court for trial. The defendant is then said to be "bound over" for trial.

Immunity

It has long been the rule that a person who receives immunity can be compelled to testify, no matter how personally embarrassing or humiliating testifying may be. As long as the prospect of criminal prosecution is absent, there is no right to "plead the Fifth." That's been the rule since 1888.[21]

Use Immunity

Use immunity
A limited form of immunity where the person's testimony cannot be used as evidence against him or her.

Immunity falls into two different categories. The first is **use immunity**. If a defendant is granted use immunity, anything he says to investigators cannot be directly used against him in a later trial. That is, the prosecutor can't use his direct words or anything the prosecution discovers that was related to the testimony. For example, assume that a defendant was granted use immunity in exchange for testimony about a murder. If the defendant testifies that he threw the weapon in the Susquehanna River, police can't dredge the river for the gun and use the weapon as evidence. However, if a bather, independent of the government, stumbles upon the gun and turns it in, the gun can be used against the defendant. The key is that independent evidence gathered by the police or others can be used even if immunity has been granted as long as it can be shown that it wasn't the testimony that led to the discovery of the evidence.

HISTORICAL HIGHLIGHT

Suspected Nazi War Criminal Must Sing

In this chapter you have learned that the right to remain silent protects defendants from having to provide testimony that can be used against themselves in a criminal proceeding. You have also learned that the rule against self-incrimination applies to the states, not just the federal government. Defendants also can't be forced to testify in a federal criminal case if they face the reasonable prospect of having that testimony used against them in a state criminal case. But what happens if the information requested places the defendant in danger of prosecution in a foreign nation? Can the defendant refuse to testify in that situation?

The U.S. Supreme Court answered that question in 1998 in *United States v. Balsys*. The real and substantial fear of prosecution in a foreign nation does not mean that a defendant can refuse to answer on the ground that his answer may incriminate him.

Balsys involved a resident alien who had been admitted to the United States in 1961 under the Immigration and Nationalization Act. All applicants for resident status under that law must provide sworn information about his or her criminal past, if he or she has one. The application Balsys signed in 1961 provided

that if he provided false or misleading information, he would be subject to criminal prosecution in the United States and face deportation. In his application, Balsys swore that he had served in the Lithuanian army from 1934 through 1940 and had lived in hiding from the start of World War II to 1944.

More than thirty-five years after his admission to the United States, the Justice Department began an investigation into whether Balsys had participated in Nazi persecution of Jews and other groups during World War II. If he had, he would be subject to deportation. When he was subpoenaed, he refused to answer questions about his alleged Nazi past on the grounds that it would subject him to criminal prosecution in Israel or Lithuania as a war criminal. He didn't claim any fear of prosecution in the United States, because the statute of limitations on falsifying his immigration application had passed. Therefore he had no valid fear of prosecution in this country.

After the Supreme Court ruling, Balsys faced the prospect of being held in criminal contempt if he continued to refuse to answer questions about his alleged Nazi past, or answering and being deported to face a war crimes trial.

Transactional Immunity

Transactional immunity is the preferred form of immunity for defendants. With transactional immunity, the government is forever barred from prosecuting the defendant for the crime from which he or she was granted immunity. No amount of independently gathered evidence can support a prosecution. The defendant, in exchange for testimony, is guaranteed that he or she will never be prosecuted for the crime about which he or she testified.

Transactional immunity
A broad form of immunity where the person cannot be prosecuted for any action related to the testimony as long as the person testifies truthfully.

Cooperation Agreements

Sometimes, prosecutors negotiate with a defendant to ensure his or her cooperation in prosecuting others involved in the same or related criminal activity. The prosecution and the defendant may then enter into a **cooperation agreement** which spells out what the defendant is expected to do and what the prosecution has promised in exchange for that cooperation. Often, that promise amounts to making a recommendation for leniency at sentencing. More often than not, the agreement is only binding on the parties and the judge hearing the case is free to accept or reject the prosecution's recommendations. Often, the agreement spells out that anything the defendant reveals while "cooperating" will not be used against him beyond the parameters of the agreement. In other words, if by cooperating, the defendant ends up admitting to other crimes, he'll enjoy immunity from prosecution for those acts.

Cooperation agreement
An agreement between the prosecution and a defendant that spells that the defendant will cooperate in the prosecution of others involved in the same or related criminal activity, usually in exchange for a recommendation of leniency to the court.

Privilege and the Right to Keep Others Silent

A concern for the sanctity and privacy of personal conversations and actions is inherent in the Constitution and the Bill of Rights. The focus on privacy can be seen in the reluctance to allow unfettered police access to our homes and possessions and in the recognition of a number of testimonial privileges that prevent the prosecution from compelling attorneys, spouses, and others from testifying about private conversations.

Attorney–Client Privilege

A privilege has long existed in conversations between counsel and client. The attorney–client privilege is one of the oldest recognized privileges for confidential communications.[22] The privilege is intended to encourage full and frank communication between attorneys and their clients. Without the guarantee that what is said to one's attorney is confidential, few faced with difficult circumstances would avail themselves of the right to counsel. The privilege applies to the attorney and anyone else on his or her staff.

In order for attorney–client privilege to apply, there must be an underlying agreement that the attorney has been retained to represent the defendant. If not, there is no privilege. Attorneys and their office staff should consult their state bar association for specific guidance on what is necessary for the formation of an attorney–client relationship and to learn under what circumstances attorneys are required to withdraw from representation if the client reveals he or she will lie under oath.

The attorney–client privilege does not extend to an attorney's participation in a crime. For example, an attorney can't hold the murder weapon in his or her safe or conceal and destroy records that have been entrusted to his or her care. The attorney–client privilege does protect notes that attorneys make memorializing client discussions and outlining the course of action recommended. The **work product rule** protects from disclosure any material the attorney created to prepare for trial.

Work product rule
The rule that protects material produced by an attorney in preparation for a trial, or the work product, from discovery.

Spousal Privilege

Another well-established privilege available to criminal defendants is the spousal privilege. This privilege is meant to protect private conversations between husband and wife and to protect marriages from the destructive effects of being compelled to testify against a husband or wife. This rule, like so many others, is not without limits.

As with many other Common Law rules, spousal privilege has a long history, springing from medieval society. Two justifications for the **marital privilege** developed over time. First, of course, was the rule that a defendant can't or shouldn't be compelled to testify against himself. Second, because husband and wife were regarded as one, and since a wife had no recognized separate legal existence, if a wife were compelled to testify, it would be the same as if the husband were the one forced to speak. Thus, what was inadmissible from the lips of the defendant's husband was also inadmissible from his wife.

Marital privilege
The right of a person to refuse to testify against his or her spouse.

For many years, courts assumed that the marital privilege meant that neither husband nor wife could be compelled to testify against each other and that each could prevent the other from testifying against the other. That changed in 1980 when the Supreme Court decided *Trammel v. United States*.[23] Elizabeth Trammel traveled to Thailand, where she bought heroin. She then boarded a plane for the United States with several ounces of heroin on her person. During a routine customs stop in Hawaii, she was searched, the heroin was discovered, and she was arrested. She made a deal with the Drug Enforcement Agency in which she received immunity in exchange for her testimony against her husband. He claimed that her testimony violated the marital privilege.

HISTORICAL HIGHLIGHT

Attorney–Client Privilege Survives Death

In 1993, shortly after the beginning of William Clinton's first term as president of the United States, employees who worked for the White House Travel Office were discharged en masse. At the time there was a great deal of speculation in the press about who ordered the firings, and why. The White House conducted its own internal investigation into the firings. Shortly after, several investigations were initiated into whether anyone in the White House involved with the investigation had committed criminal acts. Deputy White House Counsel Vincent W. Foster Jr., a personal friend and former law partner of the First Lady, was involved in the investigation.

On July 20, 1993, Vince Foster took his own life in a public park in Washington, D.C. Nine days earlier Foster had met with James Hamilton, an attorney at the law firm of Swidler & Berlin in Washington, D.C. Vince Foster sought the firm's representation, and asked whether the conversation would be covered by the attorney–client privilege. James Hamilton took three pages of handwritten notes during the meeting, all under the heading "privileged."

By December 1995, an Independent Counsel, Kenneth Starr, had been appointed to investigate potential wrongdoing by the White House, including the circumstances surrounding the Travel Office firings. At Starr's request, a federal grand jury subpoenaed James Hamilton's handwritten notes. The law firm filed a motion to quash the subpoena. A motion to **quash** is a request to a court to be excused from complying with a subpoena. The firm argued that the notes were protected by attorney–client privilege. The special counsel argued that the privilege dies with the client, and Vince Foster was dead.

The U.S. Supreme Court took up the novel question and issued an expedited opinion. On June 25, 1998, the Court issued an opinion that declared that the attorney–client privilege survives death. The Court wrote:

> Knowing that communication will remain confidential even after death encourages the client to communicate fully and frankly with counsel . . . . Clients may be concerned about reputation, civil liability, or possible harm to friends or family. Posthumous disclosure of such communications may be as feared as disclosure during the client's lifetime.

Swidler & Berlin and Hamilton v. United States, 524 U.S. 399 (1998)

The Supreme Court disagreed and ruled that a spouse who voluntarily chooses to testify against her husband may do so. The privilege belongs to the person speaking, not to the other spouse. The Court reasoned that women are no longer considered an extension of their husbands, but individual human beings. Presumably that means they can use that individuality to decide for themselves whether they will protect their spouse or cut a deal with the prosecutor.

Additionally, in state and local jurisdictions, this rule can have multiple variations. For example, Pennsylvania does not afford spousal privilege in cases

Quash
To annul.

"in which one of the charges pending against the defendant includes murder, involuntary deviate sexual intercourse or rape."[24]

Priest–Penitent Privilege

At Common Law there also existed a **priest–penitent privilege.** Its intent was to keep secret statements made in the confessional. The privilege has been mentioned in passing in several Supreme Court decisions, but the Court has never faced the question of its continued relevance. An attempt to call a priest or other religious figure to the stand to testify would likely be met with opposition. The issue may be raised in criminal prosecutions of Catholic priests accused of molesting boys in their parishes. It remains to be seen if those to whom the priests confessed within the Church hierarchy will be forced to testify later.

Patient–Counselor Privilege

Another privilege recognized by the Supreme Court, the **patient–counselor privilege**, is the right to keep confidential conversations between a patient and his or her psychotherapist. For example, in one case the Supreme Court ruled that a police officer's social worker could not be compelled to testify in a civil suit brought by the family of a man killed by a female police officer responding to a call. She had received extensive counseling after the shooting. The family had sued the officer for allegedly violating the dead man's civil rights. The Court concluded that "[t]he psychotherapist privilege serves the public interest by facilitating the provision of appropriate treatment for individuals suffering the effects of a mental or emotional problem. The mental health of our citizenry, no less than its physical health, is a public good of transcendent importance."[25]

Compelling the Production of Physical Evidence, Including DNA Testing

The right against self-incrimination doesn't apply to physical evidence. That is, the government can make a suspect produce physical evidence of guilt as long as the method used isn't unreasonably intrusive. Defendants can be made to try on items of clothing, such as a shirt or a glove.[26] But taking a suspect to the hospital and making him vomit up evidence by pumping his stomach is unreasonably intrusive.[27]

Defendants can be brought down to the police station and be made to stand in a lineup. That's because the Constitution only protects a defendant against "being compelled to testify against himself, or otherwise provide the State with evidence of a testimonial or communicative nature."[28] A lineup merely serves as a way for the police to determine if the suspect is likely to be the individual sought. The state will still have to show beyond a reasonable doubt that he committed the crime and defendants are entitled to have an attorney present during the lineup.

Defendants can also be compelled to submit to fingerprinting, photographing, and measuring. They can also be forced to provide writing and voice samples, and the results can be introduced in court.

YOU MAKE THE CALL

The Duke Rape Case: The Photo Lineup

You may recall the case of the alleged rape of an exotic dancer at a party attended by members of the Duke lacrosse team. As is typical of such cases, law enforcement officials ask the victim to identify the assailant. In this case, police demanded that all forty-six players have their pictures taken. They did.

Then the exotic dancer was twice shown a PowerPoint presentation of the photos and picked out three men as her assailants, including one who could show he was not at the party.

Defense counsel asked that her identification be suppressed, based on the fact that two other men who were at the party but were not members of the team were not included in the photo lineup. Should the identification have been suppressed?

You make the call.

> If the glove doesn't fit, you must acquit.
>
> Johnny Cochran, in closing argument to the jury, *California v. O. J. Simpson*

Breath Analysis, Blood, and DNA Evidence

Physical evidence obtained by reasonable means can be used against a suspect. For example, most state driving under the influence laws provide that motorists stopped on suspicion of driving under the influence of drugs or alcohol must submit to a Breathalyzer test or forfeit their license to operate a motor vehicle. The results of the test can be admitted at a criminal trial. He or she can also be compelled to take a blood test to determine the amount and kind of intoxicant in the body.[29]

Again, the evidence can be used for trial. However, defendants and suspects can't be compelled to take physical tests that seek to measure physiological responses that the examiner can claim indicate guilt or a state of mind. Thus, suspects can't be made to take a lie detector test.

Since the middle of this century, blood evidence compelled from a suspect has been available in court. With the advent of new, more sophisticated analysis of blood, the justice system has increased its use of such evidence. For example, DNA evidence is now routinely used to solve rape and murder cases. DNA analysis can exclude suspects altogether or provide compelling odds that the defendant committed the crime. Defendants in both civil and criminal cases are finding it hard to argue that DNA evidence doesn't prove either beyond a reasonable doubt or by a preponderance of the evidence (the criminal and civil standards of proof) that the defendant left the genetic material in question.[30]

An interesting twist on compelling physical evidence came in a recent Supreme Court case. The City of Charleston, South Carolina, decided something had to be done to combat cocaine use by pregnant women. Working with the local police department, the public hospitals in town drew urine tests on pregnant women without their consent and without a search warrant and tested for cocaine use. Positive test results were referred to the police department for prosecution. The case ended up before the Supreme Court, which ruled that nonconsensual urine tests violated the Fifth Amendment's prohibition against unreasonable searches.[31]

Plea Bargaining

Plea bargaining
The process of negotiating the settlement of criminal charges without a trial.

Not all cases go to trial. In fact, most cases are resolved through **plea bargaining**. Plea bargaining reduces case loads for prosecutors and judges in return for a reduced sentence for the defendant. Public defenders who often have more cases than they can realistically handle like plea bargaining because it lightens their load.

Plea bargaining is not always in the defendant's best interest. Sometimes the prosecutor offers a plea bargain because his case is weak. The defendant may be able to be acquitted if he doesn't agree to the deal. This is where an experienced attorney can help a defendant by understanding the prosecution's case well enough to advise the client.

Ultimately, the decision to plea or not to plea is up to the defendant. Attorneys and prosecutors can bring pressure to bear, but it is the defendant who lives with the conviction for the rest of his life.

Bench conference
A conference called among the judge and attorneys for both sides, and possibly the accused, to discuss matters without the jury hearing it.

If the defendant and the prosecutor come to an agreement, they will meet with the judge in a **bench conference**. The judge must sign off on the agreement before it becomes effective. Sometimes, the judges' record of plea agreements can become an election issue, so judges are ever mindful of the political ramifications of plea agreements.

Once the plea is agreed upon, the judge will question the defendant in open court to ensure the defendant understands the sentence he is receiving, and the rights he has forfeited, specifically the right to trial, by agreeing to the plea arrangement. The judge will also ask if the agreement is voluntary.

Plea agreements are between prosecutors and defendants. They are not binding on judges. As a result, plea agreements only contain a recommendation for sentencing. Whether that is the sentence the defendant gets is up to the judge. Most of the time, the judge will agree to the sentence in the agreement, having worked out the details at the bench conference. But defendants should understand that judges are under political pressure and do not have to take the sentencing recommendation. Cooperation agreements, discussed earlier in this chapter, often include promises to drop some charges in exchange for cooperation and a recommendation for a more lenient sentence.

Once a defendant has pled guilty, he gives up many constitutional protections. In addition to relinquishing his right to a trial by jury, he is no longer presumed innocent. Further, he no longer has the right to appeal his conviction and sentence.

Nolo contendere
Latin for "I will not contest this," also called "no contest." A plea entered that admits no wrongdoing, but allows the court to sentence the defendant as if guilty.

Instead of pleading guilty, a defendant can plead *nolo contendere* or no contest to a charge. From a criminal standpoint, the *nolo contendere* plea is substantially the same as a guilty plea. But in cases where a civil suit may arise out of the same circumstances as the criminal charge, a nolo contendere plea does not require the defendant to admit wrongdoing. A litigant could use a guilty plea as an admission of guilt, but not a nolo contendere plea. Some states only allow nolo contendere pleas for some crimes.

Alford plea
A plea entered where the accused maintains his innocence, but agrees to be sentenced as if guilty.

Another plea possibility is the **Alford Plea**, named for the Supreme Court case *North Carolina v. Alford*.[32] Under an Alford plea, the defendant pleads guilty but maintains his innocence. Defendants facing a strong government case may elect this plea to get a lighter sentence.

In the Alford case, North Carolina law at the time called for the death penalty for first-degree murder convictions unless the jury voted for life imprisonment.

Facing strong evidence of his guilt, Alford pled guilty to second-degree murder, but stated in court the only reason for doing so was his fear of the death penalty. He then appealed claiming the plea had been made under duress, specifically the state's threat of execution. The U.S. Supreme Court ruled the plea was valid even though the defendant maintained his innocence.

The Right to a Speedy Trial

The Sixth Amendment to the Constitution guarantees a defendant the right to a "speedy and public" trial. The Amendment prevents defendants from being left in jail to rot pending trial, or from enjoying years of freedom outside prison if he or she has been able to make bail.

The Supreme Court has ruled that the right to a speedy trial is flexible, with no fixed number of days or weeks dictating whether the right has been denied.[33] Instead, the Court suggested that state and federal legislatures pass laws setting time limits, if they choose. As a result, most states have laws on the books that set strict time limits for bringing defendants to trial, usually within a year of being formally charged and arrested. These statutes typically don't count any time delays caused by the defendant. For example, if a defendant requests a continuance that delay does not count toward the time limit. The Supreme Court recently considered such a case. Michael Brillon sat in jail for three years before going to trial on a felony domestic assault charge, largely because he kept firing and hiring lawyers, which delayed the trial. The Vermont Supreme Court overturned his conviction, but the Supreme Court reinstated it. The Supreme Court reasoned that the delay was Brillon's fault, not the prosecution's fault, and Brillon shouldn't benefit from delays he created.[34]

The Speedy Trial Act of 1974[35] sets strict time limits for bringing federal defendants to trial. The Act has a built-in mechanism for dealing with requests for continuances and other common delays. The penalty for violating the right to a speedy trial is dismissal of the charges.

Don't confuse the right to a speedy trial with statutes of limitations. Each state and the federal government has set time limits for the initiation of criminal proceedings against persons suspected of committing crimes. These limits range from a few years for minor crimes to indefinitely for murder. In effect, statutes of limitations set a deadline for the commencement of criminal actions, while the right to a speedy trial dictates how soon the trial must begin after a suspect has formally been charged with that crime. For example, a woman who murders her boyfriend at eighteen can be charged with that murder at age eighty, but is then guaranteed a speedy trial within her state's time limits.

CONCEPT **REVIEW AND REINFORCEMENT**

For a person charged with a crime, one of the most important constitutional guarantees is the right to counsel. Without counsel, a defendant would be left to navigate a complicated labyrinth without a guide. The right to counsel is so crucial to the legitimacy of the criminal law system that all persons, whether rich or indigent, are entitled to the services of a competent attorney. Those without adequate resources to retain private counsel are entitled to the services of a state or federal public defender or other court-appointed counsel.

A criminal suspect or defendant is also entitled to remain silent. In the American system of justice, all persons are presumed innocent until the state or federal government proves beyond a reasonable doubt that the suspect is guilty. No defendant is required to help the prosecutor prove his case through his own words. The right to remain silent and the exclusionary rule, which prevents prosecutors from using confessions or evidence obtained in violation of constitutional rights, serve to curb possible police abuses. Confessions beaten out of defendants can't be used to convict them.

The right to remain silent has several significant limitations. First, an individual who faces no possibility of having his or her words used against him or her cannot "plead the Fifth." For example, a person who has already been convicted of a crime no longer faces the possibility that his words will be used to convict. Persons granted immunity can also be forced to testify, since they don't face the possibility of having their words used against them either.

In our legal system, some relationships are regarded as inviolate. Therefore, confidences expressed in private with attorneys, counselors, a spouse, or a spiritual advisor are generally protected by a privilege against compelled revelation.

However, the privilege against self-incrimination doesn't apply to physical characteristics or evidence that is obtained in a reasonable fashion. For example, DNA and fingerprint evidence are standard fare in criminal prosecutions.

The right to remain silent and the right to counsel would mean little if persons charged with crimes were unaware of those rights. Therefore, law enforcement officers are required to tell a suspect or person under arrest that he has those rights and the right to have counsel appointed if indigent. The *Miranda* warning has become the standard method for police to convey those rights.

Defendants are also entitled to a speedy trial. Prisoners are not allowed to linger in prison awaiting trial or remain out on bail indefinitely.

KEY **TERMS**

Alford plea
Arraignment
Arrest
Bench conference
Bench warrant
Binding
Confession
Cooperation agreement

Custody
Indictment
Initial appearance
Marital privilege
Nolo contendere
Patient–counselor privilege
Plea bargaining
Priest–penitent privilege

Quash
Right against self-incrimination
Right to bail
Transactional immunity
Use immunity
Work product rule

CONCEPT **REVIEW QUESTIONS**

1. What is the *Miranda* warning?
2. When does a criminal defendant have a right to counsel?
3. When does an indigent criminal defendant have a right to counsel?
4. What is the right against self-incrimination?
5. When can a criminal defendant be compelled to testify against himself?
6. What are the attorney–client, husband–wife, and priest–penitent privileges?
7. When can physical evidence be compelled from criminal defendants without violating the right against self-incrimination?
8. What is the right to a speedy trial?
9. How does a statute of limitations differ from the constitutional right to a speedy trial?

CASE **APPLICATION**

Building Your Professional Skills

1. You work for the U.S. attorney in your jurisdiction. She is prosecuting a defendant charged with firearms possession and possession of cocaine with the intent to deliver. The defendant's federal public defender has asked for an extension of the deadline for filing pretrial motions. How is this time handled under the Speedy Trial Act? (Hint: read *Bloate v. U.S.*, No. 08-728, decided April 20, 2009)

CRITICAL THINKING **EXERCISES**

1. You are an attorney who receives a call from a client who has been arrested. You tell him to say nothing to the police until you get there. You arrive to find him chatting with the detectives and occasionally mentioning issues related to the crime they are investigating. You ask whether he had been read his rights and whether he understood them. The detectives and your client answer yes to both questions. So, why, you ask are they interrogating him. They reply that he did not tell them he was using his right to remain silent, so they began discussing the case with him. Can you challenge the admissibility of what your talkative, but not real bright, client just told the detectives?

2. You are arrested for a misdemeanor crime. You are being taken to your arraignment. You ask for an attorney. The police tell you that for such a small crime, the arraignment is just a formality and that you really don't need an attorney. You insist that you have the right to an attorney. Are you correct?

3. Given the same set of facts in Question 2, the cop finally relents and says, "Okay kid, call your lawyer." You explain that you can't afford one. The cop says, "Well kid, I guess you're just out of luck." Is he right?

4. Computer technology has grown by leaps and bounds in the last decade. As the new technologies develop, criminals are using more sophisticated encryption tools to safeguard the contents of their e-mail and the documents on their hard drive. Assuming that police had a valid warrant to seize and search a suspect's hard drive for evidence of criminal activity, can the suspect be compelled to give police the key to his encryption program so that they may have access to his records?

5. The police are interviewing your client in connection with a rape. They ask him to submit a DNA sample. He refuses. The questioning continues; your client says he is getting thirsty. The police provide a can of soda. He continues to refuse to provide a DNA sample. When you finally leave, the police take the soda can and pull a DNA profile from the saliva on the can. Will that DNA evidence be admissible in court?

6. You belong to the Church of Jesus Christ Latter-Day Saints more commonly known as the Mormons. While the church has elders, it does not have clergy in the same way that Catholic and mainstream Protestant churches do. You tell one of the elders that you committed a murder and that you want God to forgive you. Can the prosecutor compel the elder to testify against you or is what you told him subject to priest-penitent privilege?

7. You committed a crime one year and eleven months ago. The statute of limitations for the crime is two years. Just before the deadline, the state charges you with the crime. Can you argue that waiting almost two years to charge you violated your right to a speedy trial?

PORTFOLIO **BUILDING**

1. Any one who works in the criminal justice system must be fully prepared to keep up on the latest technologies and police methods. It's also crucially important to keep up on the development of criminal procedure and constitutional law at both the state and federal level. Each year, for example, the U.S. Supreme Court decides about a dozen criminal law and procedure cases. Review the following resources and summarize their usefulness for the reference section of your portfolio.

• You can follow the Supreme Court at Northwestern University's "On the Docket" web-site. The site includes background information on all the pending cases written by journalism students at the university's Medill School of Journalism. Access the site at http://docket.medill.northwestern.edu/

• You can also track the current Supreme Court term through the American Bar Association's website at http://www.abanet.org/publiced/preview/

Other good sources for the latest information on evidence, confessions, and other investigative techniques include:

• The Innocence Project—which is a nonprofit legal clinic run through the Benjamin Cardozo School of Law in New York City, http://www.innocenceproject.org/

- The Innocence Network—which tries to connect defendants with *pro bono* help, http://www.innocencenetwork.org/
- Initiative—This is a five-year program funded with $1 billion to increase the use of DNA technology in the criminal justice system. The website provides information on training and education in scientific evidence, http://www.dna.gov/

2. You work for a criminal defense attorney who has been hired to defend a young man charged with murder. When he was questioned by the police, they read the following statement:

> You have the right to remain silent. If you give up the right to remain silent, anything you say can be used against you in court. You have the right to talk to a lawyer before answering any of our questions. If you cannot afford to hire a lawyer, one will be appointed for you without cost and before any questioning. You have the right to use any of these rights at any time you want during this interview.

Your boss says that the *Miranda* warning is flawed because it doesn't specifically state that the client had a right to have an attorney present during questioning, and that the client's confession is therefore invalid. She has asked you to research the question and prepare a memo. Your research leads you to the case of *Florida v. Powell*, No. 08-1175, decided by the U.S. Supreme Court on February 23, 2010. Prepare the memo and place it in your portfolio.

3. You work for a criminal defense firm. The prosecution has presented a possible Plea and Cooperation Agreement. Read it and prepare a summary of the agreement for the client that explains her rights and obligations and those of the prosecution:

IN THE UNITED STATES DISTRICT COURT
FOR THE EASTERN DISTRICT OF NOWHERE

UNITED STATES OF AMERICA, Plaintiff, v. Jane Doe, Defendant.

No. Cr. S-998-666 LKK

PLEA and COOPERATION AGREEMENT

I.
INTRODUCTION

A. Scope of Agreement: The Information to be filed in this case charges the defendant, Jane Doe ("Doe"), with conspiring to conduct the affairs of an enterprise through a pattern of racketeering activity in violation of 18 U.S.C. § 1962(d); money laundering in violation of 18 U.S.C. § 1957; and participating in, and aiding and abetting a conspiracy to suppress and eliminate competition by allocating contracts, fixing prices, and rigging bids in unreasonable restraint of interstate trade and commerce, in violation of the Sherman Act, 15 U.S.C. § 1, and 18 U.S.C. § 2. This document contains the complete Plea and Cooperation Agreement. This Plea and Cooperation Agreement is limited to the United States Attorney's Office for the Eastern District of Nowhere and the United States Department of Justice, Antitrust Division, and cannot bind any other federal, state, or local prosecuting, administrative, or regulatory authorities.

B. Court Not a Party: The Court is not a party to this Plea and Cooperation Agreement. Sentencing is a matter solely within the discretion of the Court, the Court is under no obligation to accept any recommendations made by the government, and the Court may in its discretion impose any sentence it deems appropriate up to and including the statutory maximum stated in this Plea and Cooperation Agreement. If the Court should impose any sentence up to the maximum established by the statute, the defendant cannot, for that reason alone, withdraw his guilty plea, and she will remain bound to fulfill all of the obligations under this Plea and Cooperation Agreement. The defendant understands that neither the prosecutor, defense counsel, nor the Court can make a binding prediction or promise regarding the sentence she will receive.

II.
DEFENDANT'S OBLIGATIONS

A. Waiver of Indictment and Guilty Plea: The defendant will waive indictment by grand jury, waive venue, and plead guilty to a three-count Information charging him with conspiring to conduct the affairs of an enterprise through a pattern of racketeering activity in violation of 18 U.S.C. § 1962(d); money laundering in violation of 18 U.S.C. § 1957; and price fixing in violation of 15 U.S.C. § 1. The defendant agrees that she is in fact guilty of those charges.

B. Restitution: The Mandatory Victim Restitution Act requires the Court to order restitution to the victims of certain offenses. If such restitution is ordered, payment should be by cashier's or certified check made payable to the Clerk of the Court. The defendant understands that this Plea and Cooperation Agreement is voidable by the government if she fails to pay the restitution as ordered by the Court. Defendant further agrees that she will not seek to discharge any restitution obligation or any part of such obligation in any bankruptcy proceeding.

C. Special Assessment: The defendant agrees to pay a special assessment of $300 at the time of sentencing by delivering a check or money order payable to the United States District Court to the United States Probation Office immediately before the sentencing hearing.

D. Agreement to Cooperate: The defendant agrees to cooperate fully with the government and any other federal, state, or local law enforcement agency, as directed by the government. As used in this Agreement, "cooperation" requires the defendant: (1) to respond truthfully and completely to all questions, whether in interviews, in correspondence, telephone conversations, before a grand jury, or at any trial or other court proceeding; (2) to attend all meetings, grand jury sessions, trials, and other proceedings at which the defendant's presence is requested by the government or compelled by subpoena or court order; (3) to produce voluntarily any and all documents, records, or other tangible evidence requested by the government; (4) not to participate in any criminal activity while cooperating with the government; and (5) to disclose to the government the existence and status of all money, property, or assets, of any kind, derived from or acquired as a result of, or used to facilitate the commission of, the defendant's illegal activities or the illegal activities of any conspirators.

If the defendant commits any crimes or if any of the defendant's statements or testimony prove to be knowingly false, misleading, or materially incomplete, or if the defendant otherwise violates this Plea and Cooperation Agreement in any way, the government will no longer be bound by its representations to the defendant concerning the limits on criminal prosecution and sentencing as set forth herein. The determination whether the defendant has violated the Plea and Cooperation Agreement will be under a preponderance of the evidence standard. If the defendant violates the Plea and Cooperation Agreement, she shall thereafter be subject to prosecution for any federal criminal violation of which the government has knowledge, including but not limited to perjury, false statements, and obstruction of justice. Because disclosures pursuant to this Agreement will constitute a waiver of the Fifth Amendment privilege against compulsory self-incrimination, any such prosecution may be premised on statements and/or information provided by the defendant. Moreover, any prosecutions that are not time-barred by the applicable statute of limitations as of the date of this Agreement may be commenced in accordance with this paragraph, notwithstanding the expiration of the statute of limitations between the signing of this Agreement and the commencement of any such prosecutions. The defendant agrees to waive all defenses based on the statute of limitations or delay of prosecution with respect to any prosecutions that are not time-barred as of the date of this Agreement.

If it is determined that the defendant has violated any provision of this Agreement or if the defendant successfully moves to withdraw his plea: (1) all statements made by the defendant to the government or other designated law enforcement agents, or any testimony given by the defendant before a grand jury or other tribunal, whether before or after this Agreement, shall be admissible in evidence in any criminal, civil, or administrative proceedings hereafter brought against the defendant; and (2) the defendant shall assert no claim under the United States Constitution, any statute, Rule 11(f) of the Federal Rules of Criminal Procedure, Rule 410 of the Federal Rules of Evidence, or any other federal rule, that statements made by the defendant before or after this Agreement, or any leads derived therefrom, should be suppressed. By signing this Agreement, the defendant waives any and all rights in the foregoing respects.

E. Civil Forfeiture: The defendant agrees to sign a Stipulation for Final Judgment of Forfeiture in the pending civil action, *U.S. v. Approximately $415,000.00 in U.S. Currency seized from Bank Nowhere National Bank, et al.,* This stipulation must be signed at least seven days prior to sentencing.

F. Payment of Fine: The defendant agrees to pay a criminal fine if so ordered. The government's recommendation with respect to any such criminal fine is set forth in Section III.D of this Plea and Cooperation Agreement.

III.
THE GOVERNMENT'S OBLIGATIONS

A. Incarceration Range: The government will recommend that the defendant be sentenced to the bottom of the applicable guideline range for his offense as determined by the United States Probation Office.

B. Acceptance of Responsibility: The government agrees that a three-level reduction in defendant's offense level for his full and clear demonstration of acceptance of responsibility is appropriate under U.S.S.G. § 3E1.1, will not oppose such a reduction and will so move under § 3E1.1(b), so long as the defendant pleads guilty, meets with and assists the probation officer in the preparation of the pre-sentence report, is truthful and candid with the probation officer and the Court, and does not otherwise engage in conduct that constitutes obstruction of justice within the meaning of U.S.S.G. § 3C1.1, either in the preparation of the pre-sentence report or during the sentencing proceeding.

C. Reduction of Sentence for Cooperation: The government agrees to recommend at the time of sentencing that the defendant's sentence of imprisonment be reduced to reflect his substantial assistance to the government in the investigation and prosecution of others, pursuant to U.S.S.G. § 5K1.1. The defendant understands that she must comply with paragraph II(D) of this Plea and Cooperation Agreement. The defendant understands that the government's recommended reduction in his sentence will depend upon the level of assistance the government determines that the defendant has provided. The defendant further understands that a motion pursuant to U.S.S.G. § 5K1.1 is only a recommendation and is not binding on the Court.

Other than as set forth above, the government agrees that any incriminating information provided by the defendant during his cooperation will not be used in determining the applicable guideline range in his case, pursuant to U.S.S.G. § 1B1.8.

D. Fine: The government agrees to recommend that any criminal fine imposed on the defendant be no higher than the midpoint of the applicable fine range, given the defendant's offense level and sentencing range.

E. Other Considerations: To the extent the defendant enters a guilty plea and is sentenced on Counts One, Two and Three of the Information to be filed in this matter, the government, to include the United States Attorney's Office for the District of Anywhere, will not initiate any further criminal charges against the defendant arising out of the same facts and circumstances as the instant charges.

IV.
ELEMENTS OF THE OFFENSE

With respect to Count One of the Information to be filed in this matter, which charges the defendant with conspiring to conduct the affairs of an enterprise through a pattern of racketeering activity in violation of 18 U.S.C. § 1962(d), at trial the government would have to prove beyond a reasonable doubt the following elements:

First, that certain leaders, employees and associates of Doe Foods, L.P., and its related corporate entities ("Doe Foods"), a manufacturer and marketer of bulk tomato and other food products with principal places of business in Monterey, Williams, Ripon, and Lemoore, Nowhere, constituted an enterprise, that is, a legal entity, a partnership or group of individuals associated in fact;

Second, that Doe Foods was engaged in interstate commerce;

Third, that no later than January 2004 and continuing through at least April 2008, there was an agreement between two or more persons employed by or associated with Doe Foods to conduct Doe Foods' affairs through a "pattern of racketeering activity" as defined by Title 18, United States Code, Section 1961(a) & (5), namely, multiple acts indictable under Title 18, United States Code, Sections 1341, 1343 and 1346; N.J. Stat. Ann. § 2C:21-10 (2008); Cal. penal code § 641.3 (2008); and Tex. Penal Code § 32.43 (2008), the last of which was to occur within ten years after the commission of a prior such act;

Fourth, the defendant was employed by or associated with Doe Foods; and

Fifth, the defendant joined in the illegal agreement referenced above, knowing of its object and intending to help accomplish it.

With respect to Count Two of the Information to be filed in this matter, which charges the defendant with money laundering in violation of 18 U.S.C. § 1957, at trial the government would have to prove beyond a reasonable doubt the following elements:

First, that the defendant knowingly engaged in a monetary transaction;

Second, that the defendant knew the transaction involved criminally derived property;

Third, that the property had a value greater than $10,000;

Fourth, that the property was, in fact, derived from specific acts otherwise indictable under Title 18, United States Code, Sections 1341, 1343 and 1346; N.J. Stat. ANN. § 2C:21-10 (2008); Cal. Penal Code § 641.3 (2008) ; and Tex. Penal Code § 32.43 (2008); and

Fifth, that the transaction occurred in the United States.

With respect to Count Three of the information to be filed in this matter, which charges the defendant with price fixing in violation of 15 U.S.C. § 1 and aiding and abetting in violation of 18 U.S.C. § 2, at trial the government would have to prove beyond a reasonable doubt the following elements:

First, that the defendant entered into or aided and abetted a conspiracy;

Second, that the conspiracy was an unreasonable restraint of trade; and

Third, that the conspiracy was in or affected interstate commerce in the United States.

V.
MAXIMUM SENTENCE

A. Maximum Penalty: With respect to Count One of the Information to be filed in this matter, which charges the defendant with conspiring to conduct the affairs of an enterprise through a pattern of racketeering activity in violation of 18 U.S.C. § 1962(d), the maximum sentence that the Court can impose is twenty years of incarceration; a fine of $250,000 or twice the gross gain or gross loss resulting from the offense, whichever is greatest; a three-year period of supervised release; and a special assessment of $100.

With respect to Count Two of the Information to be filed in this matter which charges the defendant with money laundering in violation of 18 U.S.C. § 1957, the maximum sentence that the Court can impose is ten years of incarceration, a fine of $250,000 or twice the amount of the criminally derived property involved in the transaction, a three-year period of supervised release, and a special assessment of $100.

With respect to Count Three of the Information to be filed in this matter, which charges the defendant with price fixing in violation of 15 U.S.C. § 1 and aiding and abetting in violation of 18 U.S.C. § 2, the maximum sentence the Court can impose is ten years incarceration; a fine in an amount equal to the greatest of (1) $1,000,000, (2) twice the gross pecuniary gain the conspirators derived from the crime, or (3) twice the gross pecuniary loss caused to the victims of the crime by the conspirators; a three-year period of supervised release; and a special assessment of $100.

B. Violations of Supervised Release: The defendant understands that if she violates a condition of supervised release at any time during the term of supervised release, the Court may revoke the term of supervised release and require the defendant to serve up to two additional years of imprisonment.

VI.
SENTENCING DETERMINATION

A. Statutory Authority: The defendant understands that the Court must consult the Federal Sentencing Guidelines (as promulgated by the Sentencing Commission pursuant to the Sentencing Reform Act of 1984, 18 U.S.C. §§ 3551-3742 and 28 U.S.C. §§ 991-998, and as modified by *United States v. Booker* and *United States v. Fanfan*. 543 U.S. 220, 125 S.Ct. 738 (2005)) and must take them into account when determining a final sentence. The defendant understands that the Court will determine a non-binding and advisory guideline sentencing range for this case pursuant to the Sentencing Guidelines. The defendant further understands that the Court will consider whether there is a basis for departure from the guideline sentencing range (either above or below the guideline sentencing range) because there exists an aggravating or mitigating circumstance of a kind, or to a degree, not adequately taken into consideration by the Sentencing Commission in formulating the Guidelines. The defendant further understands that the Court, after consultation and consideration of the Sentencing Guidelines, must impose a sentence that is reasonable in light of the factors set forth in 18 U.S.C. § 3553(a).

B. Stipulations Affecting Guidelines Calculations: The government and the defendant agree that there is no material dispute as to the following sentencing guidelines variables and therefore stipulate and agree to the following:

1. **Offense Level for Racketeering Conspiracy Count:**
   a. **Applicable Guidelines Section:**
      with respect to the charge of conspiring to conduct the affairs of an enterprise through a pattern of racketeering activity in violation of 18 U.S.C. § 1962(d), pursuant to U.S.S.G. § 2E1.1 the defendant's base offense level is the greater of 19 or the offense level applicable to the underlying racketeering activity. In this instance, the guidelines sections applicable to the underlying racketeering activity

committed by the defendant are U.S.S.G. §§ 2B4.1 and 2B1.1. Because the guidelines section resulting in the highest offense level is § 2B4.1, and loss amounts under §§ 2B4.1 and 2B1.1 group, the offense level for the underlying racketeering activity is determined under § 2B4.1.

b. **Offense Level Under § 2B4.1:**

The offense level applicable to the underlying racketeering activity related to the defendant's commercial bribery and honest services fraud, and mail fraud is calculated as follows:

- **Base Offense Level Under § 2B4.1:** Pursuant to § 2B4.1, the base offense level is 8.
- **Specific Offense Characteristics:** Pursuant to § 2B4.1(b)(1), the parties agree that at an evidentiary hearing the government is currently in a position to prove that the amount of loss attributable to the commercial bribery and honest services fraud committed by the defendant, and relevant conduct, and the loss attributable to the mail fraud, is greater than $400,000, but less than $1,000,000. Consequently, the base offense level is increased by 14.
- **Adjusted Offense Level Under § 2B4.1:** As a result of the foregoing stipulations, the adjusted offense level applicable to the underlying racketeering activity related to the defendant's commercial bribery and honest services fraud, and mail fraud is 22.

c. **Racketeering Conspiracy Count Offense Level:**

As a result of the foregoing stipulations, the adjusted offense level for the racketeering conspiracy count is a level 22.

2. **Offense Level for Money Laundering Count:**

a. **Base Offense Level:**

Pursuant to U.S.S.G. § 2S1.1(a)(1) the defendant's base offense level with respect to the money laundering charge is 22, since that is the offense level for the underlying offense from which the laundered funds were derived.

b. **Specific Offense Characteristics:**

Pursuant to U.S.S.G. § 2S1.1(b)(2)(A), because the defendant is pleading guilty to conduct criminalized by 18 U.S.C. § 1957, the base offense level is increased by 1 level.

c. **Money Laundering Count Offense Level:**

As a result of the foregoing stipulations, the adjusted offense level for the money laundering count is 23.

3. **Offense Level for Violations of the Sherman Act:**

a. **Base Offense Level:**

Pursuant to U.S.S.G. § 2R1.1(a) the defendant's base offense level with respect to Count Three is 12.

b. **Specific Offense Characteristics:**

Because the defendant's conduct involved participation in an agreement to submit non-competitive bids, the base offense level is increased by 1 level pursuant to U.S.S.G. § 2R1.1(b)(1). Pursuant to U.S.S.G. § 2R1.1(b)(2), because the volume of commerce attributable to the defendant is greater than $10,000,000, but less than $40,000,000, the base offense level is increased by an additional 4 levels.

c. **Sherman Act Count Offense Level:**

As a result of the foregoing stipulations, the adjusted offense level with respect to Count Three is 17.

4. **Application of Multiple Count Rules in Chapter Three:**

   Pursuant to U.S.S.G. § 3D1.2(d), the offenses covered in Counts One through Three of the Information to be filed in this case merge for grouping purposes, resulting in an offense level of 23.

5. **Aggravating Role in Offense:**

   Because the defendant served as a manager or supervisor with respect to the criminal activity charged, and that activity involved five or more participants and was otherwise extensive, defendant's offense level is increased by 3 levels.

6. **Total Offense Level:**

   Pursuant to the foregoing stipulations, defendant's total offense level is 26.

7. **Acceptance of Responsibility:**

   Pursuant to § 3E1.1 and as described in more detail in paragraph III(B) above, the defendant's total offense level is decreased by three levels because of his acceptance of responsibility. The Adjusted Total Offense Level is therefore 23.

8. **Criminal History:**

   The parties agree that the defendant's criminal history is to be determined by United States Probation.

9. **Departures or Other Enhancements or Reductions:**

   The parties stipulate and agree that they will not seek or argue in support of any other specific offense characteristics, Chapter Three adjustments or cross-references, other than those contemplated in the foregoing stipulations. Both parties stipulate and agree not to move for, or argue in support of, any departure from the Sentencing Guidelines, or any deviance or variance from the Sentencing Guidelines under *United States v. Booker*, 543 U.S. 220, 125 S. Ct. 738 (2005), except: (1) pursuant to U.S.S.G. § 5K1.1; and (2) to account for the defendant's health condition at the time of sentencing. If either party breaches this provision, the other party shall be relieved of all of its obligations under this Plea and Cooperation Agreement.

VII.
WAIVERS

A. Waiver of Constitutional Rights: The defendant understands that by pleading guilty she is waiving the following constitutional rights: (a) to plead not guilty and to persist in that plea if already made; (b) to be tried by a jury; (c) to be assisted at trial by an attorney, who would be appointed if necessary; (d) to subpoena witnesses to testify on his behalf; (e) to confront and cross- examine witnesses against him; and (f) not to be compelled to incriminate himself.

B. Waiver of Appeal and Collateral Attack: The defendant understands that the law gives him a right to appeal his conviction and sentence. She agrees as part of his plea, however, to give up the right to appeal the conviction and the right to appeal any aspect of the sentence imposed in this case so long as his sentence is no longer than the top of the Sentencing Guidelines range determined by the Court consistent with the stipulations set forth above about the Sentencing Guidelines variables.

Regardless of the sentence she receives, the defendant also gives up any right she may have to bring a post-appeal attack on his conviction or his sentence. She specifically agrees not to file a motion under 28 U.S.C. § 2255 or § 2241 attacking his conviction or sentence.

If the defendant ever attempts to vacate his plea, dismiss the underlying charges, or reduce or set aside his sentence on any of the counts to which she is pleading guilty, the government shall have the right (1) to prosecute the defendant on any of the counts to which she pleaded guilty; (2) to reinstate any counts that may be dismissed pursuant to this Plea and Cooperation Agreement; and (3) to file any new charges that would otherwise be barred by this Plea and Cooperation Agreement. The decision to pursue any or all of these options is solely in the discretion of the United States Attorney's Office. By signing this Plea and Cooperation Agreement, the defendant agrees to waive any objections, motions, and defenses she might have to the government's decision. In particular, she agrees not to raise any objections based on the passage of time with respect to such counts including, but not limited to, any statutes of limitation or any objections based on the Speedy Trial Act or the Speedy Trial Clause of the Sixth Amendment.

C. Waiver of Attorneys' Fees and Costs: The defendant agrees to waive all rights under the "Hyde Amendment," Section 617, P.L. 105-119 (Nov. 26, 1997), to recover attorneys' fees or other litigation expenses in connection with the investigation and prosecution of all charges in the above-captioned matter and of any related allegations.

VIII.
ENTIRE PLEA AND COOPERATION AGREEMENT

Other than this Plea and Cooperation Agreement, no agreement, understanding, promise, or condition between the government and the defendant exists, nor will such agreement, understanding, promise, or condition exist unless it is committed to writing and signed by the defendant, counsel for the defendant, and counsel for the United States.

IX.
APPROVALS AND SIGNATURES

A. Defense Counsel: I have read this Plea and Cooperation Agreement and have discussed it fully with my client. The Plea and Cooperation Agreement accurately and completely sets forth the entirety of the agreement, and I have no reason to believe that my client's plea of guilty should not be entered.

DATED: _____ _____/s/_____
Attorneys for Defendant

B. Defendant: I have read this Plea and Cooperation Agreement and carefully reviewed every part of it with my attorney. I understand it, and I voluntarily agree to it. Further, I have consulted with my attorney and fully understand my rights with respect to the provisions of the Sentencing Guidelines that may apply to my case. No other promises or inducements have been made to me, other than those contained in this Plea and Cooperation Agreement. In addition, no one has threatened or forced me in any way to enter into this Plea and Cooperation Agreement. Finally, I am satisfied with the representation of my attorney in this case.

DATED: _____ _____/s/_____
DOE, Defendant

C. Attorney for United States: I accept and agree to this Plea and Cooperation Agreement on behalf of the government.

FOR FURTHER READING

1. Lewis, A. (1989). *Gideon's Trumpet.* Vintage Books. This book details the landmark case of *Gideon v. Wainwright* that established the right to legal counsel for everyone.
2. Leo, R. A., Thomas, G. C. III, and Thomas, G. C. (eds.) (1998). *The Miranda Debate: Law, Justice, and Policing.* Northeastern University Press. This is a collection of essays from across the political spectrum about the *Miranda* decision and its impact on law enforcement and society.
3. Horne, G. (1997). *Powell v. Alabama: The Scottsboro Boys and American Justice (Historic Supreme Court Cases).* This book is geared toward young adults, but tells the story of the Scottsboro boys in detail, and explains the importance of the case in legal and historical context.

FOR FURTHER VIEWING

1. *Gideon's Trumpet* (1980). The story of Clarence Earl Gideon's case as it went to the Supreme Court; starring Henry Fonda, José Ferrer, and John Houseman.

2. *Judge Horton* & *the Scottsboro Boys* (1976). A made-for-TV movie about the Scottsboro boys episode. The two women who claimed they were raped by the boys filed suit over this presentation. The suit was dismissed.

Chapter **thirteen**

THE CONSTITUTIONAL RIGHT TO TRIAL BY JURY

In all criminal prosecutions the accused shall enjoy the right to a speedy and public trial, by an impartial jury of the state and district wherein the crime shall have been committed.

U.S. Constitution, Eighth Amendment (1791)

The jury is both the most effective way of establishing the people's rule and the most efficient way of teaching them how to rule.

Alexis De Tocqueville, *Democracy in America* (1835)

Introduction and Historical Background

Every year, all across the United States, millions of very ordinary citizens are called to **jury** duty. For a brief time, twelve men and women gather together to render judgment on a fellow human being. Once judgment has been passed, they part company as abruptly as they came together. These ordinary men and women perform an extraordinary task that many see as an essential component of American democracy. As jurors, they are the fact finders in both criminal and civil cases. That is, they decide what witness and what evidence is worthy of belief. In this chapter, we will explore the origin of the jury system, its modern use, and its role in bringing criminal defendants to justice and judgment.

One of the earliest known uses of ordinary citizens as fact finders is the use of volunteers in ancient Greece. These volunteers were collectively referred to as the ***dicastery.*** From this pool of citizens, individual dicasts would be picked to decide the fate of fellow citizens.

The Vikings, whose warriors spread fear and destruction through Europe and the British Isles during the centuries between

CHAPTER OBJECTIVES

After studying this chapter, you should be able to:

- Define *jury*
- List and explain the provisions in the U.S. Constitution that require trial by jury in criminal cases
- Explain what attorneys do in pretrial discovery.
- Explain how the members of a jury pool are selected
- Explain the process of *voir dire*
- List some reasons a potential juror can be excused for cause
- Explain sequestration
- List some reasons for a change of *venue* and change of *venire*
- List the steps in a trial
- Understand what is permissible in opening and closing statements
- Explain what "beyond a reasonable doubt" means
- List and explain some differences between federal juries and state juries

Jury

A group of men and women from the community selected to determine the truth. *While the judge is responsible for interpreting the law, the jury is charged with the task of finding the facts of the case.* The right to trial by jury is guaranteed by the Constitution in all serious criminal cases. A jury decides what the facts of the case are, and applies those facts to the law. Juries must be convinced beyond a reasonable doubt that the defendant broke the law.

Dicastery

In ancient Greece, the group of volunteers who acted as jurors to settle dispute within the *polis*.

900 A.D. and about 1300 A.D., also had a well-developed internal system of justice. The *Thing* (pronounced Ting), a group of Viking citizens, met to mete out justice.

England traces the right to trial by jury as far back as Henry II's Constitutions of Clarendon in 1164 and the **Magna Carta** in 1215. Its usage grew and developed so that by the eighteenth century the great legal commentator, Blackstone, could write: " . . . the truth of every accusation . . . should afterwards be confirmed by . . . twelve of his equals and neighbors."[1]

Trial by jury replaced two earlier methods for determining guilt in medieval England, trial by battle and trial by ordeal. In trial by battle, the defendant and his accuser fought to the death. **Trial by battle** was essentially used when a private individual believed himself or his clan wronged by the accused in some way. These cases were generally civil rather than criminal in nature. As early as 1110, Henry I ordered lords who could not settle their differences to do so by duel. Trial by battle in the form of the duel survived well into the nineteenth century. For example, in 1801 Alexander Hamilton was killed in a duel with Aaron Burr.

HISTORICAL HIGHLIGHT

Socrates Condemned to Death by Jury for Corrupting Youth

Socrates was a Greek philosopher and teacher who lived in Athens from about 469 B.C. to 399 B.C. Students of the law may be most familiar with him through a teaching method he is credited with inventing. The Socratic Method is a staple of many law school classes. It involves the instructor questioning and challenging students to come up with answers rather than the teacher lecturing on the subject matter. Through the Socratic Method, inductive reasoning is used. Facts particular to the subject being taught are discussed. From the discussion, students draw conclusions that are general or universal, not just pertinent to the particular facts at hand. For example, a student may discuss a case that involves an automobile running a red light, causing an accident. The driver is found to have been negligent. Using the

Socratic Method, students applying inductive reasoning may conclude that any person who violates a law and, because of the violation, causes damage to another is negligent. From the specific facts the student generalizes about negligence in any case.

So popular was Socrates among young people, and so unpopular were his views, that he was brought to trial. He was charged with undermining democracy in Athens. He was tried before a jury consisting of volunteers who swore to uphold the laws of Athens much the same way a modern jury is sworn. A jury of citizens of Athens found him guilty and sentenced him to death. He died after drinking a cup of poison made from the bark of the hemlock tree, surrounded by the young people he was charged with corrupting. An account of the trial and Socrates' last days can be found in Plato's *Apology*.

Trial by ordeal involved having the accused perform some physical task. If he survived unharmed, he was innocent. For example, the accused was made to carry a red hot piece of iron for a short distance or to dip his hand in a pot of boiling water long enough to pull out a stone. After performing the feat, his hand was bandaged. If after three days there was no sign of infection, the accused was declared innocent.[2]

The right to a jury trial came to America with the English colonists. The settlers demanded that they be tried in America, not back in England. They also insisted that the jury consist of fellow colonists, not Englishmen.[3]

After the Revolution, the right to a jury trial in a criminal case was specifically provided for in the Constitution, not once, but twice. First, Article III, Section 2 of the Constitution states that "[t]he Trial of All Crimes, Except in Cases of Impeachment, shall be by Jury; and such Trial shall be held in the State Where the Said Crimes have been committed." Then, the **Sixth Amendment** reiterates the right by providing that "[i]n all criminal prosecutions, the accused shall enjoy the right to a speedy and public trial, by an impartial jury of the State and district wherein the crime shall have been committed."

Over the last two centuries, our courts have refined the right to a jury trial in many important ways. Through judicial interpretation, the right to a jury trial has been expanded and refined. It is now clear that every criminal defendant who is accused of a crime punishable by more than six months in prison can demand a jury trial. Both states and the federal government must provide juries for criminal defendants who want them. And ordinary citizens are finding it more difficult than ever before to avoid jury duty. That's because the Supreme Court has set strict standards for the composition of juries so that they reflect the philosophy that citizens must be tried by a "jury of one's peers" and that the pool from which a jury is picked was assembled in a nondiscriminatory way.

Defining the Right to Trial by Jury
Who Can Demand Trial by Jury?

The federal government has always allowed defendants in criminal cases to have their case heard by juries. In addition, every state constitution provides some type of guarantee that criminal defendants may have their case heard by a jury. But until 1968, it was unclear if persons charged with state crimes had the exact same right to a jury trial as a person charged with a federal crime. For example, some state constitutions only provided for the right to a jury trial in cases where the punishment was death or imprisonment at hard labor for a long period of time. One such state was Louisiana.

The case that firmly established that the Sixth Amendment's guarantee of a jury trial applied to the states was *Duncan v. Louisiana*.[4] *Duncan* involved a young man charged with simple battery. He asked for a jury trial, but instead was tried by a judge. The crime carried a possible penalty of up to two years in prison, although young Duncan received a sentence of sixty days. He appealed to the U.S. Supreme Court. The Court wrote that the Sixth Amendment applied to states, too, not just to the federal government. "Our conclusion," wrote the Court, "is that in the American States, as in the federal judicial system, a general grant of jury trial for serious offenses is a fundamental right, essential for preventing miscarriages of justice and for assuring that fair trials are provided for all defendants."[5]

But not every state crime requires a jury trial. Petty, or minor, offenses can be tried before a judge or even a district magistrate or justice of the peace. Generally, if the punishment possible under a criminal law is six months or less in prison, there is no right to a jury trial.[6] If the defendant faces the possibility of more than six months in prison, he or she has the right to demand a jury trial. The choices are: plead guilty, be tried by a judge, or be tried by a jury.

Recently some state legislatures have discussed changing their state constitutions to guarantee the prosecution the right to have criminal cases heard by juries. In *United States v. United States District Court*, the prosecution petitioned for a writ

Magna Carta
The "Great Charter," a document that was signed by King John of England in 1215. It guaranteed the noblemen under the King's jurisdiction life, liberty, and property. Many of the promises made in the Magna Carta became the basis of the guarantees found in the U.S. Constitution and the constitutions of the states.

Trial by battle
A method of determining guilt in medieval England. Usually reserved for civil cases, in trial by battle the winner of the battle won the lawsuit.

No freeman shall be taken, or imprisoned, or outlawed, or exiled, . . . except by the legal judgment of his peers or by the law of the land.

Magna Carta, Clause 39 (1215)

Trial by ordeal
A method of determining guilt in medieval England. In trial by ordeal, the defendant was made to perform a physical task, like holding a hot piece of iron. If the wound healed without becoming infected, the accused was innocent; if it became infected, he was guilty (and ill).

Sixth Amendment
The provision of the Bill of Rights that originally guaranteed all federal criminal defendants the right to trial by jury. It has since been applied to the states through the Fourteenth Amendment, which guarantees all citizens equal protection of the laws of the United States.

Trial by judge
A defendant may choose to be tried by a judge rather than by a jury or rather than pleading guilty. When a judge tries a case, he or she decides both the facts and the law.

Grand jury
A body of members of the community, usually twenty-three, which decides whether there is enough information to indict an individual. The standard used is "probable cause." Probable cause is a reasonable belief that the alleged facts are probably true. The right to a grand jury indictment is guaranteed in all federal criminal cases by the Fifth Amendment.

Petit jury
A trial jury. In criminal cases, the petit jury determines the facts of the case, applies those facts to the law as given them by the judge, and decides if the state has proven beyond a reasonable doubt that the defendant committed the crime he or she was charged with. Federal juries consist of twelve jurors; state juries can consist of as few as six jurors.

Probable cause
A standard of proof used to issue search warrants, and to determine if a person should be charged with a crime. Probable cause is a reasonable belief that the alleged facts are true.

Jury service is an exercise in responsible citizenship by all members of the community, including those who might not have the opportunity to contribute to our civic life.

Justice Anthony Kennedy

---

of *mandamus* to require the U.S. District Court for the Eastern District of California to grant a jury trial in a case involving sexual abuse of children. Michael and Juliette Labrecque of Fort Worth, Texas, and Allen Harrod and Irene Hunt, of Sacramento, California, were charged with ten years of ritualistic sexual abuse upon the defendants' five children. The defendants requested a nonjury trial or a **trial by judge.** District court granted the defendants' request, noting, "the heinous and repugnant conduct of the defendants, both charged and uncharged, which will be vividly apparent to the jury from the evidence to be presented, would render it 'impossible or unlikely' that ordinary jurors would be able to dispassionately listen to and consider defendants' more technical arguments." But the Ninth Circuit Court of Appeals reversed the district court's decision, granting the prosecution its jury trial.[7] The court quoted *Singer v. United States*: "There is no federally recognized right to a criminal trial before a judge sitting alone,"[8] and noted that granting a defendant a jury trial fulfills his or her constitutional rights.

If the prosecution doesn't oppose a trial before a judge, the matter can proceed. In cases like the sexual abuse trial where jurors may be swayed by the horrific nature of the charges rather than the facts determining guilt or innocence, defendants may move to have a judge hear the case. Similarly, when the trial will center on very technical issues, a judge trial may be more appropriate. One armed robbery defendant in a Pennsylvania case was asked whether he understood the difference between a jury trial and one before a judge. He replied that "in a jury trial twelve fools decide my fate and in a judge trial there's only one." He is now serving his sentence.[9]

Grand and Petit Juries

There are two types of juries: **grand** and **petit.** Each has distinct features and functions. One serves as a mechanism for bringing criminal charges, and the other decides whether the accused is guilty as charged or innocent of the charges against him.

A grand jury is a group of people selected to decide whether a prosecutor has enough evidence to charge an individual with a crime. The grand jury hears evidence and decides if the accused should be indicted and tried. If the grand jury finds there is **probable cause** to believe the defendant committed a crime, he or she is indicted. To find probable cause, the grand jurors must believe that the alleged facts are probably true. A grand jury usually consists of twenty-three members, thus the term *grand*. The Fifth Amendment to the U.S. Constitution guarantees that no person can be charged with a serious federal crime unless a grand jury authorizes a federal prosecutor to charge him or her.[10] Grand juries may meet over the course of many weeks or months on a complex case. For example, some federal grand jurors are required to meet once a week for a year to hear evidence in one or more cases that a federal prosecutor is investigating.

A petit jury is the trial jury. In a criminal case, the petit jury decides whether the government has proven beyond a reasonable doubt that the accused is guilty of the crime with which he was charged. Essentially, petit juries are fact finders; they decide collectively what the facts are in a case. Petit juries usually consist of twelve or fewer members, thus the term *petit*.

Grand juries hear requests for permission to file serious criminal charges from federal prosecutors. Some states also use their own versions of grand juries to bring charges in criminal cases or as investigative bodies. Other states give their district attorneys or attorneys general the authority to bring charges without the use of a grand jury. There is no requirement that states use grand juries to authorize serious criminal prosecutions.

Grand Jury and indictment

In most felony cases, a grand jury must issue a **true bill** charging the defendant with the felony. Grand juries date back to English law and are specifically mentioned in the Fifth Amendment to the Constitution. Grand juries are selected from the general population in the jurisdiction prosecuting the case. For example, federal grand juries are drawn from people living in the federal district. The grand jury system serves as a check on governmental power by ensuring the prosecution has evidence against the accused.

True bill
The document produced by a grand jury if it is convinced that the prosecutor's evidence is sufficient to charge the accused with a crime.

Despite its role in limiting governmental power, grand juries can be very one-sided affairs. The old saw that a "Grand jury would indict a ham sandwich" has some basis in fact. First of all, only the prosecution can present its case to the grand jury. The defense never appears.

Part of the reason for this is that grand juries are often investigatory bodies. The prosecutor presents the known facts of the crime and the evidence against the defendant. But the grand jury can subpoena witnesses, grant immunity to witnesses, and take the investigation into areas the prosecutor never intended.

The basic grand jury procedure dictates that the prosecutor presents an **indictment** to the grand jury accusing the defendant(s) of a crime or crimes. The grand jury investigates the prosecutors' claims and decides first whether it was more likely than not that a crime was committed, and secondly if it is more likely than not that the defendant committed the crime. If the answer to both questions is yes, they vote to issue a true bill.

Indictment
A grand jury's action to bring charges against an individual based on evidence presented by the prosecutor or from its own investigation.

Even though the defendant's lawyers cannot participate in the grand jury process, there are ways to combat a true bill filed against their defendant. If the defendant believes the grand jury acted in an unconstitutional manner, he or she can move to have the indictment "**quashed.**" The court will rule on the motion and if the indictment is quashed, then the charges against the defendant are dropped. Similarly, should the defense team find evidence that one of the jurors was not qualified to sit on the grand jury, it can challenge the indictment. Even if the indictment is quashed, the defendant is not out of the woods yet, though. Jeopardy does not attach just because a person has been accused. Indictments can only be quashed because of procedural issues. The grand jury can reconvene, or another one can be empanelled and issue another true bill.

Quash
To annul or set aside.

YOU MAKE THE CALL

The Duke Rape Case: Misuse of the Grand Jury?

The year 2006 was an election year in Durham County, North Carolina. District Attorney Mike Nifong faced a stiff challenge for the Democratic nomination, and in Durham County winning the Democratic nomination virtually assured winning the general election.

On March 13, 2006, two co-captains of the Duke University Lacrosse team held a party at an off-campus house. They hired two exotic dancers for $800.

(continued)

The next day one of the dancers, who was black, told police she had been beaten and raped by three white team members. The Durham County Court compelled all white team members to provide DNA samples.

Before the test results were back, Nifong labeled the assailants as "hooligans" and promised the DNA evidence would show "precisely who was involved." On April 10, the DNA test results came in and no match was found among the team members. One week after the results came in, a grand jury indicted two lacrosse players, Collin Finnerty and Reade Seligmann, charging them with rape, sexual offense, and kidnapping.

Since the defense does not put on a case before a grand jury, Mike Nifong was the only one presenting evidence to grand jury. Because grand jury proceedings are sealed, we may never know whether Nifong revealed the DNA results to the grand jury. One thing we do know is that at the time the grand jury issued the true bill, Nifong had not turned over the DNA test results to the players' defense attorneys.

On May 2, Mike Nifong won the Democratic primary election. It was only after the general election that he revealed the test results to the defense. By then he was facing sanctions from the courts.[11] Did Nifong manipulate the grand jury for political purposes? What safeguards could be put in place to prevent this behavior? Can grand juries perform their constitutional function of preventing malicious or politically motivated prosecutions if they don't hear the defense's side of the story? You make the call!

Discovery

Discovery
A formal investigation conducted before trial by both parties.

Before a trial begins, both sides gather information about the case through the **discovery** process. Discovery consists of requests from both sides for what information the other possesses. There is not constitutional mandate for discovery, but each state and the federal judiciary rely on the discovery process to streamline trials, focus proceedings, and ensure that all parties' rights are protected. Each state has its own discovery rules. Discovery in federal trials is governed by Rule 16 of the Federal Rules of Criminal Procedure.

Not everything is subject to disclosure in discovery. Under federal rules the prosecution must provide only the following items:

(A) *Defendant's Oral Statement.* Upon a defendant's request, the government must disclose to the defendant the substance of any relevant oral statement made by the defendant, before or after arrest, in response to interrogation by a person the defendant knew was a government agent if the government intends to use the statement at trial.

(B) *Defendant's Written or Recorded Statement.* Upon a defendant's request, the government must disclose to the defendant, and make available for inspection, copying, or photographing, all of the following:

(i) any relevant written or recorded statement by the defendant if:
  - the statement is within the government's possession, custody, or control; and
  - the attorney for the government knows—or through due diligence could know—that the statement exists;

(ii) the portion of any written record containing the substance of any relevant oral statement made before or after arrest if the defendant made the statement in response to interrogation by a person the defendant knew was a government agent; and

(iii) the defendant's recorded testimony before a grand jury relating to the charged offense.

(C) ***Organizational Defendant.*** Upon a defendant's request, if the defendant is an organization, the government must disclose to the defendant any statement described in sections (A) and (B) if the government contends that the person making the statement:

(i) was legally able to bind the defendant regarding the subject of the statement because of that person's position as the defendant's director, officer, employee, or agent; or

(ii) was personally involved in the alleged conduct constituting the offense and was legally able to bind the defendant regarding that conduct because of that person's position as the defendant's director, officer, employee, or agent.

(D) ***Defendant's Prior Record.*** Upon a defendant's request, the government must furnish the defendant with a copy of the defendant's prior criminal record that is within the government's possession, custody, or control if the attorney for the government knows—or through due diligence could know—that the record exists.

(E) ***Documents and Objects.*** Upon a defendant's request, the government must permit the defendant to inspect and to copy or photograph books, papers, documents, data, photographs, tangible objects, buildings or places, or copies or portions of any of these items, if the item is within the government's possession, custody, or control and:

(i) the item is material to preparing the defense;

(ii) the government intends to use the item in its case-in-chief at trial; or

(iii) the item was obtained from or belongs to the defendant.

(F) ***Reports of Examinations and Tests.*** Upon a defendant's request, the government must permit a defendant to inspect and to copy or photograph the results or reports of any physical or mental examination and of any scientific test or experiment if:

(i) the item is within the government's possession, custody, or control;

(ii) the attorney for the government knows—or through due diligence could know—that the item exists; and

(iii) the item is material to preparing the defense or the government intends to use the item in its case-in chief at trial.

(G) ***Expert Witnesses.*** At the defendant's request, the government must give to the defendant a written summary of any testimony that the government intends to use under Rules 702, 703, or 705 of the Federal Rules of Evidence during its case-in-chief at trial. If the government requests discovery related to a defense expert witness and the defendant complies, the government must, at the defendant's request, give to the defendant a written summary of testimony that the government intends to use under Rules 702, 703, or 705 of the Federal Rules of Evidence as evidence at trial on the issue of the defendant's mental condition. The summary provided under this subparagraph must describe the witness's opinions, the bases and reasons for those opinions, and the witness's qualifications.

If the defense requests and the government provides documents and objects listed under section E or examinations or tests under section F, the defense must provide any reciprocal information to the prosecution. If the defense plans to present expert testimony, they must provide the same information to the prosecution as the prosecution provided about their expert witnesses under section G.

Each category of discoverable materials is only provided upon request. Defense teams should be aggressive in asking for any and all relevant items. This forces the prosecution to either deny the items exist, explain why they are not relevant, or turn them over.

Courts have great latitude in enforcing discovery requests. If a party fails to comply courts may:

(A) order that party to permit the discovery or inspection; specify its time, place, and manner; and prescribe other just terms and conditions;

(B) grant a continuance;

(C) prohibit that party from introducing the undisclosed evidence; or

(D) enter any other order that is just under the circumstances.

Discovery is not a "once and done" process. Should either side find evidence later that was included in previous discovery requests, they must turn it over to the other side.

Exculpatory evidence is evidence that casts doubt on the defendant's guilt. Prosecutors are obligated, regardless of the status of any discovery requests, to inform the court and the defense of the evidence's existence.

Exculpatory evidence
Evidence that casts doubt on the defendant's guilt.

Pretrial Motions

Pretrial Motions
Formal requests that a judge enter a particular order prior to the start of a trial.

Once both sides complete discovery, they may find controversies that must be resolved prior to trial. These are generally resolved through **pretrial motions.** For example, assume the defense team believes certain incriminating evidence was obtained improperly. The only way to exclude that evidence is to make a motion to have it excluded. Generally, pretrial motions are written. If the issue is complicated, the judge may request the attorneys to file briefs outlining their positions citing previous case law on the point in question. For simpler issues the judge may take oral submissions and either rule immediately or take the matter under advisement and research the matter himself. For the defense team, pretrial motions serve two purposes. First, if the motion is granted, it increases the chances for acquittal. If the motion fails, the issue is preserved for appeal. Defendants may not base their appeal on issues they did not challenge during their trial.

If, following discovery, the defense thinks the prosecution has insufficient evidence to convict, it may file a motion to dismiss. The motion to dismiss may challenge an indictment, information, or some or all of the charges against the defendant. The court may force some documents to be modified rather than completely dismissed or may grant the motion. However, indictments, because they are issued only by grand juries, would be sent back to the grand jury for reconsideration.

Other common motions include:

- a **motion for change of venue or venire** (discussed at length later in the chapter);
- a **motion to sever,** where various defendants or charges are tried separately in the interest of a fairer trial;
- a **motion for discovery,** where new evidence, witnesses, or issues require further investigation before the trial can begin;
- A **motion to recuse or disqualify a judge,** where evidence indicates the judge has a conflict of interest or cannot be impartial;
- A **motion for continuance or adjournment,** when more time is needed to investigate evidence or prepare for trial; and
- A **motion in limine or for a protective order,** where certain lines of questioning that may be prejudicial but not relevant to the defendant's guilt or innocence are excluded prior to the start of trial.

While many attorneys privately lament "motions practice," motions when properly used make trials fairer and more efficient. Most pretrial motions address legal issues best handled by the judge and attorneys freeing the jury to perform its fact finding task without being bogged down by legal technicalities.

How the Jury Pool is Selected

The group of people from which a jury is selected is referred to by many names. The group is variously known as the jury pool, array, panel, or **venire.** The pool from which jurors are to be picked is drawn from the local population. The U.S. Constitution requires that jurors be selected from "the State and district wherein the crime shall have been committed," and that "such Trial shall be held in the State where the said Crimes shall have been committed."[12] In other words, the venire members must at the very least come from the state where the crime was committed. This guarantees, for example, that a Virginian will not be judged by jurors from Alaska or another distant community whose mores and standards of conduct may differ considerably. (For a discussion on change of venue and change of venire, see the discussion later in this chapter.)

The jury pool must be varied enough to allow the jury selected from the pool to be a "representative cross section of the community."[13] Selection for a federal jury is governed by the Federal Jury Selection and Service Act of 1968, which requires that both grand juries and petit juries be selected at random from a fair cross section of the community.[14]

States differ in the ways that they select community members to serve on jury duty. Most jurisdictions use a combination of methods to secure jurors for the pool. These include using voter registration lists, tax records, and driver's license records.

A Michigan court was challenged because it used the same jury pool for county and local court cases. When an African American man was convicted by an all-white jury, he claimed the jury selection process "siphoned" off the African Americans jurors to other trials. The county had originally filled local juries first, leaving the rest of the jury pool for county-wide cases. The defendant claimed that by the time the jury was empanelled for his county-wide

Motion for recusal
A formal request to have the judge turnover proceedings to another judge.

Motion to change venire
A formal request to change the trial's jury pool.

Motion to change venue
A formal request to change the trial's location.

Motion to sever
A formal request to try certain defendants or charges separately.

Motion for discovery
A formal request to investigate evidence.

Motion for continuance
A formal request to temporarily halt proceedings.

Motion *in limine*
A formal request to limit testimony so as not to prejudice a jury.

Venire
A group of individuals from the community from whom the petit jury that will hear a criminal case is drawn. Also referred to as the jury panel, pool, or array.

trial, few minorities remained in the pool. A month after his conviction, the county switched the order to address the perceived racial imbalance. The case eventually landed at the Supreme Court where a unanimous court ruled the jury selection process did not deprive him of a fair trial. The difference in the jury pools' composition was not enough for them to not be "representative cross sections of the community."[15]

At Common Law, the sheriff was authorized to conscript jurors from those passing by. States can use any method that does not exclude from selection an identifiable group or class such as women or minorities.

The Supreme Court has consistently upheld the right of all groups or classes of citizens to serve on juries. For example, in 1998 the Court decided that the apparent systematic exclusion of blacks as grand jury forepersons violated the due process clause of the Fourteenth Amendment. In that case, a white defendant challenged the Louisiana method of choosing the foreperson. The selection was made by the judge, and in the last twenty years there had never been an African-American selected even though more than 20 percent of the registered voters in the district were African-American. The Court concluded that if the selection "process is infected with racial discrimination, doubt is cast over the fairness of all subsequent decisions."[16] The decision is the latest in a long line of cases that have held African-Americans cannot be excluded from the jury pool because the Fourteenth Amendment prohibits unequal treatment and discrimination on the basis of race. As early as 1880, the Supreme Court ruled that a fair trial demanded that all racial groups be included in the pool of potential jurors and that all groups have the opportunity to serve on juries.[17]

HISTORICAL HIGHLIGHT

Don't Venture Near the Courthouse; You May End Up on a Jury!

A little-known power of county sheriffs is the right to literally "pull people off the street" to empanel a jury. This power dates back to medieval England. Modern-day usage is rare, and it often meets with an angry response.

In Pennsylvania, a retrial of a murder case exhausted the pool of potential jurors for that month. The judge ordered the sheriffs to go out in the night and bring in people scheduled for the following month's pool. When they knocked on the door of one of the potential jurors, his wife slammed the door in the sheriff's face. After some persistent knocking and cajoling, the door opened and the sheriff took the man to court.[18]

A Texas couple was at a grocery store when they observed constables roaming through the parking lot talking to people. When they were approached, they were informed that the night court needed one more juror to try a misdemeanor speeding case, and one of them would have to go. She went and was elected jury foreperson.

The constables reported that not everyone was quite as amiable. Some people had to be shown the writ issued by the judge. Others were simply incredulous that people were being brought in to try a speeding case. When the judge needed a jury for a second case, he suggested sending the constables out "shopping" again. The deputy sheriff spoke with the judge, and it was decided the trial could wait another day.

Dragging in jurors off the streets is one of the long-held powers of local sheriffs. In colonial New England sheriffs could draft townsmen to help in any emergency, and they could be fined if they refused. Although modern methods of jury pool selection make these sheriffs' surprise visits rare, it might be a good idea to avoid the courthouse area if you have plans for the evening.

Empanelling the Jury

Excusing Jurors for Hardship

The next step in the jury selection process is excluding potential jurors who can't serve for business, personal, or some other reason. Some jurisdictions allow potential jurors to request exemptions as soon as they receive written notice to appear for jury duty. Others require all jurors to appear before the trial judge to request an exemption.

Common reasons cited by potential jurors include health conditions, running a small business, being the caregiver for young children, farming during planting season or the harvest, and being in a profession such as medicine that requires long and irregular hours. Note that these reasons have nothing to do with the particular case being tried. Jurors excused from service for these personal reasons claim they can't serve on any jury because of competing obligations. Granting every request tends to concentrate those with "free time" on juries, usually the retired, the unemployed, and students. In recent years, judges have grown less tolerant of requests to be excused.

> We have a criminal jury system which is superior to any in the world; and its efficiency is only marred by the difficulty of finding twelve men every day who don't know anything and can't read.
>
> Mark Twain, Fourth of July speech (1873)

Voir Dire

Those accused of committing crimes are entitled to an impartial jury selected from a jury pool that is representative of the community. Note that the actual jury need not be representative of the community; only that the pool from which they are selected is representative. One reason for that is that it is difficult, if not impossible, to find twelve jurors who are impartial and who also mirror the racial, ethnic, sexual, and religious composition of the community for every case.

When the court or attorneys involved in a case question potential jurors about their ability to serve as impartial jurors, the process is called **voir dire.** *Voir dire* literally means "to speak the truth." Jurors are asked a series of questions about their ability to decide the case based on what they hear as evidence in the case, and not based on what they read in the paper or saw on the six o'clock news. *Voir dire* also helps weed out those who may be prejudiced against the defendant because of his race, religion, or national origin.

If, during *voir dire*, attorneys for either the state or the defense find that the answers a juror gives indicates that he or she may not be able to render an impartial **verdict,** the attorney will ask the trial judge to strike the juror from consideration. This can be done through either a challenge for cause or the use of a peremptory challenge.

Voir dire
Literally, "to speak the truth." During the *voir dire* phase of a criminal trial, the attorneys or the judge ask questions of the jury pool. These are designed to ferret out those jurors who can't be impartial, who can't serve on the jury because of illness or other obligations, and to help the attorneys in the case decide where and when to use available peremptory challenges.

Verdict
The final decision of a jury.

HISTORICAL HIGHLIGHT

The Right of Women to Serve on Juries

As a group, women have only recently begun to secure equal rights and privileges on a par with those accorded men. Women saw African-American males given equal protection of the laws long before females were granted the right to vote. It wasn't until 1920 that Congress saw fit to give all citizens a say in choosing their government. The Nineteenth Amendment to the U.S. Constitution provides that "[t]he right of citizens of the United States to vote shall not be denied by the United States or by a State on account of sex." It would be another fifty-five years before jury service by women was recognized as a fundamental privilege of citizenship. Women's quest for equal political status has met with considerable opposition over the years.

Consider the Equal Rights Amendment. The Equal Rights Amendment would have extended equal rights to women on the same basis as the Fourteenth Amendment did for African-Americans in 1868. It was passed by Congress in 1972, but never ratified by the required thirty-eight states (3/4) to become effective. It expired in 1982, just two states short of ratification. Women have had to rely on state legislatures and the U.S. Congress to provide equal rights in the workplace. Some federal statutes that protect women include the Equal Pay Act, the Civil Rights Act of 1963, and the Pregnancy Discrimination Act. The Supreme Court's interpretation of the Fourteenth Amendment's equal protection clause has also helped broaden women's rights.

Fifty-five years after women were granted the right to vote, a Sixth Amendment case provided the Supreme Court with an opportunity to address the right of women to fully participate in the nation's political life through jury service. The case was *Taylor v. Louisiana,* 419 U.S. 522 (1975). Ironically, it was a male who secured a woman's right to jury duty. He argued that Louisiana's exclusion of women from petit (trial) juries violated his right to be tried by citizens representing a cross section of the community. Until *Taylor,* female jurors were often the exception rather than the rule. Women's right to jury service evolved slowly.

In 1789, Congress passed the first law regulating the selection of juries for federal trials. Jurors were to be picked based on the rules in the state where the federal court was located. Since no state allowed women as jurors, federal jurors were also all male. As states added women to the list of eligible jurors, more federal courts also did. The first state to allow women jurors was Utah, in 1898. By mid-century, Congress changed the 1789 law. The Civil Rights Act of 1957 finally allowed women to serve on all federal juries. But many states still excluded women well into the later part of this century.

Taylor involved a male who was charged with kidnapping in a Louisiana state court. At that time, women were called to jury duty only if they asked to serve, while men were simply ordered to serve. The Supreme Court ruled that by systematically excluding a group that made up 53 percent of the population, Louisiana had violated the defendant's right to a jury drawn from a fair cross section of the community.

HISTORICAL HIGHLIGHT

Oklahoma City Jurors Make Excuses

The Search for Unbiased Jurors

Few events in recent history shocked Americans more than the events of April 19, 1995, other than those of September 11, 2001. At 9:03 A.M., as federal workers grabbed the first cup of coffee of the day and children settled into their daily routine at the on-site child care center in the Alfred P. Murrah Federal Building in Oklahoma City, Oklahoma, a powerful explosion shattered the morning calm. Before nightfall, the death toll was staggering. In all, 168 people were dead and over 500 more were injured. Like the John F. Kennedy assassination in 1963, the *Challenger* accident in 1986, and September 11, almost every American old enough to remember vividly recalls where he was and how he felt when the news broke.

How the judicial system found jurors to serve in the Oklahoma City bombing cases is a classic example of how difficult it is to guarantee all criminal defendants a trial by an unbiased jury of peers. Both Timothy McVeigh and Terry Nichols chose trial by jury. Finding willing jurors was a daunting task.

The problem became particularly acute in Terry Nichols' trial after the national publicity McVeigh's

conviction and death sentence received. Over 500 potential jurors were summoned to a state fairground for the first round of selection. There they filled out detailed questionnaires about their background, exposure to pretrial publicity, and attitudes. Apparently many of the potential jurors called for the jury pool concluded that they could avoid jury duty by providing the "wrong" answers on *voir dire.*

One potential juror announced that she was psychic and heard messages from time to time. Nichols' attorney asked that she be excused even though she had promised to tell the court if she received any messages from the hereafter. His request was granted.

Another juror expressed faith of another kind, in technology. He proclaimed that all he had to do to arrive at the "correct" decision on guilt or innocence was to put the "facts" into his laptop computer, which he conveniently carried with him. The following exchange took place between the potential juror and the court:

> **THE COURT:** Now, you know, this isn't like computers. This isn't like feeding a lot of stuff into a database and pulling it up. This involves human judgment. That's what being on a jury is. Human judgment. That's why we don't have

computers deciding cases. There's quite a difference. Do you agree?

A. Maybe we should look into computers. I would agree, yes, sir.

THE COURT: Would you like to be judged by a computer?

A. Depending on the given parameters.

THE COURT: Parameters of judgment as to whether what a witness says is true? Do you think that's a human function, to judge the truth of what another person says?

A. It would be impartial and unbiased.

Another was convinced that Nichols was hiding something, because of a particular look in his eyes. She couldn't be persuaded to set aside her belief. She was also removed from the pool.

A jury of seven women and five men was finally chosen. They spent two months together considering the evidence against Nichols before convicting him of conspiracy to bomb the Murrah building and manslaughter in the death of the federal agents killed in the blast. After the verdict, the foreperson received death threats. She explained that if she had it to do over again, she would try to avoid jury duty.[19]

The Challenge for Cause

When making a **challenge for cause,** the attorney states his or her reasons for believing that the jury pool member is unable to be an impartial judge of the facts of the case. That belief may be based on the juror's religion, nation of origin, race, gender, or relationship to the defendant, the judge, the attorneys, or the victim in the case. For example, if the potential juror is married to a police officer, and the case involves the brutal murder of a police officer, the spouse may not be impartial. The judge in a case may strike as many jurors from consideration for cause as is necessary. That's because every defendant is guaranteed an impartial jury.

The Peremptory Challenge

A **peremptory challenge** involves striking a juror from consideration as a juror for any reason, or no reason at all. No federal law requires peremptory challenges to ensure a fair trial; however every state has state laws that allow them.[20] In most courts, only a few peremptory challenges are allowed for each side. Peremptory challenges allow attorneys to help mold a jury into a group each presumes will be inclined to convict or acquit. It was designed, in the words of the Supreme Court, " . . . to eliminate persons thought to be inclined against their interests . . . ."[21] Since no reason needs to be given, an attorney defending someone charged with the rape of a young girl may try to exclude potential jurors with daughters or granddaughters the age of the victim.

A word of caution is due here, though. The courts have warned attorneys, especially prosecutors, against using peremptory challenges to strike potential jurors of one race or another in order to get a racially pure jury. For example, prosecutors can't strike all black jurors to get an all-white jury or all women to get a male jury. That would be a violation of the juror's Fourteenth Amendment right to equal protection and equal participation in civic life, and would taint the perception of the justice system as fair and impartial. It doesn't matter whether the defendant is black or white.[22]

Recently the Supreme Court considered just such a case. In *Miller-El v. Dretke*, a case involving a black defendant who faced death, Texas prosecutors allegedly followed an informal practice of striking potential jurors who were black on the assumption they were less willing to punish a black defendant. The 6–3 decision overturned the death sentence based in part on the fact that prosecutors in the case had used their peremptory strikes to exclude 91 percent of the eligible black venire members, and noted, "Happenstance was unlikely to produce this disparity."

Challenge for cause
If a juror can't be impartial because he or she knows about the case, knows the defendant's family, knows the victim or any of the people involved in the case, has already made a decision about the defendant's guilt or innocence, or admits to prejudice, he or she can be challenged for cause. There are an unlimited number of challenges for cause available. Any potential juror who can't be impartial can be stricken for cause.

Peremptory challenge
Attorneys are allowed a number of peremptory challenges when selecting jurors. The number varies from court to court. Peremptory challenges are without cause; that is, the attorney making the challenge need not state the reason for eliminating the potential juror. Caution must be used when peremptory challenges follow a pattern that seems race or gender based.

The Court also relied on the Supreme Court's 1986 decision in *Batson v. Kentucky*, which established a three-step process for evaluating whether a particular peremptory challenge violates the defendant's Fourteenth Amendment rights. The steps are as follows:

1. The defendant must make a prima facie case that the peremptory challenge was based on race.
2. If the defendant shows racial bias according to (1), then the prosecutor must offer a race-neutral basis for striking the juror in question.
3. In light of both parties' submissions, the trial court must determine whether the strike was discriminatory.

The Court was also convinced that race had been significant in peremptory strikes of two particular black jurors. Justice Breyer, concurring, wrote that the case "suggested the need to confront the choice between the right of a defendant to have a jury chosen in conformity with the requirements of the Fourteenth Amendment and the right to challenge peremptorily," and suggested it "was necessary to reconsider the Batson test, and the peremptory challenge system as a whole."[23]

In deciding *Batson v. Kentucky*, Supreme Court Justice Thurgood Marshall wrote, "The decision today will not end the racial discrimination that peremptories inject into the jury-selection process. That goal can be accomplished only by eliminating peremptory challenges entirely."[24]

While all states still allow peremptory challenges, a study by the Equal Justice Initiative may prove Marshall's point. The study noted particular problems in southern states. For example, in Alabama the study found that courts had uncovered racial discrimination in the jury selection process in 25 percent of the state's death penalty cases. The study noted a pattern of excluding blacks in death penalty cases in many states. This could be explained by the fact that a smaller percentage of blacks believe in the death penalty and are therefore not "death penalty qualified" (see Chapter 14). The study uncovered anecdotal evidence of prosecutors striking jurors because of mannerisms more common among African Americans. In one case, a South Carolina prosecutor struck one potential juror because he "shucked and jived" when he walked. The study quoted other studies showing that "racially diverse juries deliberate longer, consider a wider variety of perspectives, and make fewer factual errors than all-white juries."[25]

HISTORICAL HIGHLIGHT

Shackles Prejudice Jurors

In July 1996, Carman Deck and his sister knocked on the home of an elderly couple, Zelma and James Long, and asked for directions. The Longs invited them in and gave them the directions they asked for, but instead of leaving, Deck drew a pistol and ordered them to lie face down on their beds. The Longs did so, offering them money and whatever valuables were in the house.

After Deck finished robbing the house, he stood at the edge of the bed, deliberating for ten minutes while they pleaded with him. He shot them each twice in the head. Deck later told police he shot them because he thought they might be able to identify him later.

In 1998, the State of Missouri tried Deck. During the trial, the state required Deck to wear leg braces that were not visible to the jury. Deck was convicted and sentenced to death. The sentence was overturned on appeal.

During the second sentencing proceedings, the state brought Deck into the courtroom shackled with leg irons, handcuffs, and a belly chain. Deck's counsel objected several times to the use of the leg irons during voir dire and moved to strike the jury panel because "the fact that Mr. Deck is shackled in front of the jury ... makes them think that he is ... violent today."[26] This time, the jury recommended two death sentences, which the trial court imposed.

Deck appealed, claiming, among other things, that being shackled violated his due process rights. The Supreme Court agreed and overturned his sentence,

ruling that visible shackling undermines the presumption of innocence, and quoting from "Pleas of the Crown," which provided that a defendant "ought not be brought to the Bar in a contumellious Manner; as with his Hands tied together, or any other Mark of Ignominy and Reproach ... unless there be some Danger of a Rescous [rescue] or Escape."[27]

Death Qualifying Jurors

There are special rules for selecting members of a jury who will hear a capital case. A capital case is a case in which the possible penalty is death. A jury that will hear a death penalty case must be *Witherspoon* qualified. The term comes from the Supreme Court case *Witherspoon v. Illinois*.[28] In that case, the Court ruled that members of the jury pool can't be automatically excluded from a jury because they are conscientiously opposed to the death penalty. They must be asked whether they are able to follow the court's instructions on the law and can vote for death if the facts are appropriate. If they answer "yes," they are **"*Witherspoon* qualified."** Similarly, jurors who say they don't have a conscientious objection to the death penalty must assure the court that they won't automatically impose the death penalty.[29] (See Chapter 14 for more information about the death penalty.)

Witherspoon qualified
A jury in a capital case who have stated they will consider imposing the death penalty even if they are opposed to the death penalty.

How Many Jurors Does a Jury Make?

In federal criminal cases, a jury must have twelve members. That's been the law of the land since 1898, when the Supreme Court decided *Thompson v. Utah*.[30] *Thompson* involved a livestock thief who was tried twice. Utah was still a federal territory at the time of the first trial. The first jury consisted of twelve men. He won an appeal that gave him a new trial. Meanwhile, Utah became a state. Under Utah's new constitution, he was allowed only eight jurors. When he was again found guilty, he claimed he had been denied his Sixth Amendment rights to a jury of twelve.

When the case was heard by the Supreme Court, he argued that the theft happened when Utah was still a territory under the federal government's control. The case was therefore a federal, not a state, matter. The Supreme Court agreed. The Sixth Amendment right to trial by jury was a part of the Common Law as brought to America by the colonists. Since according to English Common Law, a jury contained twelve members, so must a federal jury.

Criminal trials in state court can use a lesser number of jurors, however. In 1970 the Supreme Court held that six jurors were a sufficient number. By the time of the decision in *Williams v. Florida*, the Court concluded that " ... the fact that the jury at Common Law was composed of precisely 12 is a historical accident, unnecessary to effect the purposes of the jury system and wholly without significance except to mystics."[31]

Five jurors are too few. That's what the Supreme Court concluded a few years later in *Ballew v. Georgia*.[32] The case involved the Paris Adult Theatre in

> For as Christ and his twelve apostles were finally to judge the world, so human tribunals should be composed of the King and twelve wise men.
>
> Credited to Morgan of Gla-Morgan, king of Wales (725 A.D.)

Atlanta. In 1973 two county investigators saw the film *Behind the Green Door* at the theater. The film was an "adult" picture featuring Marilyn Chambers, a former mainstream model. After getting a warrant, they saw the movie again and then promptly seized it as evidence. The owner was charged with violating the Georgia obscenity laws, which were misdemeanor criminal offenses. Under Georgia law, defendants charged with misdemeanors were entitled to a jury of five. Ballew argued that a jury of five couldn't be expected to assess what were the contemporary standards of the community, which is required in order to convict on an obscenity charge. He was convicted and appealed the use of a five-person jury.

The Supreme Court relied on a number of studies on jury deliberations and group dynamics. These studies concluded that as the size of the jury shrinks from twelve to fewer than six jurors, the dynamics change. In fact, one study cited by the Court found that the likelihood of convicting an innocent person rises as the size of the jury shrinks, while the risk of not convicting a guilty person rises as the size of the jury gets larger. Based upon the studies and the arguments of the attorneys in the case, the Supreme Court held that six is the minimum number of jurors allowed on a criminal petit jury.

Pretrial Publicity, Change of Venue or Venire, and Sequestration

The Media and Finding Impartial Jurors

As we have learned in this chapter, the Constitution requires that an impartial jury decide whether the government has proven beyond a reasonable doubt that the defendant is guilty of the crime he was charged with. A century ago, finding a jury that hadn't heard the details about a criminal case was relatively easy. There was no television news, no Internet news reports delivered worldwide in an instant, and no satellite communications. Today the details of crimes are known to millions of people almost as soon as they happen. If you have any doubt about the speed and distance news travels, ask yourself if you would have known the details of the following crimes and news events had you lived in the 1800s:

- The Virginia Tech massacre
- Andrea Yates' drowning her five children in the bathtub
- The kidnapping of Elizabeth Smart from her bedroom
- The Washington Beltway sniper
- The Nickel Mines Amish School shooting

Juries are obligated to judge defendants impartially. Jurors can only consider the evidence presented at trial. They can't consider what they may have learned about the case from the newspaper or television reports. The more publicity a case has received before trial, the more likely a potential juror may have prejudged the case. The ideal juror knows absolutely nothing about the defendant, the victim, or the case. But the ideal juror doesn't exist in the age of electronic communications. Few hermits are called to jury service.

The courts have come up with several ways to minimize the impact of pre-trial publicity on potential jurors, to judge whether pretrial publicity will affect a juror's ability to be impartial, and to assure that jurors decide the case only on the evidence they hear and see in the courtroom. These methods include change of venue, change of venire, and sequestration.

Change of Venue and Venire

Many crimes receive intense media coverage locally, but little mention statewide or nationally. The victim or the accused may be well known in their community, but unknown in other geographic areas. If a defendant claims he or she can't get an impartial jury, the case can be moved to another location for trial if the court agrees. This usually involves trying the case in another county if it is a state case or another federal courthouse in the same judicial district if it's a federal case. For example, the Oklahoma City bombing trials were moved to Denver from Oklahoma City. Moving the case to another geographic area is called a change of **venue.** Depending on the complexity of the case, the number of witnesses, and how long the trial will last, a change of venue can be expensive. A request for change of venue is seldom granted.

Another way of finding impartial jurors is through a change of venire. Sometimes the court concludes that impartial local jurors are hard to come by because of extensive pretrial publicity, but doesn't want to require witnesses, prosecutors, and defense attorneys to travel to another location. In that case, the simplest solution may be to bring the jurors in from another location. In other words, the jury pool or venire is brought in from out of town. This solution may be attractive when trial publicity will be extensive and the court anticipates sequestering the jury anyway. (See discussion below.)

Venue
The county or judicial district in which a case is tried. In criminal cases, the venue is usually where the crime was committed.

HISTORICAL HIGHLIGHT

Change of Venue Cannot Change Scott Peterson's Fate

On April 13, 2002, the body of a male fetus, umbilical cord still attached, washed ashore in San Francisco Bay. The next day, a partial female torso missing its hands, feet, and head washed ashore in the same area. The bodies were later identified as Laci Peterson and her unborn child, Connor. Decomposition made an autopsy difficult, but the medical examiner noted three broken ribs on Laci's body that could not have come from being dragged over the rocks in the bay. An investigation by the FBI and Modesto Police Department pointed to Laci's husband of five years, fertilizer salesman Scott Peterson. The authorities quickly discovered that Peterson had been engaged in an affair with Amber Frey, a massage therapist from Fresno. Frey told the police Peterson had implied that he was a widower, telling her he had "lost his wife" two weeks before Laci's disappearance. Frey became a critical prosecution witness and even let

investigators tape conversations with Peterson, which revealed that just days after Laci went missing, Peterson had claimed to be celebrating the holidays in Paris.

Peterson was arrested on April 18, 2003, in La Jolla, California, carrying $15,000 in cash, four cell phones, multiple credit cards belonging to family members, camping equipment, knives, a gun, a map to Frey's workplace, sleeping pills, Viagra, and his brother's driver's license. His hair and beard were bleached blonde, the effect, he said, of chlorine from swimming.

The case was circumstantial, but very convincing. It was also front-page news in Modesto and throughout the country. By the time his trial date rolled around, the hostility toward him in his wife's hometown of Modesto was so high his attorney, Mark Geragos, said his tires were slashed while he visited Peterson in jail. "The extent and intensity of the publicity in this case is of unprecedented proportions in Northern California,"

Geragos said.[33] The prosecution's argument, Geragos wrote in his request, "can be boiled down to the old adage, 'Sure we can give him a fair trial, then we will take him out and hang him.' " Stanislaus County Superior Court Judge Al Girolami agreed. The trial was moved to Redwood City, California.

In the end, the change of venue failed to change Peterson's fate. A jury convicted Peterson of first-degree murder with special circumstances for Laci Peterson's death and second-degree murder for the death of unborn Connor. Peterson's defense filed a request for another change of venue before the sentencing phase of the trial, and a change of jurors as well. Judge Alfred A. Delucchi denied the motions, saying, "Where could I send this case in the state of California that hasn't been inundated with the media coverage?"

On March 16, 2005, Judge Delucchi sentenced Peterson to death by lethal injection. He denied a defense request for a new trial and ordered Peterson to pay $10,000 toward his wife's funeral. He remains on death row in San Quentin State Prison, which overlooks the bay where Laci's body washed ashore.[34]

Sequestration

Once a trial starts, jurors are told to disregard anything they hear about the case other than in the courtroom. Jurors are told not to read about the case, not to listen to news reports about the case, and not to discuss the case with anyone until it's time to deliberate. They are also told not to discuss the case among themselves until they retire to the jury room to decide the defendant's fate. Since most trials last only a day or two, jurors generally don't have too much trouble following the court's directions. But in cases heavily covered by the media or that will take a long time to try, it may be impossible to avoid hearing about the case from other sources.

To minimize the possibility of exposure to facts outside the courtroom, juries can be sequestered. **Sequester** means to separate. When jurors are sequestered, they are housed and fed, at government expense, until the case is over. Usually sequestered jurors have only very limited contact with their families and are guarded by the local sheriff and deputies. Their mail, telephone calls, and reading materials are censored.

Sequestration is used very rarely because it is expensive and very disruptive. But some jurors have been sequestered for months or longer. For example, the jurors in the O. J. Simpson murder case were sequestered for over a year. For many, sequestration represents a real hardship, both financial and personal. Consider how hard it would be to be away from your family, friends, school, or job for months.

> "No, no!" said the Queen, "Sentence first, verdict afterwards."
>
> Lewis Carroll, *Alice in Wonderland* (1865)

Sequester
To separate jurors in order to assure that they will remain impartial during the trial and deliberations.

The Trial

The trial is the main mechanism in our system for determining the innocence or guilt of a person charged with a crime. Each defendant enters the trial with a presumption of innocence. The state must prove the defendant guilty of a charge beyond a reasonable doubt to obtain a conviction.

Trials follow a specific structure. They begin with the swearing in of the jury and the prosecutor's opening statement. The defense may make its opening statement following the prosecution's or it can wait until the prosecution has presented its entire case. Following the opening statement(s), the prosecution calls its witnesses. The prosecuting attorney asks questions in a process called direct examination. The defense attorney may ask the witness questions regarding issues raised during direct examination in an attempt to elicit evidence favorable to the defendant in a process called cross-examination. The prosecution may continue questioning, called re-direct examination, and the defense may follow up with re-cross examination. This process continues for all prosecution witnesses. Once all the prosecution witnesses have been called, the prosecution rests its case.

If the defense believes the prosecution has not proved guilt beyond a reasonable doubt, it may move to have the charge or case dismissed. In the unlikely event the judge grants the motion, the charge is dismissed. If no charges remain, the trial continues. If the defense did not present an opening statement earlier, it may do so now. The defense then calls its witnesses and the same process of direct and cross examination ensues. Once the defense rests, both sides present their closing arguments. The judge then instructs the jury. The jury deliberates until it reaches a unanimous decision on each charge. If the jury is unable to reach a unanimous verdict, the jury is hung and the judge declares a mistrial.

If the jury votes to convict, either the judge or the jury, depending on the type of case and applicable law, decides on a sentence. If the jury acquits, the defendant faces no punishment for the crimes charged.

The Opening Statement

Skillful attorneys use the opening statement to orient the jury to the evidence and issues involved in the case. Once oriented, the attorney can lead the jury through the evidence, placing it in the most favorable light for her side. The opposition's strongest arguments can be weakened by placing them in a different perspective and pointing out inconsistencies. Opening statements are an overview designed to acquaint the jurors with the case and the arguments both sides will make. Detailed or very technical discussions should be deferred until the actual trial.

The Witness List

As mentioned in the discovery section, both sides must list any expert witnesses they wish to call. Additionally, they must provide the opposition with a list of potential witnesses they may call. Individuals on the witness list may not be in the courtroom until they are called to testify in order to prevent their testimony being tainted by what other witnesses say. Savvy attorneys will include people whose presence in the courtroom may prejudice the jury against their case. For example, family members of a murder victim may react emotionally to graphic descriptions of the victim's injuries.

The Confrontation Clause

The Sixth Amendment to the Constitution reads in part, "In all criminal prosecutions, the accused shall enjoy the right . . . to be confronted with the witnesses against him, to have compulsory process for obtaining witnesses in his favor, and to have the Assistance of Counsel for his defence." This amendment provides the constitutional basis for the practice of calling examining and cross-examining witnesses. The right "to be confronted with the witnesses against him" is known as the Confrontation Clause.

The founding fathers no doubt say the Sixth Amendment as a necessary bulwark against tyranny, but they never had to deal with chemical analyses or DNA testing. As evidence has become more complex, expert testimony and the ability to intelligently cross-examine experts have become more important.

For many years, scientific reports such as chemical analyses were admitted as evidence without cross-examination. In 2009, the U.S. Supreme Court ruled this practice was a violation of the rights guaranteed by the Confrontation Clause. The prosecution must present the actual technician who completed the report to testify concerning its contents and be subject to cross-examination.[35] But the High Court also noted in a subsequent case that attorneys who fail to call or cross-examine the lab technician may not base an appeal on the lack of testimony. The state fulfills its obligation as long as it allows for the lab technician to testify.[36]

The Closing Argument

As with the opening arguments, the prosecution begins the closing argument. The defense follows, and in some jurisdiction, the prosecution may present a short rebuttal closing argument. The closing argument is each side's last chance to frame the evidence in the most positive light. A skillful attorney will weave the evidence into a story designed to persuade the jurors of their position. The jurors are generally instructed that the closing argument is not evidence. Even so, attorneys may not go too far in their summations. Courts have consistently frowned on overly religious language in closings in an attempt to show that God prefers one verdict over another.[37] Similarly, a prosecutor who told the jury that the ultimate death penalty decision in the case would be made by the Appeals Court, not the jury, was deemed to have crossed the line.[38]

If the judge determines that an attorney has so tainted the evidence that the jury can no longer be objective, he or she can order a mistrial. However, defense attorneys cannot deliberately cause a mistrial if they feel their case is lost. They may face sanctions if their behavior goes too far afield.

Jury Instructions and Forms

Once the attorneys have completed their closing arguments, the judge instructs the jury as to what issues it must consider when weighing the defendant's guilt or innocence. These instructions have been agreed upon ahead of time at a jury instruction conference. Both attorneys prepare proposed jury instructions and the legal basis for them based on relevant precedent. **Jury instructions** are tailored to the individual case reflecting both the charges and defenses raised during the trial. For instance, the instructions would not mention an insanity defense if it had not been raised during the trial.

Often in capital cases, the jury will be asked to review mitigating and aggravating factors to arrive at the sentence. Both the forms and instructions must be clear to the jury, or they, too, can become the basis for an appeal. In one case, the forms required jurors to unanimously agree on each factor before it could be used in the final analysis of whether the aggravating factors outweighed the mitigating ones. As a result, the jury voted for a death penalty even though many of them may have thought there were mitigating factors involved. With the confusing forms, mitigating factors that were not unanimously agreed upon did not enter into the sentencing decision. The Supreme Court vacated the death sentence and instructed the lower court to develop a system that reflected the true weight mitigating factors should receive in jury deliberations.[39]

Jury instructions
The directions the judge gives jurors about how they are to come to a verdict. Jury instructions typically include an explanation of the law and what must be proven to convict the defendant.

Juries are also told that they must apply the law as it is, even if they think it's an unjust, unfair, or stupid law. In other words, the jury only decides the facts, not what is the law. There have been many cases, however, where juries have seemingly ignored the law and refused to convict a defendant. This is referred to as jury nullification.

Recent rulings have indicated increasing intolerance of jury nullification among judges. In 1997, in *U.S. v. Thomas*, the Second Circuit Court ruled that jurors can be removed if there is evidence that they intend to nullify the law. The California Supreme Court took a further step in *People v. Williams*, a statutory rape case. On the first day of jury deliberations, the foreperson informed the judge that one of the jurors refused to follow instructions because he believed the law was wrong. The judge replaced the juror. The defendant appealed, arguing that jury nullification is acceptable. The Supreme Court unanimously upheld the conviction. Chief Justice Ronald M. George wrote, "A nullifying jury is essentially a lawless jury."[40] The ruling led to a new jury instruction that requires jurors to inform the judge whenever a fellow panelist appears to be deciding a case based on his or her dislike of the law.

Jury nullification
A decision by a jury to ignore the law or the judge's instructions when deliberating. For example, jurors who believe the law is unjust may refuse to convict the defendant even if it is clear that he broke the law.

HISTORICAL HIGHLIGHT

William Penn and Jury Nullification

One of the most famous jury trials in history involved William Penn, the founder of the Colony of Pennsylvania. William Penn was a Quaker at a time when England was intolerant of religious beliefs other than the Church of England's. Quakers were seen as dangerous radicals. Their religious services, held in "meeting houses," were closed by the government. They were forbidden to meet or to preach in the streets. In 1670 William Penn and a fellow Quaker, William Mead, defied the king of England and were arrested. They were accused of trying to incite a riot.

A jury of twelve men was selected to hear the case. Four of the twelve refused to find Penn and Mead guilty. The judge ordered them all to continue deliberating until they reached the proper and correct verdict. What happened next illustrates the idea of jury nullification.

Jurors are generally told by the judge before they begin deliberations that they must follow the law. For example, jurors are instructed that they cannot refuse to find a defendant guilty because they believe the law they are applying to the facts is an unjust or immoral law. **Jury nullification** occurs when a jury deliberately ignores the court's instructions to apply the law, however unjust, to the facts.

In William Penn's case, the jurors were denied food, drink, and tobacco until they reconsidered. After a few days, the twelve jurors united. Now the vote was unanimous. Penn and Mead were not guilty! The judge finally accepted their verdict, but jailed the jurors for rendering an improper verdict. They won on appeal. The case helped establish the sanctity of jury verdicts, even when that verdict seems contrary to law or common sense. A jury has the last word since defendants can't be tried again. A second trial would be double jeopardy.

Rendering the Verdict Beyond a Reasonable Doubt

What Is Reasonable Doubt?

Chapter 1 covered the essential differences between civil law and criminal law. One of those differences is the burden of proof that the prosecutor or the plaintiff must meet in order to prevail. Recall that in a civil case, the plaintiff must prove his or her case by a preponderance of the evidence. In a criminal case, the burden of proof is considerably higher. The state must prove that the defendant is guilty of a crime **beyond a reasonable doubt.** If the legal scales of justice must tip ever so slightly in favor of the plaintiff in a civil case, in a criminal case they must tip heavily in favor of guilt.

Beyond a reasonable doubt
The standard of proof in criminal cases. The prosecutor is required to prove beyond a reasonable doubt that the defendant committed the crime he or she was charged with. A reasonable doubt is a fair doubt based upon common sense.

HISTORICAL HIGHLIGHT

Can the Prosecution Put Away Two Different People for the Same Crime?

On May 14, 1984, John David Stumpf, Clyde Daniel Wesley, and a companion were traveling along Interstate 70 through Guernsey County, Ohio. Needing gas money, the men stopped the car along the highway. Stumpf and Wesley knocked on the door of Norman and Mary Jane Stout and asked to use the telephone. Once inside, Stumpf held the pair at gunpoint while Wesley ransacked the house. When Norman Stout made a move toward Stumpf, he shot him twice in the head. Mr. Stout fell unconscious, and revived in time to hear the four gunshots that killed his wife.

The third man was arrested shortly after the shooting and implicated Stumpf and Wesley. Stumpf denied any knowledge of the crime until he learned that Norman Stout had survived. He then admitted shooting Mr. Stout, but said Wesley had shot Mrs. Stout. Stumpf was charged with aggravated murder, attempted aggravated murder, aggravated robbery, and two counts of grand theft. Three of the statutory specifications of the aggravated murder charge made Stumpf eligible for the death penalty.

Stumpf accepted a plea agreement: he pled guilty to aggravated murder and attempted aggravated murder, with the other charges being dropped. In the aggravated murder charge, the prosecution dropped two of the three capital specifications. The third specification meant Stumpf was still eligible for the death penalty.

Pleading mitigating circumstances before a three-judge panel, Stumpf argued that he had participated only at the urging of Wesley and that Wesley had fired the fatal shots at Mrs. Stout. Stumpf hoped this would spare him the death penalty. The prosecution, however, argued that Stumpf had indeed shot Mrs. Stout. The prosecution also noted that Ohio law does not restrict the death penalty to those who commit murder by their own hands—an accomplice to murder could also receive it. The three-judge panel found that Stumpf "was the principal offender" in the murder and sentenced Stumpf to death.

Afterward, Wesley was extradited to Ohio for a jury trial before the same prosecutor and one of the same judges who had convicted Stumpf. The prosecution had new evidence: Wesley's cellmate testified that Wesley had admitted firing the shots that killed Mrs. Stout. The prosecution argued that Wesley was the principle offender in Mrs. Stout's murder. During the trial, the defense noted that the prosecutor had taken a contrary stance in Stumpf's trial, and that Stumpf had already been sentenced to death for the crime. Wesley was sentenced to life imprisonment with the possibility of parole.

Stumpf, with an appeal pending in the Ohio Court of Appeals, returned to the Court of Common Pleas with a motion to withdraw his guilty plea or vacate his death sentence, arguing that the state's case against Wesley had cast doubt on his own conviction and sentence. The Court of Common Pleas rejected his motion. The U.S. Court of Appeals for the Sixth Circuit, however, reversed, concluding that *habeas corpus* relief was warranted because Stumpf's plea appeared ill informed; the court believed Stumpf did not understand that he was pleading to intentionally murdering Mrs. Stout. Second, the appellate court found that "Stumpf's due process rights were violated by the state's deliberate action in securing convictions of both Stumpf and Wesley for the same crime, using inconsistent theories."[41]

The Supreme Court reinstated Stumpf's guilty plea, ruling "a plea's validity may not be collaterally attacked merely because the defendant made what turned out, in retrospect, to be a poor deal." The Court also ruled that Stumpf's conviction of aggravated murder was valid, despite the prosecution's conflicting arguments about which of the two men, Wesley or Stumpf, had shot Mrs. Stout, noting "the precise identity of the triggerman was immaterial to Stumpf's conviction for aggravated murder."

The court did rule, however, that the prosecution's conflicting theories may have more directly affected Stumpf's sentence, and remanded the death sentence for further consideration. Stumpf's case, the Supreme Court noted in its ruling, raised the legitimate question of "whether a death sentence could be allowed to stand when the sentence had been imposed in response to a factual claim that the prosecution had necessarily contradicted in subsequently arguing for a death sentence in the case of a codefendant."[42]

When a jury hears a criminal case, the jury must decide if there is enough evidence to prove beyond a reasonable doubt that a crime was committed, and the defendant did it. The court defines *reasonable doubt* for the jury before it begins deliberations. Reasonable doubt is perhaps best defined by what it is not.

It is not without any doubt. If that were the case, few convictions would be possible. Jurors are only required to decide that they are convinced that the defendant did it. Reasonable doubt is somewhere between more likely than not that the defendant did it and absolute certainty that he did. A reasonable doubt is a fair doubt based upon common sense.

Jury Unanimity, Hung Juries, and Reasonable Doubt

In federal criminal trials, the jury must reach a unanimous decision. That is, all twelve jurors must agree that the defendant is guilty beyond a reasonable doubt. But just as state criminal juries don't need to have more than six jurors, neither do state juries have to reach a unanimous verdict. The Supreme Court has upheld a state law that required only nine out of twelve jurors to agree on conviction or acquittal.[43] The fewer members there are on a jury, the more likely it is that the members must make a unanimous decision. In 1979, the Supreme Court ruled that juries of six (the smallest criminal jury allowed) must reach a unanimous decision.[44]

Most states do require a unanimous jury decision. In those states, if all jurors don't agree on the defendant's guilt or acquittal, the jury is said to be a **hung jury.** A defendant can be retried if the jury is unable to convict or acquit him or her. (See Chapter 11 for a discussion of why a retrial isn't double jeopardy.)

Hung jury
A jury that is unable to reach a verdict.

The Role of the Jury and the Role of the Judge

It is important to understand how the responsibilities of the judge differ from the responsibilities of the juror, as their roles are distinctly separate. The judge is charged with the task of interpreting and determining what is law. The jury is given the role of finding the facts in a case.

The Supreme Court ruling in *Apprendi v. New Jersey*[45] illustrates this distinction. Early on December 22, 1994, Charles Apprendi Jr. fired several shots into the home of an African-American family. He pled guilty to second-degree possession of a firearm for an unlawful purpose, which carries a prison term of five to ten years. During the sentencing phase of this case, the prosecution presented evidence to the judge that Apprendi's crime had been racially motivated, including Apprendi's confessing to police shortly after the shooting that he didn't want the family in his neighborhood because of their race. Under New Jersey law, a judge was given the ability to increase the maximum sentence for a crime motivated by racial biases. The judge sentenced Apprendi to twelve years, two more than the maximum for the weapons crime he was convicted of. The Supreme Court overturned the sentence, ruling that "The Constitution requires that any fact that increases the penalty for a crime beyond the prescribed statutory maximum, other than the fact of a prior conviction, must be submitted to a jury and proved beyond a reasonable doubt."

In *Ring v. Arizona*,[46] the Supreme Court affirmed their previous decision in *Apprendi*. Timothy Stuart Ring had been convicted of felony murder, which had taken place in the course of an armed robbery. After being convicted by a jury, the judge held a separate sentencing hearing and reviewed evidence of

Motion for judgment notwithstanding the verdict or motion for judgment of acquittal
A formal request that the judge set aside the verdict based on the weight of evidence or when the verdict clearly contradicts the law.

Motion for a new trial
A formal request for a new trial for a convicted defendant based on new evidence or a procedural flaw in the first trial.

Plea bargain
In a criminal case, an agreement between the prosecuting attorney and the defendant for the defendant to plead guilty in exchange for some benefit or advantage such as a reduction in the kind or number of charges or a reduced sentence. Most criminal cases are settled with some form of a plea bargain.

aggravating circumstances.[47] The judge then increased Ring's possible maximum sentence, giving him the death penalty. Upon appeal, the Supreme Court ruled that allowing a judge to determine aggravating circumstances, which would increase the defendant's possible sentence beyond the maximum, would violate the defendant's Sixth Amendment right to a jury trial. The Court, however, refused to apply the rule in *Ring* retroactively to others on death row sentenced under the procedure the Court found deficient in its earlier decision.[48]

Post-Trial Motions

Just because the jury has voted to convict the defendant, the defense team's job is not over. Posttrial motions serve two purposes: to contest the verdict or to preserve issues for appeal. The most common posttrial motion is for **judgment notwithstanding the verdict** or JNOV. In federal practice it is more common to use a **motion for judgment of acquittal.** Both ask the court to set aside the jury's verdict because the weight of evidence is against the verdict or if the verdict clearly contradicts existing law. These motions are rarely granted.

The defense can also file a **motion for a new trial.** The motion must cite a procedural error that occurred during the trial or present new evidence. Under federal rules, the defense has seven days to move for a new trial absent new evidence or up to three years if it has new evidence. While this motion may not be granted, it preserves the cited procedural error for appeal, even if the error was not objected to during the trial.

CONCEPT **REVIEW AND REINFORCEMENT**

Juries are an old legal tradition going back at least to the ancient Greeks. In England, the jury traces its roots to the time of Henry II and King John. When King John signed the Magna Carta in 1215, he agreed that his subjects would be judged by their peers and the law of the land rather than simply by royal command. The jury grew to be an important buffer between the people and the will of the government.

The colonists took English Common Law with them when they colonized North America. One of these traditions was the right to trial by jury. Every state constitution contains a provision for trial by jury. The U.S. Constitution guarantees the right to trial by jury in federal criminal cases in Article III and in the Sixth Amendment. This protection also extends to the states through the Fourteenth Amendment. In every criminal case where the defendant faces the possibility of imprisonment for more than six months, he or she is guaranteed trial by jury.

The right to request trial by jury rests with the accused. When charged with a crime, a defendant faces several choices. He or she can demand trial by jury, can plead guilty, or can request trial by judge. Few cases are actually tried by juries. Most defendants plead guilty, usually after making a plea bargain. **Plea bargains** are agreements between the government and the defendant that usually involve a reduction in the kind or number of charges or the length of the sentence in exchange for a plea of guilty. One advantage of plea bargaining is finality. A defendant who voluntarily pleads guilty can't appeal his conviction to a higher court. Another advantage of plea bargaining is cost. Jury trials are very expensive, especially if the members of the jury have to be sequestered.

There are two types of juries: grand and petit. A grand jury hears evidence and decides if there is enough evidence to charge someone with a crime. A grand jury may have twenty-three members. A petit jury is a trial jury. It usually has twelve members, but some states allow petit juries to have as few as six members. A petit jury actually hears the criminal case and decides if the defendant is guilty beyond a reasonable doubt.

The group from which a petit jury is selected is known as the jury pool, array, panel, or venire. The members of the pool must be selected in a way that creates a pool that is representative of the community where the defendant allegedly committed the crime. Therefore, methods of calling potential jurors that eliminate segments of the community from the pool are illegal. Many jurisdictions use methods to locate jurors that are race, sex, color, and national origin blind. Some common techniques are to use voter registration records, tax records, license records, and the like in order to create a representative jury pool.

Defendants are guaranteed that the jury pool is representative of the community, but have no constitutional right to a jury that is representative of the community. That is, it's enough that the jury pool is representative, but the actual jury picked doesn't have to mirror the community. Attorneys must be careful, though, in how they exclude potential members of the jury. A prosecutor can't, for example, strike all African-Americans from the jury through the use of his or her peremptory strikes.

Jurors can be removed from the jury pool for hardship, for cause, or through the use of a peremptory strike. Courts sometimes excuse jurors for hardships like illness, financial need, family obligations, and business obligations. Courts will eliminate jurors for cause if there is a reason that the juror can't be impartial—reasons include being acquainted with the parties or victim, having independent knowledge of the case or the evidence, and having prejudged the defendant's guilt or innocence. Peremptory challenges, in contrast, are challenges that the attorneys don't have to provide a specific reason for. Most courts limit the number of peremptory challenges to a handful. Challenges for cause are unlimited in number. A process called *voir dire* is used to select those potential jurors who will serve. During *voir dire,* potential jurors are asked questions by the court or the attorneys that are intended to identify jurors who can't be impartial.

In federal criminal cases, the jury must have twelve members, and the jury must reach a unanimous verdict. In some state courts, the jury may have as few as six members. In addition, state juries don't have to make unanimous decisions unless the jury has only six members.

Defendants are guaranteed an impartial jury. Pretrial publicity can make it difficult to find jurors who haven't prejudged the case. If the publicity has been intense, the court may change the venue, or move the case to another geographic location. Another solution is to bring in a jury pool from another location. This is a change of venire. To prevent jurors from receiving outside information about the case, the court can also sequester the jury away until the case is over.

Juries are obligated to convict a defendant when they conclude that he or she is guilty beyond a reasonable doubt. Beyond a reasonable doubt is a heavy burden, but doesn't require that the jury be absolutely certain that the defendant did it.

KEY **TERMS**

Beyond a reasonable doubt
Challenge for cause
Dicastery
Discovery
Exculpatory evidence
Grand jury
Hung jury
Indictment
Jury
Jury instructions
Jury nullification
Magna Carta
Motion for a new trial
Motion for continuance

Motion for discovery
Motion for judgment notwith-
     standing the verdict or motion
     for judgment of acquittal
Motion for recusal
Motion *in limine*
Motion to change venire
Motion to change venue
Motion to sever
Peremptory challenge
Petit jury
Plea bargain
Pretrial Motions
Probable cause

Quash
Sequester
Sixth Amendment
Trial by battle
Trial by judge
Trial by ordeal
True bill
Venire
Venue
Verdict
Voir dire
Witherspoon qualified

CONCEPT **REVIEW QUESTIONS**

1. Define *jury*.
2. List and explain the provisions in the U.S. Constitution that require trial by jury in criminal cases.
3. What do attorneys do in pretrial discovery?
4. How are the members of a jury pool selected?
5. What is *voir dire*?
6. List some reasons a potential juror can be excused for cause.
7. What is sequestration?
8. Why might someone want a change of venue or venire?
9. List the steps in a trial.
10. What is permissible in opening and closing statements?
11. What does "beyond a reasonable doubt" mean?

CASE **APPLICATION**

Building Your Professional Skills

1. Read the following edited case and answer the questions that follow.

TAYLOR v. LOUISIANA.
APPEAL FROM THE SUPREME COURT OF LOUISIANA.

No. 73-5744.

Decided January 21, 1975.

MR. JUSTICE WHITE delivered the opinion of the Court.

When this case was tried, Art. VII, 41, of the Louisiana Constitution, and Art. 402 of the Louisiana Code of Criminal Procedure provided that a woman should not be selected for jury service unless she had previously filed a written declaration of her desire to be subject to jury service. The constitutionality of these provisions is the issue in this case.

Appellant, Billy J. Taylor, was indicted by the grand jury of St. Tammany Parish, in the Twenty-Second Judicial District of Louisiana, for aggravated kidnapping. On April 12, 1972, appellant moved the trial court to quash the petit jury venire drawn for the special criminal term beginning with his trial the following day. Appellant alleged that women were systematically excluded from the venire and that he would therefore be deprived of what he claimed to be his federal constitutional right to "a fair trial by jury of a representative segment of the community . . . ."

The Twenty-Second Judicial District comprises the parishes of St. Tammany and Washington. The appellee has stipulated that 53% of the persons eligible for jury service in these parishes were female, and that no more than 10% of the persons on the jury wheel in St. Tammany Parish were women. . . . There were no females on the venire.

Appellant's motion to quash the venire was denied that same day. After being tried, convicted, and sentenced to death, appellant sought review in the Supreme Court of Louisiana, where he renewed his claim that the petit jury venire should have been quashed. . . .

Appellant appealed from that decision to this Court. We noted probable jurisdiction to consider whether the Louisiana jury-selection system deprived appellant of his Sixth and Fourteenth Amendment right to an impartial jury trial. We hold that it did and that these Amendments were violated in this case by the operation of La. Const., Art. VII, 41, and La. Code Crim. Proc., Art. 402. In consequence, appellant's conviction must be reversed.

The Louisiana jury-selection system does not disqualify women from jury service, but in operation its conceded systematic impact is that only a very few women, grossly disproportionate to the number of eligible women in the community, are called for jury service. In this case, no women were on the venire from which the petit jury was drawn. The issue we have, therefore, is whether a jury-selection system which operates to exclude from jury service an identifiable class of citizens constituting 53% of eligible jurors in the community comports with the Sixth and Fourteenth Amendments.

The State first insists that Taylor, a male, has no standing to object to the exclusion of women from his jury. But Taylor's claim is that he was constitutionally entitled to a jury drawn from a venire constituting a fair cross section of the community and that the jury that tried him was not such a jury by reason of the exclusion of women. Taylor was not a member of the excluded class; but there is no rule that claims such as Taylor presents may be made only by those defendants who are members of the group excluded from jury service. In *Peters v. Kiff*, the defendant, a white man, challenged his conviction on the ground that Negroes had been systematically excluded from jury service. Six Members of the Court agreed that petitioner was entitled to present the issue and concluded that he had been deprived of his federal rights. Taylor, in the case before us, was similarly entitled to tender and have adjudicated the claim that the exclusion of women from jury service deprived him of the kind of factfinder to which he was constitutionally entitled. . . .

We accept the fair-cross-section requirement as fundamental to the jury trial guaranteed by the Sixth Amendment and are convinced that the requirement has solid foundation. The purpose of a jury is to guard against the exercise of arbitrary power—to make available the commonsense judgment of the community as a hedge against the overzealous or mistaken prosecutor and in preference to the professional or perhaps over-conditioned or biased response of a judge. . . . This prophylactic vehicle is not provided if the jury pool is made up of only special segments of the populace or if large, distinctive groups are excluded from the pool. Community participation in the administration of the criminal law, moreover, is not only consistent with our democratic heritage but is also critical to public confidence in the fairness of the criminal justice system. Restricting jury service to only special groups or excluding identifiable segments playing major roles in the community cannot be squared with the constitutional concept of jury trial. "Trial by jury presupposes a jury drawn from a pool broadly representative of the community as well as impartial in a specific case. . . . [T]he broad representative character of the jury should be maintained, partly as assurance of a diffused impartiality and partly because sharing in the administration of justice is a phase of civic responsibility."

We are also persuaded that the fair-cross-section requirement is violated by the systematic exclusion of women, who in the judicial district involved here amounted to 53% of the citizens eligible for jury service. This conclusion necessarily entails the judgment that women are sufficiently numerous and distinct from men and that if they are systematically eliminated from jury panels, the Sixth Amendment's fair-cross-section requirement cannot be satisfied.

If the fair-cross-section rule is to govern the selection of juries, as we have concluded it must, women cannot be systematically excluded from jury panels from which petit juries are drawn. This conclusion is consistent with the current judgment of the country, now evidenced by legislative or constitutional provisions in every State and at the federal level qualifying women for jury service.

There remains the argument that women as a class serve a distinctive role in society and that jury service would so substantially interfere with that function that the State has ample justification for excluding women from service unless they volunteer, even though the result is that almost all jurors are men. . . .

The States are free to grant exemptions from jury service to individuals in case of special hardship or incapacity and to those engaged in particular occupations the uninterrupted performance of which is critical to the community's welfare. . . . A system excluding all women, however, is a wholly different matter. It is untenable to suggest these days that it would be a special hardship for each and every woman to perform jury service or that society cannot spare any women from their present duties. This may be the case with many, and it may be burdensome to sort out those who should be exempted from those who should serve. But that task is performed in the case of men, and the administrative convenience in dealing with women as a class is insufficient justification for diluting the quality of community judgment represented by the jury in criminal trials. . . .

Accepting as we do, however, the view that the Sixth Amendment affords the defendant in a criminal trial the opportunity to have the jury drawn from venires representative of the community, we think it is no longer tenable to hold that women as a class may be excluded or given automatic exemptions based solely on sex if the consequence is that criminal jury venires are almost totally male. . . .

The judgment of the Louisiana Supreme Court is reversed and the case remanded to that court for further proceedings not inconsistent with this opinion.

So ordered.

QUESTIONS

1. Prepare a brief of the case.
2. What reasons did Louisiana claim justified excluding women from juries? Do these make any sense in today's world? Did they in 1975?

CRITICAL **THINKING EXERCISES**

1. You are charged with a crime in a very small, isolated town. You hire one of the two attorneys in town to defend you (the other one is his brother, the prosecutor). You ask for a jury trial, and they bring in four people to decide your fate. Are these four a legitimate jury?

2. You represent a client accused of theft. A key witness against your client has recently suffered a stroke and cannot speak. The prosecutor wishes to read the witness' deposition, taken before she fell ill, into the record as evidence. What part of the Constitution do you cite when opposing this move and why?

3. What activity discussed in Question 2 occurred during pretrial discovery?

4. Your jury consultant advises you to avoid placing engineers on the jury because they are hard to convince. Should your pattern of striking engineers trigger any response from the judge?

5. Using the same facts as Question 4, but add that your defendant is a Pakistani and many of the engineers you struck were of Indian ancestry. Now could the judge have a problem with your peremptory challenges?

6. In which of the following situations could a juror be dismissed for cause:
   a. The juror had had business dealings with the defendant in the past.
   b. The juror's cousin's marriage to the defendant's uncle ended in a messy divorce.
   c. The juror is a close friend of the judge.
   d. The juror had edited a criminal law textbook, has a brother-in-law who is an attorney, had a state policeman as the best man at his wedding, is married to a former prosecutor, and

is in a case where the credibility of the police is a central issue.[49]

7. You are a judge in a murder case. The defendant was convicted once, but was awarded a new trial based on a technicality. When the murder occurred, six years ago, the case received quite a bit of publicity. The retrial has only warranted a few small articles in the local newspaper. You must make the choice of whether or not to sequester the jury. What factors would you weigh in making your decision?

8. Given the same facts as Question 7, you are now empanelling a jury. You quickly exhaust the jury pool set aside for this month's trial because they all have heard about the trial and formed opinions. It doesn't appear you will be able to empanel a jury using local people. What options are open to you?

9. You are a judge in a case where the defendant is an illegal immigrant accused of killing a white person in a largely white community. Which of the following statements would cause you to declare a mistrial:

   a. In the opening statement, the prosecutor says the evidence will show the defendant was motivated by racial animus.

   b. In the closing statement, the prosecutor says that convicting this defendant will send a message to all illegal immigrants considering coming to this community.

   c. In the closing statement, the defense attorney says that despite the evidence against the defendant, he is really just a hardworking immigrant like all of our ancestors who should be acquitted in order to compensate for the past wrongs committed against immigrants.

10. Is it possible to reach a verdict beyond a reasonable doubt based only on circumstantial evidence?

PORTFOLIO **BUILDING**

1. As you have done in previous exercises, locate a list of pending cases before the U.S. Supreme Court and summarize the ones that deal with jury selection for your portfolio. Be sure to include the question that the Supreme Court said it would consider and the decision below.

2. Pick one of the pending cases, locate the underlying opinion, and prepare a brief for your portfolio. Then predict the Supreme Court's decision based on what you read.

FOR FURTHER READING

1. Grisham, J. (1996). *The Runaway Jury.* Legal thriller recounting what happens when a man with a vendetta wants to be on a jury to hear a landmark tobacco liability case.

FOR FURTHER VIEWING

1. *To Kill a Mockingbird* (1962). Adaptation of the novel by Harper Lee. A small-town lawyer in the South defends a black man accused of raping a white woman. Starring Gregory Peck.

2. *My Cousin Vinny* (1992). New York lawyer goes to Wahzoo, Alabama, to defend his cousin and his friend on murder charges. Starring Marisa Tomei, Joe Pesci.

3. *Inherit the Wind* (1960). Midwestern school teacher is put on trial for teaching Darwin's theory of evolution. Starring Gene Kelly, Dick York, Spencer Tracey.

4. *Class Action* (1991). Father and daughter, both lawyers, serve on opposite sides of a case. Starring Gene Hackman.

5. *Judgement at Nuremberg* (1961). Four German judges are put on trial for compromising their integrity for the Nazis. Starring Judy Garland, Montgomery Clift, Marlene Dietrich, Burt Lancaster, Spencer Tracey, and Maximilian Schell.

6. *The Verdict* (1982). A drunkard attorney sobers up long enough to seek justice for comatose victim of a hospital's carelessness. Starring Paul Newman.

7. *Twelve Angry Men* (1957). A courtroom drama in which one jury member holds out against the rest of the jury's desire for a quick conviction. Starring Henry Fonda and Jack Klugman. If you see no other film on the jury system, see this one.

8. *The Runaway Jury* (2003). John Cusack stars in this adaptation of the Grisham book. The movie version changes the case from one about tobacco to one about guns.

Chapter **fourteen**

CONSTITUTIONAL RIGHTS POSTCONVICTION

Thou shalt give life for life, eye for eye, tooth for tooth, hand for hand, foot for foot, burning for burning, wound for wound.

The Bible, King James Version, Exodus 21:23–25

Excessive bail shall not be required nor excessive fines imposed, nor cruel and unusual punishments inflicted.

U.S. Constitution, Eighth Amendment (1791)

Introduction and Historical Background

Throughout history cultures have experimented with various forms of punishment for those who fail to conform to society's expectations. Law breakers have been punished in many ways. In ancient Rome condemned prisoners did battle with wild beasts in arenas while the public watched from the stands.[1]

Punishment in England was often equally harsh and public. During the seventeenth through the early nineteenth century criminals in England were frequently punished harshly, sometimes for what are today considered minor offenses. Dozens of prisoners were hung at a time for offenses ranging from murder to horse thievery and house breaking. In light of the penal practices of the day, it was little wonder that the criminal law was popularly known as the **Bloody Code.**[2]

Executions were often great public spectacles. Such a scene was recorded by Samuel Pepys (1633–1703), who served as the English secretary of the Admiralty. He kept a diary covering his life from 1660 through 1669. His entry for October 13, 1660, reads:

> . . . I went out to Charing Cross to see Maj.-Gen. Harrison hanged, drawn and quartered—which was done there—he looked as cheerful as any man could in that condition. He was

CHAPTER OBJECTIVES

After studying this chapter, you should be able to:

- Explain the history of the Eighth Amendment to the U.S. Constitution
- List the types of criminal punishment
- List and explain the two requirements that must be satisfied before a punishment is "cruel and unusual"
- Explain why capital punishment is not unconstitutional as "cruel and unusual" punishment
- Explain what procedural protection is required before the death penalty can be carried out
- Define aggravating and mitigating circumstances
- List the classifications of persons who may be executed
- List the crimes that are punishable by death
- Explain the Supreme Court's position on life in prison for repeat offenders
- Know the steps in the appeals process
- List and describe two current trends in punishment

Bloody Code
Popular name for England's criminal laws because of their harshness and the long list of crimes classified as capital offenses.

Transportation
The practice of exiling or expelling a prisoner from his homeland as punishment.

Cruel and unusual punishment
Punishment which violates the Eighth Amendment and which violates evolving standards of decency.

Magna Carta
Document signed by King John of England in 1215 at Runnymede in which he was compelled to grant noblemen limited civil and political liberties.

presently cast down and his head and his heart shown to the people, at which there was great shouts of joy.[3]

Prisons were reserved for very minor offenses, and stays there were short.

An alternative to hanging or a short prison stay was the practice of "transportation."[4] **Transportation** was a form of banishment or exile. Criminals were shipped to the American colonies, often for life. After the American Revolution, the colonies were no longer a practical dumping ground for prisoners so they were sent elsewhere, most notably Australia. Eventually shipping prisoners "down under" became impractical and England's temporary solution was to turn abandoned ships into floating prisons moored on the Thames.[5] It is against this background that we examine the meaning and application of the Constitution's prohibition against **"cruel and unusual" punishment.**

The Eighth Amendment's language was taken from a provision of the Virginia Declaration of Rights of 1776. And Virginia borrowed the provision from the English Bill of Rights of 1689, which was passed by Parliament upon the ascent of William and Mary. The English Bill of Rights was an attempt to curb the royal misuse of punishment in criminal cases during the reign of King James II. It provided that "excessive Baile ought not be required nor excessive Fines imposed nor cruel and unusual Punishments inflicted."[6] The law was based on an earlier document, the **Magna Carta** *of 1215*, in which the noblemen forced King John to agree that "amercements" would not be excessive.[7]

A tavern named 'The Hung Drawn and Quartered' now stands where General Harrison met his end.

The Eighth Amendment was not a part of the original Constitution as ratified in 1789. Rather, it is a part of the Bill of Rights, added in response to concerns that the new Constitution provided few protections for accused criminals. The Bill of Rights was added to the Constitution in 1791.

As we explore the meaning of "cruel and unusual punishment" you may want to keep three questions in mind. They are:

1. What types of penalties are considered "punishments" within the meaning of the Eighth Amendment?
2. What punishments are outlawed because they are "cruel and unusual"?
3. Who is protected from "cruel and unusual punishment"?

Sentencing

In the last chapter, we discussed the trial. If the defendant is convicted, the next step is to determine the appropriate punishment for the crime. From a societal standpoint, sentences protect society by deterring criminal behavior, removing dangerous people from society, and punishing them for their crimes. Society also benefits if the individual is rehabilitated as a result of punishment and can be returned to a productive role in society. To balance all of these factors, courts use the concept of **proportionality**, a term Supreme Court decisions[8] have used to describe how courts make the punishment fit the crime.

Most commonly, criminals are sentenced to **incarceration** where the convicted individual is confined to a county jail or state or federal penitentiary. Incarceration may be imposed in several different ways. For example, a person with no prior criminal record may receive a **suspended sentence** where the individual does not have to report to prison, but is placed on **probation.** Probation is a form of supervised release where the convict is required to report to a probation officer periodically. Any breach of the law while on probation will result in its revocation and the convicts return to prison.

When the court imposes sentence, it must look at all the crimes for which the defendant was convicted to determine the appropriate sentence. If the defendant has been convicted of multiple crimes, the court must determine whether the sentences for these crimes will be served **consecutively**—one after the other, or **concurrently**—at the same time. The difference is important. Someone convicted of two murders with twenty-year sentences each would have a sentence of twenty years if they were served concurrently and forty is served consecutively. The person serving the concurrent sentences would also be eligible for parole sooner.

For many years, American courts used **indeterminate sentencing** where courts had great flexibility in either keeping or releasing prisoners based on their rehabilitation. This approach led to very different sentences for people convicted of the same crime. As a result courts began to see indeterminate sentencing as leading to disproportionately punitive sentences.

To remedy the situation, many states and the federal judiciary went to **indefinite sentencing** where judges set a maximum and minimum amount of time served where the prisoner can earn early release through good behavior once the minimum sentence is served.

Proportionality
The concept courts use when evaluating whether a punishment fits the crime.

Incarceration
Imprisonment or being under a prison sentence.

Suspended sentence
The situation where a judge elects to give a convicted person probation instead of actual imprisonment.

Probation
A period where a convict is under court supervision in lieu of a prison sentence.

Consecutive sentences
Where one person is sentenced for more than one crime and the sentences are to be served one after the other.

Concurrent sentences
Where one person is sentenced for more than one crime and the sentences are served at the same time.

Indeterminate sentencing
The sentencing scheme where judges have the most flexibility in sentencing.

Indefinite sentencing
The sentencing scheme using a sentencing range where the prisoner can earn release after serving the minimum sentence by meeting certain rehabilitation goals.

Definite or determinate sentences
Fixed term sentences selected from a range determined by statute or guidelines where there is no chance of parole.

Mandatory minimum sentences
The shortest possible sentence for a given crime under an indeterminate sentencing scheme.

Enhanced sentences
Sentences lengthened by aggravating factors such as for hate crimes or the use of a firearm in commission of a crime.

Fines
Monetary penalties paid to the state as punishment for crime.

Restitution
Money paid to crime victims to help make them whole.

Not all prison sentences can be shortened through good behavior. **Definite or determinate sentences** are fixed term sentences chosen from the sentencing range, but the prisoner has no chance of parole. As discussed earlier, some statutes require prisoners to serve **mandatory minimum sentences.** For example, many states have mandatory minimum sentences for crimes committed with firearms. Certain aggravating factors can lead to **enhanced sentences.** For example, if the jury determines a crime was a hate crime, the sentence can be lengthened or enhanced.

So who actually imposes prison sentences? In most states and the federal system, judges determine the sentences and impose them. However, in the case of the death penalty many states require the jury to condemn the prisoner. In Arizona, Indiana, Kentucky, and West Virginia juries make sentencing recommendations to the judge. Juries actually set the sentences in Arkansas, Missouri, Oklahoma, Texas, and Virginia.

In addition to prison time, convicted criminals may be subject to **fines** or be forced to make **restitution** to crime victims. Also, criminals may face forfeiture of property obtained through illegal activities. For example, cars used in the commission of crimes are often subject to forfeiture. In one Pennsylvania case, a narcotics dealer attempted to launder drug money by buying investment properties. When arrested, U.S. Marshalls seized the properties as well.[9]

Cruel and Unusual Punishments

We now turn to determining what criminal punishments are cruel and unusual. The Supreme Court has held that the Eighth Amendment outlaws a punishment as cruel and unusual if the punishment itself involves unnecessary infliction of pain or if the punishment is grossly disproportionate to the nature or severity of the crime. To be excluded, a punishment must have been considered cruel and

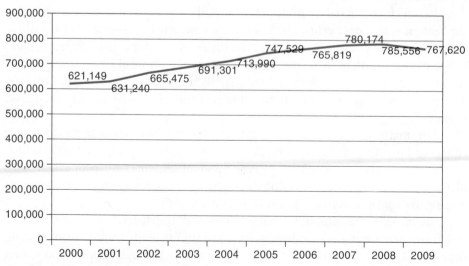

Number of Inmates in Local Jails.
Source: Bureau of Justice Statistics.

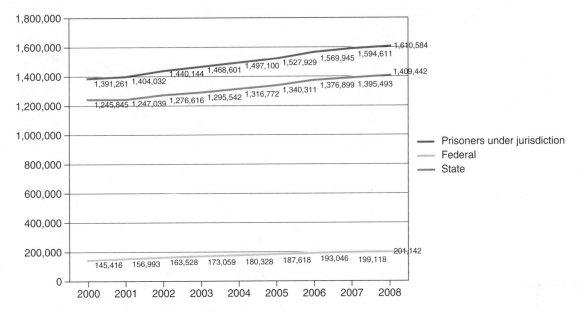

Prisoners Under State and Federal Jurisdiction.
Source: Bureau of Justice Statistics.

unusual at the time the Bill of Rights was adopted (1791)[10] or be contrary to the "evolving standards of decency that mark the progress of a maturing society."[11]

We will first consider capital punishment; second, life imprisonment; third, prison conditions; and finally, chemical castration and sex offender registration.

The Death Penalty

Capital punishment is not **per se** cruel and unusual punishment. The Constitution implicitly assumes executions are an allowable punishment. It provides that "No person shall be held to answer for a capital or otherwise infamous crime unless on a presentment or indictment of a Grand Jury. . . ."[12] Therefore, we can assume that the founding fathers accepted capital punishment.

Thirty-seven states and the federal government currently authorize the death penalty, while thirteen states plus the District of Columbia do not.[13] Generally, the death penalty only applies to cases where the defendant deliberately killed another human being,[14] or where the defendant was a major participant in a felony murder.[15] In addition, federal law authorized death for certain federal offenses such as espionage and treason. At the end of 2008, the latest year for which national figures are available, there were 3,207 individuals on Death Row. In 2009, fifty-two inmates were executed. Texas executed eighteen of them, the next closest state was Virginia with four.[16]

Death is an accepted and acceptable sanction under the Constitution. It is the way that the death penalty is carried out that is subject to scrutiny under the Eighth Amendment. As the Supreme Court wrote in *Louisiana ex rel. Francis v. Resweber,*

Per se
Latin; by itself, in and of itself.

Death is . . . different. Death is irremedial. Death is unknowable; it goes beyond this world. It is a legislative decision to do something, and we know not what we do.

Anthony Amsterdam, oral argument before the U.S. Supreme Court in *Gregg v. Georgia* (March 30, 1976)

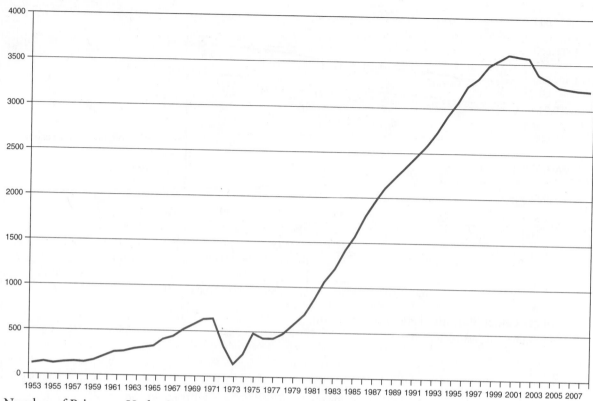

Number of Prisoners Under Sentence of Death.
Source: Bureau of Labor Statistics.

The cruelty against which the Constitution protects a convicted man is cruelty in the method of punishment, not the necessary suffering involved in any method employed to extinguish life humanely.[17]

We will consider the procedural safeguards required before an execution can take place and what methods can be used to "extinguish life humanely."

Procedural Safeguards Required by the Eighth Amendment

In recent years, the Court has focused on the procedures used by states to arrive at death as the sanction for criminal behavior rather than on the continued use of the death penalty by the criminal justice system. This is despite the fact that Amnesty International, the Roman Catholic Church, and various other human rights groups condemn death as a sanction and many modern nations have abolished it altogether.[18] For example, the European Union makes it a condition of membership that nations abolish the death penalty.

The Supreme Court has never ruled that the death penalty is always unconstitutional. The Court will, however, invalidate state statutes that do not provide enough procedural safeguards for defendants facing death. For example, in the 1972 case of *Furman v. Georgia*,[19] the Supreme Court effectively halted the death penalty, temporarily. The Court ruled that Georgia's statute was so procedurally flawed that the penalty was arbitrarily and capriciously imposed. As a practical matter, no executions were carried out between 1972 and 1976, when the Supreme Court again considered the issue.

As a result of the Supreme Court's decision in *Furman,* many states revamped their death penalty laws. In 1976 the Supreme Court again considered the death penalty, this time reviewing new state statutes designed to overcome the Court's earlier objections. The Court concluded in *Gregg v. Georgia*[20] that execution remains a constitutionally sanctioned punishment, given the existence of certain procedural safeguards. These can include:

1. A bifurcated trial, in which the jury first decides whether the defendant is guilty, and a sentencing stage, at which the jury determines punishment after hearing evidence of **aggravating** or **mitigating circumstances.** The condemned prisoner must be given an opportunity to present mitigating factors in his defense, no matter how heinous his crime. The sentence of death cannot be automatic.[21]

2. An automatic appeal to the state supreme court of all sentences of death, at least if an appeal is requested by the condemned prisoner.

The Supreme Court has considered what information jurors are entitled to receive when weighing whether a defendant should be put to death. In *Kelly v. South Carolina,* 534 U.S. 246 (2002), the Court ruled that in the penalty phase of a death penalty case where the choice is between life in prison with no possibility of

Aggravating circumstance
Act or conduct that increases the seriousness of an act, often resulting in a harsher punishment.

Mitigating circumstance
Act or conduct that lessens or reduces the punishment for a crime, such as lack of a criminal record, state of mind, or youth.

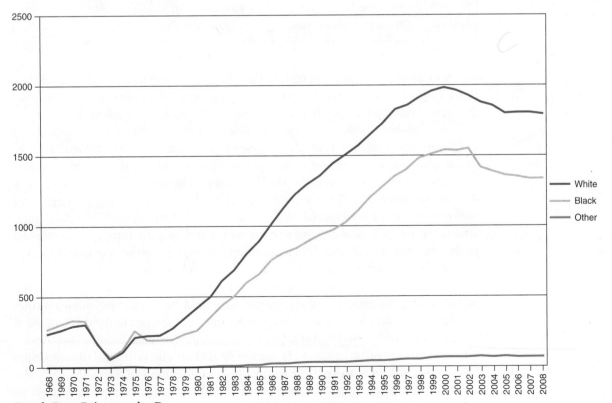

Death Row Prisoners by Race.
Source: Bureau of Justice Statistics.

Model Death Penalty
The death penalty implementation plan as envisioned in the Model Penal Code.

YOU MAKE THE CALL

American Law Institute Pronounces Death Penalty Unworkable

When the Supreme Court decided *Gregg v. Georgia*, it was largely endorsing the **Model Death Penalty** from the Model Penal Code. The Model Penal Code was created by the American Law Institute in the early 1960s to try to create uniform penal codes among the states. The Model Death Penalty was the crown jewel of the document. In many years prior to the *Furman* decision, more blacks sat on death row than whites despite the fact that they were less than 10 percent of the population at the time. (See chart: Death Row Prisoners by Race.)

The Model Death Penalty called for death only in cases of murder or felony murder and that those with diminished capacity should not be executed. Those tenets found their way into Supreme Court decisions over the decades.

Despite these successes, racial disparities lessened, but continued. DNA evidence freed many on death row who had been convicted and had their convictions upheld by Appeals Courts. The American Law Institute commissioned a study of the death penalty and ultimately arrived at the conclusion that the death penalty "cannot balance the need for consistency in sentencing with the need for individualized determinations."[22] Further, the Institute concluded there were insufficient safeguards to keep an innocent person from being executed. Many death row inmates lack attorneys and the cost of housing a death row inmate is higher than housing other types of inmates. Considering that the lack of representation delays appeals, a significant number of death row inmates die of old age or other ailments before the state ever executes them. Given all these factors, the Institute no longer advocates the death penalty. Should the United States keep its death penalty? You Make the Call.

parole or death, the jury must be told that life in prison means just that. That way, those concerned about recidivism won't feel compelled to choose death because they fear the defendant will be freed at some point, possibly to kill again.

In October 2006, the Supreme Court ruled in *Abdul-Kabir (fka Cole) v. Quarterman* that juries weighing a death sentence must be allowed "to give meaningful consideration and effect to all mitigating evidence that might provide a basis for refusing to impose the death penalty." The decision struck down jury instructions given by the Fifth Circuit Court to evaluate mitigating circumstances only on the basis of two "special issues" as sanctioned by the state of Texas for capital sentencing: one, the deliberateness of the crime, and two, the future dangerousness of the criminal. Abdul-Kabir's defense offered evidence that he was neurologically damaged as a result of childhood abuse and abandonment. The Supreme Court noted that such evidence was "double-edged" in that it was intended to reduce the defendant's culpability, but also implied he would be dangerous in the future. By allowing the jury to consider that evidence only as it applied to the deliberateness of the crime and Abdul-Kabir's future dangerousness, and limiting the jurors' responses to "yes or no" answers to each of those two questions, the Circuit Court had not allowed them to give full, meaningful consideration to the evidence.[23] The Court relied on *Penry v. Lynaugh*, which required that juries be instructed to consider a defendant's mitigating evidence and give a reasoned, moral response to that evidence in recommending a death sentence.[24]

HISTORICAL HIGHLIGHT

Governor Ryan Has Death Penalty Doubts

Following the release of a thirteenth exonerated death row inmate since the reinstatement of the death penalty in 1977, Illinois governor George Ryan declared a statewide moratorium on executions on January 31, 2002. Ryan appointed a commission to study Illinois's death penalty administration. In April 2002, the Commission on Capital Punishment presented a report suggesting over eighty changes that Illinois could implement to make their death penalty system less likely to convict and execute innocent suspects. These suggestions included establishing a panel to review prosecutorial decisions to seek the death penalty before the case goes to trial, having the police videotape all interrogations of homicide suspects rather than solely the confession, and giving judges the ability to reverse a jury's death sentence if the verdict seems improper. Best-selling author Scott Turow was a member of the commission and the work he did served as a catalyst for his latest legal thriller, *Reversible Errors*. He has also written a short book, *Ultimate Punishment: A Lawyer's Reflections on Dealing with the Death Penalty*.

In a similar situation, Maryland's release of their hundredth innocent death row inmate prompted Governor Paris N. Glendening to declare a moratorium and order a study done on racial bias in the Maryland capital punishment administration. As death penalty activists see that the Supreme Court is susceptible to arguments that evolving community standards may require it to shift its stand on capital punishment, calls for moratoriums are gaining ground.

Since the Supreme Court's decision in *Gregg* on July 2, 1976, 1,188 executions have been carried out.[25] Ten of the executed prisoners were women. The annual number rose sharply, from one in 1977 to a high of ninety-eight in 1999, and then leveled off. In 2009, fifty-two death sentences were carried out.

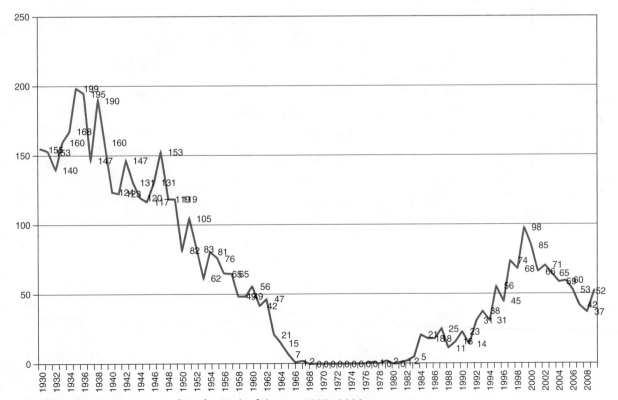

Number of Persons Executed in the United States, 1930–2009.

Appropriate Methods of Death

Generally, the sanction of death may be imposed in any way that is not unnecessarily cruel. The Supreme Court held in *In re Kimmler*[26] that "[p]unishments are cruel when they involve torture or a lingering death." Thus, firing squads are permissible,[27] as are electrocutions, lethal gas, and lethal injections. In one case the Supreme Court ruled that it was not cruel and unusual punishment to attempt to execute the same person twice. Willie Francis was convicted of murder and sentenced to death by electrocution in September 1945. On May 3, 1946, Francis was placed in the electric chair. The executioner threw the switch, but the apparatus failed. Francis was returned to his cell and a new death warrant was signed, setting his execution for May 9, 1946. He appealed this second attempt to kill him, alleging that two attempts at electrocution was cruel and unusual punishment. The Supreme Court disagreed, writing that "[t]he fact that an unforeseeable accident prevented the prompt consummation of the sentence cannot, it seems to us, add an element of cruelty to a subsequent execution."[28]

Equipment malfunctions still occasionally happen. For example, on March 25, 1997, during the successful execution of convicted killer Pedro Medina in Florida, witnesses reported that a six-inch flame erupted from the head of the prisoner, filling the execution chamber with smoke and the smell of burning flesh.[29] The Florida state attorney general commented that "[p]eople who wish to commit murder, they better not do it in the state of Florida because we may have a problem with our electric chair."[30]

The table below shows which execution methods the various states use.

Lethal Injection	Electrocution	Lethal Gas	Hanging	Firing Squad
Alabama[a]	Alabama[a]	Arizona[a,b]	Delaware[a,c]	Idaho[a]
Arizona[a,b]	Arkansas[a,d]	California[a]	New Hampshire[a,e]	Oklahoma[a,f]
Arkansas[a,d]	Florida[a]	Missouri[a]	Washington[a]	Utah[g]
California[a]	Illinois[a,h]	Wyoming[i]		
Colorado	Kentucky[a,j]			
Connecticut	Oklahoma[a,f]			
Delaware[a,c]	Tennessee[a,k]			
Florida[a]	Virginia[a]			
Georgia				
Idaho[a]				
Illinois[a]				
Indiana				
Kansas				
Kentucky[a,j]				
Louisiana				
Maryland				
Mississippi				

Lethal Injection	Electrocution	Lethal Gas	Hanging	Firing Squad
Missouri[a]				
Montana				
Nevada				
New Hampshire[a]				
New Mexico				
New York				
North Carolina				
Ohio				
Oklahoma[a,f]				
Oregon				
Pennsylvania				
South Carolina[a]				
South Dakota				
Tennessee[a,k]				
Texas				
Utah[a]				
Virginia[a]				
Washington[a]				
Wyoming[a]				

Note: The method of execution of Federal prisoners is lethal injection, pursuant to 28 CFR, Part 26. For offenses under the Violent Crime Control and Law Enforcement Act of 1994, the execution method is that of the State in which the conviction took place (18 U.S.C. 3596). In February 2008, the Nebraska Supreme Court ruled that electrocution violated the state's constitution. As of December 31, 2008, Nebraska had no authorized method of execution.

[a]Authorizes two methods of execution.

[b]Authorizes lethal injection for persons sentenced after November 15, 1992; inmates sentenced before that date may select lethal injection or gas.

[c]Authorizes lethal injection for those whose capital offense occurred on or after June 13, 1986; those who committed the offense before that date may select lethal injection or hanging.

[d]Authorizes lethal injection for those whose offense occurred on or after July 4, 1983; inmates whose offense occurred before that date may select lethal injection or electrocution.

[e]Authorizes hanging only if lethal injection cannot be given.

[f]Authorizes electrocution if lethal injection is held to be unconstitutional, and firing squad if both lethal injection and electrocution are held to be unconstitutional.

[g]Authorizes firing squad if lethal injection is held unconstitutional. Inmates who selected execution by firing squad prior to May 3, 2004, may still be entitled to execution by that method.

[h]Authorizes electrocution only if lethal injection is held illegal or unconstitutional.

[i]Authorizes lethal gas if lethal injection is held to be unconstitutional.

[j]Authorizes lethal injection for persons sentenced on or after March 31, 1998; inmates sentenced before that date may select lethal injection or electrocution.

[k]Authorizes lethal injection for those whose capital offense occurred after December 31, 1998; those who committed the offense before that date may select electrocution by written waiver.

Source: Bureau of Justice Statistics, *Capital Punishment 2008—Statistical Tables.*

YOU MAKE THE CALL

Is Lethal Injection Painless?

On January 26, 2006, at 6:00 P.M., Clarence Hill, 48, convicted of the 1982 murder of a Pensacola police officer, was strapped to a gurney, a needle in his arm, when the Supreme Court stayed his execution. While the Court refused to hear Hill's claim that lethal injection was cruel and unusual, it agreed to hear a narrower claim, which had been rejected by a federal appeals court in Atlanta, that the lethal injection formula would cause him excessive pain. That evening, the Court issued stays of execution for Hill plus two other inmates.

The next day the Court's unanimity broke down. It allowed an Indiana execution, challenged on similar grounds, to proceed, and executions by lethal injection continued, despite pleas identical to Hill's from many other death row inmates. But Hill's stay signaled the Supreme Court's willingness to consider the constitutionality at least of the lethal injection formula.

Lethal injection uses a three-drug protocol infused via intravenous lines. The first drug is sodium thiopental, an anesthetic which puts the inmate to sleep. Second, pavulon or pancuronium bromide is administered to paralyze the inmate and stop his breathing. Finally, potassium chloride is administered to stop the heart.

Though touted as painless, lethal injection can be problematic partly because medical ethics prevent doctors from administering the drugs. Instead, technicians or orderlies perform the injections, often with mixed results. In June 1997, Michael Eugene Elkins waited for an hour while executioners tried to find a suitable vein. He asked, "Should I lean my head down a little bit?" as they probed for a vein. They finally found one in Elkin's neck. In 1998, Texas inmate Joseph Cannon made his final statement, and the execution began. One of Cannon's veins collapsed, and the needle popped out. Cannon lay back, closed his eyes, and said, "It's come undone." Officials pulled back the curtain, worked on him for fifteen minutes, then reopened it. A weeping Cannon made his second final statement and the execution resumed.

Many journalists come to an execution by lethal injection expecting to see a quick and painless death, and are mortified by five- to ten-minute death throes. Florida prisoner Angel Diaz, executed in December 2006, continued to move after the first injection was administered. A second dose was administered, which took thirty-four minutes to kill him, causing Florida Governor Jeb Bush to call for an investigation into the method. Texas inmate Stephen McCoy had such a violent reaction to the drugs, including heaving chest, gasping, and choking, that a male witness fainted, knocking over another witness.[31]

Is lethal injection cruel and unusual? You make the call!

Persons whom may be Executed

Although death itself may not be cruel and unusual punishment, it has been argued that it may be cruel and unusual to impose death on particular classes of individuals. These include the mentally ill, the mentally retarded, and those who were minors at the time of the commission of the offense for which death is the sentence.

Mentally Ill and Mentally Retarded

In *Ford v. Wainwright*, the Supreme Court has ruled that a state may not execute a prisoner who is mentally incompetent at the time of execution.[32] The Court concluded that the execution of an individual who is insane violates the Eighth Amendment because the defendant is either unaware of his impending execution or the reason for it. The defendant, Alvin Bernard Ford, did not believe he would be executed because he had delusions that he owned the prison and could control the governor through "mind waves." The Supreme Court wrote: " . . . the Eighth Amendment prohibits a State from carrying out a sentence of death upon a prisoner who is insane. Whether its aim is to protect the condemned from fear and pain without comfort of understanding, or to protect the dignity of society itself from the barbarity of exacting mindless vengeance, the restriction finds enforcement in the Eighth Amendment."[33]

However, prison officials can force an otherwise mentally incompetent individual to receive medication to restore his competence even if the prisoner objects.[34] The question the Supreme Court has not addressed is whether a prisoner facing execution can be forced to take medication to restore his competence long enough to be executed. The Court refused to hear *Perry v. Louisiana,* in which the State of Louisiana argued that a defendant could be forced to receive medication to restore his mental state to normal long enough to carry out the sentence of death.[35] The Supreme Court of Louisiana later rejected that notion and concluded it was a clear violation of the Constitution to force someone to take drugs long enough to be executed.[36]

On February 20, 2002, the Georgia parole board stayed the execution of a killer who was allegedly so psychotic he believed that actress Sigourney Weaver was God. The prisoner, Alexander Williams, claimed that he had been forcibly medicated to make him eligible for execution. His attorneys had appealed to the Supreme Court, but his sentence was commuted to life in prison without the possibility of parole by the state's parole board before the Supreme Court could make any decisions.[37]

The following year, the Court did hear a case involving a man charged with less serious crimes who did not want to be medicated. The state wanted to medicate him so that he could become competent to stand trial. In a 6–3 decision, the Court ruled that the state cannot medicate a prisoner solely to stand trial, but can do so "if the treatment is medically appropriate, is substantially unlikely to have side effects that may undermine the trial's fairness, and, taking account of less intrusive alternatives, is necessary significantly to further important governmental trial-related interests." In this case, the government had not met its burden of showing that the medication would not interfere with the defendant's ability to prepare his defense.[38]

In October 2003, the Supreme Court refused, without comment, to hear the case of Charles Singleton, a schizophrenic man sentenced to death for murder. At age nineteen, Singleton had stabbed a grocery store owner during an attempted robbery in Hamburg, Arkansas. In 1997, while on death row, Singleton was diagnosed with paranoid schizophrenia. A prison review panel ordered Singleton to take antipsychotic drugs. The medication reduced Singleton's psychotic symptoms and Arkansas proceeded with plans to execute him.

Singleton's attorney filed a lawsuit arguing the state could not force his client to take medication to restore his competency in order to execute him. In October 2001, a panel of the Eighth U.S. Circuit Court of Appeals ruled that Singleton should be sentenced to life in prison without possibility of parole, but in 2004, a sharply divided full Eighth Circuit Court lifted the stay of execution. The court noted that by this time

Singleton was taking the antipsychotic medications voluntarily, and since the state had an interest in having sane inmates, the side effect of sanity should not affect Singleton's sentence. Singleton was executed by lethal injection on January 6, 2004.[39]

The Supreme Court refused to weigh in on the issue in the case of Steven Staley, a Texas death row in mate who murdered a Forth Worth restaurant manager during an attempted holdup. Staley refuses to regularly take his antipsychotic medication, claiming his doctors are trying to poison him. When off his medication, he is ostensibly delusional and incoherent. District Judge Wayne Salvant ordered that Staley be forcibly medicated to render him competent for execution. Assistant Tarrant County District Attorney Charles Mallin said, "You should not be able to circumvent the judgment of a jury by not taking your medication, and thus escape the consequences of your actions." On Staley's appeal to the Supreme Court, Mallin said, "There is no Texas law, and the Supreme Court of the United States has never decided this issue. We're out on the cutting edge here. We have nothing to lose."[40] With the Supreme Court's refusal to hear the case, the issue is still in limbo; Staley is still on death row.[41]

At one time, many states allowed the execution of the mentally retarded. Some states, including Colorado, Indiana, Kansas, and New York, prohibited the execution of defendants shown to be mentally retarded.[42] The Supreme Court had ruled in *Penry v. Lynaugh* that the Eighth Amendment did not bar a retarded individual from death, but required that he be treated like any other defendant. He could only attempt to use his retardation as mitigating evidence.[43]

Interestingly, the same case resurfaced in the Supreme Court in 2001. The defendant, John Paul Penry, whose I.Q. has been tested at fifty-six, was retried and again convicted. This time, he argued that the jury that decided whether he would live or die wasn't given enough information about his disability. The Supreme Court agreed, and reversed his sentence. His death sentence was overturned a third time since, and he still awaits resentencing. The case is *Penry v. Johnson,* 532 U.S. 782 (2001).

In 2002, the Supreme Court ruled in *Atkins v. Virginia* that executing the mentally retarded does violate the prohibition against cruel and unusual punishment. The Court found that contemporary standards of what is appropriate have changed and that the mentally retarded, with limited ability to understand the consequences of the punishment they face, should not be subjected to execution.

But *Atkins* doesn't necessarily protect mentally retarded defendants from the actions of their attorneys. A retarded Alabama man, Holly Wood (yes, that's his real name), was convicted of brutally murdering his girlfriend. For reasons unknown, his attorneys elected not to raise the issue of his mental disability. He eventually found new attorneys who raised an incompetent counsel argument on appeal. The case went all the way to the U.S. Supreme Court where a 7–2 decision said that "it is not unreasonable to conclude that . . . counsel made a strategic decision not to present to the jury" evidence of his mental deficiencies. In their dissent, Justices Stevens and Kennedy stated they could only attribute the attorney's actions to "inattention and neglect."[44]

HISTORICAL HIGHLIGHT

Executing the Mentally Retarded—Cruel or Unusual?

Terry Washington had organic brain damage. He had the mind of a six-year-old, but managed to work in a restaurant as a dishwasher. This was no easy task, for his condition would sometimes cause him to have violent seizures and foam at the mouth. Unfortunately, one night after an argument with his supervisor, Terry murdered him.

Little doubt exists that Terry Washington killed the man. The trial was an open-and-shut case, and the jury voted to give Washington the death penalty.

However, the jurors were never told that Washington was severely retarded.

Washington invoked his Fifth Amendment right not to testify during the trial. His attorneys never raised the issue, either, during the determination of guilt phase of the trial or the sentencing phase. On May 6, 1998, Washington became one of the approximately twenty-five mentally retarded people to be executed since the death penalty was reinstated in 1976.

The Supreme Court had ruled previously that the execution of mentally retarded convicts was not cruel and unusual punishment per se. But the decision left the door open when it said "a national consensus against execution of the mentally retarded may some-day emerge reflecting the evolving standards of decency that mark the progress of a maturing society."[45]

The landscape of the death penalty has changed dramatically since then with the Supreme Court's ruling that execution of the mentally retarded violates the Eighth Amendment protection against cruel and unusual punishment. Daryl Atkins, who was convicted of murder and sentenced to death, had an IQ estimated at fifty-nine. He appealed his death sentence. The Supreme Court found that a national consensus against execution of the mentally retarded had finally emerged based upon a majority of states having laws prohibiting such executions. The Court relied on information about changes to some state laws since it last reviewed a similar case. Using that information, the Court concluded that the nation's mood had changed and what was acceptable just a few years earlier was no longer acceptable.[46]

More recently, the Court rejected a Texas scheme that made low intelligence an aggravating rather than a mitigating factor in a jury's decision whether to order the death penalty or life in prison. The Court ruled that low intelligence may only be considered a mitigating factor, not a ground to execute a defendant.[47]

Minors

The Supreme Court had ruled in 1988 that it was cruel and unusual punishment to impose the death penalty on persons who committed their offense while fifteen years of age or younger. However, the next year the same Court concluded, in *Thompson v. Oklahoma,* that a youth sixteen or seventeen at the time of the offense could be sentenced to death,[48] thereby setting the lower limit for capital crimes at sixteen. That decision stood until 2005, when the Supreme Court heard the case of *Roper v. Simmons.*

Christopher Simmons, of Fenton, Missouri, was seventeen in September 1993 when he came up with a plan to break into someone's home, tie the person up, and throw the person off a bridge. Simmons recruited two younger friends to help him carry out his plan, one of whom backed out at the last minute. Simmons and his remaining friend broke into the home of Shirley Crook. They found her in bed, bound her with duct tape, and taped her eyes and mouth shut. Then they put her in the back of her van and drove to Castlewood State Park. On arriving they realized Crook had unbound her hands and removed some of the duct tape from her mouth. Simmons used her bathrobe tie, her purse strap, a towel, and some electrical wire he found nearby to bind her hands and feet. They covered her face completely with the duct tape. Then they pushed her off a railroad trestle into the river below. Her body was found the following day.

Simmons confessed to the murder and was sentenced to death. Simmons appealed on the basis of the *Atkins v. Virginia* decision, arguing that juveniles should have the same protections as the mentally retarded. His case put an end to the juvenile death penalty in the United States on March 1, 2005, when the Supreme Court ruled 5–4 that imposing the death penalty on defendants who were under the age of eighteen when they committed their offense violated the Constitution's Eighth Amendment protection against cruel and unusual punishment. At the time, seventy-one people were on death row for juvenile crimes, ranging in age from eighteen to forty-three at the time of the court's decision.[49]

Minor

A person who has not yet reached legal age, typically eighteen.

The Supreme Court based its decision on numerous factors. The court cited evidence of a national consensus against executing minor offenders similar to the consensus cited in *Atkins* against executing the mentally retarded. Thirty states had already prohibited the juvenile death penalty, the court noted, including twelve that had abandoned the death penalty altogether. Among the twenty states that still permitted juvenile executions, the practice was infrequent. The court also found that when enacting the Federal Death Penalty Act (18 U.S.C.S. § 3591) in 1994, Congress had determined that the death penalty should not extend to juveniles. The immaturity of juveniles made them less culpable, the court reasoned. The court also noted that the United States was the only country in the world that continued to sanction the juvenile death penalty.

O'Connor dissented, arguing that "the court had adduced no evidence impeaching the seemingly reasonable conclusion reached by many state legislatures that at least some seventeen-year-old murderers were sufficiently mature to deserve the death penalty." Scalia, joined by Rehnquist and Thomas, also dissented, writing that the court "had proclaimed itself the sole arbiter of the nation's moral standards" and "in the course of discharging that responsibility, had purported to take guidance from the views of foreign courts,"[50] never a popular American position.

Between 1976 and *Roper v. Simmons*, twenty-two juvenile offenders had been executed, about 2 percent of all executions during that time.

Offenses Punishable by Death

Generally, most states reserve the death penalty for murder or felony murder, at least where the defendant was substantially involved in the victim's death.[51] Whether someone is substantially involved in a murder depends on the facts of the case. For example, substantial involvement was not found in a case where the defendant did not intend to kill anyone, did not know that his codefendant would do so, and only drove the getaway car.[52] However, when another defendant, along with other family members, planned his father's escape from prison and watched his father kill and rob a family of four during the getaway, the defendant was sentenced to death. The father was serving a life sentence because he had killed a guard in a previous, unsuccessful escape attempt. The son's sentence was upheld by the Supreme Court in *Tison vs. Arizona*.[53]

Treason
Transferring loyalty or allegiance to the enemy.

A few states add **treason** as a capital offense. One state, Louisiana, specifies death for the aggravated rape of a victim under age twelve. If the rape involves an adult the death penalty is improper. In *Coker v. Georgia*, the Supreme Court ruled that death for rape is unconstitutional.[54] The defendant, while serving a life sentence for murder, rape, kidnapping, and aggravated assault, escaped from a Georgia prison and raped an adult woman. In *Coker*, the Supreme Court ruled that the Eighth Amendment bars not only punishments that are "barbaric" but also those that are "excessive." The Court wrote:

> [a] punishment is "excessive" and unconstitutional if it makes no measurable contribution to acceptable goals of punishment and hence is nothing more than purposeless and needless imposition of pain and suffering or is grossly out of proportion to the severity of the crime.[55]

Espionage
Spying; selling or giving secrets to another government.

Under federal law, death is an allowable sanction for a number of offenses, including the taking of a human life, **espionage,** terrorist acts, and treason.[56] The Supreme Court has upheld death for espionage.[57]

HISTORICAL HIGHLIGHT

Death for Corruption?

For as long as the debate about capital punishment has raged, the question of when to use it has been at the forefront. In the days of segregation, crimes committed by African-Americans were capital crimes, while the same crime committed by a Caucasian only brought a jail sentence. This clearly unfair application of capital punishment fed the movement against capital punishment in the late 1960s and early 1970s.

There are some who believe in the death penalty, but don't like the way it is applied. Some believe that chronic sex offenders should receive the death penalty, while teenagers who commit violent crimes should not. They reason that the violent teenagers are more likely to be rehabilitated than the sex offenders.

In an interesting twist in the debate, Pennsylvania Supreme Court nominee John A. Maher advocated the death penalty for corrupt politicians during his confirmation hearings in 1997. Understandably, the Pennsylvania state senators who had to confirm Maher in order for him to take a seat on the high court were less than enthusiastic about his views.

Maher was quoted by the *Philadelphia Inquirer* as saying, "I think the highest crime is the sale of office, and I am always offended as a citizen when I read the sale of office accompanied by a two-year probation. I'm not against capital punishment. I just think we should be more careful about what we give it for. The sale of office is an offense against the very existence of society."[58]

Maher's position was seen as too extreme, certainly for the politicians passing judgment on him, and he was not confirmed. At Maher's request, then Pennsylvania Governor Tom Ridge withdrew his name from consideration.

HISTORICAL HIGHLIGHT

Julius and Ethel Rosenberg Executed for Espionage

Julius and Ethel Rosenberg are the only Americans to receive the death penalty during peacetime for the crime of espionage. They were executed in New York's electric chair at Sing Sing Prison on June 19, 1953, after last-minute appeals to the Supreme Court were turned down and President Dwight Eisenhower denied a plea for executive clemency. They left behind two young sons, Robert, age six, and Michael, age ten. Both boys were later relocated and placed in an adoptive home.

The Rosenbergs were accused of giving the Soviet Union top secret information about the United States' development of an atomic bomb during World War II. The program, code-named the Manhattan Project, led to the end of the war with Japan after the atomic bomb was dropped on Japanese civilians in the cities of Nagasaki and Hiroshima. Many of the scientists working on the project were refugees from wartime Europe. One of them, German born and lifelong Communist Klaus Fuchs, provided secret data to the Russians.

Klaus Fuchs was arrested and convicted of espionage in Great Britain in 1949. He received a fifteen-year jail term in exchange for providing information about other spies. He provided authorities the name of American Harry Gold. Gold, in turn, implicated David Greenglass as another spy for the Soviets. Greenglass was Ethel's brother. In exchange for a guarantee that his wife would not be prosecuted and no prison sentence for himself, he implicated his sister and her husband, Julius. He claimed they had recruited him for the Soviets. He testified against them at their trial.

Both Ethel and Julius insisted that they were innocent, but were convicted of espionage by a jury. Although urged to do so, they would not cooperate and name others as spies. They were sentenced to death. Up until the hour of their executions they were offered clemency if they would name others in their alleged spy ring. Recently declassified information in both the United States and the former Soviet Union indicate that Julius, but not Ethel, may have been involved in low-level espionage, but does not implicate them in passing atomic secrets.

Life in Prison

According to the FBI there were 1.3 million violent crimes reported to law enforcement officials in 2008. These included 16,272 murders, 89,000 forcible rapes, and about 2.2 million burglaries.[59] The numbers of both violent and nonviolent crimes have decreased since the early 1990s and the rates of each have also declined. Still, roughly two-thirds of offenders released from prison are rearrested within three years. In response, many legislatures have passed laws requiring long sentences for recidivists. So-called "three strikes and you're out" legislation has been popular with many state lawmakers. These laws attempt to eliminate recidivism by providing that repeat offenders be imprisoned for life.

The Supreme Court has upheld some forms of repeat offender legislation as a legitimate use of state police powers, writing that states have an "interest expressed in all recidivism statutes, in dealing in a harsher manner with those who by repeated criminal acts have shown that they are simply incapable of conforming to the norms of society . . . "[60]

Prisoners have argued that mandatory life in prison for repeat offenders is cruel and unusual punishment, especially when applied to relatively minor crimes. Two such cases have reached the Supreme Court. In 1980, the Court concluded that life in prison for three nonviolent crimes was not unconstitutional as long as the prisoner was at some point eligible for parole. The case involved the following three convictions:

1. Credit card theft, $80
2. Forged check, $28
3. False pretenses, $120

Defendant was therefore given a life sentence as a recidivist for the theft of $228 over a nine-year period.[61]

However, in 1983, the Supreme Court struck down a similar law in a case where a defendant was sentenced to life in prison with no chance of parole for writing a bad check for $100, his third petty offense. Because he was never eligible for parole, the Court ruled the punishment cruel and unusual.[62]

In some cases, inmates who committed crimes as juveniles were tried as adults and ended up being sent to prison for life without the possibility of parole. Terrence Graham was arrested for armed burglary when he was seventeen. He was already on probation at the time for another violent crime. A Florida judge sentenced him to life in prison without the chance of parole. His attorneys appealed the sentence arguing that life in prison with no chance of parole for a juvenile who did not commit homicide was cruel and unusual punishment. The U.S. Supreme Court agreed and ruled that the state had to establish some mechanism where juveniles not convicted of murder would have a realistic chance of leaving prison during their life.[63]

Prison Conditions

Generally, the punishments prohibited by the Eighth Amendment are those considered to be torture or otherwise barbarous. The Constitution prohibits the "wanton and unnecessary infliction of pain."[64] Imprisonment itself obviously carries with it some control over the day-to-day lives of the inmates, including confinement and physical coercion when necessary. These are not constitutionally prohibited unless they rise to a level that can cause serious illness or injury. Thus, double bunking in prison is allowable.[65] However, conditions cannot be so poor that inmates are allowed to prey on each other and prisoners suffer malnutrition.[66] In addition, adequate medical care must be provided for inmates.[67]

Appeals

One of the fundamental features of our legal system is the right to appeal a judge or jury's decision to a higher court. Our system, for example, does not allow the immediate execution of a death sentence or allow a clearly wrong legal decision to stand without some opportunity for another review.

In both state and federal court systems, criminal defendants are allowed one **appeal as of right.** That is, every defendant may have his or her conviction reviewed by the next higher court if he or she wishes unless the conviction was the result of a guilty plea or the defendant challenges the guilty plea on grounds such as involuntariness. Typically, criminal defendants have thirty days to file an appeal with the appropriate court after a final trial court decision. That means the criminal defendant has been convicted and sentenced.

Appeal as of right
The absolute right to one appellate review of a conviction.

An appeal from a federal district court goes to the United States Court of Appeal for the circuit in which the conviction took place. As a practical matter, that means that the circuit courts of appeal are very busy courts. They cannot turn down an appeal without hearing the case unless the defendant missed a deadline.

Appeals are typically not an opportunity to present facts. That's the function of the trial courts. Instead, appellate courts determine whether the law was properly applied.

Criminal defendants who do not win on appeal can ask the next higher court to consider their case. This time, however, they are not automatically entitled to an appeal—it is a **discretionary appeal.** The appellate court has to agree to take the case, which usually only happens if the case is one of significance involving new or novel issues of law. Very few cases are accepted by the U.S. Supreme Court or by the highest courts within each state.

Discretionary appeal
An appeal allowed by an appellate court after a criminal defendant's appeal as of right.

Criminal defendants can appeal their sentence, the verdict against them, the underlying constitutionality or validity of the law they were convicted of breaking, or the constitutionality of the process that led to their conviction. The issues appealed must either have been raised during the trial or involve an obvious error.

Only errors which fundamentally would have affected the outcome of the trial require the appellate court to reverse a conviction. So-called **harmless errors** do not. For example, allowing irrelevant testimony that did not prejudice the defendant would likely be deemed a harmless error. It should not have been admitted because it was irrelevant, but it did not cause any prejudice to the defendant. Appellate courts do not require perfect trials, just fair and impartial ones.

Harmless error
An error at the trial stage which did not fundamentally affect the outcome of the trial.

When an appellate court grants an appeal and rules that the conviction or sentence was wrong, it can do one of several things. It can order the trial court to revise its decision in light of the appellate court's guidance, it can order a new trial or sentencing hearing, or it can dismiss the case entirely if the error was particularly egregious.

Once a criminal defendant has exhausted his or her appeals, there may still be avenues for having the case reviewed. The defendant may file a writ of *habeas corpus* to request his case be reviewed in the federal court system, for example. Often, such cases involve claims that counsel at either trial or on appeal was incompetent and ineffective. They may also involve claims of newly discovered evidence such as DNA evidence or a request for release based on a retroactive Supreme Court decision. Often, too, the claims are filed by the defendants themselves.

Emerging Trends

Two trends in punishment have recently received widespread press coverage and attention from state and federal legislators. Both attempt to deal with repeat offenders.

Predatory Sex Offender Registration

Every state now has predatory sex offender registration laws mandating that prisoners who are released from prison after violent sexual offenses or those involving children must register their address and make public their presence in the community where they live after release. These laws are generally referred to as "Megan's Laws." Named for Megan Kanka, a young girl who was raped and murdered by a repeat sexual offender, these new laws are causing controversy. Federal law establishes a national database at the Federal Bureau of Investigation designed to track every person who has been convicted of a criminal offense against a minor, a sexually violent offense, or who is a sexually violent "predator."

The Sex Offenders Registration and Notification Act of 2006 (SORNA) is a federal law that allows states to track registered sex offenders when they move from state to state. In 2004, Thomas Carr pled guilty to sexual abuse in Alabama and shortly thereafter moved to Indiana. Because SORNA had not yet been passed, Carr was not required to register with Indiana authorities as a sex offender. After the law passed, Carr was arrested for failing to register his new address with authorities. He appealed his conviction arguing that charging him with not registering was an *ex post facto* law and therefore unconstitutional. The Supreme Court stopped short of deciding the ex post facto issue, but did rule Carr could not be prosecuted for failing to register under these circumstances.[68]

Offenders are categorized by the severity of their crimes and the likelihood of their reoffending. Level One offenders are first-time offenders considered a lower risk to society. Level Two offenders are convicted of multiple or more serious offenses and considered a higher risk. Level Three offenders are repeat offenders or those committing the most serious offenses and are considered to pose the highest risk of reoffending. Offenders must register with the National Sex Offender Registry and keep their registrations up to date—Level One offenders for fifteen years from release, Level Two for twenty-five years, and Level Three for life. In addition, federal law requires that state and local governmental officials release relevant information deemed necessary to protect the public from predators.[69] It is up to the states to decide how much information to publish, and about what levels of offenders. Some states send photo post cards to neighborhoods to announce the presence of violent sexual predators. Each state has its own requirements for registration and most have searchable sites on the World Wide Web, many complete with pictures, names, and addresses. Some, like Maine, have been criticized for including addresses of all offenders. Pennsylvania, on the other hand, has been criticized for not giving addresses of any offenders, which some feel make its registry useless.

Recently states have been improvising ways to monitor offenders. Delaware provides for the letter "Y" to be imprinted on the driver's license of all monitored sex offenders. Some states have residency requirements that forbid sex offenders from living within a prescribed distance from schools, pools, and day care centers. After nine-year-old Jessica Lunsford was abducted, raped, and buried alive by a repeat sex offender in Homosassa, Florida, a public outcry led to the introduction of global positioning system (GPS) monitoring in Florida. Several states followed suit. Ohio's law requires GPS monitoring for life for sexually violent offenders; Oklahoma imposes lifetime monitoring on all habitual offenders.[70]

The Supreme Court has twice in the last few years addressed whether convicted sex offenders who have served their sentences can be further confined. In *Kansas v. Hendricks,* 521 U.S. 346 (1997), the Court concluded that the Kansas Sexually Violent Predator Act was constitutional. The Act allowed involuntary confinement of persons with a mental abnormality or personality disorder who were found to be dangerous by a jury. The Court also ruled that confinement after serving a sentence for sex offenses wasn't double jeopardy. Nor was the law an ex post facto law, since it was not criminal, but civil in nature. In *Kansas v. Crane,* 534 U.S. 407 (2002), the Court clarified that the state must show at a minimum that the person they want to confine must have at least some difficulty controlling his urges, but wasn't required to show that it would be impossible to control those urges.

In 2003, the Court considered whether the registration laws are in effect ex post facto laws,[71] and held that they were not.[72] So far, Megan's Laws have held up to a multitude of legal challenges.

Mandatory sentences
Sentences required by statute during which the prisoner has no chance for parole.

HISTORICAL HIGHLIGHT

Convicted Sex Offender Programs and Self-Incrimination

The state of Kansas offers convicted sex offenders an opportunity to participate in a Sexual Abuse Treatment Program (SATP), which requires participating inmates to complete a sexual history form revealing all of their prior sexual activities. This list of activities could include any activities that may constitute a criminal offense for which an inmate has never been charged. Kansas makes no promise that the information will never be used against them. Inmates who refuse to participate in the program may have a reduction in their prison privileges and could be transferred to a potentially more dangerous maximum-security area.

Robert G. Lile, a Kansas prisoner, was facing the dilemma of choosing between improved prison privileges and disclosing potentially incriminating information about his past that could lead to further criminal charges. He filed an action for injunctive relief on the grounds that participating in Kansas's SATP would violate his Fifth Amendment protection against compelled self-incrimination.

The Tenth Circuit decided that because refusing to participate in the program would result in an automatic reduction of Mr. Lile's privileges and housing accommodations, the penalty would have a sufficiently substantial impact on him that it would constitute a compelling reason to release information that could create a risk of further prosecution. However, the U.S. Supreme Court overturned this decision on appeal, stating that the consequences for refusing to participate were not great enough to compel a prisoner to abandon his/her right against self-incrimination.[73]

Corporal punishment
Punishment inflicted on the body, such as paddling, whipping, or caning.

Parole
A period of supervised release after serving a prison sentence. The parolee must follow certain rules such as reporting to a parole officer.

Chemical Castration

Chemical castration of sex offenders is also gaining in popularity. Both surgical castration and chemical castration have been used in Norway, Sweden, Denmark, and Switzerland for a number of years. Now several states here have followed suit. California[74] and Georgia[75] have passed laws making chemical castration a condition of parole for sex offenses, especially those involving a child victim. Chemical castration is accomplished by the injection of the chemical medroxyprogesterone acetate, commonly referred to by its trade name, Depo-Provera. The drug reduces the level of testosterone and decreases the male sex drive.

HISTORICAL HIGHLIGHT

Not All Sexual Predators Are Male

A Tacoma, Washington, woman is listed as a sexual predator under the provisions of that state's "Megan's Law." The lady, Laura Faye McCollum, was convicted in 1990 of raping a three-year-old girl. She completed her 51/2-year sentence in 1995 and has been housed at a treatment center ever since. She remains confined voluntarily.

McCollum is aware of her condition, but is almost helpless to stop her own actions if left unsupervised. One of her counselors described her as "an obsessive and compulsive child molester who is particularly attracted to preverbal and barely verbal children ages 2 to 4."

This type of obsessive behavior is more commonly found in males, but at least one other woman has made the sexual predator list. Minnesota also has a woman sex offender on that state's list.[76]

In fact, there were enough female sex offenders listed in the Georgia state registry that someone dedicated an Internet website to them. "Miss Georgia's Sex Offenders 2004 Pageant" featured photos of 18 female sex offenders culled from the registry, including the women's names, ages, and crimes under headings such as "Most Swine-Like," "Miss Herpes," and "Most Likely to be Mistaken for Jabba the Hut."[77]

Women make up 1–2 percent of sex offenders,[78] with 550,000 registered offenders in the United States;[79] that makes between 5,000 and 10,000 female sex offenders.

Crime
An offense against society.

Chemical castration is likely to be challenged on Eighth Amendment grounds as cruel and unusual punishment.

HISTORICAL HIGHLIGHT

What If MySpace Flagged You As a Sexual Predator?

Jessica Davis, a twenty-nine-year-old University of Colorado student, was shocked one day in May 2007 when she was kicked off of the social networking website MySpace.com on the grounds that she was a registered sex offender. Davis, as she immediately told MySpace, had no idea what they were talking about. An English major on her way to studying law, Davis insisted she had no criminal record and was not a sex offender.

Several days later, MySpace responded by saying it did not keep records of removed profiles. It took several days before Sentinel Corporation, which built the database for MySpace, acknowledged that the system had flagged her because there was a registered sex offender with the same name and a birth date two years and two days off from Davis's.[80] Sounds close, until you consider that there are over half a million registered sex offenders in this country.

MySpace had introduced the database in 2006 after journalist Kevin Poulsen published an investigative report saying he had crossed MySpace member profiles against the National Sex Offender Registry and found 744 verified matches. One registered offender was "actively trolling for underage boys," on MySpace, Poulsen wrote. That offender was later arrested. MySpace responded by hiring a background-check company, Sentinel Tech Holding Corp., to conduct a similar search.

Within the next year, MySpace removed 29,000 offenders from its website out of a total of more than 180 million profiles. After news of the Website's discoveries were made public, eight attorneys general sent a letter to MySpace expressing concern over the website's design, particularly that it did not require parental permission before minors could create a profile. The attorneys general also asked MySpace to provide the names of the regis-tered sex offenders the company had removed from the site.[81]

Jessica Davis, who hopes to work in public service someday, is concerned that her close call with the National Sex Offender Registry will come back to haunt her someday. "I don't want to have to explain to people that there's this website MySpace and they screwed this up," Davis said. "I don't want to have to defend my innocence."

CONCEPT **REVIEW AND REINFORCEMENT**

The Eighth Amendment has historical roots reaching back at least as far as the Magna Carta of 1215. Transplanted to the United States by English colonists, it serves as the minimum standard by which criminal punishments are measured.

Capital punishment has provided a fertile ground for interpretation of the ban on cruel and unusual punishment. For a brief period of time it seemed as if the death penalty would expire, beginning with the 1972 Supreme Court decision in *Fuhrman v. Georgia.* But rather than signaling its death rattle, proponents came back with new and improved legislation. In 1976 the Supreme Court revisited its 1972 decision and upheld a death penalty statute that provided procedural safeguards against arbitrary and capricious imposition of the penalty.

Life in prison is not cruel and unusual punishment for numerous offenses, including those committed by both violent and nonviolent offenders. For nonviolent offenders, a recidivism statute may not forever foreclose the possibility of parole.

Generally, prison conditions are not cruel and unusual punishment unless they reach the level of wanton and unnecessary infliction of pain.

Two areas of punishment likely to receive review under the Eighth Amendment are lifetime sex offender registration and castration of sex offenders.

KEY **TERMS**

Aggravating circumstance	Espionage	Mitigating circumstance
Appeal as of right	Fines	Model Death Penalty
Bloody Code	Harmless error	Parole
Concurrent sentences	Incarceration	Per se
Consecutive sentences	Indefinite sentencing	Probation
Corporal punishment	Indeterminate sentencing	Proportionality
Crime	Magna Carta	Restitution
Cruel and unusual punishment	Mandatory minimum sentences	Suspended sentence
Definite or determinate sentences	Mandatory sentences	Transportation
Discretionary appeal	Minor	Treason
Enhanced sentences		

CONCEPT **REVIEW QUESTIONS**

1. Explain the history of the Eighth Amendment to the U.S. Constitution.

2. List the types of criminal punishment.

3. List and explain the two requirements that must be satisfied before a punishment is "cruel and unusual."

4. Explain why capital punishment is not unconstitutional as "cruel and unusual" punishment.

5. Explain what procedural protection is required before the death penalty can be carried out.

6. Define aggravating and mitigating circumstances.

7. List the classifications of persons who can be executed.

8. List the crimes that are punishable by death.

9. Explain the Supreme Court's position on life in prison for repeat offenders.

10. Know the steps in the appeals process.

11. List and describe two current trends in punishment.

CASE **APPLICATION**

Building Your Professional Skills

1. Read the following edited Supreme Court case (citations to the record, for example, have been removed) and answer the questions that follow.

SUPREME COURT OF THE UNITED STATES
DAVID BOBBY, WARDEN, *PETITIONER v. MICHAEL BIES*

On writ of certiorari to the United States court of appeals for the sixth circuit
June 1, 2009

Justice Ginsburg delivered the opinion of the Court.

In *Atkins* v. *Virginia,* . . . this Court held that the Eighth Amendment's prohibition of "cruel and unusual punishments" bars execution of mentally retarded offenders. Prior to *Atkins*, the Court had determined that mental retardation merited consideration as a mitigating factor, but did not bar imposition of the death penalty. . . .

In 1992, nearly a decade before the Court's decision in *Atkins*, respondent Michael Bies was tried and convicted in Ohio of the aggravated murder, kidnapping, and attempted rape of a ten-year-old boy. Instructed at the sentencing stage to weigh mitigating circumstances (including evidence of Bies' mild to borderline mental retardation) against aggravating factors (including the brutality of the crime), the jury recommended a sentence of death, which the trial court imposed. Ohio's appellate courts affirmed the conviction and sentence. . . .

After this Court decided *Atkins*, the Ohio trial court ordered a full hearing on the question of Bies' mental capacity. The federal courts intervened, however, granting habeas relief to Bies, and ordering the vacation of his death sentence. Affirming the District Court's judgment, the Sixth Circuit reasoned that the Ohio Supreme Court, in 1996, had definitively determined, as a matter of fact, Bies' mental retardation. That finding, the Court of Appeals concluded, established Bies' "legal entitlement to a life sentence." Therefore, the Sixth Circuit ruled, the Double Jeopardy Clause of the Federal Constitution barred any renewed inquiry into the matter of Bies' mental state.

We reverse the judgment of the Court of Appeals. The Sixth Circuit, in common with the District Court, fundamentally misperceived the application of the Double Jeopardy Clause . . . First, Bies was not "twice put in jeopardy." He was sentenced to death, and Ohio sought no further prosecution or punishment. Instead of "serial prosecutions by the government, this case involves serial efforts by the defendant to vacate his capital sentence." . . .

For his part in brutally causing the death of a ten-year-old boy, Bies was convicted by an Ohio jury of attempted rape, kidnapping, and aggravated murder with three death penalty specifications. At sentencing, Bies presented testimony from clinical psychiatrist Donna E. Winter, who had evaluated him at the court's order during the guilt phase and again before the mitigation hearing. Bies did not qualify for a plea of not guilty by reason of insanity, Dr. Winter concluded, because he knew the difference between right and wrong at the time of the offense. Bies' IQ, she further reported, fell in the 65–75 range, indicating that he is "mildly mentally retarded to borderline mentally retarded," Dr. Winter also observed:

"[Bies] goes about the community, unassisted [and] carries out the activities of daily life fairly independently." The State responded to Bies' mitigating evidence by emphasizing the brutality of the murder and the risk of Bies' future dangerousness. Instructed to weigh the mitigating circumstances against aggravating factors, the jury recommended a death sentence, which the trial court imposed.

The Ohio Court of Appeals and Supreme Court each independently reviewed the evidence and affirmed. Neither court devoted detailed attention to the issue of retardation. Both concluded that Bies' mild to borderline mental retardation merited "some weight" in mitigation, as did his youth and lack of a criminal record. The aggravating circumstances, each court found, overwhelmed the mitigating circumstances beyond a reasonable doubt. . . .

Bies then filed a petition for state postconviction relief, contending for the first time that the Eighth Amendment to the Federal Constitution prohibits execution of a mentally retarded defendant. The trial court agreed that Bies was "mildly mentally retarded," but concluded that, under then-governing Ohio precedent, "a mildly mentally retarded defendant may be [p]unished by execution." The Ohio Court of Appeals affirmed the judgment and the Ohio Supreme Court dismissed Bies' appeal without an opinion.

Bies next filed a federal habeas petition in the United States District Court for the Southern District of Ohio. Soon after that filing, this Court held, in *Atkins* v. *Virginia*, 536 U.S., at 321, that the Eighth Amendment prohibits execution of mentally retarded offenders. Our opinion did not provide definitive procedural or substantive guides for determining when a person who claims mental retardation "will be so impaired as to fall [within *Atkins*' compass]." . . .

Ohio heeded *Atkins*' call six months . . . At an *Atkins* hearing, the Ohio Supreme Court held, a defendant must prove: "(1) significantly subaverage intellectual functioning, (2) significant limitations in two or more adaptive skills, such as communication, self-care, and self-direction, and (3) onset before the age of 18." "IQ tests," the court stated, "are one of the many factors that need to be considered, [but] they alone are not sufficient to make a final determination [of retardation]." The court also announced "a rebuttable presumption that a defendant is not mentally retarded if his or her IQ is above 70."

The District Court stayed its proceedings on Bies' federal habeas petition while Bies presented an Atkins claim to the state postconviction court. Bies there moved for summary judgment, arguing that the record established his mental retardation, and that the State was "precluded and estopped" from disputing it. Rather than proceeding with the hearing directed by the state court, Bies returned to the Federal District Court. He argued that the . . . Double Jeopardy Clause . . . barred the State from relitigating the issue of his mental condition. The District Court granted the habeas petition and ordered vacation of Bies' death sentence.

We granted certiorari, 555 U.S. ___ (2009), and now reverse.

. . . [T]here was no acquittal. Bies' jury voted to impose the death penalty. At issue now is Bies' "second run at vacating his death sentence," . . . not an effort by the State to retry him or to increase his punishment . . .

For the reasons stated, the judgment of the Court of Appeals is reversed, and the case is remanded for further proceedings consistent with this opinion.

It is so ordered.

QUESTIONS

1. Based on what you learned in the chapter, what has the Supreme Court said about executing the mentally retarded?
2. Brief the case.

3. What standards did Ohio come up with to implement the Supreme Court's ruling?

4. Why do you think Bies' attorneys don't want the state to relitigate whether he is retarded?

CRITICAL **THINKING EXERCISES**

1. The Eighth Amendment comes from a long line of limits on the power of the central government to impose penalties on citizens. Many of the punishments documents such as the *Magna Carta* and the *English Bill of Rights of 1689* targeted as "cruel and unusual" were commonplace in earlier times. What penal practices occurring today could one day be considered cruel and unusual and why? Committing sex offenders after their sentences are over? Capital punishment? Extraordinary renditions?

2. You are convicted of drug trafficking and money laundering. You will not receive the death penalty, but what other possible punishments might you receive?

3. You are an attorney representing a juvenile charged and convicted as an adult in an armed robbery. Because your client has had previous convictions for crimes committed with firearms, the laws in your state permit the judge to impose life in prison without the chance of parole. Can you challenge this sentence as cruel and unusual?

4. Since capital punishment was legal and even common in 1791, the founding fathers did not find it cruel and unusual. What conclusion or conclusions would the Supreme Court have to come to in order to decide now that capital punishment is cruel and unusual?

5. Are there crimes where conviction automatically results in the death penalty?

6. You represent a gang member who has been convicted of killing a rival gang member. Would the fact that the murder victim had, on several occasions, threatened to kill your client be an aggravating or mitigating factor?

7. Which of the following may be executed:
   a. A mentally retarded person convicted of murder.
   b. A person who committed murder as a juvenile.
   c. A psychotic person convicted of rape.
   d. A psychotic person convicted of murder.

8. At various times throughout history, the following crimes have been capital offenses. Indicate which, if any, are still capital offenses today:
   a. Treason.
   b. Rape of a white woman by an African American.
   c. Horse theft.
   d. Espionage.
   e. Rape regardless of the victim or perpetrator's race.
   f. Forced sodomy.
   g. First-degree murder.
   h. Felony murder.

9. You have a client with two felony convictions who has served his sentences. He has had trouble obtaining employment because of his criminal record. Desperate for something to eat, he shoplifts some potato chips and is caught. Under your state's law, this third offense makes him a "career criminal" who must be locked up for the rest of his life without parole. How could you challenge this sentence?

10. Does the Supreme Court have to accept an appeal in a capital case?

11. You have a client who is a serial sex offender. He has expressed the desire to stop, but seems unable to do so. What two options can you offer him?

PORTFOLIO **BUILDING**

1. As you have done in previous exercises, locate a list of pending cases before the U.S. Supreme Court and summarize the ones that deal with the Eighth Amendment and punishment for your portfolio. Be sure to include the question that the Supreme Court said it would consider and the decision below.

2. Pick one of the pending cases, locate the underlying opinion, and prepare a brief for your

portfolio. Then predict the Supreme Court's decision based on what you read.

3. Research to which court a convicted defendant would file his appeal as of right in your jurisdiction. Prepare a brief memo outlining the process, including the deadline for filing the appeal.

FOR FURTHER READING

1. Meeropol, R., and Meeropol, M. (1975). *We Are Your Sons: The Legacy of Ethel and Julius Rosenberg.* Houghton Miffllin. Written by the sons of Ethel and Julius Rosenberg, who were made orphans by the execution of their parents, this book tells the story of the trial, conviction, and execution of the Rosenbergs through the eyes of six- and nine-year-old Robert and Michael. It includes death row correspondence from their parents.

2. Prejean, H. (1993). *Dead Man Walking.* Random House. Recounts a Roman Catholic nun's work with Louisiana death row inmates. The book has been made into a major movie starring Susan Sarandon and Sean Penn.

3. Radelet, M. L., Hugo, A. B., and Putnam, C. (1992). *In Spite of Innocence: Erroneous Convictions in Capital Cases.* Northeastern UP. Studies the cases of 400 Americans who have been convicted of capital crimes and either were executed or incarcerated. The authors argue all were innocent of the crimes charged.

4. Roberts, S. (2001). *The Brother: The Untold Story of Atomic Spy David Greenglass and How He Sent His Sister, Ethel Rosenberg, to the Electric Chair.* Random House. After years of silence, a *New York Times* reporter gets Ethel's brother to confess his involvement in the Rosenberg case.

5. Turow, S. (2002). *Reversible Errors.* Farrar Straus Giroux. Tells the fictional story of a corporate attorney appointed to represent a death row inmate who just possibly might be innocent of the triple murder he was sentenced to die for committing.

6. Turow, S. (2003). *Ultimate Punishment: A Lawyer's Reflections on Dealing with the Death Penalty.* Farrar Straus Giroux. Tells of Turow's involvement with the Illinois Commission of Capital Punishment.

7. *The Green Mile* (2000). Warner. A film starring Tom Hanks and featuring life on death row.

8. *Monster* (2003). The role of Aileen Wuornos, a prostitute executed in 2002 for a series of murders in Florida, won actress Charlize Theron the 2003 Best Actress Academy Award. The film attempts to explain Aileen's horrific childhood and gradual transformation into a serial killer.

9. LaFond, J. (2005). *Preventing Sexual Violence: How Society Should Cope with Sex Offenders.* American Psychological Association.

Appendix

The Constitution of the United States of America

WE THE PEOPLE of the United States, in Order to form a more perfect Union, establish Justice, insure domestic Tranquility, provide for the common defence, promote the general Welfare, and secure the Blessings of Liberty to ourselves and our Posterity, do ordain and establish this Constitution for the United States of America.

Article One

Section 1.

All legislative powers herein granted shall be vested in a Congress of the United States, which shall consist of a Senate and House of Representatives.

Section 2.

The House of Representatives shall be composed of members chosen every second year by the people of the several States, and the electors in each State shall have the qualifications requisite for electors of the most numerous branch of the State legislature.

No Person shall be a Representative who shall not have attained to the age of twenty five years, and been seven years a citizen of the United States, and who shall not, when elected, be an inhabitant of that State in which he shall be chosen.

Representatives and direct taxes shall be apportioned among the several States which may be included within this Union, according to their respective numbers, which shall be determined by adding to the whole number of free persons, including those bound to service for a term of years, and excluding Indians not taxed, three fifths of all other persons. The actual enumeration shall be made within three years after the first meeting of the Congress of the United States, and within every subsequent term of ten years, in such manner as they shall by law direct. The number of Representatives shall not exceed one for every thirty thousand, but each State shall have at least one Representative; and until such enumeration shall be made, the State of New Hampshire shall be entitled to choose three, Massachusetts eight, Rhode Island and Providence Plantations one, Connecticut five, New York six, New Jersey four, Pennsylvania eight, Delaware one, Maryland six, Virginia ten, North Carolina five, South Carolina five and Georgia three. When vacancies happen in the Representation from any State, the executive authority thereof shall issue writs of election to fill such vacancies.

The House of Representatives shall choose their Speaker and other officers; and shall have the sole power of Impeachment.

Section 3.

The Senate of the United States shall be composed of two Senators from each State, chosen by the legislature thereof, for six years; and each Senator shall have one Vote.

Immediately after they shall be assembled in consequence of the first election, they shall be divided as equally as may be into three classes. The seats of the Senators of the first class shall be vacated at the expiration of the second year, of the second class at the expiration of the fourth year, and of the third class at the expiration of the sixth year, so that one third may be chosen every second year; and if vacancies happen by resignation, or otherwise, during the recess of the legislature of any State, the executive thereof may make temporary appointments until the next meeting of the legislature, which shall then fill such vacancies.

No person shall be a Senator who shall not have attained to the age of thirty years, and been nine years a citizen of the United States, and who shall not, when elected, be an inhabitant of that State for which he shall be chosen.

The Vice-President of the United States shall be President of the Senate, but shall have no vote, unless they be equally divided.

The Senate shall choose their other officers, and also a President pro tempore, in the absence of the Vice-President, or when he shall exercise the office of President of the United States.

The Senate shall have the sole power to try all impeachments. When sitting for that purpose, they shall be on oath or affirmation. When the President of the United States is tried, the Chief Justice shall preside: And no Person shall be convicted without the concurrence of two thirds of the members present.

Judgment in cases of impeachment shall not extend further than to removal from office, and disqualification to hold and enjoy any office of honor, trust or profit under the United States: but the party convicted shall nevertheless be liable and subject to indictment, trial, judgment and punishment, according to law.

Section 4.

The times, places and manner of holding elections for Senators and Representatives, shall be prescribed in each State by the legislature thereof; but the Congress may at any time by law make or alter such regulations, except as to the places of choosing Senators.

The Congress shall assemble at least once in every year, and such meeting shall be on the first Monday in December, unless they shall by law appoint a different day.

Section 5.

Each house shall be the judge of the elections, returns and qualifications of its own members, and a majority of each shall constitute a quorum to do business; but a smaller number may adjourn from day to day, and may be authorized to compel the attendance of absent members, in such manner, and under such penalties as each house may provide.

Each house may determine the rules of its proceedings, punish its members for disorderly behavior, and, with the concurrence of two-thirds, expel a member.

Each house shall keep a journal of its proceedings, and from time to time publish the same, excepting such parts as may in their judgment require secrecy; and the yeas and nays of the members of either house on any question shall, at the desire of one fifth of those present, be entered on the journal.

Neither house, during the session of Congress, shall, without the consent of the other, adjourn for more than three days, nor to any other place than that in which the two Houses shall be sitting.

Section 6.

The Senators and Representatives shall receive a compensation for their services, to be ascertained by law, and paid out of the Treasury of the United States. They shall in all cases, except treason, felony and breach of the peace, be privileged from arrest during their attendance at the session of their respective houses, and in going to and returning from the same; and for any speech or debate in either house, they shall not be questioned in any other place.

No Senator or Representative shall, during the time for which he was elected, be appointed to any civil office under the authority of the United States which shall have been created, or the emoluments whereof shall have been increased during such time; and no person holding any office under the United States, shall be a member of either house during his continuance in office.

Section 7.

All bills for raising revenue shall originate in the House of Representatives; but the Senate may propose or concur with amendments as on other bills.

Every bill which shall have passed the House of Representatives and the Senate, shall, before it become a law, be presented to the President of the United States; If he approve he shall sign it, but if not he shall return it, with his objections to that house in which it shall have originated, who shall enter the objections at large on their journal, and proceed to reconsider it. If after such reconsideration two thirds of that house shall agree to pass the bill, it shall be sent, together with the objections, to the other house, by which it shall likewise be reconsidered, and if approved by two thirds of that house, it shall become a law. But in all such cases the votes of both houses shall be determined by yeas and nays, and the names of the persons voting for and against the bill shall be entered on the journal of each house respectively. If any bill shall not be returned by the President within ten days (Sundays excepted) after it shall have been presented to him, the same shall be a law, in like manner as if he had signed it, unless the Congress by their adjournment prevent its return, in which case it shall not be a law.

Every order, resolution, or vote to which the concurrence of the Senate and House of Representatives may be necessary (except on a question of adjournment) shall be presented to the President of the United States; and before the same shall take effect, shall be approved by him, or being disapproved by him, shall be repassed by two thirds of the Senate and House of Representatives, according to the rules and limitations prescribed in the case of a bill.

Section 8.

The Congress shall have power to lay and collect taxes, duties, imposts and excises, to pay the debts and provide for the common defence and general welfare of the United States; but all duties, imposts and excises shall be uniform throughout the United States; To borrow money on the credit of the United States; To regulate commerce with foreign nations, and among the several States, and with the Indian tribes; To establish an uniform rule of naturalization, and uniform Laws on the subject of bankruptcies throughout the United States; To coin money, regulate the value thereof, and of foreign coin, and fix the standard of weights and measures; To provide for the punishment of counterfeiting the securities and current Coin of the United States; To establish post-offices and post-roads; To promote the progress of science and useful arts, by securing for limited times to - authors and inventors the exclusive right to their respective writings and discoveries; To constitute tribunals inferior to the Supreme Court; To define and punish piracies and felonies committed on the high seas, and offenses against the law of nations; To declare war, grant letters of marque and reprisal, and make rules concerning captures on land and water; To raise and support armies, but no appropriation of money to that use shall be for a longer term than two years; To provide and maintain a navy; To make rules for the government and regulation of the land and naval forces; To provide for calling forth the militia to execute the laws of the union, suppress insurrections and repel invasions; To provide for organizing, arming, and disciplining, the militia, and for governing such part of them as may be employed in the service of the United States, reserving to the States respectively, the appointment of the officers, and the authority of training the militia according to the discipline prescribed by Congress; To exercise exclusive legislation in all cases whatsoever, over such district (not exceeding ten miles square) as may, by cession of particular States, and the acceptance of Congress, become the seat of the Government of the United States, and to exercise like authority over all places purchased by the consent of the legislature of the State in which the same shall be, for the erection of forts, magazines, arsenals, dockyards, and other needful Buildings; and To make all laws which shall be necessary and proper for carrying into execution the foregoing powers, and all other powers vested by this Constitution in the Government of the United States, or in any department or officer thereof.

Section 9.

The migration or importation of such persons as any of the States now existing shall think proper to admit, shall not be prohibited by the Congress prior to the Year one thousand eight hundred and eight, but a tax or duty may be imposed on such importation, not exceeding ten dollars for each person.

The privilege of the writ of habeas corpus shall not be suspended, unless when in cases of rebellion or invasion the public safety may require it.

No bill of attainder or ex post facto law shall be passed.

No capitation, or other direct tax shall be laid, unless in proportion to the census or enumeration herein before directed to be taken.

No tax or duty shall be laid on articles exported from any State.

No preference shall be given by any regulation of commerce or revenue to the ports of one State over those of another: nor shall vessels bound to, or from, one State, be obliged to enter, clear, or pay duties in another.

No money shall be drawn from the Treasury, but in consequence of appropriations made by law; and a regular statement and account of the receipts and expenditures of all public money shall be published from time to time.

No title of nobility shall be granted by the United States; and no person holding any office of profit or trust under them, shall, without the consent of the Congress, accept of any present, emolument, office, or title, of any kind whatever, from any king, prince or foreign State.

Section 10.

No State shall enter into any treaty, alliance, or confederation; grant letters of marque and reprisal; coin money; emit bills of credit; make anything but gold and silver coin a tender in payment of debts; pass any bill of attainder, ex post facto law, or law impairing the obligation of contracts, or grant any title of nobility.

No State shall, without the consent of the Congress, lay any imposts or duties on imports or exports, except what may be absolutely necessary for executing its inspection laws: and the net produce of all duties and imposts, laid by any State on imports or exports, shall be for the use of the Treasury of the United States; and all such laws shall be subject to the revision and control of the Congress.

No State shall, without the consent of Congress, lay any duty of tonnage, keep troops, or ships of war in time of peace, enter into any agreement or compact with another State, or with a foreign power, or engage in war, unless actually invaded, or in such imminent danger as will not admit of delay.

Article Two

Section 1.

The executive power shall be vested in a President of the United States of America. He shall hold his office during the term of four years, and, together with the Vice-President chosen for the same term, be elected, as follows:

Each State shall appoint, in such manner as the legislature thereof may direct, a number of electors, equal to the whole number of Senators and Representatives to which the State may be entitled in the Congress: but no Senator or Representative, or person holding an office of trust or profit under the United States, shall be appointed an elector.

The electors shall meet in their respective States, and vote by ballot for two persons, of whom one at least shall not lie an inhabitant of the same State with themselves. And they shall make a list of all the persons voted for, and of the number of votes for each; which list they shall sign and certify, and transmit sealed to the seat of the government of the United States, directed to the President of the Senate. The President of the Senate shall, in the presence of the Senate and House of Representatives, open all the certificates, and the votes shall then be counted. The person having the greatest number of votes shall be the President, if such number be a majority of the whole number of electors appointed; and if there be more than one who have such majority, and have an equal number of votes, then the House of Representatives shall immediately choose by ballot one of them for President; and if no person have a majority, then from the five highest on the list the said House shall in like manner choose the President.

But in choosing the President, the votes shall be taken by States, the representation from each State having one vote; a quorum for this purpose shall consist of a member or members from two thirds of the States, and a majority of all the States shall be necessary to a choice. In every case, after the choice of the President, the person having the greatest number of votes of the electors shall be the Vice-President. But if there should remain two or more who have equal votes, the Senate shall choose from them by ballot the Vice-President.

The Congress may determine the time of choosing the electors, and the day on which they shall give their votes; which day shall be the same throughout the United States.

No person except a natural born citizen, or a citizen of the United States, at the time of the adoption of this Constitution, shall be eligible to the office of President; neither shall any person be eligible to that office who shall not have attained to the age of thirty five years, and been fourteen years a resident within the United States.

In case of the removal of the President from office, or of his death, resignation, or inability to discharge the powers and duties of the said office, the same shall devolve on the Vice-President, and the Congress may by law provide for the case of removal, death, resignation or inability, both of the President and Vice President, declaring what officer shall then act as President, and such officer shall act accordingly, until the disability be removed, or a President shall be elected.

The President shall, at stated times, receive for his services, a compensation, which shall neither be increased nor diminished during the period for which he shall have been elected, and he shall not receive within that period any other emolument from the United States, or any of them.

Before he enter on the execution of his office, he shall take the following oath or affirmation:

"I do solemnly swear (or affirm) that I will faithfully execute the office of President of the United States, and will to the best of my ability, preserve, protect and defend the Constitution of the United States."

Section 2.

The President shall be Commander-in-Chief of the Army and Navy of the United States, and of the militia of the several States, when called into the actual service of the United States; he may require the opinion, in writing, of the principal officer in each of the executive departments, upon any subject relating to the duties of their respective offices, and he shall have power to grant reprieves and pardons for offenses against the United States, except in cases of impeachment.

He shall have power, by and with the advice and consent of the Senate, to make treaties, provided two thirds of the Senators present concur; and he shall nominate, and by and with the advice and consent of the Senate, shall appoint ambassadors, other public ministers and consuls, judges of the Supreme Court, and all other officers of the United States, whose appointments are not herein otherwise provided for, and which shall be established by law: but the Congress may by law vest the appointment of such inferior officers, as they think proper, in the President alone, in the courts of law, or in the heads of departments.

The President shall have power to fill up all vacancies that may happen during the recess of the Senate, by granting commissions which shall expire at the end of their next session.

Section 3.

He shall from time to time give to the Congress information of the State of the Union, and recommend to their consideration such measures as he shall judge necessary and expedient; he may, on extraordinary occasions, convene both houses, or either of them, and in case of disagreement between them, with respect to the time of adjournment, he may adjourn them to such time as he shall think proper; he shall receive ambassadors and other public ministers; he shall take care that the laws be faithfully executed, and shall commission all the officers of the United States.

Section 4.

The President, Vice-President and all civil officers of the United States, shall be removed from office on impeachment for, and conviction of, treason, bribery, or other high crimes and misdemeanors.

Article Three

Section 1.

The judicial power of the United States, shall be vested in one Supreme Court, and in such inferior courts as the Congress may from time to time ordain and establish.

The judges, both of the supreme and inferior courts, shall hold their offices during good behavior, and shall, at stated times, receive for their services, a compensation, which shall not be diminished during their continuance in office.

Section 2.

The judicial power shall extend to all cases, in law and equity, arising under this Constitution, the laws of the United States, and treaties made, or which shall be made, under their authority; to all cases affecting ambassadors, other public ministers and consuls; to all cases of admiralty and maritime jurisdiction; to controversies to which the United States shall be a party; to controversies between two or more States; between a State and citizens of another State; between citizens of different States; between citizens of the same State claiming lands under grants of different States, and between a State, or the citizens thereof, and foreign States, citizens or subjects.

In all cases affecting ambassadors, other public ministers and consuls, and those in which a State shall be party, the Supreme Court shall have original jurisdiction. In all the other cases before mentioned, the Supreme Court shall have appellate jurisdiction, both as to law and fact, with such exceptions, and under such regulations as the Congress shall make.

Trial of all crimes, except in cases of impeachment, shall be by jury; and such trial shall be held in the State where the said crimes shall have been committed; but when not committed within any State, the trial shall be at such place or places as the Congress may by law have directed.

Section 3.

Treason against the United States, shall consist only in levying war against them, or in adhering to their enemies, giving them aid and comfort. No person shall be convicted of treason unless on the testimony of two witnesses to the same overt act, or on confession in open court.

The Congress shall have power to declare the punishment of treason, but no attainder of treason shall work corruption of blood, or forfeiture except during the life of the person attainted.

Article Four

Section 1.

Full faith and credit shall be given in each State to the public acts, records, and judicial proceedings of every other State. And the Congress may by general laws prescribe the manner in which such acts, records and proceedings shall be proved, and the effect thereof.

Section 2.

The citizens of each State shall be entitled to all privileges and immunities of citizens in the several States.

A person charged in any State with treason, felony, or other crime, who shall flee from justice, and be found in another State, shall on demand of the executive authority of the State from which he fled, be delivered up, to be removed to the State having jurisdiction of the crime. No person held to service or labor in one State, under the laws thereof, escaping into another, shall, in consequence of any law or regulation therein, be discharged from such service or labor, But shall be delivered up on claim of the party to whom such service or labor may be due.

Section 3.

New States may be admitted by the Congress into this Union; but no new States shall be formed or erected within the jurisdiction of any other State; nor any State be formed by the junction of two or more States, or parts of States, without the consent of the legislatures of the States concerned as well as of the Congress.

The Congress shall have power to dispose of and make all needful rules and regulations respecting the territory or other property belonging to the United States; and nothing in this Constitution shall be so construed as to prejudice any claims of the United States, or of any particular State.

Section 4.

The United States shall guarantee to every State in this Union a republican form of government, and shall protect each of them against invasion; and on application of the legislature, or of the executive (when the legislature cannot be convened) against domestic violence.

Article Five

The Congress, whenever two thirds of both houses shall deem it necessary, shall propose amendments to this Constitution, or, on the application of the Legislatures of two thirds of the several States, shall call a convention for proposing amendments, which, in either case, shall be valid to all intents and purposes, as part of this Constitution, when ratified by the Legislatures of three fourths of the several States, or by conventions in three fourths thereof, as the one or the other mode of ratification may be proposed by the Congress; provided that no amendment which may be made prior to the Year One thousand eight hundred and eight shall in any manner affect the first and fourth Clauses in the Ninth Section of the first Article; and that no State, without its consent, shall be deprived of its equal suffrage in the Senate.

Article Six

All debts contracted and engagements entered into, before the adoption of this Constitution, shall be as valid against the United States under this Constitution, as under the Confederation.

This Constitution, and the laws of the United States which shall be made in pursuance thereof; and all treaties made, or which shall be made, under the authority of the United States, shall be the supreme law of the land; and the judges in every State shall be bound thereby, anything in the Constitution or laws of any State to the contrary notwithstanding.

The Senators and Representatives before mentioned, and the members of the several State Legislatures, and all executive and judicial officers, both of the United States and of the several States, shall be bound by oath or affirmation, to support this Constitution; but no religious test shall ever be required as a qualification to any office or public trust under the United States.

Article Seven

The ratification of the Conventions of nine States, shall be sufficient for the establishment of this Constitution between the States so ratifying the same.

Bill of Rights

Amendment I (1791)

Congress shall make no law respecting an establishment of religion, or prohibiting the free exercise thereof; or abridging the freedom of speech, or of the press; or the right of the people peaceably to assemble, and to petition the government for a redress of grievances.

Amendment II (1791)

A well regulated militia, being necessary to the security of a free State, the right of the people to keep and bear arms, shall not be infringed.

Amendment III (1791)

No soldier shall, in time of peace be quartered in any house, without the consent of the owner, nor in time of war, but in a manner to be prescribed by law.

Amendment IV (1791)

The right of the people to be secure in their persons, houses, papers, and effects, against unreasonable searches and seizures, shall not be violated, and no warrants shall issue, but upon probable cause, supported by Oath or affirmation, and particularly describing the place to be searched, and the persons or things to be seized.

Amendment V (1791)

No person shall be held to answer for a capital, or otherwise infamous crime, unless on a presentment or indictment of a Grand Jury, except in cases arising in the land or naval forces, or in the militia, when in actual service in time of war or public danger; nor shall any person be subject for the same offence to be twice put in jeopardy of life or limb; nor shall be compelled in any criminal case to be a witness against himself, nor be deprived of life, liberty, or property, without due process of law; nor shall private property be taken for public use, without just compensation.

Amendment VI (1791)

In all criminal prosecutions, the accused shall enjoy the right to a speedy and public trial, by an impartial jury of the State and district wherein the crime shall have been committed, which district shall have been previously ascertained by law, and to be informed of the nature and cause of the accusation; to be confronted with the witnesses against him; to have compulsory process for obtaining witnesses in his favor, and to have the assistance of counsel for his defence.

Amendment VII (1791)

In suits at common law, where the value in controversy shall exceed twenty dollars, the right of trial by jury shall be preserved, and no fact tried by a jury, shall be otherwise re-examined in any court of the United States, than according to the rules of the common law.

Amendment VIII (1791)

Excessive bail shall not be required, nor excessive fines imposed, nor cruel and unusual punishments inflicted.

Amendment IX (1791)

The enumeration in the Constitution, of certain rights, shall not be construed to deny or disparage others retained by the people.

Amendment X (1791)

The powers not delegated to the United States by the Constitution, nor prohibited by it to the States, are reserved to the States respectively, or to the people.

Amendment XI (1798)

The judicial power of the United States shall not be construed to extend to any suit in law or equity, commenced or prosecuted against one of the United States by Citizens of another State, or by citizens or subjects of any foreign State.

Amendment XII (1804)

The electors shall meet in their respective States, and vote by ballot for President and Vice-President, one of whom, at least, shall not be an inhabitant of the same State with themselves; they shall name in their ballots the person voted for as President, and in distinct ballots the person voted for as Vice-President, and they shall make distinct lists of all persons voted for as President, and of all persons voted for as Vice-President and of the number of votes for each, which lists they shall sign and certify, and transmit sealed to the seat of the Government of the United States, directed to the President of the Senate; The President of the Senate shall, in the presence of the Senate and House of Representatives, open all the certificates and the votes shall then be counted; the person having the greatest number of votes for President, shall be the President, if such number be a majority of the whole number of Electors appointed; and if no person have such majority, then from the persons having the highest numbers not exceeding three on the list of those voted for as President, the House of Representatives shall choose immediately, by ballot, the President. But in choosing the President, the votes shall be taken by States, the representation from each State having one vote; a quorum for this purpose shall consist of a member or members from two-thirds of the States, and a majority of all the States shall be necessary to a choice. And if the House of Representatives shall not choose a President whenever the right of choice shall devolve upon them, before the fourth day of March next following, then the Vice-President shall act as President, as in the case of the death or other constitutional disability of the President.

The person having the greatest number of votes as Vice-President, shall be the Vice-President, if such number be a majority of the whole number of Electors appointed, and if no person have a majority, then from the two highest numbers on the list, the Senate shall choose the Vice-President; a quorum for the purpose shall consist of two-thirds of the whole number of Senators, and a majority of the whole number shall be necessary to a choice. But no person constitutionally ineligible to the office of President shall be eligible to that of Vice-President of the United States.

Amendment XIII (1865)

Section 1.

Neither slavery nor involuntary servitude, except as a punishment for crime whereof the party shall have been duly convicted, shall exist within the United States, or any place subject to their jurisdiction.

Section 2.

Congress shall have power to enforce this article by appropriate legislation.

Amendment XIV (1868)

Section 1.

All persons born or naturalized in the United States, and subject to the jurisdiction thereof, are citizens of the United States and of the State wherein they reside. No State shall make or enforce any law which shall abridge the privileges or immunities of citizens of the United States; nor shall any State deprive any person of life, liberty, or property, without due process of law; nor deny to any person within its jurisdiction the equal protection of the laws.

Section 2.

Representatives shall be apportioned among the several States according to their respective numbers, counting the whole number of persons in each State, excluding Indians not taxed. But when the right to vote at any election for the choice of Electors for President and Vice-President of the United States, Representatives in Congress, the executive and judicial officers of a State, or the members of the Legislature thereof, is denied to any of the male inhabitants of such State, being twenty-one years of age, and citizens of the United States, or in any way abridged, except for participation in rebellion, or other crime, the basis of representation therein shall be reduced in the proportion which the number of such male citizens shall bear to the whole number of male citizens twenty-one years of age in such State.

Section 3.

No person shall be a Senator or Representative in Congress, or elector of President and Vice-President, or hold any office, civil or military, under the United States, or under any State, who, having previously taken an oath, as a member of Congress, or as an officer of the United States, or as a member of any State legislature, or as an executive or judicial officer of any State, to support the Constitution of the United States, shall have engaged in insurrection or rebellion against the same, or given aid or comfort to the enemies thereof. But Congress may by a vote of two-thirds of each House, remove such disability.

Section 4.

The validity of the public debt of the United States, authorized by law, including debts incurred for payment of pensions and bounties for services in suppressing insurrection or rebellion, shall not be questioned. But neither the United States nor any State shall assume or pay any debt or obligation incurred in aid of insurrection or rebellion against the United States, or any claim for the loss or emancipation of any slave; but all such debts, obligations and claims shall be held illegal and void.

Section 5.

The Congress shall have power to enforce, by appropriate legislation, the provisions of this article.

Amendment XV (1870)

Section 1.

The right of citizens of the United States to vote shall not be denied or abridged by the United States or by any State on account of race, color, or previous condition of servitude.

Section 2.

The Congress shall have power to enforce this article by appropriate legislation.

Amendment XVI (1913)

The Congress shall have power to lay and collect taxes on incomes, from whatever source derived, without apportionment among the several States and without regard to any census or enumeration.

Amendment XVII (1913)

The Senate of the United States shall be composed of two senators from each State, elected by the people thereof, for six years; and each Senator shall have one vote. The electors in each State shall have the qualifications requisite for electors of the most numerous branch of the State legislature. When vacancies happen in the representation of any State in the Senate, the executive authority of such State shall issue writs of election to fill such vacancies: Provided, That the legislature of any State may empower the executive thereof to make temporary appointments until the people fill the vacancies by election as the legislature may direct.

This amendment shall not be so construed as to affect the election or term of any senator chosen before it becomes valid as part of the Constitution.

Amendment XVIII (1919)

Section 1.

After one year from the ratification of this article, the manufacture, sale, or transportation of intoxicating liquors within, the importation thereof into, or the exportation thereof from the United States and all territory subject to the jurisdiction thereof for beverage purposes is hereby prohibited.

Section 2.

The Congress and the several States shall have concurrent power to enforce this article by appropriate legislation.

Section 3.

This article shall be inoperative unless it shall have been ratified as an amendment to the Constitution by the legislatures of the several States, as provided in the Constitution, within seven years from the date of the submission hereof to the States by Congress.

Amendment XIX (1920)

The right of citizens of the United States to vote shall not be denied or abridged by the United States or by any States on account of sex. The Congress shall have power by appropriate legislation to enforce the provisions of this article.

Amendment XX (1933)

Section 1.

The terms of the President and Vice-President shall end at noon on the twentieth day of January, and the terms of Senators and Representatives at noon on the third day of January, of the years in which such terms would have ended if this article had not been ratified; and the terms of their successors shall then begin.

Section 2.

The Congress shall assemble at least once in every year, and such meeting shall begin at noon on the third day of January, unless they shall by law appoint a different day.

Section 3.

If, at the time fixed for the beginning of the term of the President, the President-elect shall have died, the Vice-President-elect shall become President. If a President shall not have been chosen before the time fixed for the beginning of his term, or if the President-elect shall have failed to qualify, then the Vice-President-elect shall act as President until a President shall have qualified; and the Congress may by law provide for the case wherein neither a President-elect nor a Vice-President-elect shall have qualified, declaring who shall then act as President, or the manner in which one who is to act shall be selected, and such person shall act accordingly until a President or Vice-President shall have qualified.

Section 4.

The Congress may by law provide for the case of the death of any of the persons from whom the House of Representatives may choose a President whenever the right of choice shall have devolved upon them, and for the case of the death of any of the persons from whom the Senate may choose a Vice-President whenever the right of choice shall have devolved upon them.

Section 5.

Sections 1 and 2 shall take effect on the 15th day of October following the ratification of this article.

Section 6.

This article shall be inoperative unless it shall have been ratified as an amendment to the Constitution by the legislatures of three-fourths of the several States within seven years from the date of its submission.

Amendment XXI (1933)

Section 1.

The eighteenth article of amendment to the Constitution of the United States is hereby repealed.

Section 2.

The transportation or importation into any State, Territory, or possession of the United States for delivery or use therein of intoxicating liquors, in violation of the laws thereof, is hereby prohibited.

Section 3.

The article shall be inoperative unless it shall have been ratified as an amendment to the Constitution by conventions in the several States, as provided in the Constitution, within seven years from the date of the submission hereof to the States by the Congress.

Amendment XXII (1951)

Section 1.

No person shall be elected to the office of the President more than twice, and no person who has held the office of President, or acted as President for more than two years of a term to which some other person was elected President shall be elected to the office of the President more than once. But this Article shall not apply to any person holding the office of President when this Article was proposed by the Congress, and shall not prevent any person who May be holding the office of President, or acting as President, during the term within which this Article becomes operative from holding the office of President or acting as President during the remainder of such term.

Section 2.

This article shall be inoperative unless it shall have been ratified as an amendment to the Constitution by the legislatures of three-fourths of the several States within seven years from the date of its submission to the States by the Congress.

Amendment XXIII (1961)

Section 1.

The District constituting the seat of government of the United States shall appoint in such manner as the Congress may direct:

A number of electors of President and Vice-President equal to the whole number of Senators and Representatives in Congress to which the District would be entitled if it were a State, but in no event more than the least populous State; they shall be in addition to those appointed by the States, but they shall be considered, for the purposes of the election of President and Vice-President, to be electors appointed by a State; and they shall meet in the district and perform such duties as provided by the twelfth article of amendment.

Section 2.

The Congress shall have power to enforce this article by appropriate legislation.

Amendment XXIV (1964)

Section 1.

The right of citizens of the United States to vote in any primary or other election for President or Vice-President, for electors for President or Vice-President, or for Senator or Representative in Congress, shall not be denied or abridged by the United States or any State by reason of failure to pay any poll tax or other tax.

Section 2.

The Congress shall have power to enforce this article by appropriate legislation.

Amendment XXV (1967)

Section 1.

In case of the removal of the President from office or of his death or resignation, the Vice-President shall become President.

Section 2.

Whenever there is a vacancy in the office of the Vice-President, the President shall nominate a Vice-President who shall take office upon confirmation by a majority vote of both Houses of Congress.

Section 3.

Whenever the President transmits to the President pro tempore of the Senate and the Speaker of the House of Representatives his written declaration that he is unable to discharge the powers and duties of his office, and until he transmits to them a written declaration to the contrary, such powers and duties shall be discharged by the Vice-President as Acting President.

Section 4.

Whenever the Vice-President and a majority of either the principal officers of the executive departments or of such other body as Congress may by law provide, transmit to the President pro tempore of the Senate and the Speaker of the House of Representatives their written declaration that the President is unable to discharge the powers and duties of his office, the Vice-President shall immediately assume the powers and duties of the office as Acting President.

Thereafter, when the President transmits to the President pro tempore of the Senate and the Speaker of the House of Representatives his written declaration that no inability exists, he shall resume the powers and duties of his office unless the Vice-President and a majority of either the principal officers of the executive department or of such other body as Congress may by law provide, transmit within four days to the President pro tempore of the Senate and the Speaker of the House of Representatives their written declaration that the President is unable to discharge the powers and duties of his office. Thereupon Congress shall decide the issue, assembling within forty-eight hours for that purpose if not in session. If the Congress, within twenty-one days after receipt of the latter written declaration, or, if Congress is not in session, within twenty-one days after Congress is required to assemble, determines by two-thirds vote of both Houses that the President is unable to discharge the powers and duties of his office, the Vice-President shall continue to discharge the same as Acting President; otherwise, the President shall resume the powers and duties of his office.

Amendment XXVI (1971)

Section 1.

The right of citizens of the United States, who are eighteen years of age or older, to vote shall not be denied or abridged by the United States or by any State on account of age.

Section 2.

The Congress shall have power to enforce this article by appropriate legislation.

Endnotes

Chapter 1

1. E. Durkheim, *The Division of Labor in Society* (New York: Free Press, 1933; original work published 1893).
2. K. Marx and F. Engels, *The Communist Manifesto: A Modern Edition* (New York: Verso, 1998; original work published 1848; original English version 1888).
3. D.R. Coquillette, "Ideology and Incorporation III: Reason Regulated—The Post-Restoration English Civilians, 1653–1735+," 67, *B. U. L Rev*, 289 (1987).
4. Blackstone, *Commentaries on the Laws of England,* ed. Cooley (1899).
5. Coquillette, "Ideology and Incorporation III."
6. Ibid.
7. Ibid.
8. Ibid.
9. D.L. Rhode, "Feminist Critical Theories," 42, *Stan. L. Rev.*, 617 (1990).
10. Cable News Network, *The Murder* (1995). http://www.cnn.com/US/OJ/murder/index.html.
11. Podgers, James, "COMMON GROUND: The ABA and the Obama Administration are Thinking More Alike on Detainee Policy," *American Bar Association Journal*, January 2010. 96 A.B.A.J. 59.
12. Federal Bureau of Investigation, *A Short History of the Federal Bureau of Investigation* (Washington, DC, 1998). http://www.fbi.gov/history/hist.htm.
13. Federal Rules of Criminal Procedure, Rule 29(b).
14. W. Churchill, *History of the English-Speaking Peoples* (rev. ed.) (New York: Random House, 1965).
15. E.A. Tomlinson, "Symposium: Comparative Criminal Justice Issues in the United States, West Germany, England, and France: Nonadversarial Justice: The French Experience," 42, *Md. L. Rev.* 131 (1983).
16. Ibid.
17. J.R. Schmertz Jr. and M. Meier, "Despite Requests for Stay of Execution From International Court of Justice, U.S. Supreme Court Denies Habeas Corpus Relief to Convicted Paraguayan Citizen for Citizen's Failure to Raise Violation of Consular Convention Before Virginia Courts," *International Law Update*, Vol. 4, no. 4 (April 1998).

Chapter 2

1. "Woman Who Fell from High-Rise, Boyfriend were Drinking," *The Pocono Record* (Stroudsburg, PA), February 27, 2006.
2. Michael Race, "Eckenrode Sentenced," *The Times Tribune* (Scranton), February 21, 2007.
3. Karen Arenson, "Duke Failed to See Gravity of Rape Case, Report Says," *The New York Times*, May 9, 2006.
4. Duff Wilson, "Blacks Call for Calm in Duke Rape Case," *The New York Times*, April 7, 2006. Note that the e-mail language was later revealed to have come from the book "American Psycho" by Bret Easton Ellis—which features a serial killer. It was made into a movie.
5. Dara Doyle and James Ludden, "Leeson, Who Ruined Barings, May Return to Trading," *Bloomberg News*, March 7, 2007.
6. Ken Palmer, "A Mom's Crusade; Veronica McQueen Presses on in Daughter's Memory," *The Flint Journal*, February 19, 2006.
7. Andrew Miga, "Kennedy Blames Accident on Sleep Medicine," *Washington Post*, May 4, 2006.

8. "FDA Requests Label Change for All Sleep Disorder Drug Products," *FDA Press Release*, March 14, 2007, 7–45.

9. The author was shocked when, after a shooting occurred outside her home, a neighbor who happened to be a skilled surgeon stood and watched as the victim lay bleeding from a head wound. The surgeon made no move to assist. Technically, he had no duty to do so.

10. *People v. Hebert*, 228 Cal. App. 2d 514, (Cal. App. 1964).

11. Benjamin Smith, "Linda Fairstein Changed the Way Rape is Prosecuted by Reconciling Feminist Ideals with the Dirty Work of Investigating Sex Crimes. But Will She Be Remembered for Her Pragmatism or Her Bad Publicity?" *Legal Affairs*, September/October 2003.

12. New York Police Department Report on the Central Park Jogger incident.

Chapter 3

1. Genesis 4:12.

2. T.J. Gardner, *Criminal Law: Principles and Cases,* 3rd ed. (West Publishing Co., 1985).

3. J.A. Sigler, *An Introduction to the Legal System* (Homewood, IL: Dorsey Press, 1968).

4. J.R. Nash, *Bloodletters and Badmen: A Narrative Encyclopedia of the American Criminals from the Pilgrims to the Present* (New York: M. Evans & Co, 1974).

5. *State v. Neumann,* 262 N.W. 2d 426 (1978).

6. Idaho Code § 18-4003.

7. *State v. Shuff*, 9 Idaho 115, 72 P. 664 (1903).

8. *Bradshaw v. Richey*, 546 U.S. 74 (2005).

9. *Commonwealth v. Kling*, 1999 PA Super 110, 731 A.2d 145.

10. J. Gibeaut, "Troubling Translations: Cultural Defenses Tactic Raises Issues of Fairness," *ABA Journal*, Vol. 85 (October 1999), 93.

11. A. Drell, "Witchcraft Murder Defense Fails: Judge Bars Expert Testimony on Defendant's Belief in Victim's Supernatural Powers," *ABA Journal*, Vol. 79 (May 1993), 40.

12. *Hopkins v. Reeves*, 525 U.S. 88 (1998).

13. Idaho Code § 18-4003.

14. 18 Pa.C.S. § 2502.

15. Minn. Stat. § 609.185, Minn. Stat. § 609.19.

16. *New York v. Glandman*, 41 N.Y. 2d 123 (1976).

17. *State v. Arrendondo*, 531 N.W.2d 841.

18. *Commonwealth v. Austin*, 2006 PA Super 226, 906 A.2d 1213.

19. *State v. Darris*, 648 N.W.2d 232.

20. *Commonwealth v. Matchett*, 436 N.E. 2d 400 (1982).

21. *Tison v. Arizona*, 481 U.S. 137 at 147. (1987).

22. *Gonzales v. Oregon*, 546 U.S. 243. (2006).

23. R. Phillips, *Autopsy: No Sign Schiavo was Abused.* http://www.cnn.com/2005/HEALTH/06/15/schiavo.autopsy/index.html.

24. S, Shane, "U.S. Approval of Killing of Cleric Causes Unease," *New York Times*, May 13, 2010.

25. T. Reid, "Obama Gives Order to Kill American Terror Imam," *Times* (London), April 8, 2010.

26. G. Filosa, "Orleans Jury Convicts Mab of Killing Kids in 2002 Over 'High School Drama'." *Times-Picayune*, March 11, 2010.

27. S. Horowitz, S. Higham, and S. Moreno, "Who Killed Chandra Levy?" *Washington Post*, June 23, 2008.

28. S. Horowitz, S. Higham, and S. Moreno, "Who Killed Chandra Levy?" *Washington Post*, July 24, 2008.

29. S. Higham and S. Horwitz, "Finding Chandra: A True Washington Murder Mystery," *Washington Post*, May 7, 2010.

Chapter 4

1. 2007 Crime Victimization Report. *Bureau of Justice Statistics,* http://bjs.ojp.usdoj.gov/content/pub/pdf/cvus0702.pdf.

2. Lisa Rein, "Va. House Backs Bill to Outlaw Wife Rape," *Washington Post*, February 8, 2002 and Virginia Code Ann. § 18.2-61 (B).

3. Model Penal Code § 213.1

4. Steve Lipsher, "Lawyer May Not See Humor in 'SNL' Skit; Bryant Attorney Flooded with Calls After She's Mocked on Show," *Milwaukee Journal Sentinel*, October 15, 2003.

5. Howard Pankratz, "Trial Judge Could Rule Our Testimony About Overdose," *The Denver Post*, July 22, 2003.

6. Virginia Code § 18.2-67.7

7. Katherine Finkelstein, "Deal Proposed for Defendant in Net Sex Case," *New York Times*, November 22, 2000.

8. "Focus on New York's Rape Shield Law: Court Overturns Cybersex Torture Conviction," Court TV Online, December 22, 1999.

9. Jane Fritsch and Katherine Finkelstein, "All Charges Dismissed by Judge in Columbia Sex Torture Case," *New York Times*, November 2, 2001.

10. *FBI Uniform Crime Reporting Handbook.*

11. Sharon Jayson, "Teens Define Sex in New Ways", *USA Today* at D1, October 10, 2005.

12. Child Trends' analyses of the 2002 National Survey of Family Growth, Oral Sex at http://www.childtrends-databank.org/pdf/95_PDF.pdf.

13. *Uniform Crime Reporting Handbook.*

14. Tom Hays, "Cop Gets 15 Years in Torture Case," *AP*, June 27, 2000.

15. *Uniform Crime Reporting Handbook.*

16. *U.S. v. Jerry Levis Banks, Sr.*, 556 F.3d 967, 9th Cir. (2009).

17. The EEOC's Youth@Work initiative at http:// www.eeoc.gov/eeoc/initiatives/youth/index.cfm.

18. *Uniform Crime Reporting Handbook.*

19. Alaska Stat. § 11.41.450.

20. 11 Del. C. § 766.

21. *Harmon v. State*, 11 P.3d 393 (Alaska Ct. App. 2000).

22. Peter Biskin, "Reconstructing Woody," *Vanity Fair*, December 2005.

23. *State v. Earley* (Tenn. Crim. App., 1997).

24. *McDaniel v. Brown*, 130 S. Ct. 665, (2010).

25. *District Attorney's Office for the Third Judicial District et al., Petitioners v. William G. Osborne*, 129 S. Ct. 2308, (2009).

26. The Innocence Project, http://www.innocenceproject.org (accessed May 18, 2010).

27. *Melendez-Diaz v. Massachusetts*, 129 S. Ct. 2527, (2009).

28. Ted Robert Hunt, "Charging John Doe: Tolling the Criminal Statute of Limitations in Missouri Based on the Accused's DNA Profile," *Journal of the Missouri Bar*, Vol. 66 (March–April 2010), 78.

29. The Innocence Project Website, http://www.innocenceproject.org/Content/92.php (accessed May 20, 2010).

Chapter 5

1. Ballentine's Law Dictionary.

2. 18 U.S.C. § 2113.

3. *Carter v. United States,* 530 U.S. 255 (2000).

4. S.C. Code Ann § 16–11–330.

5. Andriy R. Pazuniak, "Two Men Arrested In Toy Gun Robbery," www.TBO.com, July 5, 2007.

6. *United States v. Perry,* 991 F.2d 304 (6th Cir. 1993).

7. *McLaughlin v. United States,* 476 U.S. 16 (1986).

8. Jonathan D. Silver and Lillian Thomas, "Woman, 74, Charged in Bank Heist," *Pittsburgh Post-Gazette* (Pittsburgh, PA), March 7, 2006.

9. "Woman, 76, Gets House Arrest for Robbery," *Associated Press*, July 5, 2007.

10. 18 U.S.C. § 924(c)(1)(A)(i)(ii)(iii).

11. *Dean v. U.S.,* 129 S. Ct. 1849, (2009).

12. *Uniform Crime Reporting Handbook.*

13. Ibid.

14. 18 P.S. § 2709(b).

15. 18 P.S. § 2701(a).

16. 18 P.S. § 2301.

17. See, for example, Pennsylvania's aggravated assault statute at 18. P.S. § 2702, which affords protection to a long list of public officials including school board members, public defenders, district attorneys, and probation officers.

18. 18 Pa.C.S. § 3301.

19. Model Penal Code § 220.1.

20. Bureau of Justice Statistics, U.S. Department of Justice, Press Release, *Justice Department Releases 1997 to 1999 Hate Crime Statistics,* September 23, 2001.

21. *Apprendi v. New Jersey,* 530 U.S. 466 (2000).

22. *Virginia v. Black*, 123 S. Ct. 1536 (2003).

23. The U.S. Department of Justice News Release, *U.S. Department of Justice Announces Project Safe Childhood Initiative,* June 22, 2006.

24. California Penal Code, Section 422.6 (a).

25. Andrea J. Sedlak, David Finkelhor, Heather Hammer, and Dana J. Schultz, "National Estimates of Missing Children: An Overview," in *National Incidence Studies of Missing, Abducted, Runaway, and Thrownaway Children* (Washington, DC: Office of Juvenile Justice and Delinquency Prevention, Office of Justice Programs, U.S. Department of Justice, October 2002), p. 10, as quoted in the National Center for Missing and Exploited Children's 2008 Annual Report.

26. David Finkelhor. "What the Numbers Tell Us," in *The Front Line* (Alexandria, VA: National Center for Missing & Exploited Children, Winter 2002/2003), p. 10, as quoted in the National Center for Missing and Exploited Children's 2008 Annual Report.

27. 18 P.S. § 2901.

28. 18 P.S. § 2902.

29. 18 P.S. § 2903.

30. 18 P.S. § 2904.

31. 18 P.S. § 2905.

32. 18 P.S. § 2909.

33. 18 P.S. § 2910.

34. *Commonwealth v. Nanorta*, 742 A. 2d 176 (1999).

35. "Lindbergh Baby Kidnapped from Home of Parents on Farm near Princeton: Taken from His Crib; Wide Search On," *New York Times,* March 2, 1932.

36. "Hauptmann Guilty; Sentenced to Death for the Murder of Lindbergh Baby," *New York Times,* February 14, 1935.

37. "Federal Aid in Hunt Ordered by Hoover," *New York Times*, March 3, 1932.

38. Federal Bureau of Investigations, *History of the FBI*, online at http://www.fbi.gov/libref/historic/history/historicdates.htm.

39. 18 U.S.C. § 1201 (a).

40. 18 U.S.C. § 1201 (g).

41. 22 U.S.C. § 7102(8).

42. "What we Do: Fight Trafficking in Persons," U.S. Department of Justice, January 30, 2007.

43. V. Ortiz, "Maid Lived 20 Years in Quite Struggle; Brookfield Family and Her Family in the Philippines Manipulated Her," *Milwaukee Journal Sentinel,* January 14, 2007, p. 1.

44. "Attorney General Alberto R. Gonzales Announces Creation of Human Trafficking Prosecution Unit Within the Civil Rights Division," Press release, U.S. Department of Justice, January 31, 2007.

45. T. Opdyke, "One 'Barbie Bandit' Sentenced to 2 Years, the Other Probation," *Atlanta Journal Constitution,* March 24, 2008.

46. M. Miller, "Cumberland County Man Charged with Stalking via Fake MySpace Page," *Patriot News,* January 29, 2010.

47. 18 P.S. § 2701(a).

Chapter 6

1. Ballentine's Law Dictionary.

2. Ibid.

3. Ibid.

4. *Kelo v. City of New London*, 545 U.S. 469.(2005).

5. Ibid.

6. Ibid.

7. Ibid.

8. *Columbus-America Discovery Group v. Atlantic Mutual Insurance Company*, 1992 (974, F. 2d 450-4th Circuit 1992).

9. Richard M. Westfall, *Telepossession of Extreterrestrial Resources and Leveraged Financing of Outer Space Projects* (Denver, CO: Galactic Mining Industries, Inc.); Declan J. O'Donnell PC, United Societies in Space, Inc., Castle Rock, Colorado, and Gary Rodriguez, sysRAND Corporation, Parker, Colorado, from the website of Galactic Mining Industries, Inc., www.angelfire.com/trek/galactic_mining/Telepossession.htm.(2003).

10. National Association for Shoplfting Prevention (NASP), a nonprofit organization providing research-based shoplifting prevention initiatives including education, prevention, justice and rehabilitation programs. Visit NASP at www.shopliftingprevention.org.

11. "Looters Strike New Orleans After Storm: 'It's Insane,' Says Tourist Watching Theft in French Quarter," *Associated Press*, MSNBC.com, August 30, 2005.

12. Laura Beach, "Edward Forbes Smiley III Admits to Stealing 97 Rare Maps from US and UK Institutions," *Antiques and the Arts Online* (Newtown, CT), June 27, 2006.

13. "DEA Accuses Agent, Wife of Scheme," *Deseret News* (Salt Lake City, UT), October 1, 2006.

14. Geoffrey Fattah, "Woman Guilty of Theft in Fake Cancer Scheme," *Deseret Morning News* (Salt Lake City, UT), July 29, 2005.

15. Pamela Manson, "For Lying About Cancer, West Jordan Couple Must Pay the Feds $60,000," *The Salt Lake Tribune* (Salt Lake City, UT), June 16, 2007.

16. "'Fake Cancer' Couple Will Repay $60,000," *Associated Press*, KUTV.com (Salt Lake City, UT), June 15, 2007.

17. Brandon Ortiz, "Pair Charged with Theft from Title Fund Account," *Lexington Herald-Leader* (Lexington, KY), May 29, 2006, p. A1.

18. The author's first jury trial involved just such a case. The defendant, who represented himself, told the jury he was merely "borrowing" the grill and intended to return it after a backyard barbecue. He was acquitted.

19. David Barasch, United States Attorney for the Middle District of Pennsylvania Press Release, February 20, 2001.

20. Pegasus News, University of North Texas (Denton, TX), June 25, 2007.

21. Neil Swidey, "The Inside Job," *The Boston Globe* (Boston, MA), September 17, 2006.

22. Samantha Martin, United States Department of Justice news release (Boston, MA), February 12, 2007.

23. Insurance Information Institute, Auto Theft Statistics, 2006, www.iii.org.

24. *New Tools to Track Down Stolen Cars*, online at http://www.auto-theft.info/Plate_Check_Story.htm (accessedMay 20, 2010).

25. Data from the Insurance Information Institute located online at http://www.auto-theft.info/Statistics.htm.

26. Ibid.

27. Va. Statutes § 18 2-95. An exception to the $200 threshold is that any firearm stolen is considered grand larceny regardless of its value.

28. "LSAT Robbery Prompts Arrests," *The Daily Trojan* (UCLA), March 27, 1997.

29. "LSAT Cheaters Are Sentenced to Probation," *Corpus Christi Caller Times*, January 28, 2000.

30. 4 W. Blackstone, Commentaries 224.

31. 18 P.S. § 3502.

32. 18 Cal. Penal Code Ann. § 459

33. According to the American Psychiatric Association's *Diagnostic and Statistical Manual of Psychiatric Disorders*, Fourth Edition, patients with pyromania exhibit the following behavior: A patient must have set more than one fire, been tense or excited before setting the fire, have been fascinated by fire in the past, experienced pleasure, gratification, or relief after the fire or while watching it, and not had any of the other common reasons for setting the fire, such as revenge, political agenda, or profit motive.

34. United States Department of Justice, Federal Bureau of Investigation statistics, Crime in the United States 2008, www.fbi.gov/ucr.htm.

35. Bill Bishop, "Two Women Sentenced to Prison in 'Operation Backfire' Arson Cases," *The Register-Guard* (Eugene, OR), June 1, 2007.

36. 436 U.S. 499 (1978).

37. S. Farley, "Gun-toting Soccer Mom Is Shot Dead," *Harrisburg Patriot News*, October 08, 2009.

38. Payment Fraud and Control Survey, Association of Financial Professionals, (March 2005) reported by www.stopcheckfraud.com.

39. Minn. Stat. §609.631(2).

40. 18 U.S.C. §470 et. seq.

41. 18 P.S. § 4105.

42. Tim Wilson, "Stolen Data's Black Market," *Dark Reading*, September 7, 2006, www.darkreading.com.

43. "Alcatel-Lucent Notifies Employees and Retirees of Former Lucent Technologies of missing Computer Disk Containing Personal Information, Alcatel-Lucent news release" (Murray Hill, NJ), May 17, 2007, www.alcatel-lucent.com.

44. Revised Code of Washington. §9.35.020

45. 18 USC § 1028A(a)(1)

46. *Flores-Figueroa v. U.S.*, 129 S. Ct. 1886, (2009)

47. Federal Bureau of Investigations Internet Crime Complaint Center (IC3) Annual Report, 2009.

Chapter 7

1. The Mann Act, 18 U.S.C. § 2421.

2. *Caminetti v. United States*, 242 U.S. 470 (1917).

3. *Cleveland v. United States*, 329 U.S. 14 (1946).

4. 18 P.S. § 5902.

5. 18 P.S. § 5902(e.2).

6. 15 N.R.S. § 201.354.

7. Office of National Drug Control Policy, *The National Drug Control Strategy: 2008 Annual Report*.

8. Uniform Crime Report 2008.

9. Ballentine's Law Dictionary.

10. The DEA's HIDTA Program, http://www.justice.gov/dea/programs/hidta.htm (accessed May 27, 2010).

11. Federal Bureau of Investigations, *Uniform Crime Reports, Crime in the United States*, 2008.

12. Department of Justice, Bureau of Justice Statistics, *Drug Crime and Facts*.

13. 18 U.S.C. § 3591.

14. Felony Sentences in State Court, 2006, Bureau of Justice Statistics.

15. *Kimbrough v. United States*, 128 S. Ct. 558 (2007).

16. Matthew Ryno, *Sentence Changes Have Impact*, Telegraph Herald (Dubuque, IA), December 31, 2007, Section A, p. 1.

17. *Kimbrough v. United States*, 128 S. Ct. 558 (2007).

18. *U.S. v. Booker*, 125 S. Ct. 738 (2005).

19. Kimbrough.

20. Ballentine's Law Dictionary.

21. Utah, Tennessee, and Hawaii are the holdouts.

22. Pa. Lottery Annual Report June 30, 2009.

23. Congressional Documents and Publications, *Blumenauer Statement on Raising Revenue by Legalizing Online Gambling*, May 19, 2010.

24. States News Service, *Frank: Financial Services Committee Will Act on Internet Gambling Bill*, May 20, 2010.

25. R. Dunstan, *Gambling in California*, California Research Bureau, 1997.

26. 18 U.S.C. § 1955.

27. 413 U.S. 915, 93 S. Ct. 2607 (1973).

28. 636 F. Supp. 828 (S.D. Cal.) 1986. aff'd sub. nom. *United States v. Weigand*, 812 F. 2d. 1239 (9th Cir.), *cert denied*, 484 U.S. 856 (1987).

29. Cash, B. V. 51 Ala. L. Rev. 793, *Images of Innocence or Guilt?: The Status of Laws Regulating Child Pornography on the Federal Level and in Alabama and an Evaluation of the Case Against Barnes & Noble*.

30. *U.S. v. Matthews,* 11 F. Supp. 2d 656. District Court of Maryland. Appeal Denied (1998).

31. *U.S. v. Comstock et al.,* No. 08-1224, 2010.

32. Bureau of Justice Statistics, U.S. Department of Justice, *Intimate Partner Violence, 1993–2001 (2003).*

33. 2008 Uniform Crime Report.

34. Bureau of Justice Statistics, U.S. Department of Justice, *Violence by Intimates: Analysis of Data on Crimes by Current or Former Spouses, Boyfriends and Girlfriends* (1998).

35. 42 U.S.C. § 13981(b).

36. *United States v. Morrison,* 529 U.S. 598 (2000).

37. American Academy of Pediatrics, *Guidelines for the Evaluation of Sexual Abuse of Children,* 87 *Pediatrics* 254, 1991.

38. 18 U.S.C. § 2241(c) and 2423.

39. Assistant Attorney General Deborah Daniels, National AMBER Alert coordinator.

40. *Mormon Church v. United States,* 136 U.S. 1 (1890).

41. *Man Arrested for Tattooing Toddler.* Parentdish. com, http://www.parentdish.com/2010/02/12/man-arrested-for-tattooing-toddler/ (accessed May 30, 2010).

42. *Couple arrested for giving their kids homemade tatoos, thoughts?* Cafemom.com, http://www.cafemom.com/answers/353515/Couple_ arrested_for_giving_their_kids_homemade_tatoos_thoughts (accessed May 30, 2010).

43. 18 P.S. § 509.

44. *Kolender v. Lawson,* 461 U.S. 352 (1983).

45. Patsy A. Klaus, *Crimes Against Persons Age 65 or Older,* Bureau of Justice Statistics. Revised January 2000.

46. *Champlinsky v. New Hampshire,* 315 U.S. 568 (1942).

47. *Wright et al. v. Georgia,* 83 S. Ct. 1240 (1963).

48. Ballentine's Law Dictionary.

49. B. Hardy, "Return from Planet Pee-wee," *Vanity Fair,* September 1999.

50. *Papachristo v. City of Jacksonville,* 405 U.S. 156 (1972).

51. Ballentine's Law Dictionary.

52. Ibid.

53. 97 Miss. Code § 97-29.5.

54. N.C. Gen. Stat. § 8-57.

55. *Toncray v. Budge,* 95 P. 26.

56. 97 Miss. Code § 97-29-43.

57. *Reynolds v. United States,* 98 U.S. 145 (1878).

58. Blackstone, *Commentaries.*

59. 410 U.S. 113 (1973).

60. *Planned Parenthood of Southeastern Pa. v. Casey,* 505 U.S. 833 (1992).

61. *Stenberg v. Carhart,* 530 U.S. 914 (2000).

62. *Gonzales v. Carjart et al., Gonzales v. Planned Parenthood Federation of America,* 127 S. Ct. 1610 (2007).

63. Ballentine's Law Dictionary.

64. Code Theod. 9.7.6; Code Just. 9.9.31.

65. 25 Hen. VIII, ch. 6.

66. *Survey on the Constitutional Right to Privacy in the Context of Homosexual Activity,* 40 U. Miami L. Rev. 521 (1986).

67. *Bowers v. Hardwick,* 478 U.S. 186 (1984).

Chapter 8

1. The inscription was written by Emma Lazarus (1849–1887).

2. D. McCullough, *John Adams* (New York: Simon & Schuster, 2001).

3. *U.S. Constitution,* Article I, Section 8.

4. *U.S. Constitution,* Article II, Section 2.

5. Executive Order No. 10340 (April 8, 1952).

6. *Youngstown Sheet & Tube Co. v. Sawyer,* 343 U.S. 579 (1952).

7. E. Cray, *Chief Justice. A Biography of Earl Warren* (New York: Simon & Schuster, 1997).

8. H. El Nasser, "Papers Show Census Role in WWII Camps: Japanese-American's Data to ID them for Round-ups," *USA Today,* March 30, 2007.

9. *Korematsu v. United States,* 323 U.S. 214 (1944).

10. Blackstone, *Commentaries on the Laws of England* (1765).

11. *U.S. Constitution,* Article I, Section 9.

12. *Ex parte Milligan,* 71 U.S. (4 Wall) 2 (1866).

13. *United States v. Awadallah,* 202 F. Supp. 2d 55 (2002).

14. Curt Gentry, *Edgar Hoover: The Man and the Secrets* (New York: W.W. Norton & Company, 1991).

15. *Ex parte Quirin et al.,* 317 U.S.1 (1942).

16. *Hamdi v. Rumsfeld,* 337 F. 3d 335 (4th Cir. 2003).

17. *Hamdi v. Rumsfeld,* 124 S. Ct. 2633 (2004).

18. *Rumsfeld v. Padilla,* 124 S. Ct. 2711 (2004).

19. *Padilla v. Hanft,* No. 05-533, 547 U.S. 1062; 126 S. Ct. 1649.

20. "Terror Conspirator Padilla Appeals Conviction," *The Associated Press,* January 12, 2010.

21. *Rasul v. Bush,* 124 S. Ct. 2711 (2004).

22. Pub. L. No. 109-148, 119 Stat. 2680 (2005).

23. *Hamdan v. Rumsfeld,* 126 S. Ct. 2749, 165 L. Ed. 2d 723 (2006).

24. Pub. L. No. 109-366, 120 Stat. 2600 (2006).
25. *Boumediene et al. v. Bush,* 128 S. Ct. 2229, (2008).
26. Warren Richey, "Obama Endorses Military Commissions for Guantanamo Detainees; Obama Signed the Military Commissions Act of 2009 Wednesday. Critics Say It is an Improvement over Past Efforts But Still Offers Only Second-class Justice to Guantanamo Detainees," *Christian Science Monitor,* October 29, 2009.
27. *U.S. Constitution,* Article III, Section 3.
28. Ibid.
29. 18 U.S.C. § 2381.
30. *Stephan v. United States,* 133 F.2d 87 (6th Cir. 1943), cert den 318 U.S. 781, reh den 319 U.S. 783 (1943).
31. *Young v. United States,* 97 U.S. 39 (1878).
32. *Carlisle v. United States,* 8 Ct. Cl 153 (1872).
33. *Hanauer v. Doane,* 79 U.S. 342 (1871); *Carlisle v. United States,* 83 U.S. 147 (1873).
34. *Kawakita v. United States,* 343 U.S. 717 (1952).
35. *United States v. Chandler,* 72 F. Supp. 230 (DC Mass 1947).
36. *United States v. Hodges,* F. Cas No 15374 (CC Md 1815).
37. *Kawakita v. United States,* 343 U.S. 717 (1952).
38. *United States v. Haupt,* 47 F. Supp. 836 (DC Ill 1942).
39. *United States v. Fricke,* 259 F. 673 (DC NY 1919).
40. *Cramer v. United States,* 325 U.S. 1 (1945).
41. *Kawakita v. United States,* 343 U.S. 717 (1952).
42. *D'Aquino v. United States,* 1922 F.2d 338 (9th Cir 1951), cert den 343 U.S. 935 (1952).
43. *Miller v. The Ship Resolution* (1781, F CC Pa) 2 U.S. 1, later op (F CC Pa) 2 US 19.
44. *United States v. Chandler,* 72 F. Supp. 230 (DC Mass 1947).
45. *United States v. Burgman,* 87 F. Supp. 568 (DC 1949) cert den 342 U.S. 838 (1950).
46. *Young v. United States,* 97 U.S. 39 (1878); *United States v. Morrison,* 30 F. Cas No 18270 (1869).
47. Burr was involved in another scandal as well. He killed Alexander Hamilton in a duel.
48. W. Burger, *It Is So Ordered: A Constitution Unfolds* (New York: William Morrow and Company, 1995).
49. 18 U.S.C. § 2384.
50. Ballentine's Law Dictionary.
51. *Wright v. United States,* 108 F. 805 (5th Cir. 1901), cert den 181 U.S. 620 (1901).
52. *Skeffinton v. Katzeff,* 277 F. 129 (1st Cir. 1922).
53. *Baldwin v. Franks,* 120 U.S. 678 (1887).
54. Ibid.
55. *Wells v. United States,* 257 F. 605 (9th Cir. 1919); *Enfield v. United States,* 261 F. 141(8th Cir. 1919); *Orear v. United States,* 261 F. 257 (5th Cir. 1919).
56. *Hays v. American Defense Soc.,* 252 N.Y. 266, 169 N.E. 380 (1929).
57. 18 U.S.C. § 798.
58. 18 U.S.C. § 2383.
59. Ibid.
60. M. Sullivan and D. Rather, eds., *Our Times: America at the Birth of the 20th Century* (New York: Scribner, 1996).
61. *Holder v. Humanitarian Law Project,* Docket No. 08-1498. U.S. Supreme Court 2009 term.
62. Donald G. Rehkopf, "Commentary: Military Commissions-Shrouded in Secrecy (Again!)," *The Daily Record of Rochester,* April 13, 2010.

Chapter 9

1. Ballentine's Law Dictionary.
2. 18 P.S. § 4904.
3. 18 U.S.C. § 1623(e).
4. *United States v. Norris,* 300 U.S. 564 (1937).
5. 18 U.S.C. § 1623(d).
6. 18 U.S.C. § 1623(c).
7. *United States v. Gugliaro,* 501 F. 2d 68 (2nd Cir. 1974).
8. M. Farmer, *The Long Arm of the Law (1994),* Regia Anglorum Publications, http://www.ftecj.net/~regia/law.htm.
9. *McGhee v. Pottawattamie County et al.* 547 F.3d 922, (2008) cert. granted to U.S. Supreme Court, but dismissed before decision.
10. *United States v. Wood,* 6 F. 3d 692 (10th Cir. 1993).
11. 18 U.S.C. § 1515.
12. *United States v. Wood,* 6 F. 3d 692 (10th Cir. 1993).
13. *United States v. Cammisano,* 917 F. 2d 1057 (8th Cir. 1990).
14. "How Much Has Fred Zain Cost the State?" *Sunday Gazette-Mail,* September 23, 2001.
15. "Police Chemist's Missteps Cause Oklahoma Scandal," *Washington Post,* November 11, 2001.
16. Roadcap testified in cases the author prosecuted in the 1980s. So the author finds these later revelation particularly troublesome.
17. "'I Can Move On', Harrisburg, Man, State Settle Suits Claiming Frame-up in 1970 Murder," *Patriot News* (Harrisburg, PA), June 20, 2006.
18. Ballentine's Law Dictionary.
19. 18 U.S.C. § 401.

20. *In re Farquhar*, 160 U.S. App DC 295, 492 F. 2d 561 (1973).
21. *Floersheim v. Engman*, 161 U.S. App DC 30, 494 F. 2d 949 (1973).
22. *United States v. Seale*, 461 F. 2d 345 (7th Cir. 1972).
23. Ibid.
24. "Lessons of the 60's: 'We'd Do It Again,' Say the Chicago Seven's Lawyers," *ABA Journal*, May 18, 1987.
25. *In re Bonanno*, 344 F. 2d 830 (2nd Cir. 1965).
26. *Yates v. United States*, 355 U.S. 66 (1957).
27. *Bullock v. United States*, 265 F. 2d 683 (6th Cir. 1959), cert den 360 U.S. 909 (1959).
28. *United States v. Rollerson*, 145 U.S. App DC 338, 449 F. 2d 1000 (1971).
29. 28 C.F.R. 50.10(a).
30. J. C. Wilson, *The Politics of Truth: Inside the Lies that Led to War and Betrayed My Wife's CIA Identity*, (New York: Carroll & Graf, 2004).
31. "How it Unfolded; CIA Leak Indictment," *Seattle Time*, October 29, 2005.
32. Ballentine's Law Dictionary.
33. *United States v. Hernandez*, 731 F. 2d 1147 (5th Cir. 1984).
34. *United States v. Daniel*, 3 F. 3d 775 (4th Cir. 1993).
35. *United States v. Kim*, 870 F. 2d 81 (2nd Cir.1989).
36. 18 U.S.C. & 1961 et seq.
37. *Boyle v. US.*, 129 S. Ct. 2237 (2009).
38. *Scheidler et al. v. NOW Inc.*, 547 U.S. 9 (2006).
39. *Wilkie v. Robbins*, 127 S. Ct. 2588 (2007).
40. *Anza v. Ideal Steel Supply Corp.*, 126 S. Ct. 1991 (2006).
41. *Williams v. Mohawk Industries*, 465 F. 3d. 1277 (2006)
42. United States Constitution, Article II Section 4.
43. "Senate Convicts, Removes Hastings from Judgeship," *Wall Street Journal*, October 23, 1989.
44. M. J. Gerhardt, *Review: The Perils of Presidential Impeachment*. 67 U. Chi. L. Rev. 293.
45. 26 USC § 7201.
46. 26 USC § 7203.
47. 18 USC § 1341.

Chapter 10

1. "Wasilla Fence Fascinating for National Media Outlets," *Mat-Su Valley Frontiersman*, May 29, 2010.
2. "'They Pretended They Were God' Doctor, 2 Nurses Allededly Killed Patients with Lethal Drug Dose," CNN.com (accessed at http://www.cnn.com/2006/LAW/07/18/hospital.deaths/index.html).
3. "Foti Defends How Office Handled Investigation; Says Grand Jury Didn't See Evidence," *Times-Picayune* (New Orleans), July 25, 2007.
4. *Dixon v. United States*, 126 S. Ct. 2437 (2006).
5. S. Kiley, "Crime: After the Homemade Bomb Chained Around Bank Robber Brian Wells's Neck Exploded, Baffled Police in the Pretty Lakeside Town or Erie Found Detailed Instructions to a Bizarre Treasure Hund," *Observer Magazine*, July 22, 2007.
6. Sean D. Hamill, "Key Part of Bank Robbery Lore Is False, Prosecutors Say," *The New York Times*, Section A, p. 17, September 4, 2008.
7. *Jacobson v. United states*, 503 U.S. 540 (1992).
8. 18 U.S.C.A. 17 (2000); *United States v. Cameron*, 907 F.2d 1051, 1061 (11th Cir. 1990).
9. "Va. Moves to Limit Executions: Senate Approves Shielding Retarded," *Washington Post*, February 9, 2002.
10. *Montana v. Egelhoff*, 518 U.S. 116 (1996).
11. *Rex v. M'Naghten*, House of Lords. 10 Cl. & F. 200, 8 Eng, Rep. 718.
12. *Parsons v. State*, 81 Ala. 577. 2 So. 854 (1887).
13. *Durham v. United States*, 94 U.S. App. D. C. 228. 214 F. 2d 862 (1954).
14. *Indiana v. Jackson*, 406 U.S. 715 (1972).
15. *White v. Estelle*, 459 U.S. 1118 (1983).
16. Editorial, "1963 Birmingham Bombing: Another Man's Time to Answer," *The Durham Herald* (Durham, NC), January 7, 2002.
17. *Sell v. United States*, 539 U.S. 166 (2003).
18. *Caritativo v. California*, 359 U.S. 549 (1958).
19. N. Leavitt, "Is It Always Torture to Dismember and Eat a Conscious Human Being?" Find law commentary, http://writ.news.findlaw.com/commentary/20040108_leavitt.html (accessed August 19, 2007).

Chapter 11

1. *Camara v. Municipal Court*, 387 U.S. 523 (1967).
2. *Olmstead v. United States*, 277 U.S. 438 (1928).
3. *Buck v. Bell*, 274 U.S. 200 (1927).
4. *Skinner v. Oklahoma ex Rel. Williamson, Attorney General*, 316 U.S. 535 (1942).
5. *Griswold et al. v. Connecticut*, 381 U.S. 479 (1965).
6. *Roe v. Wade*, 410 U.S. 113 (1973).
7. *Bowers, Attorney General of Georgia v. Hardwick et al.*, 478 U.S. 186 (1986).
8. *Lawrence v. Texas*, 539 U.S. 558 (2003).

9. *Georgia v. Randolph*, 547 U.S. 103 (2006).

10. *Mancusi v. De Forte*, 392 U.S. 364 (1968).

11. *Cowles v. Alaska*, 23 P.3d 1168 (2001) cert den. 2002 U.S. Lexis 701.

12. V. Bernstein, "Police Enter Dormitory at Duke to Query Players in Rape Case," *The New York Times*, April 15, 2006.

13. *Minnesota v. Olson*, 495 U.S. 91 (1990).

14. *Katz v. United States*, 389 U.S. 347 (1967).

15. *Kyllo v. United States*, 533 U.S. 27 (2001).

16. *Brinegar v. United States*, 338 U.S. 160 (1949).

17. *United States v. Drayton et al.*, 536 U.S. 194 (2002).

18. *Pearson v. Callahan*, 129 S. Ct. 808 (2009).

19. *Chapman v. United States*, 365 U.S. 610 (1961).

20. *Carroll v. Illinois*, 267 U.S. 132 (1925).

21. *United States v. Ross*, 456 U.S. 798 (1982).

22. *Brendlin v. California*, 127 S. Ct. 2400 (2007).

23. *Arizona v. Gant*, 556 U.S. (2009).

24. *Indianapolis v. Edmond*, 531 U.S. 32 (2000).

25. *Illinois v. Lidster*, 540 U.S. 419 (2004).

26. *Brigham City, Utah v. Charles W. Stuart*, 126 S. Ct. 1943 (2006).

27. *Thornton v. United States*, 124 S. Ct. 2127 (2004).

28. *Maryland v. Pringle*, 370 Md. 525; 805 A. 2d 1016 (2002), affirmed 540 U.S. 366 (2003).

29. *Maryland v. Pringle*, 540 U.S. 366 (2003).

30. *Terry v. Ohio*, 392 U.S. 1 (1968).

31. *Brignoni-Ponce v. United States*, 422 U.S. 873 (1975).

32. *Arizona v. Johnson*, 555 U.S. (2009).

33. *Hiibel v. Nevada*, 124 S. Ct. 2451 (2004).

34. *United States v. Sokolow*, 490 U.S. 1 (1989).

35. *Illinois v. Gates*, 462 U.S. 213 (1983).

36. *The Snitch System*. Center on Wrongful Convictions, Northwestern University School of Law 2005.

37. *United States v. Banks*, 540 U.S. 31 (2003).

38. U.S. Constitution, Fourth Amendment.

39. *Illinois v. Krull*, 480 U.S. 340 (1987).

40. *Herring v. U.S.*, 129 S. Ct. 695 (2009).

41. *Olmstead et al. v. United States*, 277 U.S. 438 (1928).

42. 47 U.S.C. 605 (2004).

43. N.Y. Crim. Proc. 813-a (1958), overturned by *Berger v. New York*, 388 U.S. 41, 59 (1967).

44. *Berger v. New York*, 388 U.S. 41, 59 (1967).

45. 18 U.S.C. 2518 (3)(c) (2000).

46. 18 U.S.C. 2518 (5) (2000).

47. 18 U.S.C. 2518 (4)(c) (2000).

48. 18 U.S.C. 2516 (2000).

49. 18 U.S.C. 2518 (5) (2000).

50. *United States v. Torres*, 751 F. 2d. 875 (7th Cir. 1984).

51. Pub. L. No. 99-508, 100 Stat. 1848 (1986).

52. J. Rose, "Mayfields' Home Goes from Safe to Sinister," *The Oregonian*, December 1, 2006.

53. "Lawyer Falsely Jailed for Bombing Winds $2m," *The Australian*, December 1, 2006.

54. *Digest of Justinian*: Digest 48.2.7.2, translated in 11 Scott, The Civil Law.

55. *Ashe v. Swenson*, 397 U.S. 436 (1970).

56. *Yeager v. U.S.*, 129 S. Ct. 2360 (2009).

57. *Benton v. Maryland*, 395 U.S. 784 (1969).

58. *United States v. Lanza*, 260 U.S. 377 (1922).

59. Martin. Douglas. *Jay C. Smith, 80, Convict Later Freed in Murder Case*. Section B Obituary p. 10. New York Times. May 15, 2009.

60. *Bullington v. Missouri*, 451 U.S. 430 (1981).

61. *Sattazahn v. Pennsylvania*, 537 U.S. 101 (2003).

62. *Commonwealth v. Sattazahn*, 869 A. 2d. 529 (2006).

63. *Kring v. Missouri*, 107 U.S. 221 (1883).

64. *California Dept. of Corrections v. Morales*, 513 U.S. 1074 (1995).

65. *Stogner v. California*, 123 S. Ct. 2446 (2003).

66. C. Goodyear and P. Podger, "California Molestation Law Struck Down," *S. F. Chronicle*, June 27, 2003.

67. *U.S. v. Marcus*, 130 S. Ct. 2159 (2010).

68. *United States v. Brown*, 381 U.S. 437 (1965).

69. *Miranda v. Arizona*, 384 U.S. 436 (1966).

70. *Illinois v. Perkins*, 496 U.S. 292 (1990).

71. The author sat in on a polygraph session with another attorney's client to understand the process.

72. *United States v. Traficant*, 566 F. Supp. 1046 (N.D. Ohio 1983); *State v. Thompson*, 381 So. 2d 823 (1980); *Smith v. State*, 355 A. 2d. 527 (1976).

73. *Jackson v. Denno*, 378 U.S. 368.(1964).

74. Information provided by London Metropolitan Police officers during author's visit to London in January 2005.

Chapter 12

1. *Orozco v. Texas*, 394 U.S. 324 (1969).

2. *Brewer v. Williams*, 430 U.S. 387 (1977).

3. *Maryland v. Shatzer*, 130 S. Ct. 1213 (2010).

4. *United States v. Salerno*, 481 U.S. 739 (1987).

5. *Powell v. Alabama*, 287 U.S. 45 (1932).

6. *Gideon v. Wainwright*, 372 U.S. 335 (1963).

7. *Escobedo v. Illinois*, 378 U.S. 478 (1964).

8. *Powell et al. v. State of Alabama*, 287 U.S. 45 (1932).

9. Ibid.

10. "Famous American Trials: The Scottsboro Boys," http://www.law.umkc.edu/ftrials/scotboro, Trials 1931–1937.

11. Ibid.

12. *Dickerson v. United States*, 530 U.S. 428 (2000).
13. *Missouri v. Seibert*, 124 S. Ct. 2601 (2004).
14. *Fellers v. United States*, 124 S. Ct. 1019 (2004).
15. *United States v. Patane*, 124 S. Ct. 2620 (2004).
16. *Berghuis v. Thompkins*, 130 S. Ct. 2250 (2010).
17. *Montejo v. Louisiana*, 129 S. Ct. 2079 (2009).
18. *McMann v. Richardson*, 397 U.S. 759 (1970).
19. *Gideon v. Wainwright*, 372 U.S. 335 (1963).
20. *Corley v. U.S.*, 129 S. Ct. 1558 (2009).
21. *Hunt v. Blackburn*, 128 U.S. 464 (1888).
22. *Brown v. Walker*, 161 U.S. 591 (1896).
23. *Trammel v. United States*, 445 U.S. 40 (1980).
24. 42 Pa. C. S. § 5914, Act 16 of 1989.
25. *Jaffee v. Redmond*, 516 U.S. 1091 (1996).
26. *Holt v. United States*, 218 U.S. 245 (1910).
27. *Rochin v. California*, 342 U.S. 165 (1952).
28. *Schmerber v. California*, 384 U.S. 757 (1966).
29. Ibid.
30. For example, DNA comparison testing of a stain found on Monica Lewinsky's now-infamous navy blue dress with a blood sample obtained from President Bill Clinton revealed a probability of 1 out of 7.87 trillion that the stain was left by a Caucasian other than the president.
31. *Fergusen v. City of Charleston*, 532 U.S. 67 (2001).
32. *North Carolina v. Alford*, 400 U.S. 25 (1970).
33. *Barker v. Wingo*, 407 U.S. 514 (1972).
34. *Vermont v. Brillon*, 129 S. Ct. 1283 U.S. (2009).
35. Speedy Trial Act, 18 U.S.C.S. § 3161.

Chapter 13

1. W. Blackstone, *Commentaries on the Laws of England* (Charleston, SC: Forgotten Books, 2010).
2. V. P. Hans and L. Vidmar, *Judging the Jury* (New York: Plenum Press, 1986).
3. R. Perry, ed., *Sources of Our Liberties* (New York: William S. Hein & Co. Buffalo, 1991).
4. *Duncan v. Louisiana*, 391 U.S. 145 (1968).
5. Ibid.
6. *Blanton v. North Las Vegas*, 489 U.S. 538 (1989).
7. *United States v. United States District Court*, No. 06-72498, D.C. No. CR-03-00384-WBS, Opinion (2006).
8. *Singer v. United States*, 380 U.S. 25–26 (1965).
9. This case involved an acquaintance of the author's husband who, among other comments, told the judge he hoped to blow up the courthouse and play tiddly winks with the judge's bones.
10. U.S. Constitution, Fifth Amendment.
11. J. Mallia, "Innocent Duke Charges Dropped; 395 Days: Key Dates in the Case," *Newsday* (New York), April 12, 2007.
12. U.S. Constitution, Sixth Amendment and U.S. Constitution, Article 3.
13. *Taylor v. Louisiana*, 419 U.S. 522 (1975).
14. *Federal Jury Selection and Service Act of 1968*, 28 U.S.C. § 1861.
15. *Berghuis v. Smith*, 130 S. Ct. 1382. (2010).
16. *Campbell v. Louisiana*, 523 U.S. 392 (1998).
17. *Strauder v. West Virginia*, 100 U.S. 303 (1880).
18. As recounted by the author's husband, who served on the sequestered jury. The gentleman in question became an alternate juror.
19. However, the author would welcome the opportunity to serve on a jury. She was once sent a selection notice that asked for her occupation and responded that she was a Pennsylvania licensed attorney who had served as an assistant attorney in another county at the beginning of her career. She was never called for the jury pool. Recently she received another selection notice. This time she put her occupation as "writer." To her surprise and delight, she was called shortly after—for an eighteen-month investigative grand jury. She was selected despite revealing that she is the author of this textbook and a former prosecutor. But before the first official session, she received a note informing her that her services were not needed.
20. *Berghuis v. Smith*, 130 S. Ct. 1382 (2010).
21. *Holland v. Illinois*, 493 U.S. 473 (1990).
22. *Powers v. Ohio*, 499 U.S. 400 (1991).
23. *Miller-El v. Dretke*, 545 U.S. 231 (2005).
24. *Batson v. Kentucky*, 476 U.S. 79 (1986).
25. Shaila Dewan, "Study Finds Blacks Blocked From Southern Juries," *The New York Times*, June 1, 2010 (accessed at http://www.nytimes.com/2010/06/02/us/02jury.html).
26. *Carman L. Deck v. Missouri*, 544 U.S. 622 (2005).
27. *Deck v. Missouri*, quoting 2 W. Hawkins, Pleas of the Crown, Ch. 28, § 1, p.308 (1716–1721), section on arraignments.
28. *Witherspoon v. Illinois*, 391 U.S. 510 (1968).
29. *Morgan v. Illinois*, 504 U.S. 719 (1992).
30. *Thompson v. Utah*, 170 U.S. 343 (1898).
31. *Williams v. Florida*, 399 U.S. 78 (1970).
32. *Ballew v. Georgia*, 435 U.S. 223 (1978).
33. "Change of Venue Sought in Trial of Scott Peterson," *Cable News Network*, December 15, 2003, www.CNN.com.
34. *People of the State of California v. Scott Lee Peterson*, Case No. 1056770 (2003).

35. *Melendez-Diaz v. Massachusetts*, 139 S. Ct. 2527. (2009).

36. *Briscoe and Cypress v. Virginia*, 130 S. Ct. 1316 (2010).

37. *Commonwealth v. Chambers*, 528 Pa. 558 (1991).

38. *Caldwell v. Mississippi*, 472 U.S. 320, 105 S. Ct. 2633, 86 L. Ed. 2d 231 (1985).

39. *Mills v. Maryland*, 108 S. Ct. 1860 (1988).

40. *People v. Williams*, 01 C.D.O.S. 3577 (2001).

41. *Stumpf v. Mitchell*, 367 F. 3d 594, 596 (2004).

42. *Warden v. Stumpf*, 545 U.S. 175 (2005).

43. *Johnson v. Louisiana*, 406 U.S. 356 (1972) and *Apodaca v. Oregon*, 406 U.S. 404 (1972).

44. *Burch v. Louisiana*, 441 U.S. 130 (1979).

45. *Apprendi v. New Jersey*, 530 U.S. 466 (2000).

46. *Ring v. Arizona*, 122 S. Ct. 2428 (2002).

47. An aggravating circumstance is a fact in a case that may make sentencing more severe. Examples of aggravating circumstances may include the commission of a crime in conjunction with another crime, murder in the course of an armed robbery, past criminal record, or likelihood to present future danger to society.

48. *Schriro v. Summerlin*, 124 S. Ct. 2519 (2004).

49. This precise scenario occurred with the author's husband. He was not dismissed for cause and neither side used a peremptory challenge to dismiss him.

Chapter 14

1. L. O. Pike, *A History of Crime in England* (London: Elder & Co., 1973).

2. M. Ignatieff, *A Just Measure of Pain; the Penitentiary in the Industrial Revolution, 1750–1850* (New York: Pantheon, 1978).

3. M. R. Latham and W. Matthews, eds., *The Diary of Samuel Pepys, A New and Complete Transcription* (Berkeley: University of California Press, 1978).

4. Ignatieff, *A Just Measure of Pain.*

5. Ibid.

6. 1 Wm. & Mary, sess. 2, ch. 2 (1689).

7. *Magna Carta* (1215).

8. *Weems v. U.S.* 217 U.S. 349 (1910).

9. The author's husband worked for the real estate firm that appraised and then listed for sale those seized properties.

10. *Ford v. Wainwright*, 477 U.S. 399 (1986).

11. *Trop v. Dulles*, 356 U.S. 86 (1958).

12. U.S. Constitution, Fifth Amendment.

13. Alaska, District of Columbia, Hawaii, Iowa, Maine, Massachusetts, Michigan, Minnesota, New Jersey, North Dakota, Rhode Island, Vermont, West Virginia, and Wisconsin. Source: Bureau of Justice Statistics.

14. *Edmund v. Florida*, 458 U.S. 782 (1982).

15. *Tison v. Arizona*, 481 U.S. 137 (1987). See Chapter 14 for an explanation of the felony murder rule.

16. Bureau of Justice Statistics, U.S. Department of Justice, *Capital Punishment 2009.*

17. *Louisiana ex rel. Francis v. Resweber*, 329 U.S. 459 (1947).

18. R. Hood, *The Death Penalty, A World Wide Perspective*, 2nd ed. (Oxford: Clarendon Press, 1996).

19. *Furman v. Georgia*, 408 U.S. 238 (1972).

20. *Gregg v. Georgia*, 428 U.S. 153 (1976).

21. *Roberts v. Louisiana*, 431 U.S. 633 (1977) and *Roberts v. Louisiana*, 428 U.S. 325 (1976). Although both

cases involve an automatic death sentence for cop-killers, the two defendants are not related. They only share the same name, crime, and sentence.

22. Michael Traynor, "A Faulty Blueprint," *Los Angeles Times*, February 4, 2010.

23. *Abdul-Kabir (fka Cole) v. Quarterman*, 550 U.S. 233 (2007).

24. *Penry v. Lynaugh*, 492 U.S. 302.

25. "Executions in the United States in 2007," The Death Penalty Information Center, July, 2007.

26. *In re Kimmler*, 136 U.S. 436 (1890).

27. *Wilkerson v. Utah*, 99 U.S.1130 (1879).

28. *Louisiana ex rel. Francis v. Resweber*, 329 U.S. 459, 465 (1947).

29. D. P. Baker, *Washington Post*, March 26, 1997, p. A01.

30. M. Clay, "Flames Leap from Inmate's Head at Execution," *Los Angeles Times*, March 26, 1997.

31. "Some Examples of Post-Furman Botched Executions," The Death Penalty Information Center, May 24, 2007.

32. *Ford v. Wainwright*, 477 U.S. 399 (1986).

33. Ibid.

34. *Washington v. Harper*, 494 U.S. 210 (1990).

35. *Perry v. Louisiana*, 498 U.S. 38 (1990).

36. *State v. Perry*, 610 So. 2nd 757 (1992).

37. "Death Sentence Commuted for Mentally Ill Man," *CNN Online*, February 26, 2002.

38. *Sell v. United States*, 539 U.S. 166 (2003).

39. *Singleton v. Norris*. 319 F.3d 1018 (2003)

40. "Forced Into Sanity before Death," *San Antonio Express-News*, April 17, 2006.

41. Texas Department of Criminal Justice, *Offenders on Death Row*, http://www.tdcj.state.tx.us/stat/offendersondrow.htm, accessed June 7, 2010.

42. Bureau of Justice Statistics, U.S. Department of Justice, *Capital Punishment 1996.*

43. *Penry v. Lynaugh*, 492 U.S. 302 (1989).

44. *Wood v. Allen,* 130 S. Ct. 841(2010).

45. *Penry v. Lynaugh,* 492 U.S. 302 (1989).

46. *Atkins v. Virginia,* 536 U.S. 304 (2002).

47. *Tennard v. Dretke,* 124 S. Ct. 2562 (2004).

48. *Thompson v. Oklahoma,* 487 U.S. 815 (1988).

49. "Juvenile Defenders Who Were On Death Row," The Death Penalty Information Center, 2007.

50. *Roper v. Simmons,* 543 U.S. 551 (2005).

51. Murder committed during the commission of a felony, such as rape or armed robbery, even if not personally committed by the defendant. See Chapter 14 for a more complete discussion.

52. *Edmund v. Florida,* 458 U.S. 782 (1982).

53. *Tison v. Arizona,* 481 U.S. 137 (1987).

54. *Coker v. Georgia,* 433 U.S. 584 (1977).

55. *Coker,* at 593.

56. 18 U.S.C.§ 7794; 18 U.S.C. § 2381.

57. *Rosenberg v. United States,* 346 U.S. 273 (1953).

58. "Professor Withdraws as High-Court Nominee: Supreme Court Nominee John Maher Had Said Corrupt Politicians Deserve to Die," *Philadelphia Inquirer,* March 19, 1997. Professor Maher taught the author everything she knows about corporate and antitrust law while she was a student at the Dickinson School of Law.

59. "Uniform Crime Report 2008," U.S. Department of Justice, Bureau of Justice.

60. *Rummel v. Estelle,* 445 U.S. 263 (1980).

61. "Cookie Burglar Gets At Least 25 Years," *CNN Online,* October 27, 1995.

62. *Rummel v. Estelle,* 445 U.S. 263 (1980).

63. *Graham v. Florida,* No. 08-7412 (2010).

64. *Hutto v. Finney,* 437 U.S. 678 (1978).

65. *Bell v. Wollfish,* 441 U.S. 520 (1979).

66. *Hutto v. Finney,* 437 U.S. 678 (1978).

67. *Estelle v. Gamble,* 429 U.S. 97 (1976).

68. *Carr v. U.S., No. 08-1301.*

69. Public Law, 104–105 (April 17, 1996) and 104–236 (October 3, 1996).

70. "States Move on Sex Offender GPS Tracking," Associated Press, Jefferson City, Missouri, via FoxNews.com, August 17, 2005.

71. *Otte v. Doe,* 534 U.S. 1126 (2002).

72. *Smith v. Doe,* 538 U.S. 84 (2003).

73. *McKune et al. v. Lile,* 536 U.S. 24 (2002).

74. D. Norton, "Wilson to sign Castration Bill," *San Francisco Chronicle,* September 17, 1996.

75. G. Lucas, "Chemical Castration Bill Passes," *Augusta Chronicle,* February 12, 1997.

76. Bill Savitsky, Jr., and Pete Shellem, "Woman held as a sex predator: Designation is state's first," *Seattle Times,* January 22, 1997.

77. "Miss Georgia's Sex Offenders 2004 Pageant," www.porkdisco.com.

78. Donna M. Vandiver and Jeffery T. Walker, "Female Sex Offenders: An Overview and Analysis of 40 Cases," *Criminal Justice Review,* Vol. 27, no. 2 (Georgia State University2002), pp. 284–300.

79. "Adam Walsh Act Becomes Law," America's Most Wanted, FoxNews.com, July 25, 2006.

80. Kevin Poulsen, "MySpace Labels Innocent Woman as Sex Offender," Wired.com, May 25, 2007.

81. Kevin Poulsen, "Attorneys General Give Up Sex Offenders," Wired.com, May 14, 2007.

Glossary

A

Abduction The illegal carrying away of a person by force or coercion, generally with the intent to do harm to the victim. Today, the same criminal statute generally covers kidnapping and abduction.

Abortion The termination of pregnancy by something other than birth.

Actual possession Physically having the item on one's person, directly under physical control, or within reach.

Actus reus A wrongful action.

Adultery Sexual intercourse by a married person with someone not his or her spouse.

Advise and consent The constitutional relationship of the Senate to the president regarding the selection of federal judges and other duties.

Age of consent The age at which the individual may consent to sexual activity. Ages of consent vary from state to state.

Aggravated assault An unlawful attack by one person upon another for the purposes of inflicting severe or aggravated bodily injury. This type of assault usually is accompanied by the use of a weapon or by means likely to produce death or great bodily harm.

Aggravating circumstance Act or conduct that increases the seriousness of an act, often resulting in a harsher punishment.

Alford Plea A plea entered where the accused maintains his innocence, but agrees to be sentenced as if guilty.

Analytical School The school of jurisprudential thought that believes laws are based on logic.

Appeal as of right The absolute right to one appellate review of a conviction.

Armed robbery A theft committed by force or threat of force by a person or persons carrying a weapon.

Arraignment The stage of a criminal case at which the defendant is first formally charged with a specific crime.

Arrest The official taking of a person to answer criminal charges.

Arrest warrant Document approved by a magistrate or judge attesting that there is probable cause to believe that someone has committed a specific crime and authorizing that person's arrest.

Arson Any willful or malicious burning or attempt to burn, with or without intent to defraud, a dwelling house, public building, motor vehicle, or aircraft, or personal property of another.

Assault An act of force or threat of force intended to inflict harm upon a person or to put the person in fear that such harm is imminent.

Attorneys Licensed professionals who can appear in court to represent individuals.

B

Bail Money or other guarantee posted to assure a defendant who is released from custody pending trial or appeal will appear when called or forfeit the security posted.

Battered Wife Syndrome The condition where abused spouses refuse to leave abusive partners in the belief either that they deserve the abuse or that it will stop eventually.

Bench conference A conference called among the judge and attorneys for both sides, and possibly the accused, to discuss matters without the jury hearing it.

Bench warrant A warrant issued by a judge ordering law enforcement officers to arrest a specific person.

Beyond a reasonable doubt The burden of proof the prosecution must meet in a criminal case in order to convict the accused.

Bigamy The criminal act of marrying when one already has a spouse.

Bill of attainder A law passed that singles out a person or persons as the only individuals affected by a criminal law. Originally, a bill of attainder singled out an individual for capital punishment without benefit of a trial.

Binding An order moving jurisdiction from court where the preliminary hearing took place to the trial court.

Bloody Code   Popular name for England's criminal laws because of their harshness and the long list of crimes classified as capital offenses.

Bot   In ancient England, compensation paid for minor injuries.

Bourgeoisie   In Marxist theory, the class in society that controls the means of production.

Brady Handgun Violence Prevention Act   A federal law which requires a background check before the purchase of certain guns and prohibits some individuals from owning purchasing those guns.

Bribery   The crime of giving something of value with the intention of influencing the action of a public official.

Burden of proof   The duty to go forward to prove an allegation with facts.

Burglary   At Common Law, the breaking and entering of the dwelling house of another at night with the intent to commit a felony inside. Today, burglary is the forcible entry into a structure with the intent to commit a felony once inside.

"But for" rule   The rule that states but for the defendant's actions, the harm would not have occurred.

C

Castle Laws   Laws passed by states that allow homeowners (and renters) the right to defend their property and persons within that property from intruders, including through the use of deadly force.

Causation   The requirement that the act must cause the harm.

Chain of custody   A process by which a piece of physical evidence is tracked from collection to introduction into evidence. The chain must be unbroken.

Challenge for cause   An attorney's (either prosecution or defense) request that the judge dismiss a potential juror from serving on a jury by providing a valid legal reason why he or she shouldn't serve. Judges may dismiss potential jurors for cause as well.

Chattel   Personal property.

Checks and balances   The system of restraints built into the U.S. Constitution that prevents one branch of government from dominating the others.

Child molestation or sexual abuse   The engaging of a child in sexual activities that the child cannot comprehend, for which the child is developmentally unprepared and cannot give informed consent, and/or that violate the social and legal taboos of society.

Circumstantial evidence   Indirect evidence that requires an inference.

Clear and convincing evidence   A standard of proof normally used in civil cases higher than "preponderance of the evidence," but lower than "beyond a reasonable doubt."

Command School   The school of jurisprudential thought that posits that laws are dictated to the society by the ruling class of that society.

Commerce Clause   The clause of the U.S. Constitution that gives the federal government the right to regulate interstate commerce. Article I, Section 8, Clause 3.

Common Law   The system of jurisprudence, originated in England and later applied in the United States, that is based on judicial precedent rather than legislative enactments.

Concurrent jurisdiction   Jurisdiction shared by two or more courts.

Concurrent sentences   Where one person is sentenced for more than one crime and the sentences are served at the same time.

Confession   The act of admitting guilt or complicity to the commission of a crime.

Confirmation   The process of approval of presidential nominees by the Senate.

Consecutive sentences   Where one person is sentenced for more than one crime and the sentences are to be served one after the other.

Consensus theory   A theory developed by Emile Durkheim that postulates that laws develop out of a society's consensus of what is right and wrong.

Consent   Voluntary agreement by a competent person to another person's proposition.

Consent defense   Usually used in rape cases; argues the defendant had the "victim's" consent to perform the acts.

Consent once removed   An exception to the warrant to search requirement which says that consent to enter given to an undercover police officer or informant transfers to others in the police force who may then enter without a warrant.

Conspiracy   An agreement by two or more persons to commit a criminal act or series of criminal acts, or to accomplish a legal act by unlawful means. At common law, agreement was enough. Under the Model Penal Code and most state laws, the agreement must be followed by an overt act in furtherance of the conspiracy.

Constructive intent   The concept that some actions are so likely to cause a specific result, the law treats that result as intended whether the person meant to cause it or not.

Constructive possession   The concept that extends liability to people who have some control over an item without possessing it.

Contempt   Conduct that brings the authority and administration of the law into disrespect or that embarrasses or obstructs the court's discharge of its duties.

Controlled substance   A drug considered dangerous under the law because of its effects, including intoxication, stupor, or addictive potential.

Cooperation agreement   An agreement between the prosecution and a defendant that spells that the defendant will cooperate in the prosecution of others involved in the same or related criminal activity, usually in exchange for a recommendation of leniency to the court.

Corporal punishment   Punishment inflicted on the body, such as paddling, whipping, or caning.

Corporate liability   The legal concept that allows employers to be charged with a crime resulting from their employees' actions while carrying out corporate business.

Corpus delicti   Literally, the body of the crime.

Crime   A wrong against society or the public interest.

Criminal conspiracy   The agreement by two or more people to commit a crime. It requires at least one overt act and is punished as if the parties accomplished the objective of their agreement.

Criminal homicide   A killing that breaks the law, designated as either murder or manslaughter.

Criminal negligence manslaughter   The crime of causing the death of a person by negligent or reckless conduct.

Criminal solicitation   Under common law, a crime which occurs when one person requests or encourages another to perform a criminal act.

Crits   The school of jurisprudences that believes the legal system is arbitrary and artificial, that legal neutrality and objectivity are myths to maintain the current status quo, and that the legal system perpetuates social inequality and oppression of those not in power.

Cross-examination   Questioning a witness put on the stand by the other side following direct examination.

Cruel and unusual punishment   Punishment which violates the Eighth Amendment and which violates evolving standards of decency.

Custody   The state of being detained by law enforcement officers. A person is in custody when that person is not free to leave.

Cyber crime   Criminal act performed with the aid of a computer.

D

Deadly force   Force intended to cause death or likely to result in death.

Deadly weapon doctrine   Use of a deadly weapon is proof of intent to kill.

Defendant   In a civil case the person against whom a suit is filed. In a criminal trial, the person accused of a crime.

Defense of others   The defense used when otherwise criminal activities are done to save other people from harm.

Definite or determinate sentences   Fixed term sentences selected from a range determined by statute or guidelines where there is no chance of parole.

Degree   A measure of the severity of a crime with first-degree being the most severe.

Deterrent   An action that discourages an individual from committing a crime. Fines, imprisonment, and death are considered deterrents to crime.

Dicastery   In ancient Greece, the group of volunteers who acted as jurors to settle dispute within the *polis*.

Direct cause   The case where a clear link between the criminal act and the effect exists.

Direct evidence   Evidence based on first-hand knowledge.

Direct examination   The initial questioning of one's own witness.

Discovery   A formal investigation conducted before trial by both parties.

Discretionary appeal   An appeal allowed by an appellate court after a criminal defendant's appeal as of right has been exhausted.

District or prosecuting attorney District attorneys (sometimes referred to as prosecuting attorneys) are lawyers who typically have been elected to try criminal cases on behalf of the people.

Domestic terrorism Activities that occur primarily within U.S. jurisdiction, that involve criminal acts dangerous to human life, and that appear to be intended to intimidate or coerce a civilian population, to influence government policy by intimidation or coercion, or to affect government conduct by mass destruction, assassination, or kidnapping.

Domestic violence A person's actions designed to hurt or dominate a domestic partner.

Double jeopardy The rule, based on the Fifth Amendment, that a person can only be tried once for the same offense. The rule has several exceptions.

Duress defense The defense that a person acted under threat of bodily harm to themselves or a family member. It may not be used to justify killing. The crime committed must be less serious than the harm threatened.

Durham test Test of insanity that only requires a "substantial lack of capacity" on the part of the defendant.

Duty An obligation to perform an action.

Duty by contract A duty voluntarily assumed through an agreement.

Duty by relationship A duty expected of certain people, such as parents, by virtue of their connection with the person owed the duty, such as the parents' children.

Duty by statute A duty imposed by law.

Duty by volunteering A duty freely assumed.

Duty to render aid to persons placed in peril A duty assumed when one individual endangers another.

Dying declaration A statement made by an individual who believed death was imminent to explain the circumstances of his condition. Such statements may be admissible as an exception to the hearsay rule.

E

Elder Abuse Syndrome The condition elderly victims of abuse sometimes exhibit characterized by "learned helplessness" and the feeling they can do nothing to stop the abuse.

Elite or ruling class theory Also known as the "ruling class" theory, it is the theory put forth by Karl Marx that postulates laws exist only as a means of class oppression.

Embezzlement Theft committed by someone who has legal possession of property of another when the thief uses, converts, or retains that property for his or her own use or the use of someone other than the owner.

Eminent domain The state's power to take private property for a public use or public purpose without the owner's consent. The U.S. Constitution requires that property can only be taken after due process of law.

English Bill of Rights A precursor to the U.S. Bill of Rights, it guarantees due process and bars cruel and unusual punishment.

Enhanced sentences Sentences lengthened by aggravating factors such as for hate crimes or the use of a firearm in commission of a crime.

Entrapment A defense used when law enforcement officials lure a person into committing a crime.

Enumerated powers The powers explicitly given to the federal government in the U.S. Constitution.

Espionage Knowingly and willfully communicating, furnishing, transmitting, or otherwise making available to an unauthorized person, or publishing, or using in any manner prejudicial to the safety or interest of the United States, or for the benefit of any foreign government to the detriment of the United States, any classified information.

Euthanasia The act of causing death to end pain and distress. Also called mercy killing.

Evanescent evidence Evidence that will change or evaporate in a manner that will destroy its evidentiary value.

Exclusionary rule The "fruit of the poisonous tree" doctrine that prohibits the admission of evidence obtained illegally at a defendant's criminal trial. The rule does allow the use of evidence obtained with a technically defective warrant, but in good faith.

Exclusive jurisdiction A court with exclusive jurisdiction is the only court that can hear the case.

Exculpatory evidence Evidence that casts doubt on the defendant's guilt.

Executive One of the three branches of government; the branch charged with enforcing the law.

Executive Orders Orders given by the president or governors that have the weight of law within the operation of executive branch of the federal or state government.

Exigent circumstances   Situations that require urgent action, sufficient to excuse delay to get a warrant issued.

Ex post facto law   The rule that a person cannot be charged with a crime that became a crime after he committed the act made illegal.

Extradition   The process of returning an accused criminal to the jurisdiction in which he or she is charged.

F

Federal Circuit   One of 13 federal judicial districts, each with a U.S. District Court and a U.S. Court of Appeals.

Federal law enforcement   Law enforcement officers who Work for the Federal Bureau of Investigation (FBI), the U.S. Bureau of Drug Enforcement (DEA), the U.S. Marshall Service, the Bureau of Alcohol, Tobacco, Firearms and Explosives (ATF), and the Department of Homeland Security (DHS) or other federal agencies.

Federal system   A system of governing where government is divided into different levels.

Fee simple   The legal term for ownership of the entire bundle of rights that go with a piece of property.

Felonies   The most serious classification of crimes punishable by long prison sentences or death.

Felony murder rule   The rule that a death occurring by accident or chance during the course of the commission of a felony is murder.

Fem-Crits   A school of jurisprudence that holds the legal system perpetuates the oppression of women in society.

Fighting words   Words that inflict injury, tend to incite an immediate breach of the peace, or by their nature will cause a violent reaction by a person who hears them.

Fines   Monetary penalties paid to the state as punishment for crime.

First-degree murder   Murder committed deliberately with malice aforethought, that is, with premeditation.

First-degree offenses   Under the Model Penal Code, crimes that are committed willfully.

Forcible fondling   The involuntary touching of another person's private body parts for the purpose of sexual gratification.

Forcible rape   The carnal knowledge of a person against that person's 409will.

Forcible sodomy   Oral or anal intercourse with another person against that person's will.

Forensic accounting   An accounting subspecialty using auditing to prove fraud or other financial wrongdoing.

Forgery   The fraudulent making or altering of any writing in a way that alters the legal rights and liabilities of another.

Fornication   Voluntary sexual intercourse between two unmarried persons.

Fourth-degree offenses   Under the Model Penal Code, crimes that are committed negligently.

G

Gambling   The act of taking a monetary risk on the chance of receiving a monetary gain.

General intent   The type of intent where the person intended an action only, and not the results of the action.

Grand jury   A body of citizens whose job it is to determine if a crime has been committed and if a person should be charged with that crime based on probable cause.

Guilty, but mentally ill   Defendants who do not meet the complete lack of capacity standard but fall under the substantial lack of capacity standard are convicted and sent to a mental hospital. If they recover, they are sent to prison for the rest of their term.

H

Habeas corpus   Literally meaning "you have the body," a judicial process for determining the legality of a particular person's custody. The "Great Writ" which orders another authority to bring a person to court. It was originally used to prevent kings from simply making enemies disappear.

Harm   injury or damage.

Harmless error   An error at the trial stage which did not fundamentally affect the outcome of the trial.

Hate crimes   Offenses motivated by hatred against a victim based on his or her race, religion, sexual orientation, handicap, ethnicity, or national origin.

Hate speech   The crime of using the threat of force to willfully injure, intimidate, interfere with, oppress, or threaten any other person in the free exercise or enjoyment of any right or privilege secured to him or her by the Constitution or law of the United States because of the other person's race, color, religion, ancestry, national origin, disability, gender, or sexual orientation.

Hearsay A statement, other than one made while testifying at trial, offered in evidence to prove the truth of the matter asserted. It is not admissible.

Heat of passion The expression for a mental state on the part of a criminal defendant adequate in law to reduce the crime from murder to manslaughter.

Historical School The school of jurisprudential thought that believes that law is an accumulation of societal traditions.

Homicide The killing of a human being.

Homicide by vehicle A form of criminal negligence manslaughter reserved for a person operating a motor vehicle.

Hung jury A jury that is unable to reach a verdict.

I

Impeachment The process by which Congress may charge a sitting judge, president, or vice president with "high crimes and misdemeanors" and convict that person in a trial before the Senate. A conviction results in removal from office.

Implied consent The consent given as a condition of obtaining a driver's license to provide proof of sobriety when legitimately requested by a law enforcement officer.

Incarceration Imprisonment or being under a prison sentence.

Incest Sexual activity between relatives within a prescribed degree of sanguinity or affinity.

inchoate A class of crimes known as incomplete crimes, most notably conspiracy.

Incompetent to stand trial A person unable to understand the proceedings against him and be able to interact with his attorneys.

Indecent assault or indecent touching An attack on a person in which there is groping or other offensive touching, but no sexual act is performed or attempted.

Indefinite sentencing The sentencing scheme using a sentencing range where the prisoner can earn release after serving the minimum sentence by meeting certain rehabilitation goals.

Indeterminate sentencing The sentencing scheme where judges have the most flexibility in sentencing.

Indictment A formal charge by which the defendant has been charged with a crime, usually as the result of a grand jury inquiry.

Infancy defense The defense that a child is too young to either be prosecuted, or stand trial as an adult.

Infanticide The murder of a newborn or very young child.

Information A formal document signed and filed by a district attorney or prosecutor that charges an individual with a specific crime.

Initial appearance A court proceeding shortly after a suspect's arrest where the suspect is informed of specific rights.

In loco parentis Acting in the role of parents.

Insanity defense States that the defendant lacked the mental state to understand the nature and consequences of the crime.

Insanity during incarceration Prisoners who become insane are generally removed to mental hospitals. If they are still insane at the conclusion of their prison term, they are generally committed.

Insanity just prior to execution Most jurisdictions will not execute an insane person. Persons whose sanity returns are rewarded with death.

Intent to do serious bodily harm A defendant's plan to injure another.

Intent to kill The plan, course, or means a person conceives to take another's life.

International terrorism Activities that occur primarily outside U.S. jurisdiction, and involve criminal acts dangerous to human life, including acts of mass destruction, intended to influence the policy of a government by intimidation or coercion or to affect the conduct of a government by assassination or kidnapping.

Interstate commerce Commerce that occurs between states as opposed to strictly within a state's borders.

Intervening causes Complications that arise between a criminal act and all of its consequences.

Intrastate Occurring within a state's border.

Involuntary manslaughter The unintentional killing of a human being by a person engaged in doing some unlawful act not amounting to a felony, or in doing some lawful act in a manner tending to cause death or great bodily injury.

Involuntary intoxication The condition of a person who unknowingly ingests an intoxicating substance. Generally treated like insanity.

Irrebuttable presumption A presumption that cannot be disproved regardless of the amount or quality of evidence to the contrary.

J

Jackson-Denno Hearing   A hearing preparatory to admitting a confession into evidence where the prosecutor must prove that the confession was voluntary.

Joint tenants with right of survivorship   Form of ownership in which the joint tenant receives the property should the other die. Either may sell their share before death and the new owners then become tenants in common.

Judges   The presiding officer or officers at judicial proceedings. Judges at the trial level and above are attorneys.

Judicial   One of the three branches of government; the branch charged with interpreting the law.

Jurisdiction   The power to hear and decide a case. Jurisdiction can be divided as to subject matter, parties, or territory.

Jurisprudence   The study of law.

Jury   A group of men and women from the community selected to determine the truth; while the judge is responsible for interpreting the law, the jury is charged with the task of finding the facts of the case. The right to trial by jury is guaranteed by the U.S. Constitution in all serious criminal cases. A jury decides what the facts of the case are and applies those facts to the law. Juries must be convinced beyond a reasonable doubt that the defendant broke the law.

Jury instructions   The directions the judge gives jurors about how they are to come to a verdict. Jury instructions typically include an explanation of the law and what must be proven to convict the defendant.

Jury nullification   A decision by a jury to ignore the law or the judge's instructions when deliberating. For example, jurors who believe the law is unjust may refuse to convict the defendant even if it is clear that he broke the law.

Justifiable homicides   Those killings committed out of duty with no criminal intent.

Justification defenses   A legal excuse for committing an act that otherwise would be a tort or a crime.

K

Kidnapping   The crime of taking and detaining a person against his will by force, intimidation, or fraud. Holding the victim for ransom is not required.

Knowing possession   The condition existing when a person possesses and holds onto an item intentionally.

L

Labor trafficking   The recruitment, harboring, transportation, provision, or obtaining of a person for labor or services, through the use of force, fraud, or coercion for the purpose of subjection to involuntary servitude, peonage, debt bondage, or slavery.

Law   The body of rules of conduct created by government and enforced by the authority of government.

Leasehold rights   The rights a tenant in real property possesses through agreement with the property owner.

Legal traps   Techniques used by law enforcement to catch criminal activity that fall short of entrapment.

Legislative   One of the three branches of government; the one charged with making the law.

Letters of marque and reprisal   A letter from a government formerly used to grant a private person the power to seize the subjects of a foreign state.

Lien   A creditor's claim against a particular property as collateral for a debt.

Living will   A document in which a person sets forth directions regarding medical treatment to be given if she becomes unable to participate in decisions regarding her health care.

M

Magna Carta   The "Great Charter," a document that was signed by King John of England in 1215. It guaranteed the noblemen under the King's jurisdiction life, liberty, and property. Many of the promises made in the Magna Carta became the basis of the guarantees found in the U.S. Constitution and the constitutions of the states.

Mail fraud   Using the U.S. Postal Service in furtherance of a fraudulent scheme.

Mala in se   According to Blackstone, a category of crimes that are bad in and of themselves.

Mala prohibita   According to Blackstone, a category of crimes that are crimes because society has decided they are crimes.

Malice aforethought   An intent to kill or injure, or the deliberate commission of a dangerous or deadly act.

Malicious mischief   Also known as criminal mischief, it is defined as the criminal offense of intentionally destroying another person's property.

Mandatory sentences   Sentences required by statute during which the prisoner has no chance for parole.

Mandatory minimum sentences   The shortest possible sentence for a given crime under an indeterminate sentencing scheme.

Marital privilege   The right of a person to refuse to testify against his or her spouse.

Marital rape   The rape of one's wife.

Material evidence   Evidence that is important to the case at hand.

Military actions   Actions carried by members of the armed services under the direction of appropriate civilian authorities.

Military tribunal   A military court convened in times of emergency to try those accused of war-related crimes, such as terrorism, espionage, or treason.

Minor   A person who has not yet reached legal age, typically eighteen.

Minor judiciary   Magistrates, justices of the peace, or municipal judges who are commonly called members of the minor judiciary.

Miranda **warning**   The warning given to suspects that they have the right to remain silent and the right to counsel named for the Supreme Court case that requires police officers to read the right to suspects (*Miranda v. Arizona*).

Misdemeanors   Crimes punishable by relatively short prison sentences, or fines. Misdemeanors are less serious than felonies.

Mistake of age defense   A defense to statutory rape where the perpetrator believed the victim to be older than she actually was.

Mistake of fact   A defense used when a defendant honestly believes something to be true that isn't.

Mistake of law   A defense used when a person in good faith relied on an interpretation of law from a person charged with administering the law.

Mitigating circumstance   Act or conduct that lessens or reduces the punishment for a crime, such as lack of a criminal record, state of mind, or youth.

M'Naghten rule   Holds that a defendant "is presumed to be sane and to possess a sufficient degree of reason to be responsible for his crimes, until the contrary be proved to (the jury's) satisfaction" beyond a reasonable doubt.

Model Death Penalty   The death penalty implementation plan as envisioned in the Model Penal Code.

Model Penal Code and Commentaries   Code that attempts to unify state penal codes. Legislatures often look to it when drafting legislation.

Moral theory of law   A theory subscribed to by Natural Law adherents stating that laws are based on the moral code of the society.

Motion for a new trial   A formal request for a new trial for a convicted defendant based on new evidence or a procedural flaw in the first trial.

Motion for continuance   A formal request to temporarily halt proceedings.

Motion for discovery   A formal request to investigate evidence.

Motion for judgment notwithstanding the verdict or motion for judgment of acquittal   A formal request that the judge set aside the verdict based on the weight of evidence or when the verdict clearly contradicts the law.

Motion for recusal   A formal request to have the judge turnover proceedings to another judge.

Motion *in limine*   A formal request to limit testimony so as not to prejudice a jury.

Motion to change venire   A formal request to change the trial's jury pool.

Motion to change venue   A formal request to change the trial's location.

Motion to sever   A formal request to try certain defendants or charges separately.

Mens rea   A wrongful mind.

Mere possession   The condition occurring when a person possesses an item unawares.

Motive   The reason a person commits a crime.

Murder   The unlawful killing of a human being with malice, but the exact definition will vary by jurisdiction. See *First-degree murder*.

N

Napoleonic Code   The French System of laws developed by Napoleon I; it is the basis of Louisiana law.

Natural Law School   The school of jurisprudential thought that teaches that laws are based on morality and ethics, and that people have natural rights.

Nolo contendere   Latin for "I will not contest this," also called "no contest"; a plea entered that admits no wrongdoing but allows the court to sentence the defendant as guilty.

Nol pros **motion** An abbreviated form of the Latin *nolle prosequi*, which roughly translates as "no prosecution"; it is a motion filed by a prosecutor indicating that justice is better served by not prosecuting the defendant.

Non-deadly force Force used to subdue a criminal or prevent a crime without risking death.

O

Objective intent What a reasonable person should have known or thought at the time of the event.

Objective standard (minority rule) for entrapment Asks the question, "Would an innocent person be induced to commit the crime by the officer's acts?"

Obstruction of justice The crime of impeding or hindering the administration of justice in any way.

Omission The failure to perform a duty.

Opening statement A statement made by an attorney or self-represented party at the beginning of a trial before evidence is introduced. The opening statement outlines the party's legal position and previews the evidence that will be introduced later.

P

Parens patriae The power of the state to act as guardian for those who are unable to care for themselves.

Parental liability The responsibility parents have for the actions of their minor children.

Paralegals or legal assistants Legal professionals who assist attorneys and others involved in the legal system. These professionals can perform many of the tasks usually reserved for attorneys, with the exception that they may not represent clients in court or give legal advice.

Parole A period of supervised release after serving a prison sentence. The parolee must follow certain rules such as reporting to a parole officer.

Patient–counselor privilege The right of confidentiality accorded counselors for conversations held in the course of mental health treatment.

Per se Latin; by itself, in and of itself.

Peremptory challenge The right to dismiss or excuse a potential juror during jury selection without having to give a reason. Each party to a lawsuit is allowed a fixed number of peremptory challenges.

Perjury Giving false testimony in a judicial or administrative proceeding; lying under oath as to a material fact; swearing to the truth of anything one knows or believes to be false.

Perjury trap A situation where a grand jury subpoenas a witness for the sole purpose of obtaining perjured testimony.

Personal property All property other than real property.

Personal status as an act Generally current laws do not view personal status as an act, but historically personal status has been seen as a criminal act.

Petit jury A trial jury. In criminal cases, the petit jury determines the facts of the case, applies those facts to the law as given them by the judge, and decides if the state has proven beyond a reasonable doubt that the defendant committed the crime he or she was charged with. Federal juries consist of twelve jurors; state juries can consist of as few as six jurors.

Petition for *certiorari* Request by a litigant that the U.S. Supreme Court hear his or her appeal.

Phishing The attempt to obtain personal identifying information by posing as a bank or financial institution in an e-mail communication.

Pimp One who works to procure clients for a prostitute.

Plaintiff The party who files a lawsuit.

Plea A formal response to criminal charges. A plea may be not guilty, guilty, nolo contendere, or not guilty by reason of insanity.

Plea bargaining The practice of negotiating with a defendant and his attorney about the terms of a guilty plea.

Police power The power of a government to enforce laws and regulate the health, safety, morals, and welfare of the population.

Power to declare war The power reserved by Congress in the Constitution. Congress can declare war on a belligerent, and then the Executive Branch conducts the war.

Precedent Prior decision that a court must follow when deciding a new, similar case.

Preemption doctrine This concept that federal law must take precedence over state and local law.

Pretrial Motions Formal requests that a judge enter a particular order prior to the start of a trial.

Priest–penitent privilege The right of confidentiality accorded members of the clergy for conversations held during the ritual of confession.

Probable cause   The amount of proof required before an officer can obtain a search warrant, stop a suspect, or make an arrest. Enough evidence from which a reasonable person could conclude that the facts alleged are probably true.

Prostitution   Engaging in sexual intercourse or other sexual activity for pay.

Protection from abuse order   An order requiring a spouse accused of abuse to not contact the person filing the complaint.

Possession   Dominion or control over property.

Preliminary arraignment   An accused's first official notification of the charges against him or her. The preliminary arraignment generally occurs shortly after arrest.

Preliminary hearing   A formal hearing that is the first occasion at which the government must produce evidence against the defendant. The prosecutor must convince the judge or magistrate hearing the case that it is more likely than not that the defendant committed the crime he or she is charged with.

Preponderance of the evidence   Evidence that is more convincing than the opposing evidence; enough evidence to tip the scales of justice.

Principle of legality   The theory that an action is not a crime unless it is prohibited by law and assigned a punishment by the state.

Probable cause   A low standard of proof in a criminal case used to justify an arrest or hold a defendant over for trial after a preliminary hearing. The standard requires that there be sufficient proof to convince a reasonable person that it is more likely than not that he or she committed the crime charged.

Probation   A period where a convict is under court supervision in lieu of a prison sentence.

Proletariat   In Marxist theory, the working class who must sell their labor in order to survive.

Property   A bundle of rights, including the right to possess, use and enjoy, and dispose of something. It is not a material object itself, but a person's right to do what he or she wishes with that object, subject to limitations provided in the law.

Proportionality   The concept courts use when evaluating whether a punishment fits the crime.

Proximate cause   An act that sets in motion a chain of events leading to harm.

Public defenders   Attorneys provided by the state to defend individuals who cannot afford to hire a private attorney.

Public indecency   Lewd or lascivious conduct that is open to public view.

Q

Quash   To annul.

R

Rape   Traditionally defined as forced sexual intercourse with a woman, not one's wife. Modern rape definitions don't distinguish between male or female victims and have expanded the types of sexual contact that are included in the definition. Most states also allow at least a limited right to bring rape charges against a spouse and no longer require the use of direct force or physical harm.

Rape shield law   Codified rule of evidence that provides for the exclusion of a rape victim's sexual history unless it is directly relevant to his or her consent or other evidence in the case.

Real property   Consists of land and everything permanently attached to it. It includes land, subsurface rights, air rights, timbering and harvesting rights, and any buildings and structures permanently attached to the land.

Realists   Belonging to the Sociological School of jurisprudence. Realists believe that the purpose of law is to shape societal behavior.

Rebuttable presumption   A presumption that can be overcome by presenting evidence to the contrary.

Restitution   Money paid to crime victims to help make them whole.

Right against self-incrimination   The right embodied in the Fifth Amendment that allows an accused person to remain silent. Its corollary is "innocent until proven guilty."

Right to bail   The limited right to be released from prison pending trial after posting enough security to assure appearance at the time of trial. The right is subject to limitation in cases of murder or where release has been shown to pose a threat to the public.

Right to remain silent   The right of all persons not to testify against their own interests when suspected of or charged with a crime. The right to remain silent is rooted in the belief that it is the government's obligation to prove guilt.

Recantation   The retraction of testimony.

Recross examination   Questioning of a witness called by the other side following redirect examination.

Redirect examination   Questioning of one's own witness following cross-examination.

Referendum   The enactment of a law through a popular vote rather than a legislative action.

Regulations   A rule, adopted under authority granted by a statute, issued by a municipal, county, state, or federal agency. Although not laws, they have the force of law and often include penalties for violations. Regulations may be challenged as either exceeding the authority granted by the underlying statute or as being unconstitutional.

Released on one's own recognizance   The situation that occurs when the court does not require the defendant to post bail at the preliminary hearing. Despite the lack of bail, the defendant is obligated to return for further proceedings.

Relevant evidence   Evidence having a tendency to make the existence of any fact that is of consequence to the determination of the action more probable or less probable than it would be without the evidence.

Res gestae **theory**   Literally "the acts of the thing," the acts or words through which an event speaks.

Respondeat superior   Literally, "let the superior respond", a term indicating liability derived from an agent relationship between the superior and the person committing the crime.

Retreat rule   The rule governing when a person must retreat rather than use deadly force.

RICO   Racketeering Influenced and Corrupt Organizations Act is legislation that enables the government to prosecute individuals and organizations for a pattern of criminal activity; originally meant to target organized crime.

Robbery   A theft made by force or threat of force.

S

Schools of Jurisprudence   Various theories concerning how societies develop, maintain, and change laws governing individual behavior.

Scienter   A necessary element to prove in some crimes where the offender knew a certain fact or understood the law being broken.

Second-degree offenses   Under the Model Penal Code, crimes that are committed knowingly.

Sedition   A conspiracy to overthrow, put down, or to destroy by force the Government of the United States, or levy war against them, or to oppose the authority thereof, or by force to prevent, hinder, or delay the execution of any law of the United States,

or by force to seize, take, or possess any property of the United States contrary to the authority thereof.

Self-defense   The use of force to protect oneself from death or imminent bodily harm at the hands of an aggressor.

Self-incrimination   The act of giving testimony against one's penal interest. Generally, persons have a right to withhold information that may incriminate and to refuse to answer questions that incriminate. The right does not generally extend to giving DNA samples or submitting to blood-alcohol testing or withholding other physical evidence.

Sequester   To separate jurors in order to assure that they will remain impartial during the trial and deliberations.

Sequestration   The confining of jury members for the duration of a trial to prevent any outside influences.

Sexting   The sending of nude pictures over cell phones.

Sex trafficking   An enterprise "in which a commercial sex act is induced by force, fraud, or coercion, or in which the person induced to perform such act has not attained 18 years of age."

Sex workers   A term preferred by some working in the sex industry such as prostitutes, porn actresses or actors, exotic dancers, and the like.

Sexual assault with an object   The use of an object or instrument unlawfully to penetrate, however slightly, the genital or anal opening of another person's body against that person's will or nonforcibly when that person is unable to give consent.

Simple assault   An unlawful physical attack by one person upon another where neither the offender displays a weapon nor the victims suffers obvious severe or aggravated bodily injury involving apparent broken bones, loss of teeth, possible internal injury, severe laceration, or loss of consciousness.

Simple robbery   A theft made by force or threat of force where no weapon is used.

Sine qua non   Literally, without which, not. The Latin term for the "but for rule."

Sixth Amendment   The provision of the Bill of Rights that originally guaranteed all federal criminal defendants the right to trial by jury. It has since been applied to the states through the Fourteenth Amendment, which guarantees all citizens equal protection of the laws of the United States.

Sociological School   Adherents of the Sociological School of jurisprudence believe that the purpose of law is to shape societal behavior. Believers are called realists.

Sodomy   Sexual relations between members of the same sex, sexual conduct *per anus* or *per os* between unmarried persons of the opposite sex, and sexual intercourse with animals.

Sovereign immunity   The protection from lawsuits government agencies enjoy.

Specific intent   The type of intent where the person commits an act designed to cause a specific criminal result.

Stare decisis   To stand by that which was decided; rule by which courts decide new cases based on how they decided similar cases before.

State and local law enforcement officers   Police personnel, sheriff's deputies, and other officers who work for state and local law enforcement agencies.

Statutory rape   Sexual intercourse with a victim below the age of consent or unable to consent due to a physical or mental impairment. The crime is commonly referred to as statutory rape because it is the statute that defines what may otherwise seem to be a consensual act as a crime. The legislative presumption is that some persons cannot give meaningful consent.

Stop and frisk   Police officers may briefly stop, identify, and frisk persons reasonably believed to have committed a crime during the course of an investigation.

Strict Liability   The legal responsibility for damage or injury, even if you are not at fault or negligent.

Subjective intent   The offender's conscious intentions at the time of the crime.

Subjective standard (majority rule) for entrapment   Asks the question, "Was the defendant predisposed to commit the crime?"

Subornation of perjury   Convincing or seeking to convince another person to commit perjury.

Sudden escalation   The concept that a conflict that was not life threatening escalates to the point that it is.

Summary offenses   Minor offenses such as parking tickets, or minor traffic violations.

Supremacy Clause   The clause in the U.S. Constitution that states that the Constitution, federal law, and treaties are the supreme law of the land. Article VI, Section 2.

Suspended sentence   The situation where a judge elects to give a convicted person probation instead of actual imprisonment.

T

Tax evasion   An attempt to defeat or avoid paying a tax.

Tenancy by the entirety   The legal joint ownership in which both spouses own an undivided interest in the whole property and in which neither spouse can sell his or her interest without the consent of the other.

Tenants in common   Form of joint ownership in which each owns an undivided interest in the whole property.

Terrorism   The unlawful use or threat of violence, especially against the state or the public, as a politically motivated means of attack or coercion.

Theft   The taking and carrying away of another's personal property with the intent to deprive him or her of it permanently.

Third-degree offenses   Under the Model Penal Code, crimes that are committed recklessly.

Tort   A private or civil wrong or injury independent of contract, resulting from a breach of a legal duty.

Tort feasor   A person who commits a tort.

Transactional immunity   A broad form of immunity where the person cannot be prosecuted for any action related to the testimony as long as the person testifies truthfully.

Transferred intent   The type of intent where a person tries to harm one person and as a result harms someone else.

Transportation   The practice of exiling or expelling a prisoner from his homeland as punishment.

Treason   Levying war against the United States, or in adhering to their enemies, giving them aid and comfort. Treason must be proven by the testimony of two witnesses to the same overt act, or the defendant's confession in open court.

Treaty   An agreement with a foreign government, that to be enforceable must be ratified by a two-thirds vote of the Senate.

Trial   The examination of facts and law presided over by a judge, magistrate, or other person with authority to hear the matter.

Trial by battle   A method of determining guilt in medieval England. Usually reserved for civil cases, in trial by battle the winner of the battle won the lawsuit.

Trial by judge   A defendant may choose to be tried by a judge rather than by a jury or rather than pleading guilty. When a judge tries a case, he or she decides both the facts and the law.

Trial by jury   A trial where the verdict is determined by a jury.

Trial by ordeal   A method of determining guilt in medieval England. In trial by ordeal, the defendant was made to perform a physical task, like holding a hot piece of iron. If the wound healed without becoming infected, the accused was innocent; if it became infected, he was guilty (and ill).

Two-witness rule   The Common Law rule that requires two witnesses to testify to another's perjury in order for a conviction to take place.

True bill   The document produced by a grand jury if it is convinced that the prosecutor's evidence is sufficient to charge the accused with a crime.

U

Uniform Crime Report   An annual tabulation of serious crime in the United States issued by the FBI and based on the voluntary submission of criminal activity information from law enforcement agencies.

Uniform Crime Reporting Handbook   A guide published by the FBI to help law enforcement agencies prepare their annual Uniform Crime Reporting Program report.

Unlawful act manslaughter   Where the defendant committed a crime that resulted in the death of a person.

Unreasonable searches and seizures   The rule, based on the Fourth Amendment, that police must obtain a warrant before searching a home or arresting a suspect. The rule has numerous exceptions.

U.S. Courts of Appeal   The federal court system's intermediate appellate courts.

U.S. District Courts   The federal court system's trial courts.

U.S. Supreme Court   The highest court in the United States.

Use immunity   A limited form of immunity where the person's testimony cannot be used as evidence against him or her.

V

Vagrancy   Under modern laws, loitering with the intent of committing an illegal act.

Venire   A group of individuals from the community from whom the petit jury that will hear a criminal case is drawn. Also referred to as the jury panel, pool, or array.

Venue   The county or judicial district in which a case is tried. In criminal cases, the venue is usually where the crime was committed.

Verdict   A judge or jury's decision at the end of a trial. The verdict in a civil case must be by at least a preponderance of the evidence, while the verdict in a criminal case must be beyond a reasonable doubt.

Vicarious liability   Where one person is held responsible for someone else's actions.

Violence Against Women Act   The primary attempt by the federal government to address domestic violence.

Violent arson   Arson committed with the intent to endanger a person or persons.

Voir dire   From the French meaning "to speak the truth," it refers to the examination of citizens to ascertain their fitness for serving on a jury; during the *voir dire* phase of a criminal trial, the attorneys ask questions of the jury pool. These are designed to ferret out jurors who cannot be impartial or who can't serve on the jury because of illness or other obligations and to help the attorneys in the case decide where and when to use available peremptory challenges.

Voluntary acts   The *actus reus* element of a crime. Crimes must be voluntary acts.

Voluntary intoxication   The condition where a person knowingly ingests an intoxicating substance. Not a defense to murder or most crimes.

Voluntary manslaughter   A homicide committed with the intent to kill, but without deliberation, premeditation, or malice.

W

War on Terror   The term commonly used to refer to the aftermath of the September 11, 2001, attacks and efforts to bring the masterminds of the attacks to justice.

Warrant   A document issued by a magistrate or judge authorizing the search of a place or the arrest of a person.

Wergild   In ancient England, compensation paid to a family group if a member of that family was killed or suffered severe injury.

Wite   In ancient England, a public fine payable to a lord or tribal chieftain.

Withdrawal   The act of removing oneself from a conflict.

Witherspoon **qualified**   A jury in a capital case who have stated they will consider imposing the death penalty even if they are opposed to the death penalty.

Witness tampering   An illegal attempt to influence a witness' sworn testimony.

Work product rule   The rule that protects material produced by an attorney in preparation for a trial, or the work product, from discovery.

Writ of *certiorari*   Notice from the Supreme Court that the court will hear a case.

Writ of *habeas corpus*   An order by federal court to "bring the body" of the prisoner to the court.

Index

Note; The locators followed by 'f' and 't' refer to figures and tables cited in the text